ENOCH POWELL

By the same author

PUBLIC OPINION AND EUROPEAN INTEGRATION
A CLASS DIVIDED: APPEASEMENT AND THE ROAD TO MUNICH
IRELAND'S FATE: THE BOYNE AND AFTER
THE POWER BROKERS: THE TORY PARTY AND ITS LEADERS
IAIN MACLEOD: A BIOGRAPHY

Enoch Powell

———◆———

Robert Shepherd

HUTCHINSON
LONDON

This edition first published in 1996 by
Hutchinson

Random House (UK) Limited
20 Vauxhall Bridge Road, London SW1V 2SA

Random House Australia (Pty) Limited
20 Alfred Street, Milsons Point,
New South Wales 2061, Australia

Random House New Zealand Limited
18 Poland Road, Glenfield, Auckland 10, New Zealand

Random House South Africa (Pty) Limited
Box 2263, Rosebank 2121, South Africa

A CiP record for this
book is available from the British Library

Papers used by Random House UK Limited are natural,
recyclable products made from wood grown in sustainable forests.
The manufacturing processes conform to the environmental
regulations of the country of origin.

ISBN 0 09 179208 8

Typeset in Ehrhardt by Deltatype Ltd, Birkenhead, Merseyside

Printed and bound in Great Britain by
Mackays of Chatham PLC

Contents

Illustrations

Enoch Powell with his parents 1913 (*Enoch Powell*)
The scholarship boy (*Enoch Powell*)
Enoch Powell sketched by Freeth (*National Portrait Gallery*)
A. E. Housman (*Hulton Getty Collection Ltd*)
Powell in 1947 (*Universal Pictorial Press & Agency Ltd*)
Barbara Kennedy (*Barbara Hawkins*)
Enoch and Pamela Powell (*Universal Pictorial Press & Agency Ltd*)
Powell, Maude and Boyle
Powell as Financial Secretary to the Treasury (*Topham*)
Powell on a pogo stick (*Camera Press Ltd*)
Rab Butler and Harold Macmillan (*Hulton Getty Collection Ltd*)
With Hailsham, Soames and Macleod (*Hulton Getty Collection Ltd*)
Powell leaving the Cabinet (*Hulton Getty Collection Ltd*)
Powell travelling on the tube (*Associated Press/Topham*)
The Powells on a family picnic (*Topham*)
Newspaper headlines after Powell's controversial speech
The Powells sifting through their mail (*Topham*)
Smithfield porters march to the Commons (*Topham*)
Powell supporters in Wolverhampton (*Express & Star*)
Powell amongst his own people (*Camera Press Ltd*)
Anti-Powell demonstration (*Express & Star*)
Powell poster in Bombay (*Camera Press Ltd*)
The Powells spread the word (*Hulton Getty Collection Ltd*)
Powell supporting Heath (*Hulton Getty Collection Ltd*)
Powell backs Labour and helps defeat Heath (*Hulton Getty Collection Ltd*)
With Barbara Castle during the referendum, 1975 (*Hulton Getty Collection Ltd*)
Powell canvassing in Ulster (*Hulton Getty Collection Ltd*)
Powell in the pulpit (*Hulton Getty Collection Ltd*)
Enoch and Pamela (*Universal Pictorial Press and Agency Ltd*)
Powell in Westminster (*Hulton Getty Collection Ltd*)

Preface

This book is not an 'authorized' or 'official' biography, but Mr Powell placed no obstacles in my way. I am grateful to him for having no objection to my using the Conservative Party Archive for the period covering his career in the Conservative Party. I should also like to thank him for allowing me to draw on interviews recorded for television documentaries on contemporary history and politics.

This biography is the first one to use the papers that are now available at the Public Record Office for Powell's ministerial career until October 1963, and at the Conservative Party Archive at the Bodleian Library, Oxford, for his period in the Conservative Party until 1974.

Having had Birmingham grandfathers and Black Country grandmothers, I have long been intrigued by Enoch Powell. This early fascination was reinforced when I worked in the Conservative Research Department before the 1979 election, in the same Old Queen Street offices where Powell had worked while the Conservatives were in Opposition thirty years earlier – the furniture and fittings (and some characters) did not appear to have changed since his days there in the late 1940s. During the early 1980s, I served as special adviser to the then Secretary of State for Northern Ireland, James (later Lord) Prior, and had cause to keep a close eye on Powell during his years as an Ulster Unionist MP. I also relished the opportunity to observe Powell from the parliamentary press gallery during his final years in the Commons. In 1987, I was able to produce and direct *Enoch, A Life in Politics*, a television profile of Powell for Channel 4, and he has contributed to a number of other documentaries on contemporary history and politics that I have produced.

I should like to thank all those who have talked or written to me about Enoch Powell. Where appropriate, I acknowledge their contributions in the notes. I am also happy to record my debt to Andrew Roth and Paul Foot, two of the most assiduous and perceptive journalists, whose earlier studies of Powell remain a source of information and inspiration for any biographer.

I am grateful to Alistair Cooke for granting me permission to quote copyright material from the Conservative Party Archive; to Martin Maw, archivist at the

Bodleian Library, Oxford, for his invaluable advice; and to Colin Harris and his colleagues in the reading room for their indefatigable assistance. Crown copyright material in the Public Record Office is reproduced by permission of the Controller of Her Majesty's Stationery Office. I should like to thank David McKitterick, Librarian of Trinity College, Cambridge, and his staff for their assistance, and for allowing me to consult R.A. Butler's papers. The librarian and staff of the London Library, and also of the Royal Borough of Kensington and Chelsea, eased the task of research by their courteous and efficient assistance, as did the staff at the British Library Newspaper Library at Colindale. Mark Green of Wolverhampton's *Express and Star* kindly made available to me the newspaper's cuttings on Enoch Powell. Angela Raspin at the British Library of Political and Economic Science allowed me to consult Andrew Roth's files and the transcripts of interviews recorded for Phillip Whitehead's television series on Britain in the 1970s, *The Writing on the Wall*, produced by Brook Productions for Channel 4.

I am especially indebted to Dr Charles Webster, who generously sent me a draft of his chapters covering Powell's period as Minister of Health, from the forthcoming Volume II of his Official History of the National Health Service. I was fortunate to attend Rodney Lowe's enlightening seminar in October 1995, on 'The Conservatives and the Welfare State', at the Institute of Historical Research – he also helpfully sent me a copy of his draft chapter on the subject for a forthcoming study on the Conservatives and British society. Paul Bridgen kindly advised me on the relevant papers on Enoch Powell and the welfare state at the Public Record Office, and sent me a draft of the relevant section in his forthcoming book (with Rodney Lowe) on welfare policy under the Conservatives, 1951–64. Mark Jarvis not only gave an interesting seminar on the 1958 Treasury crisis to the Institute of Historical Research in January 1996, but provided a guide to relevant documents at the Public Record Office. Anne Colville agreed to let me read her M.S.Sc. dissertation in Irish Politics and International Conflict Areas at Queen's University, Belfast, on *Enoch Powell: His Ulster Years*. David Butler helpfully allowed me to consult interviews conducted for the Nuffield election studies during Powell's career. I also benefited from attending the witness seminar chaired by Zig Layton-Henry on race relations in the 1960s, held in February 1996 and arranged by the Institute of Historical Research and the Institute of Contemporary British History. I should like to thank Lord Jenkins of Hillhead, Lord Lester of Herne Hill, Bill Bohan and Keith Kyle for their insights.

Under the auspices of the *Prix Stendhal*, I was fortunate to be awarded a Reuter Fellowship at the University of Oxford. The advice, encouragement and friendship of Godfrey Hodgson, Director of the Reuter Foundation Programme, and Rosemary Allan, the Administrator, ensured that it was an especially memorable and rewarding experience. I should also like to thank Stephen Somerville, Director of the Reuter Foundation, and his colleagues for their assistance, and Sir Crispin Tickell, Warden of Green College, Oxford, for his hospitality and interest.

I should like to thank Tony Whittome for commissioning this book and for his encouragement and support. Michael Shaw has, as always, provided invaluable advice and help. I owe a special debt of gratitude to Gillian Shepherd for her encouragement and help with research.

ROBERT SHEPHERD
London, August 1996

1

A Driven Personality

> There must be loss to offset the advantages, such as they are, of being an only child, and probably those are deprivation of early experience of social relationships, and the relationships with equals.
>
> Enoch Powell, on being an only child.

Upbringing

Enoch Powell personified the new class of young, career-minded politicians recruited by the Conservative Party in the immediate wake of the Second World War. This new breed tended to come from less well-off backgrounds than had pre-war Tories. Lacking wealth and family contacts to smooth their paths, they had to rely instead on their intellects and own efforts. There was no better example of this phenomenon than Powell. He had been born a couple of years before the outbreak of the First World War into lower middle-class, suburban Birmingham, but by his early thirties, when he realized that his future lay in politics, he had already achieved both academic distinction, culminating in a professorship, and a rapid, war-time progression through the ranks from private soldier to Brigadier.

Yet this exemplar of post-war Conservatism, though professing himself a 'high Tory', was always something of an outsider in his party, even before his explosive speech on immigration in 1968 and his eventual break with the Conservatives six years later. There was also a touch of the outsider about another post-war recruit, Iain Macleod, who was initially a close colleague of Powell's. Powell and Macleod were independent-minded radicals, who brought a touch of devil and magic to politics and who were always able to take a detached view of their party. Perhaps not surprisingly, it was Macleod who best captured this element in his profile of Powell for the *Spectator* in which he also wrote that Powell suffered from 'an excess of logic'. This most un-Tory condition is itself a reflection of Powell's driven personality, that gives him an intensity which many have found off-putting, even intimidating.[1]

Until well into his eighties, Powell sustained a prolific speaking and writing career, and remained a controversialist who continued to capture the headlines. This achievement is a tribute to his upbringing. It was to his father that Powell attributes his skill of oratory. As he has recalled, his father

> believed that one of the important things, if not the most important thing in life, was to write and speak good English. He would frequently read to me, books and passages, and he encouraged me to read books and passages, saying, 'Now that's real English; to write like that, that's an achievement.'[2]

Powell was an only child, and this had a crucial bearing on his personality. He had mixed feelings about his lack of siblings, but was able to identify some benefit:

> I am not quite sure whether I wish I had not been an only child, so one explores the advantage of being an only child. And one is that one is brother and sister to one's mother and father; that one is treated as a brother or sister by adults. One joins in to some extent in adult life at an earlier stage.

However, as he has acknowledged in the words quoted at the head of this chapter, there are disadvantages. The most important one for Powell's personality was the 'deprivation of early experience of social relationships, and the relationships with equals'. Although he claimed that 'from the earliest time that I can remember I have made friendships very easily, and friendships have been very important to me', his insight about the absence of relationships with equals is revealing. The lack of this early social experience, combined with the upbringing he received from his parents, particularly his mother, helps to explain the solitariness that is Powell's outstanding characteristic – or 'temperamental isolation' as the astute Tory writer, T.E. Utley defined it. Although Powell made some close friendships, and became less prickly as he aged, he has never been a man whom it is easy to befriend. A recurring feature of Powell's life and one that has marked his politics has been his difficulty in handling his relations with other people.[3]

John Enoch Powell was born on the thundery night of Sunday 16 June 1912, in a three-bedroom house in Flaxley Lane, Stechford, a nondescript suburb to the east of Birmingham. Stechford was never particularly fashionable, but it suited Powell's school-teacher parents who had met in 1907 and had been married two years later. Powell's father, Albert Enoch, was thirty-seven when he married, and his mother, Ellen Mary, was twenty-three. The street in which Powell was born and where he spent his first six years overlooked the old London and North Western railway between Euston and Birmingham New Street, and today the modest red-brick houses where Powell began his life can be glimpsed from the Inter-City express.

'I was born a Tory', the adult Powell has been wont to declare. In party political terms, his father's political sympathies were Liberal, with radical inclinations, whereas his mother's loyalties lay with the Conservatives, or

'Unionists' as they were then known, especially in the Chamberlainite stronghold of Birmingham. But Powell's deliberate choice of the term 'Tory' implies more than a party label. As far back in his boyhood as he could remember, Powell had a strong reverence for the English past. Aged about eight, during a visit to Caernarvon Castle, he suddenly doffed his cap in one of the rooms, and explained to his puzzled father that it had been the birthplace of the first Prince of Wales. And in 1919, when seated with his parents in the front seats of the otherwise empty top deck of a Birmingham tramcar, 'I start up singing my favourite (was it my only ?) song, "God Save the King!".' His mother had scolded him, 'Don't sing that here.' 'Oh, let the boy sing it,' his father had enjoined, 'he may not be able to much longer' – a reference to the republican threat that many people feared from socialist activists in areas such as Clydeside and the increased number of Labour MPs elected in 1918, following the enfranchisement of working-class men.[4]

Probably his parents' strongest influence on their son was in giving him his didactic character. He was nicknamed 'the Professor' at the age of three, because he used to stand on a chair and tell visitors the names and give a description of the stuffed birds that his grandfather had shot and which were displayed in his parents' home. His father once told him that if he 'were not a teacher, it would be contrary to the laws of biology ... and I suppose looking back over my misspent political life, perhaps I have been teaching after all'. Few people can have been brought up in a family home better suited for a life of teaching, speaking and writing than Enoch Powell's.[5]

Metal-bashing and municipal reform had been the twin forces that had shaped the early twentieth-century Birmingham into which Powell was born. They had also influenced his family background. The Powells originated in Radnorshire, the Welsh border county, but in the early nineteenth century his great-grandfather migrated to the industrial coalfields of the West Midlands to find employment in West Bromwich, at a 'gin-pit' where a horse walked round and round raising and lowering buckets. The metal-bashing trades that earned Birmingham and the neighbouring Black Country their reputation as 'the workshop of the world', consisted of numerous small firms and foundries, and the Powells became part of a bustling, entrepreneurial community in which class divisions between 'boss' and worker were generally less severe than in the great northern mill-towns, the east-end docks of London, or Britain's large-scale mining areas. Powell's grandfather, Enoch Powell, was an iron merchant and general dealer in Smethwick, to the west of Birmingham. The name Enoch – pronounced 'Aynuck' in the local dialect – was one of several biblical names that were common in the Black Country, especially among Methodists. As it happens, 'Aynuck' is the name of a mythical hero in local folklore, who, with his friend 'Ayli' (Eli) features in many dialect stories. 'That acme of incomprehensibility', as Powell described his fictional namesake, 'who put his pig on a wall – the actual wall used still to be exhibited in Upper Gornal – "to watch the band go by".' Explaining to readers of the *Spectator* that 'Awd

Aynuck' (Old Enoch) is 'a bit stupid, ignorant and illogical but tough and enduring', Powell reported a typical Old Enoch story:

> 'So ah says, "dom the Pope", and Ayli sloshed I.'
> 'But Aynuck, yo knowed as ow Ayli am a Catholic.'
> 'Ah, but ah day know as ow the Pope wor.'

Powell's father, who was born in Smethwick in 1872, was christened Albert Enoch, and when his son was born, he wanted to perpetuate the family christian name. Although Powell's mother was not fond of the name 'Enoch', she accepted it as her son's second name – the young boy was always known as 'Jack'.[6]

Instead of following his father into the iron trade, Albert Powell made teaching his career. Manufacturing in Birmingham and the Black Country had been badly hit by the great depression of the 1870s and increasing competition from Germany and the United States, whereas the opportunities in schools had expanded following the introduction in 1870 of elementary education for all children – the cause that had brought Joseph Chamberlain into politics. Albert began as a pupil-teacher in Birmingham in the 1880s, and at the age of sixteen he was in control of classes of sixty children. Having survived this baptism of fire, he became established as an elementary school-teacher. By the time his own son, Jack, was in his teens, Albert Powell had become head-master of the George Dixon School, a higher grade elementary school that had been named in honour of the former Birmingham Mayor, who had also campaigned for state elementary education.[7]

Albert Powell had been brought up as a Methodist, but he had converted to Anglicanism during his teens. Although he had become a volunteer in the Royal Warwickshire Regiment, when the South African War came he supported the Boers – a radical act, defying what his son was to deride almost a century later as 'the forced and foolish patriotism' that had been whipped up by the erstwhile champion of Birmingham Radicalism, Chamberlain. At the outbreak of the First World War, Albert was already in his forties and, unlike the younger fathers of young Jack Powell's contemporaries, did not go to the trenches. However, the Great War impinged on his little son's consciousness, since one of Powell's earliest memories was sheltering under the stairs during a Zeppelin raid on Birmingham.[8]

The impression among Powell's school contemporaries of his father's having a distinctive bearing was enhanced by Albert's age – he turned fifty the year after his son had started secondary school. As an acquaintance of his son's recalled: 'Powell's father was a very distinguished-looking man with a somewhat ruddy complexion set off by white hair and carefully trimmed white moustache, very upright . . . He looked more like a soldier than a schoolmas-ter.' In addition to kindling his son's passion for good English, Albert fostered Jack's interest in nature and the outdoors – Powell was to remain an inveterate weekend picnicker and rambler. Albert also made his son conscious of his Welsh roots, especially during Whitsun and summer holidays that were often spent exploring Wales and the Welsh borders.[9]

Albert's occupation as a teacher, and later, headmaster, brought a steady income into the home. Although teachers' pay had been relatively low before 1919, when national rates were introduced with the Burnham negotiating machinery, by the 1920s an experienced male teacher could earn up to £300 a year, and a headmaster up to £450 a year, while the average male manual worker's wage was about £150 a year. In keeping with the conventions of the day, Albert Powell's salary was sufficient for him to support his wife and child – lower middle-class couples enjoyed a relatively comfortable standard of living, provided that they limited the size of their families and kept a close watch on their spending. Self-control and deferred gratification were the watchwords of the milieu in which Powell was brought up – he remained teetotal until his forties, and had a lifelong aversion to gambling. But it was a secure upbringing. His father never faced the prospect of unemployment and Jack Powell never saw his parents worried about whether a job would last, or when the next one would come.

The Powells kept themselves very much to themselves. They were regarded as a charming couple, if rather remote. But it was a happy home, not a solemn one, and the Powells were devoted to each other and to their son. 'If I could remake it and reconstruct it,' Powell once observed, 'I wouldn't know what to do to make it better.' Albert was more approachable than his wife, and if he was in the garden would happily chat to the neighbours – he volunteered, without being asked, to help coach one of their daughters when he realised that she would soon have to sit her examinations. Powell remembered his father as having been 'by nature an easy-going man. He couldn't see that things had to be pushed beyond a certain point and this made for an agreeable temperament – though not one, in this respect, that was very intelligible to me.' Powell's mother had a different personality. She was the stronger, aspirational influence on her son. 'My father was, as it were, a warm presence and another boy around the place,' Powell has recalled, 'but my childhood is very much my mother.' She was somewhat reserved and shy, but with a beautiful speaking voice. She was slim, and tended to dress in a rather old-fashioned style for her age.[10]

Powell's mother, Ellen Mary Breese, had been born in 1886 in the Toxteth Park area of Liverpool. She was the daughter of a police constable and granddaughter of a journeyman tailor from Newport in Shropshire. As a schoolgirl she had taught herself Greek, partly to explore the meaning of the New Testament – Powell's controversial new interpretation of the St Matthew Gospel, completed after he had turned eighty, was rooted in the burning curiosity and sheer drive of this late-Victorian Liverpudlian girl. She became a teacher, and met Powell's father while she was supply teaching in Birmingham. She had lost her religious faith for some time when her son was born, but she ensured that he had a Christian education in order to enable him to make his own mind up.[11]

Like other women of her time, Ellen Powell gave up her state teaching job when she married. Instead, she became young Jack's first teacher:

> I suppose some of my earliest recollections are of my mother putting up the alphabet round the kitchen wall so that I could learn it and saying the most elementary lessons to her standing on a chair in the kitchen while she worked on the stove or the sink. And, from the very beginning right up to the sixth at grammar school she took a part in my learning, encouraging me and helping me and very much working with me.

Powell 'could read reasonably by the age of three'. In his words, his mother 'taught me how to work'. His early learning and school homework were conducted to the accompaniment of his mother's injunctions: 'What you start, you must finish' and 'Your motto ought to be "*Thorough*"!' He had been born with the brains to maximize his opportunity, and rapidly showed a precocious intelligence that brought him outstanding scholastic success. He imagined that he would be a scholar. The image of a demanding teacher, hovering over his shoulder, was to remain a powerful goad for Powell throughout his life. His mother's ambition was that her son should be a happy man, but his acquisition of his mother's application and drive left him unable fully to understand others, including his father, who lacked them.[12]

Powell was not sent to a council elementary school, although both parents had taught in state schools. In 1918, the Powells moved from Stechford to a leafier suburb to the south of the city, King's Norton, where they lived at number 52 Woodlands Park Road. There were still fields on either side of the road, and a neighbour recalled that 'there was no council school nearer than Bournville, well over a mile across a lonely field-path'. A local woman, Mabel Pane, had started holding classes in her front room, and these had proved so popular that she had taken over the little village hall, near to the Powells' new home. Jack Powell attended this small, private school until he was nine years old, and always remembered Mabel Pane as 'a great teacher'.[13]

In Powell's case, Miss Pane was only supplementing what he was learning at home. Despite the Powells' careful budgeting and their enjoining Jack to watch his every halfpenny, they had never stinted on books. By the age of eight Jack was already familiar with a large part of this treasure trove on his parents' shelves, as a local girl who used to visit the Powells discovered. 'There was such an array of books!' the girl recalled:

> I remember there were a number of Jack London's. I – not an avid reader by any means – was invited to select one, read it and bring it back next week and choose another. This I did, and to prove that I *had* read it he would ask me a lot of questions about it. I was four years older, and it felt terrible if I couldn't answer the questions correctly, or got one book mixed

up with another whereupon he would quote chapter and verse for my special benefit.

She and Powell were 'very good friends' and she was sometimes invited to tea, but it says much about the Powells that although tea (with Bourbon biscuits) was served modestly in the kitchen, they none the less had a room that their visitor described as a 'library'.[14]

Contemporaries of Jack Powell remember him as a serious-minded and rather withdrawn child, who was always studying and seemed older than his years. One neighbour recalled him as a young boy, 'appearing from a cold bedroom, where he was doing his homework, wrapped in an eiderdown'. Another remembers him standing on the kitchen table, practising his speeches as prime minister. Since the local shops were about a mile or so away at Cotteridge, the local children used to make their own sweets, hold their own flower shows and set up their own club, with about ten members. They put on plays, and Jack played the Wizard in their version of *Cinderella*, wearing 'a long black cloak, a pointed black hat and, to make it all more realistic, he made himself long plasticine claws to fit on his fingers'. He also used 'a roaring voice, nearly frightening to death some of the younger members of the cast'. They also used to take it in turns to give a talk on some subject of their own choosing. 'For most of us', one of them recalled, 'this was quite a task, even choosing a subject, let alone talking on it for, say, twenty minutes.' But not for Jack. When his turn came – he was eight years old at the time – he said his subject was to be 'Bacon or Shakespeare'. By the end of the evening, his audience were in no doubt that Francis Bacon wrote *Henry V*, *A Midsummer Night's Dream*, and other plays usually attributed to Shakespeare.[15]

But Jack Powell rarely joined in rough-and-tumble games with other boys, and was sometimes a target of other children's mischief. Woodlands Park Road was a tobogganner's paradise in winter, as it ran down a steep hill from its southern end to the foot of a valley and up the other side towards Bournville. One of the older boys owned a large sledge, that carried him and four or five younger children, while he held a smaller sledge in front to help him steer. A girl who used to act as a weight by sitting on the front, smaller sledge recalled the exhilaration of 'bumping into the ruts and potholes, whizzing through the freezing air at ever increasing speed as the track became harder, down the hill and up the other side'. One day, Jack Powell, who was several years younger, was persuaded to take a turn. 'He was not used to this sort of caper,' the girl remembered. 'By the time we arrived at the end of the track he was stiff with fright and as white as a ghost.' On the long walk back up the hill, he disappeared into his house. A few days later, however, 'not wishing to be outdone or thought afraid, Jack appeared with his own sledge and proceeded, with something of a flourish', to a slope in a nearby field that was a softer and safer ride.[16]

When Jack was older and was travelling daily to school in Birmingham, he and a neighbour's son decided to test which was the quickest of the two possible routes by foot and train to the city centre. Powell took what was likely to be the quicker one, and was astonished when he arrived second. The other boy did not admit to having run instead of walking, and was much amused that it never seemed to occur to Powell that he had cheated.[17]

Powell's introduction to life came mainly through books. His first encounters with facts, emotions and opinions during his reading as a child and an adolescent frequently recur in his later speeches and writing. In recapturing these memories, he reveals a bias towards romantic adventures and eccentric authors. When he reviewed Wilfred Thesiger's *Arabian Sands* in 1959, the 'haunting and the fascination flowed back like a tide after forty years', and he revealed that he still had the maps that, at the age of nine, he had 'meticulously copied from the works of the Arabian travellers'. Commending *George Borrow, Eccentric*, Michael Collie's biography of the English nineteenth-century romantic writer and linguist, as one of his books of the year in 1982, Powell rejoiced 'that a boyhood favourite and inspirer is coming back into recognition and popularity'. Asked in 1986 to nominate his two favourite books, he nominated 'an unlikely pair' from his early years – Richard Jefferies' *Bevis*, that captured magically the combination of practicality with pretence which every boy likes to find in his adventures', and *The Harmsworth Encyclopaedia*, that had been published as a part-work. His maternal great-grandfather had bought the bindings and given it to his grand-daughter, Powell's mother. As Powell observed some seventy years later, the *Encyclopaedia* 'displayed to me an illimitable vista over the ocean of knowledge and many of its illuminated entries remain indelible memories'.[18]

The recollection of his early days when he was trying to satisfy his vast appetite for knowledge and the images that his search stimulated were etched in Powell's mind. Endorsing Nietzsche's observation 'that the memory of big experiences in the world of books is flavoured with the tang of the physical setting in which they happened', Powell recalled, when he was about fifteen,

> the detonation of *Sartor Resartus*: I still hear, when I recall the first reading of those intoxicating pages, the gentle hissing of the incandescent gas mantle above the table where homework was done, and the tone of my father's voice saying that I would find Carlyle as great an experience as he had done at the same age.

In addition, Powell also revealed that

> the long avenues of thought that have led from Frazer's *Golden Bough* seem to start physically in front of the dining room fireplace of the home where as a boy of fifteen I sat hour after hour absorbing first the one-volume abridgement and then the three-volume edition. I cannot imagine how different my mental and religious life would have been if the impact of J.G. Frazer had come at another time or not at all.

His encounter with the *Golden Bough* was the most powerful intellectual experience of his boyhood. More than any other influence, it set him adrift from the Church of England, by demonstrating, 'beyond all doubt', that the Christian belief in the killing, eating and resurrection of Christ was merely one variant of similar belief-systems throughout human history. 'Christ, Christianity and the Church had crumbled and vanished,' Powell later wrote, 'or rather, they were now dried and labelled specimens in a large case in the museum of anthropology.' But Powell's temperament was such that he regarded agnosticism as 'only a lazier form of superstition'. He was ready to welcome and to propagate Nietzsche's atheistic declaration that 'God is dead'.[19]

As Jack Powell pored over the great tracts of red in his atlas, devoured his books and scoured his encyclopaedia for facts, his sense of the unique power of the British Empire became as strongly imprinted in his mind as had the physical setting of his parents' home. Yet Powell had not gleaned this image of imperial might from his parents. As he later explained, the world in which he was brought up, 'where Britain was the greatest power because she was also India, was, by historical standards of brief duration. It was as improbable to the generations born before about 1890 as it was inevitable to those born since.' Remembering how his father used to quote to him, 'without disapproval, John Bright's famous ejaculation, "Perish India!"', Powell noted, 'It was not that I did not agree: I did not understand; for between my father's birth in 1872 and mine in 1912 it had become synonymous with "Perish Britain!"' At the age of seventy-nine, Powell evoked the enduring impact of this image of Britain's imperial power to a gathering of historians, who listened in amazement 'as that air-raid siren voice' – in Peter Hennessy's phrase – 'its West Midlands cadences adding, as always to the effect, rose higher with increasing intensity'. Powell told his startled audience,

> I [also] know that, on my deathbed, I shall still be believing with one part of my brain that somewhere on every ocean of the world there is a great, grey ship with three funnels and sixteen-inch guns which can blow out of the water any other navy which is likely to face it. I know it is not so. Indeed, I realized at a relatively early age that it is not so. But that factor – that emotional factor ... will not die until I, the carrier of it, am dead.

The emotional factor was always central to Powell's understanding of politics, but he knew why historians had ignored it:

> It is unquantifiable. It is rather shameful and it is difficult to handle. But without the emotional factor, I do not think one can understand the turn around which occurred in this country or some of the most surprising things which this country did in the second half of the twentieth century.

And without it neither can one understand Powell.[20]

Scholarship boy

In 1921, Jack Powell left the security of Mabel Pane's small school and entered the more boisterous environment of the nearby council secondary school for boys, where he joined most other nine- to thirteen-year-olds in King's Norton. He spent four not particularly happy years there. But having been programmed by his mother as a 'prize-scholarship winning, knowledge-eating' being, he achieved the rare distinction for a boy at a council school of winning a coveted 'King Edward Scholarship' to the prestigious King Edward VI High School for Boys, Birmingham. The school, whose former pupils include Edward Burne-Jones, the pre-Raphaelite artist, Professor Benjamin Kennedy, the renowned nineteenth-century Cambridge classicist, Field-Marshal the Viscount Slim, and Professor J.R.R. Tolkien, the author of *Lord of the Rings*, was then located in the city centre that Joseph Chamberlain had reconstructed between 1876 and 1885. The great Victorian thoroughfares of Corporation Street and New Street, with their arcades, passageways and shops, became Powell's schoolboy haunts. But by the 1920s, it was, as Powell later recognized, 'no use attempting the romantic pretence that it was the ideal environment for a great school'.[21]

More than forty years after he had left King Edward's – and over thirty years after the school had moved to Edgbaston – Powell could still recapture vividly 'Barry's Gothic building in New Street, cramped and darkened by the rise of commercial buildings around it and noisy with the swirl of traffic in front and the main railway station behind'. As a boy he had known neither 'ancient' nor 'rural loveliness' in a school and would have been prepared to 'extol the advantage of a city school in a city centre', but in adulthood, he readily conceded the drawbacks: 'four train journeys a day, with the resulting disruption of classes by fog and other delays; the impossibility of extending or improving the facilities for teaching; and the almost total lack of even playground space'. Despite these severe handicaps, the masters at King Edward's had 'achieved the superb standards of academic attainment which were taken for granted'. During his five years at the school, Powell became one of its star pupils.[22]

However, Jack Powell made an inauspicious start. When he first enrolled as a 'King Edward Scholar' on 16 September 1925, he was put in the Lower Fifth form, on the science side. Ellen Powell had overdone his science coaching for the scholarship examination, having recognized it as his weakest subject. But after a term, he was moved to the classical side, which happened to be under strength. Although the boys he joined had already been studying Greek for two and a half years, Powell was unperturbed:

When I was transferred from one desk to another in big school, where we all assembled in the morning, I was greeted somewhat quizzically by the classical form that I had joined. I remember informing them that after two terms I would be top of the form. I was.

His mother enabled him to fulfil his boast – he won the form prize three years in succession. Self-taught in Greek as a schoolgirl, Ellen Powell woke him earlier each morning in order to give him extra coaching before he left to catch his train.[23]

Although Powell denied ever having 'any sense of separation' or feeling 'a sense of superiority' to others because he was an academic child, attending King Edward's set him even further apart physically and socially from the vast majority of his contemporaries in suburban King's Norton. As one of them recalled:

> I can still picture him arriving home – much later than the rest of us because of the long journey from King Edward's – with his dark blue cap with the light blue rings round it pulled well down over his forehead and his bulging satchel under his arm.

Yet 'Scowelly Powelly', as he was nicknamed at his new school because of his habit of frowning, also seemed somehow set apart from his fellow pupils at King Edward's. Whereas some boys, such as Raymond Lyttleton, a future Professor of Astronomy, regarded Latin and Greek classes as being miserable almost beyond endurance and were never able 'to muster the smallest interest in "Sailors sacrificing bulls on the altar of the goddesses"', Powell excelled. 'He was in the back row of the Sixth Form when I was in the front row,' C.F. Evans, a classmate who was later at university with Powell, remembered:

> He'd come streaking up from the lower forms at a tremendous pace and, although he was two years younger, he was already arrived in the back row of ... a rather powerful Sixth Form ... and those of us in the front row ... were I think – at least I was – pretty frightened. I think he was a very formidable scholar ... in classics even at that age.

Powell's teachers were similarly impressed, notably the young 'Duggie' Smith, who had recently obtained a double first in Classics at Trinity College, Cambridge, and who was Powell's form-master in the Lower Classical Sixth in 1927–28, and his principal classics master in the Upper Sixth during 1928–30. 'Of all my pupils', Smith later recalled,

> he always insisted on the highest standards of accuracy and knowledge in those who taught him. Woe betide the careless young master, as I was, who was guilty of a rash statement because, from the back bench of the Upper Sixth would come a voice, 'But, sir', followed by a long quotation from an author. He was a pupil from whom I learnt more than most.[24]

Yet it was not only his academic prowess that distinguished Powell. Despite his repeated claims to 'have always been happy in a collective environment', the recollections of him by his school contemporaries reflect an impression that was to be shared by almost everybody else who was to become a colleague of Powell's – at Cambridge, in the army, in the Conservative Party, and in the Commons. Lyttleton, for example, did not think that anyone knew Powell 'closely' at King Edward's. 'He was agreeable and polite,' another school contemporary remembered, 'but he was completely self-sufficient; he did not seem to want to share his life; he didn't encourage anyone to encroach on his privacy.' C.F. Evans described him as having been

> really unlike … any other schoolboy one had known. He was austere. One seldom, if ever, had seen him standing up against a wall with his hands in his pockets, just talking. He didn't play games, though I gather he had quite a capacity for gymnasium. He was either at his books, or he was walking purposefully from A to B with a goal in mind, with either his books or his clarinet under his arm, pale, head rather forward, shoulders slightly stooped. He was … quite a phenomenon.'[25]

By way of getting some exercise, Powell had taken up gymnastics, and, characteristically, won a school prize – the Bronze Medal. He never had any interest in team games like soccer or rugger. During compulsory games, he used to stand on the playing field without joining in and made an arrangement with a boy on the other side to avoid their having to change ends at half-time. Neither did he join in other collective pursuits, such as the Boy Scouts or bicycling, although his mother would have preferred that he did. He also declined to join the school's Officer Training Corps. And although like most other boys at King Edward's, Powell travelled between his home and the school by train, he is remembered as a solitary, rather forbidding figure. Rowland Ryder, a contemporary, and later a biographer and cricket commentator, recalled that although he must have shared a compartment with Powell well over a hundred times, 'never once in those four years did I hear him speak'. On one occasion, Ryder 'was indulging some mild horse-play when I was flung against him as he was reading in a corner seat. I was terrified and apologized profusely. He grunted amiably and went on with his reading.'[26]

In his own memory, Powell was not only tolerant of schoolboy mischief, but also joined in more than has been remembered by his contemporaries – nobody can escape 'original sin', whether a latter-day vandal or young Jack Powell. 'When I was young,' Powell has recalled, 'my friends weren't bored or idle or particularly poor; but we still took it out on the rolling stock of the Midland railway and vandalized it frequently.' He also used to delight in leaning out of the carriage window as his train left New Street station in an effort to knock the porters' hats off – a risky game, since Ford, the station's head porter, reputedly knew by which train every boy travelled.[27]

Less surprisingly than his recollection of youthful mischievousness, Powell's schoolboy rummaging in Birmingham's second-hand bookshops evoked strong memories in the adult man. When he was forty-eight, he discovered among the desolation of a city centre that had been ravaged by war, slum clearance and redevelopment,

> a second-hand bookshop, one of half a dozen which the street had once boasted. As a schoolboy I used to make my way along it once or twice a month in the lunch-hour, to rummage in the penny boxes and scan the sixpenny shelves. This particular shop, it was commonly agreed among us of the classical sixth, had an exceptionally good penny box in those days, and more than one leather-bound volume out of it stands on my shelves to this day. There is something special for a schoolboy – and perhaps not only for a schoolboy – about a second-hand book picked up really cheap. It tends to get read and studied with more than ordinary loving care, and I am sure that a disproportionate share of my classical knowledge when I left school had come not out of prescribed textbooks, but out of the second-hand bargains which I bought and studied 'on the side'.[28]

Powell's main relaxation from books during his first couple of years at King Edward's was playing the clarinet. He played in a school orchestra – a collective act that was a rare exception to his usual solitariness. So enthusiastically did he embrace music, that when he was fifteen he entertained thoughts of making it his life and seeking a scholarship at the Royal Academy of Music. However his parents thought this unwise and he was dissuaded. Instead, his goal became winning a place at Cambridge. In itself, this decision was not all that surprising, particularly in an aspirational, lower middle-class family for whom the risks of an artistic life almost invariably appear prohibitive. Not that Powell's future was being viewed in narrowly mercenary terms. As he later recalled:

> This was how one got on and up. One was certainly not saying, 'Well if I go to Cambridge I can get a degree in so-and-so and then I can have a career as a this or a that.' That wasn't it at all. It was much more that here is an opportunity, an opportunity to rise, I'm sorry the word must seem so crude but that I'm sure is how I saw it – get on has too much of a connotation of economics, get on would understate it but rise is the best I can do to describe it.[29]

Powell's reaction to the decision that he should not pursue a musical life was drastic. Instead of continuing with his clarinet as a hobby, it was immediately abandoned. Listening to music was to continue for some years, until that too eventually ceased. His reasoning had a blinkered feel:

> It's not unnatural to think: 'Well there are only a certain number of things I can do, and if I'm to do them I must concentrate'. If so, there must, alas, be a whole part of one's experience, of one's emotional development and all the rest of it, which must be renounced.

The consequences were bleak. 'I don't like things which interfere with one's heart strings,' he later confessed when asked why he rarely listened to music. 'It doesn't do to awaken longings that can't be fulfilled.'[30]

However, at about the time that he discarded his clarinet other longings were awakened in this intense and solitary schoolboy. He experienced the first of his extreme enthusiasms for an idealized, almost Utopian, view that he developed of a particular culture or society. On at least two occasions, this susceptibility to such idealized impressions rendered him vulnerable to profound psychological shock, when his visions were suddenly smashed on the rocks of reality. The first such instance of his idealizing occurred when he began learning German at King Edward's. In his determination to excel in the classics he had sought extra lessons in Greek, but his teachers advised that he should instead learn a modern language – and since some of the leading classical scholarship was then being produced in Germany, any would-be classicist should be able to read the language. But whatever the practical merits of learning German, Jack Powell approached his task with all the excitement that one of his favourite authors, George Borrow, a linguist, experienced when he discovered a new language and that he described in his novel, *Lavengro*. In Powell's case, the German language unleashed an emotional explosion:

I remember, as sharply as Keats recalled first looking into Chapman's Homer, the moment – it must have been in 1927 – when I opened my first German book. Here was the language I had dreamt of but never knew existed: sharp, hard, strict but with words which were romance in themselves, words in which poetry and music vibrated together.

The effect was to last for the rest of his life. 'When I speak German,' he was to reflect fifty-five years later,

I become a different person. I become a more emotional person. There is a band of expression, of temperament, what you will, for which German is a vehicle but for which Greek – though it may have been the educator of the English – is not.[31]

Jack Powell 'dived into' this new language 'like into a familiar body of water and I could swim right away'. And mingled with his love of the language was the thrill of discovering a spiritual homeland:

This linguistic experience was accompanied by all possible romantic and exciting feelings. I experienced what Thomas Carlyle and the other friends of Germany at the height of the Victorian age must have experienced. Their works came to life for me, and expressed in English what I myself wanted to say about this miracle which had occurred to me. My experience, like theirs, was two-fold: the discovery of a dual world – of fantasy and romantic magic and a world of mental strength and philosophical courage.

The first German book that he read of his own volition was Wagner's libretti, 'not exactly the highest rung of German literature but somehow still of central significance'. It was 'the springboard toward German poetry, toward Goethe, toward Heine, toward Hoelderlin, and George and to German philosophy – Fichte, Hegel, Schopenhauer ... and especially it was for me the springboard toward Nietzsche.' For the next seven years, Powell was to remain in uncritical awe of German culture. His eventual disillusionment, when it finally came, was to be shattering.[32]

Yet Powell never allowed these deep emotions to distract him from his objective of winning the scholarship that would enable him to go to Cambridge. Indeed he could not resist chasing any academic prize and became something of a 'pot hunter' at King Edward's. Besides winning the annual form prize, he twice won the Badger Prize for English Literature, and was awarded the Lee Divinity Prize and the Lightfoot Thucydides Prize. In addition to all his scholastic pursuits, Powell also performed his duties as a prefect and as Comptroller of the Cot Fund – the boys raised money each year to help finance beds for children in a local hospital. All Powell's studying only served to whet his appetite for an even harder task. He had found the existing translations of Herodotus unsatisfactory, and while still at King Edward's began working on his own version. When his retranslation of the whole of Herodotus, the historian of the fifth century BC, finally appeared some twenty years later, Powell acknowledged his debt to his mother, 'who was my first Greek teacher as well as my first teacher, and who in the earlier stages of the work assisted me substantially in checking and revision'.[33]

There was never any question that one of the brightest King Edward's classicists would study anywhere other than Trinity College, Cambridge. The two masters who were to have the most lasting effect on Powell had both been classicists at Trinity. Cary Gilson, the headmaster during the first four years of Powell's five years at King Edward's, was the fifth headmaster in succession to have been a Fellow of Trinity, and 'Duggie' Smith, Powell's classics master, had obtained his double first there. Gilson devoted his teaching of the Classical Sixth form

> to subjects outside the prescribed necessity. It was an outline of economics one term, comparative religion or the history of science another, or in a third the Epistles of St Paul. I have been astonished to discover how many of the memorable sayings and moments of those crucial years in the Sixth occurred in the extra-curricular hours with Cary Gilson.

Smith, in contrast to the headmaster, was, in Powell's time, 'quite near in age to the boys whom he taught, and the relationship was often that of an elder brother, with laughter and good fun never far below the surface'. Many years later, Powell could still picture Smith's 'peculiar habit of rubbing his gown between his knees in glee when we hit upon some specially elegant or convincing solution to a problem of grammar and criticism'. Smith also maintained the 'closest personal contact' with Trinity.[34]

Powell's exceptional industry was rewarded. The examination for a scholarship to Trinity College involved translating a passage from Bede. He translated it into Platonic Greek but still had plenty of time left. 'In the remaining hour and a half,' he later recalled, 'I tore it up and translated it again into Herodotean Greek – Ionic Greek (which I had never written before) – and then, still having time to spare, I proceeded to annotate it.' At a time when the Government awarded only about two hundred university state scholarships, Powell became both a State Scholar and a City of Birmingham Major Scholar. He later discovered, as he told the television political biographer, Michael Cockerell, that his parents had made arrangements without telling him to ensure that even if he had failed, he would none the less have been able to afford to go to Cambridge.[35]

In the autumn of 1930, aged eighteen, Powell left Birmingham to take up his place at Trinity College, Cambridge. He was already determined to become the foremost classicist, but there was another classicist by the name of Powell, a Fellow of St John's College, Oxford, who signed his articles, 'John U. Powell'. In deciding how to distinguish his own work from his near namesake's, Powell does not disguise his self-confidence as a schoolboy. 'This is going to be awkward,' he remembers thinking, 'because I am going to be a classical scholar and writing articles much better than his; I must make sure that there's no confusion between us.' From that moment onwards, Powell always wrote 'Enoch' out in full. It was to be a fortuitous decision. 'The fact that I came years later to represent a constituency in Enoch's own Black Country,' he has since explained, 'has nothing to do with it; you do get the bonus occasionally in life.'[36]

2

Scholar-Poet

He became an abiding presence, so much so that in intellectual or even moral difficulty it is the voice which I sometimes think I can hear. For there emerged from Housman's lectures a moral precept. And the moral precept is that if you don't understand, admit to yourself that you do not understand; if you have a problem, say there is a problem here which I have not solved. Do not be frightened, do not be put off because others appear not to see it, others appear not to have confronted it. Do it yourself. Apply your own mind to it.

Enoch Powell, on the life-long influence of Professor A.E. Housman's lectures at Cambridge in the early 1930s.

Loner and textual critic

The young classics scholar, J. Enoch Powell, had been primed for academic excellence, but the freshman who entered Trinity College, Cambridge, was unready for any other aspect of university life. Socially he was a fish out of water. In those days, the great majority of young men at Cambridge and Oxford (and the undergraduates were predominantly male) came from well-off families, and had attended fee-paying public schools. There was an unbridgeable gulf between those privileged students and the intelligent and intense Entrance Scholar from lower middle-class Birmingham whose knowledge of life came almost entirely from books. 'I went up to Cambridge in a sense ill-prepared,' Powell acknowledged rather wistfully in later life, during a return visit to Trinity:

I thought the only thing to do was to work. I thought that was what I was going to Cambridge for, because I never knew of anything else. That had been the terms upon which I had arrived. And I was astonished to discover fellow undergraduates at Cambridge, who had been at public schools, who were admittedly not so good as I was at Latin and Greek, but nearly as good, and they had so much else in addition. It was a lesson I never forgot.

But the lesson took a long time to have any perceptible effect on Powell's behaviour. As an undergraduate, he saw his life almost entirely 'as a simple continuation of the prize-scholarship-winning, knowledge-eating process of the working side of my school life'.[1]

Despite his evident suitability for academic study, Powell never felt that life at Cambridge was meant for him. More than thirty years after leaving Trinity, he could still remember 'the sense of ... well suffocation would hardly be too strong a word ... which I used to feel as an undergraduate when I went under the Great Gate at Trinity'. Powell always felt that he 'was going out of the world into something enclosed, that all my instincts were to get out of what was enclosed into the world'.[2]

Whatever his feelings about Cambridge, Powell knew that he had to succeed as there would be no second chance – unlike many of his contemporaries, he had neither a family business nor contacts, nor private means to depend on afterwards. He shut himself in his rooms, behind a 'sported oak' – meaning that he kept his outer door closed to indicate that he did not wish to receive visitors – and concentrated on his classical studies. The solitariness to which he had become accustomed was second nature to him, and to all intents and purposes he became a recluse. He claimed that 'this was not because I disliked my fellows', but they could have been forgiven for thinking otherwise. Old Edwardians at Cambridge had their own club, the Tudor Society, and its secretary, C.F. Evans, who was then in his second year but who had been in the Classical Sixth form with Powell, called on him in his room. 'I went to ask him to tea,' Evans recalled,

> and climbed up the stairs of those garret rooms at Trinity and knocked on the door and Powell said, 'Come in.' I opened the door and I think I'm right in saying that it was ... in the middle of November and very cold; the room was quite bare except for the College furniture; as I remember it there was no fire, there were no pictures, Powell was sitting in his overcoat with a rug across his knees and the whole of the table was ... he was surrounded by eighteenth-century folios. I said: 'Hello, Powell, would you like to come to tea?' and he said 'No.' I'd never met this response before and so to recover my wits I walked over to his mantelpiece and leant on it and took out a cigarette and he said, 'Would you mind not smoking.' And so I left.[3]

At Trinity, Powell's reclusive behaviour became legendary. He 'never dined in hall beyond the statutory number of nights', a contemporary recalled. 'He had nothing to do with the rest of us. He liked to be on his own.' His conviction that he was there to work led him to flout one of the college's hallowed social traditions. Each year, freshmen were invited by the Master's wife to dinner with her and her husband in the Master's Lodge, but when Powell's turn came in 1930 he declined on the grounds that he would be too busy working. Such self-induced isolation in a collective environment might betoken shyness. But this was not Powell's problem. He was 'terribly wrapped up in what I was doing' and he was ignorant of aspects of life that other students of his age regarded as everyday: 'college was a social life completely unfamiliar to me – even the sheer mechanics of it, of how to tie a bow tie, were unknown to me.' It was a revealing comment, and one that underlines the limiting nature of his lower middle-class upbringing, where black-tie functions were so rare as to be virtually unknown.[4]

Remarkably, for a man who was to become one of the finest parliamentary performers of his generation, he never attended a debate at the Cambridge Union. He became a life member of the Union, an option which was open to any member of the university, to humour his father, who had been anxious that he should join. He sometimes dined there and read the German newspapers. Even Powell's method of daily exercise betokened an ascetic, almost monastic approach to life. He took a regular evening walk to the railway station and back, although on Sundays he enjoyed a more scenic route along 'the Backs', where the colleges back onto the Cam, and might venture to the neighbouring village of Madingley. During his early university vacations, Powell used to take walking holidays alone in England and Wales. It is an arresting image to picture the lonely figure of this young undergraduate in the early 1930s, with his slightly stooped shoulders and earnest face peering ahead, stepping along the countryside roads at a steady $5\frac{1}{2}$ miles per hour (about half a mile an hour slower than his normal speed for short distances), often sleeping on railway platforms or in barns to save money on lodgings and eating inexpensively wherever he could. Although he travelled up to London with a companion during his second year, in the winter of 1931–32, to try and get into the Covent Garden Opera – they had to console themselves with a visit to Noël Coward's *Cavalcade* at the Drury Lane Theatre – he made few friends at Cambridge. It was not until his third year that he met Edward C. Curtis, who was at Clare College. Curtis became a life-long friend, and was to be Powell's best man and godfather to one of the Powells' daughters.[5]

Compounding Powell's social inhibition was the impact that Cambridge's formidable classicists made on a young man for whom academic achievement was the be all and end all. Cambridge was then the bastion of English classical studies, and Trinity College was revered as the acme of classical scholarship. But it was a particularly painstaking form of scholarship in which Powell was tutored, since its principal task was the restoration of surviving Greek and Latin texts that had often been corrupted during their transmission down the centuries (somewhat in the manner of Chinese whispers) to as close to their original state as possible. This approach, in which 'a formidable grasp of the language and a minute study of all available relevant manuscripts' were paramount, was epitomized by A.E. Housman, a Fellow of Trinity and Kennedy Professor of Latin at Cambridge since 1911. He is now better remembered for his poems, notably *A Shropshire Lad*, but his five-volume revised text of the works of the Latin poet, Manilius, published over a period of eighteen years, was regarded as one of the great academic feats of the day. 'Knowledge is good, method is good', Housman had once said of the qualities needed in a textual critic, 'but one thing beyond all others is necessary; and that is to have a head, not a pumpkin, on your shoulders, and brains, not pudding, in your head.' Patently, Powell passed this test. And in addition, as he noted himself, his 'habit of slow and intensive reading, not gladly missing a footnote or a misprint (and usually officiously proof-correcting, regardless of ownership), was perhaps the foundation of an early and continuing taste for textual criticism'.[6]

Powell never forgot his anguish at the reaction of his tutor, Andrew Gow – a protégé of Housman's – to the list that, as a new student, he had been required to present of his reading in his chosen field of study. 'Well, I must say,' Gow had remarked, 'for a scholar of the College [Trinity] this reading list is excessively thin.' Over thirty years later, Powell could 'still hear the drawling disgust of A.S.F. Gow ... as he surveyed the gaps in my classical reading.' This wounding criticism only intensified Powell's belief that he dare not slack. The fact that Powell was a slow reader made repairing the gaps even more demanding.[7]

The intense and solitary Powell came to regard the ascetic and increasingly frail figure of Housman, who was by then in his seventies, as something of a hero. It was an odd choice for a young undergraduate, and made all the more so by Powell's regarding Housman's chief characteristic as his 'cheerlessness' – though Powell sympathetically acknowledged it as that of a man who understood things that others did not. But Housman struck a chord with the solitary and over-conscientious young Powell. Housman's example helped him to survive his time at Cambridge, particularly to withstand the raw cold of the Fenland winter as the arctic gales blew from the North Sea across flat countryside. On even the bleakest of days, Powell used to see the aged Professor returning to climb the steps to his rooms in Whewell's Court, a gloomy neo-Gothic building on the opposite side of the street to Trinity's Great Gate, to continue his laborious work. If Housman could do it, Powell used to tell himself in self-exhortation, then so could he.[8]

Powell was spell-bound from the moment in his second year at Cambridge (the 1931–32 academic year) that he first heard Housman lecture. He never forgave his supervisor for having failed to inform him of the Professor's lectures during his first year and thereafter attended each term's twice-weekly lectures. Housman 'looked like death warmed up' as he strode down King's Parade just before ten o'clock in the morning, among the milling crowd of undergraduates, to the lecture-room. After using the window-pole to exclude any draught, Housman would begin a scholarly exposition on Latin writers such as Persius, Lucan and Horace. His lectures were better suited to his fellow dons than to students, and of his audience of between twenty and thirty, several were themselves lecturers. As a brilliant scholar, Powell relished these occasions. Housman's 'face as he read was expressionless, and the effect, especially with the heavy overhanging moustache and bald cranium, was of a voice proceeding from the mouth of one of those masks which the actors wore on the Greek tragic stage'. Housman's voice sometimes choked with emotion as he recited a poem in Latin, but he would translate it none the less. Powell was struck by 'the severity not of passionlessness, but of suppressed passion, passion for true poetry and passion for truthfulness'. The overriding impression was one of tension, between suppressed emotion and the logical analysis of a text. At the end of the lecture, which was always precisely fifty minutes in length, Housman 'donned his mortar board and stalked impassively back to his fastness above the Jesus Lane entrance to the repellent pile of Whewell's Court'.[9]

Housman's influence was to have a powerful effect on Powell for the rest of his life, as he made clear in the comment quoted at the head of this chapter. Much of what came to be regarded as Powell's approach to political discourse can be traced directly to the school of classical textual criticism at Cambridge between the wars. Under Housman's spell, Powell's forensic, textual analysis acquired a new dimension. 'For Housman textual criticism was the exercise of moral self-discipline', Powell recalled. 'The phrases remembered over the years were flashed from the inner furnace of passion for truth and logical thought, and of indignation against every interest of influence which could corrupt it.' This marrying of close analysis – whether of a classical text, a parliamentary bill, a white paper, or a speech – with an impassioned, sometimes indignant moralizing was to become Powell's trade-mark. 'Under the radiation of this display of a great critical mind in action,' Powell recalled, 'one's own powers, such as they might be, developed – above all, the spirit of bold but temperate self-reliance without which no criticism is possible.'[10]

It was Housman's voice that Powell used to hear over his shoulder:

When I've been tempted to fudge it, when I've been tempted to pretend that, 'Yes, I do understand that; yes, I do agree with that,' I've heard a kind of voice behind me, a kind of stirring, which is Housman from the lectures at Cambridge from 1930 to 1933. And that I suppose has lived with me all my life, and will die with me.

And it was Housman who, in Powell's words, 'drew out in me the consciousness that I was endowed with an instrument and the courage to use that intellectual instrument'. This lesson was one for life, 'wherever and however life was going to be lived. And the mere fact that my life was lived for forty or fifty years in politics did not make Housman more or less relevant.' But a corollary is Powell's self-confessed intellectual arrogance – as he has admitted, he has 'a strong conviction in my own capability of being right when everybody else is wrong. I have a savage reliance on the working of my own intellect, which renders me impervious to intellectual isolation.' The schoolboy and student who won all the prizes was unlikely to be an easy colleague. Housman's influence accentuated this trait. Behind Powell's dogged espousal of an unfashionable brand of Toryism many years after he left Cambridge was the same disdain for conventional wisdom that had once led Housman to denounce scornfully the belief 'that the fashion of the present, unlike all fashions heretofore, will endure perpetually and that its own flimsy tabernacle of second-hand opinions is a habitation for everlasting'.[11]

Despite Housman's reputation for demolishing other scholars, Powell, in his final year as an undergraduate, wrote to him proposing an amendment to Virgil's *Aeneid* – the epic Latin poem from which Powell was to quote some thirty-five years later in a speech that transformed his political career. In reply to the young student's letter, Housman commented: 'You have analysed the difficulties of the passage well and your emendation removes them.' Powell was never sure whether or not Housman approved of his suggestion, 'but at least it was not a put down'. Yet Powell had virtually no opportunity to learn anything in direct conversation with Housman, since in those more formal days there was almost no personal contact between a lecturer and an undergraduate. By the time that Powell had become eligible as a Fellow of Trinity to sit at High Table and join other Fellows in the Combination Room, the ageing classicist was approaching the end of his life and was uncommunicative. Their exchanges at High Table were mainly limited to Powell's requests, such as, 'I'll trouble you for the cheese, Professor'. Such comments as Housman made mainly concerned the college food, and Powell was wont to recall that 'the correct use of red pepper was the only actual piece of learning I ever imbibed from him in personal intercourse'. As to the possibility that Housman's homosexuality might have caused the older man to find the young classicist attractive, Powell was 'unaware of any such vibration'. Housman died in the spring of 1936, aged seventy-seven, while Powell was still at Trinity.[12]

Whereas Powell admired Housman's uncompromising approach, others found him arrogant and forbidding. Another Old Edwardian and Cambridge classicist, Professor F.H. Sandbach, who was a little older than Powell, felt that Housman had a bad influence upon Latin studies because his remoteness and ferocity frightened off younger classicists and led them to become Hellenists as opposed to Latinists. But as far as Powell was concerned, Housman's 'gibbetings always bore a moral message: the dangling corpses were specimens of intellectual sloth, of thoughtless prejudice, of arrogant pomposity, of blatant bad logic, of dishonesty in exposition'. Many years later, Powell's own intellectual arrogance, his intolerance of what he regarded as these same qualities of sloth, prejudice, pomposity or dishonesty, and the unsparing ferocity of his criticisms, seemed to have a similar effect among his fellow Conservatives. Like Housman, he attracted some devotees and disciples, but others appeared wary of him.[13]

'Compulsions'

Although there had been a revival of interest in *A Shropshire Lad* during the 1920s, and Housman's *Last Poems* had also sold well, Powell was ignorant of his Professor's poetry when he first arrived at university. However, he became inspired to compose poetry during the seven years that he eventually spent at Cambridge. But he was not merely copying his hero, and later wrote of the 'compulsions under which they were written'. Although Powell thought that Housman 'was greater as a Latin textual critic – greater in intellectual achievement and in the moral dimension – than as poet', there are similarities between Housman's poems and Powell's 'short lyrics', both in their ordered style and in some of the subject-matter. This is not so surprising, since Housman acknowledged among his main influences *Ballads from Herodotus*, Heine and Shakespeare, and much of his other reading also became familiar to Powell. Perhaps Powell also felt a personal affinity because Housman had been born and brought up near the Worcestershire town of Bromsgrove, only ten miles or so over the Lickey Hills and a few stops along the old Midland railway line from Powell's King's Norton home. He was not conscious of Housman's having had a West Midlands accent, but there was an echo of Powell's own childhood in Housman's images of Shropshire, the county from which Ellen Powell's forebears had hailed and that Powell used to explore with his parents.[14]

During the 1930s, Powell found an emotional release in composing poetry. As Powell later reflected, 'In Tennyson's and Housman's Cambridge, I was not ashamed to break off my work on Greek lexicography to "cry out" in the vein they had made available, as a hungry workman might lay aside his tools to snatch a mouthful of bread and cheese.' What particularly caused Powell to 'cry out' was his need to give expression to 'the sheer almost physical agony which is caused in youth by the passage of time, when the turning of spring into summer arouses pain as lively as the pain of toothache.' His vision of the succession of the seasons as 'a recurrent inescapable catastrophe, which sweeps away what is young and beautiful, and what is beautiful because it is young', inspired his early poetic lyrics:

> Through all the burning summertime
>   And through the day's decrease
> And through the months of mist and rime
>   I saw and held my peace.
>
> But when the spring to hill and coomb
>   Returned in warmth and rain,
> The torture of the trees in bloom
>   Stung me to speech again.[15]

This opening poem of the 'fifty short lyrics' that comprised his *First Poems* published in 1937, gives a striking echo of Housman's poem, the second in *A Shropshire Lad*, that begins, 'Loveliest of trees, the cherry now / Is hung with bloom along the bough'. In later life, Powell nominated Housman's poem as his favourite lines. Although acknowledging that it 'may be conventional and I fear that it "dates" me', none the less it was 'redolent for me of the memory of the interwar 1930s, when life seemed so evanescent and so tragic'. As he commented after his emotional reciting of the poem during a radio programme when he was in his eighties, he found it 'irresistible' – for Powell, 'it says it all'. Appropriately, the *First Poems* were 'turned into cherry trees', although they have, in Powell's words, long since 'gone the way of all cherry trees'. He had been lent a hundred pounds to meet the cost of printing by a senior colleague at Trinity, the Rev. F.W. Simpson, who, when in due course repaid, 'applied the money to planting cherry trees along the Coton footpath behind the Backs'.[16]

'In Mr Powell's verse', noted *The Times Literary Supplement* of his second collection, published in 1939, 'lyrical feeling, reflection, and an epigrammatic conciseness are pleasantly balanced, and he is particularly happy perhaps in saluting the blossoms of spring'. But *Casting Off, and Other Poems* contained some love poems, including these highly erotic lines:

> I did not speak, but when I saw you turn
> And cross your right leg on your left, and fold
> Your hands around your knee, I felt a flow
> Of white-hot lava seething up the old
> Volcano-shaft. That selfsame attitude,
> Though not of yours, it was which long ago
> Fired me, an innocent, unknowing boy,
> And led me on to sin and on to learn
> And onwards to the very fount of woe ...

Powell regarded this as 'a perfect love poem', and has said that it was written, 'as an exercise', to nobody in particular, and was a work of the imagination. But its subject-matter is lust rather than love. Sex is presented as a sin, and there is obvious annoyance at a lack of self-control. According to Powell, however, he had no social life as an undergraduate and felt that women 'didn't exist'. He even wondered what they were doing at university, because – as he asserted in a caricature of sexual stereotyping – 'the analytical faculty is underdeveloped in women'.[17]

Powell said of Housman's poems that they afford 'irrefutable evidence' of his 'emotional homosexuality', as they often depend 'for full intelligibility upon homosexual implications'. Some of Powell's poetry suggests sexual ambiguity:

> While yesteryear I tarried
>   In a garden in the south,
> I met a youth who carried
>   A rose-bud in his mouth
>
> I gave him chase and caught him,
>   And would not set him free,
> But held him and besought him
>   To give the flower to me.

> He smiled, and broke a petal
> And laid it in my hand –
> It seared like molten metal,
> And here is yet the brand.

Powell was steeped in classical literature, and the Greeks idealized male beauty and composed homo-erotic poetry. Some of his poems reflect this influence, but as the *TLS* reviewer observed, 'his more personal lyrics are apt to be too private and confidential to communicate their feeling to the outsider'. Powell's 'simple and sensitive' verse reflected Housman's style, but he failed to express personal feeling as effectively as his mentor.[18]

As an undergraduate, Powell remained as besotted with Germanic culture as he had been while at school. The magic he sensed in Germany was reinforced by the academic imperative of knowing German. According to his academic supervisor, Powell 'had already something of the air of a German *gelehrte* [scholar] and no doubt he realized early that a serious scholar must keep abreast of the Germans.' His proficiency in German was outstanding, because it was the language of his spiritual homeland. 'I used simultaneously not only the methods of German linguistics for my work as a classicist,' he recalled, 'but I also used German to express my thoughts. My first contributions in the classics were written in German and appeared in German [professional] publications.'[19]

Even Powell's choice of music was Germanic. For some relaxation from his academic work while at Trinity, Powell used to listen to Beethoven and Wagner. In Beethoven, he found the musical counterpart to Goethe and Carlyle, recognizing in his compositions 'that marriage of logical statement and intellectual precision with the ardour and infinitude of Romantic poetry which haunted me like a passion in all things German'. After the 1930s, Powell never felt that he had sufficient time to devote to listening to music. His appreciation of music was to remain limited to the Germanic composers. When, more than fifty years later, he appeared on *Desert Island Discs*, his eight choices of records comprised four pieces by Wagner, three by Beethoven and one by Haydn.[20]

It was during this exploration of German culture, that 'like some traveller who, in the moonlight clearing of a forest, comes across another human being pursuing the same journey,' Powell 'fell in at this point along my road with a certain young scholar of my own age.' He had discovered the work of Friedrich Nietzsche. The German thinker 'was destined to be my companion through every published scrap of his writing from the opening bars of *The Birth of Tragedy* right on into the ultimate explosion into insanity of *Ecce Homo*'. Powell had strong affinities with the German scholar. Nietzsche had become a Professor at the age of twenty-four, an achievement that the brilliant and self-confident young Powell sought to emulate. The German thinker's declaration, 'God is dead!' also chimed with Powell – his mother had lost her religious belief, and Powell had come to regard himself as an atheist. Nietzsche's views on the development of human culture were based on his analysis of the history of Greek tragedy, an approach that had resonance for any classicist. And his belief in the superiority of action over discussion had obvious attraction for a young man anxious to escape Cambridge. Powell appeared to echo Nietzsche's 'morality of strenuousness' in one of his early poems, that was later to be seized on and quoted against him – although the final lines suggest not so much Nietzsche as Powell's characteristic expression of the sheer, physical agony of youth:

> I hate the ugly, hate the old,
>   I hate the lame and weak,
> But more than all I hate the dead
> That lie so still in their earthen bed
>   And never dare to rise.
>
> I love only the strong and bold,
>   The flashing eye, the reddening cheek,
> But more than all I love the fire
> In youthful limbs, that wakes desire
>   And never satisfies.[21]

Like Nietzsche, Powell was to become disillusioned with German culture. But as regards any lasting influence, Nietzsche's belief that 'This world is the will to power and nothing else besides', finds a strong echo in Powell's views in later life on issues such as race relations and Northern Ireland. Unlike many other British politicians and commentators, who tend to see such problems as more complex phenomena, he has been uncompromising in viewing them first and foremost as intense struggles for power.[22]

Powell's intellectual brilliance and his exceptional power of application yielded as rich a harvest of academic prizes at Cambridge as it had at King Edward's. In 1931, he achieved the rare distinction for an undergraduate of winning the Craven scholarship for classicists, thereby supplementing his income of £300 a year from his existing scholarship with an additional £100. The award also brought Powell to the attention of a wider public for the first time, since the *Birmingham Post*, the respected morning newspaper in his native city, devoted a substantial report to his achievement. He was also Percy Pemberton prizeman, Porson prizeman, Yeats prizeman and Lees Knowles exhibitioner – the prestigious Porson prize for Greek verse was commemorated by an engraving of a Greek scholar that Powell was later to keep above his desk at his South Eaton Place home. In the Classical Tripos, Part I, Powell won a distinction in Greek and Latin. His winning the Members' prize for Latin prose and the First Chancellor's Classical Medal as top classicist were among the achievements that led, in 1932, to the granting of a half-day's holiday at King Edward's. In March 1933, he was awarded the Cromer Greek essay prize of the British Academy, having written on the subject of 'Thucydides, his moral and historical principles and their influence in later antiquities'. The same year, he first caught the attention of a Tory leader. As Powell read his winning composition as Sir William Browne medallist in the Cambridge Senate House, the then Chancellor of the University and Lord President of the Council in the National Government, Stanley Baldwin, commented in an aside to the Master of Trinity, Sir J.J. Thomson, 'Powell reads as if he understands'.[23]

In addition to the extra effort required to win all these prizes, Powell had continued working on his re-translation of Herodotus, the project that he had begun before leaving King Edward's, and completed his first draft before graduating. None the less and predictably, three months later in his final examinations, Powell gained a first class with distinction, as he had in Part One of the Classical Tripos. His graduation from Cambridge University was a proud day both for him and, above all, for his elementary school-teacher parents. Despite his scholarly pre-eminence, Powell had long looked forward to leaving Cambridge, but his departure was not yet imminent.

Under the shadow of war

Powell's distinction as an undergraduate, as shown by the array of prizes that he won and his single-minded dedication to his academic work, appeared to cast him as the perfect candidate for continuing at Cambridge and becoming a don. Yet he had always felt that he was in an enclosed world at Trinity. As he later commented, 'the question of a classical career never really existed in my mind'. While a student, he began looking for a career in the diplomatic service, although his mind was not set on 'a diplomatic career specially, but something, for God's sake, outside' – the possibility that the young Powell might have entered the Foreign Office, with unknowable consequences for his future, is an intriguing thought.[24]

Despite Powell's impatience to escape the cloistered world of Cambridge, the 'outside' had to wait a few more years. After his graduation in the summer of 1933, he stayed at Cambridge for a further academic year as a research scholar and Craven Student, and in October 1934, aged twenty-two, was elected a Fellow of Trinity College – an honour that was again recognized by the granting of a half-day's holiday at his old school. 'If I can take off the shelf being a Fellow of Trinity,' he remembered thinking, 'very well then I will, so be it.'[25]

Powell contributed to German scholarly periodicals – '*Das Niltal bei Herodot*' was published in *Hermes* in 1933 – but in the summer of 1934, he suffered a devastating psychological blow. It was to prompt the first of several great reappraisals that Powell was to undertake during his life. On each occasion, one set of ideals was abandoned, and an opposing set of beliefs was adopted and maintained with the same deep-dyed conviction and inexhaustible vigour with which he had upheld the first set. On Sunday 1 July, news reached Britain of the 'Night of the Long Knives', Hitler's purge of the Brown Shirts, his radical storm-troopers, and the assassination of their leader, Ernst Roehm.

The British press was full of the details – Hitler's allegations of homosexuality among the Brown Shirts, the shooting of Roehm and the dozens of arrests and summary executions. Powell's Germanic idyll, that had entranced him ever since he first read the German language seven years earlier, was shattered. As Nietzsche had become disillusioned with German culture in the 1870s, so Powell became disillusioned sixty years later. Powell was on a walking holiday with a friend in Cornwall when he first heard of the atrocity. 'I still remember clearly how I sat for hours in a state of shock,' Powell later reflected,

> shock which you experience when, around you, you see the debris of a beautiful building in which you have lived for a long time ... So it had all been illusion, all fantasy, all a self-created myth. Music, philosophy, poetry, science and the language itself – everything was demolished, broken to bits on the cliffs of a monstrous reality. The spiritual homeland had not been a spiritual homeland after all, since nothing can be a homeland, let alone a spiritual homeland, where there is no justice, where justice does not reign.[26]

Overnight, Powell was left only with his 'geographical homeland' of England, but realized that this itself was threatened. It was a watershed in Powell's early life. His patriotism, that had been strong within him ever since childhood, became the sole focus for his deep sense of emotional commitment that had previously been shared with his former spiritual homeland. Certainly by 1935, 'what mattered to me, more than anything that could happen to me personally was the outcome of that war that was to come for the existence of the nation'. At this stage, Powell 'saw the nation in the framework of the British Empire', but it was from this period that the young man who had hitherto been preoccupied through his classical studies 'with mankind and their thoughts but at a distance of time', now became equally concerned with 'this nation, Britain, my nation'.[27]

What was happening in Europe, Powell realized, was bound to come to war. He saw 'that it would happen very soon. About the enemy and about what was at stake there was no doubt. The enemy was to be Germany and at stake was the freedom of England. From then on Germany, although still an abstraction, was for me the enemy.' He redirected his understanding of German culture into preparing for the conflict that he believed was unavoidable: 'And everything which I knew about her [i.e. German] language, her spirit and her literature remained only material with which to comprehend the enemy, which one needs to be able to stand your ground in a fight'.[28]

Powell was better informed than many people about events abroad during the mid-thirties, because his various awards and scholarships had enabled him to spend some time on the Continent, where he visited museums and historic monuments, and libraries where he tracked down and studied items for his work on Herodotus. He also learned more about contemporary events as a result of attending international conferences on classical studies and through the contacts he made with European scholars. It was while visiting Rome in

1936 to read manuscripts in the Vatican Library that he met H. Andrew Freeth, almost his exact contemporary and also from Birmingham. The young artist had been awarded a 'Prix de Rome' scholarship. They became lifelong friends, and Freeth's portraits of Powell give a good impression of the emerging man.[29]

Powell's sensitivity to international events surfaced in a lecture on 'The War and its aftermath in their influence on Thucydidean studies', that he delivered to the Classical Association in January 1936 and that was reported in *The Times* under the headline, 'Thucydides in the Trenches: Hitler as Pericles'. According to Powell, the Germans had found Greek civilization in general, and Thucydides in particular, 'exceptionally congenial':

> The intensely political outlook of Thucydides may be made serviceable to a doctrine which asserts the absolute domination of the State over every phase of individual existence; and, as the more striking figures of Caesar and Augustus had already been captured as prototypes by Mussolini, Hitler might well be made to look very like Pericles – or Pericles, rather, to look like Hitler.

In contrast to other branches of classical research, the study of Thucydides had not suffered by the 1914–18 War. 'Many a pocket edition of Thucydides', Powell testified 'from personal information, went into the trenches on both sides of the line in the late war.'[30]

For more than five years, from the age of twenty-two, Powell 'lived under the shadow of the conviction that the hostilities temporarily suspended in November 1918 would presently be renewed on a similar scale of brutality and intensity'. However, as Powell was to be reminded by his visit to the 1995 London revival of Noël Coward's early 1930s' musical, *Cavalcade*, most of his fellow countrymen 'still saw 1914–18 as a climax and trusted it would be a turning point'. '*That* was the England which welcomed *Cavalcade*', Powell noted, 'England in a world where war was no longer possible'. Powell held the opposite perception at the time. Some contemporaries who shared his oppressive awareness of the inevitability of war pursued an aimless hedonism, while others took to campaigning against appeasement, and in some cases, fighting in the Spanish Civil War. The Italian invasion of Ethiopia in the autumn of 1935 almost led Powell to abandon Cambridge and volunteer on the side of the Ethiopians. In 1936, he offered his services to the Commander of the Officer Training Corps at Cambridge, but had to admit that he had received no previous training. He found the Baldwin and Chamberlain governments 'utterly unattractive' and was appalled that his compatriots could remain 'wilfully blind'. But the nearest he came to any radical gesture was in 1937 at a Trinity College Feast. When the guest of honour stated that 'Our government is doing its best to prevent war', Powell shouted from the Fellows' table, 'but we *want* war'. And during the same year, driving to Boar's Hill, near Oxford, with the philosopher, Gilbert Murray, Powell told him, 'There's no hope for us unless we go to war with Germany.' Powell recalled Murray looking him straight in the eyes and replying, 'I think so too.'[31]

Powell's fatalism failed to douse the emotional fire that raged within him at the prospect of war. His early poems were about 'the pangs of growing old', and after the events of 1934 this human predicament had an added poignancy:

> To-night on years I shall not see
> My thought more warmly runs:
> Clearer to-night is borne to me
> The murmur of the guns.

'Youth doomed by the passage of time was subsumed by youth doomed to die as youth not many years before had died in Flanders,' he later recalled. 'The young soldier or soon-to-be soldier was its type.' The influence of Housman, whose poems celebrated the soldiers who had left his beloved Shropshire for the Boer War, was unmistakable. Housman had expressed in *A Shropshire Lad* his envy of 'The lads that will die in their glory and never be old'. Powell, echoing these sentiments, planned to volunteer the moment war came and was convinced this 'meant that I would not survive'. His *First Poems* included the following verses:

> With twinkling eye the cloudless sky
> Looks through the sombre larch,
> And rotting mould is turned to gold
> By suns of March.
>
> Now tame and wild are all with child;
> With vital hope and fire
> The world is rife; yet not for life
> Is my desire,
>
> But first to close the eyes of those
> Who brought me to the light,
> And then before my youth is o'er
> To die in fight.[32]

In 1935, and as anxious as ever to leave Cambridge, he began applying for the top posts in other universities. His warning of his intention to enlist on the outbreak of war raised some eyebrows, but greater surprise was caused by his seeking professorships when he was still so young. As far as Powell was concerned, Nietzsche had won his first chair at the age of twenty-four, and he could see no reason why he should not do the same. 'Never, I think, having been guilty of underestimating my claims,' he later observed, 'I didn't consider myself suitable for being a Lecturer or a Reader. So I thought I'd better get a chair. I put in for Professorships and quite a number of them went jolly well until they discovered that I was only twenty-three, and then there was a marked coolness.' Although he failed to emulate Nietzsche, his ambition was not denied for long. He was twenty-five when, in the autumn of 1937, the University of Sydney appointed him Professor of Greek.[33]

Powell's main research project was a lexicon to Herodotus that would serve as a new dictionary to the writings of the ancient historian. Powell was encouraged by his senior colleagues and former supervisors at Trinity, Gow and Ernest Harrison, who promised him help from the college's Rouse Ball Fund towards publishing the book. But while wrestling with this demanding task, he contributed articles to academic journals, both English and German, on an array of subjects.[34]

When Powell embarked on his new lexicon to Herodotus, he was already translating the Rendel Harris Papyri. He had first learned of these papyri (manuscripts on papyrus) in 1932, from Dr James Rendel Harris, a noted archaeologist, who had acquired them in Egypt some twenty years earlier. The papyri were written in Greek and dated from 200 to 400 AD, but little was known about their contents. By the time that Powell heard of them, they had lain virtually forgotten in the library of Woodbrooke College, in Selly Oak in his native Birmingham, only a couple of miles from King's Norton. At Rendel Harris's prompting, Powell proposed to the trustees of the college that he should translate the papyri and that they should be mounted and the translations published. The trustees agreed and Powell's work revealed that the papyri consisted of contemporary documents, including census lists, contracts and tax receipts, that provided fresh insight into the society of the period. By the spring of 1935 Powell was able to deliver a paper on the papyri to the Congresso Internazionale di Papirologia at Florence. The following year, his translation was published.[35]

On Sundays, Powell used to let himself into the magnificent Wren library at Trinity with the Fellows' key, and look through the collection of manuscripts. He discovered a Welsh medieval text that intrigued him, and set about studying the text, a task that led him, unaided, to develop his rudimentary knowledge of Welsh into a good understanding of medieval Welsh. As a conscientious academic, he reported his find in May 1936 in the relevant journal, *The Bulletin of the Board of Celtic Studies*, and wrote a further contribution in November 1937. His work excited the interest of the Welsh scholar, Stephen Williams, of Swansea University, who contacted Powell. Their collaboration was interrupted by Powell's going abroad and the coming of war, but finally, in 1942, they published *Llyfr Blegywryd*, a study of the laws of the Welsh king, Howell the Good.[36]

All the while, Powell continued his voracious pursuit of knowledge. He later remembered 'the excitement with which, as a Fellow of Trinity as yet untinctured with economics', he first read the *Essay on the Principle of Population*, written in 1798, by Thomas Malthus, a Fellow of Jesus College, Cambridge, and a wrangler, 'upon the recommendation of an older member of High Table, also a wrangler, who had retired after a career as a judge in India'. Malthus propounded an iron law that the potential increase in population was geometric, but of resources at best only arithmetic, and advanced the grim thesis that the only alternative to 'prudence' in maintaining a balance between a society's population and its resources was 'misery'.[37]

The work of Malthus was a stark induction into political economy, and it is a striking thought that within a stone's throw of Trinity was King's College, whose First Bursar, the economist, John Maynard Keynes, published his seminal work, *The General Theory*, in 1936. Keynes's reputation as the scourge of *laissez-faire* theory and conventional 'balanced budget' economics had already spread beyond the academic world following his critique of Britain's ill-fated return to the Gold Standard in 1925, *The Economic Consequences of Mr Churchill*, and his work on *The Yellow Book* in 1929. Yet Powell, the young classicist at Trinity whose knowledge of political economy at this time barely extended beyond Malthus was, less than twenty years later, to emerge as a fierce critic of Keynesian economics. His readiness to criticize Keynesian economics, when he had no training as an economist, reflected his self-confessed intellectual arrogance, encouraged by his Housman-like refusal to accept what others said at face value. Powell's training as a classicist reinforced these traits. 'The distance lends not proverbial enchantment, but universality', he once said of having studied Greek and Latin civilization and literature: 'if they, who are so remote, so different, are nevertheless so much the same, then indeed here is humanity itself, eternally unchanging, displayed before our gaze and speaking to our minds and hearts.'[38]

Finally, in the autumn of 1937, Powell completed his new lexicon of Herodotus. His contact with German classicists had provided a major breakthrough in May 1935, when he acquired the entire collection of word-slips on Herodotus that had been compiled during 1912–14 by Ludwig Kalpars and Fritz Nawak. Their scholarship speeded Powell's daunting task of noting every occurrence of every word or name used by Herodotus, and providing a translation and references classified by meaning and construction. Powell devised an entire system of signs to indicate variants, spurious words, and so on. His work was made more demanding by including not only the accepted texts of Herodotus, but also the various versions that Powell had studied in the libraries of Florence and Rome.[39]

Powell's exhaustive *Lexicon to Herodotus* was published by the Cambridge University Press in 1938, replacing the only other known lexicon, a German work, that Powell derided as a 'pretence' because it ignored 'more than twelve hundred words used by Herodotus'. The self-confident disdain that he showed for an unsatisfactory work had been the hallmark of his late mentor, Housman. The response to the lexicon among Powell's colleagues was more qualified. Conceding that it was 'a very valuable and much needed tool for scholars', one classicist dismissively observed that 'it demanded punctilious accuracy and long labour rather than originality'. But Powell, in his meticulous concern to establish an accurate foundation for understanding Herodotus, had adhered rigorously to the tenets of classical study that had been exemplified by Housman.[40]

Pacific perspective

In February 1938, Powell embarked on the gruelling journey by air to Australia, eventually arriving 'by the first flying boat to come through with passengers to Singapore, then on by Qantas de Havilland to Sydney – fourteen days from Southampton, not counting stops for engine-trouble.' He spent the time reading *Ecce Homo*. As he later told the political biographer, Michael Cockerell, the journey was a revelation and gave him a lesson in imperial geography, as he saw the British Empire spread out in front of him. Landing five times a day, nearly always on British territory, was an experience that he was never to forget. Although Powell's imperialism had been stirred, his mind at this stage was still dominated by the impending conflict that he foresaw in Europe. The certainty of his conviction and his determination to 'wear the King's uniform' shook his new acquaintances. 'I still remember the look on the Vice-Chancellor's face,' he later recalled, 'when, at my first interview with him, I told him I intended to leave the day the United Kingdom declared war.' Powell vividly recaptured his feeling that he was alone in detecting an almost physical sensation: 'I felt I could hear the German divisions marching across Europe and I could hear this drumming coming through the earth and coming up again in Australia, where no one else could hear it.' The month following his departure from Britain brought the *Anschluss* as Hitler's troops occupied Austria.[41]

Powell sought, during his inaugural lecture as Professor of Greek at Sydney on 7 May 1938, to show the relevance of classical scholarship to the modern world. He readily accepted that the purpose of teaching Greek was not to produce increasing numbers of classicists. 'The true Greek textual critic is so excessively rare a bird,' the twenty-five-year-old Professor asserted, 'that Trinity College itself has hardly produced more than half a dozen of them in three centuries' – with an implication that despite his stringent taxonomy he might be included among the select few. Instead, he identified the benefits of studying Greek irrespective of whether or not it led to an academic career. Essentially, Powell portrayed Greek scholarship as a powerful antidote to the poisons of the modern world. As he caustically observed, 'We do not live in a world where independent judgment is a superfluity or healthy scepticism a disadvantage.' And he launched into a powerful condemnation of the contemporary political scene and its values:

> Day by day the newspapers of all allegiances present their readers with the statement, in almost so many words, that black is white; and only too many of those readers are thoughtless or trusting enough to accept the perilous falsehood as truth. Year after year political parties secure a return to power by promising the electorate that they will do what any one of those electors, with a few minutes of clear and dispassionate reflection, could perceive to be either impossible or disadvantageous. Stranger still, the world has recently been treated for nearly a decade to the unusual spectacle of a great

empire deliberately taking every possible step to secure its own destruction, because its citizens were so obsessed by prejudice, or incapable of thinking for themselves, as never to perform the few logical steps necessary for proving that they would shortly be involved in a *guerre à l'outrance* which could be neither averted nor escaped.

Although Powell was to decide to enter politics only after his subsequent experiences of war and the Raj, his eventual abandonment of academic life is understandable in the light of his heart-felt diatribe against what passed during the 1930s for press reporting, political leadership and public understanding. It was also in Sydney that Powell had his first experience as a radio pundit, when the Australian Broadcasting Commission gave him his own regular half-hour talk about 'antiquity in the news'.[42]

Powell later claimed that he 'fell in love with Australia', but there was never any question in his mind of his settling there for any length of time, as he could have done. He was homesick – 'the dull pang I had known and shared in Sydney University ... the heartache of the exile, the oppressive sense of being remote, so remote, from everything that ultimately mattered, from all that gave one birth.' Within a year of his arrival in Sydney, he had been appointed to a chair in England – he was due to take up his post as Professor of Greek and Classical Literature at Durham in 1940. During his year and a half in Australia – 'those few months of crowded experience' – Powell astonished his new pupils by his enthusiasm for the outdoors, and for the outback. 'When a Greek class went uninstructed one Monday morning,' he later recounted, 'because the professor had been "bushed" and had to spend the night in a cave by a gumstick fire, more were surprised by the taste for exploration than by the getting lost.' His missionary zeal as a classicist took him round New South Wales in term-time, and round the continent in vacations. 'Unless there were unintentional omission,' he recalled, 'every school where Greek was taught, or ever had been taught, was visited.' In little over a year, he reckoned that he had made friends with all his classical colleagues in Australia's other five universities in the 1930s – Adelaide, Brisbane, Hobart, Melbourne, Perth. Yet the new environment had not fundamentally changed Powell. He was still neither outgoing nor sociable, and at Sydney he was generally regarded as a lonely and rather eccentric figure.[43]

Until war came, Powell continued his duties as a classical scholar, and in 1939, his *History of Herodotus* and his translation of *Herodotus, Book VIII* appeared. In his preface to the former study, Powell emulated Housman's disdain for some other scholars. 'As I care more about the soundness of my reasoning and conclusions, acknowledgement to predecessors is rare,' he wrote, and added that, 'I have, besides, profited much more often from their mistakes than their successes.' Yet he was under 'no illusions about the unpopularity to which a work of dissection is doomed, in England especially', and confidently expected that he would find himself 'face-to-face with the whole forces of prejudice and thoughtlessness'. Even as an academic, it seems,

Powell cast himself in the role of the persecuted loner, ploughing his furrow for truth. The *Classical Review* found that in the *History of Herodotus*, Powell's 'reasoning is subtle and compact and the conclusions are stated with admirable clarity'. Although it was 'open to doubt' whether Powell had always been as careful as he claimed 'to distinguish between possible, probable, and certain inferences', the reviewer none the less concluded that his work 'will certainly form the basis of all future study of the subject'.[44]

Powell made innovations in his teaching in a way that would have been unimaginable at Cambridge. Although beginners' classes in Greek might contain up to thirty or forty students, only ten to a dozen students entered for the honours degree, and he therefore converted his lectures 'into informal encounters between students and professor'. Powell had to admit that the 'going was heavy at first'. But he claimed that his students came to enjoy sessions at which they began with a Greek text that contained a single corruption, 'and then, picking on one student, not necessarily the brightest, take him on from one deduction to another, always asking questions but never answering them, until he produced the emendation which restored the sense and explained the error'.[45]

But this ordeal appears to have been less popular with those students who had no intention of devoting their lives to textual criticism of Greek – especially since Powell seems to have chosen them as his victims. 'Just out of nappies and as arrogant as hell', was the verdict passed on the earnest, young English professor by one such student, Gough Whitlam, later Prime Minister of Australia, who gave up Powell's lectures because they were 'as dry as dust'. Whitlam is also credited with having dubbed Powell as a 'textual pervert'. This latter epithet reflected Powell's awkwardness with women students – the trait of an only male-child, who between the ages of thirteen and eighteen attended an all-male scholastic hot-house where relations with girls were actively discouraged, and who had subsequently spent seven years at all-male Trinity. Curiously, however, Powell made a lasting impact on Sydney by persuading Princess Radziwill to sell to the university 'a replica of the famous monument of Lysicrates, the so-called lantern of Diogenes, which an Athenian erected to commemorate his provision of prize-winning plays'.[46]

During the winter of 1938–39 Powell returned to Britain to make arrangements to take up his professorship at Durham at the start of 1940. He took the opportunity to make a brief visit to Germany, and more than forty years later was able to recall 'my sensation of embarrassment on producing a British passport at the German frontier in December 1938'. It was less than three months since Neville Chamberlain and Adolf Hitler had signed their agreement at Munich, and a month since the *Kristallnacht* attacks on Jews in Germany had made cruel mockery of the British Prime Minister's boast of having brought back 'peace with honour'. While in Germany, Powell made a point of visiting Paul Maas, the Jewish-German classicist, whom he had first met in Florence in 1935 and who had become a friend. Powell helped obtain a

British visa for Maas through the British consul in Berlin. Maas delayed using it until the last minute, arriving in Britain on 31 August 1939.[47]

Under the shadow of war, Powell's 'compulsions' to write poetry had continued, and were if anything intensified by his sense of exile. 'All this mass of painful emotion struggling into verse', as he later recalled, had 'crossed the world ... to Australia, not undiminished, but rather heightened by the sensation of living amongst those to whom the sound of impending doom appeared to be inaudible.' In Powell's second collection of poems, *Casting Off, and Other Poems*, published in 1939, 'the backdrop of an Asiatic as well as an Australasian tapestry largely replaced the English scenery of *First Poems*'. On the 6th of June that same year, the bayoneting to death of an Englishman, R.M. Tinkler, in Tientsin by the Japanese in the course of the Sino-Japanese war, provoked Powell to produce one of his most bitter condemnations of his country's craven attitude towards foreign aggression. But at the same time, Powell sensed that the tragedy had brought the war he had long expected a step nearer:

> Murdered, deny who can,
> Here lies an Englishman;
> The steel that through him ran
> Was tempered in Japan.
>
> Who then the murderer?
> England, that would not stir,
> Not though he died for her;
> England, the slumberer.
>
> His cry she would not hear
> Because insensate fear
> Had stopped the mother's ear;
> But now revenge is near,
>
> For while his land forgets
> And bends the knee to threats,
> His vengeful spirit whets
> The German bayonets.[48]

'One never knows', Powell recalled of the outbreak of the Second World War, 'exactly how that which is inevitable actually starts.' When Germany's invasion of Poland finally triggered the war that he had long foreseen on 3 September 1939, Powell was 'still on board ship, coming across to Australia from New Zealand', where he had been on leave. He was anxious that nothing should prevent him from returning home to fight. He resigned his chair and managed to get on the flying boat back to Britain. His Australian sojourn was at an end. 'One last picture of all is cast on the screen,' he later wrote as he reflected on his memories: 'evening at Darwin, huge hermit crabs on the beach, the gaunt deserted canning factory of Vesteys, the "digger" hat and bayonet of a sentry. The aircraft which took off a few minutes after was flying towards the war.'[49]

But the perspective of the world as viewed from Sydney was now imprinted in Powell's mind, and was to have a crucial bearing on his future career. As he later explained, 'The familiar 1914–18 shape of the impending doom I now perceived increasingly in terms of the Pacific'. And this new perception was given emotional force during Powell's homeward flight, 'after my last parting at Changi airfield in Singapore in 1939 from a younger friend who was in fact, as we foreknew that he would be, killed by the Japanese on the Johore Straits in 1942'.[50]

3

A Purpose in Life

But then I woke, and recollection came
That I for ever and alone remain
On this side of the separating flame.
Enoch Powell, *Dancer's End*, 1951.

'With hope no more denied'

For Powell, the war came as 'an almost unhoped for release and relief', after years in which he 'had feared that Britain would go under without fighting, that the steam-roller would drive over us and that we would find means of submission'. If Britain went down, it would at least now be with a fight, and he would have the chance to put on the uniform in which he thought he would probably be killed. On his return from Sydney he visited Cambridge, and in the quadrangle of Pembroke College bumped into a couple of young dons, who were surprised when he told them that he had quit his chair in Australia in order to fight. Powell's explosion of relief at the prospect of active service was expressed in a remarkable poem that he had written, in which he universalized his personal feelings and likened men joining up at the outbreak of war to 'bridegrooms going to meet their brides':

The fisher lays aside the hook,
    The farmer leaves the plough,
The student rises from his book:
    Their day and hour is now.

Their faces all, both man and boy,
    With a lover's flush are fired;
They haste with swinging steps of joy
    To meet their long-desired;

And every eye is glistening
    With hope no more denied;

> For now the marriage-morn will bring
> The bridegroom to the bride.

'That's how joining up was to me,' he recalled, but in his exaltation there was little recognition that others might have accepted their duty to fight with very heavy hearts – particularly those who, unlike this ascetic bachelor, were having to bid farewell to their flesh-and-blood brides.[1]

On 20 October 1939, Powell enlisted as a private in the Royal Warwickshires, the same regiment in which his father had been a volunteer. But he was almost thwarted in his ambition, since the lack of immediate action during the 'phoney war' had led the authorities only to recruit men who had received some military training. Powell, who had declined to join his school's Officer Training Corps, did not come into this category. However, he had heard that Australians were exempted from this rule as their High Commission had intervened to ease the plight of those who had sought to enlist and who were now unable to make ends meet. Powell duly passed himself off as an Australian, obtained the necessary certificate and, in keeping with the terms of their exemption, was accepted immediately at the lowest rank. Had Powell waited, with his academic qualifications he would have been virtually guaranteed a higher rank, but he wanted to begin as an ordinary soldier. 'I enjoyed best of all being a private soldier,' he later recalled, 'It's the nicest thing there is to be.'[2]

'It was with a sense of joy that I managed to put on the King's coat,' Powell remembered. But his joy was not only because he now had the chance to fight, and to die, for his country: in addition, this temperamentally isolated personality had a seemingly paradoxical desire for belonging to corporate institutions. He loved and honoured his school and his college, and likewise now felt pride for his regiment. 'I found that I enjoyed the Army,' he explained. 'I enjoyed its discipline; I enjoyed its institutionality; the framework in which men understand one another because they live subject to the same conventions, the same rules. It's the kind of environment in which I've always flourished – Commons, college, or regiment.'[3]

How to explain this loner's love of the corporate body and his sense that, for him, 'being shoulder to shoulder with other human beings is very powerful'? As far as Powell is concerned there is no paradox. In contrast to Margaret Thatcher, who famously doubted the existence of society and recognized only individuals, he saw man as a collective, social animal. And the army, in particular, 'is to a man a fairly natural form of existence. For a man is a herd animal, a hunting animal, perhaps a fighting animal. I don't mean an individual fighting animal but a man who fights collectively, and an animal who fights collectively. So there is an instinct in most men to which the army appeals.' But even by Powell's notion of an instinctive liking for the army, his own passion for it is exceptional – 'the framework of discipline, the exactitude of rank, the precision of duty was something that was almost restful and attractive to me'. And despite this passion, he has never been seen by his fellow 'hunters' as a team player, and always seemed anxious to distinguish himself from the herd. This solitary only child, who never had to mix with a brother or sister from early childhood and relied heavily on books to learn how people behave, seemed happiest in corporate institutions, in which formal rules govern predictable relationships and casual, unpredictable informality is minimized.[4]

As a new recruit, Powell was first stationed at Warwick, for which he was to retain a special affection for the rest of his life. He was an exemplary soldier and 'took great pride in smartness at drill', remembering all his life the 'absurd compliment' paid him when his platoon sergeant told the company commander that he was the smartest soldier in the company. He was thrilled to earn rapid promotion to Lance-Corporal. 'It was the biggest kick-up I've ever had. Perhaps becoming a Privy Counsellor was comparable. But for the sheer crossing of a barrier I don't think I've ever known anything otherwise quite like it.' When he had a day's leave, he went rambling to local haunts such as Kenilworth castle, four miles to the north of Warwick, but even this pastime had a more demanding purpose. In order to improve his map-reading skills, Powell began studying the Ordnance Survey maps and was soon detecting errors – in his seventies, when the latest edition of the Ordnance Survey maps appeared, he was still correcting them.[5]

However, Powell's spell in the ranks was short-lived. Early in 1940, as Powell was doing kitchen duties, an inspecting brigadier had asked him how he liked his work. Powell replied with a Greek proverb. The brigadier happened to be a Greek scholar, and Powell was duly posted to an Officer Cadets Training Unit (OCTU) at Aldershot. Among his fellow trainees was Hardy Amies, later the Queen's dressmaker, who became a lifelong friend. Powell passed out top of his OCTU course in April 1940, and was despatched on a field security course at Sheerness, in north Kent. His striking appearance has been recaptured by the journalist and writer, Malcolm Muggeridge, who happened to be on the same course. 'I remember this strange-looking man who had a rather remarkable moustache – it was almost a soup-strainer moustache,' Muggeridge later recalled. 'I asked him why afterwards, and with his usual honesty he replied that he grew it to convey an impression of Nietzsche. He was an extraordinary young man.' Powell's father, however, had a moustache, and it seems likely that his son had simply followed suit.[6]

Next came a course in military intelligence at Swanage, on the Dorset coast, where Amies was again among Powell's colleagues, along with James MacGibbon, later a publisher, David Hunt, the future diplomat, and Michael Strachan, an upper-class Scot who was to serve with Powell for much of the war. They were greatly impressed by Powell's reading, in the original German, of the classic early-nineteenth-century military and political treatise, *On War*, by the Prussian soldier and writer, Karl von Clausewitz. But Powell's self-confidence caused some amusement. During a walk one evening, Amies and MacGibbon could not help laughing as Powell said, 'When I am a brigadier ...' But what struck others as arrogant was, for Powell, only a statement of fact.[7]

Powell was commissioned as a second lieutenant. But on his first posting, to the 1st (later the 9th) Armoured Division, at Guilsborough, nine miles north-west of Northampton, he was given the rank of captain and appointed third ranking General Staff Officer, assigned to intelligence. It was one of the most frustrating and anxious periods of the war. Britain stood alone against Hitler but was beleaguered and desperately short of the right military equipment. Powell, like many other soldiers, was left kicking his heels on the home front – on one occasion having to do so in the guard-room after he returned to camp singing the Nazi anthem, the *Horst Wessel* song, and the sentry suspected him of being a spy. Powell's feeling of powerlessness as his nation lay under siege, its fate hanging in the balance, and his acute sensitivity to a national consciousness, are palpable in the poem that begins, 'From Guilsborough to Northampton, all the way / Under a full red August moon, / I wandered down'. Although there was no sound of aircraft or gunfire, or of anybody else on the road, none the less the night air,

> Seemed thronged and teeming, as if hosts
> Of living presences were everywhere;
> And I imagined they were ghosts
> Of the old English, who by tower and spire,
> Wherever priest and sexton's spade
> In church or graveyard round about the shire
> Their unremembered bones had laid,
> Now in the warm still night arising, filled
> The broad air with their company,
> And hovering in the fields that once they tilled,
> Brooded on England's destiny.[8]

While Powell had also been 'brooding on England's destiny' during this demoralizing period, he had occupied himself by learning Russian – 'the modern language of that country which stands in the same relation to Byzantium as we of the West of Europe do to Rome' as he had described it in Sydney when advocating its inclusion in the ideal university curriculum. Perhaps because of his special consciousness of Russia he foresaw that Hitler would cast aside the Nazi–Soviet pact and attack Russia – as happened in June 1941. He also believed that for economic reasons the United States would enter the war. In these circumstances, Germany's defeat was inevitable. When Powell first formulated his theory, his commanding officer, Major-General Montagu Burrows, who thought highly of him, saw that it offered a welcome fillip to morale. At Burrows's invitation, Powell lectured his fellow officers on the likely course of the war. It was not only Powell's prediction of how the Nazis would meet their downfall that overcame their initial scepticism of the young professor with a Midlands accent, it was the manner of his delivery. 'It wasn't just what he said,' one of his audience at Guilsborough later recalled, 'it was the way he put it all. He made his conclusions not merely convincing, but inevitable. You kicked yourself for not seeing it all before. And you felt shamefaced if you had even the tiniest reservation, so overpowering was he as a lecturer.' It was a method and a style that years later Powell was to make his own on the public platform.[9]

For Powell, it had seemed only natural that, as a soldier who intended to reach a senior rank in a war against a European enemy, he should read the classic texts on European military history and strategy. He had been surprised that his concern to learn all that he could about continental military theory was not shared by his superior officers, but he was hoping to find like-minded thinkers at the Staff College at Camberley, where he was sent in 1941. However, Powell's 'surprise was repeated ... when I arrived with Clausewitz, Jomini, the textbooks on the American Civil and the Russo-Jap, etc., already devoured in barrackrooms and billets, to discover that the war of nations, *la grande guerre*, was not the passion and the life interest of highly talented and professional instructors'. At heart, the British army remained a colonial army, not a continental one. Powell used to jest at the Staff College that the regular British officer was uneasy with any unit larger than a brigade, 'but the notion that there were such things as armies and groups of armies was abhorrent to him. That was not a world in which he would wish to live. Unfortunately, that was the world with which the United Kingdom was threatened.' There is a certain irony in Powell's having taken the view that the imperial perspective, enhanced by the carnage of 1914–18, had rendered Britain wilfully ignorant of thinking across the Channel, since his experience during the latter part of the Second World War was to convert him for some years into an ardent imperialist.[10]

The view from Cairo

Powell had hoped that after Staff College he would see front-line combat, but with his academic background and bookish learning he was destined to be kept in Intelligence. In October 1941 he was posted to Cairo, serving initially as a Major in Intelligence and Plans Division of the Middle East Forces. The circumstances were inauspicious. The British were on the defensive in North Africa, where the German General, Erwin Rommel, was leading his Afrika Korps in a brilliant desert campaign, in which his marshalling of limited forces and supplies and his use of subterfuge and surprise were unrivalled. The British in Cairo also feared that it was only a matter of time before the Germans overcame Russian resistance and pushed across the Caucasus, into the Middle East. There was every prospect of the collapse of British power in the region, with the loss of Egypt, the end of any effective role in the eastern Mediterranean, and the severing of the vital link with the empire in India and the Far East.

Powell became Secretary to the Joint Intelligence Committee, Middle East and – with promotion to the rank of Lieutenant-Colonel – took charge of the intelligence unit that had the key task of providing all services with assessments of Rommel's position and his likely plans. Powell's unit began work at 04.00 hours each day in order to brief the Chiefs of Staff at their daily 09.00 hours meeting. They based their assessments on the latest batch of German messages that had been decoded and translated at Bletchley Park – Powell took boyish delight in correcting the translations. As head of a unit, he was martinetish and intolerant of fools, of whatever rank. Michael Strachan, a former colleague from Swanage and Guilsborough, who served as a Major under Powell in Cairo, 'witnessed more than one explosive scene, when the offenders had been very senior officers indeed and had not taken kindly to his blunt exposure of their brainlessness.' Powell also took pride in the reputation that he earned for his unshakeable belief in his own correctness. 'When I was in the Army,' he later recalled, 'a fellow officer described me as the most bloody-minded officer in the Middle East. I think it was a great compliment.' And in an echo of his unsociable behaviour at Cambridge, he greeted an OCTU acquaintance who had looked him up while passing through Cairo en route to India with the words, 'I can give you three minutes!' Yet Powell was more forthcoming with his time with Andrew Freeth, his artist friend, who had been posted to Cairo, and also when Nick Hammond, a fellow Cambridge classicist who had fought with the guerillas in Greece, visited him.[11]

For months, 'daily and even hourly', as Powell later recalled, 'I had to try to see the situation as Rommel saw it.' By the middle of 1942, the war in North Africa was hanging in the balance. On 30 June, 'Rommel arrived at the defences of the Alamein position – what there then were – with twelve serviceable tanks. If the number had been 112, or even much less, then there is little room for doubt that within a week or two he would have reached Alexandria and Cairo, and the British would have evacuated Lower Egypt.' As it was, the British began burning official papers in Cairo and making plans to retreat into Palestine. 'Rommel's success had been a matter of mathematics' – in Powell's vivid words, 'It was not for nothing that an estimate of "runners", or serviceable tanks, formed the core of our intelligence appreciations in those weeks.' By September 1942 – a month or so before the battle of El Alamein – Powell felt sufficiently confident to tell Nick Hammond that 'Rommel was finished and the Germans would be out of Africa soon.' His forecast was proved correct, and the British – strengthened by American Sherman tanks – won a famous victory, although Rommel was to remain a serious threat in North Africa for a further four months.[12]

El Alamein stirred mixed, and often painful, emotions in Powell. It marked a turning-point in the war, and he began seriously contemplating the world that would emerge after the enemy's defeat. He was enjoying his role in intelligence, but it denied him his wish to fight for his country, and after this victory it was highly unlikely that he could ever hope to see active service. His expectation of being killed in uniform was almost certain to remain unfulfilled. Far from rejoicing at his own good fortune, Powell felt anguish at being separated from his colleagues who had given their lives. 'A veil had been drawn between them and us, between friend and friend. It must be my own fault: I must be guilty.' He again felt the compulsion to write poetry, that offered at least some emotional release:

> I dreamt I saw with waking eyes the scene
>   So often in imagination wrought,
> The flame-wall in the night at Alamein
>   Before the attack. And I was glad, and thought:
> 'My sorrow and despair was after all
>   Some evil dream. It still is not too late,
> My friends who passed before me through that wall
>   Not lost, nor I for ever separate
> From them condemned to live. I break to-night
>   As they did through the fire, and so again,
> Knowing and known, shall pass into their sight.'
>   But then I woke, and recollection came
> That I for ever and alone remain
>   On this side of the separating flame.

More than forty years later, during a radio interview, Powell was reduced to tears as he read this poem, and spoke of all soldiers who come home alive carrying 'a sort of shame with them to the grave'. When his interviewer, Anne Brown, asked how he would like to be remembered, Powell replied simply, 'I should like to have been killed in the war.'[13]

While El Alamein was the focus of Powell's anguish at his own survival, the dramatic events that followed were to colour his future attitude to the world that was to emerge from the war. A fortnight after the battle, an Anglo-American invasion – 'Operation Torch' – was launched along the Algerian and Moroccan coast, heralding full-scale American involvement in the North African war. Powell, like many other British officers who were used to having to manage with limited resources, was appalled at the Americans' overweening confidence in their sheer fire-power. One incident in early 1943 always stuck in Powell's mind. Rommel, who was caught between Montgomery's advancing Eighth Army in the east and the invasion force in the west, counter-attacked the Americans at Gafsa, capturing about fifty tanks. The British staffs 'were almost as aghast as if the war had been lost,' Powell recalled. 'After fighting the Germans in the desert for two years, we knew what Rommel could do with a few captured tanks. The Americans couldn't understand. "Hell," they said, "there's plenty more where those came from".'[14]

Powell had particularly good reason to be sensitive to Rommel's wiles after Gafsa, since the German commander had nearly cut short Powell's career in Intelligence. At the start of February 1943, Rommel and 'RO-RO', his wireless call-sign, had disappeared suddenly from the battlefield when circumstantial intelligence reports arrived saying that he had been wounded in an air-raid and had died in a Tunis hospital. Although the reports were groundless, Powell 'swallowed them, and told an officer to draft for issue a full obituary informing all whom it might concern'. Fortunately for Powell, however, he disagreed with his officer's appraisal of Rommel and, 'after some argument, decided to leave the thing over till the next day. Next day, Rommel attacked and broke through the American lines at Gafsa.'[15]

Powell, who had scrutinized Rommel's movements and supplies more closely than anybody, judged that he was 'the ablest General of any army during World War II' and had 'taken the right decision in every major crisis of the North African campaign'. Ultimately, the German commander was doomed by Britain's intelligence capability: Rommel's orders to counter-attack the advancing and exposed Eighth Army were in Montgomery's hands within hours, enabling the British General to avert disaster and instead inflict the final defeat on Rommel in North Africa. In Powell's view, Rommel's 'failure, and the causes of his failure, only raise him into a great tragic figure as well as a great military one.'[16]

Powell was gazetted by his superiors for the military M.B.E. and received the order in 1943. When Prime Minister Churchill visited Algiers in late May that year and discussed future strategy with senior Allied Generals, Powell was on hand to provide Intelligence support. Although Powell had no part in the discussions, he had already developed his own distinctive thinking on strategy. He was against opening a 'second front' in Europe, gave short shrift to Soviet complaints that they were having to bear the brunt of German aggression, and was unpersuaded of the supposed advantages of an assault on southern Europe. Instead, he had become what he later termed a 'Lansdowne man' – in 1917, Lord Lansdowne, 'the last of the Whigs' and the former Foreign Secretary and Conservative leader in the House of Lords, had concluded that since it was obvious to all sides that the Central Powers in the Great War could not win, they should behave like rational human beings and negotiate a settlement instead of continuing the destruction. Likewise, by 1943 Powell was arguing for the same conclusion to be drawn in the case of the war in Europe. 'It was perfectly clear by then', he later explained, 'that the Central Powers of World War II couldn't win. Let them settle scores with their unsuccessful regimes, let them deal with the dictators that had brought them to that pass, but no need to carry on the chess game to the point of sweeping all the pieces off the board and smashing the board up as well into the bargain. But apparently we had to go on.'[17]

It is striking that a man who so loved life as a soldier and positively rejoiced at being in the army should, none the less, have come to this view as early as 1943. But it was typical of Powell that, having seen what he believed was an inevitable outcome, he drew logical conclusions – even though it bore little relation to reality. The prospect of Hitler and Mussolini, who then controlled most of continental Europe, accepting that their defeat was inevitable and simply surrendering the vast tracts of the European mainland under their control was unrealistic. And why would they readily surrender if, as Powell so confidently argued, their certain reward would be their own people's wrath? Arguably, Allied indications of a readiness to contemplate something less than unconditional surrender might have encouraged other elements in the German and Italian leadership to overthrow Hitler and Mussolini, but there was no certainty that this would happen – the dictators would almost certainly have portrayed such overtures as demonstrating that the Allies were not prepared to see through the fight, in the same way that they had been prepared to appease rather than resist during the 1930s. At any rate, the question was much less black-and-white than Powell allowed.

Having become certain in his own mind that there was no longer any question of an Allied defeat in Europe, Powell's thinking turned to the future of the British Empire. His travels through south-eastern Asia and his eighteen months in Sydney had heightened his consciousness of Britain's Asian and Far Eastern empire. Hong Kong, Burma and Malaya, including the strategic base of Singapore, had all been occupied, and the Americans had become the dominant power in the war in the Pacific. He was convinced that the Empire's survival depended on recovering these territories before they were occupied by the United States, and was determined to play his part in his country's coming struggle. He became set on obtaining a posting from Cairo to Britain's next theatre of conflict, Burma and the Far East.

Powell's return journey from Algiers to Cairo during the latter half of June 1943 was fortunately chronicled in brilliant and comic detail by Michael Strachan, his long-standing army colleague who had accompanied him to Algiers. Powell and Strachan had estimated that it would take them about fourteen days to drive the army lorry that they had to take with them some three thousand miles back across North Africa. Strachan's hilarious account of their adventure, entitled 'Teaching the Professor', was first published in *Blackwood's Magazine* in May 1949 under the initials, 'M.F.S.'. Powell was the 'Professor', whose true identity was not revealed, while their battered, thirty-hundredweight truck was called 'Pinafore', after Gilbert and Sullivan's fictional operatic ship, symbolizing Strachan's view that their plan was never practicable. However, Powell had been determined that their plan should not dissolve into a day-dream, and Strachan was soon witness to a bizarre spectacle at half-past six on a June morning, in a disused railway cutting sixty miles east of Algiers. 'Breakfast was not a success,' Strachan's story began, ominously.

> The fire smouldered dejectedly until the Professor teased it with a gill of petrol, and then it sprang up in a fury and singed his moustache; when he assaulted the sausages the tin counter-attacked and cut his finger; the water refused to boil, and while he was not looking tipped itself over into the fire. 'Oh the malice – the cursed, diabolical malice of inanimate objects!' muttered the Professor ferociously between clenched teeth. 'Here, let me help,' I said. 'You keep away,' he snarled. 'If they want to be bloody-minded, I'll show them, by God I will,' booting the empty sausage tin into a cactus bush.

Informing his readers that 'the Professor' was his senior officer, Strachan provided a vivid thumb-nail portrait of Powell as a young war-time officer, noting that:

> if he was a singular and in some ways unorthodox Lieutenant-Colonel, he certainly looked more like a soldier than an absent-minded scholar. He was still in his early thirties, stockily built, with a pale face and brown hair *en brosse*. His eyes were greenish, very penetrating and rather sinister; they indicated something of their owner's intellectual brilliance and something of his force of character.

In the disaster that had resulted from Powell's determination to cook breakfast unaided on their first day on the road, Strachan detected one of his companion's central characteristics:

> The sausages were cold and flabby, tea-leaves floated on the top of a grey, tepid liquid which I tactfully consumed with feigned relish. But the Professor was not deceived and went about shaking his head muttering, 'Bloody inefficient! Bloody inefficient!' too angry to eat. If he had a failing it was an overbearing intolerance of stupidity and inefficiency. People less acute and less energetic than himself, that is practically every other human being with whom he came into contact, were very liable to excite his wrath.

But this was something new – Powell was angry with himself. Strachan had never seen this before, because he 'had never before seen him make a fool of himself'. Powell was having to contend with aspects of life that he had never encountered – instead of joining the Boy Scouts and cooking camp-fire breakfasts, he had preferred his books and clarinet.

Neither had Powell learned to drive. Although he possessed a certificate stating that he was authorized to drive any Government road vehicle, he readily confessed to Strachan that it had been presented to him by an over-optimistic Sergeant-instructor before his one and only driving lesson. Since then he had displayed courage, but great ineptitude, in trying to master an army motor-bicycle. None the less, Strachan was confident that he could teach Powell to drive without much difficulty. When 'the Professor' took his first spell at the wheel, he was 'piqued' that Strachan 'insisted on pointing out which was the accelerator and which was the brake', but as his new instructor discovered Powell's 'difficulties were much more complex than being unable to distinguish one pedal from another: they involved problems which would not even have occurred to a normal beginner'.

> The main difficulty, according to the Professor, lay in the steering. His diagnosis was at least partly correct, as I discovered when we had to turn back on to the main road. Instead of slowing down he suddenly accelerated, at the same time swaying about in his seat as though wrestling for possession of the wheel. We turned neither to the right nor left, but shot

straight on towards a stone wall on the far side. We stopped with a lurch a few inches short of the wall and I found that I had subconsciously pulled the handbrake hard on.

'You see what I mean?' asked the Professor, quite unperturbed.

'Yes, I see,' I replied, wiping the sweat off my hands, determined to be equally composed. 'Now to turn her it's no good just shifting your weight about in the seat; you must take a grip of the steering-wheel and turn it like this.'

'Of course, of course, I quite understand. I must remember I am not on that motorcycle,' he said.

'Take it easy, don't be in a hurry, reverse her and try again.'

He reversed without much difficulty, but in two seconds we had shot back across the road and were again facing the wall.

'Never mind,' I said, wiping my hands again, 'just take it steady – try again.'

'I'll manage it,' muttered the Professor with the most ferocious look of resolution. Next time he certainly did manage it. We turned a good deal more than the necessary right-angle and narrowly missed the ditch on the wrong side of the road.

'Done it!' beamed the Professor as we swerved back to the centre of the road. I was too unnerved to make any comment.

Powell insisted on taking an exactly equal share of the driving along what were at times treacherous roads. Despite the wear and tear on Strachan's nerves caused by several accidents and numerous hair-raising scrapes, in which either driver and passenger or hapless Arab pedestrians nearly came to their grief, the two men settled into a daily routine. By nature, Powell was a stickler for routine, and even in the desert had lost none of his obsession with smartness. 'The Professor was habitually an early riser,' Strachan noted,

and I always awoke to find him offering me a mug of tea while still polishing away at what he called his collection of brass. I, like other normal people, wore a shirt and shorts and nothing much else. The Professor, who spent most of the war in Egypt and Africa or places even hotter, invariably wore a shirt with collar and tie, long drill trousers and boots, a tailored drill jacket with brass buttons and regimental badges, and a Sam Browne [belt].

As Powell explained to his puzzled colleague, 'wearing his full uniform kept up his morale, and it certainly did not seem to make him feel the heat more than other people.'

It was in these unlikely surroundings that Powell's great passion for fox-hunting was first aroused. As they pressed on across the desert for hour after hour, conversation sometimes ran dry, and they might fall silent for two or three hours. In order to relieve the boredom, and to prevent the driver falling asleep, Strachan suggested that the long hours in their hot cab should be employed in Powell's remedying his junior officer's ignorance of ancient history – they encountered the remains of the Roman occupation of North Africa dotted along their route. Powell only agreed with the proviso that whenever Strachan was not driving, he in turn should improve Powell's knowledge. Strachan was hard put to find a subject about which he knew more than 'the Professor', but the discovery that Powell had never ridden horseback resulted in Strachan's talking about horses and riding. The history of the Punic Wars, the philosophy of Aristotle, and the story of the Odyssey were interspersed with episodes from Surtees' 'Mr Sponge's Sporting Tour'; tales of the daredevil Regency squire, Jack Mytton; and a detailed account of working a pack of hounds. 'By Jove, what I've been missing!' Powell exclaimed one day after a 'more or less true account' of an eventful day's hunting, '"The image of war without its guilt and only five-and-twenty per cent of the danger!" I believe that fellow Jorrocks knew what he was talking about.' Quite solemnly, Powell added, 'I've made up my mind. I shall hunt.'

As they made supper on their last night, 'the Professor' asked whether his instructor would pass him fit to drive. Strachan was unsure, but suggested a final, stiff test – if Powell could drive 'Pinafore' from the Pyramids to GHQ 'without hitting anything and without turning my hair grey', he would certify that he could drive. To Strachan's astonishment, Powell's handling of 'Pinafore' during the final hour was 'masterly', as he weaved through 'all the hazards and navigational uncertainties of the teeming streets'. Within a few hours of their arrival, 'the Professor had done the round of the bookshops and purchased three Surtees and a Whyte-Melville' to feed his new passion. Powell insisted they have tea at Gezireh, where Strachan was almost overwhelmed by the contrast of the luxuriousness of the clubhouse after their gruelling drive 'through lands thronged with ghosts and saturated with blood'. But still bursting with energy, Powell proposed heading for the polo ground where he wanted Strachan to explain the game. 'Presently,' murmured his companion, and promptly dropped off to sleep.[18]

'A great delusion'

After twenty months in the Middle East and North Africa Commands, Powell was restless on his return to Cairo. 'I wanted to get into the war against Japan as soon as the crisis of the war with Germany was past, with a view', as he used to put it, to 'getting to Singapore before the Americans.' So eager was he to go east, that he jumped into the taxi carrying Orde Wingate, the legendary commander, through Cairo, to beg a place with the Chindits in Burma, but Wingate was killed before Powell 'cashed the cheque'. Although Powell only had to wait till August 1943 for a new posting, he was transferred to India, and not to one of the territories occupied by the Japanese. Until he arrived there, he saw the sub-continent merely as a stepping-stone to his real objective, further east.[19]

The precise circumstances that had led to his posting remain uncertain, but

Powell had mentioned to Nick Hammond almost a year earlier that he was going to India because there was an important job to be done, which suggests that a move there had been in the offing for some time. General Auchinleck, the commander-in-chief in North Africa, who was transferred at Churchill's behest to take command of the army in India, was later to claim responsibility for Powell's posting. But according to Powell he had, off his own bat, 'persuaded General Cawthorn, a 16th Punjabi, the Director of Military Intelligence (India) to take me on his staff to organize joint service intelligence'. Shortly before his promotion to full Colonel, Powell was appointed Secretary to the Joint Intelligence Committee for India and South-East Asia Command. It was a commission that was to change his life, setting him on a path that eventually led to the House of Commons.[20]

'The love affair started on my first night in India,' Powell was to recall almost forty years later. 'With the sights, the sounds and the odours' during those first hours spent on a platform at Delhi railway station, he 'drew in a new intimation'. India 'claimed' him almost from his first moment there: 'I started to love, and to learn thirstily. I bought and read omnivorously – anything about India that I could lay my hands on.' But Powell's passions were not aroused solely by the sub-continent. 'I was in India in time to touch the hem of the British Raj', he once commented reverentially, and it was the unique phenomenon of the British Raj that immediately captured his emotions in 1943 and blinded him to reality. As Powell later recalled, 'by the time Lord Mountbatten in 1944 moved South-East Asia Command HQ from Delhi to Kandy (Sri Lanka), I had fallen hopelessly in love with India, and I refused a transfer to Mountbatten's staff'.[21]

Powell has since freely admitted that 'India I suppose was my great delusion, but then India was a great delusion for the Indians as well as for the Europeans'. He was in accord with the *aperçu* made by an earlier politician, that the British Empire in India was the greatest wonder of the world, because it was the equivalent of a block of granite weighing fifteen tons in mid-air without any means of suspension. None the less, 'it was a dream which was dreamt by millions of people, and the wonder of this, and its apparent inevitability to those who dreamt the dream, caught me up. And I dreamt the dream too, and I thought it was a dream that could go on, and it was a good dream.' The dream to which Powell succumbed 'was that there could be a connection between the United Kingdom – a political connection – and the hundreds of millions of inhabitants of the sub-continent of India' that did not depend upon 'the ultimate principle of the government of the United Kingdom', namely representation in the British parliament.[22]

Powell subsequently recognized that the notion of being able to rule India through the parliament of the United Kingdom 'was a fallacy, it was a demonstrable fallacy, it was a fallacy which had been demonstrated before in British history, in the rebellion of the American colonies'. But the thirty-one-year-old officer who had left North Africa because of his concern to preserve the British Empire in the east was not in the frame of mind to detect such a fallacy. He was not alone, of course, and whereas his father had echoed Bright's nineteenth century antipathy to the building of the Indian empire, Powell readily identified with the paternalistic tradition exemplified earlier in the twentieth century by Lord Curzon, who had seen the task of governing India in the twentieth century as a noble and righteous duty, and whom Powell regarded as the greatest Viceroy of India.[23]

Yet the Curzon tradition was already well-dated by the 1940s, and although Powell assumed that his own attitude typified his generation, he was anachronistic – in the 1930s Winston Churchill had been widely regarded as hopelessly out-dated and out of touch in his opposition to the Government's granting of Dominion status to India. The rising tide of Indian nationalism since before the war and Gandhi's ability to evoke massive non-violent protest rarely, if ever, seemed to intrude upon Powell's consciousness in the way that it had upon many others. 'The word I constantly recur to,' he later wrote,

> when I attempt to describe the atmosphere up to a mere fifteen months of the sudden (and catastrophic) British withdrawal in 1947 is 'inevitability'. Whatever the politicians were saying and the papers were writing, the British seemed – seemed, I say, for all is hallucination – a natural part of the scene. The moon rose, the cow walked through the village, the British magistrate or officer went about his duties, as if from time immemorial. In fact, in parts of Bihar within the present century the British were called 'the Muslims', so natural was their identification with the dynasties of the past.[24]

Powell had written about the seeming 'inevitability' of British rule after having read E.M. Forster's *A Passage to India* in 1982 – almost forty years after his own 'passage' there, and nearly sixty years since the book's publication. He was riled, at first, by Forster's portrayal of the British characters, which he felt 'read like a deliberate caricature', even after he had taken into account 'the fact that most of the book was written during the aftermath of the massacre in the Jallianwala Bagh, Amritsar'. It simply rang false to him that the National Anthem 'was the Anthem of the Army of Occupation', or that various British characters would make comments such as the Indians gave them 'the creeps', or that their job was 'to hold this wretched country by force'. However, Powell also appeared to go some way to acknowledging that fewer people than he had imagined had shared his dream. Despite his initially hostile reaction, on second thoughts Powell recognized that Forster had captured 'that sense of hallucination that pervades India' and that there was 'a core of truth beneath the crudity and bias' of the book.[25]

In this latter recognition lies an explanation of Powell's response to India. In the novel, Forster writes that Fielding, the English schoolmaster, 'had discovered that it is possible to keep in with Indians and Englishmen, but that he who would keep in with Englishwomen must drop the Indians. The two wouldn't combine.' As Powell noted, the social conventions that governed the life of Indian women 'raised between them and European women (and therefore European mixed society) a barrier to which no obstacle between European and Indian men was in any way comparable.' Only on those occasions when European women took on roles analogous to men – in the camp, on tour, or in medicine or missionary work – would they 'ever be in India other than a stranger at a distance in a strange land.' Powell's experience of India had been that of a bachelor officer, who immersed himself in the Indian Army and had every interest in the new culture in which he found himself and little concern for 'European mixed society'. As he finally accepted,

> The dream that the British and the Indians dreamed together for so long, a dream unique in human history in its strangeness and its improbability, was bound to break one day. Even India, the land of hallucinations, could not preserve it for ever from its contradictions. This the wisest of the British in India had seen and known all along, though some of us, under the influence of our love affair, dared to believe otherwise. Yet the dream was always imperfect; it was a dream that only the men would ever dream.[26]

The incompatibility of Forster's perception and his own view stemmed, in Powell's belief, from the novelist's virtual exclusion of the Indian Army from his story. For the Indian Army was Powell's passage into Indian culture. 'Unlike any other native army of the European colonial powers,' he noted, 'the Indian Army was quite deliberately and self-consciously Indian: its language was Urdu, its European officers were on an extraordinarily low cadre ... and success, promotion and opportunity lay for them through deep and thorough knowledge of the people and the country.' He was taken through his interpretership in Urdu by a poet and nephew of one of the great Urdu poets, Hali. Powell learned to ride a bicycle, and he and his tall bearer, sporting a henna-dyed beard, travelled by train with their bicycles in the luggage van, exploring the United Provinces (Uttar Pradesh) and the Gujerat in search of the more celebrated examples of Islamic architecture. Such was Powell's immersion in Indian culture that when, during the winter of 1945–46 while cycling near Muttra, he was offered hospitality by a Brahmin family, he knew that he should smash the rough earthen tumbler from which he had drunk – '"He is a Hindu," they said to one another with a smile,' Powell later recalled, and added, 'there is a sense in which it had been true: the British were married to India, as Venice was married to the sea.'[27]

As he had done at King Edward's, and in Cambridge, Guilsborough and Cairo, Powell seemed determined to set himself apart from his colleagues. Glyn Daniel, another Cambridge don and an archaeologist who was to become a television celebrity in the 1950s, served with Powell in Delhi and asked him on several occasions to have a drink or dinner. But Powell declined, saying that he could not waste time on social occasions because he wanted to devote every minute outside his military duties to studying the poet, John Donne. Daniel even found it impossible to interest Powell in the Greeks or Romans in India. Everything about Powell seemed deliberately different. Philip Mason, an official in the Indian Civil Service, was startled when Powell first entered his office, demanding to see a secret document:

> There before me was a figure that a Japanese cartoonist might have drawn if he wished to portray a British officer. His uniform was formally correct – but it was not what people wore. Others in GHQ at that time of the year kept as cool as possible; they wore shorts and soft brush shirts of cotton twill with badges of rank in worsted. This man was in starched khaki drill, with a tunic, long stiffly creased trousers, a collar and tie; he looked as if he were going to a ceremonial parade. His badges of rank were of burnished brass and heraldic antelopes pranced in brazen splendour on the lapels of his tunic. He looked very uncomfortable.

So surprised was Mason that he rang military intelligence to check that Powell was genuine. 'You thought I was a spy,' Powell joked with him later, but it had not been as definite as that – Mason simply felt that Powell 'looked *wrong*' [his emphasis]. But Mason was fascinated by his studied distinctiveness and came to the conclusion that Powell had

> made up his mind that he would not – like most wartime officers – try to behave as though he too had been to Cheltenham and Sandhurst. No, he would not be like other soldiers, he would be what he was, an exceptionally gifted boy from the West Midlands who had become a Professor of Greek at Sydney and who could do a military job better than a soldier.[28]

Some of Powell's odd remarks appear to confirm Mason's view, as does the element of self-mockery that Powell sometimes evinced. A year or so after their first meeting, Mason happened to comment that the mid-afternoon in Delhi in the hot weather, when temperatures in the shade might approach 120 degrees fahrenheit, was not the best time for hard mental work. 'On the contrary,' Powell remarked, 'I find it a very good time for work – provided that I have had a sufficiently heavy lunch'. When Mason inquired what he meant by 'heavy', Powell replied with a smile, 'Steak and kidney pudding followed by jam roly-poly'. On another occasion, Mason arrived at the military base at Dehra Dun to find the officers' mess deserted, except for Powell. 'Will you have whisky and soda?' Powell inquired, before adding, 'I have observed that is what an English gentleman considers suitable after a journey.' It was all part of his pose as 'the incorruptible plebeian'.[29]

Others found Powell infuriating. In Delhi, he chaired a committee that was planning the capture of Akyab, an island off the coast of Burma – mainly, it was presumed, as a training exercise for the later capture of Rangoon and Singapore. Serving on the committee were Glyn Daniel, Peter Fleming and Orde Wingate. Daniel discovered that Wingate, like Powell, eschewed all social contact, but he also realized as their meetings progressed that Powell and Wingate did not get on. One day, as Daniel was walking along the corridor,

Wingate stopped him and, furious, shook the big Irish blackthorn knobkerry that he always carried, and said, 'Daniel, one day I want to beat the brains out of that stupid man Powell. Will you restrain me? Will you see that I don't make a fool of myself?' It seems unlikely that had Wingate lived, he would have granted Powell's request that he had made in the taxi in Cairo to join the Chindits in Burma.[30]

In the summer of 1944, Powell conceived a fresh ambition. This new goal was rooted in the same desire to prevent the seemingly imminent disintegration of the Empire that had caused the Far East to beckon. But now his fascination with the Indian empire prompted him to look back towards Britain. His profound unhappiness with imperial policy in India and elsewhere prompted a 'blinding revelation':

> I can remember the day – it was the day the monsoon broke – in Delhi, in June 1944, when suddenly I said to myself: 'You're going to survive. There'll be a time when you won't be in uniform; painful though it may be, you've got to face it. True, Japan is not yet defeated, but the chances are mounting that there will be a lifetime for you, and a lifetime not as a soldier.' This was the opening of the door from one mental room to another and there was the answer. 'Of course you'll go into politics, in England.'

Powell had remembered 'how Burke had said one hundred and sixty years earlier that the keys of India were not in Calcutta, not in Delhi, they were in that box – the Despatch Box at the House of Commons. I decided at that time I must go there.'[31]

The die was not yet finally cast, although Powell informed Durham University that he would not, after all, be taking up the chair that they had kept vacant for him during his war service. In the winter of 1944, he was still contemplating a role in the Far East and wondering how he might participate in the attack upon Sumatra and Malaya that was planned for 1945. And for a further eighteen months, until the winter of 1945–46, the possibility remained that Powell might not return to London. In December 1945, he was still undecided, telling Glyn Daniel over dinner at the Gymkhana Club in Delhi that his choice for the future lay between staying in the army or going into politics. 'Having achieved what I have achieved in this war,' he told Daniel with typical self-assurance bordering on arrogance, 'I should be head of all military intelligence in the next.' As Daniel discovered, Powell's view that America's interests would be antipathetic to the British Empire after the war had hardened into the conviction that 'the next war will not be between America and the West versus Russia. It will be between Russia and Europe versus America.' Powell concluded that 'the key area to understand is Central America', and told Daniel: 'I shall go underground for a year or so and get to know everywhere from Mexico to Peru.' If not the army, Powell would apply to the Conservative Party – 'I think I have a good chance of becoming Prime Minister'. But as Powell wrote thirty-seven years later, 'If in 1946 there had been a foreseeable future in the Indian Army, I would have opted to "leave my bones there".[32]

Had Powell had his way, he might well have guaranteed himself a future as an officer in the Indian Army. In 1944, Major-General Walter Cawthorn, his commanding officer, 'who became almost a second father' to Powell, had recommended that his protégé should serve as secretary of the Re-organization Committee set up by Auchinleck to report on the size of army India would need after the war. The thirty-two-year-old Powell was promoted to Brigadier and transferred to the Committee's headquarters at Dehra Dun, about one hundred and twenty miles north-east of Delhi, in the Himalayan foothills. Powell's approach and the way in which he came to dominate the committee were to become familiar hallmarks in his political career, although if his conclusions had been accepted Powell might never have left the army. According to Philip Mason, who served on the committee, Powell 'behaved beautifully at meetings', but he dominated its work 'by getting up very early in the morning and drafting the next chapter'. There is one other incident that occurred at this time and which is important in the light of the allegations of racism that were made against Powell a quarter of a century later. Powell was reminded of it in 1986 by another member of the committee, and later first chief-of-staff of the Indian Army, General K.M. Cariappa, who remembered that during their visit to Poona together in 1944 Powell had refused to stay at the Byculla Club when it became clear that Cariappa, as an Indian, would not be allowed to stay there.[33]

However, there was another aspect of Powell's approach on the Re-organization Committee that Mason remembered 'because it illustrated a habit of mind which is surely dangerous'. The subject concerned the number of officers that the Indian Army would require. Powell first weighed the threats that India might face after the war and estimated the forces needed to meet them. From this, it was possible to calculate the required number of officers. But an officer must have a certain educational qualification. During the war, there had been in India so many men of military age with that qualification, of whom only a certain proportion held commissions in the army. This gave a fixed proportion from which to work. Now, another committee had just reported that the total number of men with the right educational qualification could not increase by more than two per cent a year, which meant that the total number of young men suitable to be officers could not increase by more than two per cent either. Powell concluded that it would take twenty-five years before all officers in the army were native Indians. In the meantime, the Indian Army would need to draw on Britain for up to half of its officers.[34]

The argument had proceeded logically, according to certain assumptions and on the basis of supposedly immutable, fixed relationships. Yet, as Mason observed, 'it reached a conclusion that was absurd if one took into account human factors. India was not going to wait twenty-five years for independence, and no independent country would agree to accept half her officers from abroad. The conclusion being outrageous, a more flexible mind would have questioned the earlier links in the chain.' In Mason's view, it was likely that a higher proportion of young Indians would join the forces of an independent India, and Powell should have realized that predictions by committees about rates of growth are not infallible. Auchinleck dismissed this chapter as being wide of the mark, and it discredited the other recommendations too.[35]

But the disagreement between Auchinleck and Powell ran deeper than mere technicalities. Whereas the commander-in-chief accepted the political reality of early post-war independence for India, Powell epitomized those old India hands who predominated among the British officers in the army and who wanted only the most cautious and gradual political change. Auchinleck's repudiation of the Re-organization Committee's report meant that there was no guaranteed future for Powell and other British officers in the Indian Army, and finally confirmed Powell in his view in the winter of 1945–46 that, if he were to play a part in saving the British Empire, he had to return to Britain and enter the House of Commons. But his new purpose in life was not to turn out as he had expected.

4

'My Time Will Come'

Such is the result of socialism in action in imperial affairs that it has threatened the eclipse of the whole Empire, which is the structure on which we are dependent for our very existence. If there is a way for the Empire to survive, and if that great chain of British territories round the world is to remain united, it can only be because through Britain is liberty and independence preserved. If that is not true, then we will perish in proving it otherwise.

Enoch Powell, on the pre-eminent need to preserve the British Empire, Normanton by-election, January 1947.

Learning the ropes

In late February 1946, aged thirty-three, Powell returned to civilian life and England with a new mission. On landing at Brize Norton in Oxfordshire, after almost four and a half years in Africa and India, his first sight of green fields caused him to weep. But despite the emotions that were evoked in him, his homecoming was motivated not by a wish to return to his roots, but by his resolve to do all in his power to prevent the dissolution of British rule in India, which he regarded as the lynch-pin of the Empire. If he was to stand any chance of helping to preserve British rule in the sub-continent, Powell realized that he had to become a government minister. To achieve this, he had to join a major political party and become a Member of Parliament. Within twenty-four hours of his arrival at Brize Norton, Powell 'looked up "C" in the telephone directory, "C" for "Conservative"'.[1]

Although Powell had been 'born a Tory', there were reasons why, in 1945, an ambitious young officer planning a political career might instead have looked up 'L' for 'Labour'. As Powell later recalled, he had felt 'total antipathy to the Conservative Party and successive Conservative Governments as I had known them before 1939'. Moreover, his experiences in India had convinced him that if he was to help preserve the British Empire he had to secure office as quickly as possible, and a call to Transport House would therefore have seemed a safer bet than to Central Office. Labour had won a landslide victory in the general election of July 1945, with every prospect that they would remain in office for at least two parliaments – until the middle of the 1950s. However, having realized that he needed 'a vehicle and a framework for what I imagined I would be doing' in politics, Powell knew that 'it had to be the Conservative Party'.[2]

Quite simply, Powell regarded himself as a Tory. By this, he meant 'a person who regards authority as immanent in institutions'. As he explained,

> I had always been, as far back as I could remember in my existence, a respecter of institutions, a respecter of monarchy, a respecter of the deposit of history, a respecter of everything in which authority was capable of being embodied, and that must surely be what the Conservative Party was about.

In addition, Powell believed that the Conservative Party 'would be a party which did not believe in always starting afresh over and over again, it would be a non-innovatory party, a party which chimed in, therefore, with my own prejudices and nature.' But Powell was never a mere conservative reactionary: he was a High Tory – a 'Church and King Tory'. His colleagues in India had been puzzled by his claim that he was an 'Anglican atheist', but such was his reverence for traditional authority as embodied in the English constitution that he used to assert: 'I think nothing of religion, but I think there ought to be an established Church and the King ought to be its head!' These innermost political beliefs had intruded in his choice of a 'vehicle and framework' for his imperial mission. Yet he was to continue in British politics long after his mission had been rendered impossible.[3]

Within a fortnight of his having telephoned Conservative Central Office at its wartime offices in Old Queen Street, Westminster, Powell was on the party's panel of speakers; the candidates' list – 'it was easier in those days'; and was employed in the new Conservative Parliamentary Secretariat, accommodated at 24 Wilton Street, a private house near Buckingham Palace. The Secretariat had been created in the aftermath of the Conservatives' 1945 election rout in order to help restore the effectiveness of a much-reduced parliamentary party and front bench. The then Chairman of the Party Organization, Ralph Assheton (later Lord Clitheroe), had found the money to launch it and had persuaded David Clarke, who had been appointed Director of the separate Conservative Research Department, to set it up. Miss Marjorie Maxse, a party vice-chairman, with whom Powell had spoken at Central Office, had passed his name to Clarke, who was urgently recruiting talented staff for the Secretariat – at the end of 1945, three officials, including Reggie Maudling, were having to service twenty-three party parliamentary committees.[4]

Powell attended his interview in full uniform, and Clarke was never to forget the experience of vetting an immaculately dressed Brigadier for a job that largely involved taking minutes at committee meetings and preparing briefs for debates and speeches. However, for young men like Powell, recently demobilized from wartime service and eager to enter politics as Conservatives, the Secretariat offered a golden opportunity. During the next four years, Powell was able to overcome his ignorance of domestic politics and learn the ropes of parliamentary government before embarking on his political career. And in his case, it was a process of instruction that was to foster a new and lasting devotion to an institution – the House of Commons.[5]

By the middle of March 1946, Powell was briefing and servicing the Conservative parliamentary party and front bench on defence and India, the two subjects that he knew most about. However, the Secretariat was still so over-stretched that he also had to tackle other subjects and service other committees, including – improbably for an Englishman of Welsh ancestry – the Scottish Unionists. The arrival of another new recruit, Major Iain Macleod, a month later on 15 April, came as a great relief to Powell, since Clarke handed responsibility for the Scottish Committee to this Yorkshireman of Scottish islander descent. But Powell was somewhat taken aback at their first meeting. Having welcomed his new colleague, he made to gather the Scottish papers from his desk and hand them over, only to discover that Macleod had already helped himself. It was the start of a curious relationship between two of the brightest and most gifted of modern Tories. As Macleod reflected in his *Spectator* profile of Powell almost twenty years later, 'our paths have run together, diverged and come together again'. By the time of Macleod's untimely death in 1970, they were estranged.[6]

As had been the case at King Edward's, Trinity and in the army, Powell's distinctive attitudes and behaviour, bordering at times on eccentricity, made him a legendary figure at the Secretariat, firstly in Wilton Street and from late 1946 at numbers 24 and 34 Old Queen Street, premises that were shared with the Research Department. Recently demobilized officers were known at first by their military titles – Brigadier Powell, Major Macleod, and so on. Later, as most of them gradually returned to being addressed as 'Mister', Powell remained 'Brigadier'. This helped to distinguish him from a Mr Powell who worked in Central Office, but the military title suited the austere and hard-working figure in the Secretariat. Brigadier Powell had no small talk and never passed the time of day with junior staff. On one occasion, he was discovered at the start of the day's work sweeping the floor of his office – he reckoned that the cleaner's efforts were unsatisfactory, and so had arrived early in order to do the job himself.[7]

Adding to the legend that developed about 'the Brigadier' or 'the Brig', as he was nicknamed, was Powell's refusal to allow the fact that he was living in central London to prevent him from fulfilling his ambition, ever since Strachan's talk about horses in 1943, to ride to hounds. He had learned to ride at Dehra Dun, as one of the 'perks' of the Indian Army. By the time Macleod joined the Secretariat, Powell used to travel from Earl's Court on a workman's ticket at some unearthly hour of the morning in his hunting clothes, to revel in a day's hunting. A couple of years later, on a December evening, Strachan happened to bump into his old army colleague on a London-bound underground train. 'I could not have missed that pale face and those arresting eyes,' Strachan wrote. He would in any case have taken a second look because Powell 'was wearing a bowler hat with a mud-smeared dent in it, a black cutaway coat with a muddied shoulder, a stock with a fox-head pin, and mud-spattered breeches and boots'.[8]

Powell told Strachan that he had done what he had said he would do and now hunted every Saturday, getting to and from the meets 'somehow – by train, bus, horse-box or pony trap. The other day I walked the last six miles in my boots in just under the hour.' On this particular day, he had taken 'four tosses ... but the last two were at jumps'. And in a reference to Strachan's earlier tales about the thrill of hunting, Powell remarked that 'judging by the number of bowlers I've smashed I'm inclined to think that "five-and-twenty per cent of the danger" is an underestimate, but my luck holds and "all the time is lost wot is not spent in 'unting".'[9]

Powell got on well enough with his near contemporaries in the Parliamentary Secretariat, although he did not join Macleod and Maudling for their protracted lunches at Macleod's club, Crockford's, or at their evening discussions over a drink. Crockford's had no appeal for a man who never gambled and who was teetotal – in addition, these two future fellow parliamentarians and ministers of Powell's both lived with their families in north London, which made it easier for them to socialize. Sometimes, however, if it suited Macleod to spend the night in central London he would stay at Powell's maisonette, number 34a Earl's Court Square, and the two men would sit up till the early hours discussing their ideas. But Macleod was never likely to tolerate an evening spent entirely in earnest discussion, and he introduced Powell to the films of the Marx brothers. Powell became a lifelong fan of their zany logic, and they were one of the few American influences that were ever to have any appeal to him. Maudling shared an office with Powell for two years, and remembered 'those times with considerable affection'. 'I do not think I had any real arguments with Enoch in those days,' he noted, 'they came later.' And, as Maudling added, he could

> not recall meeting anyone else with a mind that had such a power of acquiring knowledge. At one stage when Enoch was detailed to become the expert on town and country planning, he acquired the standard textbook and read it from page to page, as an ordinary mortal would read a novel. Within a matter of a few months he was writing to the author of the textbook, pointing out the errors that he had made.[10]

This impressive feat had occurred within a couple of months of Powell's having started at the Secretariat, when the Labour Government introduced their New Towns Bill. He was also soon handed housing and local government. Unlike defence and India, these were subjects about which he knew virtually nothing and he had to teach himself about them while briefing MPs and the front bench. But as Maudling's recollection suggests, Powell relished the new challenge, since he liked nothing better than learning about a new field of knowledge. He also knew that he had to master such aspects of domestic policy if he was to make his way in his new career. On 3 May 1946, Brigadier Powell circulated six pages of 'Notes on the New Towns Bill' to Conservative MPs who were to discuss the proposed legislation at a joint meeting of the party's health and housing and town and country planning committees prior to the second reading debate. Powell's training as a textual critic was evident in his detailed analysis of both the Bill and other, related, legislation.[11]

Also evident in Powell's first paragraph of his briefing on the New Towns Bill was the approach that was to become his hallmark over the coming decades – his insistence at the outset of any debate that the basic principles should be identified. Although the Bill was 'concerned only with the agency for establishing new towns', he urged the need for the Government to state their position on 'certain major matters of principle' – 'these include the location of industry, proposed scope of the new towns scheme, and compensation and betterment'. Powell's free-market convictions can already be detected in the clarity and force with which he warned of the Government's intention to create, within a mere decade, economically and socially balanced communities. 'The production of such balanced communities,' he argued, 'by natural forces operating over a lengthy period is perfectly feasible.' However, nothing similar had ever been attempted in Britain on the timescale envisaged, 'and there are grounds for seriously doubting whether it can be accomplished without dictatorial powers on the part of Government to control and direct both population and employment.'[12]

But as Powell's minute of the joint committee meeting reveals, Conservative MPs were mindful that the wartime Coalition Government had approved the study of a new towns scheme, and that the proposal to found a town experimentally had been put to (though not considered by) the Cabinet of the all-party 'caretaker' Government in July 1945. In consequence, the Conservatives decided not to oppose the Bill on second reading, but instead to seek a number of assurances from the Government. From mid-May until the start of July 1946, Powell sustained a weekly flow of briefing on clause-by-clause amendments as the New Towns Bill passed through the standing committee and its remaining Commons' stages. Later in July, as the acute housing shortage persisted and the Conservatives seized on one of their first opportunities to attack the alleged failings of socialist planning in a Commons' debate on housing and building materials, Powell circulated a meticulous thirteen-page briefing to Conservative MPs. In mid-October, an equally thorough nine-page note, supplemented by copies of articles from the *Economist* and the *House Builder*, issued from Powell's desk for a further debate on housing.[13]

Yet India and the British Empire remained the cause that was closest to Powell's heart. While he had been at his busiest in the Secretariat, he had also been preparing himself for the day when he might assume high office in India by continuing to study for a diploma in Urdu at the School of Oriental and African Studies. However, the writing was already on the wall for his beloved Raj. On 16 May 1946, the Prime Minister had declared his plan for a united, independent India, and the following December announced talks on independence for Burma – a statement that prompted Churchill's condemnation of the pace of British withdrawal as a 'scuttle'. Many years later, Powell was to describe Burma as 'that anomalous stepchild of the Indian Empire', but within a month of his leader's outburst in the Commons he launched his own, deeply felt, public attack on Labour's hasty dissolution of Britain's Asian Empire.[14]

New worlds

Powell's growing mastery of the mechanics and detailed aspects of domestic politics was, however, a means to an end – entering parliament. Whereas Macleod and Maudling had both fought seats in 1945 and had since been adopted as prospective parliamentary candidates in north London constituencies, Powell had never fought an election. He urgently needed to overcome his lack of political experience if he was to stand a reasonable chance of securing a winnable seat before the next general election. In late 1946, he seized a golden opportunity to be 'blooded' when he put his name forward as prospective parliamentary candidate for a by-election in Normanton, a safe Labour mining seat in West Yorkshire. Brigadier Powell won the Conservative nomination, helped by his pedigree as a member of the party's Parliamentary Secretariat and having as a referee Rab Butler, the Chairman of the Research Department.[15]

Powell's relationship with Butler was not as close during this period as has sometimes been suggested, to Powell's irritation. But the young Brigadier was certainly no stranger to Butler. Although the Secretariat had recently left Wilton Street to share numbers 24 and 34 Old Queen Street with the Research Department, Powell and his colleagues servicing the parliamentary party had less to do with Butler, who had an office on the third floor of number 24, than their Research Department counterparts who focused on policy work. But Powell had agreed to speak in Butler's Essex constituency during January 1947, and although the meeting turned out to be a flop, Butler was grateful and assured him 'how much I value this friendly act'. In addition, Powell received his 'best wishes for your success at Normanton, realizing what a tough fight it is', while Butler's solicitous final comment – 'I hope you are looking after yourself' – suggested that he knew Powell sufficiently well to be concerned at the bachelor's tendency to drive himself hard.[16]

During late January and early February, Powell campaigned tirelessly in Normanton, but as Frank Barber, a reporter who met him during the by-election, wrote, 'he had not the slightest prospect of winning, he was merely polling-fodder to give the Conservatives a show'. The campaign was fought within weeks of the Government's much-vaunted nationalization of the pits that had been welcomed throughout the coalfields. Conditions were atrocious, as the severe cold weather that hit the country on 24 January developed into a great freeze, exacerbated by the winter's crippling coal shortage. 'It was a horrible winter,' recalled a Yorkshire Conservative MP who helped in the campaign. 'Everything was frozen up. The fight was hopeless. You either had hundreds turning up to jeer you – or no one. Powell impressed you as dedicated, decisive and madly keen, even if he had little warmth or humour.' However great the hardships, Powell never allowed himself to lose sight of his objective and his longer-term reason for fighting Normanton. As Barber remembered, when he found the young Conservative candidate 'huddled in a chilly room' and asked him what he thought he was doing there, Powell 'fixed me with a cold stare and said: "My time will come"'.[17]

At Powell's adoption meeting on 11 January, he echoed the gaffe that Churchill had made during the 1945 campaign, and warned that already a Labour 'Gestapo, as yet in a mild form and under the reassuring title of inspectors or enforcement officers, pry into private lives'. Powell even claimed that parliament was becoming a 'rubber-stamp Reichstag'. The country was suffering from the 'moral and material consequences of state socialism'. In another Churchillian flourish, he lambasted Labour's withdrawal from empire as 'a desire to get out of the troublesome difficulties at whatever sacrifice of future safety'. It was a cause that was close to his heart, and, in the comment quoted at the head of this chapter, he adopted the portentousness of an oracle in some classical tragedy.[18]

Apart from these stirring interventions, Powell generally reiterated unexceptional Conservative propaganda. While Conservatives supported a fair distribution of the golden eggs laid by the goose of private industry, he argued that Labour would kill the goose. But the fuel crisis gave added weight to his claims that 'the Socialist Government' had put 'the wrong things first' and that there was 'no sign' that they had 'seriously considered those urgent and practical steps which one needs to put this country on its feet again'. When polling took place on 12 February, there was little surprise that Labour held the seat comfortably, but their majority had fallen by about 8,000 to 14,827. The fuel crisis appeared to have taken its toll, enabling Powell to score the first by-election 'swing' against the Attlee Government.[19]

Eight days after his defeat at Normanton, as Powell sat in the official box in the chamber of the House of Lords (where the Commons met while their chamber was being rebuilt after the war), he witnessed the historic moment when Attlee told MPs that the transfer of power in India would take place not later than June 1948. 'There was a moment in the late 1940s when it could have gone either way,' Powell was later to reflect on the course that Indian independence took. 'It could have happened that we would have needed to maintain some development of the existing connection for five, [or] ten years.' Instead, 'we precipitately cleared up'. As the India Independence Bill passed through parliament, Anthony Eden, *de facto* deputy leader of the Conservatives, made sure that, as far as possible, Churchill was kept away from the

Commons for fear that he would use his position as leader to jettison his party's acquiescence and commit them to outright opposition.[20]

It had been the Conservative Party that Powell had chosen as the 'vehicle and framework' by which he would seek the highest office in India, but it was not to be the last time that the party would fail to live up to his expectations. Neither was it to be the last time that his sentiments were shared by an element in the Labour Party, since Powell would have found a receptive ear for his views on India from Labour's Foreign Secretary, Ernest Bevin. As we now know from the official papers, this formidable former trade union leader strongly objected to Attlee's setting an early deadline for independence, echoing Lord Curzon on the indispensability of India to Britain's status as a world power. Attlee, however, overruled his friend and ally. In doing so, he had also destroyed Powell's greatest ambition.[21]

'It was a shattering moment, a shattering undeception', was how Powell remembered vividly the instant when he realized the inevitability of India's rapid transition to independence. The shock of being woken so abruptly from the 'dream' of the India that he had known, and that he had thought would last for the foreseeable future, was traumatic:

> The bottom had dropped out of my world. And the assumptions and presumptions with which I had returned to this country from India and out of uniform had gone, and I had to find my way in a new world. I remember I wandered round the streets in London that night, sitting on doorsteps with my head in my hands, wondering what to do and where to go.[22]

Powell's evident despair at the precipitate ending of the Raj gave credence to a story that entered Old Queen Street folklore. According to T.E. Utley, it was said that after Powell had been to see Churchill to assist in the preparation of a speech on India, the party leader rang up the Research Department to ask, 'Who is that young madman who has been telling me how many divisions I would need to reconquer India?' However, no trace of any such proposal by Powell was found by the present author in the surviving papers of the Secretariat or the Research Department. It is possible that since Powell's suggestion and Churchill's complaint were alleged to have been made orally, they were never minuted. In addition, Cosgrave – who 'utterly' rejects the story – identifies its chief disseminator as having been Rab Butler, but although Butler had a mischievous sense of humour he was unlikely to have indulged in a complete fabrication, and it would almost certainly have been he, in his capacity as Chairman of the Research Department with his office in Old Queen Street, whom Churchill would have telephoned. None the less, Powell's denial of having made any such proposal to Churchill rings true. Recalling the year he had spent in India on the committee 'studying the future of the Indian Army under the assumption that there would be a continued British connection', he suspected that 'probably the report of that committee and the reference to it was the basis for the false report that I recommended to

Churchill in the late 1940s that we should conquer India with ten divisions – something which no sane person could imagine'. By Powell's account, it seems plausible that Churchill, having misunderstood a reference to the report on the Indian Army, complained – unjustifiably – to Butler about 'that young madman'.[23]

In common with Lord Curzon and Ernie Bevin, Powell had regarded India as the corner-stone of the British Empire. As he wrote some thirty years after its independence, 'it was for the sake of India, or rather of the supposed necessities of that link with India, that literally every other possession in the Old World was acquired and maintained'. It therefore followed that with the loss of India, there was little point in Britain's retaining the rest of its colonies. Yet Powell was to remain a strong imperialist for about another five years. None the less, the loss of India was to mark one of the most important steps in the development of his concept of the nature of his nation, its policies, and its role in the world.[24]

'Now India has gone,' Maudling told Powell, 'I don't think politics will hold you any longer.' But Maudling was wrong. Powell insisted, because of his strong opposition to Conservative policy, that he should no longer be responsible for briefing the party on India. But although he found that it 'was a tremendous challenge' to accept that the purpose for which he had come into politics had become an 'unreality', another fascination had already taken hold. He had, in his own words, 'been sufficiently entranced by the political process of the United Kingdom, sufficiently captured even as a spectator by the House of Commons, no longer to wish to escape'.[25]

Powell's letter of resignation as secretary of the Tory back bench India committee, in protest at Conservative policy, was one of the first letters typed for him by a new secretary, Pamela Wilson. Pamela was in her early twenties when she began working as Powell's secretary during the spring of 1947, and had recently returned from America, where she had worked for just over a year with the military staff of the United Nations, high up in New York's Empire State Building. She had loved her time in New York and was fed up at having to return to Britain because of the dollar crisis. In those days, the Research Department's secretaries were recruited by Miss Avis Lewis, who felt not only that Pamela's obvious competence would meet Powell's high standards, but that her cheerful disposition might even make 'the Brigadier' smile. Unlike some of the other secretaries, Pamela was unlikely to be intimidated by his military bearing – she was the daughter of a Colonel in the Indian Army and had worked for a Naval Captain in New York. Almost 50 years later, Powell told the political biographer, Michael Cockerell, that he had been beguiled when he interviewed Pamela by a brooch that she wore on her hat, depicting a champagne bottle in a bucket. She found him formal and more serious than her boss in New York, but thought that he was easy to work for and was grateful when he helped her to understand references to arcane reforms in a speech that Harold Macmillan had dictated to her about India. Research Department folklore has it that she was the first secretary who survived working for Powell without suffering a nervous breakdown and that she was the only one who was prepared to share with him the cramped and rickety lift at Number 24. She was eventually to bring out a more humorous and sociable side in his personality, but it was several years before their romance developed.[26]

'The Brigadier' and policy

Powell's appetite for work remained insatiable. After his expected defeat at Normanton his search for a seat continued, as did his speaking engagements – on the evening of Friday 4 July 1947 he spoke on housing in Bexley, where Edward Heath was shortly to end his long quest for a constituency. In the Secretariat, Powell was more industrious than ever, attending the weekly meetings of the parliamentary party's committees on housing and local government, town and country planning, defence, and the army, and doing his full share of briefing on the Attlee Government's flood of legislation. His main pre-occupation in the first half of 1947 was the Town and Country Planning Bill, on which he demonstrated his tactical awareness.[27]

Powell's minute of the Conservative back bench town and country planning committee meeting on 20 January noted that although Tory MPs felt that the legislation contained 'a number of highly objectionable features', they accepted that it represented an attempt to consolidate and improve existing law, and declined to oppose it outright. He had sensed their likely response beforehand, and had already advised Central Office that although the Bill was likely to give a further impetus to 'grandiose and objectionable' town planning schemes, 'we shall not take the field against the planning mania as such but rather wait until its consequences are more evident to the public at large through one or two practical demonstrations of failure'. Powell prepared about forty briefing notes on the legislation between January and August 1947, including a thirty-seven page summary of proceedings at the committee stage, in addition to his briefings for debates on house-building, rural housing and local government finance, among others, during the same period.[28]

This prodigious output of Powell's, on an array of subjects, was maintained during the rest of 1947 and for most of 1948. In August 1947, following some confusion in ministerial pronouncements on the size of the army, Powell 'felt obliged to get the figures straightened out'. In the autumn, he briefed on the Local Government Bill that was designed to equalize the burden of the rates. At around the same time, when reform of the House of Lords was mooted by the Government, he discovered that there was no authoritative account of the early years of the upper chamber, as distinct from histories of parliament. Despite his punishing workload and the time spent outside office hours making speeches and seeking a seat, he decided to embark on such a study. This project was to be repeatedly interrupted by the pressures of a political career, including periods of ministerial office, but characteristically Powell never gave up, and the final results were to be published more than twenty years later.[29]

Like others in the Secretariat and Research Department, Powell's war service influenced his relationship with front bench spokesmen and MPs. When Brigadier Head, a front bench spokesman, thanked Powell in December 1947 for having been the 'main prop and stay' of the army committee and sent his best wishes for the New Year, he was writing to an officer of equal rank. 'As a Parliamentary Spiv,' he quipped, in the vernacular of the time, 'I salute the workers of Old Queen Street and hope they don't start a union.' Powell's generation sometimes dispensed their advice with a self-assurance that was seldom to be surpassed by their successors, who tended to be younger and lacked similar experience. Lord Egremont, who as John Wyndham worked in the Research Department, personally found Powell 'gentle, considerate, good-humoured and good-natured,' but recalled that when a member of the Tory front bench complained at some action by the Research Department, Powell simply replied: 'There is a reason for everything.'[30]

On another occasion, Powell was consulted by Central Office about the advice given by John Hay, chairman of the Young Conservatives and a candidate in Brixton, over a war disability pension case. Powell advised that 'the candidate has been very foolish ... to refer to a mythical "compassionate pension" or to raise the man's expectations' – Hay was later to become a close political ally and friend of Powell's. Similarly blunt advice was despatched to Churchill's staff about a young officer in the Dragoon Guards who had written about the hardship of being married. Powell had 'no reason to suppose' that the party disagreed with the policy 'that there should be no inducement to Regular officers to marry in the early twenties'. As he elaborated, 'nobody obliged Lieutenant [X] ... to marry at the age of twenty or less, when he was perfectly aware of the financial consequences and was intending a career as a Regular Officer. He has therefore no complaint.'[31]

Even senior front-benchers were liable to receive forthright comments from Powell. As Eden discovered towards the end of the 1940s, Powell's self-assurance, allied with his conviction on imperial policy, was a formidable combination. Having called on Eden to brief him on housing for a passage in a forthcoming speech in Nottingham, Powell had seized his moment as their meeting ended, and asked, 'Well, I've told you what I know about housing, may I speak to you on another subject on which you know a great deal and I know nothing?' 'Yes, what is it?' Eden replied. 'In the Middle East our enemy is not Russia,' Powell declared, 'it is the United States.' Some years later, Eden recalled this incident to an artist who was painting his portrait and confessed, 'Do you know, I couldn't think what he was talking about.' As Powell wryly observed almost forty years after the Suez débâcle, after 1956 Eden knew what he had meant. Powell had become convinced by the time that he left Cairo in 1943 that the Americans 'were our chief enemy. That the United States was fundamentally antipathetical to Britain as an imperial power, and committed in a sense by its very nature to the destruction of Britain as an imperial nation.'[32]

Powell became more involved in policy making from the start of 1948, the mid-point of the Labour-dominated Parliament, as the Conservatives began to step up their work on new policies ready for the next election, due by the summer of 1950 at the latest. Although policy making had traditionally been the preserve of the Research Department, Powell and his fellow members of the Secretariat had developed formidable expertise in their subjects. This merging of roles was confirmed in October 1948 when the Secretariat and the Research Department were combined, and Powell was appointed joint head, with Macleod, of the enlarged Department's new Home Affairs Section, based in 34 Old Queen Street.[33]

Wales provided one of Powell's first opportunities to make a distinctive contribution to party policy – appropriately, because of his family origins, and, as with defence and India, it was a subject with which he had a special affinity. Moreover, his contribution to the party's approach to Wales is important because he reveals an acute sensitivity to political and social factors, and a recognition that they should not always be subordinated to *laissez-faire* economics – the doctrine that he was later to expound with impassioned fervour. The catalyst for Powell's work was the resolution passed at the Conservative Conference at Brighton in October 1947, that called on the party 'to formulate and declare a policy for Wales', and the Labour Government's attempt to demonstrate its special commitment by publishing a White Paper on the Principality. In the light of these developments, Powell spent ten days in January 1948 during the parliamentary recess meeting 'representative Conservatives' throughout rural Wales. On his return to Old Queen Street, he compiled an eleven-page paper 'to ascertain in what general directions, so far as rural Wales is concerned, a Conservative policy for Wales should be sought', and sent copies to Rab Butler, Central Office, front-benchers and MPs closely concerned with Wales.[34]

'The all-embracing practical object of policy', in Powell's submission, had to be 'to enable the inhabitants of rural Wales to live, work and prosper in their native country, or even in their native districts, and to assure the like prospect for succeeding generations.' This is not the language of market forces, and when he claimed that his objective was 'consistent with the historic outlook of Conservatism', he was evoking the paternalist tradition associated with Disraeli. Powell was explicit in his concern to prevent a repetition of the 'drift from the land' of a century earlier, and the loss of the 'most socially valuable and stable elements' of rural life. To this end, he identified practical, low-cost proposals to assist agriculture and industry – in order of importance, on roads, water supply, hill-farming, housing, education, electricity, afforestation, land for training, quarrying and minor industries, including tourism. Among his suggested 'sentimental' recommendations, he favoured steps to demonstrate the party's 'sympathy with the Welsh language', including Welsh-speaking candidates in Welsh-speaking areas.

Yet the key recommendation was Powell's strong endorsement to calls by 'Conservatives of all shades that separate Ministerial representation for Wales is a *sine qua non*'. He found no demand for greater devolution or a separate Welsh Department on the lines of the Scottish Office, but identified as the real need 'the provision at the centre of some single authority in, or with access to, the Cabinet and charged with ensuring attention to Welsh interests in all spheres of government'. He thought this function could be combined with some other office, such as Lord Privy Seal or Lord President, 'provided the relationship to Wales was explicitly recognized'.[35]

So favourable was the report's reception that within two months of its completion, the General Director at Central Office, Sir Stephen Pierssené, instructed his Cardiff office to help Powell arrange a similar fact-finding visit to industrial south Wales. In his call for 'a comprehensive policy, social and industrial' for south Wales, Powell identified the 'pivot' as being housing – a popular demand among the Tory rank and file at the time – and suggested that the back-log of construction from the 1930s justified special measures 'to stimulate house-building'. Better transport was also vital, and, within the resources available, Powell urged the 'linking of the coastal plain with the valleys by faster and cheaper road and rail services', and the 'improvement of the road connection with areas in the West and South Midlands'. Moreover, he deplored the lack of frankness by major industries about their plans and their impact on employment, and declared that it should be accepted as 'fundamental' that where large-scale reorganization was planned, 'the Government has the duty to be publicly satisfied' that minimum social dislocation would occur, and that the 'appropriate authorities' would minimize the effects upon 'the lives and well-being of the individuals concerned'.[36]

Powell's reports formed the basis for Conservative policy in Wales. In the appropriate setting of Llandudno, Rab Butler drew heavily on Powell's work in setting out the principles of Conservative policy for Wales, and announced the future publication of a policy statement. *The Statement of Policy for Wales and Monmouthshire*, the so-called 'Welsh Charter', was finally launched on St David's Day, 1 March 1949, with simultaneous press conferences in Cardiff and London. As Powell had also suggested, the Charter was published in both English and Welsh, and generally received full coverage in the Welsh press, where the proposal for separate Ministerial representation for Wales attracted most attention.[37]

The Conservatives' emphasis on freeing Britain from the mass of post-war controls and regulations, some inherited from the war, others imposed by Labour, was also reflected in Powell's policy work. In May 1948, he was concerned at the lack of thinking given to town and country planning, and warned that the 1947 Act was likely to present a Conservative Government with 'the most difficult of all its administrative and legislative problems'. The legislation had 'effected what is virtually the nationalization of the land, since it transferred to the ownership of the state all rights of property in land except the right to continue its existing use'. But Powell was not advocating a free-for-all, since he accepted the need for some curb on development.[38]

The controversial question of housing rents provided the clearest example of Powell's pursuing a free-market argument on an issue with which he was to become closely identified. At the time, the rents that most private tenants paid were restricted, and landlords had to charge a 'fair rent', that was settled by a tribunal. He was dismayed to discover in August 1948 that the policy committee on housing had omitted to seek the approval of Rab Butler, in his role as policy overlord, to include the contentious issue of rent restriction in their study, but so 'pervasive' was the influence of these Acts 'on the whole housing problem that without considering their effect the whole study would be rendered unreal'. Butler gave his assent. When the committee reported to the Shadow Cabinet in March 1949, priority was given to increased house-building. Although the committee proposed moving towards the abolition of rent restriction, they avoided any mention of such plans in their draft statement. The Conservatives were aware of the political sensitivity of rents, and it was some years before they attempted the fundamental reform in which Powell was to play a central role.[39]

The roots of large-scale, non-white immigration into Britain – an issue on which Powell was to play an even more controversial role than on rents – can also be traced back to 1948, at the very moment when the Labour Government introduced their British Nationality Bill. The first influx of post-war immigrants, in the shape of about 500 Jamaicans, arrived at Tilbury on board the SS *Empire Windrush* on 21 June 1948, to the Government's consternation, while the Bill was still under consideration in the Lords and before it reached the Commons. But neither Powell's briefing nor the parliamentary debates focused on the issue of possible future mass immigration. The widely-held assumption remained that any significant movement of population was more likely to involve emigration from the United Kingdom to the Empire and Commonwealth. Britain could continue its policy of no restrictions, and, in the tradition of imperial Rome's *civis Romanus sum*, could safely uphold the doctrine of *civis Britannicus sum*. One of the criticisms of the Bill made from the Conservative front bench in the debates on the Bill on 7 and 13 July – and echoed in the Research Department briefing – was the threat that it posed to this doctrine. Indeed, proudly proclaiming the lack of 'colour bar restrictions' on immigration into Britain, Sir David Maxwell Fyfe (later Lord Kilmuir), a future Conservative Home Secretary, reiterated that 'we must maintain our great metropolitan tradition of hospitality to everyone from every part of our Empire.'[40]

The need for the new nationality legislation had been triggered not by fears of mass immigration but by the need to coordinate Commonwealth policy. Citizens of the Empire and Commonwealth had shared common status as British subjects, because they had been born 'within His Majesty's allegiance' – self-governing countries in the Commonwealth had remained monarchies under the British Crown. But in 1946 Canada's new Citizenship Act changed this principle by declaring that 'a Canadian citizen is a British subject'. In theory, it became possible for Canada to renounce its allegiance to the Crown and become a Republic, but for its citizens to remain, in the eyes of Canada, British subjects. However, what was only a remote possibility in the case of Canada seemed certain to happen in India, which was likely to become a Republic after independence. In response, a conference of Commonwealth experts in 1947 agreed 'that each independent Commonwealth country would determine its own nationality laws, but all Commonwealth countries would recognize that citizenship of any Commonwealth country was a sufficient qualification for a common status of Commonwealth citizen, or British subject'. The enactment of this agreement was the main purpose of the 1948 British Nationality Bill. The Bill also established that although the Irish Free State had declared itself a Republic and was recognized to be no part of the British Empire, its citizens were to be treated as though they were United Kingdom citizens.

Powell's chief concern at the time, and one that was voiced by Conservative spokesmen, was the Bill's impact on the unity of the British Empire and Commonwealth. Underlying this issue lay the principle of shared allegiance to the British Crown, on which the unity of the Empire and Commonwealth, 'as evinced by the common status of its peoples', had been based. The Research Department's briefing advised that, by extending the change of principle incorporated in the new Canadian Act to the whole Commonwealth, the Bill 'destroys the existing bond of union and substitutes a purely statutory connection' – a British subject was defined as a person who was a citizen of either the United Kingdom and Colonies, or of one of a list of self-governing territories. It therefore became possible 'for the first time' for territories whose governments do not recognize the British monarch as their sovereign to remain in the Commonwealth. Such a development might be 'desirable', and on the eve of the formulation of a new Indian constitution, the Government 'may regard the change as convenient and hope that it will slip by unobserved'. However, the change represented a 'constitutional revolution' that ought to be recognized:

There is an essential difference between union dependent upon allegiance to a common hereditary sovereign and union dependent on a series of statutes equating one status with another. The recognition by two nations of the same hereditary monarch is an assertion of the expectation and intention of permanent association. It differs essentially in character and in value from a connection resting upon statute and therefore dissoluble by statute.

Powell's concern at the change in the nature of the union between Commonwealth countries reflected his Tory respect for 'immanent authority', embodied in the British sovereign, and sowed the seeds of the contempt in which he came to hold the Commonwealth.[41]

Later in his career, Powell was frequently to criticize the 1948 Act for having facilitated large-scale non-white immigration into Britain. Faced with the prospect of India's becoming an independent republic, Britain had attempted, in what Powell was to describe in 1987 as 'a posthumous flight of fantasy', to maintain the fiction of a dead Empire in the form of an enlarged Commonwealth:

> So the question arose, are we going to accept, are we going to be prepared to accept that there was an Empire, there were eight hundred million British subjects all round the globe, and are no longer? Are we capable of accepting that the only subjects in a political sense are those who live under the Parliament of the United Kingdom of Great Britain and Northern Ireland. And we wouldn't face it, so we said let's pretend, and in order to pretend we altered the basis of our law of citizenship. We said we will alter the law, it is no longer allegiance, it is no longer those who were born in the allegiance to the Crown, it will be those who are the citizens of a list of countries ... and we thus created a citizenship of the United Kingdom – and this only applies to the United Kingdom – we thus altered our own law in such a manner that persons who had no connection with us, no allegiance to, no commonality with the United Kingdom, were in the law of the United Kingdom indistinguishable from those born here and belonging here. It was a deliberate act of self-humbug which we did in order to maintain the fiction that the Empire had passed into an equally great and glorious Commonwealth.[42]

But Powell appears, in his 1987 explanation of events of almost forty years earlier, to have been blessed with 'twenty-twenty hindsight', in the phrase used by Lord Roll in another context. In 1948, Powell had himself been primarily concerned about the threat to the unity of the Empire and the Commonwealth. A year after the passage of the 1948 Act, the Conservatives explicitly accepted the prospect of non-white immigration in their policy document, *The Right Road for Britain*. The document was drafted by David Clarke, a joint Director of the Research Department in which Powell still worked (albeit on a part-time basis), and re-affirmed that, 'there must be freedom of movement among its members within the British Empire and Commonwealth. New opportunities will present themselves not only in the countries overseas but in the Mother Country, and must be open to all citizens.'[43]

A bumpy road to Wolverhampton

Having been 'blooded' at Normanton in February 1947, Powell had taken up the search for a winnable seat in earnest. His quarry proved elusive, and he was to suffer nineteen rejections over a period of almost two years before he finally succeeded. It was a frustrating time, but Powell remembered 'particularly kindly' the encouragement he received from Iain Macleod, his colleague in the Secretariat. 'When I was going to be interviewed for a constituency,' Powell later recalled, 'he used to talk me through the questions likely to be put to me and to brief me on the manner in which to handle them.' Much though he appreciated this assistance, Powell sensed a difference between them. Macleod 'was playing a game and playing it to win. He wished me to play the game and play it in order to win.' The implication is that Powell was not as cynical in his approach to politics, whereas Macleod 'was always a gamesman'. Yet Macleod's career was to demonstrate that although he was calculating, he was not a mere cynic and was prepared to court unpopularity on causes in which he believed. The extent to which Powell was calculating needs to be assessed in the context of his career, but in T.E. Utley's judgement, although Powell considered the morality of what he was doing, 'few men calculate more closely the effects of their words and actions'.[44]

Powell's prospects were not helped by his austere, intense and reserved manner that often gave a forbidding impression. He was regarded by constituency agents, whose opinions carried weight in the selection process, as a 'poor mixer', and 'not a good man for the bar parlour'. His modest social background also counted against him. Another ambitious, but socially awkward, would-be candidate of lower-middle-class origins who had had a good war, Lieutenant-Colonel Edward Heath, MBE, was having the same trouble as Powell in finding a seat. Despite the determined efforts of the party chairman, Lord Woolton, to encourage a wider cross-section of candidates, local parties often continued to opt for applicants with traditional public school backgrounds.[45]

In the more urban parts of his native West Midlands, however, Powell's origins were unlikely to count against him and were even something of an asset. From a Conservative agent in the region came a suggestion that he should seek the nomination at Brierley Hill, but he decided not to apply – this Black Country seat, located to the south of Dudley and home to many workers at the large Round Oak steelworks, was not won by the Conservatives until their 1959 landslide. During the autumn of 1948, and following the re-drawing of constituency boundaries, Powell became interested in a new seat, Wolverhampton South-West, an industrial and residential area to the north of the Black Country, that had been created mainly from the old Wolverhampton West, and part of the Cannock division. The Central Office Agent for the West Midlands, the party's senior professional in the region, Colonel Ledingham, reckoned that 'given a good candidate and reasonably favourable conditions, [that] we could win the seat'. Wolverhampton West already had a candidate, Patrick Stirling, a London-based barrister, who was the son-in-law of the president of the association, Sir Charles Mander. But at a meeting of the committee formed to bring the new association into being, representatives from neither Cannock nor Wolverhampton West were prepared to recommend Stirling, although they agreed to include his name on a list of candidates for consideration by the new selection committee.[46]

Noting the wish by Tories in Wolverhampton South-West to have 'candidates with some political experience, preferably those who have fought a seat at the General Election', Ledingham warned J.P.L. Thomas (later Viscount Cilcennin), the party vice-chairman responsible for candidates, that 'unless we can produce one or two good names, Patrick Stirling will be re-adopted'. Experienced names were thin on the ground when many new constituencies were having to seek candidates, but Thomas did not think that his list for Wolverhampton South-West 'could be bettered'. Among those about whom Central Office had 'recently had excellent reports' were Lieutenant-Commander Ronald Bell, who was to become a long-serving back bench MP and exponent of market economics; and Major Angus Maude and Mr John Peyton, both of whom were eventually to rise to Cabinet rank. Brigadier Powell was among seventeen names on Thomas's list, that included two highly recommended women candidates.[47]

What happened at the selection meeting in Wolverhampton on Friday 4 December was to become the subject of some dispute. Powell's bid began inauspiciously when, as he was about to meet the executive council, its chairman told his colleagues, 'Now I just want to say to you before the next candidate comes in, don't be put off by appearances.' As Audrey Rose, who was chairman of the Young Conservatives, recalls, Powell 'had very piercing eyes and this very short haircut – I do mean terribly short'. But although he seemed 'rather dour and serious', he was 'very commanding', had a 'real presence' and was 'terribly sincere'. The Young Conservatives 'were absolutely convinced' that Powell should become the candidate, but the older members of the selection committee were less sure. In the end, however, youth won the day and Powell was adopted.[48]

But Stirling, who had been the candidate in Wolverhampton West for some eighteen months, was sore at being unhorsed and wrote an intemperate letter to the party chairman, Lord Woolton, claiming that Powell had enjoyed an unfair advantage as a party employee. Whereas Stirling had to earn a living in London, and could only attend in the evening and on Fridays and Saturdays, he alleged that Powell had said that he had been authorized to say that although he was employed in the Secretariat, he could spend four full days a week (including Saturdays) in Wolverhampton. No sooner had Stirling's letter of Sunday 12 December landed on Lord Woolton's desk than the matter threatened to escalate into a public row, that would be damaging to the party and also to Powell, whose formal adoption meeting was due in a few days' time. Reports of Powell's selection and his promise to spend a great deal of time in the constituency appeared on Monday 13th in Wolverhampton's *Express and Star* and two days later in the *Daily Telegraph*'s 'Peterborough' column, then edited by Bill Deedes, himself a Tory candidate. Mark Chapman-Walker of the Central Office publicity department liaised with Henry Hopkinson, a joint Director of the Research Department, to check what undertakings Powell had given. Powell explained that when Rab Butler had invited him to become joint head of the new Home Affairs Section, he had said that he hoped soon to be adopted as a candidate and the calls on his time in the constituency might make it necessary for him to work only part-time, or else resign from the Research Department. In those circumstances, if Butler preferred, he would decline the offer of the new post. However, Butler had been sure that arrangements could be made so that Powell could devote whatever time was necessary to the constituency. Accordingly, when asked by the Executive Council in Wolverhampton South-West how much time he could devote, Powell had said 'he would give whatever was necessary to do the work. If it proved to be necessary, he would either give up the whole or part of his present job. On being called back and asked to state a definite period, he said that in view of his assurance already given this was not necessary, but if he had to state a period he would say four days a week averaged out during the year.'[49]

Powell had behaved properly and had been prepared either to give up his job or accept a cut in salary, but in making his offer to the selection committee he had taken full advantage of having such an understanding employer. Butler's sympathetic behaviour, and Powell's action, lends credence to the widely-held impression that Butler was a political patron to would-be politicians in the Research Department. Certainly, Powell was in a more fortunate position than most contenders for a seat. Although Stirling had not been a popular candidate in the old seat, and his accusations against Powell were wide of the mark, few candidates could have matched Powell's promise to spend so much time in the new seat. It also helped Powell that, at the age of thirty-six, he had led an abstemious life since leaving home and could contemplate working part-time, or living off his savings for a year or so.

On Friday 17 December, only three days after his colleague, Macleod, had been confirmed as the Tory candidate in Enfield West, Powell was formally adopted as the prospective Conservative candidate for Wolverhampton South-West. In proposing Powell as the new candidate, the association chairman made an exceptionally long speech, and left the seconder, Audrey Rose, with little to add. But on the spur of the moment, she realized the local significance in the Black Country of Powell's second name, Enoch, and declared, 'Let's get our "Aynuck" into Parliament!' After this, there was never any question that Powell would be introduced not as John, but as 'Enoch' to his constituents, and eventually to the wider world. In February 1949, he agreed to a further change of *persona*. 'Mr J.E. Powell has agreed to drop his title of Brigadier in the Division,' Colonel Ledingham informed Central Office in London, implying that Powell had had to be persuaded of the change. But Powell was happy in his constituency. 'I found myself very much at home there,' he was to recall. 'After all it was the part of the country I came from, where I'd grown up.'[50]

In his adoption speech, Powell warmed to the theme that was to inspire the Conservative campaign at the next election – setting people free from controls and regulations, while preserving a welfare state. He warned that if Labour were to be re-elected, socialism would be extended to the retail trade, distribution and other things close to people's lives. But as Powell was to note several years later, a political party, 'especially in a two-party state, is immensely embracing and can include within its limits diametrically opposite opinions on almost all subjects except the one or two which happen to be the immediate ground of party conflict at the particular time'. His own iconoclastic approach to political issues was evident in his early journalism, mainly for the *Birmingham Post* and the *Newcastle Journal*. He made little effort to conceal his contempt for the American character in his review of Eisenhower's memoirs for the *Sunday Sun* on 2 January 1949, when he wrote witheringly of 'that lack of subtlety and of appreciation for the complex and problematic which often makes it appear to the Englishman crude and naive.'[51]

Even more striking was Powell's early questioning of the assumptions shared by the Government and Opposition front benches on Britain's possession of the atomic bomb. 'The atom bomb may not be used', he declared in an article for the *Newcastle Journal* in July 1949, and asked whether it was worth it and necessary. In the first place, it would be 'some years before any nation likely to be our enemy is ready to wage war with atomic bombs' – in fact, within two months, President Truman delivered the shattering news that the Soviet Union had tested an atomic bomb, and in March 1950 the Soviet military confirmed that they possessed atomic bombs. As to the future, 'when atom bombs are a stock line in the principal arsenals of the world, the absolute certainty of reprisals reduces the likelihood of their being used, though it cannot, of course, eliminate the possibility'. Powell was always to harbour doubts about Britain's being an atomic power.[52]

Until the spring of 1949, Powell continued working full-time in London. Who better, in February, to brief on the Anti-Blood Sports Bills that were being introduced, than the fox-hunting Brigadier? But there was no echo of Jorrocks or Squire Mytton in his two-page briefing note, which virtually ignored the usual arguments about the role of blood sports in countryside tradition or pest control and instead offered Conservative MPs a philosophical treatise on the concept of 'cruelty' to animals. Powell's expertise was eagerly sought on other, more mainstream political subjects. He was co-opted to serve on the London County Council's housing committee at the suggestion of Henry Brooke, who had served in the pre-war Research Department and who had been deputed to lead the Conservatives on the LCC after losing his parliamentary seat in 1945 – the association between the two men on housing policy was to last many years.[53]

But from May 1949, Powell began working part-time in the Research Department. In June, he resigned his post as joint head of the Home Affairs Section. Although he remained as a part-time adviser, his colleague, Philip Bremridge, spoke for others when he noted that 'the quality and value of papers on defence questions have deteriorated since Brigadier Powell gave up these subjects'.[54]

Powell quickly established an equally impressive intellectual reputation in Wolverhampton, although there were some doubts about his personality. 'A very enthusiastic and hard working candidate', was Colonel Ledingham's verdict on Powell in his constituency report for August 1949. 'His keenness tends to make him tense', the Central Office Agent added, 'and that, coupled with a rather shy personality, does not make him a good mixer. His political knowledge is brilliant and he puts his case across well in a very convincing manner. He is canvassing every house in the constituency.' Ledingham's assessment of the party's prospects in Wolverhampton South-West was optimistic. 'The local government election gave a good indication of the trend of public opinion in this division. Taking the results into account and bearing in mind the strength of the organization and the ability of the candidate, this seat should be won.'[55]

Powell had taken a small flat in the centre of Wolverhampton, on the top floor of 17 Chapel Ash, above a dentist's surgery. 'I like it here', he told a visiting journalist from the local paper. 'It's very quiet, the rent is reasonable, there's plenty of sun and it's ideally situated in the division. I do most of my writing here.' The reporter, who had arrived to find Powell frying sausages for breakfast, was reminded, by the camp bed and rough grey blankets that he saw, of 'an army officer's temporary billet'. Apart from politics, Powell admitted to no interests other than reading and writing, 'a spot of journalism', and riding and fox-hunting. 'But I don't suppose I've ever had any interests apart from my work,' and, as if further testimony were needed, his translation of *Herodotus* was also published in 1949.[56]

But it was during his early months in Wolverhampton that Powell underwent a profound change in his life. 'One night in Wolverhampton I was coming from the station', he recalled almost forty years later:

The bells of St Peter's were ringing for evensong and I went in. It was the first time I had been into a church for worship, to a service, for fifteen years or more. I sat down in a dark corner, just by the south door, hoping I wouldn't notice myself, because I didn't know what I was doing and I was rather ashamed of it. As I listened, the language of it all came back to me.

Powell has attended church on almost every Sunday since. But characteristically, he was content neither to remain merely a regular attender, nor to become the type of Anglican for whom religion is primarily a social activity, and port and stilton with the vicar at Christmas is the highlight of the calendar. The following Easter, Powell told himself, 'Look, you can't stay here, you either go back or you go forward.' He knew that he could not go back, 'so forward I went', and at 6 a.m. on Easter Sunday 1950 he took communion. In Powell's view, the Christian gospel can only be a matter of private conscience and has no practical bearing on particular political decisions. But his devout belief in Christ and the resurrection as the prerequisite to salvation were to remain essential to his private being.[57]

5

Straws in the Wind

An able and most hard working Member but quite inhuman and arrogant in personality with little or no knowledge of human psychology. His political worth is esteemed in Wolverhampton but his real friends are few.

Colonel Ledingham, Conservative Central Office Agent for the West Midlands, commenting on Enoch Powell, 7 May 1951.

Invoking Disraeli

British politics was transformed during the 1950s. When Powell first participated in a general election, in February 1950, electioneering was still characterized by vibrant debate in the constituencies. Within a decade, this was no longer so. 'The public meeting was killed stone dead by television,' he recalled more than forty years later. 'I saw it die, I saw it expire. But the public meeting was still alive and real in 1948–49–50. A meeting, successful or unsuccessful, really mattered.' Although Powell was to demonstrate to greater effect than any modern politician that, even in the age of television, a compelling speaker with a dramatic message could excite an audience and attract the media, his general point is valid – his exception as a platform speaker proved the rule, since it was to take quite extraordinary circumstances between 1968 and 1974 for Powell to breathe a last gasp of life into the old-style public meeting. When asked in his eighties whether his distinctive style of speaking had been fashioned by his early experience of public meetings, Powell stressed the importance to him of the chemistry between speaker and audience: 'I need to be talking to somebody, I need to be talking to heads in front of me.'[1]

Viewed from afar, the politics of the first half of the 1950s can appear deceptively calm. By 1950, the Conservatives were committed to the essentials of the post-war settlement, embodied in a mixed economy and a welfare state, that the 1945 Labour Government had introduced. And on foreign and defence policy both front benches shared the common assumption that Britain remained a world power. Yet the political climate into which Powell first ventured as an elected politician was anything but tranquil. In many ways, it was a formative period, in which politicians were groping their way forward in a new world with new problems. During Powell's first spell as a back bench MP, between 1950 and 1955, issues were raised that were to preoccupy him and dominate British politics over the following decades – Britain's role in the world, whether as a European or an imperial power; the nature and scope of the welfare state; the role of sterling; and immigration; to name but a few. In some cases these straws in the wind roused little political excitement although they gave concern behind the scenes in Whitehall, but on occasion some of them provoked lively, even anguished, public controversy. Among the new generation of Conservative MPs, few debated as confidently or energetically as Powell.

Devaluation of the pound in September 1949 – sterling crises were to become a recurrent event – provided an auspicious backdrop to Powell's first election campaign in Wolverhampton. A general election had to be held by the summer of 1950, but only four months after the value of the pound had been reduced from $4.03 to $2.80, Attlee decided to go to the country. With the psychological scars of devaluation fresh, and people suffering the immediate impact of higher prices but not yet reaping the rewards of increased exports, an early election favoured the Conservatives. Yet despite this boon and widespread frustration at the continuation of rationing, queues and the housing shortage, the prospect of Labour's 146-seat majority being overturned seemed remote. The more realistic test was how much of an inroad could the Tories make, and how many marginal Labour seats could they capture?

In the newly created marginal of Wolverhampton South-West, the young Tory high-flyer with the distinctive local Christian name of 'Enoch', who had been 'born in Birmingham 37 years ago of a Black Country family' – as his election address told voters – skilfully pitched his appeal to people's grievances. Powell wrote to his electors on 6 February 1950 from 17 Chapel Ash, his flat in the constituency,

In the last four years, I, like you, have watched the price of nearly everything rise and major shortages continue – or get worse. Other countries, even those invaded or defeated, have found themselves able to bring controls and rationing to an end; but for us the prospect seems, if anything, bleaker in 1950 than in 1945. We have watched, too, our country's strength and reputation in the world going to pieces in these years immediately after victory.

Powell was cleverly weaving together the dissatisfaction at home with the damage inflicted on national pride by devaluation and the loss of Britain's Asian Empire, although he made no explicit reference to these events. His patriotic appeal was strikingly emphasized by the use of red and blue ink for headlines and cross-heads in his election address, but this also reflected a

merging of local tradition and modern practice, since red was the Conservatives' colour in Wolverhampton, while blue represented the national party's
modern colour (though locally it was claimed by the Liberals).[2]

Disraeli was explicitly invoked by Powell, reflecting not only the soul-
searching in the party after the electoral catastrophe of 1945, but also revealing
his brand of Toryism. In post-war politics, harking back to Disraeli was to
become synonymous with 'One Nation' Conservatism, with which Powell was
to be involved, but which, over the years, came to be identified with leftish
Conservatives who tended to support state intervention. When Powell cited
the Victorian party leader in Wolverhampton in 1950, however, he was
affirming that his Toryism accorded as much importance to the British
constitution and a robust imperialism as to economic and social policy – 'the
objects of Conservatism' he declared, in the words of Disraeli's 1872 Crystal
Palace speech, were: 'the maintenance of our institutions; the preservation of
our Empire; and the improvement of the condition of the people'.[3]

Set free from his responsibilities as a party functionary, Powell enthusiastically played to the Conservatives' theme of 'setting the people free'. After a
decade of 'big government' during the war and immediately afterwards, a
reaction was to be expected in the shape of more liberal policies. Liberal
economics has long represented a strand within the Conservative Party, and
Powell was to come 'to see the market process as a means whereby a society
takes instinctively its own decisions and works out its future as it goes'. He
advocated increased competition, denationalization and tax cuts. 'Nothing
sends up prices like monopoly; nothing brings them down like competition',
he asserted, promising to 'denationalize the *iron and steel industry* and *road
transport*, re-open the *commodity exchanges*, end *bulk buying* and break the
State's *monopoly over land*'. [Powell's emphasis] However, in some respects,
Powell also echoed his party's pragmatism, acknowledging that 'where it is too
late to denationalize, we shall see that the State monopoly is run on *sound,
competitive lines*.' More optimistically, he predicted that taxation could be
reduced by 'saving hundreds of millions of pounds wasted by the Government
trying to do the other man's job'.[4]

The Conservative manifesto, *This is the Road*, had earned plaudits from the
Manchester Guardian for its 'enlightened' stance on social policy, 'from full
employment to education and the social services', but Powell was guarded in
his welcome for the welfare state. Whereas Iain Macleod in Enfield West was
happily embracing the goal of maintaining and improving the social services,
Powell prescribed the defeat of inflation as the priority in this area. 'Only if
prices are brought down', he wrote, emphasizing his message in bold type,
'will the pensions and social services which Conservatives introduced or
planned regain their value.' He made no mention of full employment, the
corner-stone of post-war social policy: quite what impact bringing down prices
would have had on jobs was left unstated. On housing, however, an area in
which he was 'specially interested', he was sensitive to the damaging charge
that the Tories were not fully committed to the public sector. 'Our idea is not

to build fewer council houses,' he reaffirmed, 'indeed, we are determined to *restart slum clearance* straightaway.' But in addition, 'a lot more houses must be built for other people as well, and costs and prices thus brought down'. The only sure way in which supply could match demand was by deregulation – 'the building industry, which *should be giving twice the present output of houses*, is hamstrung by interference and control'.[5]

Although Powell was as aware as anybody that bread-and-butter issues would settle the election and highlighted tax-cutting, house-building and price-reduction in his programme, he also stressed that 'there is another side, too, to all this'. The stock Conservative line, when Labour still espoused equality and nationalization, that people's liberty depended on the right to own property was extended by Powell to incorporate the long-established institutions of the British state as bastions of individual freedom. 'Nor can we have liberty,' he proclaimed, in the guise of a latter-day Lord Salisbury, 'without our constitution, our hereditary monarchy and House of Lords, a free and unfettered House of Commons, and the Rule of Law.'

But even a stout defence of the constitution was not, in Powell's view, sufficient safeguard of Britons' liberties and well-being. 'The United Kingdom can only be prosperous and safe as part of a great Empire,' he declared. Notwithstanding the loss of India, he was an avowed imperialist. Not for him the mere stewardship of Britain's imperial legacy: instead, his tone was expansive. 'To preserve, strengthen and extend our Empire', he waxed, 'is the mission of the Conservative Party.' Neither was there any premonition of the end of empire in his commitment to 'firm, just and enlightened rule' in the colonies, although it betokened the high standards of administration and justice upon which Powell was always to insist for all British territories. Nor was there any doubting his commitment to the Commonwealth in his reaffirmation that '*With the Dominions we want unity* in defence, in economic policy and in foreign affairs'. [Powell's emphasis] He apparently saw no contradiction in championing economic liberalism at home while expressing such Chamberlainite sentiments, that underpinned protectionism, or 'imperial preference', in the British Commonwealth and Empire.[6]

Campaigning – whether electoral or military was immaterial to Powell – had to be conducted with ruthless efficiency and a single-minded will to win. He spent months beforehand canvassing his constituency, street-by-street and door-to-door, and pulled no punches during the campaign in his scare-mongering about Labour's socialist intentions. His energy was rewarded, for among the 298 seats that returned Conservative MPs on 23 February 1950 was Wolverhampton South-West. Powell received 20,239 votes and defeated the Labour MP, M.D. ('Billy') Hughes, who had represented the old constituency of Wolverhampton West, by a majority of 691. Nationally, Labour's majority in the House of Commons was slashed to a mere six seats. Powell had no doubt as to the cause of the big swing against Attlee's Government. 'They overdid it', he recalled, and it's always dangerous in English politics to overdo it. They overdid the principle of nationalization. They overdid the principle of the free universal service, free universal benefits ... There had to be a reaction. Was it Disraeli who said, 'reaction is the law of English politics'?

However, there were two clouds on Powell's horizon. His constituency was one of three seats in the West Midlands in which the Liberals had polled well, winning over 4,000 votes. Privately, the Tory area chairman, Martin Lindsay, MP for Solihull, warned Central Office that 'all these three seats may well be lost if there is no Liberal candidate next time'. The more serious threat was self-inflicted. In his drive to win, Powell's habit of treating party volunteers, who included respected local figures, as military subordinates created ill-feeling in his constituency association that continued to fester while he began trying to make his mark at Westminster.[7]

At 6.21 p.m. on Thursday 16 March, just fifteen days after the opening of the new parliament, during a debate on defence, Powell rose to deliver his maiden speech in the House of Commons. It was an appropriate choice for a former Brigadier who had briefed his party on the subject, and in his sixteen-minute speech, he took up the defence of the Empire, on which he believed everything else in Britain depended. Despite his imperial theme, however, he sympathized with a concern voiced on the Labour benches – not the only, neither the last, time that he was to do so during his parliamentary career. Echoing Dick Crossman, whom he followed and who had spoken of the financial strain, Powell warned of 'the staggering burden' of the defence effort, especially in its demands on manpower. Britain's defence forces were 'approximately double the size they were in 1938', but the burden had more than doubled because it was being met by conscription, 'the least efficient and most dislocating to the national economy of any use of manpower'. Moreover, since 1938, Britain had lost the Indian Army while having to commit more forces in the Middle and Far East, and in Europe.[8]

Powell's prescription was two-fold. In the first place, he argued, 'if we are an Empire defending the Empire, we must draw far more than we do on the vast resources of Colonial manpower within the Empire.' It was 'imperative' that a replacement for the Indian Army should be created, primarily from 'our Malayan and our great African territories'. In addition, Australia, Canada and New Zealand had a smaller proportion of their manpower engaged in defence than Britain, and could afford to shoulder more of the burden. Powell went on to suggest that 'if what we are defending is indeed a unity – and the Tory Party at all events asserts that it is a unity', more than manpower was needed. He had in mind an ambitious proposal for a unified, Commonwealth defence organization – equivalent, at least, to the North Atlantic Treaty Organization (NATO), created in 1949. 'We require', Powell argued, 'instead of mere consultation, mere machinery of co-operation, usually left somewhat vague, a real recognition of a truly joint responsibility amongst all His Majesty's Governments for the defence of His Majesty's Dominions.' In his desire to build on the Dominions' shared allegiance to the Crown, he seemed ready to contemplate some loss of national sovereignty (already reduced by membership of NATO), acknowledging that 'such a demand raises far-reaching political implications'. But, he believed, 'unless we summon to the defence of this worldwide Empire all its resources, be they European or non-European, we shall fall under the load which we are attempting to bear.'[9]

However, Powell's proposals were anachronistic. Even when similar ideas had enjoyed wider currency half a century earlier, Joseph Chamberlain's hopes of building common imperial institutions had foundered on the lack of sufficient common interest among the Dominions. Moreover, like many of his British contemporaries, Powell was oblivious to a new, regional consciousness in the Dominions. As Lord Hunt, a former official in the old Dominions Office, has recalled, the signing by Australia and New Zealand of the ANZUS Pact with the United States in 1951 came as a great shock to many people in Britain.[10]

One Nation

The 'class of 1950' were one of the most impressive Tory intakes. Powell, Macleod and Maudling from the party's Secretariat were joined by Julian Amery, Robert Carr, Edward Heath, Angus Maude and Christopher Soames. Moreover, it was a propitious time to enter the Commons. 'We had the God-sent opportunity', Powell was to recall, 'with a narrow majority in the House, when one's services were in demand.' The newcomers were encouraged from the front bench and whips' office to harry the Government at every turn, but a number of them were dissatisfied that, despite a manifesto commitment to the welfare state, their party's handling of social policy was inept. The idea of setting up a ginger group had occurred to Cuthbert ('Cub') Alport, who ran the Conservative Political Centre (CPC), the party's political education organization, and who had identified Angus Maude, a deputy director of the research body, Political and Economic Planning (PEP), as a likely ally. Events moved fast. Gilbert Longden, Robert Carr, Richard Fort, John Rodgers, Edward Heath and Iain Macleod were also soon involved.[11]

When the new group met for their first lunch at PEP's office at 16 Old Queen Street, Macleod suggested another recruit: 'we've got to have Enoch,' he is reported to have urged. Powell became the ninth member. 'Presumably he regarded me as having a creative approach to party policy,' Powell commented years later on Macleod's action. Powell was to prove 'creative' in the same way as grit in an oyster. Although the new group initially had no name, their first meeting yielded a project when Macleod suggested that the CPC pamphlet that he had been asked to write on the social services should become a collective production. Each member was delegated to write a chapter, and, after their first meeting, the author of whichever chapter was under discussion usually took the chair. The authorship of each chapter was to remain anonymous. Appropriately, in view of his role in the Secretariat, Powell wrote about housing.[12]

The nine MPs eventually became known as the 'One Nation' group, and Powell's membership has puzzled many people who regard him as a scourge of the centrist Conservatism, commonly associated with fellow members of the group such as Heath and Macleod, and often characterized as 'One Nation Toryism'. The explanation is to be found in the genesis of the group in 1950, and the drifting apart of its members over the years as their differing interpretations of Toryism were accentuated by events – Alport, for example, left the Conservative Party in the 1980s to join the Social Democrats. It was not until the summer of 1950 that the name 'One Nation' originated, when a title had to be chosen for their first pamphlet, that was due to be published in time for October's party conference. One of the joint editors, either Macleod or Maude – there is dispute over who first had the idea – was inspired to suggest 'One Nation' by Disraeli's novel, *Sybil, or the Two Nations*, in which the social divisions created by unfettered *laissez-faire* capitalism were condemned. As a strong adherent of Disraeli's definition of Conservatism, Powell was unlikely to object. After publishing their work on social policy in October 1950 the nine MPs together were known as the One Nation group.[13]

'I knew what we were about in One Nation', Powell claimed many years later, 'was providing a philosophical justification for what an Opposition was in any case going to do.' And in his view, what the Conservatives were set on doing was 'both to accept and to criticize the social legislation of a Labour Government'. Powell's hindsight, reflecting a world-weary cynicism, understates the element of idealism that existed among the group. They were motivated by a desire to demonstrate that the new generation of Conservatives were inspired by a distinctive Tory vision of social policy. Powell was as unimpressed as his colleagues by lamentable front bench performances. And although he was coming increasingly to favour the 'market process', he 'believed that the welfare state was an expression of the community nature of society, that was defensible and only defensible on those grounds'. These views informed the fierce scrutiny and impeccable logic that he brought to the group's meetings. Their debates helped him formulate his own thoughts, and as Lord Carr has recalled, in those days Powell was ready to compromise and agree a common position. 'I've brought you a long way,' Powell would say to his colleagues, 'but I can't bring you any further.'[14]

Two events occurred in June 1950, as the group thrashed out their drafts for their first pamphlet, that were to have a profound impact on the course of post-war politics. Both raised awkward questions for Powell. On 1 June, the British Government received the ultimatum sent by the French Government, giving other countries until 8.00 p.m. the following day to decide whether or not to join the European Coal and Steel Community (ECSC). The ECSC had been proposed by the French foreign minister, Robert Schuman, in his plan to integrate Europe's economies, and entailed ceding national sovereignty in coal and steel production to a supranational body. When the Labour Cabinet rejected the French ultimatum, the Conservatives attacked the decision during a two-day Commons debate on 26–27 June, and, with Liberal support, urged the Government to enter the Paris talks on the Schuman Plan subject to the same conditions as the Dutch, namely that they would preserve their freedom of action if the plan were shown not to be practicable. Powell was among the half-a-dozen Conservatives who rebelled against their party's pro-European stance, by defying a three-line whip and abstaining. Labour won the vote with a majority of twenty instead of the expected five. Powell's action, he later recalled, 'was enough for me to be sent for by the chief whip the following morning, and warned sadly that that had done for my chances of forming part of the new administration which it was then confidently expected was round the corner – as indeed it was.' It was no idle threat.[15]

It would be wrong to see Powell's rebellion in 1950 as the first action of a consistent opponent of European integration, although this is an impression that Powell has encouraged. 'I was aghast that Winston Churchill should propose to support such a proposition,' he recalled more than forty years later,

> a proposition which would remove responsibility for an important sector of the economy, from the Parliament and the electorate of a United Kingdom. It was essentially my first act as a Euro-sceptic. It was my first act of rebellion against the handing over to European authorities of responsibility for the governance of England.

Yet in the early 1960s Powell was to support Britain's application for membership of the European Economic Community. In 1950, Powell's anti-European motivation owed as much, if not more, to his conviction that Britain's future depended on its role as head of an Empire. Like the other rebels, Powell was an imperialist.[16]

The debate on Britain and the ECSC had also revealed a rift among the nine Tory newcomers. Although they could agree on social policy, there was never any prospect of their working together on foreign policy. Whereas Powell was deeply committed to the Empire and rebelled against his party, Heath made his maiden speech in the debate, arguing that Britain's future lay in Europe. The Tory back bench rebellion might have attracted more attention, but the same night Attlee announced the Cabinet's decision to honour Britain's obligation to support international resistance to the communist invasion of South Korea, and placed Royal Navy ships in the Far East under the joint command of the United Nations and the United States. The Korean War presented a fresh problem for Powell as the front benches pursued a bipartisan policy that amounted to backing the Americans in a cold war showdown under the guise of an international peace-keeping operation. Ever since the Second World War, he had viewed America's interests as antipathetic to the British Empire, and privately had said as much to Eden. But he avoided another public disagreement with his party on a fundamental question of policy after his revolt on the ECSC.[17]

Equally as striking as Powell's silence on Korea is his readiness and that of his colleagues in the new Tory ginger group to complete and publish their work on social policy largely undeterred by the economic ramifications of the war. When the extent of British involvement became clear, they had spent months discussing and refining their draft chapters. Faced with increased defence spending, they might have been expected to accept cuts in spending on the social services, especially since they had based their review of social policy on the premise that Government spending was already too high and that the level of taxation, at 40 per cent, had to be reduced. However, when *One Nation* was published on the eve of the October 1950 Conservative Conference, Powell and his fellow authors sought to square the circle by suggesting that the additional needs of defence should be met and the welfare state maintained primarily through additional output. 'Whether this increase in production can be obtained or not', *One Nation* argued, 'will [therefore] depend to a large extent on all those engaged in industry.' Although they accepted that rearmament would impose extra demands, they added, 'We must call on them for a great effort to save the social services.' Such optimistic sentiments were plainly at odds with the Gladstonian rigour on public finance with which Powell was to be associated. They were a reflection of the One Nation group's recognition of the extraordinary public support that existed for the welfare state.[18]

One Nation's commitment to the fundamentals of the reformed post-war welfare state was reflected in its enthusiastic endorsement of the 1942 Beveridge Report. 'The wall of social security has been built at last,' the nine co-authors declared. 'Here and there stones need shifting or strengthening, here and there we could build better and more economically.' Although in a few, limited respects, *One Nation* was more radical than anything attempted by any future Conservative Government – for example, by proposing hospital charges – its overall message was the need for Conservative reforms to underpin, not demolish, the welfare state. Priority was given to education and housing, the chapter on the latter subject being drafted by Powell.[19]

In few other areas of social policy than housing was there greater scope for expanding the role of the private sector. Few other Tories could have argued the case as convincingly as Powell. His remedy for tackling the desperate housing shortage was to boost house-building to pre-war standards – as Powell noted, 'in the five years 1934–38 an average total of 335,000 houses was built each year in Great Britain'. This was to be achieved by ending the licensing system for building that was run by local authorities, and easing the control on development imposed by the Town and Country Planning Act. Powell still assumed considerable political interference in the market. Emphasizing that such an approach would not entail 'the cessation of council building', he urged that priority in the public sector should be shifted from providing houses that often only the better-paid applicants on the waiting list could afford, and should focus instead on slum clearance, that had 'been virtually at a stand-still since 1939'. Local authorities were to be required to submit a five- or ten-year building programme, 'based upon a systematic plan to deal with slums and with acute overcrowding'. In the private rented sector, landlords were to be allowed to charge higher rents, provided that they undertook repair and maintenance, and a right of appeal was to be introduced into rent tribunals pending their eventual abolition.[20]

With the prospect of the Conservatives returning to office in the foreseeable future, the press were hungry for hints of Tory thinking and constituency workers were anxious for evidence that the party was ready for government. 'The authors believe that the next advances in the social services should be planned now,' reported the *Express and Star*. Although the Wolverhampton-based newspaper noted that Powell and his colleagues believed that it was necessary to 'search the social services and to insist that the most urgent needs are met first', *One Nation* was not perceived as some radical right-wing tract: 'among many things the publication urges are the claims of teachers and doctors for higher pay, the necessity of re-establishing the school dental service, the urgent importance of slum clearance and a higher rate of house-building'. *One Nation* had an immediate impact, selling 8,500 copies within a couple of months, an impressive figure for a political publication. Powell's chapter gave further ammunition to the campaign for the Conservatives to pledge themselves to a target of building 300,000 houses a year – a commitment that the leadership were forced to concede at the party conference, only days after publication.[21]

The Muse departs

Powell's early months as an MP coincided with great turmoil in his personal life. The end of the Second World War had induced an emotional crisis in him. As he later explained, 'something was released in me. Because a lifetime lay ahead. I saw women for the first time.' His experience, although it is difficult to appreciate in the more easy-going era since the 1960s, was by no means unique among the generation of men who were demobbed after 1945 – especially those, such as Powell, who were reserved and had not mixed with women. Powell had been an only son, and in addition, had attended a boys' school; had spent seven years as an undergraduate and Fellow at an all-male college; pursued an academic career when few women did likewise; and served in the Army for the duration of the war. But although he 'saw women for the first time' after 1945, it was not until he was in his late thirties, after his selection as a Tory candidate in Wolverhampton, that he first dated a woman.[22]

Following his adoption in Wolverhampton, Powell's bachelor status prompted immediate local interest. The following month, in January 1949, a local woman learned of his plan to retrace his father's walk, made many years earlier, along the canal towpath from Wolverhampton to Birmingham, and wrote under the *nom de plume* of 'Salome' offering to accompany him. But he hastily assured the *Express and Star* that he had done the walk the previous weekend, 'so "Salome" is too late. However, I appreciate her offer.' A year later, 'this handsome politician with the Clark Gable moustache', as the local paper described him (in contrast to previous comparisons with Nietzsche's moustache), fended off a reporter's query about marriage plans. 'I've been looking after myself for about twenty years now,' he replied, before adding: 'A wife? I suppose I've been too busy for courting – but I'm still an "eligible" bachelor.' Powell did not reveal, however, that he was deeply in love with his first girlfriend and wanted to marry her.[23]

Powell's first experience of love was 'intense and mysterious', and prompted the muse to return. 'Like a powerful hallucinatory drug', this transformation in his life 'unsealed again the necessity and capability to write poetry. Dawn after dawn the stuff rose in my throat and would have choked me, had I not got it down and licked it into shape in *The Wedding Gift*.' But during the summer of 1950, his verse was given an added edge, even bitterness, after the woman whom he loved had decided to marry somebody else. The title's ironic meaning and the identity of 'B', to whom Powell dedicated the poems when they were first published in 1951, were known only to a small circle of friends.[24]

'B' is Barbara Hawkins – Barbara Kennedy as she then was – whom Powell met when he began taking up his new-found enthusiasm for hunting in the Shropshire and Staffordshire countryside, and joined the Albrighton hunt. She was in her early twenties, attractive, self-assured and vivacious. The daughter of a Colonel, she belonged through her mother to the Moncktons, one of England's long-established aristocratic families, and had spent her childhood between the family farm in Yorkshire and the Staffordshire estate of her uncle, Major Reginald Monckton. Powell's romance with her began when Barbara was staying with her uncle at Stretton Hall, near Brewood, to the north of Wolverhampton. She was a member of the hunt's social committee, and had chatted casually to Powell on the ride back from a day's hunting. Afterwards he telephoned her and asked her out. She knew him as John, not Enoch. On their first date, they went to a music hall in Wolverhampton, by bus. She told him at the end of the evening that if he wanted to take her out again, he would have to get a car. 'To be fair,' she later reflected, 'John was not practised with girls.' He told her on their first date that she was the first girl he had ever taken out. 'John was very nice, very intelligent, but rather quiet, very reserved and desperately shy. He was very handsome with piercing, penetrating eyes. He had an intense look. I suppose he was fascinating because I didn't know what was going on in his brain half the time.'

They started to see more of each other. Although Barbara was very much one of the county set, and Powell, like other newcomers and less established members of the hunt, used to hire his horse, it would be misleading to exaggerate the class difference. Although some members of the hunt tended to keep their distance from those who rode a hired horse, Powell was a young Brigadier who had become the local Tory candidate and seemed destined to reach the top in politics. Their time together revolved around hunting and politics. She was struck by how excited he was about hunting, while she had become interested in politics through her uncle, who was very active in the local Conservative association. After Powell's adoption in Wolverhampton, she used to see him at local meetings, and she started driving him to and from his speaking and other party functions. But sometimes they also went to classical concerts in Wolverhampton.

Powell got to know some of Barbara's friends, although he never mixed much with her set. But she had 'a lot of boyfriends in those days', and while she was seeing Powell, she would go with other men to balls and social events. Whereas she was having a profound effect on Powell, he failed to have a lasting impression on her. 'I suppose at one time we were actually dating,' she later recalled, explaining that 'John was passionate, but it was more emotional than physical. He wasn't the sort to crawl all over you. Ours wasn't a sexual relationship.' But, as Barbara has pointed out, 'you'd never have sex before marriage in those days. After all, you might get pregnant. There was no provision made for that sort of thing.' She realized that Powell 'was serious though, you could see it in his eyes. His eyes were very expressive.'[25]

As an expression of his emotions, Powell wrote several poems for her. 'Tiger Hill', which he was later to publish in *The Wedding Gift*, was set in India. She found it rather obscure. Written on a single sheet of embossed pale-blue folded paper, the copy that he gave her was dated 1 April 1950, 9.30 p.m. But Powell had greater success with another poem that was prompted while Barbara was working temporarily in the Middle Temple, London, where a tulip tree that rarely bloomed, suddenly burst into blossom. Powell was inspired by this coincidence to suggest that her effect on the tree had been similar to her effect on him:

> The tulip-tree
> Scarce once a century
>   Puts on its blossoms white;
> But this year in the spring
> The tree was blossoming,
>   A breathless sight.
>
> The passers-by
> Came, saw and wondered why
>   It suddenly had power
> After so long a sleep
> And wintriness so deep
>   To wake in flower.
>
> But I could sense
> The hidden influence
>   That touched the flowerless tree:
> Her presence there had brought
> This thing to pass, who wrought
>   The like for me.

Easter 1950 was an intensely emotional time for Powell. Not only was he deeply in love, but he had also fallen under the spell of ritual worship. At six o'clock on Easter Sunday morning – the day on which he dated the poem about the tulip tree – he took communion for the first time in twenty years. Having dedicated himself fully to his restored Christian faith, he began exploring the meaning and the content of the Mass.[26]

Partly as a result of his poetry, Barbara became more aware of the depth of Powell's feelings. She was also conscious that he was desperately keen to have children and a family – many years later, he was to write that, having survived the war, he had walked 'out of a nightmare world into a waking world … a world in which there would be "marrying and giving in marriage", children and the rearing of children'. Barbara began seeing less of him, but it was not long after she had received his poems that her engagement was announced to Paul Hawkins, a local businessman and one of her set. Powell was irate. 'He came to my uncle's house and told me I was making a great mistake,' she later recalled. 'He said I'd agreed to marry him, but I don't ever recall him proposing. I think he was so intense and had his head so much in the clouds that he wanted to marry me but never told me.' She only realized later that he had asked her to marry him. 'I didn't understand a word he was saying. He was so erudite. I was gobsmacked when he said it was a proposal afterwards.'[27]

Barbara never had any intention of marrying Powell, although she has fond memories of their time together. 'You couldn't really compare him with other people because he stood out as a loner,' she recalls. She admired his intellect, but he was too much of an intellectual for her. 'It was marvellous. He is such a classical scholar that he was streets ahead of anybody, particularly me. Being a country girl born and bred, dogs and horses were my life.' In addition to the poems, Powell gave her some books in Greek, although she could not read them. 'He was one of nature's gentlemen, but also a dedicated career politician,' she also reflects. Despite her interest in politics, she would never have chosen to marry a politician. 'I remember he used to get very annoyed when I used to fall asleep at the back of the hall when he was giving a speech,' she remembers. 'I know that sounds unkind but if you've had a good dinner on a warm summer's day and you've heard it all five or six times before …' In short, as Barbara recognizes, 'we were like chalk and cheese'.[28]

Barbara married Paul Hawkins in September 1950. Powell did not attend their wedding, but he sent her a gold cigarette case as a gift. But when the cigarette case was opened, it revealed the head of a snarling fox. 'It was horrible, really,' she recalls, 'but it showed that he had a sense of humour.' Powell was to confess of his first, lost love: 'I failed. I was not satisfactory. That's it.' But the emotions that he had experienced and his sense of anguished disappointment had an enduring effect. During the summer of 1950, he was again compelled to express his feelings in poetry. Now, however, his verse was also tinged with the new religious experience that he was undergoing at the same time, as in the following poem that he recited with evident emotion on the radio almost forty years later, when he spoke of his 'premature' attempt to break into the full life of marriage and having a family:

> I dreamt that on a mountain-crest
> As in the sheep-cropped grass we lay,
> The words that ever at my breast
> Leap and are striving to be spoke
> Suddenly I began to say.
> Yet words not those I purposèd
> From lips and heart impassioned broke
> But, as it seemed to me, I said:
> 'Therefore with all archangels I,
> All angels and Heaven's company
> Thy glorious name
> Do magnify,
> Thee praising and for evermore
> Saying –' and from your mouth reply
> Not such as that I waited for
> In whispered tones mysterious came
> But – 'Holy Thou, of hosts the Lord,
> Full of Thy glory earth and sky,
> Glory to Thee,
> O God most high!'
> You ceased. The wind that through the sward
> With steady-breathing passion swept,
> From flower and grass and heather blent
> 'Amen' to that strange sacrament;
> And silent, as it seemed, we wept.

When he was eighty-three, and forty-five years after he had last seen Barbara, Powell broke down in tears reading this poem on television. 'You mustn't put me in a situation in which I'm so overcome by emotion,' he told Michael Cockerell – 'old emotion; but re-summoned by the poetry written under the spell of that emotion.'[29]

Although *The Wedding Gift* was to mark the end of Powell's life as a poet – apart from the poem that he writes each year for his wife on their wedding anniversary – in his mind, the same compulsion that had led him to compose poetry also led him to make speeches. As his poetry dried up, his speech-making began to flow. 'If there was a river, the river went underground,' Powell reflected in later life, 'but underground it must have been flowing still.' For more than forty years after his last poems, he was 'to harangue, lecture, cajole, admonish my fellow countrymen', as he obeyed an ex-poet's 'imperative necessity to speak'.

There is, in this explanation of Powell's, perhaps an element of rationalizing his failure to achieve more in practical terms by portraying himself as the political equivalent of an oracle, a politician who had to speak the truth regardless of its consequences. Yet there is also a key insight into Powell the poet and academic, turned parliamentary candidate. 'I had to explore', he recalled, 'as one not unaccustomed to addressing audiences, though of a different character, the presumptions upon which I addressed my fellow citizens in political meetings.' He 'was already conscious of the great assumption of the politician addressing his fellow countrymen, namely the identity of introspection, the identity of insight'. Powell realized that if a politician was to have any success in persuading his audience, he had to appeal to them upon the basis of common, shared assumptions that exist between him and them, and that are often unstated. As Powell put it, 'I assumed that my fellow countrymen felt and thought as I did about their country.'

In this respect, his poetry and his speeches performed the same function: 'poetry is something which you say to other people in the conviction that they will feel the same if they hear those words, thus arranged and thus ordered. And I suppose in politics, that's what I've been doing. I have been saying to people, "This is how I feel, you surely must feel the same".' The story of his career as an elected politician is largely the extent to which he succeeded, or failed, in identifying with, and appealing to, people's feelings about their country. But it is also about Powell's social awkwardness and his difficult personality. These latter traits almost led Powell, during the emotional aftermath of losing his first love, to quit Wolverhampton and, as a result, risk leaving politics before his new career had barely begun.[30]

'Persecution mania'

During his first year in parliament, Powell deservedly won a reputation as one of the most assiduous and talented of the Conservative 'class of 1950'. He impressed as a constituency member. In June 1950, his complaints about the spray of a cooling tower that kept much of Wolverhampton damp secured an amendment to the Wolverhampton Corporation Bill and steps by the British Electricity Authority to remedy the problem. During the 1950–51 winter recess, Powell spent his time calling on voters in his constituency – his only break was to spend Christmas with his parents, who were living at Southborough, near Tunbridge Wells. The following February, he put information gained from his house visits to good use when he raised the plight of elderly people who had run out of coal to heat their homes and urged the creation of small, local coal banks to deal with such emergencies. In the party, his appointment in the summer of 1950 as chairman of the West Midlands CPC was recognition of his role as one of the most promising Conservative communicators and thinkers. His membership of the One Nation group further enhanced his reputation as a rising star.[31]

It therefore came as a bombshell when, on 13 November 1950, *The Times* reported that Powell had decided not to stand as a candidate at the next general election. 'Still only thirty-eight, Mr Powell has the kind of intellect that burns more fuel than a frail frame can contain,' reported the *Daily Telegraph* the following day. 'He has been burning it fast since February 1950. It might be better for him and Wolverhampton if he turned for a while to one of his two recreations – fox-hunting and writing poetry.' Behind Powell's astonishing decision lay a bitter row with some members of his constituency association, that developed in the months after he had lost his first love, Barbara Kennedy. There is no direct evidence that Powell's personal anguish affected his behaviour, but his sense of loss went deep and may have made him more inclined to feel like quitting Wolverhampton. But new light is shed upon this extraordinary episode in Powell's career by the Conservative Party records of the incident, which are now available. They show him at his most exasperating and reveal that, contrary to the widely held assumption, he did not have his own way in the matter. Indeed, the Conservative papers demonstrate that the party's professionals were fully aware of the paradox of Powell from his earliest days in the Commons – that although he could be the best of politicians, he could also be the worst.[32]

Trouble had first arisen between Powell and his constituency party before the February 1950 election. According to a private report by Colonel Ledingham, the Central Office Agent for the West Midlands, some of the elected officers in the local wards felt that Powell had been dictatorial and wanted to run the organization himself. 'There is no doubt that Mr Powell took a very active part in the day-to-day work of the agent and in the association', Ledingham noted, 'and was at times, in his eagerness for efficiency, rather intolerant.'[33]

Things came to a head during the February 1950 election campaign. Technically, from the day that a candidate is officially nominated, the constituency association is dissolved and the candidate is responsible for anything done in his or her name. In practice, most candidates – particularly when they are fighting a seat for the first time – rely heavily on the agent and local party officers, and need to retain their goodwill and sustain their morale. Local parties also contain influential and respected figures in the community, whose tendency to feel self-important needs handling with great diplomacy. Powell's sole concern was to win the seat, and he expected party members to jump to his command. Ledingham reported that 'the association officers were pretty well frozen out', and that Powell had forced the resignation of his chairman, Councillor T. Griffin Williams, who had been mainly responsible for building up the association after 1945.[34]

In September 1950, the committee of the Graiseley ward in Powell's constituency party passed a resolution referring to the 'bad feeling' that had existed in the association during the previous election, and blamed his interference in the association. Powell had been criticized in Graiseley ward for his undemocratic methods. The ward committee complained that during the election he 'by-passed the normal ward organization', forcing some polling district officers 'to give up control of their districts' and had 'spreadeagled the team and its spirit which had taken four years to build up'. They demanded provocatively that 'our next prospective candidate (we hope Mr Powell) should be asked *now* to give his assurance that for the next election he plans no second coup d'état'. In future, they requested that Powell should work through the ward committees, and asked that he should signify his acceptance of this. As Ledingham noted, 'the resolution was couched in unfriendly terms', and had probably been inspired by James Beattie, a senior councillor, former candidate in Wolverhampton West, and proprietor of the town's largest department store, 'who did not see eye to eye with Mr Powell'.[35]

'You will realize,' Powell responded icily to his constituency chairman that 'the resolution is such as no Member or candidate could regard otherwise than as a severe and deliberate censure upon himself.' He asked that the association's executive council should 'repudiate this resolution in its entirety', and should 'take steps to secure for Graiseley ward a committee and officers with whom I shall be able to cooperate'. Unless his demands were met, he would 'feel obliged to withdraw now from the candidature at the next election'. Powell incorporated his demands in a draft resolution that he expected the executive to pass. When Ledingham advised him that forcing his executive to dissolve a ward committee and prohibit the re-election of its ex-officers and committee was not only unwise but also unconstitutional, Powell 'would not agree and was quite adamant that the matter must go forward in the way he desired, "they must be disciplined"'. When the executive met a week later, Ledingham, who attended on Powell's behalf, had to intervene in Powell's support 'when the meeting looked like getting out of hand'. After a 'very acrimonious discussion', a compromise emerged when the council agreed not to consider the Graiseley ward resolution and decided, at Ledingham's prompting, that Powell should be invited to meet the constituency's seven ward chairmen, with Ledingham, 'in an effort to resolve the difficulties in a friendly manner'.[36]

However, Powell rejected the compromise, an action that Ledingham judged 'unfriendly and unwise'. Powell remained unbending at an emergency meeting of the executive on 2 November, chaired by Sir Robert Bird, a highly respected figure in the West Midlands, who had become president of the new constituency association the year before. The old constituency of Wolverhampton West had been something of a family seat for the Birmingham custard-making dynasty, having returned Sir Robert's father as MP for the first two decades of the century, and Sir Robert for the next twenty-five years. But there was no meeting of minds between an old-style patrician like Sir Robert and the self-made, uncompromising newcomer. Despite Sir Robert's best efforts, the impasse remained. Eight days later, when the matter was raised at the association's annual general meeting a vote was forced against Sir Robert's advice. The result was a tie, but Sir Robert declined to use his casting vote. It was after this meeting that Powell's intention to stand down at the next election was reported in the press. Central Office suspected that the source had been Sir Robert Bird.[37]

Powell's attitude was exasperating. 'I am dealing very firmly with Mr

Powell at this end,' the party vice-chairman for candidates, J.P.L. Thomas, told Sir Stephen Pierssené, General Director at Central Office. Writing to Powell, Thomas warned that 'you really are not justified in digging your toes in'. Urging Powell to reconsider his position, he warned that it would be difficult for him to secure another seat, 'as any constituency to which I send your name will obviously make enquiries as to what happened in Wolverhampton and when they hear the true facts I am pretty certain they will consider that you ought never to have resigned'. Briefing the party chairman, Lord Woolton, on the trouble in Wolverhampton, Thomas reported that he had told Powell, 'both in writing and in speech, that he is an unmitigated fool'. But he seemed doubtful of any change of mind on Powell's part. 'We shall be sorry to lose Brigadier Powell in the House of Commons', Thomas added, 'as, in spite of his idiosyncracies, he is quite outstanding.'[38]

From the Central Office Agent in the West Midlands had come confirmation of Powell's intransigence. In a further conversation with Sir Robert Bird, Powell had given the impression that he 'did not care very much whether he went on or not in South-West Wolverhampton' and had 'suggested that he wanted a constituency where the majority was such that the association did not matter very much'. According to Ledingham's note, Sir Robert felt that Powell 'showed a hatred for all those who did not support him and seemed to suffer from a persecution mania that everyone was his enemy'.[39]

However, Powell was convinced that the tide was turning his way. A special meeting of the executive, called by the new chairman of the association, Alderman Bowdler, who supported Powell, backed his demands by voting to dissolve the Graiseley ward branch and ban its ex-officers and committee from election to the re-formed branch. This decision split the association and was almost certainly unconstitutional, but Powell informed Bowdler that these steps would enable him to stand as a candidate at the next election, and he assured J.P.L. Thomas that things were a good deal better in Wolverhampton. But it soon became clear that the re-formed Graiseley ward were likely to defy Powell and the executive by re-electing their former officers and committee. This prompted a former chairman of the ward, Councillor Morrell, to write to Powell, offering to 'make a final gesture to reconciliation' and negotiate a settlement of the dispute. Thomas wished that he could 'watch Brigadier Powell and the Graiseley Ward "gesturing" at each other'.[40]

By this stage, Alderman Bowdler was becoming worried at the damage being done to the Conservatives in Wolverhampton, particularly since they held the council by only three seats and faced elections in the coming May. He therefore struck a deal with Conservative councillors, including Beattie and Morrell from the Graiseley ward, and summoned a meeting of the ward for 2 January – Powell wanted only members residing in the ward to attend, thereby excluding three councillors, but Bowdler insisted on inviting all ward members. The meeting re-elected the ward's former officers, but, in keeping with the deal arranged with Bowdler, they immediately stood down in favour of Powell's nominees.[41]

The feeling that the dispute had ended harmoniously was short-lived. Bowdler's deal came undone at a further meeting of the ward on 19 January, called to elect a new committee and to hear a speech by Powell on 'The Situation Abroad'. Bowdler had agreed that the former officers who had given way to Powell's nominees should be eligible for the new committee, but Powell would not accept this. The ward chairman complied with Powell's view and refused to accept the re-nomination of the former officers. There was 'complete uproar' as alternative nominees were declared elected. When the chairman invited Powell to address the meeting, there were 'renewed uproar and boos', and as Powell began to speak 150 people walked out, leaving an audience of only twenty-five.[42]

'On the face of it', Ledingham noted at the end of January 1951, 'Mr Powell would appear to have won the battle.' But the Central Office Agent warned party headquarters that the situation was 'deteriorating' in the constituency. 'Despite Mr Powell's assertion that the situation is in hand and that the association has never been so happy,' Ledingham reported that 'South-West Wolverhampton is split from top to bottom, and this goes for Conservatives generally in the constituency and not only members of the association.' He reckoned that 'as many are against the Member as are for him.'[43]

The turning point came on 3 February when some home truths from Ledingham crystallized Powell's thinking. Ostensibly, Powell had called on his regional party agent in Birmingham to report that all was quiet in his constituency. When Ledingham disagreed and warned him that 'there was a very strong and dangerous under-current operating against him', Powell 'bridled', but after a while his 'tense, almost fanatical intransigence changed'. Powell admitted that 'the present calm was surface deep'. Ledingham explained that it was difficult to help because of Powell's 'unbending attitude'. But he suggested that Powell should re-establish contact with his most influential opponents, Councillor Beattie, who was almost certain to become Lord Mayor of Wolverhampton, and Councillor T. Griffin Williams, his ex-chairman. 'Rather to my surprise,' Ledingham noted, 'he seemed to jump at the idea.' And when told that his constituency executive 'might be only too glad to receive some indication of a less unbending attitude', Powell agreed to think over possible means of reconciliation. 'I promise I will not wreck the future' was the gist of Powell's parting comment as he left for Wolverhampton.[44]

From the moment he reached his constituency, Powell was conciliatory. Later in the day, he telephoned Ledingham to report that he had had 'a very friendly meeting' with two members of the Conservative group on the council, and would be inviting Councillor Beattie to lunch. Initially, Beattie looked set to spurn Powell's olive branch, but with Ledingham acting as go-between, the two sides finally met. Such was Powell's readiness to compromise that Sir Robert Bird, whom he had bruised earlier in the dispute, observed that 'he (Powell) does not want to retire from South-West Wolverhampton, and that, notwithstanding his words to me, he never did really wish to retire, if his end were not to be attained.' Eventually, Powell climbed down on his key demand. On 25 February, he informed his constituency chairman, Alderman Bowdler, that he felt the ban on the re-election of former officers and committee members of the Graiseley ward should be lifted from the end of 'the current constituency year'. Moreover, he hoped that in the meantime, the ward committee would co-opt the ward's councillors – who included Powell's main opponents. Powell's about-turn angered his loyal chairman in Graiseley ward: 'Mr Powell told him to take one line in sacking the late officers, and now he wants him to take them all in again.' But Powell's bluff had been called. By February 1951, he had become too deeply attached to life in the Commons to want to give it up, and had been made to abandon any fond notion that if he deserted Wolverhampton he would easily find another seat.[45]

'An uneasy armistice rests over the association,' Ledingham wrote of Wolverhampton South-West in May 1951. But he was in no doubt of the damaging impact of the row between Powell and some of the local party, or of the main cause of the problem. 'This was a very well organized Association with plenty of workers willing to pull their weight in an election campaign,' but the dispute 'has weakened its efficiency and dampened the enthusiasm of the workers to such an extent that many may stand aside when the election comes.' Ledingham reckoned that 'with some movement in our favour the seat should be held', but without 'a national swing towards our party' he was less sure. But Ledingham felt that Powell 'considers the Association his own personal appendage,' and constantly intervened in its affairs: '"They must be disciplined" is a phrase of his which is a true reflection on his outlook towards the voluntary worker.' Ledingham's pen portrait, sketched by a close and experienced observer and quoted at the head of this chapter, was to be echoed by others down the years.[46]

Needs and Means

After the publication of *One Nation* in the autumn of 1950, Powell had argued against the group's continuing. But he was outvoted, and as reward for his dissent was given the task of writing the weekly minutes. For the next five years, *One Nation* was to serve Powell as sounding board, stimulant and support group for developing, testing and trying to propagate his brand of Toryism against a background of rapidly unfolding events. Equally important, as Powell's minutes of the group's weekly meetings make clear, was *One Nation*'s role as a Tory commando unit that planned assaults on the ailing Labour Government in the Commons. Powell was adept in the guerilla warfare of adjournment debates, private members' motions, praying against statutory regulations and putting questions to ministers. In addition, the group acted as a cell on their own side of the House, agreeing their line before Conservative back bench committee meetings and supporting each other, or other like-minded MPs, in the election of committee officers. Powell was elected secretary of the party's back bench committees on legal affairs and town and country planning during his first, five-month parliamentary session.[47]

Powell was in his element in the House of Commons, although – perhaps because – he was rarely seen in those parts of the Palace of Westminster where MPs socialize. The tea-room and dining-room were treated as mainly functional, and the smoking-rooms and bars (he was still tee-total) were 'no-go' areas. His slightly stooped figure became a familiar sight – as it was to remain, apart from one brief break, for thirty-seven years – walking briskly through the members' lobby as he made his way between the Commons library, where he worked on his speeches, and the chamber, or treading purposefully along the committee floor above. He took his constituency mail with him, despatching it in odd moments as he moved between rooms and subjects. His love of institutions was fully realized in the Commons, where procedure is everything, and he could conduct his relations with others on the basis of time-honoured conventions, rules and regulations. Month by month, he grew more attached to the Commons, and could imagine no life other than as an MP.[48]

Whereas most MPs specialized in a few areas, Powell busied himself with many subjects, including defence and imperial affairs, housing and local government, town and country planning, constitutional and legal matters, health and social services, and even Welsh affairs. This unparalleled range of interests and his depth of knowledge led the whips to encourage Powell as a back-bencher on whom they could rely as a supporting speaker in the Commons and a member of standing and select committees – during his first two years in the House he served on the estimates committee that vetted the Government's annual spending plans.[49]

Although Powell was respected for his erudition, he tended to be too didactic and prone to conduct a forensic dissection of the subject under debate, in the manner of a textual critic. This approach created a cold and uncaring impression that rankled with Labour MPs, even when his interest had been inspired, in part at least, by his deep romanticism. As a Tory representing an English seat, his regular interventions in Welsh business in the Commons further irritated the large contingent of Labour MPs from the Principality. Significantly, Powell was ready to subordinate market forces to overriding political or cultural factors, as he had recommended following his tours of Wales over two years earlier. But in expressing this pragmatic view, Powell none the less contrived to appear ideological and patronizing, with the result that he was misunderstood on the Labour benches. Economically, he argued, it would be better for Welsh people to leave Wales, but culturally it was better to sacrifice the optimum economic position and help keep a bigger population in the Principality. George Thomas, the Labour MP, who immediately followed him, objected to his talk of 'sacrifice' and claimed that he 'had done his cause a great deal of harm', while Ness Edwards, the Postmaster-General, took exception to his talk of 'economic man'. It was in vain that Powell sought to explain that he had referred to economic logic in order to argue that, in this instance, it should be overruled.[50]

Despite Powell's having no standing as a party spokesman on Wales, his expertise on policy and his continuing interest prompted a request by Conservative Central Office that he should attend a special meeting of Welsh Tories in Ludlow in late May 1951. Powell readily agreed, although it was arranged for a Sunday on which he already had a morning engagement in Cheltenham (Powell was later to set aside Sunday as a day of rest). The meeting reflected concern among Welsh Tories that party policy to assign special responsibility for Wales to a Cabinet minister was no longer sufficient, especially in the light of a campaign that had been organized for a Welsh parliament. Reporting on the meeting to Central Office, Powell recommended that the party needed to clarify the status and duties of the proposed Minister (though Rab Butler's speech in Pembrokeshire less than 48 hours before the meeting had largely done this); and that a handy guide should be produced, debunking the arguments for devolution. In addition, Powell repeated his plea for the party 'to associate itself even more, when occasion offers, with manifestations of sympathy with the Welsh language and culture'. At a weekend school for Welsh Tories at Swinton College in June, Powell's suggestion that the proposed Minister for Wales should be assisted by a junior minister (with the rank of parliamentary secretary) and that either the minister or parliamentary secretary should spend most of their time in Wales, 'was greeted with much pleasure'. Few other Conservative MPs were as well qualified as Powell for this junior post, but subsequent events were to suggest that he was not drafting his own job specification.[51]

Increasingly, the Korean War was shaping the political climate in which Powell tested his mettle and developed his thinking. He steered clear of public debate on the war as such – his anti-Americanism was at odds with Churchill's approach, that was, if anything, more strongly pro-American than Attlee's. Instead, he sniped at Labour's record and tactics, claiming that they would use re-armament as yet another excuse for their inaction in other areas. In February 1951, he joined other Tory ex-officers in forcing their front bench into a vote of censure on the Government on the way that the 'Z reserve', consisting of almost all men demobilized at the end of the Second World War, were being called up. But Powell again demonstrated an unsureness of touch in the spring. In addition to accusing the defence minister, John Strachey, of breaking Attlee's pledge that only 'in certain cases' would Second World War reservists be called up, he claimed in his constituency that statements made by Strachey and Attlee were 'quite untrue'. But after Strachey had rebutted Powell's allegation in the *Express and Star*, Powell suggested that the disagreement had been due to inadequate Government information.[52]

The cost of rearmament became the dominant issue. Powell's pre-occupation with its repercussions revealed, on the one hand, the depth of his commitment to certain social services, but on the other hand, his tendency to submerge his argument in meticulously researched detail. As befitted the son of state school teachers, he joined with other members of the One Nation group to oppose the Labour Government's increase in the price of school meals from 6d to 7d, to help pay for rearmament. Powell argued that increasing the price of school meals was bound to lead to 'a sharp and permanent reduction in the number of them taken by children', as had been the case in Wolverhampton following the last 1d. increase in January 1950. 'It is perfectly proper', Powell maintained, 'that we should regard the provision of a midday meal in school as an essential part of the education service, as it ensures that the children are in a condition, and in a frame of mind, to benefit from their instruction.'[53]

The imposition of charges on prescriptions, spectacles and dentures in Hugh Gaitskell's April 1951 budget was political dynamite, provoking the resignations of Nye Bevan and Harold Wilson from the Cabinet, and of John Freeman, a junior minister. Powell regarded Labour's policy as 'a turning point in the history of the development of the social services in this century'. In the debate on Labour's National Health Service Bill, that extended the power to levy health charges, he explained that transforming the NHS from a free service to one that was to become subject to a means test represented a fundamental change. His objections were two-fold, and revealed much about his thinking. In the first place, he appeared to want a more radical approach, arguing that he would have preferred to see saving 'over a much wider field'.[54]

At the same time, Powell criticized Labour's method of means testing. His concern was rooted in his thrifty, lower-middle-class background in Birmingham, and in the similar values shared by many people in his Wolverhampton constituency. They were often decent, hard-working and proud, yet nothing in life had come easy for them. They would no more dream of claiming national assistance – the basic, subsistence-level state benefit – than accepting 'poor relief', its hated predecessor. 'The people who are not going to be helped, who are not going to pass this means test', he claimed, 'are precisely, in many cases, the most deserving. They are the people, the old-age pensioners, people just on a living wage, who are going to say: "This is a pretty stiff sum I have got to pay, but I will be dashed if I am going to the National Assistance Board to argue the toss about it".'[55]

This same concern for the values of personal responsibility and thrift explains why Powell was exercised by the increasing inadequacy of the national insurance scheme. His concern was highlighted by the National Insurance Bill, another of Labour's 1951 cost-cutting measures. Beveridge's intention had been to provide security during sickness, unemployment and old age through a national insurance scheme funded by contributions – and the contribution principle is consistent with Conservative thinking, since it is tantamount to compulsory saving and enforces on everybody the middle-class value of thrift. However, national insurance was not working as Beveridge had intended, and more people were seeking national assistance, which was funded through progressive taxation. Conservatives had always suspected Labour of wanting to fund the social services increasingly through progressive taxation as a means of creating an egalitarian society.[56]

In the light of these developments, Powell readily agreed to Macleod's suggestion to renew their collaboration and produce a new study on the social services. The two men discussed the underlying principles on which state aid was distributed during their many hours at the Commons in the spring and summer of 1951 as the Tories increased the strain on ministers of governing with a slender majority by waging a war of parliamentary attrition. On nights when the House sat into the small hours, Macleod sometimes stayed overnight at Powell's Earl's Court flat, where their discussions continued. They completed their work in December 1951, and *The Social Services: Needs and Means* was published the following month. Most of the drafting of the thirty-five-page pamphlet was done by Powell, especially after Macleod began writing a book on bridge. Their study is often seen as the seminal argument in favour of means testing, but it suggests virtually no practical reform and does not recognize the danger of creating a 'poverty trap' as people receiving means tested benefits are discouraged from trying to earn more. The reason for its lasting impact is to be found in the question posed early in the pamphlet, that was mentioned approvingly in *The Times*'s editorial comment. Powell and Macleod began by accepting that redistribution was basic to the social services – an arresting assumption for two Tories. From this, they deduced the 'general presumption' that such services will be rendered 'only on evidence of need, i.e. of financial inability to provide each particular service out of one's own or one's family's resources'. It followed that 'the question therefore which poses itself is not, "Should a means test be applied to a social service?" but "Why should any social service be provided *without* test of need?"'[57]

Casting the issue in these terms was a radical step in itself in early 1950s Britain. But the remaining thirty pages were overwhelmingly unradical. Powell and Macleod shied away from identifying the social services to which they thought means testing could be extended. Indeed, much of their pamphlet explains why such a policy was unsuitable for vast tracts of the welfare state. They accepted that means testing could not be applied to family allowances (these were already subject to tax), national insurance, food subsidies and rent restrictions. They endorsed the free education service. Despite a suggestion that the NHS should be funded on a contributory basis, like national insurance, it would remain available in any individual case without contribution conditions. Only in the case of subsidized housing did they expect a return of means testing. And although their historical survey of the welfare state demonstrated that means testing had been integral to the social services, by 1951 it was limited principally to children's and old people's services, university education and national assistance.[58]

Powell and Macleod contended that there 'was a crisis in the social services, a crisis all the more dangerous for being unrecognized'. The cause of this crisis was the spread of the National Assistance Board means test, since this threatened to reverse the principle that had previously been established – 'the application of different means tests, well above the subsistence level, to different social services through the agency of the authorities respectively administering them'. However, Labour's health charges had extended the National Assistance Board's means test into the NHS at the expense of the free service principle. 'If the principle of charges based on means is to be extended farther,' they argued, 'it is imperative that the test of means should be applied upon a considered basis fixed *well above subsistence* and separated sharply from the administration of the subsistence minimum for the purposes of national assistance.' [present author's emphasis][59]

The most serious aspect of the new crisis, according to Powell and Macleod, was the increasing reliance on national assistance. Insurance benefits had been set below subsistence level and their value had been eroded by inflation, with the result that over two million people had been forced to depend on means tested national assistance in 1950 – more than had been receiving 'poor relief' in 1900. However, economic measures 'to give stability to the pound' were beyond the study's remit. Powell and Macleod also eschewed any radical solution. Instead, they came to the sobering conclusion that national insurance could be restored only by increased contributions – whether by employers, employees, or the Exchequer.[60]

Powell's thinking on the welfare state has generated much debate, but the clearest expression of his ideas came in a talk on the BBC Third Programme, broadcast only three months after the publication of his joint pamphlet with Macleod. Powell was responding to Richard Titmuss, the respected social policy expert, who had welcomed their work as 'a serious study' but argued that the main problem for the social services stemmed from the extra demands created by a post-war baby boom and increasing numbers of pensioners, not inflation. Titmuss also maintained that the social services would 'lose their citizenship quality' if they were limited to the poor and needy, and became 'a new version of the nineteenth-century poor law'. Powell's reply is striking for the strength with which he reiterated his commitment to national insurance, state education and the NHS. He emphasized that he and Macleod 'wanted to see insurance restored because we wanted to limit as much as possible the sphere of national assistance and the test of means'. Moreover, 'the so-called free social services, namely education and health, stand in a class by themselves'. These services were afforded without means testing, because 'they are viewed as a service to the community at least as much as to the individual', and, in the case of health, included an element of insurance.[61]

Equally striking is Powell's argument that the views that he and Macleod held reflected an underlying 'Tory' philosophy on the social services, that was distinct from either a 'socialist' or 'classical liberal' philosophy. Although he caricatured Titmuss as an egalitarian socialist instead of defining him as a social democrat, as would have been more accurate, his depiction of three distinctive philosophies helps throw his own thinking into relief. He recognized common features between the various strands. Whereas the socialist and Tory philosophies derived 'the social services from an idea of society', the liberal, 'both in its economic and its humanitarian aspects, sets out from the individual'. But because he was responding to Timuss, Powell focused on the difference between the socialist concept on the one hand, and Tory and liberal views on the other. The socialist approach 'means that ideally the needs of individuals and families will be met to a common standard from common resources', thus leading to the elimination of private education and medicine. Since 'the badge of citizenship' is participation in social services, they must be made universal. The system of social security therefore becomes 'one of these universal benefits to which those who need it have access, as the children to free education and the sick to free health'. And as a result, 'the importance of the principle of insurance which seems so great to Tory and liberal is much reduced'.[62]

Powell also accepted that 'for Tory and liberal alike, redistribution is of the essence of the social services'. However, for the socialist, he argued, redistribution was 'only incidental to the social services as a means to an end' – in other words, social policy was subordinate to the goal of total equality. Whereas the socialist regards a 'common standard' as the aim of the social services, the Tory seeks 'the guarantee of a minimum standard'. 'So far from spreading and generalizing benefits,' Powell argued, 'the aim for the Tory must therefore be to concentrate them where they are needed.' Ascertaining need, he maintained 'may take other forms than those which have given the term "means test" its emotional and political constant today'. None the less,

> a means test and a pure social service go together. But precisely from this fact derives the anxiety to concentrate and limit the area of need and to render as wide a section of the community as possible self-providing in the basic needs of the individual and the family.

Powell never deviated from his 'Tory' philosophy on the welfare state that set him apart in important respects from consistent free-market critics of the welfare state with whom he was, in other respects, in sympathy.[63]

6

For Queen and Country

We in this House, whether we are the humblest of the back-benchers or my right hon. Friend the First Lord of the Treasury himself [Winston Churchill], are in ourselves, in our individual capacities, quite unimportant. We have a meaning in this place only in so far as in our time and generation we represent great principles, great elements in the national life, great strands in our society and national being.

Enoch Powell, House of Commons, 3 March 1953.

Acceptance and refusal

The victory of the Conservatives at the general election held on 25 October 1951 and their return to office with a majority of seventeen seats raised hopes of early ministerial preferment among the Tory intake of 1950. In Wolverhampton South-West, Powell benefited from the general swing against Labour and, in the absence of a Liberal candidate, substantially increased his majority to 3,196. However, he was to wait longer than his former colleagues in the party's Parliamentary Secretariat, Macleod and Maudling, for promotion as a minister.[1]

Powell's appeal to the voters was much as it had been twenty months earlier, causing him to claim after his victory that he had 'fought the election without compromising a single principle of the Tory Party'. If anything, he laid even greater emphasis than previously on the importance of the Empire. His reaction to the takeover of the formerly British-owned Abadan oil refinery, following its nationalization by the Persian prime minister, Dr Mohammed Mossadegh, and to a comment in an Egyptian newspaper that the British had got used to being driven out, was to declare that the only way to deter anti-British attacks was to end the retreat from Empire. 'Without the Empire,' he proclaimed, 'Britain would be like a head without a body.' Yet before he next faced his electors, Powell was to undergo a complete change of mind on the British Empire.[2]

It was, however, for a personal reason that the October 1951 election campaign was most important to Powell. His former secretary, Pamela Wilson, had worked in Strasbourg at the Council of Europe after the 1950 election, but she had returned to London and wanted to see something of grass-roots politics. She and Powell had kept in touch, and when the 1951 election was called, she went to Wolverhampton to help him in his campaign. When Powell had been her boss, Pamela had found him 'very attractive – his eyes were very blue and very mesmeric and he was great fun', and his local party workers now sensed that she had fallen in love with him. They used to go out together on Sundays in his small car, but their relationship became much closer one foggy Sunday night. Pamela had returned to London for the weekend, and her train back to Wolverhampton was badly delayed. When she finally arrived, hours late, she was amazed to find Powell still waiting for her on the platform. She realized then that his concern signalled something more than common courtesy.[3]

Their romance began in earnest after the campaign, and in a matter of weeks Pamela accepted the thirty-nine-year-old bachelor's proposal of marriage. 'We had dinner at a Chinese restaurant and I knew that he was going to ask me and three days later he did ask me,' she later recalled. Powell proposed to her at his Earl's Court maisonette, kneeling on a blanket. In one sense, however, he was distinctly unconventional, telling her that he could not promise anything except a life of grinding poverty on the back benches. As Pamela has commented, 'I knew politics, I knew exactly what that meant.' Pamela's mother, with whom she was living, was pleased that her only daughter was to marry a man who obviously loved her, and who was both intelligent and a Tory MP. 'Ten years with Enoch', Mrs Wilson reportedly told Pamela, 'will be the equivalent of a University course.' Colleagues of Powell's were astonished by the news. 'They tell me Enoch's getting married,' Macleod commented to Eve, his wife. 'I can hardly believe it.'[4]

Enoch and Pam Powell were married on 2 January 1952 at the parish church in Lancaster Gate – they had hoped to wed in the crypt of the Palace of Westminster, but it was closed for repairs. Their three-week honeymoon was spent driving through France and Spain in their small car, nicknamed 'Gabrielle'. They crossed the Pyrenees in the snow, and went by boat to Mallorca. A few weeks after they had returned, Pam went to meet her husband at the House of Commons, and was waiting for him in the crowded Central Lobby when she saw him arrive and start looking for his new wife. 'I watched him going all the way round,' she remembers, 'wondering which one he'd married and been on honeymoon with.' But Powell's romantic side was reflected in his wish to sleep in a four-poster bed when he got married, and in his sending his wife a poem on their anniversary, with a red rose for each year of their marriage – though eventually, as the years passed the number of roses had to be reduced.[5]

Married life began in Powell's Earl's Court maisonette, where Pam worked as Powell's secretary in the morning and, after completing this work, did shopping and housework in the afternoon and evening while he was at the Commons. But as Pam later revealed, 'everything to do with our home we agree on jointly. Home-making should be a joint effort.' Powell had already installed bookshelves, but he developed his practical, do-it-yourself skills, fitting sliding cupboards and other improvements. When redecoration was needed, the Powells went to the shops together: 'my husband is terribly good as a carpenter and painter,' Pam told the *Express and Star*, 'but he can't put the paper on without me.' The change in Powell after his marriage was perceptible. He began drinking the odd glass of sherry or wine, having been told by Pam that her father would never have allowed her to marry a teetotaller. And despite his passion for fox-hunting, he gave up the sport since she did not ride to hounds, although he continued to ride into his sixties. Many people noticed a distinct softening in his behaviour towards them. As Colonel Ledingham, the party's Agent in the West Midlands, observed, 'since his marriage, some gleams of humanity have brightened his rather sombre personality'.[6]

The Powells lived on his MP's annual salary of £1,000 (about twice the average pay of a manual worker), supplemented by his earnings from journalism, that included an increasing number of radio broadcasts. He had been impressive as a presenter of BBC Radio's 'The Week In Westminster', and, for the BBC's overseas broadcasts, he had the advantage of being able to speak German and Urdu. But Powell had not entered parliament as a route into the media, however useful the extra income and opportunity to express his views were. By early 1952, his political prospects were good. The new Churchill Government had promoted hardly any of the up-and-coming Tory MPs from the 'class of 1950' to ministerial rank – Heath was an exception in the whips' office – but it was widely thought that Powell would soon be appointed to the front bench. The *Sunday Express* told its readers that he was 'a Tory to watch ... a short, brisk man with a prodigious memory', while the Labour MP, J.P.W. Mallalieu, vividly portrayed him in *Tribune* as one 'whose white-faced intensity betokens a nervous determination that at least one person on his own side should show up well in argument'. During the Commons' debate on Welsh affairs in February, James Callaghan (the future Prime Minister) chided Powell that 'when the Right Hon. Gentleman reaches the stage of becoming a minister – as I am quite sure he will one day – he will see just how far his theorizing falls short of practice'. A fortnight later, his local paper suggested that Powell might be named as a junior defence minister, with a salary of £1,500. 'He has exceptional attainment as a parliamentarian, and his prestige, as one of the most promising of the younger Conservatives, is high,' reported the *Express and Star*. 'There are other names mentioned, but none as frequently as Mr Powell's.'[7]

However, Powell's ambition was to be thwarted by an odd combination of chance and parliamentary convention that worked to the advantage of his close colleague and – as with any political friendship – rival, Iain Macleod. The outcome was to leave Powell feeling bitter and briefly estranged from Macleod. With the support of fellow members of One Nation at the start of the new parliament in November 1951, Powell and Macleod had been elected vice-chairmen respectively of the party's back bench committee on housing and local government and of the health and social security committee. One of the benefits of a vice-chairmanship was the increased likelihood of catching the Speaker's eye in debates and questions in the House. Macleod's chances of being called to speak were further enhanced when he became chairman of the health committee in February 1952, after his predecessor had suddenly been promoted to the front bench, at the very moment that health was becoming a political hot potato. He was virtually certain of being called early in the second reading debate on 27 March of the Conservatives' controversial National Health Service Bill, that imposed additional health charges, but Powell also intended to try and speak.[8]

Because of the close interest taken by Macleod and Powell in social policy, MPs had grown used to the sight of them both leaping to their feet to catch the Speaker's eye. Sometimes they were mistaken for one another, as happened early in the NHS Bill debate, when Dr Edith Summerskill, the Labour shadow health minister, referred to Powell's constructive contributions in earlier national insurance debates but referred to him as 'the Hon. Member for Enfield'. 'Yes,' Powell exclaimed, 'but I sit for Wolverhampton.' Had matters gone as expected during the debate, it might have been Powell, and not Macleod, who had the opportunity of taking one of the biggest scalps in politics and being rewarded by promotion as a minister.[9]

By convention, the Speaker endeavours to call MPs from opposing sides of the House in turn, beginning – when the debate is on a Government motion – with the Government and Opposition front benches respectively, and thereafter alternating between Government and Opposition back benches. On this occasion, the Minister of Health, Captain Harry Crookshank, was followed by Dr Summerskill for the Opposition, and since no Conservative privy counsellor or former minister sought to speak, Macleod would normally have followed Dr Summerskill. However, the deputy speaker, Sir Charles MacAndrew, who had taken over in the chair, realized that a new Tory MP, Philip Ingress Bell, was anxiously waiting to make his maiden speech, and called him instead of Macleod. After Bell, MacAndrew called Aneurin Bevan, the former Labour Minister of Health, founder of the NHS and one of the most formidable debaters in the House. As a result, Macleod, who followed next, was presented with a golden opportunity and, discarding his prepared notes, attacked Bevan with a savagery that no other Tory had dared attempt. Powell immediately realized that Macleod had 'scooped' the day's debate, put his speech away and limited himself to intervening in the speech of Bevan's successor as Health Minister, Hilary Marquand.[10]

Powell recaptured the drama of Macleod's triumph over Bevan many years later with a characteristic classical analogy, likening it to Polyphemus's being attacked by Odysseus – the giant taken on by the unknown. But had Macleod preceded Bevan, Powell might well have had the opportunity to play the Tory Odysseus. Whether he could have seized it as effectively must be doubtful. Although his expertise approached Macleod's on health, his dependence on carefully researched speeches robbed him of the passion and spontaneity that had invigorated Macleod's performance and also makes it unlikely that he could have spoken impromptu as well as Macleod. Moreover, at this stage in his career, Powell lacked Macleod's political bite and killer instinct in debate.[11]

However, judging by his reaction to the consequences that were eventually to flow from Macleod's speech, Powell had not yet accustomed himself to the fact that in politics, in contrast to his academic and military experience, luck, a good speech and a well-placed patron are much more important than any amount of hard work and careful preparation in winning the big prizes. Both Macleod and Powell were appointed to the committee that considered the NHS Bill clause by clause, and played an active part during April in counter-attacking Labour's onslaught of amendments. Yet when Powell spoke during the third reading debate on 1 May, he appeared to strike an almost ministerial pose – as though he were rehearsing for the part – in stressing the common ground between the approach of both front benches. Within a week, the resignation through ill-health of the Transport Minister, John Maclay, occasioned a reshuffle in which Crookshank was also moved. But any hopes of promotion that Powell harboured were dashed when Churchill appointed Macleod as the new Minister of Health on the recommendation of James Stuart, the influential Scottish Secretary and former chief whip, who had known Macleod from the latter's days in the Parliamentary Secretariat.[12]

Powell was shocked that Macleod, who was a year younger, had won the great prize of becoming a privy counsellor and head of a department, and had not even had to serve an apprenticeship as a junior minister. The pot-hunting automaton from Birmingham and Cambridge, the youthful professor and brigadier, was not used to seeing somebody else walk off with the biggest prize. 'There is a distance between a minister in office and a back-bencher,' he lamely ventured, 'which arrives quite suddenly upon the appointment of a minister.' But Macleod was deeply hurt by Powell's sudden coldness towards him. Although he reacted calmly, he could not fathom 'what the hell had got into Enoch'.[13]

The first, brief estrangement lasted only six weeks. It ended as suddenly as it had begun after Powell reacted with practical generosity to the personal tragedy that hit the Macleods when Iain's wife, Eve, was struck down by meningitis and polio. As Macleod sat in his room at the Commons, 'wondering desperately how to cope' and trying 'to conjure up a hundred solutions for all our family worries, Enoch strode into the room and threw a key on my desk. "There's a room ready in my flat," he said. "Come and go as you wish." And the door banged behind him.' With good reason, Macleod characterized Powell as being, 'abrupt and shy, gruff and gentle', and reflected that 'sometimes he seems to take great pains, almost delight, in hiding the fact that he is a kind and generous person'. Powell could never shake off his decent but unostentatious upbringing.[14]

The unexpected sequel to the slight suffered by Powell was equally revealing. He continued to toil as industriously as ever on the wide array of subjects in which he took a close interest, playing an active role in the Commons and behind the scenes at party back bench committee meetings, especially on housing, and continuing his journalism – in March, he had been one of the panellists when an edition of BBC Radio's *Any Questions* was broadcast from Westminster. In June, he demonstrated his desire to see the Government push ahead with deregulation of land control when he intervened at the 1922 Committee, attended by about 140 Tory back-benchers, to complain that Lord Woolton, the former Party Chairman, had disavowed the Conservative election manifesto by suggesting during a debate in the Lords that the Government's reforms to the Town and Country Planning Act would not be drastic – with the backing of the back bench housing and local government committee, Powell also wrote to the Chief Whip. In addition, he joined other Tory MPs in a policy sub-committee to review national insurance.[15]

In the summer of 1952, Powell succeeded Macleod as the part-time Director of the London Municipal Society, that serviced Tory councillors on the London County Council and the London boroughs, along the lines of the Conservative Research Department. His appointment brought an additional salary of £500, that, together with his pay as an MP, gave him the same income as a junior minister. Working from a dingy basement in Bridge Street, opposite the Palace of Westminster and across the river from County Hall, then headquarters of the LCC, Powell supervised the Society's research and edited its journal, *The Londoner*. There was none of the martinet about him, and he was modest and conscientious. The Powells became good friends of the Society's administrator, Miss Phyllis Gelli, a middle-aged spinster, who later helped as a baby-sitter, and whom they sometimes took with them to social functions.[16]

When another minor ministerial reshuffle occurred in the autumn of 1952 without Powell's gaining promotion, he began to attract sympathy for being overlooked yet again. Powell had always been bracketed with his former colleagues in the Parliamentary Secretariat, Macleod and Maudling, as being among the most talented Tories of their generation, yet he was apparently left languishing on the back benches as first of all Macleod won promotion, and then in November Maudling was appointed to the coveted post at the Treasury of Economic Secretary. However, those who sympathized with Powell's plight were not to know, and were not told by Powell, that Churchill had offered him a position in the Government in November. Moreover, the job that had been earmarked by the whips' office was one that seemed tailor-made for him. As the party had promised, on their return to office in 1951 the Conservatives designated a cabinet minister, Sir David Maxwell Fyfe, the Home Secretary, as having responsibility for Wales. News that a Scot sitting for a Liverpool constituency was to represent Wales provoked anger and shock. The Tories sought to counter this by appointing the young Welsh Tory, David Llewellyn, as a parliamentary under-secretary responsible for Welsh affairs – a post suggested by Powell, who defended the appointment of ministers to deal with Scottish and Welsh business regardless of their nationality within the United Kingdom. 'Once we begin jealously investigating the nationality of individual members of the administration', he warned MPs in February 1952, 'and saying that only Scotsmen can concern themselves with the affairs of Scotland and Welshmen with the affairs of Wales, we shall be starting on the road which, at any rate, leads to the dissolution of the United Kingdom.'[17]

Notwithstanding his English constituency, Powell seemed an ideal replacement when Llewellyn left the Government through ill-health the following November. On the advice of the Chief Whip, Sir Patrick Buchan-Hepburn, the Prime Minister offered Powell the post. However, Powell refused. The episode was not disclosed for some years, which suited everybody involved, particularly since there was a touch of Whitehall farce about it. While Powell was with Churchill, the Prime Minister's private secretary, Jock Colville, learned that Powell's appointment would bring the number of ministers in the Commons to 71, exceeding the then permitted maximum of 70. On Powell's departure, Colville rushed in to explain the problem, to which Churchill retorted, 'In that case you are in luck, because he has just turned it down!' Instead, a member of the House of Lords, Lord Lloyd, was appointed.[18]

Powell's refusal was almost unthinkable for an aspiring MP. What made it especially eccentric and perverse was that he had already turned forty and had seen younger rivals appointed to the front bench. However, their success in securing positions at the heart of government helps explain his extraordinary behaviour. He was prepared to hold out for a post that was more suited to his talents and was in the mainstream of British politics. But prime ministers and whips do not like having their patronage spurned, and they were unlikely to rush to make Powell a new offer. The rest of Westminster was to remain puzzled for more than three years at the apparent neglect by his party leadership of Powell's undoubted talent.

The beginning of the end for the imperial dream

Powell had prolonged his time as a back-bencher by refusing to accept a junior position in Churchill's Government, and the next two years were to mark a crucial transition in his career. His speeches improved, and in 1953 he delivered what he came to regard as his best parliamentary performance. By the autumn of 1954, the essential elements in what was to emerge a decade later as 'Powellism' had begun to take root. At the heart of this process was his complete change of mind on the Empire. Having been the champion of its indispensability to Britain, he became reconciled to its speedy dissolution, a transformation that saw him move from one extreme in the stormy debate in the Conservative Party to the other.

During the autumn of 1952, Powell succeeded in remaining on safe ideological ground. Addressing the annual party conference for the first time at Scarborough, he urged support for the Government's planned de-nationalization of road transport. After the legislation was included in the Queen's Speech, he put himself in the forefront of the party battle by speaking in the second reading debate and serving on the committee, where he combined mastery of technical detail with relish for the dogfight, sharpening his political teeth in clashes with Sir Hartley Shawcross and James Callaghan on the Opposition benches. In addition, he served on the committee stage of another deregulatory measure, the Town and Country Planning Bill, that decontrolled land for development purposes – a policy that he had long espoused.[19]

Although Powell had only been in the House for fewer than three years, his election to the dozen-strong executive committee of the Conservative 1922 Committee by his fellow Tory MPs on 11 November signified that he was coming to assume the status of a senior back-bencher. But he was not one to rest on his laurels and seemed to step up his prodigious work-rate. He combined his work on standing committees and his regular attendance at weekly back bench committees on housing, health and other subjects, with membership of the specialist select committees on statutory instruments and delegated legislation – the following year he was appointed to the prestigious public accounts committee and private bill procedure committee. Moreover, his local paper, Wolverhampton's *Express and Star*, revealed that during the first week alone in December 1952, he had sought, unsuccessfully, to speak on four subjects in the Commons – he reckoned that each twenty minute speech took him a day to prepare, and 'he prepares for four or five times as many speeches as he gives'. In January 1953, he appeared on BBC's *In the News*, the Sunday afternoon discussion programme, in place of the controversial historian, A.J.P. Taylor, but he was subdued by comparison with previous panellists, who had included Bob Boothby and Michael Foot. And all the while, Powell continued his work at the London Municipal Society, cranking up the Tory machine in the hope that a good performance at the borough elections in the spring of 1953 would bring him deserved but long overdue recognition.[20]

However, during the winter recess of 1952–53, Powell's strong commitment to the Empire prompted Julian Amery to invite him to the Eaton Square house of his father, Leo Amery, the imperialist statesman, to join in what Powell later called 'colloquies, not to say cabals', of Conservative MPs who believed that Government policy in Egypt amounted to the appeasement of nationalism and the abandonment of British interests. The 'Suez Group', of which Powell was to become a member, was formed by Julian Amery and Harry Legge-Bourke in order to resist the view of the Foreign Secretary, Eden, that Britain's large military base in the Suez Canal Zone was untenable because of political realities in Egypt and the cost to Britain, and was unnecessary in the age of jet aircraft and nuclear deterrence. In a wave of violently anti-British sentiment, the Egyptians had demanded the British evacuation of the Sudan, where Britain and Egypt had exercised joint control under the 1899 condominium, and the withdrawal of Britain's 80,000 troops from the Canal

Zone Base, which they held under the terms of the 1936 Anglo-Egyptian Treaty.[21]

Eden had been made aware in February 1952 of the anxiety felt by Tory MPs at his plan for rapid Sudanese independence, but they restrained their public criticism while warning against any withdrawal from the Canal Zone. The Foreign Secretary's reassurance that he was seeking Anglo-American solidarity in the Middle East provided no comfort for Powell, who had warned Eden some years earlier that the Americans were Britain's real enemies in the region. But following the Egyptian coup in the summer of 1952, Eden had felt sufficiently encouraged by the abandonment of Egypt's claim to the Sudan by the new leader, General Mohammed Neguib, to transfer the headquarters of the Middle East command from Egypt to Cyprus and begin negotiations for the withdrawal of British troops in the Canal Zone, much to the chagrin of Powell and other Tory imperialists.[22]

Yet it was a quite different, and apparently arcane, matter that provoked Powell in early March to launch his fiercest condemnation of what he saw as the Government's disregard of the Empire and British Commonwealth. There had been a foretaste more than a year earlier of his eagle-eyed opposition to even the most seemingly innocuous legislation that he regarded as weakening imperial unity when he attacked the Diplomatic Immunities Bill. This legislation extended to Commonwealth High Commissioners the legal immunities enjoyed in the United Kingdom by foreign ambassadors, but Powell saw it as another step towards loosening the 'old basis' of imperial unity, 'which was our duty of allegiance to our common Sovereign'. On 3 March 1953, he savaged the Royal Titles Bill as the culmination of this steady erosion of imperial and Commonwealth unity. Most MPs treated this legislation as a formality, since it gave effect to an agreement reached at the Commonwealth Conference the previous December that each member-state should use a form of royal title appropriate to its own circumstances. Both front benches supported the Bill on second reading, and Powell made the only speech against it from the Government benches. It was not only a matter of deep principle for him, but it also brought together his three great, romantic Tory and imperialist preoccupations – the Monarchy, the Empire and Commonwealth, and British citizenship.[23]

Powell detected in the Bill 'three major changes, all of which seem to me to be evil'. In the first place, the Bill was undermining imperial unity. The British Empire had been a unit 'because it had one Sovereign. There was one Sovereign; one realm.' Following the growth of self-government in the Empire (in Australia, Canada, and so on), the Sovereign had ruled his or her Dominions 'upon the advice of different Ministers, but the unity of the whole was essentially preserved by the unity of the Crown and the one Kingdom'. This would all be changed by the Bill. 'That unity', Powell declared, 'we are now formally and deliberately giving up, and we are substituting what is, in effect, a fortuitous aggregation of a number of separate entities.' These various 'entities' would define the identity of their Sovereign differently. Moreover,

Powell perceived a deeper threat to the institution of the Monarchy. 'By recognizing the division of the realm into separate realms,' he suggested, 'are we not opening the way for that other remaining unity – the last unity of all – that of the person [of the Sovereign] to go the way of the rest?'[24]

The Bill's suppression of the word 'British' from the description both of the colonies and the Commonwealth further roused Powell's suspicion. 'Why is it then', he queried,

> that we are so anxious, in the description of our own Monarch, in a title for use in this country, to eliminate any reference to the seat, the focus and the origin of this vast aggregation of territories? Why is it that this 'teeming womb of royal Kings', as Shakespeare called it, wishes now to be anonymous?

Powell argued that the answer was to be found in the next part of the Queen's proposed new title, as 'Head of the Commonwealth'. Returning to an old concern of his, he traced the origin of this title to the 'immense constitutional revolution' that he claimed had been brought about by the 1948 British Nationality Act. In keeping with this Act, India had been able to renounce its allegiance to the Crown and become a republic, without having to leave the Commonwealth. India's new status, however, was 'ungraspable' in law and in fact. Observing that the Indian Government recognized the Queen as the head of the Commonwealth, Powell commented, 'I recognize the Right Hon. Member for Walthamstow, West, [Attlee] as Leader of the Opposition, but that does not make me a Member of Her Majesty's Opposition.' At this protestation, a Labour MP interjected, 'Thank God.'[25]

The question of India's relationship with other dominions brought Powell to the kernel of his argument. In his view, India's position was being kept deliberately vague. It was therefore necessary, Powell argued, to define what constitutes unity, and apply this definition to India's position. 'I assert that the essence of unity', he continued, 'is that all the parties recognize that in certain circumstances they would sacrifice themselves to the interests of the whole.' Applying this yardstick to India – 'that former part of Her Majesty's dominions which has deliberately cast off allegiance to her' – he denied the presence of 'that minimum, basic instinctive recognition of belonging to a greater whole which involves the ultimate consequence in certain circumstances of self-sacrifice in the interests of the whole.' According to Powell, it followed

> that this formula 'Head of the Commonwealth' and the declaration in which it is inscribed, are essentially a sham. They are essentially something which we have invented to blind ourselves to the reality of our position.

Powell was to continue speaking for some minutes, but his dismissal of the new formula 'Head of the Commonwealth' as a sham marked a critical development in his thinking, paving the way for him to abandon his belief in Britain's role at the heart of a united Empire and Commonwealth.[26]

Powell was ready to accept the Bill's proposed changes if they were 'demanded by those who in many wars had fought with this country, by nations who maintained an allegiance to the Crown, and who signified a desire to be in the future as we were in the past'. He regarded these nations as 'our friends', and was ready to listen to them. But 'the underlying evil of this is that we are doing it for the sake not of our friends but of those who are not our friends. We are doing this for the sake of those to whom the very names "Britain" and "British" are repugnant.' He was clearly referring to the Indian Government. When the moderate Tory MP, Godfrey Nicholson, reminded him of India's past sacrifices in blood and treasure, Powell retorted that having had 'the advantage and privilege of serving with the Indian Army in the war', he was 'not likely to be unmindful of it'. Crucially, however, it had been an army that had owed allegiance to the Crown. 'That allegiance', he declared, with absolutist finality, 'for good or for evil, has been cast off, with all that follows.'[27]

Although Powell was under no illusion that his attack on the Royal Titles Bill would have any immediate effect, he concluded by emphasizing – in the words quoted at the head of this chapter – that he had a duty, as an MP, to express great principles and traditions in society. In a moving final passage, he encapsulated the romantic Tory view that motivated him, even when he knew that he was in a minority:

> Sometimes, elements which are essential to the life, growth and existence of Britain seem for a time to be cast into shadow, obscured, and even destroyed. Yet in the past they have remained alive; they have survived; they have come to the surface again, and they have been the means of a new flowering, which no one had suspected. It is because I believe that, in a sense, for a brief moment, I represent and speak for an indispensable element in the British Constitution and in British life that I have spoken. And, I pray, not entirely in vain.

Powell's speech irritated his front bench. He caused further annoyance by voting against the Bill, despite the Chief Whip's blandishments, with 38 other MPs, including Tory traditionalists and Labour left-wingers. Neither did it help him when the radical weekly, the *New Statesman*, ridiculed Sir David Maxwell Fyfe's criticism of him at the end of the debate as 'the sort of rebuke which is usually uttered only by Emperors to those who draw attention to their absence of clothes'.[28]

In his speech, Powell had taken a major step towards renouncing the romantic imperialism that had drawn him into politics, but his journey of conversion was not finished. Although he 'was aware of the self-deception of the Commonwealth', it would take him a little longer to conclude 'that we were applying the salve of the Commonwealth pretence to shield ourselves from the insight of the changes in the status of Britain in the world.' In view of the romantic nationalism that was to supersede his romantic imperialism, there is a certain irony in Powell's recollection that he had attacked the Bill because it perpetuated a 'fiction'. By the same token, however, Powell is well qualified to appreciate the importance of myth in politics. When he also sought to explain why so many people were seduced for so long by 'the fiction that the Empire had passed into an equally great and glorious Commonwealth', he observed that 'it may be that self-deception is part of being a nation, that a great deal of self-deception has to be fed into national feeling and national self-consciousness.' This was true, he thought,

> particularly perhaps for the British, who have this aptitude for deceiving themselves, for 'mugging' themselves, and the creation of a Commonwealth with the Queen as head of it was a means of self-deception ... Anyhow, this was a British self-deception; a characteristic self-deception. Let's use a form of words. We can make a reality of it here in our own country, the others don't have to do anything, we can do it to ourselves. We can pretend – let's go in a corner and pretend.[29]

Although Powell's comments betray his disappointment with his fellow citizens, they illustrate perfectly his ability to stand back from events and, in this instance, to perceive the role of myth-making in politics. This talent is rare among practising politicians. It was informed by his academic cast of mind and his having entered politics as an outsider – somebody who had come late to the compromises and conventions by which Britain is governed, and who always remained something of an observer because he was not born or brought up to take them entirely for granted. But the paradox of Powell is his own susceptibility to myth and romanticism. This, too, is deep-rooted in his temperament and upbringing, and is evident in his unswerving loyalty to the British constitution, and in particular, to its hereditary element – the Monarchy and the House of Lords.

From romantic imperialist to romantic nationalist

In the spring of 1953, however, Powell was a practising politician who was hoping for a renewed offer of promotion to the front bench. He knew that he could not afford another rebellion following his outspoken assault on the Royal Titles Bill. Yet three weeks later, he was again in major disagreement with the Government, this time over their legislation to establish the Central African Federation, that comprised the colonies of Nyasaland, and Northern and Southern Rhodesia (respectively, the future Malawi, Zambia and Zimbabwe). Today, this subject seems arcane, but the Government invested enormous hope in the concept and saw it as the means of resolving conflict between Africans and Europeans, that might serve as the model for the entire continent. During the 1950s the Federation became an article of faith for

Conservatives, on a par with Labour's 'clause four' of their constitution. Criticism was regarded as little short of heresy. Powell 'badly wanted to make a speech', explaining that the Central African Federation was 'an absurdity', but as he later recalled,

> I remember saying to myself, no you mustn't make that speech, because if you go against the Government on Central Africa as well, then they will say, 'Take no notice of Enoch. Enoch's somebody who's always against everything.'

As a result, he 'quite deliberately' kept quiet. 'I always regretted it afterwards', Powell confessed: 'if only I'd gone on the record in 1953 as saying the Federation was a mistake, in how much stronger a position I'd have been.'[30]

Significantly, while Powell's preoccupation continued with the imperial implications of the Government's Middle East policy, he devoted time, especially during the parliamentary recess in the summer of 1953 and the winter of 1953–54, to drafting the first half of a new book that outlined the creation of Britain's national consciousness. Written jointly with Angus Maude and finally published in 1955, the *Biography of a Nation* was a 200-page potted history of the country and its people. In a scathing review in the *Spectator*, Henry Fairlie described Powell as the 'more old fashioned' of the co-authors, adding that 'he simply believes in Order and Authority and is always prepared to offer a half-brilliant, half-mad, intellectual defence of them'. The book's mixed reception and its necessarily much-simplified narrative are less important than the coincidence of this expression of Powell's fascination with the idea of a nation as a living being and the powerful notion of 'national consciousness', while he was exercised about policy in Egypt and its ramifications for Britain's role in the world. These concerns and preoccupations were to bear fruit with profound consequences for his whole political outlook in July 1954.[31]

None the less, Powell's romantic imperialism gushed as hot and strong as ever during the remainder of 1953. In August, he fulminated against what he described as the 'most menacing and insistent demand among the Tories', namely the desire 'to get rid of Empire'. The Suez Group were buoyed up by the strong show of support for Julian Amery at the party conference in Margate, and despite Eden's having sought to reassure Tory MPs at a private meeting on 21 October, Powell threw down the gauntlet at the start of the new parliamentary session, by warning that the removal of British troops from the Suez Canal Zone would be a 'fatal step' with 'almost illimitable repercussions'. According to Powell,

> It would have repercussions in the Mediterranean, in the Middle East and in Africa. In the Middle East all our positions would thereby become insecure. Our positions in Cyprus, in Malta and in Gibraltar would be called in question by the fact that we had been eliminated from the focal

point, for the sake of which most of those positions have been taken up and maintained.

He was uncompromising in opposing concessions to Egyptian nationalists. 'It is by holding out the prospect of a reward for threats,' he argued, 'that we encourage and promote that very terrorism and those very threats.' Such was the strength of Powell's conviction, that Leo Amery reckoned in December 1953 that of the forty or so potential Suez rebels, only his son Julian and Powell were prepared to 'go to the point of risking the Government's existence'.[32]

A notable feature of Powell's attack was the ferocity of his anti-Americanism. American policy over the past decade, he claimed, had been 'steadily and relentlessly directed towards the weakening and destruction of the links which bind the British Empire together'. For although the United States had 'a very considerable economic and strategic use' for Britain, he argued that it saw 'little or no strategic use or economic value in the British Empire or the British Commonwealth'. It was 'against that background' that Powell asked MPs 'to consider the evidences of advancing American imperialism in this area from which they are helping to eliminate us'. Such outspoken hostility to the United States was largely limited to the pro-Soviet Communist Party, and prompted the Labour MP, Maurice Edelman, to comment that he had been 'astonished' to hear Powell 'using language which might have come directly from the *Daily Worker*'.[33]

When the *Economist* analysed the complexities of policy in the Middle East, and noted that American support for Greece and Turkey complemented Britain's role in the region and also that United States' policy had become more realistic, Powell retorted in legalistic detail, accusing the magazine of having misread the 1936 Anglo-Egyptian Treaty. A few months later in the journal, *Twentieth Century*, Powell further demonstrated the depth of his anti-Americanism and his imperialism. Britain's post-1945 participation in the United Nations and NATO was criticized as an unnecessarily defeatist departure from its previous overriding objective, namely 'the wellbeing and the power of the British dominions'. Moreover, Powell contended that the UN and NATO 'have in effect proved to be instruments in the expression of the power and influence of the United States'. He urged instead that 'the two great objects of British foreign policy ought to be to facilitate the defence by air-sea power alone of the British territories, and to secure a stable balance of power in Europe *without* Britain.' [his emphasis][34]

At the start of 1954, Powell still assumed that the imperial powers could defy both the rising tide of nationalism and the intense super-power rivalry. He believed that Britain's most pressing need was to give an 'open and practical recognition' of its 'natural community of interest with France in south-east Asia'. Powell's proposed strategy for Britain entailed weakening the main pillar of west European security with an increasing involvement in the Far East. A few months later, the Tory imperialists were to regard Eden's role at the Geneva conference on south-east Asia as another sell-out. As it was, the Foreign Secretary helped avert a super-power confrontation. Responding to Powell's article, Denis Healey, the young Labour front-bencher, chose a quotation that was appropriately arcane:

'The owl of Minerva only flies abroad when the shades of night are gathering.' Speaking for Conservatism, Hegel was right. And nothing proves the point better than the post-war crop of Tory intellectuals, sprouting like mushrooms in the damp cellars of Abbey House [Central Office]. Mr Enoch Powell's essay is a case in point.

Criticizing Powell's 'quaintly old fashioned' assumptions and his 'romantic chauvinism', Healey suggested that he had at least rendered 'explicit the assumptions unconsciously held by a certain type of politician whom Sir Winston most superbly represents'. But Healey cuttingly concluded that 'although the owl speaks clearer, the bulldog keeps his feet on the ground'.[35]

The Suez Group maintained a rumbling barrage of discontent during the 1953–54 parliamentary year, bursting into a crescendo of dissent whenever the Government seemed about to clinch an agreement with the Egyptians. At a Conservative back bench foreign affairs committee meeting on 2 December, Brigadier Powell (as the minutes still described him) argued that since Ministers had addressed the committee in October, the Foreign Secretary had felt bound to protest strongly against the Egyptian breach of faith in the conduct of the Sudan elections. This put the negotiations with Egypt in an entirely different light. If, Powell argued, Britain were to conclude an agreement on Suez of the character apparently contemplated, it would do so in the face of all the evidence that the Egyptian Government were false to their pledges. Before Christmas, Powell was in the forefront of the Group's campaign to prevent any sudden agreement being rushed through during the winter recess. After the reports in February 1954 of a coup against Neguib and the emergence of Colonel Nasser, Powell asked whether it was 'reasonable to suppose that Colonel Nasser or whatever regime succeeds Neguib, or whatever regime succeeds that, will fulfil the terms of the agreement in amity and concord with Britain?' In June, he took issue with the Cairo correspondent of *The Times* for having suggested that a new Anglo-Egyptian agreement would be advantageous to Britain.[36]

By the time that matters finally came to a head with the announcement, at the end of July 1954, that Britain and Egypt had reached agreement on the Suez Canal Base, Powell had completed the intellectual journey that marked his personal retreat from Empire. None the less, he opposed the agreement under which Britain would evacuate its troops within twenty months, but the base would be maintained by British civilians for another seven years and would be reactivated for use by British troops in the event of an attack on an Arab state or Turkey. Churchill's argument to Tory MPs that the recently developed H-Bomb had rendered such bases obsolete was unlikely to dissuade

Powell, who was a sceptic of nuclear deterrence, from rebelling. But even the appeal from the Chancellor, to which Powell might have been more sympathetic, that it would cost £50 million a year to maintain troops at the base left him unmoved. Having failed to speak in the debate on the agreement, Powell voted against the Government, together with more than two dozen Tories.[37]

'It's humbug and it's a lie and I won't tell that lie', was Powell's subsequent, explosive recapitulation of his reaction to the agreement. Britain had 'proceeded to humbug itself by saying that there was something just as good' as holding the Suez Canal Base, in the shape of a deal with Egypt that entailed evacuating British troops from the Canal Zone to Cyprus, Kenya and Jordan. As Powell recalled,

> if we were saying we would march out with drums beating and flags flying, if that was the judgement, that it couldn't be held, well so be it. But we were deceiving ourselves if we left on the assumption that we could re-occupy at will.

It was his objection to this latter assumption that lay at the heart of Powell's opposition. But a revolution had occurred in Powell's attitude to Empire, as he had revealed in early July 1954.[38]

This revolution in Powell's thinking was prompted by events that typified his political career. As an exceptionally intellectual Tory MP, who had somehow failed as yet to become a minister, he was an ideal choice to be appointed as chairman of the party's National Advisory Committee on Political Education. In this capacity, he approached with characteristic earnestness his task of delivering a lecture on 'The Empire of England' at Wadham College, Oxford, to the CPC summer school, that had for its theme the 150th anniversary of the birth of Disraeli. In drafting his speech, Powell pulled together constitutional and historic threads that had run through his earlier speeches, but the pattern that he wove marked a sensational shift in his thinking. Moreover, at the heart of this new departure is the importance that he accords to three themes that were to preoccupy him, at various times, during the remainder of his political career – the concept of sovereignty; the supremacy of parliament in the British constitution; and relations with the non-British and non-European populations of British colonies.[39]

The brief, preliminary definition of 'sovereignty' with which he began his lecture was to inform not only his new thinking on the Empire, but was also to underpin, many years later, his approach to European integration and to Northern Ireland. It was as though Powell could only jettison his romantic imperialism by rationalizing his romantic impulse in politics and finding a new object for his affection and loyalty. Asserting that mankind, at any moment, is divided into sovereignties, Powell defined a sovereignty as 'a group to all of whose members, but to no others, a single authority is able to give commands'. This did not rule out subordinate authorities, whose commands apply to some of the group only, but 'the existence of a single common authority competent to command, at least on some subjects and in some form' was a universal characteristic of the human species. Additionally, in Powell's view, sovereignties 'may maintain a continuous identity over centuries', against which 'geography, race, constitution can be powerless' – he cited the Roman Empire as an instance. And crucially, with sovereignty and its sense of continuity 'are associated mental images which provide an important motive to men's acts' – for example, 'the savage' who submits to sacrifice 'to avert a taboo from his tribe', or 'the mayor and city fathers unveiling a memorial to those who "fell for their country"'. This powerful, emotional – and to Powell, unavoidable – dimension to sovereignty was to remain at the core of his philosophy.[40]

The revolutionary flavour of the rest of Powell's lecture can be gauged from the quotation by, appropriately, Disraeli, that adorns the printed version of his text: 'these wretched colonies will all be independent in a few years and are a millstone round our necks'. At the crux of his argument was a 'simple but fateful dilemma' that resulted from the simultaneous emergence in Britain of parliamentary government and the acquisition of an overseas empire. 'The one kind of authority', he argued, 'which in the end must prove unacceptable to a community is that of a representative body in which it is not represented itself.' The 'ultimate alternatives' were only two: either representation had to be extended to include all the King's dominions, or British sovereignty had to be reduced 'to the limits of the representation of the Parliament of Great Britain'. In short, the choice lay between establishing an imperial parliament, or the inevitable, eventual 'dismemberment' of the Empire.[41]

Significantly, in presenting his analysis of how the demise of the Empire had eventually become inevitable, Powell drew a crucial distinction between colonies dominated by Europeans, and those where non-Europeans predominated. For many years, the inherent instability in relations between Britain and its colonies had been disguised by the circumstances of the time – Britain's power and the advantages of the Empire when set against the realistic alternatives. But during the latter half of the nineteenth century, as Canada and Australia moved towards self-government and Britain faced new challenges from America and Germany, the notion developed of a federal system of imperial government, with an imperial parliament, as a means of preserving unity between Britain and its colonies of European stock. However, the federal dream never materialized, and the First World War shattered the remaining anomaly of the British Government's running defence and foreign policy for the self-governing colonies.[42]

In describing how the independence of the self-governing, European-dominated colonies had been formalized by the Statute of Westminster in 1931, Powell reversed the position that he had held with such conviction on the Royal Titles Bill only sixteen months earlier. In that speech, he had emphasized the overwhelming importance to imperial unity of the common allegiance to the Crown, re-affirmed in the Statute of Westminster. But in his lecture, he declared that 'this common allegiance was already in 1931 practically devoid of content. It was indeed only possible precisely *because* it was devoid of content.' Having turned his previous argument on its head, Powell could reconcile himself to the inevitable sweeping away by the British parliament over the previous six years of every vestige of a common sovereignty between the United Kingdom and its former self-governing colonies.[43]

The importance that Powell accorded to culture, race and colour in politics is evident in his explanation of the final stages of the Empire's demise. In his view, this process had been accelerated by the existence of colonies 'with large populations unconnected in origin with the United Kingdom and potentially antipathetic to it by tradition or colour'. The 'simple but fateful dilemma' of non-representation in the ruling, representative assembly had raised itself in a different way in colonies where the population was non-European, or the territory was strategically important. Rule by force was ultimately incompatible with rule by representative assembly, but representation for these colonies in an imperial parliament had been 'dismissed out of hand as impracticable, because implying greater homogeneity in the electorate than can subsist between a European and a non-European territory'. Disraeli had squared the circle in the largest non-European colony by having Queen Victoria declared Empress of India, but this solution became untenable during the twentieth century.[44]

The British Empire could no longer withstand what Powell had identified as the inevitable logic of parliamentary representative government. As he argued,

A representative assembly which finds itself ruling by force a population other than that which it represents can only escape from that position, without denying the assumptions on which its own claim to authority rests, by creating in the dependent territories representative institutions in its own image.

The Westminster model was exported. But the British parliament was 'on hopeless logical ground' in trying 'to ration and subject to a timetable' its granting of authority to assemblies that it had created in its own image. 'By its very nature the transfer of sovereignty through the creation of representative institutions is bound to be a self-accelerating process.' Moreover, after the defeat inflicted on the British Empire by the Japanese,

it was henceforward clear that the realization of self-government in the dependent territories would end, as it had done in the self-governing colonies, in complete political separation. That separation would not even leave behind it the sentiment and tradition of common origins and mutual goodwill, but instead the heightened sense of racial and cultural difference and the saga of a 'struggle for freedom'.[45]

Powell had constructed an impressive, logically consistent explanation of decolonization that rivalled Marxist theory in its deterministic inevitability. But by presenting the process as 'the inevitable consequence of the political institutions of the United Kingdom and the character of its former and present dependencies', he had contrived to overlook the great historical changes – economic, political and social – that were eroding the old bonds of empire throughout the post-war world. Powell was set on the intellectual path that was to lead him to define the nation as 'the ultimate political reality', even though, 'what it is cannot be determined scientifically, you cannot pick it up, you cannot measure it. You can't survey it on the map.' So total was Powell's renunciation of empire that, when recalling the post-war imperialist cause of which he had been such a staunch supporter, he later declared that, 'no such political entity as the Empire nor the possibility of its unity existed'.[46]

There was nothing to keep Powell in the imperialist camp after he had concluded that what was surprising was not that the sovereignty of the British Empire had been dismembered, 'but that its dismemberment was so long postponed'. When parliament resumed after the summer recess at the end of October 1954, his old Suez Group allies again sought his support, but after British withdrawal from the Canal Zone he regarded 'the Egyptian question' as belonging to the past. Earlier that month, at the Blackpool party conference, the old Chamberlainite imperialists had suffered a further heavy defeat when the Conservatives consigned another legacy of Empire to the history books by supporting an impassioned plea from Peter Thorneycroft, the then President of the Board of Trade, to abandon imperial preference in favour of Britain's continued participation in the General Agreement on Tariffs and Trade, that was designed to promote a system of wider trade and payments. Powell had already deserted the imperialist cause, and Britain's new economic strategy accorded with his generally strong support for market economics.[47]

'Change Is Our Ally'

By the autumn of 1954, the key elements in what was later to be described as 'Powellism' were becoming discernible, although some aspects were more readily apparent than others: a deep attachment to parliament and the constitution; a romantic nationalism; and a strong commitment to market forces. In this latter respect, within four months of the Tories having won the October 1951 election, Powell had criticized the similarity between the economic policies pursued by the Labour and Conservative Governments. His attack had been prompted by Rab Butler's January 1952 restrictive economic package, that he compared with previous Labour measures.[48]

Governments of both parties faced problems in maintaining Britain's commitment to a fixed exchange rate. After their return to office, the Conservatives began to refer to 'freeing the pound', and secretly, during the first half of 1952, ministers and officials considered a scheme for a floating exchange rate (the so-called 'Robot' plan). Such a policy lay at the heart of the free-market approach that Powell supported – he later wrote of Butler's having 'suffered the crucial key of a free exchange rate to be wrenched from his hands'. Some seventeen years later, when Powell made a floating exchange rate a central plank in his alternative Tory economic policy, he condemned the Conservative Governments of 1951–64 for having failed to implement it. 'Robot' was finally rejected in Whitehall principally for fear that it would be tantamount to devaluation, causing prices to rise, and also because of sensitivity to international reaction, especially in the Commonwealth, since it entailed freezing certain sterling balances – Britain's massive debts to former colonies and existing dependent territories.[49]

Powell's impatience for more radical economic policies was shared among the new breed of Tory MPs. Many of them did not necessarily have Powell's enthusiasm for market economics, but they increasingly felt that the Conservative Government were failing to address the new challenges that Britain faced as the war receded and the defeated powers, Germany and Japan, began to recover and look for markets. Powell later revealed something of his frustration at the time in his caustic comment on Churchill's peace-time administration that, 'it was all coming to pieces, with Winston's failing health and failing control, and failing Prime Ministership. It was a Government in disarray.'[50]

Again, it fell to the One Nation group of Tory MPs to voice the concern of young Tories, and to propose a new approach. In 1950, they had reflected the anxiety felt about their party's failure on social policy, and developed a 'Tory approach to social problems'. In 1951, the group had planned a new book on 'The Revival of Britain', but it never saw the light of day – among the proposed chapters, Powell was to write two (on the Church and the Monarchy); Macleod was to write on the Welfare State, and Richard Fort and Heath on the United Kingdom. But the parliamentary battles during 1952–53 over the de-nationalization of road transport and iron and steel, and the de-control of land for development, shifted the political spotlight onto the future of the nationalized industries and the mixed economy. Believing 'that nothing less was at stake than the ability of British industry itself to evolve and therefore to survive', the One Nation group sought to devise an industrial policy that 'would facilitate and encourage economic change rather than resist and be broken by it'. This theme, they argued in *Change Is Our Ally*, published in May 1954, 'ran through every debate, whether on privately-owned or publicly-owned industry, on controls or taxation, on wheat or on coal'.[51]

The imprint of Powell's thinking is unmistakeable throughout *Change Is Our Ally*, of which he was co-editor with Angus Maude (Maude's previous co-editor, Macleod, had left the group on his appointment as Minister of Health). According to Powell and his colleagues, during 'six years of war and six of Socialism', the important truth that economic change is 'the normal environment in which nations live and successful adjustment to it is a condition of their wellbeing' had been 'dangerously obscured and overlaid'. In fact, the first half of the book, entitled, 'The retreat from *laissez-faire*', also denounced the active state intervention, principally through rationalization and nationalization, practised by the Conservatives during the inter-war years. The message to their own Government could hardly have been more explicit. 'We doubt', they declared of the urgent need for economic change, 'if it yet claims sufficient attention.' It was because of such criticism that Rab Butler, who was not only Chancellor of the Exchequer but had also served in the inter-war Governments, declined to write a foreword, as he had done for *One Nation*.[52]

In Powell's view, market economics offered the most effective method of achieving, and adapting to, economic change. The radical thrust of the recommendations in *Change Is Our Ally* was captured in the title of the book's second half, 'The return to a free economy' – that could also have served for Powell's alternative Tory economic programme in the 1960s. In keeping with One Nation's impatient tone, the de-nationalization and de-regulation measures since 1951 were regarded as only a beginning, and emphasis was placed on the need to encourage competition. However, in a notable qualification, decentralization as opposed to denationalization was recommended for the coal industry, while the retention of a national minimum wage for miners was seen as 'an economic advantage to the industry', since it would help force up productivity.[53]

In almost every other aspect of industrial policy, the group accepted intervention only on social or strategic grounds as opposed to economic reasons. They proposed the removal of the few remaining price controls, including rents; the ending of indiscriminate subsidies, particularly in housing; the relaxation of controls on industrial location; and lower levels of taxation. Centralized economic planning was eschewed as a means of co-ordinating resources in favour of 'the exercise of consumer choice based on economic costs competitively determined'. And, in anticipation of the party's rejection of protectionism the following autumn, the One Nation group emphasized the desirability of 'the so-called liberalization of trade'.[54]

One of the most fascinating aspects of *Change Is Our Ally* is that it appeared several years before Powell played a key part in the great split in Conservative ranks on the role of public spending and borrowing in managing the economy. But a difference of emphasis already existed between, on the one hand, Tories who accepted the approach advocated by the economist, Keynes, of managing the economy by adjusting the levels of taxation and public spending in order to mitigate the impact of the business cycle; and, on the other hand, those who clung to traditional economic nostrums, such as balancing the budget, and tended to attach greater weight to curbing inflation. Powell never embraced Keynesian economics, but in 1954 (when inflation was virtually non-existent as prices were rising at only two per cent a year), he was prepared to join his One Nation colleagues in rejecting a 'pure *laissez-faire* economy' and reiterating the state's role in preventing deflation and unemployment by fine-tuning the economy – 'raising or lowering the economic temperature', as the One Nation group expressed it. However, the careful wording in *Change Is Our Ally* shows that the difference of emphasis within the party was mirrored in the group. 'The most desirable instruments of such intervention', they argued, 'are budgetary and credit policies, because they exert a general influence on the economic temperature rather than introduce artificial distortions into the pattern of production.' Although the Tories had placed greater reliance on interest rates as a tool of policy since 1951, the reference to 'credit policies' could be taken to include an old-fashioned policy of 'dear money' (high interest rates) to dampen inflation, thereby satisfying Tories like Powell.[55]

The extent of Powell's differences with his One Nation colleagues had been clearly demonstrated shortly before the publication of *Change Is Our Ally*. In early 1954, Thorneycroft, then President of the Board of Trade, introduced legislation to permit federal organizations to be created in badly-organized industries, and to make levies on member firms to foster efficiency, research and export effort. Thorneycroft's corporatist approach was in the tradition of the Labour Government's Development Council and inter-war notions of self-government in industry. Not surprisingly, it commanded the general support of the Labour front bench, but this fact gave added force on the Tory right to Powell's criticism of it as a 'surrender to socialism'. Faced with having to depend on Labour votes against determined opposition from a group of back-benchers organized by Powell, the Government abandoned the Bill.[56]

When consulted in July, in his capacity as a representative of the 1922 Committee on the party's advisory committee on policy, about a statement on employment and industrial relations for the next election, Powell peppered the draft with deletions that he 'would athetize [sic] as "gup" or "un-Tory"'. The rejection of 'the socialist conception of a wages freeze' was insufficient. 'Ought we not to condemn a "wages policy" as well as a "wages freeze"?', he queried, asserting that 'both are socialism and open to all the same objections'. 'For the future', Powell urged, 'the really strong point is that a Conservative economic policy *in itself* [his emphasis] breeds good conditions of employment and industrial relations'. Yet a year later he publicly commended Sir Walter Monckton, Churchill's emollient Minister of Labour, for having handled industrial relations 'so successfully' – Monckton was later to be regarded as something of a *bête-noire* by Tory right-wingers for having appeased the unions during the early 1950s.[57]

Powell was an instinctive right-winger on economic policy, but had not given it anything like the same thought as he had social policy. He was a natural supporter of the campaign run by Ralph Assheton, the Tory MP and former party chairman, to cut public spending, and therefore opposed the hefty increase in the borrowing powers of the public sector electricity and gas authorities. At this time, Powell wrote a review for the *Spectator* of *Capitalism and Historians*, a collection of essays edited by the free-market economist, Hayek. Unsurprisingly, Powell drew attention to the claim that historians had misinterpreted or suppressed evidence on the industrial revolution to serve left-wing ends. Less predictably, however, he took issue with some of the authors for having made 'unsubstantiated assertions' of their own. Even

Hayek's claims for the wealth-creating impact of 'the competitive order' and 'the freedom of economic activity' in eighteenth-century England were said by Powell to 'contain assumptions less crude but not necessarily less debatable than those which the book is devoted to demolishing'. In view of Powell's predilection for making assertions on economics, there was a certain irony in his criticism of Hayek, in what appeared to be an attempt to distinguish his Toryism from pure, *laissez-faire* liberalism. Similarly, in his review of *The Economist in the Twentieth Century* by Lionel Robbins, the liberal economist, Powell was at pains to emphasize the limited role of economic principles in explaining, let alone influencing, political action.[58]

In the summer of 1954, a new edition of *The Social Services: Needs and Means*, was published, updated and marginally revised by the hyper-active Powell. Yet he had already undergone a conversion on a central feature of the argument that he and Macleod had advanced. Although they had argued in 1952 that 'it was imperative to restore the principle of insurance', he had become convinced that the insurance principle could no longer be applied to old age pensions. Powell's thinking had developed during his membership of a small policy sub-committee that had been set up in March 1952 under the auspices of the Tory back bench health and social security committee to review national insurance benefits. The sub-committee's final report in 1953 highlighted the consequences of the decision that was made in 1946, with all party support, that pensions and other benefits should be paid in full to very large numbers of people who were either too old to earn contributions or whose contributions would never cover the full cost of their benefits. As a result, from 1954–55, the insurance fund would be increasingly in annual deficit, rising from £100 million in 1957–58 to £420 million by 1977–78. As each year's deficit had to be met by an Exchequer 'block' grant, Powell and his colleagues warned that this growing annual charge would make it difficult to maintain the insurance principle, and a future Government might 'decide that the growing liability of non-actuarial pensions cannot be met from the Exchequer without the imposition of a needs test'. The sub-committee shied away from recommending anything as radical and politically controversial as replacing the old age pension with a means tested benefit. In what smacked of a compromise between its members, they concluded that for the time being the contributory insurance scheme should continue, and any future decision would depend on economic circumstances at the time.[59]

Avoiding or fudging the issue, however, was never going to satisfy Powell. Like the Commonwealth, the insurance principle as it applied to the retirement pension, had become a fiction. He was convinced that the pensions conundrum could best be solved through means testing. At a private meeting of the Conservative back bench health and social security committee on 5 May 1954, Powell warned of the implications of the Government's intention to restore the purchasing power of the retirement pension to its 1946 level. Such an increase, he argued, would not help those most in need, and would be unpopular with poorer pensioners on national assistance who had little or no other means. Powell now evinced no sympathy for those who were too proud to apply for national assistance, suggesting that their numbers were exaggerated and that policy could not be based on people who declined to use a publicly provided service. But his greater anxiety, reflecting his work on the policy sub-committee, was that any increase in the pension would inevitably increase the deficits in the national insurance fund, and the extra cost would fall on the Exchequer.[60]

This latter concern informed Powell's speech six months later, during a Commons debate on old age pensions called by the Labour Opposition, in which he demolished the conventional assumption that the old age pension was based on the insurance principle. In reality, he argued, people's contributions were not being saved to fund their pensions, but were merely another tax that paid for current pensions. Indeed, Powell advocated a subsistence pension paid from general taxation, and then taxed if the recipient was a taxpayer, in the same way that the family allowance was paid. But with a general election imminent, the Tories were not about to embark on radical reform, and within the month introduced legislation that would substantially increase national insurance benefits, including the old age pension, in return for a modest rise in contributions.[61]

Intriguingly, the strongest echo of Powell's speech was heard at Labour's annual conference at Margate the following October during a debate on pensions, in which Aneurin Bevan attacked the national insurance scheme. As it happened, Powell witnessed Bevan's speech in his capacity as a presenter of the radio series, 'Straight from Conference', that was broadcast on the BBC Light Programme each evening during the main party conferences. Powell's co-presenter at Margate, and in Bournemouth at the Conservative conference, was the thirty-year-old Labour MP, Anthony Wedgwood Benn, a choice that reflected the BBC's concern to recruit two of the most able, up-and-coming party politicians for the nightly discussions. Yet the selection of Benn and Powell by the BBC is not without irony in that although they went on to become cabinet ministers, they eventually emerged as mirror images of one another on the left and right of British politics – the most senior and outspoken critics of their party leaderships since the end of the Second World War, and leading opponents of British membership of the European Community.[62]

During their 1955 radio series, Benn and Powell tended to reflect their party's respective positions, but at Margate they found common ground on pensions. Bevan had denounced the 'insurance' scheme as a 'misnomer', arguing that the contributions made in a compulsory and universal system were a 'poll tax'. 'You know, Benn,' Powell observed, following this extract from Bevan's speech, 'I've got a great deal of sympathy with that point of view,' and later recalled that in his Commons speech the previous November he had 'attacked the insurance principle very much along Mr Bevan's lines.' When Bevan proposed instead that 'the finances should be found by the general Exchequer', Powell not only concurred, but blamed a former Tory

Minister of Health, Neville Chamberlain, for having made the original mistake, in 1925, of extending insurance to pensions. 'I really think it's phoney and we've got to change it,' Powell told Benn and their listeners.[63]

But not everybody in the Labour Party was happy with Bevan's argument. Opponents were concerned that, although Bevan was against means testing, there was a danger that replacing the pension by a state benefit would lead to means testing being introduced. Warning of this danger in replacing the pension by a state benefit, Sir Alfred Roberts, chairman of the TUC's social security committee, clearly had Powell in mind and to underline his fear quoted the question that had been posed by Macleod and Powell: 'why should any social service be applied without a means test?' In response to Roberts's argument, Powell recalled suggesting in his Commons speech that, 'if you went away from the contributory principle then you could means test the pensions like you do means test the family allowances, through taxation on the total income of the people who receive them'.[64]

At the end of that night's programme, Powell was able to tell Benn that 'this is the first time when I don't think I can complain of your party and your platform not having got their policy yet'. For he readily acknowledged that 'without the agreement of the trade unions and the vast mass of public opinion which they represent neither your party nor my party can make any change in this matter'. Before thanking Powell 'for a very enjoyable discussion', Benn teased him that 'it was a historic day for you, not only because you were quoted at a Labour Party conference, but because Labour policy of next year will be the Tory policy of twenty years hence, and I feel now that you're in at the start.' Powell had been an astute Tory observer of national insurance since the post-war system's enactment in 1946, and he was to argue within his party for many years for the radical reform of state benefits for the elderly.[65]

7

Reaching the Despatch Box

I know everything that can be said against him and in particular perhaps the fear that he might resign over a minor issue. I do not believe this is a true view: indeed I know it is not. His ability of course is not in doubt, only his judgement.

Iain Macleod on Enoch Powell, in a letter to R.A. Butler urging that Powell should be appointed to the Government, 20 July 1954.

Loyalist with a conscience

In its Christmas edition of 1954, the *Economist* assessed the impact of what it called the 'Class of 1950', the 96 Conservative MPs, including Powell, whose entry into the Commons had heralded the eventual demise of Attlee's Government and the beginning of a new Tory dawn. However, as the weekly magazine reported a month after Prime Minister Churchill's eightieth birthday celebrations, the 'class of 1950' were deeply frustrated. Although forty of them had, at one time or another, been ministers or parliamentary private secretaries, there were still too many outdated, aristocratic figures in the Government. The new breed of modern Tories, who were more in tune with young, aspiring voters in dormitory towns and suburbs, were being largely overlooked. By the end of 1954, Powell, whom the *Economist* mentioned for having left 'no shred of empire' in that year's CPC summer school lecture, had become by far the most glaring example of wasted talent on the Tory back benches.[1]

Powell's claims to a place on the front bench had been most recently ignored in a minor reshuffle at the end of July 1954, despite an extraordinary plea by his former colleague, Iain Macleod, who by then had been running a department for more than two years. Writing to Rab Butler, the Chancellor, on 20 July 1954, from the Ministry of Health in Savile Row, Macleod confessed that although he had 'not the slightest idea if the general view that there will be a "shuffle"' was correct or not, it was clearly possible 'and certainly the P.M. will be consulting you'. Since he had not seen Butler 'for more than a moment or two' lately, he thought that he 'should write personally' to Butler about Enoch Powell. 'I hope very much that he will be included,' Macleod wrote, adding the words that appear at the head of this chapter. Quite why Macleod felt so confident about Powell's disinclination to resign is not clear, but his acknowledgement of the doubts about Powell's judgement reveals Powell's reputation among the party hierarchy.[2]

Although Macleod did not always agree with him, especially on economic policy, he had no doubts about Powell's ability. He was also more aware than most ministers, through his role on the research study group that was devising policy for the next election, of Powell's real contribution to party thinking. When the group had met representatives from the Tory back bench committees in April, Powell made the hard-headed appraisal that housing would be played out as an electoral issue by 1955, but urged that Labour's vulnerability on controls and monopolies should be exploited by a vigorous presentation of plans to sweep away remaining war-time controls and that the Tories should not set their face against further denationalization. In a tactical assessment of the kind that Macleod relished, Powell was minuted as having outlined the 'three essentials' for the next Tory manifesto:

i) an attack on Socialism; ii) to tell the success story of the present Government – remembering that the best legislation passed may not always be the most popular; iii) to produce 'pies in the sky' which would be definite, characteristic, and on points (e.g. taxation) where we would not be outbid by the Socialists.

But Powell's contribution went much wider than his conscientious work behind the scenes. As Macleod told Butler,

No one – except yourself – has done as much in the country and the House for the true Tory thinking approach to our problems as he has done. All his recent contributions, to the Transport debate, the rating and valuation Bill and others, have been distinguished as they always are.

In addition, there was 'a very strong desire in the party to see him on the front bench'. But was Macleod's remarkable letter part of an old pals' act? 'I do not write this to you particularly out of friendship for Enoch,' Macleod explained. 'Indeed, I have hardly seen him these past two years and we rarely even talk'. But as he concluded, 'we were both your lieutenants for some years and I would not feel happy if I did not bring this question of his promotion to your notice.'[3]

Macleod's exceptional and impressive plea on Powell's behalf was in vain. While Powell was again left lingering on the back benches, Sir Edward Boyle, another bright young Tory MP from a West Midlands seat, who had held Birmingham Handsworth for the Conservatives at the by-election in November 1950, was appointed to the Ministry of Supply. Although Powell had opposed the Suez Agreement, its signing gave him a new opportunity to improve his standing with the party hierarchy. Whereas he had missed many previous meetings of the party's advisory committee on policy, under Rab Butler's chairmanship, because they were often held on Fridays when he was in his constituency, he played an active part in the committee's discussions on 1 September (a Wednesday). On housing policy, he agreed with Henry Brooke, newly promoted to the Treasury in the re-shuffle, 'that slum clearance was something that we could and must stress'; on agriculture, he countered Lord Hawke's call for more canneries and deep freeze storage plant by arguing that it should be left to private enterprise; and, on the question of 'help for the middle classes', he supported the view that encouraging private education or medicine was best done through income tax relief. During late September and early October, he made a series of speeches for the party in the East Midlands and southern England. When the Commons reassembled, his desertion from the Suez Group and his tendency to speak in debates on non-controversial matters strengthened the impression that he was anxious to demonstrate his eagerness for office.[4]

Powell was forty-two years old, and unless he became a minister within the next few years, he was in danger of being type-cast by the whips as a permanent back-bencher. He had also experienced profound changes in his personal life, that had forever closed a door on his youth. The death of his sixty-six-year-old mother from cancer in May 1953 deeply affected him. He owed her everything. Many intelligent women of Ellen Powell's generation had transferred ambitions that they might have had for themselves onto their children. As the only child, Powell had been the sole recipient of all his mother's devotion and fierce determination. 'My mother and I were not gentlemen,' he recalled in his old age.

> My father was a gentleman in all his instincts, and this was something that I felt I didn't share. There was something harder, more aggressive in my character, which I shared with my mother: the feeling that we had to fight for whatever we were going to get.

In an echo of *Sons and Lovers*, D.H. Lawrence's autobiographical novel of another upwardly mobile Midlands scholarship boy, Powell added, 'I was close to my mother, possibly too close. I only realized when she died that my father and I were jealous of one another for my mother's love.' At least one close acquaintance of Powell's felt that Pamela, his wife, increasingly came to take his mother's place.[5]

Powell had also assumed the family responsibilities that often accompany middle age. In January 1954, Pamela had given birth to their first child, a daughter, Susan Mary. In London, the family still lived in the Earl's Court maisonette that he had bought as a bachelor, and Powell's skill at do-it-yourself again came in useful as further modernizations were made to accommodate the baby. Specially grooved rails were commissioned by Powell from a Wolverhampton firm to allow the baby's perambulator to be wheeled safely down the rather steep steps into their back garden. Instead of going on holiday to France in the late summer, as they had the previous year, the Powells stayed in Britain with their baby. Not only did Powell take the opportunity to make his show of loyalty to the Government, he also bought a house in his constituency. The flat in Chapel Ash was no longer adequate for their needs, and, in addition, the Powells were anxious to care for Powell's father. The Victorian house that the Powells bought – number 79 Merridale Road – was situated in a residential area to the west of the city, and served as Albert Powell's home and as their family base at weekends and during parliamentary recesses. Powell was proud that it was furnished with some of his parents' Edwardian furniture, although the house is remembered as having looked rather gloomy.[6]

The new house in Wolverhampton cost £1,500, which was the amount that Powell earned from his £1,000 a year salary as an MP and his £500 part-time post as Director of the London Municipal Society. He also received extra income from his broadcasting and journalism. Financially, the Powells were not badly off for the time (average manual earnings were around £550 a year), and they made a point of saving something every year towards their retirement. But although Powell's means were modest by the standards of many wealthier Tory MPs, he had resolutely opposed the calls made in February 1954, following the recommendations of a select committee on MPs' pay and pensions, to provide an extra £500 a year for MPs to help cover their expenses – at the time, the parliamentary salary included neither free postage nor free travel for a spouse. Although the Commons chose, in a free vote, to ignore ministerial opposition and vote for the extra money, continued pressure from Powell and other Tories persuaded the Government to defer any increase. When Powell saw the Prime Minister as one of a deputation from the Tory back bench 1922 Committee, Churchill fixed him with his eye and, glaring at him, growled, 'You would be against me if I put the salary up.' 'Winston was right,' Powell later recalled,

> I had gained the prize; membership of the House of Commons, that I had been working and arguing for since the war. That – with the remote chance of office – was more than enough. I would live, plus what I could make by occasional writing, on a scale that would enable my wife and me to face defeat or (if, unimaginably, it were to come) resignation.

Powell was opposed in principle to any improvement in MPs' pay during the course of a parliament. This was to remain his position for the rest of his parliamentary career. Since MPs are the only people who can vote themselves an increase out of public funds, he never thought it right to accept any pay increase until his electors had had an opportunity to decide whether or not he should continue to serve them.[7]

The year 1954 was also to assume great importance for Powell, because of a major change that was beginning to occur in some parts of Britain's inner cities. 'For over ten years, from about 1954 to 1966,' he was later to write, 'Commonwealth immigration was the principal, and at times the only political issue in my constituency of Wolverhampton.' By the mid-1950s, the numbers of West Indians settling in certain areas, especially in London and Birmingham, was already being raised as an issue by a number of MPs, local politicians and party activists – Labour, as well as Tory. In the autumn of 1955, West Midlands Tories had a heated debate on immigration from the Commonwealth and the Republic of Ireland, and unanimously passed a resolution demanding the introduction of control that was forwarded to ministers in London. Yet there were, in fact, only about 1,000 West Indians living in Wolverhampton by 1956. Powell was not among the small number of Tory back-benchers who began calling publicly for control of Commonwealth immigration, although his conversion from imperialism to nationalism had led him to denounce the trappings of Empire, of which Britain's 'open door' immigration policy for the Commonwealth was one.[8]

In the course of Powell's July 1955 Conservative Political Centre summer school, however, he developed an argument that was to inform his later approach on immigration. In view of the direction that his thinking on the Empire had taken, it was unsurprising that he should talk about 'Nationalism', and this led him to discuss decision-making in the nation state, and the potential divisiveness of majority decisions. In discussing the 'lines of fission' along which societies can become divided, Powell argued that it might be 'racial',

> provided that difference of race, in the absence of religious or linguistic differences, is marked by plain and visible distinctions, such as colour; for men assume that those who look differently from themselves have different interests – there could scarcely have been anti-Semitism as we have known it unless Jews were recognizable at sight.

In short, as a nationalist, Powell saw racial difference as a potentially divisive factor in politics. It was to be this line of thinking that was to lead him, more than a decade later, to predict violence, and even civil war, in Britain.[9]

At this stage, however, Powell still seemed happy with the open-door policy on immigration. Just a few months after his lecture on 'Nationalism', one of his evening radio broadcasts from the October 1955 Conservative conference at Bournemouth included an extract from a speech in which Alan Lennox-Boyd, the Colonial Secretary, urged Tories 'to help the members of this great imperial family, not only the 10,000 colonial students, but the colonial immigrants who are just as much citizens of the United Kingdom, as their passports will show you, as are you and I'. Lennox-Boyd also argued for accepting increased economic competition from the colonies, as opposed to resisting it. In response to this powerful evocation of the doctrine of *civis Britannicus sum*, Powell declared, with evident approval, to his co-presenter,

Anthony Wedgwood Benn, 'Well, Benn, I don't see how you could have a more modern or forward looking exposition than that.'[10]

The left-right political spectrum is a dubious aid to understanding at the best of times, but as Powell's opposition to capital punishment demonstrates, he defies any simple classification as being 'right-wing'. In February 1955, he was one of only eighteen Tory MPs to support the call by the Labour MP, Sydney Silverman, to suspend capital punishment for five years, following the report of the Royal Commission on Capital Punishment. Although Conservatives had been allowed a free vote, the Home Secretary, Gwilym Lloyd George, had urged that they should oppose suspension of the death penalty. Powell later explained his anti-hanging vote in his constituency. His position was informed by a liberal, humanitarian approach on certain moral issues.[11]

In the same month as Powell's liberal stand against hanging, he demonstrated his commitment to state intervention on social grounds. The appalling smogs of the early 1950s, in which many people had become ill or died from respiratory problems in Britain's smoke-laden cities, had led to demands for curbs on air pollution. When the Government failed to act on a report on clean air to the Ministry of Housing and Local Government, Powell co-sponsored and helped draft the private member's bill, introduced by the Tory MP, Sir Gerald Nabarro. Informing MPs during the Clean Air Bill's second reading that he not only represented a Black Country constituency, but that his family had lived in the area 'for generations', Powell recalled Dickens's graphic description of the Black Country's 'tall chimneys, crowding on each other' as they 'poured out their plague of smoke, obscured the light, and made foul the melancholy air'. Although the 'conditions of that full horror' had ceased to exist, Powell none the less argued that 'the time is ripe now for a drastic step which within a measurable period – let us say of ten or fifteen years – will make the description "Black Country" once and for all obsolete.' This particular Bill did not become law in 1955 because a General Election was called, but the Clean Air legislation that Powell eventually steered onto the statute book in 1956 brought a huge improvement in people's health and in their physical environment, by restoring the light to their towns and cities, and by any standards represented a great social reform.[12]

Hopes of early recognition for Powell when Eden finally succeeded Churchill as Prime Minister were dashed when the new administration was formed in April 1955. Yet again during a re-shuffle, Powell remained an onlooker as his colleagues and rivals moved up the ministerial ladder. Another former colleague, Maudling, joined Macleod as the head of a department (Supply), while Sir Edward Boyle, ten years Powell's junior, replaced Maudling as Economic Secretary to the Treasury. The becalming of Powell on the back benches was even more remarkable in view of his exceptionally well-informed speech on the Government's Requisitioned Houses Bill on 15 February, and his role as Director of the London Municipal Society in April's London County Council elections, when he seized the initiative at the outset of the campaign by condemning Labour's record on slum housing in a letter to *The Times*.[13]

Presenting himself again to his electors at the May 1955 general election that followed the Tories' local election successes, Powell appeared as an impeccably loyal supporter of the Government. Gone was the heady rhetoric of Empire. In contrast to his previous election addresses, imperial policy received no mention. Moreover, despite his intemperate criticisms of Eden's conduct of foreign policy, Powell felt able to reassure his electors that the Government's record, including 'peace in South-East Asia', gave 'confidence for the future'. On domestic policy, Powell naturally highlighted the Government's record on denationalization, deregulation and lower taxation, but he was also quick to argue that the 'prosperity and expansion' of the previous three and a half years 'would be worth little unless the advantages had reached everybody through the social services'. There was not a hint of his misgivings about certain aspects of welfare spending as he emphasized (in bold print) not only that NHS spending had increased and extra school places had been provided, but also that 'retirement and other pensions, insurance benefits, family allowances, have been increased by 50 per cent or more'. Moreover, on 18 May, he reassured a meeting of Conservative women that he was an unashamed believer in family allowances, and wanted to see further measures passed to the advantage of those who accepted the burden of raising a family. And, notwithstanding his enthusiasm for a market-oriented approach to housing, Powell was proud to claim that '1,000,000 new homes – *three-quarters of them let at subsidised rents* – have been built'. [present author's emphasis][14]

In a national swing to the Conservatives on polling day, their majority in the Commons was increased from seventeen seats to 58. In Wolverhampton, Powell's majority more than doubled to 8,420, assisted by the transfer of a Tory ward from the neighbouring Labour seat. There followed, however, perhaps the most frustrating period of all for Powell, as Eden deferred his expected post-election re-shuffle for many months. Powell remained as active as ever. In August, he recorded three talks on the House of Lords for BBC Radio's Third Programme, that were broadcast during early September while he and his family were on holiday. The programmes were a spin-off from his work on a history of the upper House, first begun in 1949. He had sufficient self-confidence to try and inject a sense of spontaneity by preparing only half a page of notes for each broadcast and addressing his comments to a producer, from whose reactions he judged which points were difficult to understand and needed elucidation. While travelling from Bournemouth to Margate in order to co-present the nightly radio reports on the 1955 party conferences, he broke his journey to deliver a lecture in German to foreign students at Wilton Park. And in November, at the party's advisory committee on policy, Powell argued strongly against any proposal to link wage negotiations with productivity, on the grounds that 'there was little the workers could do to increase productivity', and 'the more we associated labour with any other responsibility' in addition to its function of wage bargaining, 'the less free was the play of the economy'.[15]

By this time, the argument for promoting Powell had become virtually irresistible. In July 1955 he had been re-elected to the executive of the 1922 Committee, and when the chairmanship fell vacant the following autumn on the appointment of Derek Walker-Smith (later Lord Broxbourne) to the front bench, he was pressed to stand against the vice-chairman, Major John Morrison. Although he demurred, his subsequent election as a vice-chairman of the '22 – notwithstanding a scrutineer's report that members had had trouble putting their crosses in the right place – demonstrated the strong regard for him in the parliamentary party. Within six weeks, Powell's display of loyalty finally bore fruit and brought the recognition that his reputation and talent deserved. Appropriately, in view of his specialization in housing policy since 1946, this subject provided his passport to the front bench.[16]

'Best ever Christmas box'

Within two months of Eden's general election triumph in May 1955, Powell, as chairman of the Tory back bench housing and local government committee, echoed a strong desire in the party for a new approach to housing policy. 'The very success of the Government's housing policy', he is minuted as having warned his back bench colleagues, 'was taking us further into socialism in housing'. Although other Tories might not have expressed the thought with quite the same ideological flourish, Powell's desire for a major re-direction of policy was widely shared in the party. Over the previous ten years, both Labour and Conservative Governments had given priority to tackling the acute housing shortage, but the 1953 housing white paper and the 1955 Conservative manifesto had outlined a shift in priorities, whereby local councils were to concentrate on slum clearance and re housing, while owner-occupation and private renting were to be encouraged.[17]

Powell was to play a significant role in the enactment of these plans in the first eighteen months of the 1955 parliament. As a result, however, he became a hand-maiden to the disastrous boom in 'high-rise' building in Britain's cities and introduced a rent reform that was to become a political millstone round his party's neck. Given Powell's relatively junior position at the time, it would be wrong to attribute too much of the responsibility to him. None the less, he had specialized in housing and contributed to policy-making since 1946, and was never shy as an MP of displaying his mastery of the most arcane legislation and regulations. He might have been expected, therefore, to be aware of some of the likely pitfalls and problems of some of the Government's policies. Yet despite his detailed knowledge, his ideological preconceptions sometimes blinded him to realities on the ground.

Since first entering the Commons, Powell had attended weekly meetings of the back bench housing and local government committee, serving as its vice-chairman from 1951, and as chairman from 1954. His contributions blended an ideological commitment to the de-control of land, house-building and rents with an unrivalled expertise that ranged from leasehold reform to rating revaluation. He played a key role in coordinating detailed Tory consideration of their own Government's legislation and, as early as the 1951–52 parliamentary session, took the chair of the back bench committee during discussions on the reform of Labour's Town and Country Planning Act. Indeed, he regarded the abolition of Labour's development charge on land as 'the most important measure of denationalization carried out by the Government in this 1951–55 parliament'.[18]

Ministers were able to rely on Powell's staunch support as they legislated during 1953–54 to encourage landlords to make repairs by allowing those who did so to increase rents. His speeches and interventions were well-researched, but his ideological edge sometimes provoked fierce clashes with Labour MPs, who often knew a lot about housing problems and regarded the provision of state housing and protection from profiteering slum landlords as bulwarks of the welfare state. For his part, Powell was perturbed that council house rents were still too high in places. He was also concerned that slum dwellers often could not get on a housing list, and when their house was pulled down they had to take the first one offered, whether or not they liked it or could afford it. Ultimately, Powell's remedy was to extend market forces in housing as the only sure way to match supply with demand. But he agreed with giving slum clearance utmost priority and, in 1954, persuaded other Tory MPs that housing subsidies should not be reduced until the Minister had settled his slum clearance programme.[19]

Laudable though 'slum clearance' was as an objective, the manner and method of its implementation during the latter half of the 1950s and the early '60s created one of the worst social disasters to befall post-war Britain. 'Slum clearance' often became a euphemism for the wholesale demolition of housing that merely needed refurbishment and modernization, while many of the former inhabitants, who had little say in the matter, were 'dispersed' to towns many miles away or re-housed in high-rise flats. Although the Conservative Government, mindful of their party's county and rural support, reformed planning criteria in order to discourage the extension of urban local authorities into rural areas and the expansion of the New Towns, Powell accepted the need for some dispersal of population as an essential element in re-housing. In 1953, he admonished Tory MPs from the home counties, who were anxious at the consequences for their majorities, that although 'it was frightening, it was a fact that the Conservative Party is "overrepresented" in [the 1951–55] parliament, and if one de-centralizes one is sure to influence adversely the majorities in less densely populated areas'.[20]

In Powell's view, the concern of rural Tories would be best met by addressing the ratio of local authority and private enterprise building in the receiving areas. Although at least one colleague thought it was already too late, Powell suggested that if the satellite towns were expanded by private enterprise, the inflowing population would be more likely to be Conservative. Arguably, however, it was in the inner cities where his belief in an expanded private sector could have helped preserve a more balanced population. The damaging exodus of aspiring white-collar and skilled workers might well have been stemmed if, during the years after the war, they had been able to become owner-occupiers in their traditional, urban neighbourhoods.[21]

Yet the growing emphasis on high-rise building was to prove a much more destructive force for inner-city communities than the lack of private housing. Its development reflected a strong body of opinion among architects, builders, planners and Labour politicians, that reinforced the strong bias against the dispersal of urban populations among Conservatives, many of whom – unlike Powell – represented county and rural seats. The latter group included MPs such as Viscount Hinchingbrooke, who lobbied vigorously against any dispersal of inner-city populations to rural areas and advocated instead the building of high-rise flats 'on the continental model' in the inner cities.[22]

Recalling the vogue for high-rise flats, or 'tower blocks', Powell commented many years later that he had 'witnessed with dumb astonishment the earlier stages of the frenzy as a co-opted member of the LCC housing committee for 1949–52'. Indeed, *One Nation* had warned against 'the building of such family nightmares as blocks of flats without balconies and gardens'. But although the Conservative Party papers show that Powell was not a mindless follower of the 'frenzy', he appears not to have queried the policy effectively. In response to a call from a fellow Tory MP to build 'upwards' in the cities, Powell echoed the shallow prejudice, typically voiced by urban-based Tories (as opposed to their rural counterparts), that 'blocks of flats breed socialism', and thought that Conservatives should be 'chary of urging flat development indiscriminately'. None the less, he suggested that flat-building was 'desirable' in the 'big, provincial city centres', where fewer people lived in flats than in London, but not in the smaller towns. Bearing in mind his views on the political impact of flats, it seemed that Powell was prepared to concede the inner cities to Labour.[23]

Moreover, the real 'frenzy' for high-rise building occurred between 1956 and 1965, as a direct – if largely inadvertent – consequence of the shift in Tory priorities immediately after the 1955 election that Powell helped bring about. Steering the Tory back bench discussion in July 1955 on the prospects for the expected four-year term of the new parliament, Powell 'stressed the importance of the problem of the Rent Acts and housing subsidies'. Rent control 'made true rents appear too high' and, in effect, subsidized tenants at the expense of landlords, while local authority house-building was 'provided through an indiscriminate all-round subsidy' funded by taxpayers and ratepayers. In the autumn, Eden's Government moved to restrict council house-building. Local authorities were no longer allowed to borrow from the Public Works Loans Board, which offered a low rate of interest, and instead had to turn to the money markets and incur higher interest charges. The following month, the Minister of Housing and Local Government, Duncan

Sandys, advised Powell and his colleagues of his plan to end indiscriminate housing subsidies.[24]

The Housing Subsidies Bill was designed as a cost-cutting measure. Its main purpose was to reduce the general housing subsidy paid to local councils to £10 per house, as a preliminary step to its eventual abolition – a measure that was bound to increase council house rents. The subsidy for slum clearance was to be continued and, in addition, the Exchequer subsidy for re-housing in New Towns and expanded towns was to be increased by nineteen shillings (95p) to £24. Significantly, the subsidies for flat-building were fundamentally re-structured and a new progressive storey-building subsidy was introduced – the subsidy per dwelling rose steeply up to six storeys and by a further increment with each further storey. Announcing this change, Sandys had bemoaned the tendency for local councils to build flats of only three, four or five storeys, which, he had added, 'are most monotonous'. His intention was to reduce subsidy costs, but the effect was to give the green light to a boom in high-rise flats and transform Britain's urban skylines within a decade.[25]

Unsurprisingly, the continued subsidy for 'overspill' was one of the issues that Tory MPs regarded as being most controversial when they met to discuss the Bill in November 1955, prior to its second reading. The Government's attempt to appease its rural and urban MPs by continuing to subsidise both overspill building in rural areas and high-rise building in inner cities was criticized as a contradiction, with Hinchingbrooke and his allies pressing the case for high-rise. Powell, as chairman, agreed to raise the issue of the increased overspill subsidy, among other points, in a letter to the Minister, but thought that the best that MPs could hope for was pegging the subsidy at its existing level. He had to report back, however, that Sandys regarded the increase as 'unavoidable', since the New Towns and the expansion schemes in small towns had no pool of prewar houses and rents would be high without a subsidy.[26]

As far as Powell was concerned, the Bill had to be viewed as part of a grander scheme on housing, and it made the reform of rent control even more pressing. Sandys accepted that rent reform could not be shirked, but sensing the political dangers wanted first 'to break the ice' by having a review, and told Powell and his colleagues that since the structure of rents was linked to the valuation of houses any reform had to await the completion of new valuation lists. In Powell's logical mind, however, the only alternative to the Housing Subsidies Bill, 'coupled with a revision of the Rent Acts, was the Bevan solution of local authorities taking over all rent-restricted property'. Returning to a familiar theme, he argued that 'it was impossible to raise the rents for some four million council houses and leave untouched the "pegged" rents of some seven million rent controlled houses'.[27]

This same search for an all-encompassing, market-oriented solution to the inconsistencies and unfairnesses that Powell perceived in the housing system informed his speech in the Commons on the second reading of the Housing Subsidies Bill on 21 November 1955. It was to be a turning-point in his career.

Beforehand, he had taken the precaution – with the authority of his colleagues on the back bench housing committee – of consulting the Government Chief Whip to make certain that it would be a wide debate, in which matters such as the future of rent control could be raised. On the day, Powell benefited from the same good fortune that Macleod had enjoyed more than three and a half years earlier, in the speech on the NHS that had launched him on his ministerial career. Like Macleod, Powell caught the Speaker's eye immediately after Bevan had spoken. And likewise, with his opening words Powell took on the greatest debater of the day, dismissing much of Bevan's speech as irrelevant. He countered Bevan's accusation that he 'was a past-master in the art of sub-editing history' to suit his own argument by reminding the House that as Housing Minister in 1946, Bevan had introduced legislation for the progressive reduction of subsidies. Interventions from other Labour MPs, who were riled by Powell's ideological onslaught on the combined effect of rent control and housing subsidies, enabled Powell to demonstrate his command of every detail of housing legislation.[28]

Powell's real targets, however, were the policies that distorted the housing market, thereby creating new problems. 'Whatever view one takes of the purpose of housing subsidies and rent restriction,' he told the House,

> it is recognized that this situation involves gross anomalies and injustices; anomalies and injustices as between owner-occupiers and tenants, the one subsidized if in a council house and the other not; anomalies and injustices between the tenants of privately owned houses and the tenants of council houses; injustices and anomalies within each of these groups, since the rent which a person pays, whether in a privately owned house or in a council house, has no ascertainable relationship either to the value of the house or the means of the tenant; injustices and anomalies, finally, in the source of the subsidy, which is drawn haphazard either from the rates and the taxes in the case of a council house or from the capital of the owner of the house in the case of rent restriction.

He put Labour's protests in context by pointing out that one-third of British families had television, at twice the cost of the general housing subsidy. Powell made no reference to the re-structuring of subsidies for flat-building. He concluded, predictably, by arguing that the private sector, if given the opportunity, could meet the country's housing demands.[29]

Although his performance was timely, since it had put his name in the limelight shortly before Eden's long overdue re-shuffle of his Government, Powell needed a further piece of luck to avoid being overlooked yet again. Among the ministerial changes announced on 20 December was Macmillan's transfer from the Foreign Office, where he had been Secretary of State only since April, to replace Butler at the Treasury, while two of Powell's contemporaries won major promotion – Macleod entering the Cabinet as Minister of Labour and Heath becoming Chief Whip. Powell had not featured in the initial plans, but these went awry when Sir Hugh Lucas-Tooth, a junior minister at the Home Office, realized that he was not about to be promoted and resigned. His place was taken by Bill Deedes, who was moved from his junior post at Housing and Local Government. Powell was the obvious candidate to fill the unexpected vacancy. But being pestered by the press for confirmation of his appointment made an anxious wait even more difficult to bear, three long years after he had snubbed Churchill's offer. When the summons eventually came, the Prime Minister offered Powell his first ministerial post as parliamentary under-secretary of state at the Ministry of Housing and Local Government. But Powell's acceptance could hardly be described as appropriate to the occasion, as he recalled their clash over the Suez Agreement. 'I would have done anything to defeat you in 1954,' he told Eden with a startling candour, 'and here I am and I'm ready to serve your Government.'[30]

The 'best ever Christmas box' was Pam Powell's more ebullient response. Powell's speech on housing subsidies had 'won him high praise', the *Express and Star* reported on his appointment, and 'undoubtedly clinched his claim for office'. He clearly thought that he deserved his promotion. 'My brains are my wealth and my right,' he told the *Wolverhampton Chronicle*, 'just as inherited material wealth is the right of those who have that as their birthright.' The new post brought an annual salary of £2,000, comprising £1,500 as a junior minister and a £500 MP's allowance. The Powells had plenty to celebrate at Christmas and the New Year holiday, and Powell's eighty-three-year-old father travelled down from Wolverhampton to join his son, daughter-in-law and little grand-daughter in Earl's Court, where Pam's mother also joined them for Christmas dinner.[31]

Albert Powell was in good form, but later in the holiday he suddenly collapsed and died. Mourning his family's loss, Powell deferred settling in to his new job and instead arranged for his father to be buried with his mother at Worthing, following a service at St Mary's, Goring-by-Sea. His gift of a cover to the font of the church was inscribed: 'Given by John Enoch Powell in memory of his mother, Ellen Mary, and his father, Albert Enoch, to the church they entered last for those who will enter it first'.[32]

Thrown to the lions

It had taken Powell almost ten years since he returned to London and entered politics to reach the despatch box of the House of Commons. He had thought that he would find the key to India there, but by 1956, when he first spoke from the front bench, Britain's greatest imperial possession had long since gone its own way and he was dealing with the parochial subject of housing. None the less, despite his detailed grasp of the legislation and his ability as a speaker, Powell found the experience of addressing the House as a minister a daunting one. As Wolverhampton's *Express and Star* revealed shortly after his debut, 'his emotion when speaking from the despatch box for the first time was to compare himself with a Christian in the amphitheatre surrounded by lions and Romans'. The sensation, as Powell had helpfully explained, was caused by standing on the floor of the House with benches rising away from one, both before and behind. But wisely, he chose not to elaborate on his pointed analogy about MPs – assuming that the 'lions' occupied the Labour benches, the implied suggestion that his fellow Tories were 'Romans' captured the ruthlessness with which a minister's own party could round on him or her.[33]

As a junior housing minister, Powell had plenty of practice at the despatch box. He often had to answer the half-hour adjournment debates at the end of the day's main business, when an MP could raise a constituent's grievance with the relevant minister. Sometimes, these debates were delayed till the small hours, but Powell and the MP concerned had to stay on after virtually everybody else had left. In the first nine sitting days after the winter recess, Powell spoke twenty times on five different matters, most of them in the committee stage of the Housing Subsidies Bill, which, as a controversial item of legislation, was taken on the floor of the House.[34]

Although the Bill halved the general housing subsidy, it retained certain specified subsidies – housing for the elderly, for instance. It fell to Powell on his debut to defend one such subsidy, for housing miners who were moving into a new district. The idea was to increase the numbers who could leave declining pits for expanding ones, and Powell argued that without this subsidy councils would continue giving priority to people who lived in their own districts, thereby inhibiting labour mobility. 'I represent a constituency under which coal is mined,' Powell told the House, arguing that this gave him 'experience' and 'sympathy' in tackling the problem. The irony of Powell's position – the advocate of market economics having to justify state intervention – was not lost on Labour MPs. Bevan was unable to resist twitting him, and looked forward to 'a number of other conversions from him'.[35]

Powell, however, was concerned at the scope for exploitation of the new subsidy for housing workers who moved into a new district. As he knew from a busy industrial centre like Wolverhampton, new industries were always moving in, but under the legislation as it had been drafted, councils would be allowed to request a subsidy on that basis. Powell persuaded Sandys of his concern, and on 1 February was able to inform MPs that the terms for granting the subsidy had been tightened, so that the minister would have to give his approval. Spotting the change to a more restrictive policy, Bevan chided Powell. 'It is always a delight to listen to the Parliamentary Secretary,' he observed. 'He is always so lucid that the weaknesses of his own case become apparent as he proceeds.' But Powell retaliated in the increasingly ill-tempered exchanges on the Bill, when he opened the third reading debate and reminded the House of Bevan's comment to the 1950 Labour Party conference, that: 'You must always remember, when you are talking about council rents, that the rate subsidies are being paid by the people that have worse houses to keep down the rents of people who have better homes.'[36]

Bearing in mind the enormous impact that the changes in the flat-building subsidies were to have, there was remarkably little discussion of the matter during the Bill's passage. Sandys and Powell were wary of being drawn by Labour's Ben Parkin, MP for inner-city Paddington and an advocate of high-rise, into a stronger public endorsement of the policy. Powell met the same MP's call to help councils buy expensive city sites for housing by arguing that it would be cheaper to transfer Paddington's population to overspill areas in the country. This latter argument disturbed some of the 'Romans' on the benches behind Powell, though Hinchingbrooke, the arch Tory opponent of dispersal, sought comfort by suggesting that the new minister's shrouding of his explanation 'in metaphysical planning language' indicated a lack of sympathy for dispersal.[37]

It had been a difficult Bill for a new minister to handle, but the most striking feature of the whole episode remains the contrast between Powell's apparently bemused attitude towards the high-rise boom and the very clear impact of the changes that he helped take through parliament. The progressive storey-building subsidy rapidly became what Patrick Dunleavy, in his study of mass housing, described as 'the dominant means of central government support for central urban development'. In 1953, only three per cent of public housing approvals had been high-rise flats; by 1960, the proportion had quintupled to fifteen per cent. In 1956, the number of high-rise dwellings built had been 6,000; by 1961, this had almost trebled to 17,000, before doubling again to reach 35,000 in 1964, when the Conservatives left office.[38]

Powell's self-confessed tendency to be too didactic served him ill in his early months at the despatch box. This was commented upon by the *Express and Star*, whose reporter thought that his 'logical thought and his mastery of any subject' were 'so overwhelming that they have done him more harm than good'. But Powell's problem was that 'the House does not like to be lectured. He lacks the human touch and has, up to now, failed to evoke the Members' sympathy.' Fortunately for Powell, however, during the spring of 1956 he was able to speak on two Bills that enabled him to appear in a more sympathetic light. At the end of March, he was again justifying the payment of a subsidy, on this occasion to the owners of unfit houses, 'for whom in equity, if not in strict justice and logic, some special treatment is called for'. The Slum Clearance Bill was designed to compensate people who, as a result of the housing shortage caused by the war, had bought houses subsequently condemned as unfit. When such houses were acquired by a local council, however, the owners often suffered great financial loss. As a remedy, Powell outlined the Government's plan for the owners of such houses, bought between the outbreak of the war and the end of 1955, to be paid the price of the houses as though they had not been declared unfit. At the same time, he helped pilot through the Commons a new Clean Air Bill – successor to the Bill that had been lost when the 1955 election was called – and earned plaudits for his role in the reform. The Bill's sponsor, Sir Gerald Nabarro, attributed the measure 'largely to the advice' that he had received from Powell, while

Powell's departmental boss, Duncan Sandys, spoke admiringly of his junior minister's 'profound grasp' of 'pretty well every other measure even remotely connected with the Bill'. But it was in his allusion to the legendary railway timetable which is a by-word for organization, that he best captured Powell. 'He seems to have a Bradshaw mind,' Sandys observed.[39]

Powell's relationship with Sandys at the Ministry was never close. They had little in common and could both be difficult. Sandys, the wealthy son of a Tory MP, had served in the Diplomatic Service, fought in Norway in 1940, married Churchill's daughter, Diana, and, in his approach to life, was anything but a puritan. He was passionately pro-European, and although his political sympathies generally lay towards the right, he regarded Powell as being too intellectual and not sufficiently political. Sandys was slow on his feet, but was doggedly persistent in argument and used to base any decision on painstaking attention to detail. He thought nothing of keeping his officials in seemingly interminable meetings that might last until the small hours. Powell was on the receiving end of his insensitivity when Sandys suggested that his personal aide, Colonel Kenneth Post, might share Powell's office at the Ministry.[40]

Most of the civil servants found Powell to be extremely courteous, hard working, highly principled and disputatious. He had ideas and would argue his case in a donnish manner – like Richard Crossman, later a Labour housing minister – although Powell's officials sometimes felt that 'his feet were planted in mid-air'. But his over-reaction to an official's error concerning a compulsory purchase order was typical of his attitude at the Ministry. Local authorities had to apply to the minister for permission to purchase land compulsorily, and mostly these requests were handled by officials, with only the most controversial cases being referred to the minister. After the error, however, Powell insisted that he should see every such application, even though he was warned that the numbers made this impracticable. Officials tried, unsuccessfully, to persuade Sandys to intervene, and when they eventually approached the permanent secretary, the formidable Dame Evelyn Sharp, they were told, 'Swamp him!' Every application was duly brought to Powell's office. After some weeks, hundreds of these files were still stacked round the walls, awaiting his attention. Eventually, the old method was quietly resumed.[41]

Moreover, Powell took it upon himself to be more radical than Sandys in pursuing the Government's policy of restricting the acquisition of land by local councils and encouraging instead private development. Whereas his departmental boss sought a gradual approach, Powell had a mission to restore market forces in housing. He treated local authority deputations in a brusque manner and rejected many councils' applications for land purchase orders out of hand. Warnings from his officials that he was going beyond Government policy were brushed aside, but when they went over his head to Sandys, Powell seemed to suspect that they were deliberately trying to thwart his mission. He was at risk of becoming an isolated figure at the Ministry, but outside events intervened to give him a central role in the department's next great legislative reform. It was a cause that was near to his heart.[42]

Actor and spectator

Powell's long hours at the Ministry and his evenings spent at the Commons, sometimes followed by a late-night adjournment debate, meant that he saw little of his wife and young daughter except on Sundays. But the small amount of time that he allowed himself away from politics was devoted to his domestic life, which plainly brought him fulfilment and happiness in his middle age. At the start of September 1956, Enoch and Pam announced that they were expecting their second child. Jennifer Helen was born on 17 October and, like her elder sister, was christened in the crypt of the House of Commons.[43]

Gardening had become a new pastime for Powell. He devoted his Whit holiday in 1956 to the garden of 79 Merridale Road, which he had constructed from the wilderness that he and Pam had found when they moved in a year earlier – though Powell had to remain on constant call from the Ministry, since Sandys was out of the country on a visit to Russia. Even gardening was approached with a rare attention to detail, as a close neighbour of the Powells in Wolverhampton, Mary Whitehouse, noticed over the years. While Susan and Jennifer Powell watched from their nursery window as the Whitehouse children built a tree house, Powell's activities in his 'tiny garden' created equal interest among the Whitehouse family, who 'observed with fascinated interest and respectful awe the care with which he planted out his lettuce seedlings. We felt he must be almost counting the specks of soil between each, so meticulous was he.'[44]

Part of Powell's problem has been that although he always thought that his behaviour was perfectly logical, and was therefore quite natural, it surprised other people who were not accustomed to his ways. Mary Whitehouse recalled one such incident, when three workmen who had been making some alterations to their house, were sitting in the garden eating their lunch. Suddenly, she heard them

> making almost unprintable remarks about 'that chap on the wall shaking the fruit off the tree'. They didn't know who 'that chap' was, sitting astride the dividing wall, and we didn't share their dismay because to us the falling apples simply demonstrated the direct Powellian approach to the immediate problem.[45]

Powell has often been equally baffled by the behaviour of his fellow men. The most striking instance occurred when Nasser nationalized the Suez Canal Company on 26 July 1956 and triggered a crisis that was to eclipse every other issue in British politics for the rest of the year. It was an odd experience for Powell, the former imperialist and ex-member of the Suez Group, who had abandoned the cause after the signing of the Anglo-Egyptian Agreement and the withdrawal of British troops. 'I couldn't think why people were surprised,' Powell later recalled of his reaction to British anger at Nasser's take-over. As he elaborated,

I couldn't think what had got into them. I had a lonely job of it in that second half of 1956. It was like being in a world where everyone else was a stranger, and I couldn't understand why they were fussing. Didn't they expect this?[46]

Powell had once had the temerity to express his views about British power in the Middle East, but he now accepted that, in his deadpan comment, 'a parliamentary secretary at the Ministry of Housing and Local Government has very limited powers of influencing foreign policy.' Moreover, Sandys, his departmental boss, adhered rigorously to Cabinet secrecy. As the fiasco of Suez unfolded like some latter-day Greek tragedy, Powell was fortunate to be able to remain 'hunched in a remote and subordinate cranny of government', and, as he confessed, 'was not disposed to go overboard'. Although Suez stole the limelight during the autumn, it also brought Powell a new opportunity to make his mark as a minister. Inevitably, he came to play a more important role at the Ministry as his senior minister was increasingly distracted by the crisis – although Sandys was not engaged in the detailed management of Suez, he had to devote an increasing amount of time to the discussions in Cabinet, and had to attend extra meetings. But the day-to-day work of government had to continue, and Powell concentrated on matters in the department, in particular the great housing reform for which he had long lobbied.[47]

In the summer of 1956, almost five years after the Tories had returned to office, the Government finally announced their intention of tackling rent restrictions on the six million or so houses and flats that were let to private tenants. Powell had consistently urged scrapping rent controls on the basis that only by allowing landlords to increase rents would new accommodation be attracted onto the market, thereby helping overcome the housing shortage. Thereafter, the increased competition would offer the tenant protection against excessive rents. Such was his determination to eradicate every vestige of rent controls that he had warned Tory colleagues who favoured improving the workings of the rent tribunals that 'if the final object was to abolish rent tribunals it would be harder to abolish an improved Conservative tribunal than an unimproved Socialist tribunal'. Powell's well-known commitment to market forces, however, was less important in the decision to reform rent control than the failure of the limited steps taken since 1951 to revive private renting.[48]

'I would rather see the houses go up first before the rents go up,' Harold Macmillan had commented when Housing Minister in March 1952. His maxim reflected a well-founded caution on rents and had become the Tory watchword on the subject. Conditions in privately rented housing were frequently appalling – about one-third of its households lacked hot water – but millions of tenants had grown used to low rents, with real earnings having outstripped rent rises three-fold since 1938, the year before rents had last been frozen. As Conservative Research Department briefs of the early 1950s never hesitated to point out, 'at least ten' of the dozen or more acts passed since 1915 to control rents and still on the statute book had been passed by majority Conservative Governments. The 1950 manifesto had echoed the 1949 policy document, *The Right Road for Britain*, by accepting that rent control had to continue 'until there is no housing shortage at any given level', and promised merely to keep the matter under review. Neither the 1951 nor 1955 manifestos included any specific reference to rent de-control, and during the 1955 campaign the Research Department had specifically rejected a rumour that the Conservatives were planning to remove protections for tenants. Macmillan's rent reform, the 1954 Housing Repairs and Rents Act, had offered only modest incentives to landlords.[49]

By the time that Powell entered the Ministry of Housing and Local Government, its officials had already become convinced that something more radical was required. The 1954 Act had failed to bring extra accommodation onto the market, many older properties were continuing to degenerate into slums, and landlords who had repaired their property tended to sell it for owner-occupation instead of re-letting. A stronger dose of the de-control medicine seemed the logical answer. Confirming this prescription at the October 1956 Conservative conference at Llandudno, Sandys announced the Government's intention 'progressively to abolish rent control altogether'.[50]

Early November's opening of the 1956–57 parliamentary year, in which rent reform was to be a key feature of the legislative programme, was completely overshadowed by the international drama in the Middle East. Since returning from Llandudno, Sandys had become increasingly unable to concentrate on the final preparations of the Rent Bill as intensive diplomatic activity during the latter part of October had been followed by the Israeli attack on the Egyptian army on 29 October. The bombing of Egyptian airfields by British and French planes two days later sparked a furious debate over future British involvement. Powell was correspondingly able to occupy the driving seat on rent reform. But despite his lack of involvement in the Suez fiasco, he was unable entirely to escape its malign influence.

Events came to a head in the first week of November. After a weekend of agonized debate within the Cabinet, the decision was taken to invade, and British troops began landing at Port Said. Powell's earlier puzzlement at British reaction to Nasser's seizure of the Canal was intensified by his incredulity at the sheer folly of the invasion. 'It was a weird time', Powell later remembered,

> for someone who was as penetrated as I was by 1956 with the conviction that our whole position in the Middle East was untenable, physically untenable. It was a weird position actually to see the contrary being

asserted. I remember having the sense of being a spectator of a drama in which I played no part, an incomprehensible drama.

Powell's incomprehension stemmed from the evident impracticality of the Anglo-French invasion:

The impracticality of Suez is that if we had gone to Suez from Port Said, and occupied the Canal, which we physically could have done, we would have had to occupy Cairo. And if you occupy Cairo you have to govern Egypt, but we knew we couldn't govern Egypt, we'd said we couldn't govern Egypt. So it was a drama to which there was no intelligible conclusion.

Powell had discovered that 'you can become a spectator in your own country'. He found that it was 'a weird and miserable experience, not to share'.[51]

Even at the more prosaic level of parliamentary business, Powell was unable to escape from the long shadows cast by Suez. Following Eden's announcement to the Commons on Tuesday 6 November of the Government's fateful decision to call a ceasefire in Egypt, the rest of the day's main business was abandoned, and the scheduled adjournment debate, that Powell had to answer, was suddenly brought forward. While the rest of Westminster was the scene of animated discussion among politicians and journalists about Eden's future and the mounting world crisis, Powell debated with Hackney's Labour MPs, in an otherwise deserted chamber, the extent of financial aid for houses that had been requisitioned in the war, and that the Government required the council either to buy or to release for sale.[52]

A fortnight later, the second reading of the Rent Bill marked the pinnacle of Powell's ten-year career as a Tory housing expert, but Suez again overshadowed the two-day debate and presaged major changes both for British politics and for Powell. Unusually on a major item of Government legislation, the responsible Cabinet minister, Sandys, allowed his junior departmental minister, Powell, to open the debate. For Powell, there was no prouder moment in his life than when he rose at the despatch box on 21 November 1956 to speak on the Rent Bill, since it represented a first step towards his long-held ambition of decontrolling rents and restoring competition to private renting. Sandys's action reflected his confidence in Powell's ability and the key role that his junior had played in finalizing the details over the previous month, but there was no reason why he should have wanted to do Powell a favour and other motives probably played a part. There was something to be said for letting Powell speak first, since Sandys could moderate Powell's ideological edge when he wound up the debate. And there was even more to be said from the point of view of an ambitious and pragmatic middle-ranking Cabinet minister such as Sandys for not becoming personally identified with one of the most contentious Government measures of the parliament, and instead letting Powell take most of the political flak. Indeed, Sandys had warned Tory MPs on the eve of the second reading debate, that 'the Government would suffer adverse reactions from the public before the favourable consequences of the Bill became apparent'.[53]

The circumstances surrounding Powell's speech on the Rent Bill could scarcely have been less auspicious. The Suez crisis again drew MPs from the chamber, as Conservatives were plunged into panic by the announcement of the Prime Minister's departure from the country for a spell of rest, and by the looming prospect of a humiliating withdrawal of British troops from Egypt. Persevering, none the less, in a thinly attended chamber, Powell delivered an uncompromising argument for removing rent controls. The words, 'supply and demand', that are part of market economists' argot, tripped off his tongue four times within the first couple of minutes, setting the ideological tone and provoking the Opposition. So frequent were the interventions from the Labour benches that it took Powell fully an hour to complete his speech.[54]

For somebody who had paid such close attention to housing for more than a decade, Powell based his argument for removing rent control on an extraordinarily simplistic assertion. 'We are now', he boasted to MPs, 'within sight of, and should in twelve months' time or so be level with, an equation of the overall supply and demand for houses.' He had derived this statement from various housing statistics, and had proclaimed Britain's record of having built between 2.5 million and 2.75 million new houses since the war. The problem, however, as Powell should have realized, was not to be found in the aggregate figures but lay in the mismatch between housing needs and the availability of suitable accommodation in different areas. He focused on the avowedly temporary nature of the 1939 restrictions and highlighted the 'evils' caused by holding rents at pre-war levels – waste of accommodation, disrepair, the loss of housing stock available for rent, and a bar to labour mobility. In addition, there was the 'injustice' that many landlords were, in effect, being forced by rent controls to subsidize the income of their tenants.[55]

The Bill was made to sound more sweeping than it was in practice by the fundamentalist rhetoric of Powell's opening comments. But even he accepted that after so many years of rent restrictions, 'decontrol cannot be sudden or immediate'. Rents at the top end of the market, affecting about half a million dwellings with a rateable value above £30 (£40 in London), were to be decontrolled over three years; any dwelling was to be decontrolled if the tenancy changed; and rents in five million dwellings were to be increased to enable landlords to make repairs and a reasonable profit, but were to remain controlled. Staged decontrol, however, meant that the full impact would not be felt for some years, and this political time-bomb kept ticking under the Tories until the 1960s.[56]

Powell was to play no further part in the Bill's remaining parliamentary stages, and it fell to Henry Brooke and Reginald Bevins, who succeeded Sandys and Powell at the Ministry, to face Labour's onslaught. But Powell's reputation as an apostle of decontrol and his vigorous speech on second reading ensured that his name was identified with the 1957 Rent Act. This was more of a hindrance than a help. Already in the summer of 1957 as the Bill finally completed its stormy passage through parliament, the respected political correspondent, Harry Boyne, reckoned that the Rent Act cast 'the longest shadow over the next election', and the Tories would therefore delay going to the country until the summer or autumn of 1959.[57]

The Rent Act tilted the balance of power in the landlords' favour, and where accommodation was scarce they took advantage. Several million tenants who remained in controlled dwellings faced an average rent increase of 60 per cent (rises varied between 50 and 75 per cent). The effects were worst in London, where Powell had been badly mistaken to be sanguine about the impact of decontrol on higher-valued properties that were rented mainly by professionals. London also saw some of the worst cases of harassment of tenants, as unscrupulous landlords exploited the provision for decontrol when a tenancy ceased. The political time bomb of the 1957 Act finally exploded at the worst possible moment for the Tories in the wake of the Profumo scandal in 1963, when revelations about the intimidation of tenants by Perec Rachman, who had owned properties in London at the end of the '50s, gained sensational coverage and added to the Government's woes. Despite Powell's confident expectations, the Tory experiment with decontrol failed to revive the private rented sector.[58]

On the second day of the Rent Bill debate, Thursday 22 November 1956, Powell had witnessed an incident that was, indirectly, to lead to his early departure from the Ministry. With the Conservative parliamentary party on the brink of mutiny over Britain's humiliating withdrawal, at America's behest, from Egypt, junior ministers were 'specially invited' to attend the weekly meeting of the 1922 Committee – a gathering usually limited to Conservative back-benchers. Accordingly, Powell absented himself from the chamber of the Commons, and at 6.00 p.m. joined about 250 other Tories who had packed into committee room number 14, where they were to be addressed on the Suez crisis by Rab Butler, the Lord Privy Seal, who was running the Government in Eden's absence and consequently suffered the obloquy for Britain's humiliation, and Harold Macmillan, the Chancellor of the Exchequer, who had begun as the strongest hawk but had been chastened by the collapse of confidence in sterling following the Anglo-French invasion and become a dove – 'first in, first out', in Harold Wilson's telling epithet. Whereas Butler talked briefly about Tory publicity (he was also to take questions), Macmillan was expansive and uplifting, and delivered 'a real leadership speech'. 'I had held the Tory Party for the weekend', Macmillan commented cynically later that evening, 'it was all I intended to do'. Acknowledging that Macmillan had 'put Butler in the shade', Powell later recalled the incident:

One of the most horrible things that I remember in politics was seeing the two of them at that 1922 Committee meeting – seeing the way in which

Harold Macmillan, with all the skill of the old actor manager, succeeded in false-footing Rab. The sheer devilry of it verged upon the disgusting.[59]

Seven weeks later, when Eden resigned as Prime Minister, Macmillan was the overwhelming choice of the Cabinet to succeed him. Perfunctory consultations among the rest of the party by the Chief Whip (Heath), the Party Chairman (Oliver Poole) and the Chairman of the 1922 Committee (Morrison), reportedly confirmed the Cabinet's view. Powell, however, like many other Tories, was not consulted. Macmillan 'kissed hands' with the Queen on 10 January 1957 and began forming his administration. The Macmillan era was to open new opportunities for Powell, but the two men had a fundamentally different approach to politics. It was on the anvil of Macmillan's Toryism that 'Powellism', as it emerged in the 1960s, was finally beaten into shape.[60]

8

At Odds with Macmillan's Court

The year at the Treasury was a very important year. The year in which three politicians, almost in isolation from the theories of the civil service found themselves obliged to address their minds to the question of inflation, its causes and its remedy, and came up, although very different personalities and dealing with very different subject matter, with what was essentially the same answer. And I suppose the development of that answer which has come to be known as monetarism has occupied my mind and my speeches ever since in the last thirty years ... Certainly that was an important formative year, and it was a year from which lines of force ran out through the rest of my political life.

    Enoch Powell on the importance of his year at the Treasury (1957–58) with Peter Thorneycroft and Nigel Birch.

'Country' Tory

Despite Powell's 'weird and miserable' experience during the Suez crisis and his disgust at Macmillan's display at the 1922 Committee, his career prospects improved immediately after the new Prime Minister's arrival at Number 10. On 14 January 1957, Powell was summoned to Downing Street, where Macmillan offered him the ministerial post at the Treasury that he had long coveted. Only two ministers then worked with the Chancellor of the Exchequer, and although Powell remained outside the Cabinet, he became, on his appointment as Financial Secretary, the Chancellor's deputy and the highest ranking junior minister in the new administration. Within a few weeks, Powell also had been recruited by Iain Macleod to the new Policy Study Group that Butler had initiated within days of the formation of the new administration, and that was charged with coordinating and developing Tory policy for the next election. As a Treasury Minister and a member of Macleod's small policy team, Powell was at the heart of Conservative politics. Yet his spell at the centre of the Tory web was to last less than twelve months as a result of a clash over economic policy that has since assumed symbolic importance.[1]

'The Suez fiasco cut deep into the consciousness of the British people,' Powell argued thirty years later. 'It had the same sort of effect as a nervous breakdown, similar to what America experienced after the Vietnam war but more severe.' He came to regard Suez and its aftermath during 1957–58 as the crucial turning point in post-war Britain. In an important sense, he was right. Suez delivered a deep shock to British confidence and prompted a reassessment among decision-makers of Britain's role in the world that was long overdue, and for which Powell himself had argued. Powell had also been impatient for a more radical approach on domestic matters. During the first year of the Macmillan Government he was engaged in a vital debate in Whitehall that centred on the control of inflation and the Tory commitment to full employment and the welfare state. Unfortunately for Powell, however, his *bêtes-noires*, Keynesian economics and the Anglo-American relationship, emerged stronger than ever.[2]

Powell later explained the defeat of his beliefs in terms of everybody else's defeatism. In his days as a post-war imperialist, Powell had detected a defeatist strain in the assumption of total British dependence on the United States and the retreat from empire. This defeatism had been exacerbated by Suez. The British people 'no longer felt sure of themselves', he later asserted. 'They disbelieved that they could any longer be a nation, with all that meant in terms of independence, pride and self-confidence.' Indeed, Powell recalled Macmillan, in his 'leadership' speech to the 1922 Committee during the Suez crisis, 'trotting out for the dozenth time his tired simile comparing the British and the Americans with the Greeks and the Romans respectively' – the point being that the British, like the ancient Greeks, had once been the greatest power in the world, but had to reconcile themselves to a new role as a civilizing influence on their successors, the Americans, as the Greeks had with the Romans. Britain's defence policy, its membership of Europe and its approach on Northern Ireland were all explicable to Powell, in his later life, in terms of Britain's subservience to American strategy.[3]

During the spring of 1957, Powell took a jaundiced view of the British people. In the privacy of Macleod's policy group, he warned of the difficulties of ensuring that the results of successful policy were (in the words of the minute) 'apprehended by an electorate determined to look for trouble and to regard itself as victimized'. From this bleak perspective he drew a tough-minded moral. He urged that the Tories 'must infuse a higher percentage of realism into what we did, and not be driven by panic' into adopting image-conscious gimmicks. But Powell was to feel badly let down by Macmillan, whom he came to regard as the ultimate cynic in politics and the personification of all that was wrong.[4]

Powell later castigated his former leader as a 'Grand Whig', and accused him of having possessed the 'essentials' of Whiggism:

> cynicism, agnosticism, bread and circuses (provided that they are held at a decent distance from the ducal estate), European combinations, a readiness

to try any wheeze (provided it helps to keep in power) and a contempt for principle in politics (though some of Mr Locke's ideas might come in handy).

Yet there was more to Powell's contempt than either 'the natural antipathy between congenital high Tory and the congenital grand Whig', or the chip on the shoulder resentment of the Birmingham scholarship boy for aristocratic connections, that might be implied from the gibe about 'the ducal estate'. The difference between Macmillan and Powell reflected another historic fault-line in British politics – that which divided 'Court' and 'Country' elements in both Tory and Whig parties in the eighteenth century.[5]

Powell was not opposed to natural office-holders in principle, since he respected Butler as a fellow 'congenital Tory' and as a great servant of state. He, himself, was to spend the bulk of his time in the Macmillan Government, in which he was to serve for more than four years, including fifteen months as a Cabinet Minister, administering the health service. But Macmillan epitomized the 'Court' element of professional politicians who wanted power and were anxious for office at almost any cost. This aspect of Macmillan stirred in Powell an affinity with the 'Country' element of natural back-benchers who cared little for office, who could not always be trusted to support the political ambitions of their leaders, and who were hostile to what they regarded as the excessive power of the executive and the corrupt tactics of the Court. The Walpole in Macmillan was to agitate the Bolingbroke in Powell. This tension simmered beneath the surface during Powell's time in Macmillan's administration, erupting once, but only emerging into open contempt on Powell's part long after Macmillan's political demise.[6]

'Country' politics also had a moralistic strand, and a similar trait was evident in Powell. It combined with his Gladstonian austerity towards government spending to explosive effect at the start of 1958, and was again evident five years later in his reaction to the handling of the Profumo scandal. It was more generally reflected in Powell's tendency to idealize institutions and to judge his own actions and those of others against these models. By the late 1950s, the British constitution and market economics had become the latest in a line of idealized institutions, after Germanic culture, the Army, the Raj and the Empire. Scarcely anybody or any real-life institution could measure up to the high standards set by Powell. Yet this moralistic aspect, that matured in counter-point to Macmillan's 'Court' politics, was to enable Powell, at the end of the 1960s and in the early '70s, to strike a chord with millions of voters who had become disillusioned with the political system – on the left, Tony Benn has evoked a similar 'Country' appeal.[7]

But what were Powell's hopes for the future direction of Tory policy when Macmillan became Prime Minister? On 13 February 1957, Powell outlined his thinking in a letter to Macleod, in the latter's capacity as head of the new Policy Study Group. Macleod had immediately recruited Powell to his six-man team, and before their first meeting circulated Powell's letter. 'First I put without hesitation external relations,' Powell wrote, replying to his own question about 'the main pieces of mental work before the Party'. Macmillan had already made the repair of Anglo-American relations his priority, and there was no explicit trace of Powell's anti-Americanism in his letter. But in his search for a 'salve that must be applied to the deep Suez wound', Powell reflected the hostility felt by Conservatives towards the United Nations [UNO] – an organization, in Powell's eyes, that the Americans had used to sanction their intervention in Korea and to pursue their interests in the Middle East and elsewhere by exploiting the increasingly strong majority against the old imperialist powers, especially Britain. Instead, the nation state had to remain the basis of international relations. 'The Tory Party', he wrote, 'must find the means to interpret its membership of international organizations in a manner which shall not be repugnant to its deep sense of nationhood and shall also not be verbiage and humbug.' Powell recognized, however, that although people were disillusioned with UNO, it did not necessarily follow that they would 'go with us in a dispassionate debunk of it. We should not demolish UNO, but perhaps develop it as a forum of opinion.'[8]

Powell was especially concerned that Conservatives should follow his example and cast off every last remnant of imperialism – though before his own *volte face*, he had suspected his party of being weak on the Empire. None the less,

> the Tory Party must be cured of the British Empire, of the pitiful yearning to cling to relics of a bygone system (and fight for them if necessary at the barricades and in the wrong division lobby), while at the same time proclaiming the wonders of a new system whose foster parents were Attlee and Nehru.

He was later to tell Macleod and his colleagues that the Tories 'had been on the wrong track' as regards the Commonwealth 'since 1947'. 'Economically and politically', Powell maintained, 'we need what the Younger Pitt of 1784 stands for: what (and why) the Empire was and what (if anything) the Commonwealth is, must be made clear to ourselves till it hurts no longer.' In a juxtaposition that became his trademark, Powell appealed to logic while asserting a romantic nationalism:

> The courage to act rationally will flow from the courage to see things as they are. The Tory Party has to find patriotism again, and to find it, as of old, in 'this England'. This too will be a salve to the wound of Suez.

Powell's subsequent bitterness reflected a growing sense that the wrong conclusions were drawn in the post-Suez reassessment of Britain's world role – though for most of the 1960s he was to support British involvement in

Europe, which was integral to Macmillan's 'Grand Design' for a revived post-imperial Britain.[9]

The future of the welfare state was the other main concern of Powell's. His Tory pragmatism on some aspects of social policy, especially education and health, caused him to accept – and on occasion to advocate – the enhanced role for the state that was to emerge during the Macmillan administration. In this respect, there was an implicit contradiction with his Gladstonian attitude towards government spending. But in other aspects of social policy, Powell's radicalism was to the fore. Certainly this latter quality inspired his comment to Macleod that, 'the whole machinery of social security has to be overhauled', because the architects of the welfare state, 'Lloyd George, [Neville] Chamberlain and Bevan have had their day: their theories and their system, on which we are living still, were the delayed reaction to Victorian poverty.'[10]

Even before the group had been set up, Macleod and Powell had discussed 'some administrative consequences and retrenchments which should flow' from an administrative shake-up, though Powell's talk of 'retrenchment' suggested a different emphasis from Macleod's desire to see ministers responsible for social policy given a stronger voice in the Cabinet. 'About education up to school leaving age and the National Health Service,' Powell told Macleod,

> I obstinately refuse to lose any sleep: in neither do I envisage any radical change of system, and with complacency strange in a Treasury Minister I contemplate them reaching their zenith in due course, guided, but not distorted, by financial disciplines.

His Tory acceptance of public provision for education and health kept him unradical on these issues, but in his 1957 policy survey, Powell was less happy about education above the school-leaving age of fifteen:

> there indeed we must establish both principles and policy: at present we have neither. The way we are drifting into State universities and German High Schools is frightening. Wanted: a Conservative theory of higher education.

Some months later, Powell was to advocate, to the consternation of his colleagues, the effective nationalization of the universities. He suggested the introduction of 'free university education', since some 75 per cent of undergraduates already received state aid and the extra cost of abolishing fees would not be large. Moreover, 'the standard of university entrance was now so low', he waspishly observed, 'that the present rights of parents to educate their more stupid children would only be marginally affected.' Although Lord Hailsham, the then Education Secretary, thought that Powell's idea was a possible development, he was 'appalled at the idea of a State monopoly', as were Macleod and Maudling.[11]

Yet the fields of social policy that had long preoccupied Powell – housing, national insurance and pensions – remained the focus of his radicalism. Housing policy, he thought, 'if we have the determination to follow out Duncan's [Sandys] course to its logical conclusion, will make itself'. On pensions, he planned a separate paper. This was a more pressing matter, and was the first substantive item on the agenda at the group's first meeting, since Labour's shadow minister, Dick Crossman, had been working on a new plan that reportedly would guarantee 'half pay on retirement'. Although John (later Lord) Boyd-Carpenter, the Minister for National Insurance and Pensions, was well advanced on his own plans, they were unlikely to go as far as Crossman's. Powell, however, thought that it was 'premature to consider supplementary pension arrangements before taking decisions about social security in general'.[12]

Powell had long believed that the insurance principle had broken down and that many people were forced to live on national assistance. But his main criticism was that the existing scheme would 'run into steeply mounting annual deficits rising over some two decades to a maximum of £500 million a year'. In the past, these deficits had been mitigated by the original over-estimation of unemployment, and the effects of inflation. Powell was uncertain whether, in view of the prospective deficits, the cost of the scheme would continue in a steady ratio to national output. But this yardstick was no longer sufficient for Powell – an early sign of the fierce battle that loomed on government spending during the first year of Macmillan's Government. Warning that 'we should no longer allow ourselves such flattering unction', he declared that,

> Our hope for the future must surely be that the existing services will represent a *declining* fraction of a rising national income and so leave room for their expansion, for new services, and above all for the increased investment which alone will yield the increased production.

Powell's argument, however, and the severe economies that it implied in government spending, ran counter to the growing sensitivity of other Tories, notably Macleod and members of the Conservative Research Department, to the growing demand in an affluent society – and especially among the middle class – for enhanced public provision. In this clash of ideas lay the seeds of a major dispute that was to rock the Macmillan Government only a year after its formation.[13]

Yet Powell demonstrated inventiveness in his proposal to meet the pressing problem of providing better pensions. The only solution, he argued, was 'to move over on to the basis of need' and guarantee

> to all in retirement a minimum income which could and should be substantially above the present National Assistance scales, and to finance

the far lower cost of doing so by 'contributions' which would be as unashamedly a social service poll tax as the National Health Service 10d [4p].

In Powell's view, the cost of his scheme would 'be automatically and progressively reduced' through the growth in occupational pensions and other methods that encouraged saving for retirement. Although his reform would entail a means test, this would be 'far less of a difficulty' than the existing situation, in which insurance pensioners had to go to the National Assistance Board. Moreover, 'the very universality of the test would negative our old friend the "stigma of the Poor Law".' Some of Powell's claims for the reform were debatable, and the idea of a guaranteed income in old age was shelved after a few months following a ministerial meeting at Chequers. None the less, Powell was to revive the idea after the 1959 election, and it presaged what has been described as the 'holy grail' of the 1960s and '70s – a negative income tax that would target benefits on those in need without stigma.[14]

With the temporary demise of his idea for a means-tested, guaranteed income, Powell saw some attraction in Labour's approach on pensions. His interest was triggered by a chance meeting with Dick Crossman, author of Labour's policy, at a Cambridge Union debate. As Crossman noted in his diary, Powell looked 'passionately interested and bewildered when I said that our scheme would produce net national savings'. Contrary to Powell's expectation that Labour's plan would add to government spending because of the heavy cost of increased pensions, Crossman revealed that people's graduated contributions would be high, since 'our aim is to make people sacrifice present consumption'. This aspect appealed strongly to Powell, but Maudling and Michael (later Lord) Fraser of the Research Department pointed out that graduated contributions towards an increased, but still flat-rate, benefit, were 'just another form of taxation'.[15]

The search for economies also motivated Powell's call to put 'the crazy system of subsidies' for farmers on the group's agenda. 'No quantity of guarantees, pledges, farmers' votes, White Papers, Agriculture Acts, front bench speeches, etc.' he argued, could save them from having to think about the problem. Yet Powell was anxious to steer Macleod away from an early general discussion of economic policy, arguing that 'exchange, monetary and fiscal policy, as I see it, come later. Until we know the possibilities of retrenchment and budgetary action up to April 1958, I believe policy study in this field is premature.' As a newly appointed Treasury minister, Powell had a special interest in preserving his new department's domain, and the group readily demurred to the Chancellor's traditional authority. But the debate in Government over 'the possibilities of retrenchment and budgetary action up to April 1958' was to disrupt Powell's ministerial career and shape the development of economic and social policy during the remainder of Macmillan's administration.[16]

Praetorian guard at the Treasury

So great was the Government's vulnerability in the immediate wake of the Suez débâcle, that Macmillan had told the Queen at his first audience, 'half in joke, half in earnest', that he could not answer for his new administration lasting more than six weeks. Macmillan's skill in restoring confidence and reviving Tory fortunes was to ensure that his Government eventually lasted more than six years, but at the outset the position was precarious. His own *volte face* over Suez had been prompted by a sterling crisis and the prospect of devaluation that had only been averted by acceding to American demands and accepting military, as opposed to financial, humiliation. Since his Government were extremely unlikely to survive another sterling crisis in the immediate future, Macmillan took care to choose ministers at the Treasury who would follow his cautious example as Chancellor – despite his expansive rhetoric, he had damped down demand following Butler's 1955 pre-election boom.[17]

At the same time, Macmillan saw the urgent need to modernize Britain and give his party new inspiration. His vision of an 'Opportunity State' envisaged a dynamic economy, in which incentives would be given to people who wanted to better themselves and to businessmen, who would create the extra wealth for improved social services. This meant that in addition to restoring confidence, the ground also had to be prepared for tax cuts. In these respects, the appointment of Peter (later Lord) Thorneycroft as Chancellor, and Nigel Birch (later Lord Rhyl) as Economic Secretary, in addition to his choice of Powell as Financial Secretary, seemed to suggest good judgement. Yet Macmillan was to get more than he bargained for.

As Powell later observed of the Treasury team, 'it would be difficult to find among the Government three more diverse individuals in personality, temperament and background.' Thorneycroft, the Chancellor, was the scion of a wealthy family of Staffordshire ironmasters and soldiers, who had entered the House in 1938. He was approachable and amiable, even jovial (an impression that was enhanced by a trace of the now defunct upper-class Cockney accent in his speech), and had a talent for painting. Although he was not an intellectual, he was a highly effective speaker and had been a driving force during the 1940s in the progressively-minded Tory Reform Committee, a ginger-group of young Tory MPs who were concerned to ensure that the Conservatives took an enlightened view on social policy. After Churchill had brought him into his Cabinet in 1951, he had served as President of the Board of Trade for more than five years. His principal achievement was to steer Britain away from protectionism towards a more liberal trade policy, and he was a stronger European than Macmillan in the 1950s. At the Treasury, he missed the advice of Sir Frank Lee, with whom he had developed a good working relationship at the Board of Trade. Moreover, the Permanent Secretary, Sir Roger Makins (later Lord Sherfield) had been an appointee of Macmillan's at the Treasury, having served him in North Africa during the Second World War.[18]

Any possibility that Thorneycroft might take too much of a risk with the economy in the immediate aftermath of Suez was prevented by Macmillan's appointment of Birch and Powell to serve as the Chancellor's praetorian guard. Birch was an acerbic character, who relished the outspoken independence that came with wealth – partly inherited, partly amassed in the pre-war City, and partly obtained through marriage. He could view with equanimity his cut in salary from £5,000 a year as Air Secretary to £2,000 as Economic Secretary – the same salary that Powell received as Financial Secretary. Although Birch was already troubled by the ill-health that affected his eyesight and eventually led to blindness, he was delighted with his move because he had little time for the new Defence Secretary, Sandys, and held trenchant views on the strong pound and the need to curb government spending.

But it was Powell, as Financial Secretary, who had prime responsibility for controlling spending by vetting the annual estimates of each government department. He seemed well qualified for the task by his Gladstonian disposition, and had served on the Commons' estimates and public accounts committees. Powell relished his task. 'It's a great job – a wonderful job!' he enthused, adding that he had 'always wanted' to be Financial Secretary because 'it has responsibilities claimed by no other junior ministry. I may be biased, but I rate it one of the best, most important jobs in Government.' In contrast to Birch's asperity, Powell's courtesy and politeness were appreciated by civil servants in the Treasury. Although Powell was initially rather guarded and worked hard at mastering his briefs, after he had settled into the job his officials were left in little doubt about the strength of his belief in market economics. He used to arrive at the Treasury at about 9.15 a.m. and work until around 7 p.m., depending on circumstances, but he took care to keep in touch with the Commons, taking lunch there and making a point of joining other Conservatives each evening over dinner. 'We Tories team up four or eight to a table,' he told the *Express and Star*,

> and have a 'frank opinion' session. It's a pure relaxation for me, refreshing and invigorating for a junior minister whose job tends to keep him out of touch with things. No lonely hot-milk vacuum flasks for me![19]

Powell entered the Treasury as the annual battle on the estimates of government spending for the coming financial year, 1957–58, was reaching its climax, ahead of April's budget. The economic strategy for 1957 had already been set by Macmillan, and entailed a retrenchment in government spending. Accordingly, Thorneycroft and Powell agreed that they should take 'a very tough line this year and that the general doctrine should be no expansion'. But since education was to be expanded in the new 'Opportunity State', other social services were earmarked for economies. Powell threw himself into the task with the keenness of a ferret leaping into a rabbit warren. He proposed that £15 million could be saved from the health service estimates and suggested developing a ceiling on the Exchequer's liability to the NHS as a guide to future spending.[20]

There was fierce resistance from John (later Lord) Boyd-Carpenter, the Minister for National Insurance and Pensions, to the Treasury's demand for the abolition of family allowance for the second child. As Boyd-Carpenter pointed out, the proposal contradicted recent election pledges and the Government's policy of increasing family allowances to compensate for withdrawing food subsidies. The idea was dropped, but it was to re-surface the following year, with dramatic consequences for Powell, his Treasury allies and the Government.[21]

By February 1957, the Chancellor was able to announce economies of £35 million in the social services, mainly through increased charges for school meals and welfare milk, and by raising the NHS contributions. In 1951, Powell had spoken out against increasing the cost of school meals, but there was no question of his resigning as Financial Secretary. These savings helped bolster the Chancellor's credibility when he cut the Bank Rate from 5.5 to five per cent to counter a bigger than expected increase in unemployment. In addition, Sandys's unveiling of a new defence strategy based on the nuclear deterrent heralded substantial savings in conventional forces as the number of men in the services was to be cut by 65,500. Powell was later to condemn the 1957 shift in defence policy, but at the time he remained in office.[22]

Powell received mixed notices in his early months as Financial Secretary, but he had the opportunity to improve his standing during the debates on the 1957 budget, since it was primarily his responsibility to pilot the annual Finance Bill, that contained the detailed tax changes, through the Commons. This process usually lasted from the spring, when the budget used to be delivered, until the summer recess. In those days, moreover, the committee stage, at which the Chancellor's reforms were closely scrutinized, was held on the floor of the House. When the budget was unveiled on 9 April, cuts of £95 million in defence spending and a limited increase in civil estimates of £189 million enabled Thorneycroft to reduce taxes by £130 million in a full year. The 1957 budget was among the least expansionary of the 1950s, but the Chancellor was able to deliver an upbeat speech and give the Tories a much-needed fillip. Opening the third day's debate on the budget, Powell was positively Gladstonian in his concern to demonstrate that the tax cuts were consistent with financial probity. In his painstaking defence of the Chancellor's tax reliefs, he spoke as though the highest purpose of public life was to leave more money in people's pockets. Although praising Powell for the presentation of the Government's case, the *Economist* considered that his 'survey of the minutiae of the Exchequer accounts – the sort of speech that could have been made in any pre-war budget debate – was a really rather startling reminder that the new Financial Secretary to the Treasury is a former Professor of Greek.'[23]

Behind the scenes, Powell urged the Tory leadership to adopt a Gladstonian approach as the basis of their appeal at the next election. When Rab Butler suggested to Macleod's influential Policy Studies Group on 6 May that the Tories should base their philosophical appeal on 'the defence of the individual against the repositories of power' (the unions, monopoly capitalism, the nationalized industries and the state), Powell added to the list 'the Gladstonian concept of allowing money to fructify in the pockets of the people'. This idea plainly worried Macleod, who countered that the Tories 'should not ignore the Shaftesbury tradition', and suggested a package of reforms to improve employment protection and pension requirements that could be presented as 'a good employer' policy. Butler, however, thought that Macleod's suggestion 'did not seem in harmony with the mood of the party', and Maudling and Powell suggested that this would remain the case as long as there was full employment.[24]

In July, when the Prime Minister sought the group's views, Powell again identified taxation as 'the most promising field: a reduced burden was the one thing the electorate could not expect from the other side'. Macmillan, however, was pre-occupied by 'the reconciliation of full employment with a stable cost of living', which he saw as the 'key problem', and wondered whether 'either could be said to be electorally more important than the other, and what balance or margins of tolerance should we aim at?' His remarks presaged his speech at Bedford, five days later, during which he declared that 'most of our people have never had it so good' – the origin of the damaging phrase that was to haunt him: 'you've never had it so good'. Macmillan's real concern, however, was whether the new prosperity that accompanied an expanding economy and full employment was 'too good to last' because of the constant problem of rising prices. It was on this dilemma of economic management that the Treasury team came to disagree fundamentally with Macmillan and his Cabinet.[25]

Myth and reality of a monetarist experiment

In several respects, the summer of 1957 was a good time for Powell. The Finance Bill had a relatively easy run, partly due to the signs of economic recovery and a record performance on exports. Although Powell was baited for the obscurity of his language, his mastery of technical detail on the whole served him well, and on 19 July the Bill received its third reading with only minimal amendment. Such criticism prompted a good-natured response from him in the *Express and Star*, when he explained that

> if there is a concession to be made or a pleasant answer to give, the Chancellor speaks; if the answer is at least intelligible, but not necessarily pleasant, the Economic Secretary to the Treasury gives it. If the answer is both unpleasant and unintelligible it falls to the Financial Secretary to do what he can with it.

Powell even managed a smile in the Commons, causing Arthur Moyle, a Black

Country Labour MP, to quip that 'the Spartan look is very acceptable occasionally, but a pleasant smile does much good in relation to the psychology of the House'. Powell's local paper acknowledged that 'with his somewhat lofty ascetic air, he gives the impression at times of not caring very much what the rest of the world thinks about him', but was confident that such faults of manner could be corrected and that he was bound to go to the top.[26]

Earlier in the summer, junior ministers and MPs were finally awarded the salary increase that had been delayed since the previous parliament. The rise in Powell's income from £2,000 to £3,250 was especially welcome, since the arrival of a second child necessitated a move to a larger house. The Powells' new home, number 33 South Eaton Place, was one of many terraced town houses built by Thomas Cubitt from the 1820s in the area now known as south Belgravia. It was a narrow house, with comparatively small rooms, a front door that opened on to the street and a small back-garden – the unearthing of human bones in a neighbouring garden in 1987 confirmed that the site had once been occupied by a military hospital. The interior required Powell to apply his skill at do-it-yourself whenever he could spare the time. 'When the family was growing up,' he later recalled, 'the house had to be fitted and refitted and I was often busy with carpentry.' South Eaton Place remained the family's London home.[27]

At the Treasury, however, Powell faced a much less propitious outlook by mid-1957. After the tough battle over the 1957–58 estimates, he and his fellow ministers were deeply perturbed by what they saw as profligacy in government spending. Powell's Gladstonian austerity as Financial Secretary gave his cost-cutting drive a moralistic edge, while Thorneycroft, like Macmillan, was preoccupied by inflation and fearful of a sterling crisis. The country's seeming inability to conquer inflation was to prompt a reassertion by the Treasury team of older economic orthodoxies, especially monetarism, or the 'quantity theory of money'. The notion that inflation is caused by an increase in the amount of money in the economy, or the money supply – bank deposits plus notes and coins in the hands of the public – had been an important assumption in pre-war economic policy. Keynes's demolition of the theory had led to its abandonment by post-war policy-makers, but monetarism still had its supporters, and by the mid-1950s was enjoying something of a revival.

In 1951, Ralph Assheton had made a monetarist attack from the Tory benches on Labour's budget, and, later in the year, the liberal economist, Lionel (later Lord) Robbins, launched an influential counter-attack on Keynesian thinking that prompted a revival of interest in monetarist thinking. In January 1956, Oscar Hobson, city editor of the *News Chronicle*, argued that long experience proved that proper control of the money supply was the only way to curb inflation. In the same year, a joint inquiry by the Treasury and the Bank of England, prompted by the Government's alarm at their inability to control bank lending, reported among other things that Governments which failed to finance their spending out of taxation or long-term borrowing inevitably lost control of the money supply. This variant of monetarism influenced Powell's thinking. In early 1957, a special committee was established under Lord Radcliffe into the working of the monetary and credit system.[28]

During the summer and autumn of 1957, Treasury ministers increasingly echoed a monetarist-inspired dissent. Although they also appeared sometimes to advocate crude, old-fashioned deflation, the monetarist experiment upon which they wanted Macmillan to embark was to lead to their resignations and cause a major political crisis. Powell always regarded 1957–58 as a turning-point for the post-war economy, after which financial prudence was cast aside and inflation steadily increased. He was always to remain a monetarist, and claimed that he and his colleagues were the originators of the theory that is usually attributed to Professor Milton Friedman of the University of Chicago. 'We didn't borrow it from Chicago,' Powell asserted, adding – with tongue only partly in cheek – 'indeed, we really thought it was rather unfair that the Nobel Prize, which was awarded to the Chicago School, was not shared with Thorneycroft and his colleagues.'[29]

Leaving aside the fact that this ignores the role of Robbins and others in reviving British monetarism, Milton Friedman was already developing a modified monetarism that took account of Keynes's critique of the old quantity theory of money. But Powell and his colleagues were not espousing this new theory. Neither were they proposing the adoption of monetary targets as the basis of economic policy, which was the approach pursued by the Thatcher Government – incidentally, the information to measure 'sterling M3', Thatcher's chosen monetary indicator in 1979, was not available until 1964. The Treasury team's approach during 1957–58 amounted to a return to a more traditional monetarism.[30]

Powell's view that 1957–58 marked a turning-point for the British economy has, however, been mythologized by Margaret Thatcher and her monetarist heirs on the new right. They have demonized Macmillan's Government as an inflationist and, in effect, a socialist, regime, while portraying Powell, Birch and Thorneycroft as heroic martyrs. But Thatcherite mythology caricatures Macmillan's approach, misrepresents the economic facts about his premiership (the country enjoyed full employment, relatively low inflation and respectable growth), and does not accord with the evidence that is now available in the official papers. These show that Macmillan was acquainted with and, to an extent, sympathized with monetarist thinking, but that for sound economic, political and social reasons was not prepared – and neither were his Cabinet – to abandon the post-war commitment to full employment and a comprehensive welfare state. Indeed, the Treasury ministers would have inflicted overkill on the economy had the Cabinet approved their plans to cut government spending.[31]

As to the suspicion among Macmillan's supporters that Powell had a Svengali-like hold over the Chancellor, Powell has suggested that he, Birch and Thorneycroft, reached the same conclusions about inflation quite independently of each other. 'As this inflationary year ticked by,' he recalled, all three 'started to drop in one another's rooms and hold conversations and it turned out that we were arriving at the same conclusions as to the causation of inflation.' In short, they 'converged upon' the view that inflation was self-inflicted by the Government's spending too much and having to borrow from the banks – 'we are doing it ourselves all the time and must stop doing it', as Powell recalled. This view, however, was not new and before the Second World War had been known as 'the Treasury view'. According to the 1950s' variant of this view, the Government's raising funds through taxation, private saving or by selling gilt-edged securities to the public, was not inflationary. But when the Government borrowed from the banks by selling Treasury bills, the money supply was increased. This process is sometimes known as the 'monetarization of debt'. The money supply increases directly as a result of bank lending to the Government, and indirectly because the resulting banks' holding in Treasury bills increases their liquidity and thus their ability to lend to the private sector. And the resulting increase in the money supply, according to monetarist theory, causes inflation.[32]

'I don't mind it being said that Enoch influenced me', Thorneycroft remarked shortly before his death, 'I'm sure he did. But I wouldn't like to underestimate the influence of Nigel Birch, who is less talked of but was a brilliant man, and he certainly held the same view as I and Enoch.' These recollections, however, underestimate the influence of their outside advisers – as will be seen, at two crucial moments in the crisis, Thorneycroft and Powell summoned prominent monetarist economists to advise them. But Powell's role was crucial since he became a firm adherent to monetarism, whereas Thorneycroft was essentially a pragmatist who had come to believe in tougher economic policies on the grounds that the country's commitments were putting too much strain on its resources. Thorneycroft, towards the end of his life, dismissed any idea that he and his colleagues had been 'proto-Thatcherites'. Instead, he maintained that they had stood for economy and balancing the books – in other words, a return to pre-war economic orthodoxy and its monetarist assumptions. Characteristically, however, Powell invested the monetarist element with a theoretical certainty. On government spending – the issue that triggered the final crisis – his attitude was unbending. By late 1957, his Gladstonian predisposition was reinforced by a fervently monetarist commitment to curb government borrowing. Thorneycroft's experiment in applying pre-war monetarism to post-war Britain was transformed into a crusade.[33]

This monetarist experiment began because although inflation in the 1950s was low by the standards of the 1970s and 1980s, it had troubled the Conservatives since 1955. The annual rate of price increases had risen sharply to 3.5 per cent, while wages were increasing at 4.5 per cent. It was generally assumed that the inflation was wage-driven and, in March 1956, the Government began actively seeking pay restraint. These initial efforts, however, were undermined by the impact of Suez. Petrol rationing brought higher transport costs and bus fares, and in turn prompted a renewed escalation of wage demands. By the spring of 1957, strikes over pay had halted the shipbuilding industry and were intensifying in the engineering industry, while industrial trouble loomed on the railways and in the docks and mines. Economic disruption on this scale would have triggered the sterling crisis that the Government were desperate to avoid after Suez. As the industrial crisis deepened at the end of March, Macmillan kept in constant touch from Bermuda, where he was meeting President Eisenhower in an attempt to repair Anglo-American relations. The immediate crisis was defused when Macleod, as Minister of Labour, set up Courts of Inquiry into the shipbuilding and engineering disputes.[34]

Although there was anger among employers that ministers had failed to back them up, the pace of wage inflation began to slow down during 1957. None the less, Macmillan and his ministers still anguished over the difficulty of trying to maintain both full employment and stable prices. Macmillan hankered after talks with the TUC to link pay with productivity, and at the start of June announced that Thorneycroft and Macleod were to consult on pay policy. Macleod had already taken up with Macmillan and Thorneycroft an idea put forward by Professor Jack, who had headed the Courts of Inquiry, for an 'authoritative and impartial body' to consider 'the general economic position of the country as affected by wages, profits and prices'. Thorneycroft wanted the new body to issue a 'guiding light' figure for pay increases that was compatible with stable prices. In view of events over the coming months, it is ironic that the Cabinet, who feared that a guiding light would simply become a minimum benchmark for wage increases, had to restrain the Chancellor's zeal for an incomes policy.[35]

Despite this setback, Thorneycroft set up the three-man Council on Productivity, Prices and Incomes at the start of August, in the hope that they might exert some influence on pay bargaining. The most interesting appointment among the 'three wise men', as they were known, was that of the economist, Sir Dennis Robertson, who had worked with Keynes at Cambridge, but who had become disillusioned and increasingly favoured a monetarist approach. Sir Robert Hall (later Lord Roberthall), the Government's chief economic adviser, was to note in his diary following a conversation with Bryan Hopkin, secretary to the Council, that Robertson 'gets a dogged look whenever the words "full employment" are mentioned and is determined to take no account of their existence in his terms of reference'. Robertson was to become an important influence on Powell, who had known him at Cambridge. 'In the last few years,' Powell acknowledged in March 1960, 'I have enjoyed and (I hope) profited from the advice and instruction of Sir Dennis Robertson.'[36]

During the summer of 1957, Thorneycroft also began to push harder for the second leg in his anti-inflationary strategy, namely allowing no increase in government spending. This aspect was much closer to Powell's heart, and by the autumn had become sacrosanct in Treasury ministers' thinking – indeed, by making no allowance for inflation they were, in reality, proposing to cut spending. They had a variety of motives, including the traditional Treasury function of controlling the departmental estimates. There was also concern that excessive spending would trigger a sterling crisis. In addition, Powell was eager to make room for tax cuts. In July, Makins, the permanent secretary, minuted Powell that the Chancellor was planning to put a paper to the Cabinet, in which 'he wants to argue your general point, namely, that unless we are very tough on government expenditure, there will be precious little room for further tax remission in the next budget.' But above all, the Treasury ministers were convinced that cutting government spending would curb inflation.[37]

This uncompromising attitude created a growing rift between Treasury ministers and their senior officials. As early as May, despite optimistic indications from the Treasury's budget committee, Thorneycroft had warned Macmillan of the risk of an 'economic collapse', and urged that there should be no increase in government spending for fear of a 'progressive decline – even ultimately the collapse – of the currency and the dramatic and world consequences which must follow'. Officials feared that the Chancellor was overdoing things, and in July, Bruce Fraser minuted the chief economic adviser, Sir Robert Hall, that government spending had 'been stable, if not actually reduced' in real terms between 1954–55 and 1957–58, adding that it was 'difficult for anyone to pretend that Government supply expenditure has been leading the inflationary gallop'.[38]

Over the months that followed, Treasury ministers became isolated within the Government. During the summer, they increasingly disagreed with their senior officials. At this stage, Macmillan backed his Treasury ministers, though with some reluctance. But their disagreement with their officials had a crucial bearing in creating the sense among the Treasury team that they had to depend on each other. This mentality, that they would either stand or fall together, was to colour their reaction as Macmillan's Cabinet turned against them.

Despite signs of Thorneycroft's tougher approach, the range of measures for countering inflation that he proposed to the Cabinet on 19 July were in accord with the Government's 'existing framework' of economic policy. They included the stabilization of the level of government spending and public investment, in addition to the continuation of credit restrictions and the setting up of the new body on pay and prices. As the Cabinet conclusions noted, 'no other course was open to them unless they were prepared to adopt a wholly different approach to the problem of inflation'. Taking over direct control of the money supply from the Bank of England was specifically ruled out.[39]

By the end of July, however, Thorneycroft had adopted an avowedly monetarist stance. 'Our ends will be defeated', he minuted Macmillan, 'if the Exchequer is financed by methods which add to the money supply.' The Chancellor's argument reflected the traditional Treasury variant of monetarism. 'The only resolute action which is really within the power of the

Government', Thorneycroft accordingly warned Macmillan, 'would be to restrict the supply of money, to the point where cost and price increases were checked by severe unemployment.' If this were politically impossible, the Chancellor suggested, the only alternative was to continue the squeeze on credit and on government spending and investment – a straightforward deflation.[40]

The monetarist bias in Treasury ministers' thinking was reflected in the Chancellor's minute of 7 August to his officials. He wanted to 'consider limiting the increase of bank advances' to the increase in production, since 'this would at least make it harder to finance wage increases unrelated to production'. Crucially, in the public sector, he suggested examining a new approach, and suggested that, 'if necessary we should abandon the accepted tradition that the banks will provide cash against unlimited Treasury Bills'. At this stage, Thorneycroft argued that he was not proposing 'a full-blooded deflation on the lines of 1930', and envisaged an unemployment figure of 2–3 per cent – about double the average at the time. On the same day, Hall, the chief economic adviser, minuted that the Chancellor wanted urgent study on the means of bringing about 'a further measure of deflation' in order to steady prices, and that he envisaged further restrictions on the supply of money.[41]

Allowing no increase in government spending was seen by Treasury ministers as being crucial in restricting the supply of money, since government borrowing had to be curbed. In early August, Macmillan endorsed Thorneycroft's demand that the departmental estimates for spending in the next financial year, 1958–59, should be kept to the same level as the current year, 1957–58. This went against the advice of Treasury officials and represented an exceptionally tough policy. Without any allowance for either inflation or for any additional spending incurred during the current year, it would mean a savage cut in government spending. Moreover, the Government were already set to spend an additional £150 million in 1958–59 on pensions because of a long-standing commitment that would bring large numbers of elderly people into the national insurance scheme for the first time. No sooner had Macmillan agreed to his Chancellor's demand than a sterling crisis reinforced the shift towards a deflationary and monetarist approach.[42]

The September Measures

The defining moment in the collapse of trust between Treasury ministers and their senior mandarins occurred during August. When the Commons rose for the summer recess at the start of the month, the Powells took a short holiday with their young daughters. Basing themselves at their Wolverhampton home, they toured the country and Powell indulged in a favourite pastime of visiting old churches. But by the time that he returned to the Treasury later in August, there had been an alarming run on the country's reserves. His fellow Treasury minister, Nigel Birch, was especially alarmed because of his passionate commitment to a strong pound and to the sterling area. Before he left for a holiday on the grouse moors, Birch told Thorneycroft that he would resign unless strong measures were taken against inflation.[43]

Official Treasury advice, however, was more sanguine, since the problem had been caused by a flight of 'hot' money and there was a comfortable surplus on the balance of payments. This was little consolation to Thorneycroft. He had never got on with his permanent secretary, Makins, and he was now at odds with Hall, his chief economic adviser. Hall was driven twice to offer his resignation during this period, and reflected on 27 August that the Chancellor's 'holiday seems to have increased his conviction that it is too much money which is at the root of all our troubles'. Thorneycroft had turned elsewhere for reassurance and summoned Robbins, whom he knew and respected, from his holiday in Austria, to see what he thought. It is significant that Thorneycroft should turn to this prominent monetarist during the crisis, and his subsequent response was to reflect monetarist thinking. During the autumn, Robbins even joined a Treasury and Bank of England working party on monetary policy, chaired by Birch, that was established because of the Chancellor's deep concern at the authorities' apparent inability to control directly the activities of the banks.[44]

But it was not only the Chancellor and his ministers who were influenced by Robbins's monetarism. Macmillan, who had served as Chancellor before becoming Prime Minister, had been brooding over the differences between the economists on the causes of inflation – on the one hand, Roy Harrod, the Keynesian, who peppered him with advice, and on the other hand, Robbins. 'There are two theories about inflation,' he wrote in his Cabinet memorandum of 1 September, noting that whereas Harrod argued that it was 'caused by the power of the unions to demand ever-increasing wages', Robbins suggested that its cause was 'too much money created in an attempt to do too many things at once'. As Macmillan stated, 'the economists may argue; we have to decide'. This was clearly easier said than done. He was attracted by Harrod's call to boost demand by cutting taxes, but for the most part he 'broadly adopted the Robbins view' and discussed methods for 'reducing the total volume of money which comes into the system'. That Macmillan shared this monetarist perspective is striking, although there was an indication of the coming conflict in his Cabinet when he counselled that 'there is nothing very substantial to be squeezed out as regards current expenditure' in the public sector – 'the lemon is pretty dry'.[45]

The apocalyptic mood that was gripping Treasury ministers was evident in the Chancellor's comments to his officials and in his paper for the Cabinet. 'The Chancellor told me plainly at an office meeting,' Hall noted of a discussion on Britain's economic problems, 'that it was nonsense to say it was not the supply of money because everyone knew it was.' But when Thorneycroft commented in his Cabinet paper that 'a great number of people who are suffering from inflation are just the people who form the hard core of the Tory Party', it appeared that his monetarist inclinations had political as much as economic motives. After suggesting to the Cabinet that both

Keynesian and monetarist explanations of inflation had some truth in them, the Chancellor concluded that 'the continual increase in wages and prices rests in the last resort on the belief in the country that the Government will always make enough money available to support full, and indeed over-full, employment.'[46]

His response amounted to a combination of deflation and monetarism. The 'essence' of his proposal was to 'limit the level of money available in the economy' by cutting back Government spending – a deflationary measure. But there was also a strong monetarist element. 'What is needed in addition', he continued, 'is to make it rather harder to make money but rather easier and rather more rewarding to save it. Until we have done this we shall not be able to meet more of the Government's needs by borrowing from the public' – i.e. from private savings and not from the banks, since the latter source increased the money supply. Thorneycroft envisaged unemployment rising to three per cent, from its average of one per cent.[47]

'The key to the problem lay in restricting the supply of money,' Thorneycroft told the Cabinet on 10 September. The following week, he reiterated that 'it was essential that the supply of money should be restricted if the inflationary pressure was to be contained'. Ministers were worried about the effect on full employment and the risk that workers might submit higher compensatory pay awards. There was little comfort in Thorneycroft's view that the Government might lose the next election anyway, but a tough economic policy would be more likely to ensure that they returned to office, 'perhaps quite soon'. This was hardly the way to win the full-hearted backing of a Cabinet that wanted to win the next election and avoid any risk of being condemned to the political wilderness.[48]

None the less, the Chancellor was finally able to announce his 'September Measures' on Thursday 19th. He raised the Bank Rate from five to seven per cent, its highest level since 1921, cut public sector investment, limited the level of bank advances and intensified the credit squeeze. The Chancellor also made public his intention to halt the rise in government spending. Although the catalyst for the measures had been a bout of currency speculation, the measures were addressed to the problem of domestic inflation. At this stage, Macmillan backed his Chancellor, though not without anxiety on the Bank Rate. Powell thought that if Thorneycroft had made a mistake, it was in raising the Bank Rate, since this 'distracted vision from the rate of government expenditure'.[49]

Hall, the chief economic adviser, who was excluded from final discussions of the September Measures, noted privately that the Chancellor's package 'was done by ministers and they would not listen to any suggestion that what they were saying did not make much sense as economics'. Thorneycroft had argued that the 'control of the money supply' was the basis for any remedy to inflation, but the Governor of the Bank of England, Cameron (later Lord) Cobbold, told him on 9 October that it was wrong to assert that the authorities had failed to control the money supply since the war. In particular, bank advances to private borrowers had increased by only five per cent over the past six years and were likely to be held steady for a further year. In fact money supply had fallen rapidly as a proportion of national output for several years before Thorneycroft's measures, and increased more quickly in the year *after* September 1957 than in the year before.[50]

In Cabinet, Powell's longstanding wish for a floating pound had been taken up by David (later Viscount) Eccles. Although this was a non-starter following the rejection of Robot five years earlier, the crisis of 1957 must rank as a lost opportunity. It was probably the last occasion for more than a decade, as Samuel Brittan has argued, when a floating rate could have been presented as something different from devaluation.[51]

A few days after the announcement of the September Measures, Powell had to deputize for the Chancellor, who was attending the International Monetary Fund in Washington, by fielding a demand by Harold Wilson, the Shadow Chancellor, for an official inquiry into an alleged leak about the rise in the Bank Rate. A leak had supposedly prompted heavy sales in Government securities shortly before the Bank Rate rise. Powell replied to Wilson, on the basis of assurances by the Governor of the Bank of England, that there was neither evidence nor any serious suggestion of a leak. But Wilson persisted, and the Prime Minister eventually conceded after Thorneycroft and Poole, who had been implicated in the alleged leak, demanded an inquiry. The Parker Tribunal provided a fascinating insight into the close-knit world of the Bank and the City, but failed to unearth any evidence of a leak.[52]

Powell came into his own when he spoke in support of the Chancellor during the debate on the economy at the October 1957 Tory conference in Brighton. His enthusiastic cry for cuts in government spending proved to be an early warning of the ideologically charged battle between the Treasury and the spending ministers over the coming year's estimates. This annual Whitehall ritual was likely to be bloodier than usual as a result of the Chancellor's commitment to halt the rise in government spending. Powell reiterated for the party's benefit the political message that he had privately pressed on Butler and Macmillan. Referring to the falling share of national income taken by taxes, he added that it would be brought down further, and declared that 'those who affect to believe there is no substantial difference between us and our opponents should ask themselves if they ever heard that demanded by a socialist conference or from a socialist platform.'[53]

In his speeches on the economy during the autumn, Powell took an openly monetarist line. At Wednesfield in October, he asserted that 'if inflation was to be stopped, then the increase in the supply of money had to be halted without delay'. Addressing the Penn ward of his constituency in November, he argued that Britain had made the mistake of 'putting more money, not more goods into circulation'. The extra money had been put into circulation by the banks, by increasing their overdrafts; and by the Government by increasing its own overdraft with the banks – thereby increasing the floating (short term) debt.[54]

In a demonstration of his tough-mindedness a month later, Powell contrived to display yet again his extraordinary lack of political touch. Justifying the saving of £16 million by scrapping a concession on tobacco tax for pensioners that Hugh Dalton, the Labour Chancellor, had introduced in 1947, Powell appeared to imply, without saying so directly, that abuse lay behind the apparent dramatic increase in the proportion of habitual smokers among pensioners. In a state of high moral dudgeon, Dalton attacked Powell's 'dirty little smear'. Whatever the reason for the increased demand for tobacco by pensioners, Powell had again shown his insensitivity and unhappy knack for provoking people. He and the acerbic Birch were not the happiest choice of lieutenants for the usually more urbane Thorneycroft as the tense battle on government spending began.[55]

Pitched battle

In early October, the Prime Minister had fired a warning shot across his Chancellor's bows when he wrote in a Cabinet memorandum that 'we must make it clear that while we will not finance inflation, we are not attacking employment. We are asking for a pause, not a retreat.' Macmillan's comment reflected not only his own concern, but also that felt by many in the Cabinet at the severity of the September Measures. But Thorneycroft and his lieutenants were convinced of the need for a tougher policy on a long-term basis.[56]

When the Treasury collated the provisional departmental spending bids for 1958–59 at the start of December 1957, it was found that they were £276 million above the original estimates for 1957–58. In absolute terms, this was the largest increase recorded in peace time, but as Thomas Padmore, the senior official dealing with the estimates noted, 'as a percentage of the total it is about the same as the £212 million increase in 1954–55'. The following day, Powell reported to the Chancellor the comment by Padmore that the provisional estimates represented 'the largest increase in peacetime' and the biggest rise since 1954–55, but he failed to put it in perspective by making the real comparison with 1954–55. Hall, the chief economic adviser, identified the main cause of the increase as the extra pensions burden and increased prices, but Powell was quick to point the finger at Government policies, and was determined to make no allowance for inflation.[57]

Powell wanted drastic action, Padmore and Makins, the permanent secretary, did not. Urging that 'we cannot go blundering on as we are at present', Powell lined up in his sights a shooting gallery of departmental programmes and vested interests that would have provoked a major political storm if he had been allowed to pull the trigger – he proposed facing up to the farmers; scrapping civil defence; slashing colonial, Commonwealth and foreign aid; halting public building; and imposing health charges, introducing hospital boarding charges and making other economies in the NHS. But Treasury officials denied that the problem was as grave as he claimed. Far from 'blundering on', policy decisions had reflected 'political and economic forces which are real and compelling', and 'violent action' risked making matters worse. When Sir Douglas Allen (later Lord Croham), at the time an assistant secretary at the Treasury, asked Thorneycroft whether the Cabinet were backing him, Powell replied that all the Cabinet were in favour. Allen suspected that this answer had a certain amount of false prophecy about it. It seemed that Powell, who was convinced in his own mind of the need for tough economies, assumed that other ministers would agree – or perhaps he thought that they would have to agree.[58]

The Treasury team's search for economies, however, was conducted in the wake of a wholesale review in Whitehall of spending on the welfare state. The Conservatives had set up the ministerial Social Services Committee after the 1955 election in response to the Treasury's concern that welfare spending was growing too fast. But the Treasury's alarmist presentation and misguided emphasis on narrow financial criteria back-fired badly. By the time that Powell and his colleagues entered the Treasury, the review had prompted other ministers to develop a robust defence of welfare spending. Moreover, when Thorneycroft and Powell pressed for immediate economies in the winter of 1957–58, they repeatedly returned to options that had already been discredited in the Social Services Committee. In response, the Cabinet reiterated the main objections that had been rehearsed in the earlier review.[59]

There were early signs of ministerial resistance to the Treasury team's demands. Thorneycroft regarded the extra spending that had been sanctioned during the current year in the supplementary estimates for 1957–58 as 'a major defeat'. He also felt – 'quite rightly' in Hall's view – that increased spending on the scale of the departmental bids submitted for 1958–59 would 'make the statement of September 19th look very silly', as his message then had been that the Government 'would not go on pouring out more money to meet inflated prices'. Erroneously, however, he believed that a renewed wage-price spiral was beginning, and that this would lead to uncontrolled inflation. The Chancellor therefore demanded £200 million of cuts in the 1958–59 estimates, that would have resulted in a real cut in government spending, since no allowance was made for inflation or the extra expenditure on pensions. At the Cabinet committee convened to consider spending, Thorneycroft won general support, but Powell's desire for radical changes in policy was torpedoed by the conclusion that any measures must be consistent with the Government's long-term programme.[60]

Powell, however, sought to stiffen Thorneycroft's resolve by issuing a stern monetarist warning. Reporting that the Chancellor's 1957 budget plan for funding the Government's commitments by taxation and non-inflationary borrowing was being achieved, because higher than expected spending was being met by higher than expected taxation, he added, however, that 'the situation has remained gravely inflationary'. Looking to 1958–59, Powell counselled that 'you have no right to assume that a larger volume of non-inflationary lending to the Government will be available; indeed it would be prudent to count on less rather than more'. In other words, the Chancellor could not rely on private saving to cover the Government's borrowing, and he therefore had to reduce the need to borrow instead of running the risk of having to resort to the banks, i.e. inflationary lending.[61]

Initially, on 16 December, Powell identified cuts of £175 million in the civil estimates. He thought that £115 million could be saved from the family allowance; hospital boarding and minor charges; school meals; welfare milk and other welfare foods. Another £55–60 million could come from civil defence; foreign and Commonwealth spending; and capital payments. Cutting the family allowance had been one of the previous year's most controversial proposals, but Powell's plan to save £65 million by scrapping it for the second child had made it a key issue. 'I don't see how he [Thorneycroft] is going to get much money,' Hall observed from his ring-side seat, 'except if he cuts the family allowances which the FST [Powell] wants him to do.' Powell fully appreciated the importance of reducing family allowances in order to secure his target of cuts, but he signally failed to understand the political impact, arguing that this change 'is the only one which offers a large saving by a single (*and not entirely unpopular*) decision'.[62] [present author's emphasis]

Powell's proposed cut in the family allowance would have deprived an estimated five million families of their allowance. Not only would the proposal re-open the battle with Boyd-Carpenter, it was bound to be highly controversial with other ministers and MPs, especially since family allowances had been introduced to increase the gap between the income of those in work and those on national assistance, and thereby maintain work incentives. And it would be deeply unpopular among lower-middle- and upper-working-class parents – especially mothers, to whom the benefit was paid – whose support the Conservatives urgently needed to recover if they were to stand any chance of winning the next election. In Powell's last election address to his electors in Wolverhampton, he had included the family allowance in his list of benefits that the Conservatives had increased by more than 50 per cent.[63]

Moreover, in the budget debate only six months earlier, Powell had commended the increase in tax relief for children and praised 'the general approach' of the budget in 'recognizing and assisting with the burdens which are undertaken by a family with dependent children'. By the same token, suddenly scrapping the family allowance for the second child would represent a dramatic *volte-face* – fortunately for Powell's argument, he had been thwarted from doing so in 1957. In turn, reducing the family allowance was likely to provoke higher wage claims as compensation. Hall noted in his diary that a moderate wage round would enable the Government 'to let up a bit' on monetary and fiscal policy, but 'the Chancellor is now conducting a ferocious anti-expenditure drive and probably going to take away the child allowance for the second child which will add something to the view that this Government really is the enemy of the welfare state'.[64]

Thrashing out agreement between the Treasury and spending ministers is a delicate matter at the best of times, but what was bound to be a difficult process in the winter of 1957–58 was made even more fraught by an unusually tight deadline. Whereas the bargaining over the estimates frequently lasted during January and into February, on this occasion the Prime Minister's scheduled departure on 7 January for a six-week tour of the Commonwealth meant that all the outstanding issues had to be resolved before Macmillan left. Any irritation that Powell felt at the hurried negotiations, and at ministerial resistance to his proposed economies, was likely to be exacerbated by the priority that the Prime Minister was giving to the Commonwealth as opposed to the control of government spending. Indeed, there is a suggestion that Treasury ministers tried, in the last resort, to force Macmillan to delay his departure.[65]

On 20 December, parliament rose for the winter recess and Powell was never to return to the despatch box as a Treasury Minister. The Chancellor's meeting with the Prime Minister and senior ministers on 23 December revealed deep opposition to Powell's idea of removing the family allowance on the second child. Thorneycroft, however, indicated that he was considering resignation. Macmillan urged support for his Chancellor, but warned about the impact of economies in social services on wage demands.[66]

After only the briefest of breaks for Christmas with his wife and daughters, Powell returned to the Treasury to resume what was fast turning into a pitched battle on government spending. By 27 December, Thorneycroft and Powell had revised their final target for cuts in the spending plans from £200 million to £153 million. This would still mean a real reduction in government spending and involve pruning the existing estimates; removing the family allowance for the second child, or other health and welfare economies; and cutting defence spending. Reiterating the monetarist analysis that underpinned these spending cuts, Thorneycroft echoed Powell's earlier warning that 'it would be unwise to count on a greater volume of non-inflationary lending to the Government', and argued that 'in fact we are still in an inflationary situation'.[67]

Thorneycroft's reiteration of his arguments for making economies won general support from senior ministers on 31 December, but they were divided on specific proposals. In a comment that might have sent a warning signal to Treasury ministers, the Prime Minister urged no rigid adherence to the target of £153 million. Macmillan again voiced his priority of a moderate pay round and not putting the Government in a 'politically indefensible position'.[68]

The next two days, 1 and 2 January 1958, witnessed a hectic round of negotiations. Thorneycroft, often accompanied by Powell, or sometimes by Birch, repeatedly trooped through the passage from Number 11 Downing Street to join the Prime Minister for talks with spending ministers. That the Treasury team were driven by monetarist assumptions is clear from Powell's minute of 1 January on a long discussion at the ministerial group on the estimates of the possibility of financing the £40 million increase in the deficit on the national insurance fund 'out of the reserve fund'. 'The Chancellor pointed out', Powell noted, 'that the proposal to meet the cost of pensions "out of the reserve fund" was equivalent to meeting it by increased borrowing, i.e. in present circumstances by inflation'.[69]

The official papers reveal how close these ministerial discussions came to bridging the gap between the Treasury team and their colleagues, but also indicate Macmillan's concern at the political impact of the proposed economies. Privately, the Treasury team even considered a minor reduction in their demands, when Powell minuted Thorneycroft on 2 January, accepting that the £153 million target 'may (confidentially) be revised downwards to £141 million'. But it was at this stage that Powell's option for cutting the family allowance was controversially pressed. Without consulting Boyd-Carpenter, the Treasury informed his department of the Chancellor's intention to remove family allowances for the second child.[70]

The Treasury team's unbending attitude was reflected in the Chancellor's display at the Cabinet meeting on the morning of Friday 3 January. Despite the narrowness of the gap between the two sides and the fact that Thorneycroft looked set to achieve two-thirds of his target, and possibly even more, his hectoring manner and intransigent insistence on further economies infuriated his colleagues. Although Sandys, the Defence Minister, had already reduced his plans below the previous year's estimates, he was still under pressure to make further cuts. Sandys resisted any further reductions and won Macmillan's support.[71]

Boyd-Carpenter attended the Cabinet to discuss Powell's proposed cut in the family allowance, and was so strongly against the idea that he brought with him his letter of resignation. His recollection on this point captures the huge gulf that had developed between the Treasury team's determination to meet their target at all costs, and the political considerations that still weighed with their Cabinet colleagues. 'Family allowances of course were an essential part of the whole Beveridge concept,' Boyd-Carpenter later recalled,

> and the Conservative Party has always prided itself on its concern with the family. And therefore it seemed to me that to knock, as was proposed, £50 million off that would be very damaging indeed to our system of social security. It was certainly not a position that I was prepared to accept ... the whole thing was quite ridiculous because it was £50 million, which was extremely important from the point of view of family allowances, but in the totality of the national finances was really quite marginal.

The Prime Minister made it clear that the Treasury team could not expect to achieve their full target. 'If, in the event,' Macmillan suggested, 'a total saving of the order of £100 million or more could be achieved, the residue of some £50 million, representing an increase of no more than one per cent in Government expenditure, could perhaps be regarded as defensible in itself and consistent with the Government's broad purpose of maintaining a firm control over the supply of purchasing power in the economy.' Eventually, with no agreement reached, Friday's Cabinet meeting was adjourned until 4.30 p.m.[72]

At the Treasury, according to Hall, Makins confided that 'tempers were rising at the Chancellor's determination to get the estimates down at any cost'.

The permanent secretary also reportedly suspected that Thorneycroft 'was being egged on by Birch and Powell, who in their different ways are both rather mad'. Hall, too, was 'getting uncomfortable' about Thorneycroft's rigidity, and thought that his 'bad errors of judgement' were 'based in the end on a sort of *laissez-faire* morality' – a trait that Powell shared, and was likely to encourage in the Chancellor. While Hall regarded Birch as 'an extreme right-wing Tory who felt that it was much better to go down fighting for this (very right-wing) position', he found Powell 'a very queer man indeed, fanatically holding principles of economy and austerity which he does not understand in the least'.[73]

At Friday afternoon's Cabinet, the wrangling over the different options continued. When Macmillan asked the Chancellor if he would stay if he got economies totalling £113 to £117 million, Thorneycroft replied that he was in a difficult position, and wanted time to consider. The Cabinet adjourned again. At 6.30 it resumed, initially without the Chancellor while the Lord Chancellor outlined Thorneycroft's conditions. But there was confusion over the details, and the Chancellor was summoned. When Macmillan suggested pruning £30 million from the civil estimates, Thorneycroft insisted that he wanted £30 million from welfare spending and the freedom to seek other economies. Macleod accused Thorneycroft of 'Hitler tactics', while Boyd-Carpenter objected to welfare spending being singled out. Macmillan then adjourned the Cabinet, saying that if, following a further meeting on Sunday 5 January, there was still no agreement, he would have to consider submitting his Government's resignation to the Queen. Macmillan, of course, never intended to quit, and was manoeuvring to ensure that if anyone resigned it would be Thorneycroft.[74]

At Sunday's Cabinet, Thorneycroft dug in his heels by telling ministers that he saw it as his duty not to accept estimates for spending in 1958–59 that exceeded government spending in 1957–58. His overriding priority was to support sterling, and it was therefore essential that wages and government spending should be held down. Despite misgivings by ministers about Thorneycroft's rigid £153 million target, Macmillan again tried to see if it could be achieved. Macleod reiterated the difficulties in making economies in welfare spending, but suggested savings of £30 million (£20 million by increasing the NHS stamp and £10 million by cutting the welfare milk subsidy). The Prime Minister ruled out abolition of the family allowance for the second child as being 'neither politically nor socially desirable. It would be contrary to the tradition of the Conservative Party; it would represent to three million households a reduction of five per cent in their weekly income.' Moreover, he felt that even Macleod's suggested savings were too risky in the short run, for fear that any benefits from such economies would be lost if they caused economic stagnation or industrial unrest. Macmillan reiterated his view that savings of between £76 million and £110 million would keep the increase in planned spending for 1958–59 to only one per cent above spending in 1957–58, and would demonstrate the Government's commitment to the

Chancellor's policy. Thorneycroft, however, was unconvinced and stuck to his £153 million target.[75]

The dénouement was at hand. At the Treasury, Makins and his fellow permanent secretary, Sir Norman Brook, had tried hard to persuade their ministers to stay in the Government and continue to fight for their policy from the inside, where they would wield more influence than if they resigned. But Thorneycroft, Birch and Powell were listening to monetarist advice from outside the Government. In the immediate aftermath of August's sterling crisis, Thorneycroft had summoned Robbins: on this occasion, it was Sir Dennis Robertson who received the call. Robertson's meeting with the Treasury ministers was unlikely to encourage a mood to compromise. There was an idiosyncratic cameo by Powell when Thorneycroft consulted him and Birch on the Cabinet's resistance. According to Powell,

> It was the following morning that he [Thorneycroft] told us:
> 'They won't face it, they won't do it, it's no good. And what we have to decide', said he, 'is whether it's good enough.'
> And I said, 'Shall we follow the procedure in the House of Lords where the junior baron speaks first?'
> And he said, 'Yes.'
> And I put my hand on my left breast and said, 'It won't do.' And Nigel Birch said, 'I don't think it will do either.' And Peter Thorneycroft said, 'No, it won't do.'

Thorneycroft said that he intended to tender his resignation, but Birch and Powell were under no obligation to do the same. It was little surprise, however, that they followed suit. At 10.30 a.m. on Monday 6 January, their three resignation letters arrived together at Number 10, only 24 hours before Macmillan was due to depart for his six-week Commonwealth tour.[76]

Were the Treasury team trying to call the Prime Minister's bluff? According to John Wyndham (later Lord Egremont), Macmillan's political secretary, they 'had been muttering to each other for some time about resigning over government expenditure, and suddenly found a splendid opportunity for putting a pistol to the Prime Minister's head'. Some of Macmillan's private secretaries, Wyndham claimed,

> getting wind of what the Chancellor and his colleagues had in mind, had ventured to suggest to Mr Thorneycroft that their behaviour was perhaps not what it ought to be. Mr Thorneycroft looked embarrassed but took the line that the short time available would enable Mr Macmillan to concentrate his mind on the issue in dispute.

Similarly, in the view of Lord Sherfield (formerly Sir Roger Makins), the Treasury ministers felt that 'they must insist on the principle', and thought that 'if they threatened resignation, they would create a Cabinet crisis, [and] they would stop the Prime Minister, who was just about to leave on a Commonwealth tour, from going away.' Such a gesture would enable them to make their point about the primacy of controlling government spending. This interpretation is compatible with Thorneycroft's contentious resignation letter, that Macmillan recognized as a threat to sterling and to the Government's credibility on inflation.[77]

Macmillan, however, saw that postponing his departure and resuming the discussions on spending risked a deeper crisis in his Cabinet than the loss of his Treasury team. Thorneycroft, Powell and Birch had played into his hands as a result of their intransigence. Thorneycroft was in a minority of one in the Cabinet and the three of them were isolated in the Government. 'It was a great miscalculation' by Thorneycroft, Birch and Powell in Lord Sherfield's view, 'because they had in fact no support. They had exhausted all their influence in these Cabinet discussions and their colleagues thought that they'd gone as far as they possibly could do to meet them.' The wider significance was captured in an incident involving Robbins, who was at his club when news of the Treasury resignations came through. 'This is the best news for years,' a young economist commented, deliberately loudly, 'it is the death of the quantity theory of money.' The official verdict on the attempted monetarist experiment was finally pronounced in 1959 when the Radcliffe Report concluded that such a policy could not have much useful effect on the level of demand 'unless applied with a vigour which itself creates a major emergency'.[78]

Fall-out

Macmillan famously dismissed the major shock of losing his entire Treasury team as 'little local difficulties', before departing for his Commonwealth tour on schedule. The Treasury ministers' resignations had been unexpected by the press and public, especially since journalists were misinformed that Sunday's Cabinet meeting had discussed international affairs. Having read the extensive and excited coverage of the crisis in the morning's papers on the way to the airport, Macmillan nonchalantly asked Heath 'to look after the shop' as he boarded his plane.[79]

Because of the winter recess, it was more than a fortnight before the Commons could debate the resignations, under the pretext of a debate on the economy. Although Powell and Birch were present, only Thorneycroft spoke. In an impressive speech that avoided recrimination and eschewed theorizing, the former Chancellor reiterated that, since 1945, Britain had sought to do more than its resources allowed by trying to be a nuclear power and by maintaining an expensive welfare state. In the process, the country had gravely weakened itself. Despite instinctive Tory sympathy for Thorneycroft, the new Chancellor, Derick Heathcoat Amory, was a reassuring figure who epitomized the virtues of honesty and financial probity.[80]

Powell had taken the unusual step of calling a special meeting in Wolverhampton three days after his resignation to explain himself to his constituency party. There was no question of his being censured for disloyalty, and he had no intention of saying anything that would damage or weaken the Government. None the less, in a carefully measured statement, Powell was determined to put his position on the record. He began by reading Thorneycroft's letter of resignation, and explained his responsibility, as Financial Secretary, since it was in his name, not the Chancellor's, that the estimates were presented to parliament. Like the Chancellor, he explained, he had not cast away his position in the Government 'for any light cause'. 'To be Financial Secretary of the Treasury was one of my aspirations,' he told his audience, 'and I felt proud to occupy that place. I did not decide to give up quickly, lightly or hastily.'[81]

Following Macmillan's lead, the Government and party machine had dismissed the difference between the Treasury team and the Cabinet as a trivial matter. Powell had to counter this charge without laying himself open to accusations of widening the division and re-opening old wounds. His reply pointed to a fundamental difference of approach.

First, the issue was not over £50 million or any other specific sum, although I do not personally regard £50 million or one per cent of the national expenditure as a triviality ...

Second, the issue was not family allowances or any other specific item of welfare or other expenditure. The issue was whether Mr Thorneycroft felt he had the necessary minimum support from his colleagues for *the policy to which he and they were committed*. He was forced to the conclusion that he had not that support. Neither Mr Birch nor I could avoid coming to the same conclusion.[82] [present author's emphasis]

For Powell, the resignations had been about the failure by Macmillan and the rest of the Cabinet to make a continuing commitment to the monetarist and deflationary medicine that had been prescribed in the September Measures. 'It was a difference of comprehension, not a difference of detail,' Powell argued some thirty-five years later, claiming that the figure of £50 million was only 'the ultimate residual of a package which had already broken down before Thorneycroft resigned'. But this claim misses the central point that the package had collapsed because the Treasury's target had been shown repeatedly to be politically unrealistic.[83]

Macmillan, despite his outward display of sang-froid, was deeply worried that, in his absence, the former Treasury team might rally Tory support to their cause. He thought that his Treasury ministers had engineered the crisis, and Sir Edward Heath continues to believe that Thorneycroft and his allies were motivated by their ambition for power, claiming that they had long wanted 'to get rid of Macmillan'. This is not a view, however, that is supported by other witnesses of the crisis, who are convinced that the reason was a genuine difference over economic policy. But is it possible that

Macmillan, having suspected a plot, had been determined to remove the Chancellor and his allies?[84]

This view appears, at first sight, to be supported by events in the Cabinet during the weeks after the resignations. The new Chancellor, Heathcoat Amory, revealed that the 1958–59 estimates were likely to be even higher than Thorneycroft had expected, because of a reduction in the contributions by the Federal German Government to defence costs and a further increase in the deficit on the national insurance fund. This was politically awkward, since Macmillan had made much in public of the fact that the difference between the Cabinet and the former Treasury team had been only £50 million – this extra spending would nearly double the gap to £90 million. As a result, Heathcoat Amory pressed for, and eventually secured, a further £40 million of savings, only £10 million less than the final difference with Thorneycroft. Moreover, ministers agreed to raise the NHS contribution by eight pence – a measure that they had previously resisted. This raises the question of whether Macmillan might not have done more to prevent Thorneycroft from resigning by accepting these cuts in the first place. He might well have done, had Thorneycroft and his colleagues been equally concerned with the politics of the situation and less dogmatic in their approach. Moreover, after the resignations, the Cabinet were anxious to defend Macmillan over the £50 million gap and were willing to give Heathcoat Amory the cooperation that his predecessor had been signally unable to elicit. The extra £40 million of additional savings agreed during January 1958 highlights the failure of Thorneycroft, Powell and Birch.[85]

During 1958, Macmillan increasingly came to suspect the former Treasury team's motives as Heath, his Chief Whip, repeatedly warned him that the ex-ministers posed a threat to his premiership. But the Cabinet had remained loyal after their trying experiences over the 1958–59 estimates. In addition, Thorneycroft, Birch and Powell, for their part, saw that any hopes they might harbour of eventually returning to office would be ruined if they were seen to indulge in the factionalism that had characterized the Bevanites since Labour's split over the 1951 budget.[86]

Many years later, after the Thatcher Government's monetarist experiment, Powell claimed that he and his allies in the 1950s had been exceptionally far-sighted. 'We said the [government's] borrowing requirement is what makes inflation,' he recalled, adding that 'we were talking a language which no one understood at that time.' Some thirty-five years after his resignation, he was at pains to stress that

It's difficult to realize now how strange and unfamiliar to people in politics was the fact that if you borrow from the banking system instead of from the public, a certain excessive amount, you're in for inflation – in fact, that inflation is a creature of government. It was that principle which the Treasury ministers discovered in 1957, and which they believed themselves to be implementing by endeavouring to hold down the level of public expenditure to an arbitrary figure. The figure had to be arbitrary. Any figure to which one holds down expenditure is arbitrary.

This ideological attitude of Powell's explains the bafflement felt among the rest of the Cabinet at the Chancellor's uncompromising stand. Hall heard from Makins that it had been Thorneycroft's 'extreme rigidity which succeeded in the end in turning a Cabinet which begun on his side unanimously against him'. Thorneycroft's successor, Heathcoat Amory, had found it 'impossible to understand how they had got to this stage since there was (in the minds of the rest of the Cabinet) very little between them and Peter Thorneycroft. They saw it as a matter of practical judgement'.[87]

Indeed, Heathcoat Amory's budget in 1958 was extremely close to the approach that Thorneycroft and his allies had had in mind, since it was even more cautious than Thorneycroft's had been in 1957. A policy of deflation, however, was misguided since the economy was already moving into recession. By exacerbating the downturn, this error subsequently prompted Macmillan to over-react. The Tories were badly shaken by the loss of the Rochdale, Glasgow Kelvingrove and Torrington by-elections in early 1958, and by the autumn the Cabinet were bordering on panic as unemployment reached two per cent and looked set to rise to a then post-war record of 750,000 in the spring of 1959. This reaction gives an idea of the political storms into which the Treasury team's approach would have driven the Government. Macmillan, who feared the return of mass unemployment and saw the next election looming, soon cajoled his anxious Chancellor into rapid reflation.[88]

As far as Powell was concerned, Macmillan's reflation before the 1959 election confirmed him as a ruthless cynic, who gambled with the economy in order to stay in power. The 'Country' element in Powell was shocked by Macmillan's 'Court' politics. In 1971, however, Powell was to suggest another motive for Macmillan's reflation. 'I do not believe now,' he wrote,

whatever I thought at the time, that the Prime Minister cold-bloodedly planned, two years in advance, to fight and win an election at the boom point of a deliberately contrived inflation. There is too much evidence that he was still influenced by what proved to be the groundless anticipation of a slump as a practical possibility. [present author's emphasis]

Powell later stressed the impact on Macmillan of the mass unemployment that his former leader had witnessed between the wars in Stockton, the northern town where he had served as an MP. 'Macmillan was a man of the '20s and '30s', Powell observed. 'He never survived into the '50s. He still lived in Stockton in the 1930s. That was real to him.' But in the end, Powell returned to his original, cynical interpretation of Macmillan. As he told Alistair Horne, Macmillan's 'love of the winning trick predisposed him to a theory [Keynesianism] which hallowed this winning trick – e.g. buying votes for 1959.' While admitting that he was 'an unsympathetic witness', Powell continued, 'the trickster element in Macmillan was always very repugnant to me. He saw politics as a game ... pure Whiggery.'[89]

There is a double irony in Powell's caustic comments about Macmillan. In the first place, Butler, whom Powell greatly admired and whom he was to support for the leadership, was as passionately opposed as Macmillan to the Treasury team's attempt 'to overturn in the course of a few days policies in education or social welfare to which we have devoted the service of our lives'. Secondly, as Powell acknowledged in 1971, his resignation and those of his allies 'came at the right point of time' for Macmillan to demonstrate, early in his premiership, that he could 'dispense with any colleague, whoever he may be'. After the Treasury resignations, Powell's great adversary enjoyed a political ascendancy that lasted for five years. Powell and Thorneycroft were to return to Macmillan's administration in 1960, after the 1959 election victory that had, in Powell's mind, been bought by inflation.[90]

Thorneycroft later doubted the wisdom of his and his allies' resignations, and felt that 'we probably made our stand too early'. His second thoughts suggest that events might have taken a different course had he, as Chancellor, been able to draw on the advice of a Financial Secretary who was more politically astute than Powell and, while fighting hard for the maximum economies, would have used his influence to ensure that the Treasury ministers continued to press their view where it mattered most – in the Government. But Powell was not that sort of political animal. His inclination, once he had established a position of theological certainty – in this case, on government borrowing – was to worry at any disagreement and to regard any concession as a major defeat.[91]

The fact that Thorneycroft was not as ideologically committed to the theory as Powell was confirmed by an incident in January 1981, when Thorneycroft was Party Chairman. Following a seminar at Conservative Central Office given by Friedrich von Hayek, the free-market philosopher, Thorneycroft hosted a lunch at which Hayek expounded more fully on the virtues of monetarism. Unemployment had already almost doubled during the first two years of the Thatcher Government to 2.2 million and was still rising. As Hayek extolled the virtues of company bankruptcies, Thorneycroft was heard to confess, in an allusion to the 'dry' and 'wet' labels of Tory factions at the time, that he (Thorneycroft) regarded himself as a case of 'rising damp'.[92]

Powell, however, had 'no doubt' that in 1957–58 'those who took part regarded the clash of personalities as being also a parting of the ways in some historical sense'. In his eighties Powell claimed a final vindication. 'We'd lost the argument but we'd won the theory,' he asserted.

The theory was right, the theory was indefeasible. The theory was going to prevail. We might lose the argument, but the theory was there. We'd established the theory, at least to our own satisfaction. And the theory lives.

Yet by the time that Powell was proclaiming the correctness of monetarist theory, the monetarist experiment of the 1970s and early 1980s had been widely discredited, principally because it had proved impossible to control the money supply. Moreover, the socially corrosive side-effect of long-term mass unemployment, that Macmillan had sought to prevent, had again become apparent in many parts of Britain. In 1957–58, when folk memories of the 1920s and 1930s were potent (not only in Macmillan's mind), and two-thirds of the electorate were working class, it had been vital for the Conservatives to avoid being labelled as the party of unemployment and the enemy of the welfare state. Powell and his allies should not have expected the Cabinet suddenly to abandon the Tory commitment to the post-war settlement on the basis of such a politically maladroit and poorly presented argument. Paradoxically, their dogmatic approach had the opposite effect to the one that they had intended. Their resignations were crucial in determining the centrist direction of Conservative economic and social policy in the late 1950s and early '60s.[93]

9

'Coming Home to Mother'

The curious thing that's happened to me every time on the first occasion afterwards that I went back into the chamber of the House of Commons, a quite extraordinary sensation which I can only describe like coming home, almost like coming home to mother. I felt like saying, 'Well, here I am, I'm back.'

Enoch Powell, on his feelings whenever he resigned office or refused to serve, July 1987.

Liberty versus ambition

Having waited longer than his former close colleagues and rivals, Iain Macleod and Reggie Maudling, to become a minister, Powell had lasted barely two years in the Government. Only the previous autumn, Powell had been tipped as a possible Minister of Health, but now he had consigned himself to the back benches while Macleod and Maudling established themselves in the Cabinet. At forty-five years of age, Powell's ministerial career should have been blossoming, but instead, his prospects of returning to the front bench in the foreseeable future were remote. His resignation confirmed many Tories in their long-held doubts about his judgement – it was difficult to imagine Macleod's repeating the private reassurance about Powell that he had given Butler in 1954. But Thorneycroft, Powell and Birch were also able to evoke natural sympathy among Tory MPs and middle-class party activists for their tough stand on inflation, with the result that Macmillan and Heath, the Chief Whip, who suspected their motives, anxiously watched their every move.[1]

The uneasiness between the former Treasury team and the Tory leadership had its comical side. In early February, Powell joined other MPs at the memorial service to the late Walter Elliot, a former Tory minister. As Powell delighted in telling the *Express and Star*, the lesson, a passage from Ecclesiasticus which begins, 'Let us now praise famous men', was read by Butler. All went smoothly until he came to verse 16, that runs, 'Enoch pleased the Lord, and was translated, being an example of repentance to all generations'. In another incident, Macmillan briefly visited Wolverhampton during one of his regional tours in the run-up to the next election. Conversation between the Prime Minister and Powell was somewhat stilted, but in the Town Hall Macmillan tried to break the ice by asking Powell about the identity of an imposing statue. Powell had to explain that it honoured a former local iron-master and mayor of Wolverhampton, by the name of Thorneycroft – an ancestor of the former Chancellor.[2]

Yet there was a part of Powell that only felt truly at home on the back benches. As he was to recall in the quotation at the head of this chapter, following his resignation in 1958, and after each time that he refused office (he was to do so three times), he had the same odd experience. Bearing in mind Powell's exceptionally close bond with his mother, this self-revelation provides the strongest possible testimony to his deep, emotional attachment to the House of Commons. Ministers, of course, sit in the Commons, but in Powell's view 'they don't belong'. And since returning to the back benches for Powell brought 'a sense of coming back where one belonged', he also suggested that 'there must be something about me which needs the kind of liberty which a member of Parliament not corruptible by ambition of [or] by office enjoys'. This tension runs through Powell's career more powerfully than through those of his contemporaries in politics. At this stage, the ambition for office was still uppermost, although the liberty to speak out could not be entirely suppressed. But he had few illusions about the impact of speech-making, as he acknowledged during a talk on BBC Radio's Third Programme in November 1958. Arguing that great movements of public opinion originate at levels deeper than politicians can plumb, still less reach, Powell expressed the modest view that when they made speeches, they were

not the cause, nor the masters, of changes of opinion, but the exponents, representing to the public, in a kind of dialectical drama, what is passing in its own mind. 'What a dust do I raise!' said the fly as he sat on the hub of the wheel. What a dust![3]

Little more than a month after his 'coming home to mother', the Government's reform of the House of Lords, that had been foreshadowed in the 1955 Conservative manifesto, provoked Powell into giving free rein to both his 'Country' and his Tory sentiments. Indeed, such was the force of his onslaught that it raises the question of how Powell could have envisaged remaining a member of a Government that introduced such legislation. 'I believe that the House will make a mistake if it passes the Bill into law,' Powell declared after he had risen to speak on the first day of the two-day debate on the second reading of the Life Peerages Bill. The reform was intended to strengthen the upper House by enabling the creation of non-hereditary peers, who would be appointed for life, thereby increasing the number of peers who took part in the work of the Lords, while improving the representativeness of the upper chamber. Powell, however, saw the introduction of non-hereditary peers as a cynical manipulation by Macmillan of an institution that was in no need of reform. In his speech, he defended the Lords as an integral feature of Britain's evolutionary constitution, the virtues of which had been expounded by Edmund Burke, a founding father of modern Conservatism, in reaction to the French Revolution. 'There is no possibility of arguing that the present composition of the House of Lords can be justified either by logic or by reference to any preconceived constitutional theory,' Powell continued. 'It is the result of a long, even a tortuous, process of historical evolution. Its authority rests upon the acceptance of the result, handed down to our time, of that historical process.'[4]

In this respect, the House of Lords was no different from other institutions that were integral to the constitution, such as the Monarchy or the House of Commons. 'Neither logic nor statute nor theory', he declared, 'is the basis of that other hereditary institution by which it comes about that a young woman holds sway over countless millions.' Powell had implicitly raised the spectre with MPs that after the reformers had tinkered with the House of Lords, there was no reason for them to stop, with the risk that they would destroy people's historical acceptance of the constitution, and with it their sense of national identity.[5]

This was an alarmist response to a modest and practical reform that was, by any standards, to prove a success. Powell was perilously close to adopting an ultra, die-hard stance to any change whatsoever, while apparently being prepared to accept every change in the past that had enabled the constitution to evolve into its present form. He sought to defend himself against any such charge by denying 'that one should never alter or interfere with an institution of this kind', and acknowledging that there were 'many cases where a change has, in fact, resulted in preserving, and even enhancing, the institution in question'. One such instance was the creation of barons by royal patent, which, he claimed, had helped preserve the Lords 'through the last four or five centuries' – this innovation, that separated the status of a baron from the tenure of an estate, had been made in 1441. But in his view, reform should only be made when necessary 'for the avoidance of an evil which is clear and imminent'. He certainly saw no need for such a fundamental change as the modification of the hereditary principle.[6]

Having delivered his stinging attack on the idea of life peerages, Powell took no further part in discussion of the Bill. Instead, he resumed his research on the medieval House of Lords, retiring to his familiar place in the House of Commons library to which he had returned after quitting the Treasury. In November 1958, he wrote to *The Times* to correct a statement by its parliamentary correspondent that abbesses had once sat in the Lords, when, as Powell pointed out, although summoned, they had sent male proxies. Powell's opposition to the Life Peerages Bill was to have far-reaching effects. His speech presaged the devastating attack that he was to launch a decade later when the Wilson Government introduced plans for thoroughgoing reform of the Lords. And almost thirty years later, after Powell had lost his seat in the Commons in 1987, he paid a heavy personal price. He could not, in all consistency, accept a life peerage, and he was unable to join the throng of former MPs who have occupied the red benches 'in another place'.[7]

The personal cost of Powell's resignation from the Treasury had been immediate. His salary fell from £3,250 to £1,750 a year, only months after the family had moved to their new home in Belgravia. But he was soon supplementing his income by resuming his journalism and broadcasting, although he refused to say any more about his resignation. In April 1958, he again began his weekly broadcasts in Urdu to Pakistan – Patrick Gordon Walker, the Labour MP for Smethwick, who took over every three months, had to have his talks translated. Powell gave another broadcast in Italian. In the autumn of 1958, he gave two talks on the BBC's Third Programme on the history of the House of Lords and the House of Commons, and in November visited Germany to lecture (in German) on 'Current Problems of the Welfare State'. During 1959, he presented twelve descriptions of great parliamentary occasions from the fourteenth century onwards, a series that became the basis for his book, *Great Parliamentary Occasions*, that was published in 1960. From his freelance media work, Powell could earn around £1,000 a year, but a more reliable source of income eventually came with his appointment to the board of the Bestwood Company, through the offices of the Tory back-bencher, Colonel Claude Lancaster. He was paid £500 a year and focused on financial aspects, an expertise that he developed by taking directorships with a number of unit trusts, including the Commonwealth Unit Trust Fund, of which Thorneycroft was chairman. By the 1959 election, Powell was probably earning more than he had at the Treasury.[8]

Politically, Powell and Thorneycroft were in a tricky position. They hoped to return to office – Birch's failing eyesight was thought to rule him out – and had to avoid being seen constantly rocking the boat or plotting. Yet silence on their part would be taken as a tacit admission of defeat in the argument about inflation. During 1958, Powell busied himself with his research in the library, while making occasional re-statements of his economic beliefs. These sometimes appeared in *Crossbow*, the journal of the Bow Group, a ginger group of liberal-minded younger Tories, and he also ventured his thoughts on the future of Toryism at CPC summer schools. During his period on the back benches, his free market brand of Conservatism increasingly became an inspiration for a younger generation of articulate Conservative graduates, including John Biffen, who was to become an MP in 1961, and Geoffrey (later Lord) Howe, who was first elected in 1964.[9]

A couple of months after his resignation, he was approached by Ralph Harris (later Lord Harris of High Cross), who with Arthur Seldon ran the recently established free-market Institute of Economic Affairs (IEA). But there was little possibility of Powell's becoming a vigorous, high-profile champion of the IEA. Harris urged him to write a pamphlet for them about his experience at the Treasury, or about financial and monetary policy, and Powell finally wrote *Saving in a Free Society*, that was not published until 1960. It was certainly no polemic, and Harris regarded it as being akin to a PhD thesis.

Since the IEA was then based in Eaton Square, round the corner from Powell's home, Harris and Seldon 'got really quite pally with him'. But their meetings were characterized by rather severe intellectual exchanges. In particular, they strongly disagreed over the health service, which Powell was studying in the light of his concern as Financial Secretary at the cost of the NHS, to see how it might be managed more efficiently. Whereas Harris and Seldon believed that market principles could be applied to the health service, as to any other social service, Powell put the NHS in a separate category.[10]

Powell had not spoken in the Commons on the economy since his resignation, but April's debate on the 1958 budget provided him with a justifiable opportunity to expound his views without being accused of looking for trouble. Indeed, he gave every impression of a man who had a duty to speak, as he argued that government spending for 1958–59 was set to rise, compared with both the original estimates and the final level of actual spending for 1957–58. Remarkably, despite Heathcoat Amory's extreme caution in his budget, Powell warned MPs of the risk of imminent inflation – though the following year, he had to concede that government spending had grown by only two per cent during 1958–59, as had been predicted. Reiterating that stable money and expansion were not alternatives, but that the former was a precondition of the latter, Powell quoted a recent article by Robbins, the economist whose views had influenced the Treasury team. Robbins had drawn attention to the 'smart rates of growth and high levels of employment' that were being achieved in West Germany, combined with a 'steady price level'. Pointedly, Powell repeated Robbins's concluding question, 'Is it not the bankruptcy of statesmanship and national morale to argue that this sort of thing is impossible for us?'[11]

Although Powell did not speak again in the Commons until the following autumn, he reincarnated Mr Gladstone for the City of London Young Conservatives on 23 April 1958, and the readers of the *Daily Telegraph* on 9 June. Since the state effectively guaranteed people a minimum income, he advocated scrapping the subsidies on school meals, welfare milk and council house rents – he had suggested cutting the latter item in his CPC summer school lectures while still Financial Secretary, on the grounds that rents in the private sector had been decontrolled. Yet even these economies would not finance cuts in income tax, and other savings would need to be found, some of which could be found by re-organizing the NHS and abolishing the regional hospital boards, thereby creating a more direct relationship between the minister and the hospital management committees. He also urged a shift to other taxes, since progressive income tax had become 'positively harmful' in its impact on 'producers' – though as Financial Secretary, Powell had dismissed as impracticable a proposal from the Conservative Research Department for cutting income tax by introducing a sales tax, on the grounds that the latter would only yield as much as existing taxes if it included food and was levied at five or ten per cent.[12]

In the *Daily Telegraph*, Powell reversed his earlier position by advocating longer-term planning of government spending instead of relying solely on annual estimates. He now believed that such an approach was essential in curbing public sector costs. In addition, he reckoned that government spending should be cut by between two and five per cent a year. And in an echo of the Treasury team's demands, he argued that these reductions should be made in money terms, i.e. without allowing for inflation, since making estimates in real terms was to 'assume inflation' and 'to surrender one of the Government's weapons against it'.[13]

During the spring of 1958, a pay deal for the railwaymen, which many Tories saw as a sell-out, and back bench anger at Sandys's re-organization of the armed forces, raised the spectre of an anti-inflationist, anti-nuclear alliance on the Tory back benches. Birch was known to oppose the Government's shift to nuclear deterrence. Speculation about Powell's views had been excited by Thorneycroft's reiteration in the *Daily Mail* of his misgivings about the cost of nuclear weapons. But Powell kept his scepticism about the Bomb to himself. The notion of a new faction evaporated as Thorneycroft welcomed the Government's modest expansionary measures for the economy – the reflationary overkill was to come later. Powell's continued advocacy of deflationary policies was seen as perverse. Less than a month after printing his thoughts on government economies, the *Daily Telegraph* judged that Powell was 'never likely to be forgiven' by the Tory leadership. 'The only future he can confidently look forward to is to sit on a Tory back bench for ever and ever.'[14]

As Tory fortunes revived in the wake of Macleod's symbolic victory over Frank Cousins, the transport union leader, in the London bus strike, Powell and his former Treasury allies were eclipsed. After a family holiday at Saint Jacut, a fishing village near Dinard in Brittany, Powell had the mixed pleasure of welcoming the Prime Minister to Wolverhampton and hearing him tell the press that the Government was tackling unemployment by putting its foot gently back on the accelerator. Over the coming year, Macmillan was to put his foot through the floor, but the isolation of the former Treasury team was complete at October's Tory conference in Blackpool. Apart from an exposition to hospital finance officers at Oxford in September and an academic-style BBC Radio Third Programme broadcast on 'Movements of Political Opinion' in November, little was heard from Powell for the remainder of 1958. During the autumn, Thorneycroft left for a four-month trip to Australasia, the Middle East and the Soviet Union, while Powell ended his year with a family Christmas in Merridale Road, combined with a week of canvassing new houses in his constituency.[15]

Not even the eruption of non-white immigration as a major issue in the latter months of 1958 stirred Powell from his relative restraint. Race riots at the end of the summer in Notting Hill, Nottingham and Dudley – the latter being graphically reported in the *Express and Star* – shattered the complacent assumption that Britain was free of the racial tensions that were troubling the United States. Many years later, Powell recalled only that he was 'unsurprised' by the riots, but 'wouldn't put it higher than that'. John Biffen, who had got to know Powell while living and working in Birmingham in the late 1950s, and who stood as a candidate in Coventry in 1959, recalls having talked with Powell during this period about the emergence of immigration as an issue in the West Midlands. But although Powell was aware of the concern that was felt by some whites in urban areas about increased non-white immigration, he declined to join other Tory MPs in their campaign for immigration control.[16]

Exactly two years before the race riots, Powell made a statement on immigration that is the only one by him on the subject available on published record before 1964. He was asked about immigration control at a meeting of the Wolverhampton branch of the Institute of Personnel Management on 31 August 1956, and loyally kept to the Government line. 'A fundamental change in the law is necessary', he explained,

> before there can be any limit to West Indian immigration. It would be necessary to define a citizen of the British Isles by his place of birth and race. Such a definition would put in the category of 'the rest' many British subjects, white, yellow and black, and would bring with it the necessity to discriminate against classes of citizens and to accord this or that class certain privileges. There might be circumstances in which such a change of the law might be the lesser of two evils. There would be very few people who would say the time had yet come when it was essential that so great a change should be made.

Powell's phraseology is important, because while ruling out any change in the law at the time, he did not deny the possibility of future action.[17]

Powell's qualified answer is given added significance by the fact that the official papers show that during 1956 he was attending meetings of the Cabinet committee on colonial immigrants. As housing minister at the time, it made sense for him to be included in the discussions, but oddly he was attending in an *ex officio* capacity, since Sandys, his boss at the Ministry of Housing and Local Government, was not a member of this particular Cabinet committee. It is clear from the minute of the second meeting on 25 April 1956, that ministers were split between those who supported the introduction of immigration controls, and those who were opposed. But it is not possible to confirm whether Powell supported controls during this discussion. The conclusion of the meeting clearly formed the basis for Powell's statement the following August. According to the official minute, it was 'the general view of the committee ... that steps to impose control would not be justified at present. On the other hand, there seemed little doubt that some form of control would become necessary in the long run'. The committee agreed that the situation would need to be reviewed again in a year's time – by then Powell was no longer the housing minister.[18]

A year later, however, on 1 August 1957, Powell was present at a meeting of Macleod's party policy group when the issue of immigration was discussed.

But it was not Powell who raised it, and there is no note of his having intervened to express any strong opinion. During a discussion of the Commonwealth and colonies, Powell is minuted as having raised only the problem of reconciling in the manifesto 'the changes in the Commonwealth with the fundamental prejudices of the rank and file of the Party'. It was left to Jock (later Lord) Simon, who was then at the Home Office, to point out 'that people in Britain were worried by immigration from the Commonwealth'. But according to the minute, 'while this was agreed, it was felt that the present scale of the problem was not such as to warrant restrictive legislation'. There is no record of Powell's having disagreed.[19]

The 1958 race riots crystallized a three-way split in the Conservative Party. At one extreme were those who were strongly urging the Government to impose immigration controls on non-white immigration from the Commonwealth. Although this group was small within the parliamentary party and very much centred on the efforts of the MP Sir Cyril Osborne, it attracted stronger support among the Tory faithful. In the immediate aftermath of the race riots, the Conservative conference snubbed the Cabinet's rejection of immigration control by voting for such action by a substantial majority. At the other extreme were those Tories who were wedded to the notion of Britain at the heart of a multi-racial Commonwealth and regarded control of immigration on racial grounds as beneath contempt. This group included both Sir Alan Lennox-Boyd and his successor as Colonial Secretary, Macleod. In view of his caustic attitude towards the Commonwealth, Powell was never likely to belong to this group. Indeed, earlier in 1958, before the race riots, Lennox-Boyd, who took responsibility for immigrants' welfare in Britain, contacted him about alleged racial discrimination against a West Indian family who had been denied a house on an estate near Wolverhampton (the case was outside Powell's constituency). Powell replied, in his own words, 'very sharply that it was no good dealing with the details when the real issue, the citizenship laws, was not changed'. But although he appeared sympathetic to the case for control, Powell continued to take a cautious approach, as was evident during an incident in the spring of 1958, when the manager of a Wolverhampton ballroom began banning non-white boys who did not have dancing partners with them. The dispute rumbled on for months, and the local Labour MP, John Baird, introduced a private member's bill to outlaw racial discrimination, but Powell refrained from becoming involved.[20]

At some point after the 1958 race riots, Powell was approached by Sir Cyril Osborne who asked him to support his campaign against coloured immigration by raising the matter in the Commons and at the 1959 election. Powell declined, but his subsequent reasoning was diametrically opposed to the attitude that he took ten years later. 'The more the harouche,' he explained, 'the more difficult it is to do it. It was a tactical problem. I thought that such a fundamental change in the law of the country was a monkey which was easier caught softly.' A Birmingham Tory MP, who sensed the strength of feeling among his white constituents at the 1959 election, placed Powell in the uncommitted group on the immigration issue. 'Enoch was one of these,' the MP commented. 'I recall his listening sympathetically to me in the early days, but not saying anything in reply.'[21]

The Commons in his hand

The most revealing insight into Powell's mind comes not from his silence on immigration in 1958, but in his emotional speech on a quite different subject in the House of Commons in July 1959, only three months before the election. This latter performance was to mark his emergence as a politician who could muster not only logic but also passion to his cause. Viewed in the context of his concern to avoid any further trouble with the leadership as his hopes of returning to office grew, his action was exceptional.

Powell's conviction that inflation would revive was only confirmed as the Government's reflation gathered steam during 1959. In January, in his first speech in the Commons since the previous spring, he objected to the size of a planned £1,000 million increase in the borrowing powers of the nationalized electricity authorities, especially the proposal that the new powers would last for six or seven years without any need for parliamentary approval in the meantime. But he was not looking for trouble – though sometimes he seemed to attract it. In February, his alleged comments at a CPC meeting for industrialists and selected trade unionists in Coventry caused a stir. The engineers' leader, Sir William (later Lord) Carron, complained to the Prime Minister, claiming that Powell had said that it was the true function of a Tory Government to stand up to the unions, and if necessary to oppose them. Powell refused to comment on the grounds that it had been a private meeting.[22]

Behind the scenes, Powell received a clear signal that he might be viewed more favourably by the Tory leadership. His membership of the Policy Study Group had ceased after his resignation from the Treasury, but in February 1959 Macleod invited him to rejoin, writing that 'this would give me a good deal of personal pleasure, quite apart from the fact that I would be happy to have your mind with us when we study our programme for the next election'. Powell's pleasure in accepting was reflected in his witty reply, apologizing for his delay (it was only eight days) with a topical allusion to a diplomatic snub that the Soviet leader, Khrushchev, had given Macmillan during the Prime Minister's visit to Moscow. 'I have been guilty of almost Muscovite discourtesy in not replying sooner to your letter of 19 February about the Policy Study group, which I shall now be pleased to rejoin,' Powell wrote, signing himself, 'Yours, Enoch'.[23]

Although Powell's rejoining was highly significant for his longer term prospects, his immediate impact on policy was extremely limited. By this stage in the parliament, the major policy issues had either been settled or were being considered by Macmillan's Steering Committee of senior ministers. Macleod's group were mainly concerned with drafting the manifesto. Macmillan's management of the economy was plainly at odds with Powell's view, and the general thrust of domestic policy was not as radical as he had hoped. In August 1957, Powell had urged Macleod's group to reject the report of a policy subcommittee that had recommended only a few, minor measures of denationalization and instead 'to consider the possibility of another wave of denationalization, to be carried out in the next Parliament if we got in again'. Although he accepted that 'in present financial circumstances it was not feasible, and that coal and railways would have to come last', he none the less maintained that 'the idea of a free economy was irreconcilable with this great block of capital investment which was unrelated to the general economic situation except by arbitrary decision'. But his call for an election pledge to radical denationalization was rejected.[24]

The state's role had been reduced most effectively in housing, as Powell had advocated. The 1957 Rent Act, in which he had played a key role, decontrolled many private rents, and the 1959 Town and Country Planning Act implemented another of his aims by requiring local councils to purchase land at its full market value. Powell's mind was already turning to the next steps. At weekly back bench housing committee meetings, he urged that, following decontrol in the private sector, the subsidies on council house rents should, in all consistency, also be reduced. Yet Powell's free-market approach was already causing qualms in the party. Following the Tory losses in by-elections and local elections in the spring of 1958, the Government introduced the Landlord and Tenant (Temporary Provisions) Act, to give a respite to tenants under notice to quit decontrolled homes. And whereas Powell had expected that decontrol would increase people's mobility by reviving private renting, others realized that it would encourage home ownership instead – as Michael Fraser of the Research Department pointed out, people who were able to buy were likely to do so when a rent-restricted letting was removed from them.[25]

Powell had also urged a radical approach on pensions, but the Government rejected his critique of the national insurance scheme and expanded it significantly. In 1958 and 1959, ministers raised insurance and national assistance benefits higher than was justified by price rises, and gave the right to contract-out of the state scheme into a private occupational pension. The 1959 manifesto also promised pensioners a share in the higher standard of living produced by an expanding economy. Significantly, the 1959 legislation breached Beveridge's principle of flat-rate contributions for flat-rate benefits further by introducing for employees on or just above average wages, earnings-related pensions in return for earnings-related contributions – Powell had advocated only earnings-related contributions, while keeping flat-rate benefits.[26]

Tactically, Heathcoat Amory's expansionary April 1959 budget presented the trickiest challenge of all for Powell and his former Treasury allies. On the one hand, the logic of their disagreement with the Cabinet demanded that they should attack the rip-roaring reflation, but on the other hand, shattering Tory unity as an election loomed would gain them only their party's opprobrium.

Choosing his words with care, Powell suggested that the quadrupling of government borrowing to £721 million must have caused Heathcoat Amory 'more anxiety and more thought than all the other budget decisions together'. How much of this would the Chancellor borrow from the public and how much from the banks, as the latter would expand the money supply? Instead of taking a risk with inflation, Powell argued that 'we ought to rely, and that we must rely, primarily upon other forces and other sources for the renewal and carrying forward of the expansion of our economy'. With the Tories wanting to hear an upbeat message, Powell's implicit preference for tax cuts as opposed to extra spending had managed to avoid sounding too austere. This speech was the last that MPs were to hear of Powell on the economy until after the election, and he was equally cautious in a series of articles for the *Financial Times*. Eschewing outright criticism of the Government, he pointed out instead that economic policy had less effect than was imagined – unemployment was falling in Britain, the United States and West Germany, despite their different policies.[27]

Powell kept to his uncontroversial approach on issues other than the economy in the first half of the summer, rejoining the One Nation group in June, and regaling the Tory back bench housing, local government and public works committee in mid-July on the increasing importance as an issue of sewage. But less than a fortnight after this latter intervention, and with an election looking imminent, Powell was suddenly provoked into abandoning all caution and making an explosive speech in the Commons that was much more damaging to the Government's case than the furious attacks launched from the Opposition benches. The occasion was a late-night debate on the Hola Camp affair, that centred on the deaths of eleven Kenyan African detainees who had resisted compulsory work. At first, it was suggested that the deaths were the result of drinking contaminated water, but a subsequent inquiry disclosed that the detainees had been killed brutally. The Tory whips had deliberately timed the debate for late at night, on the eve of the summer recess, in order to avoid undue embarrassment for the Government. But Powell was not to be deterred from making an impassioned speech because he believed that the affair had given an affront to a key constitutional principle.[28]

The Labour Party had been raising allegations of brutality in detention camps since early 1958, and the vindication of their campaign in the inquiry into Hola Camp inspired a fierce attack in the Commons debate from Barbara Castle. But Powell, who spoke immediately after Castle and whose speech was even more coruscating, condemned the failure to adhere to the principle on which parliamentary government is based – the government's responsibility to answer for its actions to parliament. 'Hola Camp was not about the British Empire, it was about ministerial responsibility,' Powell explained many years later.[29]

Although Powell exonerated the Colonial Secretary, Alan Lennox-Boyd (later Lord Boyd) from any personal blame for the affair, he none the less insisted that 'the responsibility is recognized and carried where it properly belongs'. So far, that had not happened, but the responsibility 'cannot be ignored, it cannot be burked, it will not just evaporate into thin air if we do nothing about it'. The 'real heart of my anger', as Powell later put it, was the abdication of responsibility by the executive for what had occurred and, in view of the Governor's failure to take responsibility, especially the failure of the Colonial Secretary to take responsibility in the House of Commons.[30]

Whereas other back bench Conservatives who spoke in the debate saw their first duty in political terms as being to defend the Government and sought to excuse the colonial authorities by suggesting that they had been guilty of little more than an error of judgement, Powell saw his first duty in constitutional terms. 'I was just a back bench member who read the report,' he recalled of his reaction to the inquiry, 'and as a Member of Parliament I said, "but the responsibility is not being taken to this place which after all is responsible, whether it wants to be or not, for what happens in East Africa".' In Powell's mind the issue was clear-cut. 'The affair of Hola Camp was a great administrative disaster,' he told MPs when he spoke shortly after 1.15 a.m. As such, he later explained, it was 'an event for which responsibility must be taken. If it's not taken by the Governor, it must be taken here in this House. That's what I was saying.'[31]

Moreover, the efforts by Powell's fellow Conservative back-benchers to plead mitigating circumstances served only to intensify Powell's deep sense of indignation. As he later recalled,

> I was also stirred by the attempt to pretend that responsibility could be diluted or affected by the nature or circumstances of the persons concerned. If Parliament is responsible, parliament is responsible, and it's responsible for everybody. It's responsible for everything that is done in its name, and with the power and the money which it supplies.

In particular, Powell was affronted by the suggestion from another Tory MP, that the African detainees were 'sub-human', countering that 'that cannot be relevant to the acceptance of responsibility for their death'. As he told MPs,

> In general, I would say that it is a fearful doctrine, which must recoil upon the heads of those who pronounce it, to stand in judgement on a fellow human-being and to say, 'Because he was such-and-such, therefore the consequences which would otherwise flow from his death shall not flow.'[32]

In a moving peroration, that was to have a strong influence on his fellow Tories, Powell fused the enlightened paternalism that had once informed his imperialism with his emotional commitment to parliamentary government:

> Finally it is argued that this is Africa, that things are different there. Of course they are. The question is whether the difference between things

there and here is such that the responsibility there and here should be upon different principles.

He could not imagine that the way 'to plant representative institutions' in Britain's former colonies was to be seen shirking the 'acceptance and the assignment of responsibility, which is the very essence of responsible government'.

> Nor can we ourselves pick and choose where and in what parts of the world we shall use this or that kind of standard. We cannot say, 'We will have African standards in Africa, Asian standards in Asia and perhaps British standards here at home.' We have not that choice to make. We must be consistent with ourselves everywhere. All Government, all influence of man upon man, rests upon opinion. What we can do in Africa, where we still govern and where we no longer govern, depends upon the opinion which is entertained of the way in which Englishmen act. We cannot, we dare not, in Africa of all places, fall below our own highest standards in the acceptance of responsibility.[33]

'I remember sitting down and crying,' he later recalled, at which 'Peter Thorneycroft got up and walked over and sat down beside me.' Thorneycroft said nothing, but for Powell it was 'one of those things you never forget'. Powell's speech was always to remain his 'most powerful memory' from a career in the Commons that extended over thirty-seven years. It was one of his proudest moments,

> not so much because of the content, as because it was one of the occasions in which I have as an individual dominated the House. One of the exhilarations of being a member of the House of Commons, if you experience it, are the moments in which you actually have it in your hand, in which you play upon it like an instrument. They don't often happen, and one ought to be humbly grateful when they happen.

Moreover, Powell always regarded the occasion as a testimony to the qualities of both parliamentary politics and of the Conservative Party that, as a Tory back-bencher, he had been able to criticize his own Government without recrimination. Indeed, he was always to remember the Colonial Secretary coming up to him afterwards and 'saying we are closer friends than ever before'. In terms of content, however, his speech against the Royal Titles Bill six years earlier retained Powell's personal accolade as his best.[34]

But the content of his Hola Camp speech was to assume a new significance as a result of Powell's vehement statements on immigration only nine years later, and in particular the 'racialist tone' – in Sir Edward Heath's phrase – of his speech in Birmingham in April 1968. Humphry Berkeley, in his study of Powell, referred to Powell's final plea in his Hola Camp speech for maintaining the highest standards of British government 'in Africa of all places', and stated that 'no racialist could have uttered those words'. It is, indeed, impossible to imagine a racialist bigot being as angered as Powell had been by another MP's reference to the African detainees as 'sub-human'. Powell was primarily motivated by a basic constitutional assumption. As he later explained, as an MP, he 'accepted a duty and a responsibility to everyone in Kenya as long as the responsibility for the government of Kenya rested with the House of Commons'. In the same way, he accepted that as a Member of Parliament in Wolverhampton and later in County Down, he had a duty to represent his constituents in the House of Commons, whatever their origin.[35]

Powell's speech had little immediate effect on the point at issue. Although the Colonial Secretary acknowledged that it had been the best critical speech, he would not accept that the Kenyan Ministers should be held responsible and conceded only that the detainees would be removed from the care of the Prison Department. The longer term effects, however, were more significant. Macleod regarded it as 'a very fine speech ... which made a very deep impression on the House, and indeed upon me'. Powell's withering attack on colonial maladministration in British Africa helped contribute to the mood for rapid decolonization after the 1959 election. Yet the strongest effect was on Powell's own career. Any calculation of the likely impact beforehand would have suggested that Powell could only damage his prospects by launching such an onslaught against the front bench. Yet such was the force and – crucially – the passion of his speech, that Powell won new respect. Previously, he had been seen as a cold fish who was almost unrelievedly logical. But after this speech, he was seen as a more emotional figure. The combination of logical argument and passionate emotion was a heady mix, and Powell had experienced its potent effect. From this moment, he was regarded as one of the more substantial Tory politicians of his generation, and he was aware of his potential as an orator.[36]

A personal appeal

When the October 1959 general election was called, Powell's experiences during the 'eventful years' since the last contest prompted him to adopt a distinctively personal tone in his election address. Whereas previously he had used the common conceit of a letter to his electors as a means of conveying party propaganda, spiced with his own preferences, he now struck a different note. Instead of merely sounding like the person who happened to be the Conservative candidate, he claimed to be acting in the national interest and to be ready, if necessary, to act above other interests. This personal appeal was to become his trade-mark in Wolverhampton South-West.[37]

Not that Powell was above dissembling. On Suez, Powell declared that he had 'supported the course then taken' by Eden, a claim that is consistent with his having remained a member of Eden's Government, but that scarcely accords with his privately-held views on the folly of the venture. 'But for that action,' he further assured his electors, 'our American allies would not now be committed with us to the defence of the Middle-East, and Russia might well have stepped in our place.' This was a stock Tory justification of Suez, but it cannot be squared with his long-held view that the United States was Britain's real enemy in the region. Either Powell had temporarily abandoned his deep distrust of American objectives – which seems highly improbable – or he had chosen to toe the party line.[38]

The latter course made sense on tactical grounds, since he was more forthright in his economic views, and sticking his neck out on two issues would have been asking for trouble. 'Being convinced', he boldly told his electors, 'that restraint on government expenditure is the key to complete and lasting success in the battle against inflation, I followed Mr Thorneycroft when he resigned on that issue in January 1958.' Powell's inclusion of 'the continuance of full employment' and 'rising production' in his list of economic gains that had been made possible by the deflationary 'September Measures' was, to put it mildly, stretching a point. The matter of Macmillan's subsequent reflation was let pass. But all this was by way of a prelude to his justification of his resignation. 'I can only say', he told his electors,

> that if I had the decision to take again, it would be the same one. There could be no faith in government nor decency in public life if it were thought that Ministers hesitate to prefer the national interest, as they see it, to their own.[39]

Powell assured his voters that since his resignation he had 'continued to support from the back benches the Conservative policy under which this country has made such immense progress' – note his emphasis on supporting 'policy', as opposed to supporting the Government. The Government deserved a pat on the back to the extent that it had given 'the nation the freedom and the opportunity' to create extra wealth. Powell's message chimed with the mood in the West Midlands, as its economy boomed. Although parts of the region had suffered a scare over jobs in 1956, when automation in the car industry caused redundancies, Powell made no mention of his party's manifesto pledge to 'remodel and strengthen' their powers for tackling local unemployment. 'The basic issue of the general election', he asserted during the campaign, 'is simply whether the country wants a free economy or a planned economy.'[40]

Despite the race riots having occurred little more than twelve months earlier, immigration was scarcely mentioned during the campaign. Powell's Labour opponent, Eric Thorne, and his supporters had been 'disconcerted' by Powell's stand over Hola Camp and 'were all impressed by Powell's refusal to get involved in what was, even then, an explosive issue in Wolverhampton'. Powell made no mention of the issue in his election address, and Conservative policy was still against control. He later claimed that he had not planned a major speech on the issue because he had expected it to be raised in a question at one of his meetings. Although there is no record of Powell's having spoken publicly on the issue, whenever it was raised with him personally he stuck to his 1956 line by pointing out that nothing could be done until the citizenship law was changed. The issue featured more prominently in some Birmingham constituencies. After the election, however, when a group of MPs from the city began meeting to press for the introduction of immigration controls in the new parliament, Powell kept his distance from them.[41]

Powell was confident that on economic policy he would be proved right and, in the meantime, did not want to wreck his prospects of an early return to the Government. 'When I *am* back at the Treasury ...' he had remarked in the spring of 1959 in reply to a question about his approach if he were to become Chancellor of the Exchequer, implying that he set his sights as firmly on the key to Number 11 as he had once set them on the key to India. His ambition was helped by an unprecedented third successive Tory election victory, in which he emerged as one of his party's leading politicians in the West Midlands. Powell increased his majority to 11,167, with a swing of 3.9 per cent to the Conservatives, above the regional swing of 2.5 per cent in the West Midlands and much higher than the national swing of 1.2 per cent, although not as high as in Labour-held Wolverhampton North-East. Nationally, Macmillan's landslide triumph on 8 October and his increased, 100-seat majority in the Commons confirmed the Prime Minister's dominance. 'Supermac' was in the ascendant.[42]

'Mr Powell in new sensation', ran the *Express and Star* headline a fortnight after the election, 'refuses job in Government'. In Macmillan's post-election re-construction of his administration, the Prime Minister decided to recall Powell. There was no place, however, for Thorneycroft. Powell was offered only the post of parliamentary under-secretary for Education, but declined on the grounds that he had resigned with Thorneycroft, and that he could not return to the front bench until the former Chancellor was also restored. It was a remarkable act by any standards, but especially since the forty-seven-year-old Powell wanted to return to office, and had seen his contemporaries and rivals promoted in the re-shuffle – Macleod, at the age of forty-five, became Colonial Secretary; Maudling, aged forty-two, became President of the Board of Trade; and Heath, aged forty-three, entered the Cabinet as Minister of Labour.[43]

Whereas Powell's first refusal to accept a ministerial post in 1952 had remained secret, news of his second refusal soon leaked out. 'Mr Powell is a politician with an inflexible, almost quixotic code of conduct,' reported the *Daily Telegraph*. 'Whether his judgement was faulty remains to be seen,' the paper added, but suggested presciently that 'his evident self-sacrifice will enhance the respect in which he has always been held in the House of Commons'. Macmillan paid him an unintended compliment by acknowledging that Powell had attracted a band of admirers in the Commons, despite his disdainful dismissal of any idea that they would 'linger for long beside his lonely camp fire in the wilderness'. Powell, however, lost no time in the new parliament in staking out his position. Speaking in the opening debate of the new parliament, he reiterated his opposition to state intervention, again urging that subsidies for council house rents should be cut.[44]

But if Powell was to avoid being deserted in the wilderness, he needed to do more than merely re-state his views. His position as a former Financial Secretary in the previous parliament was of diminishing influence, and he needed to demonstrate that he counted for something in the new parliamentary party. This objective he quickly accomplished by securing re-election to the executive of the 1922 Committee on 12 November, a position he had had to relinquish when he joined Eden's Government. On 17 November, his election as chairman of the influential Conservative back bench finance committee was widely seen as a warning shot across the bows for Macmillan and his run-away boom. Two days later, Powell's response to the Radcliffe Committee's report on credit and monetary policy was published on the editorial page of *The Times* as the first in a series of articles. But instead of attacking Radcliffe's failure to endorse monetarist theory, Powell voiced the opposition of most Tories to the idea of replacing the existing links between the Bank and the Treasury by a standing committee.[45]

Powell sustained his campaign during the winter of 1959–60 and into the following spring. In particular, he attacked the Government's misguided efforts at Keynesian fine-tuning of the economy in the *Financial Times*, and called for de-nationalizing the giant steel company, Richard Thomas and Baldwin – a proposal that had been shot down by his colleagues on the Policy Study Group before the last election. His moralistic edge struck a chord among some Conservatives, but it grated on others. When he proclaimed that 'the council house system today is immoral and socially damaging', he was taken to task by the *Daily Telegraph*. The paper's editorial acknowledged Powell's points on the need for consistency and the folly of Labour's dogmatism, but wondered, 'is not Mr Powell's policy a trifle dogmatic also?' Moreover, Powell's radicalism prompted a display of consensus politics in this most Tory paper, in its recognition that since subsidies were spread over sixty years, 'their abolition would come perilously close to a breach of contract'.[46]

Yet by devoting an editorial to Powell, the *Daily Telegraph* had demonstrated the success of his campaign. He had done more than merely resist the danger of being left high and dry on the back benches, and had enhanced his standing on the right of the party and re-established himself as a contender for high office. For the third year since their resignations, Powell and Thorneycroft approached the budget with immense care. It was increasingly clear that the economic boom would have to be reined in, and they wanted to encourage a measure of deflation. But if they appeared to be fighting old battles or seemed too tough they would only annoy Macmillan and lose back bench support. In the budget debate, Powell repeated his familiar refrain that government spending was too high, but he did more to further his prospects as the Commons debated the Finance Bill during the spring and summer. His preoccupation with parliamentary power over finance – the root of parliament's ability to exercise any form of control over the executive – was reflected in his opposition to the betting levy, a new tax that would not require annual approval. In addition, he successfully championed his finance committee's crusade against the excessive powers of discretion that had been given to the Commissioners of the Inland Revenue in clamping down on tax advantages.[47]

Macmillan finally ended the speculation about Powell and Thorneycroft by bringing them back into the Government in his re-shuffle at the end of July 1960. They returned very much on the Prime Minister's terms, and their new posts reflected shrewd judgement on his part. Powell was appointed Minister of Health, while Thorneycroft became Minister of Aviation. The vacancy at Health occurred because of Derek Walker-Smith's decision to quit the Government – with hindsight, there is a supreme irony in the fact that Powell's promotion was facilitated by the departure of a staunch opponent of British membership of the European Economic Community. Moreover, Heath's move to the Foreign Office in the July re-shuffle was to presage, a year later, Britain's historic decision to apply for membership of the EEC.

'An organization which had amalgamated all the previously existing channels of health care,' Powell recalled many years later, 'was not the choice of a politician identified with the limitation of public expenditure and already interested in exploring the scope for the restoration of market economics.' Yet the forty-eight-year-old Powell fared better than he could have dared hope the previous autumn by becoming head of a major department, although he remained outside the Cabinet. Thorneycroft's acceptance of Aviation, albeit with a seat in the Cabinet, represented a serious demotion for a former Chancellor. More to the point, not only had Macmillan kept both men away from the Treasury, he had put these two arch hawks on government expenditure in departments where they would be among the biggest spenders in Whitehall. It was the touch of a master in man-management, and of a Prime Minister with a wry sense of humour.[48]

Powell's appointment was widely welcomed. 'The Ministry of Health should give scope to the humanity which, I suspect, lies beneath his odd exterior,' was one comment in the *New Statesman* – many on the left had been influenced in their estimation of Powell by his Hola Camp speech. Powell had expected beforehand that he might be offered education or health. In April, he had delivered a timely reminder of his Tory attitude on both elements in the welfare state in his article for *Crossbow* – its title, 'The Limits of *laissez-faire*', might almost have been commissioned by Macmillan. 'In founding a university or instituting a universal free medical service,' Powell wrote, 'a Government does not act on economic criteria. It acts on the ground that it is a "good thing" for its subjects to be well-educated or to be cured of their ailments if humanly possible.'[49]

Yet since his resignation, Powell had worked hard to devise plans for re-organization in the health service that he claimed would achieve significant economies. So, how successful would the former Financial Secretary be in curbing health service spending? Would he be a reforming minister or would his Tory inclinations prevail and result in his leaving the NHS largely as he found it?

10

Arch-Planner

The power of initiative is early lost. The political head, though he must cope with everything that is thrown in his path, can only take personal control and initiative on very few fronts at once. He must select his points of attack and throw all his available weight and attention there.

Enoch Powell, on the limits on a minister's power, 1966.

New vistas and an old battle

'To deal with certain immediate difficulties, an immense task lies before you, both psychological and practical,' the Prime Minister wrote to his new Minister of Health, only days after Powell had first entered the department's offices in Savile Row. 'There is really the future of the Service, which way it will go,' Macmillan added, indicating that he had put Powell in charge at a key moment. Despite their differences over economic policy, Powell had exempted the near-monopoly state health service from his advocacy of market forces, and his study as a back-bencher of its organization demonstrated his concern for a cost-effective NHS. Macmillan regarded the major problems that faced his Government on the health service as a challenge that demanded Powell's characteristic 'energy and integrity of mind'.[1]

After allowing himself a brief holiday on the Isle of Wight with Pam, six-year-old Susan and three-year-old Jennifer, Powell had three months before parliament resumed in which to come to grips with a massive nationalized organization that had an annual budget in 1960–61 of £860 million and a workforce of 400,000. The Ministry of Health would not have been his choice, but as he told the *Observer* in February 1961, he took to politics mainly because he rejoiced in the dispatch of business. 'I think that's quite a good phrase for describing it – I love to see business done,' he remarked, appearing to 'smack his lips at the idea'. This attitude enabled him to respond to the challenge that Macmillan had given him with the same thoroughness and zeal that he had brought to bear, sixteen years earlier, to the re-organization of the Indian Army.[2]

By 1960, the health service needed to be redirected as urgently as the Indian

Army had had to be remodelled in 1944 for the post-war world. The Conservatives had been responsible for the National Health Service for nine of its first dozen years. As the creation of Aneurin Bevan, the most socialist member of a Labour Government, the NHS had been viewed sceptically by many Conservatives. Partly for this reason, and partly because of the Treasury's persistent concern about its cost, the NHS was a prime target for economies in government spending. But its popularity with the voters, who saw it as the epitome of the welfare state, enabled ministers such as Macleod, first as Health Minister and subsequently in the Cabinet, to resist drastic cutbacks and to consolidate the NHS.

Consolidation, however, was no longer sufficient, especially in the hospital service. At a time of rising public expectations, many new and expanding towns either had no hospital or were poorly served, while existing hospitals were being rendered obsolete by medical and technological advances. This was the major problem that Powell would have to address, while somehow containing costs. His response was to reflect well on his mastery of detail and skill as an administrator, but he was quite incapable of acquiring the political touch that was essential for success in such a sensitive post.

'I was a lucky man', Powell later recalled, 'to come to the Ministry of Health at a critical time – when there was room for big thinking and long vistas.' He was, in fact, doubly fortunate, because shortly before his arrival, the Ministry had acquired a new permanent secretary, Bruce Fraser, and a new chief medical officer, Sir George Godber, both of whom were also seized of the need for 'big thinking and long vistas'. Powell, Fraser and Godber were to form a dynamic triumvirate which masterminded a new phase in the development of the NHS. The three men were highly intelligent, relished a challenge and enjoyed each other's respect. Fraser, like Powell, had read classics at Trinity College, Cambridge, but more importantly, they had worked together at the Treasury, where they got on well and Fraser had appreciated Powell's conscientiousness and intelligence. Moreover, as a result of his work on government spending, Fraser felt that public provision in capital projects such as hospitals and roads had been neglected. As a former Treasury senior official, he continued to enjoy the trust of his ex-colleagues and was well-placed to make the most of the new system of long-term planning of government spending, that followed the Plowden Report of 1961.[3]

Godber was equally important to Powell. He was a radical egalitarian who, in the words of Professor Rudolf Klein, the NHS expert, 'had never lost sight of Bevan's hope of universalizing the best'. His advice on the practical side was invaluable because he kept abreast of the latest research, but his role went much further than this because of the special position of the medical professions in the NHS. Powell quickly discovered 'the intense resistance of the professions to anything that could even be misinterpreted as lay invasion of clinical and scientific judgement'. As a result, he needed 'a bodyguard and a lightning conductor', a role that was fulfilled by his chief medical officer, 'who had therefore to think as a professional, feel as a professional, and advise as a professional'. When, shortly after Powell's appointment, a patient died due to a surgeon's 'undeniable and gross incompetence', Powell told Godber that although it was a clinical matter, he, as Minister, felt responsible. Godber, however, took care of the case and was able to assure Powell that the surgeon would never operate again. 'It was the paradigm of a great truth', Powell later noted. 'The Government and the politicians responsible for the National Health Service can accomplish anything (humanly speaking) *with* the medical profession and *nothing* against it.'⁴

Powell's approach to the NHS was differentiated from that of Conservative Ministers of Health since the 1980s by another early lesson. He had 'grabbed at' the meticulously prepared and voluminous NHS statistics 'with the same glowing expectation as I imagine every other newcomer to the job has felt'. They included every conceivable detail – cost per patient for laundry, catering, hospital pharmacy; overall cost per patient day in hospital; number of beds for different speciality per thousand of the population served; length of stay per patient, and so on. But Powell's hopes that they were the 'instrument for testing efficiency of performance' were quickly dashed. When he enquired why there were 'such wide variations between Nuneaton and Southport, or between Norfolk and Lancashire', he discovered an important truth. 'Search for the answers revealed evidence neither of inefficiency nor of waste,' he later explained. 'The impression of a precise, uniform and impartial standard, which the statistics conveyed, was a delusion.' Indeed, the figures 'concealed and often falsified the realities', since they took no account of the 'profound and often subtle variations' between catchment areas.

The moral that Powell drew from this realization would send a shiver down the spine of latter-day exponents of 'performance indicators'. 'There was no method of measurement', he judged, 'which would identify good hospitals and bad hospitals, efficient medical care and inefficient medical care, humanity or inhumanity of service.' Instead, the NHS's various 'teams' were 'continuously adapting their methods and their resources to changing demand and changing medical perspectives'. Although in some sense, the Minister was the ultimate leader, he could only give 'moral encouragement to the process: he could not enforce it by exacting quantitative performance'.⁵

One incident taught Powell the danger of relying on official interpretations of statistics, and also revealed his method of working. He had been approached by an obscure medical man, who had used statistics other than those issued by the department and warned Powell of the real extent of the emigration of young doctors. The Minister summoned his expert advisers, who told him that the statistics were faulty and the problem exaggerated. As John Rowan Wilson recalled, Powell

listened carefully to their analysis and was convinced by it. From that moment there seemed to be no means known to man by which his opinion could be changed. He directed all the powers of his exceptional mind, all his formidable personality and capacity for dialectics, to demolishing these alarmist predictions. Only one thing marred this supremely logical sequence. The predictions, as it turned out, were perfectly right.

Some years later, Powell was to become the scourge of ministers and officials at the Home Office on the immigration statistics, issuing his own dire predictions.[6]

Powell had mixed results in trying to inculcate a sense of teamwork. In the Ministry, this ethos was encouraged by his evident lack of *amour propre*. He was unconcerned to have the best office, and when – as was often the case – he worked as late as 10.30 p.m., he travelled home by underground or walked rather than have his official driver wait. As an *Observer* profile of him while he was at Health noted, the would-be musician and young poet in Powell had given him a manner – 'gentle, courteous, almost shy [that] comes as a shock to those who know only his fire-eating political reputation'. At the same time, 'the ferocious pedant, the terrier-like hunter of facts' in him, that had made him a noted textual critic and translator, could transform him into 'a terror to his civil servants'. He 'asserted his authority from the very first day', as Bryan Rayner, one of his private secretaries, recalls. Immediately after Powell's appointment, his officials had given him an extensive brief to read overnight ready for a Cabinet committee meeting the following morning at which the main item was to have been a paper by his predecessor on 'an abstruse, complex and detailed area of public health legislation'. Powell, however, shook his officials the next day by informing them that he had asked leave for the paper to be withdrawn as there were some aspects with which he disagreed. At a meeting that afternoon with the officials who specialized in the subject, Powell went through the paper, raising his objections. As Rayner remembers, 'the officials looked at each other, shuffled their feet and would say, "Yes, Minister, we think you're right." News of that shot round the Department, and had a profound effect on his future relations with it.'[7]

Powell's position vis-à-vis the NHS presented a difficult challenge – although it had 'a direct vertical line of responsibility up to the Minister', he exercises that responsibility through persons and bodies, whether lay or professional, 'who are not his to command'. Powell's intention was to bypass this problem through close consultation with the regional hospital boards. But his announcement shortly after his appointment that he wanted to meet the fourteen board chairmen as soon as possible, and to hold regular monthly meetings, raised eyebrows among his official advisers.[8]

Yet Powell's personality, for all the courteous aspects of his nature and his vision of the NHS as a team, could create awkwardnesses. He was less chatty and informal than other ministers on his hospital visits, although his *ad hoc* discussions at the end of a ward, often in the sluice room, 'where a concentrated input from all ranks and grades becomes available', helped in his drive to humanize the NHS. At times, he could be insufferably condescending, as a young worker with the Sheffield regional hospital board discovered. The young man, Roy Hattersley, later to become a Labour MP, accompanied a party of champion blood donors who were to receive their 'gold awards' from the Minister. Powell entertained Hattersley's 'Good Samaritans' with a selection of Roman opinions on blood and bleeding. 'The translation was, in one sense, essential,' Hattersley has recalled, 'for there was not one classical scholar amongst them. But it would not have been necessary if Mr Powell had resisted the temptation to use the original Latin.'[9]

An oft-quoted comment of Powell's about the NHS could be taken as a confession of his failure as its team leader. 'One of the most striking features of the National Health Service', he observed, 'is the continual, deafening chorus of complaint which rises night and day from every part of it.' Yet his point was not addressed exclusively to his personal experience, but referred to the unavoidable consequence of state funding of the NHS. 'The universal Exchequer financing of the service', he explained, 'endows everyone providing as well as using it with a vested interest in denigrating it, so that it presents what must be the unique spectacle of an undertaking that is run down by everyone engaged in it.' Complaint was seen as the most effective method of securing resources within the NHS. 'The unnerving discovery every Minister of Health makes at or near the outset of his term of office', Powell also observed, 'is that the only subject he is ever destined to discuss with the medical profession is money.'[10]

Unsurprisingly, money was at the root of the first controversy to erupt after Powell's appointment. The issue was one that had long rankled with Tories and was to mark a defeat for Powell, but it none the less served as a pointer to developments during his tenure at Health. It concerned the cost of drugs to private patients. From the beginning of the state system in 1948, NHS patients received drugs free, whereas private patients had to pay the full cost. According to Powell, in the autumn of 1949, the idea occurred to some of those drafting the Conservative policy document, *The Right Road for Britain*, to promise that private patients should also have their drugs free. Almost immediately, however, the Labour Government introduced the principle of charges on prescriptions and other items. Not wanting to be seen to be proposing a subsidy to private patients while supporting a charge for NHS patients, the Conservative leadership sought to omit the proposal. 'But it was too late,' Powell recalled, 'the policy document was already in print.'[11]

Although the promise was never repeated in any subsequent Conservative election manifesto, many Tories continued to object strongly to charging private patients for their drugs on the grounds that it was one thing to pay for consultation, but quite another to pay for drugs, since private patients had already paid for them through taxation and the NHS stamp, if they worked. The influential British Medical Association were also exercised about the issue, since GPs were unable to build up private practice because of the deterrent effect of the cost of drugs. But none of Powell's five Tory predecessors at Health had sanctioned the concession of free drugs for private patients, because it would have added to NHS costs while appearing to undermine the Government's commitment to the NHS. In early 1959,

Walker-Smith proposed making the concession at a cost of £2 million, but ministers feared that it would increase the pressure for similar concessions on school fees while provoking Opposition accusations of Tory bias against NHS patients.[12]

When Powell arrived at Health in the summer of 1960, however, the issue was again an urgent priority. The campaign had been renewed earlier in the year, when many Conservatives, buoyed by their 100-seat majority in the Commons, looked to ministers to press ahead with policies that they had previously avoided. Despite enormous pressure from two-thirds of Tory back-benchers to make the concession to private patients, the Cabinet again deferred a final decision. As chairman of the Tory back bench finance committee, Powell had undertaken not to put his name to any measure that involved extra state spending and had not signed the Commons motion in support of the concession before he was appointed to Health. The issue was still unresolved by late summer, but Powell was anxious to announce the concession at October's annual Conservative conference at Scarborough.[13]

On 20 August, in his first submission to the Prime Minister since his appointment, Powell argued that the Government's failure to act had soured relations between the Health Minister and the party, and urged that 'the concession should be made, and made now'. Macmillan merely directed Powell to the Cabinet's home affairs committee. Despite strong opposition from the Financial Secretary, Sir Edward Boyle, ministers supported the concession at a cost of £2.5–3 million. But a week before the Conservative conference, Powell's plan suffered a severe setback. He was summoned to the Cabinet on Wednesday 6 October – having appeared at Cabinet for the first time earlier that day for an item on the 'investment programme' – but ministers baulked at approving his concession because they were also considering an increase in the NHS component of national insurance. To concede free drugs to private patients at the same time as a hike in the NHS stamp would be portrayed as taxing the poor to fund hand-outs to the rich. Powell's plan would have to await a decision on the NHS stamp, but there was a feeling that the issue should be resolved once and for all.[14]

The Cabinet's caution put Powell in an awkward position when he addressed the Tory faithful at Scarborough on 15 October. The resolution for the health debate not only criticized the provision of free medical treatment for foreigners when there were no reciprocal arrangements for British tourists abroad, but also contrasted this with the fact that private British patients, unlike other taxpayers who used NHS doctors, could not secure free drugs. In his reply, Powell had no trouble in accepting the first part, arguing that the NHS was intended for the people of Britain 'and not intended to be exploited by the foreign visitor', although he defended the right to give emergency 'Good Samaritan' treatment. The second part, however, was extremely difficult for him. Although Powell supported the concession to private patients, he dare not even hint as much, as he would be in an impossible position if the Cabinet were to overrule him. His response was simply to ignore it. But this outraged one of the leading campaigners for the concession, the right-wing Yorkshire Tory MP, Geoffrey Hirst, who tackled Powell privately before publicly accusing him of having insulted the conference.[15]

Opinion in the Cabinet, however, was hardening against the concession as ministers increasingly felt that it was ruled out by any increase in the NHS stamp – of those unable to attend on Monday 18th, Brooke backed Powell, but Eccles, Macleod and Maudling were strongly opposed. Finally, on 27 October, Powell's proposed concession to private patients was rejected by the Cabinet as impracticable. Almost seventy Conservative MPs had marked the new parliamentary session by renewing their demand for the concession, but at his first appearance as Minister before sixty MPs at the party's back bench health and social security committee on 15 November, Powell had to explain its rejection by the Government.[16]

It was an extraordinary performance, as Powell made clear his own disappointment, while justifying the Government's decision on purely political grounds. Accompanied by his parliamentary under-secretary, Miss Edith Pitt, a Birmingham MP, he readily admitted that 'he had long been in favour of "free" drugs for private patients'. But pointing to the supplementary estimates of £42 million for the NHS that he had presented only the previous day, he warned that the 'present rate of increase in the cost of the National Health Service indicated that it would be necessary for the Government to take some far from palatable steps before long to restrain it'. Powell explained that the Government were bound to conclude that it would be 'politically impracticable to combine these two developments with what would be regarded as a "sectional concession" in some quarters'.[17]

Of the thirteen Tory MPs minuted as having spoken following Powell's opening remarks, eight strongly attacked the Government. Among the five MPs who voiced their doubts about the concession, Sir Alexander Spearman, a fellow advocate of market economics, reminded the Minister that the most effective way to cut spending was to confine free services to those who could not afford them, and warned of the danger of 'extravagant prescribing by the medical profession', with the risk that the need for supervision might weaken private practice. Powell thought that a way had been devised with the BMA of supervising prescriptions. But his sanguine comment that he 'would try to say nothing that would tie the Government's hands in the future', sat oddly with his revelations to the same committee only a fortnight later. Reporting on the NHS's escalating drugs bill, he commented that 'there was a tremendous sales effort without any consumer resistance, and that the prescriber and consumer had no direct interest in the cost of prescriptions. In a word, there was no "market" in the field of drugs.' It is difficult to reconcile these remarks with Powell's wish to supply more drugs free of charge.[18]

Powell's contorted logic had enabled him to support, at the same time, both a £3 million concession to private patients and the Government's rejection of it. Some Tory MPs were as impressed as others were puzzled. The issue of free drugs for private patients had, in Powell's words, 'stuck to successive

Conservative Governments and Ministers of Health like flypaper', but it was about to be killed stone dead in the much bigger controversy on NHS costs. Five years later in *Medicine and Politics*, Powell was dismissive of the arguments for free drugs, and concluded that the proposal amounted to 'a subvention for private medical care in addition to, and not in substitution for, nationalized medical care'. He was right, but he gave no hint that as Minister of Health he had pleaded with Macmillan to be allowed to make the concession.[19]

Planning and axeing

Notwithstanding Powell's attitude on subsidized drugs for private patients, no other senior post-war politician was as committed as Powell to *laissez-faire* economics. And even when he accepted that the state had a role, as in health and education, he was unrivalled in his insistence on economy in government spending. Yet on Tuesday 29 November 1960, twenty Conservative MPs witnessed the sudden transmogrification of this Gladstonian-liberal incarnate into the epitome of the state planner. Addressing a private meeting of the Tory back bench health and social security committee, Powell vouchsafed that in his four months as Minister (in the words of the minute)

> one conviction had been growing in his mind, that it was urgently necessary for the Government to plan ahead for hospitals and the health service over the next fifteen years. No shorter period was worth considering.[20]

This was state planning with a vengeance – even the Soviet rulers in their heyday had planned only five years ahead. Powell explained that he 'aimed to put on paper, now that more funds were available for hospital building, what the general picture in this field would be in 1975'. Unabashed in his new role as state planner, he claimed that 'a co-ordinated central scheme would also stimulate more public support'. Even when he had warned, in a speech a month earlier, of 'the dangers implicit in a monolithic state health service', he had declared that, 'if Leviathan tends to be rigid and centralized, at least he can combine great power and force with singleness of purpose'. But perhaps Powell the planner was not such a paradox after all, for there were shades of Brigadier Powell, the military strategist, as he sought to map the future of the NHS. And as the words quoted at the head of this chapter show, Powell believed in concentrating his efforts on very few fronts. The hospital plan was to be his major initiative, although its main elements had been devised by Fraser, his permanent secretary.[21]

The key to Powell's enthusiastic embrace of planning lay in the Conservative 1959 manifesto commitment on hospital building. Noting that there were already 'sixteen new general or mental hospitals and some fifty major extension schemes under way', the Tories pledged to 'double the amount being spent within five years' – on average, capital spending on hospitals had reached £20 million a year by the late 1950s. Although the Treasury identified the health service as a prime target for cuts immediately after the election, the Chancellor, Heathcoat Amory, finally acknowledged in early 1960 that the NHS would take a bigger share of the country's resources because of commitments on hospital building and pay – doctors and dentists were due a substantial rise. None the less, he was anxious that the growth in health spending should not exceed what could be afforded and sought a new formula for financing the NHS. Little progress had been made when Selwyn Lloyd moved in to Number 11 in July, but it was Powell's arrival at Health that broke the deadlock – on the Treasury's terms.[22]

Powell approached his first annual negotiation as a spending minister as though he was still Financial Secretary to the Treasury. At a stroke, he reversed the Ministry's traditional resistance either to increased contributions and charges or to cuts in the estimates. He not only accepted Selwyn Lloyd's suggestion to raise the NHS stamp by one shilling, but in addition, volunteered to cut £45 million from the forecast estimate of spending for 1961–62. The effect would be to push the share of NHS revenue derived from contributions and charges (as distinct from taxation) above the 20 per cent limit that the Macmillan Government had imposed on themselves – this had been the level set for contributions by Beveridge before charges were introduced.[23]

Strong objections were raised in Cabinet when Powell supported the Chancellor's proposed increase in the NHS stamp. In particular, Boyd-Carpenter, the Minister for National Insurance and Pensions, was concerned that it would hit the low-paid very hard, especially since it would coincide with heavier deductions for many workers in the new graduated system of national insurance contributions. Many other ministers were alarmed at the prospect of raising the stamp at the same time as announcing economies on the scale that Powell envisaged. Finally, after two further Cabinet meetings in late October, ministers agreed to increase the NHS stamp by one shilling to 3s/4d, yielding £50 million. The announcement was to be made with the publication of the 1961–62 estimates in February 1961.[24]

Powell, however, was not satisfied that this controversial increase in contributions would be sufficient. He was concerned, as he had been as Financial Secretary, to keep current spending virtually constant, with no allowance for inflation. His immediate aim was to reduce the NHS estimate for 1961–62 to the same level as the original estimate for the current year, 1960–61. Actual spending in 1960–61 exceeded the original estimate by £42 million, and the estimate for 1961–62 had incorporated this excess spending. Powell would have none of it. But he also had a longer term objective in proposing that the 1961–62 estimate should be reduced by £40 million. In return for stringent control of current spending, he expected in the future to secure the promised increase in capital spending.[25]

Powell subsequently reduced his target for economies to £27 million, but in order to achieve even this figure he envisaged cutting the subsidies on welfare milk and foods; increasing the charge for dentures and the price of spectacle lenses; raising the cost of amenity beds in hospitals; and doubling the prescription charge from one shilling to 2s/- per item. Although some members of the Cabinet's home affairs committee were concerned that the measures were too severe, most ministers supported Powell's proposals. Despite Macmillan's qualms that the Government were attempting too much, and serious misgivings about the political risks from Eccles and Macleod, Powell's package was finally approved by the Cabinet. Powell had achieved his immediate aim. Taken together, the increase in the NHS stamp and his economies would yield about £60 million, thereby reducing the estimate for 1961–62 to the level of the original estimate for 1960–61 – though this excluded the cost of the pay award for doctors and dentists, for which his Ministry had to seek £37.6 million from Parliament in December 1960. Following press speculation about Powell's plans to cut NHS spending, he was depicted by Vicky, the cartoonist, in the *Evening Standard*, wielding an axe. Vicky was to repeat the image when Powell came to announce his stringent economies in early 1961 and triggered a political explosion.[26]

Yet at the same time Powell was preparing to launch the ambitious and expensive hospital plan that he had trailed privately with Tory MPs in late November. The plan was the culmination of professional aspirations (in 1959 the BMA had proposed a ten-year, £750 million building programme); years of lobbying the Treasury by the Ministry of Health for a longer-term commitment on capital spending; and the new vogue for planning. Fraser, the permanent secretary at Health, had played a key role in smoothing the way with the Treasury and preparing a practical scheme, with the result that Powell was able to unveil the hospital plan to the chairmen of the fourteen regional hospital boards on 20 December. Powell told Rab Butler that the plan would be a 'durable asset politically'. 'We all felt the Minister of Health had done an excellent job,' Butler commented to Macmillan, who wrote to congratulate Powell.[27]

Almost six months into his stewardship of the NHS, Powell explained his thinking on NHS spending and planning to the Conservative Research Department's policy committee on the future of the social services. He saw the NHS as 'simply the method in this country of channelling resources into medical care'. His duty, as the Minister, was to see that spending on the NHS did not rise out of proportion with the growth in the national income, since if it became necessary to retrench, 'the result would be a worse service than the country would otherwise have had'. But there was neither a 'right amount, nor an economic one, to be spent on the NHS'. '*L'appetit vient en mangeant*' – demand was unlimited. 'On strict economic grounds the absolute minimum of National Health Service was probably desirable.'

On the future of the NHS, however, Powell shared the perspective of the medical profession. The resulting hospital plan would not come cheap. 'The predominant movement of modern medicine', he told the research department committee, 'was from the general practitioner to the hospital', with the emphasis on 'increased specialization and expensive apparatus'. Powell saw this as 'the central fact' in the development of the NHS 'to which other considerations were secondary'. The expansion of the hospital service, that he was about to announce, 'would mean not only a simple increase in the number of beds, but the replacement of our present hospitals by a smaller number of beds in really modern hospitals'.[28]

It was in this context that Powell stumbled on 'Powell's Law'. As he later took great delight in explaining, Powell's Law states that 'there is no such thing as a bed'. There is, however, one exception to it, namely, 'except when planning a new hospital'. An estimate had to be made of what hospital capacity should be provided for a given catchment population. The 'bed' was merely the unit that was used in assessing 'how many patients would be receiving the various sorts of hospital treatment at any one time', and had no relationship with the real object, which was the effectiveness of the treatment and patients' subsequent recovery. Powell had long been aware of the importance of this distinction, since as a back bench MP in 1953, he had drawn the attention of his fellow Tory back-benchers to a 'snap test' in Birmingham, where hospital overcrowding had been reduced by sending home patients who were able to rely on local authority services. But he had to grow accustomed to talking about hospital capacity in numbers of beds, and the provision of various forms of care in terms of beds per thousand of population in a hospital catchment area.[29]

The hospital building plan was given a high-profile launch on Tuesday 17 January 1961, with Powell claiming that it represented 'the beginning of a new phase in the history of the hospital service and therefore the National Health Service as a whole'. His press conference offered the incongruous sight of the former scourge of Whitehall spending departments proclaiming that his ten-year plan might cost about £500 million in total. The Treasury's concern to control costs required an annual re-assessment of the programme and regional hospital boards were to receive firm figures for only two years in advance. On the same day, regional health boards were asked to submit their proposals for hospital building work to be started by 1970–71. These proposals were to be prepared on the 'tentative' assumption that hospital capital spending would rise to about £50 million a year by 1965–66. The maximum cost of individual projects that boards were to be allowed to undertake was to be doubled from £30,000 to £60,000. Accompanying the circular were detailed Hospital Building Notes, drawn up centrally by Powell's officials. These directions stipulated that the NHS should be based on a network of District General Hospitals, each equipped with the main medical specialities and with 600–800 beds, serving a catchment population of 100,000–150,000. As a result, most examination and treatment was to be performed at one site, and the average number of beds for acute cases was to be reduced from 3.8 per thousand population to 3.3.[30]

Yet Powell's launch of his capital investment programme in the NHS was overshadowed by rumours of what he might be about to do to the existing

NHS. During January, it was reported that Powell had attended the Cabinet to finalize details of his expected statement on the NHS budget. 'Apart from the impending first budget of Mr Selwyn Lloyd,' noted David Wood, political correspondent of *The Times*, 'Conservative back-benchers await no revelation of Government policy in the next few weeks and months with a sharper appetite than they do Mr Enoch Powell's financial proposals for the Health Service.' And in a comment that, with hindsight, has a certain irony, Wood continued, 'Conservative back-benchers are sure that these are to be Health Estimates with a difference, if only because Mr Powell is a Minister of Health with a difference who is believed to have been given the department by Mr Macmillan to see what impact new and strong-minded management can make on a stubborn problem.' The measures that Powell was about to announce were certainly financial proposals with a difference, but instead of giving new hope to the Tories they revived the Opposition. Labour's third successive election defeat and the factional warfare that split the party following their conference vote in favour of unilateral nuclear disarmament in October 1960 had allowed the Tories an easy ride since October 1959. All this was about to change.[31]

Hero or villain?

The sense of anticipation was heightened before Powell rose at the despatch box on 1 February 1961 to make his statement on 'National Health Service (Increased Charges and Contributions)', because it was his first appearance at a major set-piece occasion in the Commons since his appointment the previous July. Apart from the routine matters of answering oral questions and seeking approval for supplementary estimates to cover increased pay for doctors and dentists, his only other appearances had been to speak on non-controversial legislation, such as the Human Tissues Bill that clarified the law regarding tissue and organ transplants. Cutting the NHS budget while increasing NHS charges and contributions was of a different political magnitude. The occasion was bound to be highly charged, but Powell's statement was to mark a turning point in the 1959–64 parliament.[32]

It was no matter that Powell began by stating that the forecast estimate of health spending for the coming year, 1961–62, had shown that there would have been an increase of eleven per cent, following increases of eight per cent in the current year and six per cent the year before. Neither was his reiteration of the Government's commitment to a long-term programme of hospital modernization any help. Powell's explanations of the need to take 'certain steps to reduce the net estimates' primed MPs to fear the worst. There was shock at his increasing substantially the charges for dentures and spectacles, and the doubling of the charge for amenity beds. Angry cries of 'shame' and 'disgraceful' greeted his doubling of the prescription charge. 'They never had it so good,' mocked an MP as Powell announced the hike in contributions. Further cries of 'shame' accompanied him as he sat down, having revealed that his measures would cut £65 million in a full year from the net health estimates.[33]

Powell had provided Labour with a heaven-sent opportunity to find a crusade on which they could re-unite after their schism over nuclear weapons. The NHS was the perfect salve for Labour's wounds, while Powell, who looked and sounded the part as a flinty-faced die-hard, was the perfect target. The Opposition seized the political initiative from the moment that Kenneth Robinson, the shadow health spokesman, replied to Powell's statement by attacking the increase in 'a poll tax' (the NHS stamp), that would hit those least able to bear it, and taunting Powell, in a reminder of his earlier resignation, by suggesting that he should have resigned as Health Minister rather than accept increased NHS charges. 'I would have been betraying my trust if I had,' Powell retorted, arguing that without economies, the future development of the NHS would have had to be curtailed. To Powell's contention that the choice lay between his measures or limiting the NHS, Labour MPs chorused 'No!' These exchanges set the tone for a series of fierce clashes on the measures as Labour sustained their attack over the following month and won widespread coverage in the press for the issue. Pressing home their advantage, they tabled a censure motion against the Government that was debated a week after Powell's statement, and mounted a vigorous fight against the legislation that was necessary to give effect to his measures.[34]

Many Conservatives welcomed Powell's economies as a sign that, with their large majority, the Government were finally prepared to grasp the nettle of what they regarded as the heavy burden of the welfare state. But a significant number of Tories were deeply perturbed. Although Powell was contemptuous of a motion signed by 26 Tory MPs that called for relief to low wage-earners, he was left in no doubt of the concern felt on the Conservative back benches over the increase in charges when he faced the party's health and social security committee on the eve of Labour's censure debate. By far the most damaging criticism was made publicly by Sir Derek Walker-Smith, the former chairman of the 1922 Committee and Powell's immediate predecessor at Health. Commenting in the *Daily Telegraph*, Walker-Smith observed that the measures were 'the sort of proposals which Chancellors have been urging on Health Ministers at times of financial pressure from the start of the Health Service'.[35]

Powell had to face a rumbustious sixty-six-minute diatribe from George Brown, Labour's deputy leader, who was undeterred in his attack on a 'monstrous policy' by the presence, at his side, of Hugh Gaitskell, whose imposition of NHS charges in 1951 had split the Labour Government. The flavour of Brown's emotional assault can be gleaned from his comment on Powell's raising NHS charges instead of taxing the profits of the pharmaceutical industry. 'The Minister finds it easier to take it out of mothers, their children and the sick', Brown declared, 'than to take on this vast, great industry.' And for good measure, he wound up by quoting from Powell's early poems the following lines:

I hate the ugly, hate the old,
I hate the lame and weak.[36]

In his reply, Powell ignored Brown's onslaught, but his speech confirmed his poor reputation as a debater – a weakness that the *Observer* had highlighted only the previous Sunday. 'Both in private conversation and while addressing the Commons,' the paper commented, 'he still tends to lecture, as if explaining complicated matters to an undergraduate audience – he has been accused, in fact, of being lucid to the point of incomprehensibility.' On this occasion Powell was at least lucid. But though he sought to concentrate on 'the human element', his reply was packed with references to committees and statistics, and sounded like a report by a company secretary or economic analyst. The kernel of his case was clear enough – the decision to 'adjust' the financing of the NHS in the light of rising costs meant that the service was 'underpinned', not 'undermined'. He was unable, however, to summon either the passion that had inspired his Hola Camp speech, or the heart-felt conviction that had informed his attack on the Royal Titles Bill. Powell ploughed on remorselessly, to a rising chorus of complaint from the Labour benches as he refused to take an intervention from Margaret Herbison – she later reminded MPs that in April 1951 Powell had attacked Gaitskell's measures on the grounds that the 'most deserving', especially pensioners, would decline to reclaim their prescription charges from the National Assistance Board. 'Austerity fits him like a hair shirt,' the shadow health minister, Robinson, declared of his opposite number. The Government won a majority of 90 at the end of the censure debate, but with tempers already frayed Labour sought to block the financial resolution that would bring the new NHS charges into effect. The Opposition's anger and their frustration at the chair's handling of the vote finally boiled over, and the sitting ended in uproar at 1.21 a.m.[37]

The impact of the NHS measures had proved the Labour MP, J.P.W. Mallalieu, right in his prediction of the previous September in the *New Statesman* that Powell 'could blow the close corporation of present-day politics wide open, to the dismay of his leaders and the delight of his followers. He could even reinvigorate the Labour Party.' Later in February, the Labour front-bencher, Richard Crossman, noted in his diary that the 'morale' of the parliamentary party and of the party in the country had been 'enormously improved' by the all-night sittings on the Health Service. As the political editor of the *Sunday Times*, James Margach, wrote of the row over the NHS, there had been 'nothing like it since Suez'. The debate was inevitably personalized, because of Powell's high-principled approach and his well-known enthusiasm for cutting government spending. The Government had to resort to using the procedural device known as the 'guillotine', in order to limit the debate on the NHS measures and overcome Labour's opposition – the first use of the 'guillotine' since the Rent Bill during 1956–57, another item with which Powell was closely identified. From the outset of the controversy, as Peregrine Worsthorne pointed out in the *Sunday Telegraph*, opinion was polarized between, on the one hand, centre and right-wing Conservatives, and, on the other hand, the Labour Party – 'the former sense that they have discovered a genuine hero and the latter a genuine villain'.[38]

But the official papers and party archive for the period reveal that the crude characterization of Powell as either 'hero' or 'villain' on the NHS is wide of the mark. If he was a villain, he was a singularly inept one since the political storm over his measures ruled out any further increase in charges or contributions during the remaining three and a half years of Conservative Government. After February 1961, any extra spending on the NHS would have to be financed from general taxation.

This unintended limitation on Powell's freedom of manoeuvre in funding the NHS reinforced his strong predisposition, when setting future estimates of spending, to act as though he were Financial Secretary. In July 1961, he acceded to the Treasury's demand for a limit of 2.5 per cent as the maximum increase in departmental spending for the coming financial year, 1962–63. Although this figure was only about half the average rate of increase in health spending over the previous four years, it was incorporated in the new system of long-term planning for government income and expenditure (PESC). Health spending would therefore only be allowed to rise by a total of £80 million over the next four years (until 1965–66). In order to meet this target, hospital running costs would have to rise by only 2 per cent a year. Powell's officials doubted that these targets were feasible – the overall limit of 2.5 per cent became known as Powell's 'contract' with the Treasury.[39]

The problem with Powell was his failure to reconcile satisfactorily the dual role that he adopted as Minister of Health – on the one hand, as a surrogate Financial Secretary on NHS spending, and, on the other hand, as an arch-planner on hospital building. Every minister has to strike a balance in the conflict between keeping within budget and satisfying wider demands. But striking a balance was not Powell's strong point. Instead of trying to reconcile this conflict and find some sensible compromise, Powell acted as though his best approach was to adopt two quite distinct roles and to pursue them both as vigorously as possible. As a result, he sought to impose the tightest possible control on current spending while pressing on with an ambitious hospital building plan that was bound to prove highly expensive. Powell deserves great credit for the modernization of Britain's hospitals, but he stored up trouble by failing to resolve satisfactorily his conflicting duties as a minister.

One incident perfectly illustrates the dichotomy in Powell between Treasury hawk *manqué* and spending minister. In September 1961, he became *plus royaliste que le roi* when he wrote to the Chancellor, objecting to the Plowden report's recommendation that forecasts of government income and expenditure should be prepared and published for a period of years ahead, instead of relying on the existing system of a Budget and estimates that only related to one year ahead. Three years earlier, Powell had advocated longer-term planning of government spending, but he had coupled it with a call for planned reductions in the level of spending each year. Whereas the Treasury accepted that Plowden's proposed new system, known as PESC, would lead to firmer control of government spending by confronting ministers with the need for priorities and the implications of their decisions, Powell dismissed it as 'an exercise in escapism'. He argued that it would be 'destructive of Treasury control and will strongly tend to the increase of public expenditure and inflation' – politicians would base their forecasts of government income on optimistic assumptions about growth; they would promise to expand existing services; they would find it virtually impossible to forecast a decline in the share of national income spent on public services; and they would build in inflation, since any rise in prices would lead to demands for extra cash from the Chancellor to honour the long-term plans that had been made in 'real' terms.[40]

There was rich irony in Powell's opposition to planning government finances for even four or five years ahead, since he was passionately committed to pressing ahead with his *fifteen-year* hospital plan. Indeed, he was about to begin a fierce battle with the Treasury over his insistence on publishing a White Paper, that put flesh on his massive programme of hospital moderniza-tion, and his demand to increase future spending plans on hospital building. Presumably, this was one reason why Powell wrote to Selwyn Lloyd about the Plowden report 'as a colleague and not in a departmental capacity'. But the point was not lost on Otto Clarke, the Treasury official who drafted a note for the Chancellor to send to Powell. As Clarke counselled, the Government were, in effect, already committed several years ahead in the field of defence and social services, whether this was formally recognized or not. 'The problem here (not least in the hospital service) is to provide a sufficient degree of assurance ahead to enable proper and economical planning to be carried out.' It was a classic piece of Whitehall drafting – rarely has the bracket been used to such telling effect.[41]

Although Powell failed to dissuade the Chancellor from introducing the PESC system, he won his main battle on the hospital plan. At his insistence, the modernization programme was described as a 'ten-year plan'. Finally, on 23 January 1962, Powell published his White Paper. 'The Hospital Plan for England and Wales' totalled nearly 300 pages, the bulk of which set out detailed building proposals for the regional health boards, based on the submissions that had been requested from their chairmen twelve months earlier. The plan made a commitment to build 90 new hospitals, substantially modernize another 134 and introduce 556 other big projects. A separate Scottish plan was published on the same day. In a truly remarkable comment, Powell proudly proclaimed that the new hospital plan 'marked one of the most important days of the health service, because it gave the opportunity to plan the hospital service on a scale not possible anywhere else, certainly on this side of the Iron Curtain'.[42]

In ebullient mood, Powell told a meeting of the Tory back bench health and social security committee two days after publication of the hospital plan, that (in the words of the minute) 'he had been very pleased at the reception which it had been given by the public and the press, especially by the British Medical Association, whom they had "done proud"'. Casting aside his Gladstonian *persona*, Powell declared that whereas the BMA had proposed spending around £750 million, the plan 'included schemes worth £700 million in England and Wales and over £70 million in Scotland to be started in the first ten years'. By referring to the total value of the schemes that were due to be *started* during the ten-year programme, Powell was quoting the highest possible figure for total spending – the agreed forecast total for the first ten years of the plan was £500 million, of which £200 million was allocated for the first five years. The Treasury regarded these figures as estimates for planning purposes, but Powell could justifiably claim that, in crude terms, the net effect of the complete programme would be to replace about one half of the existing English and Welsh hospitals – between one-quarter and one-third within the first ten years.

When Powell turned to briefing MPs on how best to deal with criticisms of the plan, he revealed something of the optimistic assumptions on which he was heavily dependent for its ultimate success. Arguing, not unreasonably, that it was the turn of the hospitals to have the same priority in building that had previously been given to housing and schools, he claimed that 'the long-term plan was in itself a form of financial control in that it put the hospital building programme on a firm financial basis'. This latter point was essentially the same as the one that had been made by Clarke at the Treasury in his rebuttal of Powell's critique of PESC. Powell, however, went further in his claims for the plan, suggesting that it 'could also be defended as an instrument of actual economy, insofar as the replacement of old hospitals by new ones which could be run more efficiently was the best kind of economy'.[43]

This last assertion raised two problems. The first concerned 'the replacement of old hospitals', since this was another way of describing hospital closures, the aspect of Powell's plan that had most worried ministers. The draft White Paper had explicitly acknowledged that the plan involved the closure of a large number of hospitals, and Powell had argued that the public would understand that the advantages of new hospitals would outweigh the disadvantages of closures. But other ministers feared the reaction, especially since in many Tory county strongholds, Tory supporters were active in voluntary work for their local 'cottage' hospitals. As a result, the wording in the White Paper was changed from 'some hospitals would be closed' to 'the use of some hospitals would be changed'. When Tory anger mounted as the reality of closures became apparent, Powell countered unsentimentally that 'the patient of the second half of the twentieth century would look for all the facilities provided by a central hospital. The cottage hospitals all dated from the "horse and buggy" age.' Although Macmillan was unimpressed by his reasoning, Powell insisted to Tory MPs in 1963 that he had 'greater qualms about retaining hospitals than closing them, in view of the all too frequent deaths that might have been avoided by removing patients to the district general hospital'. He could only promise to 'do everything in his power to minimize the inevitable political friction' caused by closure.[44]

The second problem concerned the vexed issue of running costs. This was a bone of contention between the Ministry of Health and the Treasury. Powell had told the Commons in February 1961 that 'the modernization of the hospital service should reflect itself in genuine economy in the running costs of the hospitals', but the Treasury were sceptical and expected that current spending would increase. Indeed, their view was reflected in the White Paper's assumption of a real increase in hospital running costs by the 1970s 'due ... to a higher standard of service'.[45]

This difference on running costs reflected the deeper problem that came to confront Powell on the hospital plan and NHS spending in general. The July 1961 limit of 2.5 per cent on annual increases in the total health service budget proved unrealistic, and by 1963 it was clear that the limits would have to be breached. The Ministry expected hospital running costs, that had been set at 2 per cent, to increase by at least 2.5 per cent during the next five years. In a reversal of roles, Powell, the former Treasury hardliner, had to go cap in hand to Boyd-Carpenter, the former champion of welfare spending who had become the first Chief Secretary to the Treasury, to seek extra funds. Unless the money was forthcoming, Powell indicated, 'there would not only be a great deal of ill feeling and criticism but ... essential maintenance would be skimped'. As a result, a supplementary increase in NHS spending was made in 1963, and again in 1964.[46]

More ominously, it soon became clear that NHS capital spending was rising because the cost of the hospital plan was escalating. This was partly due to an increase in the scope of projects, as a wider range of facilities was incorporated in the new hospitals, but there had also been serious under-estimation of costs. This excess spending would lead to delays as regional hospital boards struggled to keep within budget. When the first up-dated hospital plan was published in 1963, the ten-year spending total increased by 20 per cent to £600 million (in his address to Tory MPs Powell again preferred to use the higher figure for the value of schemes that would be started – this was now £800 million). Publicly, Powell proclaimed the plan's rising cost as a triumph. When a television interviewer mistakenly mentioned the initial £500 million estimate, Powell interjected,

> it's up since then. You've been looking at the first edition. The hospital plan has been revised and carried forward another two years since then. And the new ten years is a £600 million programme – that's England and Wales.

Powell also added that, 'this is going to happen, and no-one, short of generating a world war, can stop it'. This last comment showed scant respect for the Treasury's effort to exert some control over spending by insisting that the total figure was a conditional planning estimate, not a firm commitment.[47]

By 1964, after Powell had left the Ministry, the estimated ten-year cost of the hospital plan had leapt by a further £150 million to £750 million, and there was growing evidence that the final cost might be considerably higher. Yet none of this should detract from Powell's achievement. As Sir Kenneth Robinson, who served as the first Minister of Health in the 1964 Labour Government, commented in 1993, the hospital plan was Powell's 'great achievement'. He also suspected that possibly it could only have been achieved by Powell, as an ex-Treasury Minister with a 'dry' reputation. 'Previously', Robinson recalled, 'you never knew whether you were going to get any capital money the year after next.' Although Fraser, the permanent secretary at the time, should also share much of the credit, Powell's role had been crucial in giving the plan his full ministerial backing and insisting that it should cover at least ten years. It is extraordinary that the politician who was most strongly opposed to 1960s-style state planning should have erected one of its most practical monuments.[48]

Hypocrite on immigration?

It has become almost a commonplace to say that, despite his anti-immigration stand at the end of the 1960s, as Minister of Health during the early years of the decade Powell deliberately recruited large numbers of black and brown immigrant nurses from the Commonwealth and colonies to work in Britain's hospitals. 'It gives a certain amount of wry amusement', Lord Hailsham has remarked, 'that the person who imported the Asian [sic] nurses was the Minister of Health at that time, who was Mr Enoch Powell, and he was the one who was the architect of that.' It has also been alleged that the nurses' pay dispute of 1962 was attributable in part to Powell's using the recruitment of immigrant nurses to hold down wages. Geoffrey (later Lord) Rippon mischievously suggested during the Shadow Cabinet's weekend talks at Selsdon in early 1970 that the Macmillan Government had 'listened to Enoch's argument about not paying the nurses more because of the black girls'.[49]

When later questioned on the number of immigrants working in the NHS in the early 1960s, Powell stated that, 'recruitment was in the hands of the hospital authorities, but this was something that happened of its own accord given that there was no bar upon entry and employment in the United Kingdom to those from the West Indies or anywhere else [in the Commonwealth or colonies]'. He 'had no power to dissuade them [the hospital authorities]', and had not wished for any such power, since 'this was part of a whole picture'. The 'whole picture' to which Powell referred was the law on British nationality – control of Commonwealth immigration only came into effect in July 1962, two years after his appointment as Minister.[50]

Powell must have been aware of the importance to the NHS of immigrant nursing and medical staff from his hospital visits as Minister. In addition, at the end of 1961, the papers prepared by his officials on nursing recruitment and wastage should have acquainted him with the facts. In one respect, he very much welcomed the presence of immigrant nurses and doctors, namely on condition that they were temporary workers, training in Britain and subsequently returning to their own countries as qualified doctors and nurses. In particular, he faced a serious shortage of doctors, principally as a result of a disastrous underestimate of the future supply of doctors by the Willink Report in 1957, which explains his readiness as Minister to acknowledge that almost 2,000 Commonwealth and foreign doctors came to Britain each year for temporary work, and filled 34 per cent of junior hospital posts. When the issue of 'recruitment from overseas' was raised with Powell during the nurses' strike, at a meeting of the Tory back bench health and social security committee on 26 March 1962, he tried to play it down. He is minuted as having stated that

> the best available figures showed that less than seven per cent of nurses came from the Commonwealth; but this proportion had not been increasing at all fast in recent years and many of them were student nurses.[51]

During his early months at Health, Powell was concerned about another aspect of immigration that affected the health service, namely the extra demands made on the NHS by immigrants. Shortly after his appointment, Powell specifically asked Butler, the then Home Secretary, that he should be appointed to the ministerial committee, chaired by Lord Kilmuir, that kept a watching brief on the need for immigration control and that was about to be re-constituted. Matters of health, in addition to problems of housing and schools, were among the social considerations that were raised by immigration, but it was primarily because of Powell's experiences in Wolverhampton that he was anxious to serve on Kilmuir's committee. 'It is understood', the Cabinet Secretary, Sir Norman Brook, minuted Macmillan on 24 November 1960, 'that the Minister of Health would like to be a member of the committee because the problem arises in a particularly sharp form in his constituency.' Powell's request was granted, and he became one of nine ministers whose discussions during 1961 led to the first imposition of controls on Commonwealth immigration. As the papers reveal, however, Powell favoured a more drastic measure than was finally adopted.[52]

Pressure on the Government to introduce controls became almost irresistible as the economic boom drew 58,000 immigrants to Britain during 1960. The increased numbers arriving in Britain from the Caribbean and the Asian sub-continent since the mid-1950s had generated resentment in the industrial areas where they settled among working-class and lower-middle-class residents, who felt that their neighbourhoods were being changed without their consent. The title of the re-constituted Kilmuir committee, the Committee on Commonwealth Migrants, was euphemistic and the minutes reveal the contortions into which ministers were driven as they fretted over methods of controlling the numbers of black and brown immigrants without appearing to be racially motivated.[53]

Even before the Kilmuir committee's first meeting, Powell sought to impress upon his colleagues the problems associated with Commonwealth immigration. On 11 January 1961, he circulated a letter that he had received from the Town Clerk of Wolverhampton, Mr R.J. Meddings, expressing the view of the council's health committee 'that for a number of reasons the immigrants do make a disproportionate claim on the Health Services of the town'. In particular, Meddings stated, immigrants occupied properties in the centre of the town 'more intensively than is customary in this country', and made heavier demands on both TB and ordinary hospital beds, and on day nurseries, and frequently received 'priority for the allocation of hospital beds for confinements'. Meddings concluded that his health committee 'would urge that before an immigrant is allowed to settle in this country he should at least have been declared as medically fit'.[54]

Powell kept up the pressure at the committee's first meeting in February with a radical suggestion that immigration should be curbed from Britain's remaining colonies as well as from independent Commonwealth countries. He proposed a fundamental change in Britain's citizenship law and was asked to explain his idea in writing. The argument took him back to the British Nationality Act of 1948, on which he had briefed the Tory front bench when he worked in the party's Parliamentary Secretariat. In his paper, submitted on 11 April 1961, Powell argued that if 'we desire to impose limitations or conditions on the entry of coloured British subjects into this country', it was essential to replace the existing legal definition of a British subject by creating a new citizenship of the United Kingdom. Under existing law, British subjects who had a right of entry into Britain consisted of the citizens of independent Commonwealth countries listed under Britain's nationality law, and the citizens of the United Kingdom and Colonies – this latter category was 'an *omnium gatherum* containing all the denizens of the Commonwealth'.[55]

Powell argued that his plan would put United Kingdom citizenship on the same footing as that of other independent Commonwealth countries, who had restricted the full privileges of citizenship, including free entry, to their own citizens. Crucially, it would also divide the existing 'citizenship of the United Kingdom and Colonies' into a 'citizenship of the United Kingdom' and a separate 'citizenship of the Colonies'. The full privileges of citizenship, including the right of entry, would be attached only to the new United Kingdom citizenship. Powell accepted that if it were desired to retain for Irish citizens their existing freedom of entry, it would be necessary to equate their status in the United Kingdom not with that of 'British subjects', but with that of the new United Kingdom citizenship.

The effect of Powell's proposal would have been to create two classes of British subjects, with different rights of entry. His purpose was manifest: to deny the right of entry not only to the citizens of independent Commonwealth countries, but also to those of Britain's remaining colonies. He pointed out that Jamaica, where many immigrants came from, was still a colony. He accepted that his plan would involve minor amendments to the citizenship law in other Commonwealth countries, and 'would therefore have to be taken in concert'.[56]

Plainly, Powell's proposals would have caused a major ruction in the colonies if they had ever been adopted, however much he might argue that other Commonwealth countries had their own citizenships and that a citizenship of the United Kingdom was only a 'natural further development' of the concept of 'British subject'. A colonial row was unlikely to have worried Powell, given his hostility to the idea of empire. But, an inter-departmental working party that examined in detail various proposals for controlling immigration, warned the Kilmuir committee that creating a new, distinct United Kingdom citizenship 'would tend to weaken the ties between the United Kingdom and Colonies'.[57]

Of much greater significance, however, was the working party's additional objection to Powell's plan, namely that 'some other classes of citizens of the United Kingdom and Colonies, such as Europeans in Kenya, might resent being deprived of their citizenship'. Although independence might bring about Kenyan citizenship for such people, the working party, in best Whitehall tradition, thought it preferable not to force the pace at this stage. As it turned out citizenship was to become a crucial issue for non-African minorities (both European and Asian) at the time of Kenyan independence, and the decision of the Kilmuir committee to keep the category of citizen of the United Kingdom and Colonies was to have far-reaching consequences when, in 1967–68, large numbers of Kenyan Asians who had not opted for Kenyan citizenship took up their right to emigrate to Britain.[58]

In early 1961, however, the inter-departmental working party had made little reference to Kenyan Asians, and, indeed, the issue of immigration from East Africa was considered to be of minor importance. Most immigrants were coming from the West Indies and the Asian sub-continent, and it was these people that Butler, the Home Secretary, had in mind when he warned the Kilmuir committee in May that the projected intake of immigrants for 1961 had soared to an estimated 150,000, and possibly 200,000, and that by the end of the year the coloured population would number 500,000.[59]

By the summer of 1961, Powell and his colleagues agreed that the housing problems and social tension being caused by this large-scale non-white immigration could no longer be ignored. Faced with an expected surge in numbers, ministers were virtually unanimous on the need to act – even the liberal-minded Macleod came to accept that legislation was a 'sad necessity', and only Sir Edward Boyle, who was not a member of the committee, but who attended in July, remained strongly opposed. Accordingly, the Kilmuir committee finally recommended to the Cabinet that the balance of advantage had shifted in favour of controls on Commonwealth immigration. The form of legislation that was proposed, however, was less drastic than Powell wanted, since citizenship of the United Kingdom and Colonies was to be retained, and immigration control was to be introduced on the basis of different categories of passport holders. This difference between Powell and his colleagues in 1960–61 was to widen the disagreement between them on immigration after the party lost office in 1964, culminating in 1968 in one of the most vivid political explosions in modern times.[60]

11

Humanizing the NHS

There they stand, isolated, majestic, imperious, brooded over by the gigantic water-tower and chimney combined, rising unmistakable and daunting out of the countryside – the asylums which our forefathers built with such immense solidity to express the notions of their day.

Enoch Powell, on the Victorian mental hospitals that he planned to close, March 1961.

Care in the community

Like Macleod before him at the Ministry of Health, Powell was concerned to humanize the NHS. In this respect, his public statements rarely did him justice. No matter how much he might stress the 'human aspect', he rarely succeeded in injecting it convincingly into his speeches. Yet there was one startling exception. The problem of mental illness evoked a strong response in him. In his first speech to the Conservative annual conference as Minister of Health, he admitted to 'a personal bias' for more generous attention to the mentally ill. In January 1961, his launch of the new hospital plan presaged a new approach to their treatment, and two months later, Powell delivered an impassioned plea on behalf of the mentally sick. His radical comments were to have a profound impact on the treatment of mental illness in Britain.[1]

Powell's dramatic pronouncement was made at the annual meeting of the National Association of Mental Health in London on Thursday 9 March 1961 – only three days after the 'guillotine' debate in the Commons on the Bill to implement his controversial increases in NHS charges. His unsuspecting audience of 900 members of the association had grown used to hearing fine platitudes from politicians, but Powell used the occasion to announce a revolution in official thinking on the mentally ill that was inspired by humanity, insight and passion.

As Powell informed his audience, he had 'intimated to the hospital authorities', who were drawing up proposals for the hospital plan, 'that in fifteen years' time there may well be needed not more than half as many places in hospitals for mental illness as there are today'. His words implied 'nothing less than the elimination of by far the greater part of this country's mental hospitals as they exist today', and he spoke of Britain's many outdated asylums in the chillingly evocative passage quoted at the head of this chapter. Powell was in no doubt that 'the powers of resistance to our assault' had to be overcome. He spoke of setting 'the torch to the funeral pyre' of the mental hospitals – imagery that he was to use again seven years later in an even more apocalyptic speech – and declared that 'if we err, it is our duty to err on the side of ruthlessness'. The passion of Powell's condemnation of the old asylums seemed to unlock in him an ability to express an humanitarianism that he was rarely able to convey and sometimes seemed to lack. The logical conclusion of Powell's policy was clear. As he argued, the hospital plan made no sense

> unless the medical profession outside the hospital service can be supported
> in this task by a whole new development of the local authority services for
> the old, for the sick and for the mentally ill and mentally subnormal.

Powell had committed the Government to care in the community.[2]

'I thought he had gone over the top,' was the reaction of Sir George Godber, the Government's chief medical officer, when he first saw the draft of the speech. But there was no doubting the force of either Powell's conviction or of his message. 'The whole mood was of being startled,' recalled Edith Morgan, who had been in the audience,

> We all sat up, looked at each other and wondered what had happened.
> Because we'd been struggling for years to get the idea of community care
> and the eventual closure of mental hospitals on the map and here it was
> offered to us on a plate.[3]

What had motivated Powell's declaration of intent? The cynical explanation is that care in the community seemed to offer a much cheaper option for central government than the alternative of renovating or replacing the many Victorian asylums that were in a bad condition by the 1960s. In reality, however, several factors lay behind Powell's championing of community care. The development in the 1950s of new antipsychotic drugs in some cases offered the prospect of treatment for, and sometimes cure from, mental illness without recourse to hospital. The major reforms introduced in the Mental Health Act of 1959 reinforced the system of voluntary treatment and tightened the procedures and safeguards for compulsory detention and treatment. Government statistics also showed that the number of occupied beds in mental hospitals had declined since 1954, and a new spirit of partnership was developing between local government and the Health Service. These changes all accorded with the thinking behind the hospital plan. At its launch in 1961, Powell had stressed the importance of modernizing the hospital service in tandem with local health care – Birmingham's experimental scheme in 1953 had greatly impressed him.[4]

Yet the importance of Powell's personal feelings about the treatment of the mentally ill should not be underestimated. He was deeply shocked, as he recalled some thirty years later, at the 'horrifying overcrowding' that he saw for himself in the larger mental hospitals. At the same time, he was impressed by the efforts of some medical superintendents to create a new system of care outside the hospital, and also by the dramatic improvements that intensive training could produce among some of the mentally handicapped. 'The need of the acute hospitals was, as always, voracious,' Powell remembered,

> but I was so struck by the need to support the mental health services that I even shifted a few million [pounds] up a line or two in one region's plan just before it was published, so bad were their services for these people, something I had never done before or since.

In a further indication of his concern, Powell took the opportunity of the prestigious Conservative Political Centre lecture at the 1961 Tory conference to suggest that funds spent on housing subsidies could be re-allocated to other programmes, including prisons, the treatment of juvenile offenders and mental hospitals.[5]

The closure programme for the old Victorian asylums was officially launched with the publication of the hospital plan in January 1962. Powell's objective of halving the numbers in these massive mental hospitals by 1975 had been derived simply by extrapolating the decline in bed needs on the basis of the trend between 1954 and 1959. This forecast was to prove remarkably accurate, but the medical officers who prepared it had not foreseen the huge increase in the numbers of old people and the impact these would have on the future demand for beds. As a result, many of the mental hospitals lasted longer than Powell had predicted and closures were not effected on a significant scale until the 1980s. None the less, the policy had an enormous impact over a 35-year period. When Powell made his speech, there were about 140,000 beds in mental hospitals. By 1996, the total had fallen to about 40,000.[6]

Latterly, however, care in the community has become synonymous for many people with an increase in the numbers of mentally disturbed people on the streets and some terrible tragedies involving the mentally ill. Notwithstanding the widespread recognition of the inhumane conditions in many of the old asylums and the wholly laudable desire to create a more decentralized and intimate system of care, this has inevitably led to a questioning of the policy, and of Powell's part in giving it such impetus. It should be noted that neither Powell nor any other proponent of care in the community ever envisaged allowing patients to leave hospitals who might be a danger to themselves or to others. But even in 1961 Powell's call for far greater reliance on community care was greeted by some of his audience with scepticism. Their doubts were expressed the following day, when Powell's old adversary on the welfare state, Richard Titmuss, pointed out that as things stood, community care was largely a fiction. This concern was shared across the political spectrum. 'There is no doubt that the Minister's pronouncement was in part sketchy,' the *Sunday Telegraph* commented in October 1961, 'and he was assuming a massive framework of psychiatric service and community aid organized by local authorities and financed by ratepayers, which does not exist'.[7]

Powell, however, repeatedly emphasized that the hospital plan only made sense in the context of what was happening in the local community. It could, he argued, 'be thought of as "an essay on the unity of the National Health Service"'. He had sought to bring the local authorities into his confidence at an early stage, and he echoed the remark by one of their representatives that the hospital plan was 'a charter for the local health and welfare services'. As requested, local authorities submitted their ten-year development plans by the end of October 1962. The following April, *Health and Welfare: the Development of Community Care* was published as a white paper, simultaneously with the first revision of the hospital plan, and was hailed by Powell as representing the first attempt by local authorities to plan their health and welfare services.[8]

Money, however, as Titmuss and the *Sunday Telegraph* had warned, proved to be the bugbear. 'The new forms of care', Powell later wrote, 'were going to require more money than the old.' The local authorities' plans outlined in *Health and Welfare* envisaged, in the following ten years, 'capital expenditure of well over £200 million and an increase of 45 per cent in the staffs employed'. But since the NHS was funded from general taxation, whereas local authorities were funded by rates and government grants, Powell's reforms 'implied there had to be a massive transfer of money *from* central government *to* local government. That was the assumption on which everything rested: that was where disaster befell.'[9]

Largely as a result of Powell's efforts, community care had become official policy in 1962. He bears some responsibility for its subsequent problems. Despite having argued that community care was integral to the hospital plan, he gave overriding priority to hospital building. As the cost of hospital modernization escalated, extra resources were committed to the building programme that could have been spent on community care. From 1962, he accepted Treasury economies in forecast spending on local health and welfare. The Health Visitors and Social Workers Training Bill introduced by Powell in 1962 was symptomatic, because while the Bill marked an advance, Powell was widely criticized for his reluctance to give national grants.[10]

Moreover, an unintended consequence of the predicted large-scale closure of mental hospitals was that too little was spent on their repair and maintenance, resulting in a number of scandals as they lasted longer than had been expected. After 1964, successive Governments were beset by economic problems, and community care fell between the stools of cash-strapped local authorities and central government – by 1974, there were 60,000 fewer people in mental hospitals, but very few were cared for adequately by local services. During the 1980s, the policy fell victim to the 'open warfare' that raged between central and local government. Powell could not have foreseen these last developments, and he deeply regretted them. These latter years were the period when the worst disasters associated with care in the community occurred.[11]

Yet Powell's humanitarianism in respect of the mentally ill cannot be gainsaid. This aspect of his character was illustrated in a revealing incident when he visited Broadmoor Hospital on its centenary in June 1963. Broadmoor was under the Minister's direct management, and after announcing a £1.25 million programme of rebuilding and improvements, Powell added that he planned a further change. On his visits to the hospital, he had been struck 'by the prison-type uniforms of the male nursing staff'. But designing a new uniform that met the needs of security and enhanced the morale of the staff would be, he had realized, an exceptionally difficult task, 'and thinking that nothing but the best would do for Broadmoor I approached my old wartime comrade, Hardy Amies'. Powell had no need to explain that Sir Hardy Amies was, of course, dressmaker to Her Majesty the Queen. As a result of this surprising and imaginative initiative, Powell was able to announce that 'greatly improved modern uniforms' would be issued the following year.[12]

Powell had a genuine desire to humanize the NHS. In April 1961, he issued a 'Mother's Charter', following a report by the Ministry's standing committee on maternity and midwifery that had found too much loneliness, too many bullying attendants and too many insults to personal dignity in maternity wards. Powell forwarded the report to every hospital management committee and regional board, making clear that they should not regard it as just another circular, and demanding that they should report by the end of July on what action they were taking to implement it. 'The hospital exists for the convenience of the patient and not of the staff,' he told the annual meeting of the Hospital Matrons' Association in June, and urged the ending of the 30-minute limit on visiting time in children's wards. In July, speaking in the Commons, he called for an end to the 'blind spot' that made it difficult to see that patients had 'the right to be treated as intelligent persons.' Powell accepted, however, that he had to retain the sympathy of the professions and could only go as fast as they would allow. But he tried to maintain a steady tempo by bringing issues such as 'noise' and 'food' in hospitals into the limelight for limited periods. As he was minuted as having told Tory MPs privately in July 1962, humanizing the hospitals was 'worthwhile and redounded to the credit of the Government'.[13]

Scares and scandals

Powell's rational mind enabled him to keep a sense of proportion and to avoid over-reacting to the health scares that confront any Minister of Health. He was commendably level-headed in his response to the panic that ensued after a Pakistani girl with smallpox had entered the country and triggered an epidemic during the winter of 1961–62. This incident prompted Harold Gurden, the Birmingham MP, a strong supporter of immigration control, to attend the Tory back bench health and social security committee when Powell spoke about the hospital plan in January 1962. Gurden urged that stronger powers should be taken in the Government's Commonwealth Immigrants Bill, that introduced controls and was then being considered by the Commons. Powell, however, resisted this demand, since he already 'had all the stringent powers for taking precautions'.

None the less, the panic over smallpox led to demands by some Tory MPs for compulsory vaccination for all children. As Powell pointed out, however, there was only a remote risk of catching smallpox and immunization against polio, a disease that was far more prevalent, was not compulsory. Yet the demands persisted, and in February Powell had to appear before the 1922 Committee in order to try and impart a sense of proportion into the debate.[14]

Ignorance and irrationality equally typified the debate over the addition of fluoride to water in order to prevent dental decay. On this issue, Powell, despite his sympathies for individual freedom against the state on economic issues, had no truck with those who objected to fluoridation on ethical grounds. 'I am completely satisfied that these scruples are unfounded and groundless,' he told MPs when he announced limited measures to encourage fluoridation in December 1962. Under growing pressure to act from local health authorities and professional bodies, Powell proposed to the Cabinet a way in which fluoridation could be encouraged without laying the Government open to the charge that they were seeking to impose it as general policy. His plan was to invite local authorities to submit proposals under existing NHS legislation for fluoridation, thereby obviating the need for immediate legislation, and to indemnify them against hostile legal suits. But Powell's method had very little success. By April 1963, only eight local authorities out of 1,800 had submitted schemes. The following September, in Wakefield, Powell commended the Labour-controlled county council for agreeing to make arrangements for fluoride to be added to the water supplies – a move that was condemned by West Riding Tory councillors. His outburst at 'cranks who are trying to hold up fluoridation by scare-mongering and misrepresentation', reflected his frustration at having failed to grasp the nettle and legislate.[15]

Powell was similarly over-cautious in his response to one of the thorniest issues of preventive care – smoking. In early 1962, Powell received the report on *Smoking and Health* by the Royal College of Physicians, that identified smoking as a severe danger to health in general and not only through a greatly increased risk of lung cancer. It led Powell, himself a non-smoker, to ponder the attitude of his fellow countrymen and women who continued smoking in their millions, but who were reduced to panic by the extremely remote possibility of contracting smallpox. Powell took the dangers of smoking very seriously, and was deeply concerned that 25,000 people a year were dying from lung cancer when he had information that might help prevent so many deaths.

At a personal level, Powell declined to have ashtrays in his room, although he would provide one if somebody asked to smoke. But he anguished over what he could reasonably do as Minister of Health to discourage smoking: 'You cannot forbid people to do something which is not regarded as a crime or as calling for prohibition as punishment'.[16]

In March 1962, Powell acted on his belief that he had 'a clear duty to make my knowledge known', and proposed to the Cabinet that they should respond to the physicians' report by launching an anti-smoking campaign. In a separate paper, Powell's officials had argued that 'all tobacco advertising can be regarded as contrary to Government policy', but the Treasury opposed any control – their unusual concern for individual freedom explicable by the significant revenue that the Government received from tobacco tax. Tory Ministers were also wary of imposing controls on commercial advertising, and there is no evidence that Powell pressed hard for such interventionist action in Cabinet. As a result, he could only promise MPs an increase in health education campaigning. The new health warnings against smoking were hard-hitting, but Powell's failure to impose curbs on tobacco advertising drew sharp criticism. Powell was subsequently able to claim that he had persuaded advertisers to stop targeting the young and inculcating smoking itself rather than recommending one brand.[17]

Drugs raised the spectres of both scare and scandal, and again presented Powell with similarly awkward commercial and ethical issues. He had to contend with the appalling legacy of the Thalidomide tragedy of the late 1950s and early 1960s, in which babies had been born without some or all of their limbs, as a result of their mothers having taken the drug as a sleeping pill during pregnancy. There were about 450 such children in Britain. In responding to this intensely emotional issue, he appeared consciously to steel himself to remain dispassionate. In the words of his minuted private comments to Tory MPs in July 1962, 'he had resisted any sentimental treatment of the present situation, which he saw as only one type of maternal tragedy – others being mongol and subnormal babies'. He had ensured, however, that GPs had been reminded of the facilities available for dealing with the situation, and of the steps they ought to take to meet it.[18]

The Thalidomide tragedy and the scandal of the drug's being prescribed to pregnant women raised deep concern about the testing of new drugs and the legislation that governed their safety. Initially, Powell appeared ready to take tough action on drug safety. In July 1962, he told Tory MPs that he regarded the existing legislation as out-dated, but was seeking guidance from his standing medical advisory committee, chaired by Lord Cohen of Birkenhead. In April 1963, the Cohen committee recommended the creation of a safety committee to advise on new drugs. Powell accepted their recommendation, but despite his earlier comment rejected a minority report by two members calling for new legislation – one of the dissenters who favoured legislation was Sir Hugh Linstead, the Tory MP who was a qualified pharmaceutical chemist and a member of the Pharmaceutical Society and of the Medical Research Council.

On 24 April, Powell told members of the pharmaceutical industry, who were relieved that he had resisted the strong pressure to legislate, that 'no absolute security' was to be had on drug safety, and that it would be 'irresponsible' to suggest that even his new drug safety committee could rule out dangers.[19]

Powell's blunt approach and his rejection of new legislation caused deep concern among some Tory MPs who felt that more had to be done to prevent a repetition of the Thalidomide tragedy. His comments to Tory MPs at a meeting of their back bench health and social security committee on 30 April about his decision to refer the matter of drug safety to the Cohen Committee did little to reassure them. In Powell's view,

> it would have been the theoretically right course to have admitted that Thalidomide could not have been avoided and to have maintained that the incentives to administering it safely were already as great as possible, but this had not been possible in the excited state of public opinion.

Powell's response to the Thalidomide tragedy had been based on the widely held assumption that Thalidomide had been properly tested according to the knowledge of the time. But the senior medical officer who briefed him on this point later admitted that he himself had been briefed by a medical adviser to Distillers, the company that had manufactured the drug under licence from the originators of the drug, Chemie Grunenthal, of Germany.[20]

The question of how best to allay the public's fears was the source of a heated, private row between Powell and some of his own back-benchers. Powell claimed that Cohen's proposals 'did, in fact, have teeth and gave the medical profession the whiphand', while importers would also have to have their new drugs cleared by the new safety committee. His comment that 'he would not be happy at the present time to legislate for toxicity and clinical trials' provoked Sir Hugh Linstead to counter that the proposed voluntary system merely postponed the need for legislation. But Powell appeared to concede that tougher action on drug safety might come – as Sir Hugh had urged – since he commented that 'the voluntary system would enable them [his advisers] to make a better job of possible eventual legislation'.[21]

Safety was not the only unresolved issue on drugs that Powell bequeathed his successors at the Ministry of Health. The soaring NHS drug bill had long worried the Government. On Powell's appointment, Macmillan had written to him of the 'terrible expense' of the NHS, 'especially in the form of the drug bill'. The post-war pharmaceutical revolution was making many new drugs available and was offering doctors and their patients the prospect of improved treatment. The NHS, however, was left to foot an ever-rising bill, while the drug manufacturers were suspected of making excessive profits. Tackling the problem raised complex ethical, commercial and legal problems. In the first place, a Minister could not easily interfere in the clinical judgement of the medical profession. Secondly, the drug companies were anxious to secure a return on new drugs in order to cover their expensive research and development costs. They therefore charged high prices for their latest products, especially as they were likely to remain the best in their field for only a few years. In these circumstances, deciding what constituted excess profit was not always easy.[22]

Powell's predecessors had sought to curb costs by relying on a voluntary approach to put pressure on the drug companies and the medical profession. In April 1957, after protracted negotiations between the Ministry and the pharmaceutical industry, the Voluntary Price Regulation Scheme (VPRS) was introduced for a three-year period. Its results were disappointing, but some tightening up was agreed and, in January 1961, Powell announced an extension of price regulation for a further three years. Although significant economies were never likely to be forthcoming through the VPRS, it provided Powell with a guarantee against rocketing prices and political embarrassment.[23]

The second leg of the voluntary approach that Powell inherited was an agreement made in February 1960 with GPs on a code of voluntary restraint on prescribing. As part of the scheme, however, the then Minister, Walker-Smith, had agreed that if this method succeeded in controlling the drug bill, the Government would consider whether it justified abolishing the prescription charge. But this scheme was destroyed in February 1961 when Powell doubled the prescription charge and GPs responded by increasing the quantities prescribed (though the doubling of the charge reduced the number of prescriptions by more than the seasonal drop in February from 22 million to 17.5 million). The following month, however, Powell made a fresh attempt to encourage doctors to be more economical by supporting a suggestion of the Cohen committee on the classification of proprietary preparations, that a doctor should be called upon to justify his actions if he prescribed medicines outside the approved lists of standard, new and therapeutic drugs. In addition, Powell issued more authoritative guidance for doctors in a new *Prescribers' Journal*, with the hope that it would help them withstand the sales pressure from drug companies.[24]

The need, however, for something more drastic than these modest measures was demonstrated by the evidence that emerged across the Atlantic during 1960 of the extent of drug companies' excessive profits in the investigation conducted by the United States Senate sub-committee on Antitrust and Monopoly. In some cases, companies were recording profit margins of more than 90 per cent. The hearings had a knock-on effect in Britain, where the Commons' Committee on Public Accounts highlighted the profits made by the drug companies.[25]

At the end of April 1961, Powell fired a warning shot across the drug manufacturers' bows in a speech to the Association of the British Pharmaceutical Industry. Analysing the problem of the NHS drug bill in terms of its unique customer-supplier relationship, he explained that in the NHS, the three activities of a normal customer were divided between three sets of people. 'I pay the bill', Powell declared, 'but I don't order the goods; and I don't consume them either' – the doctor orders, the patient consumes, but the Minister pays. At the same time, the drug industry, for a large range of its products, was 'confronted in the home market with virtually a single customer' – the NHS. Powell urged, as near as possible, 'a straightforward customer-supplier relationship'.[26]

Within three weeks of his speech, Powell delivered a bombshell that shook the industry. He went to the heart of one of the main methods by which drugs companies were able to charge a high price and prevent competition – the law on patents. Powell's chosen weapon was the highly interventionist 1949 Patents Act, that had been devised, in the event of war, by Sir Stafford Cripps, the senior Labour politician and barrister in patent law. The idea behind Cripps's scheme had been that if the Government needed a patented product in wartime but were being held to ransom, they could obtain the product from an unlicensed supplier while the original patent-owner would receive an agreed royalty. Powell announced on 17 May that he would apply section 46 of the Act, in order to enable companies other than those that owned patents on three antibiotics – tetracycline, chloramphenicol and chlorothiazude – to supply them to the Government. His Ministry would put these drugs out to tender, and, if necessary, reimburse patent-owners by adjudication through the High Court. Under the terms of the legislation, however, his initiative was limited to hospitals, that accounted for only £14 million of the annual £110 million NHS drug bill.[27]

None the less, Powell's announcement was an assault on the assumption that British patent law afforded virtually cast-iron protection to the drug companies. In addition, Powell was prepared to seek cheaper drugs from companies that imported them from countries such as Italy that did not allow patents on drugs, or from behind the Iron Curtain, where Western patents were not recognized. In 1962, he gave one such company, DDSA, a contract to supply tetracycline to NHS hospitals at about one-tenth the price charged by Pfizer, the company that held the patent. Pfizer, a British subsidiary of a US manufacturer, took the fight to court, but two years later lost narrowly in the Lords.[28]

Powell had proved himself tougher than any of his Conservative predecessors in tackling the cost of drugs. His concern to cut NHS current spending was such that he was prepared to resort to price regulation, and in using Cripps's legislation, he was deploying the power of the state to inject greater competition in the supply of NHS drugs. But Powell launched no major new initiative on drug costs after his first year at Health, with the result that the issue of profiteering by drug companies at the taxpayer's expense continued to embarrass the Tories in the run-up to the next election. None the less, his overriding determination to cut NHS current spending and his readiness to use the power of the state to do so had an even more damaging impact on the Government in another politically sensitive area – nurses' pay.

Taking on the nurses

Powell entertained hopes that, after his spell at Health, he might succeed Selwyn Lloyd as Chancellor of the Exchequer. It is doubtful if this was ever a realistic possibility while Macmillan remained Prime Minister because of the differences between the two men – for much the same reason, Tim Bligh, Macmillan's private secretary, had scotched a suggestion that Powell might be appointed as a ministerial chief of staff inside Number 10. But Powell was tipped in the press as a candidate to become Chancellor during the spring of 1961 and again a year later. His undoubted integrity and unquestioned intellect qualified him for the job. Yet his formidable reputation was also his Achilles' heel, since he was seen as lacking the human touch.[29]

During the early part of 1962, Powell sought to remedy this perceived weakness by encouraging photographs of himself to appear in the press – these included an hilariously staged photo-opportunity during which Powell, immaculately turned out as always in his black homburg hat, suit and overcoat, hopped along the pavement near his Belgravia home on a pogo-stick, watched by his admiring wife and two young daughters. 'Evidently Mr Powell is not as immune from the tug of ambition as once he seemed,' 'Crossbencher' suggested in the *Sunday Express*. 'He, too, sees his chance of getting to the top.' The new, more approachable, Powell also granted a television interview to his former war-time colleague, Malcolm Muggeridge, in which he revealed that he wished he had rebelled by speaking out against the creation of the Central African Federation nine years earlier. Making his comment when he did, after the troubles in Nyasaland and the Rhodesias had preoccupied the Government for three years, and only days before Macmillan appointed Rab Butler to head a new Central African Department, Powell's revelation of his own earlier doubts about Federation helped foster the impression of a rising Tory star who was far-sighted and progressive.[30]

But no amount of photo-opportunities or self-revelatory interviews could repair the damage that Powell was about to inflict on his prospects of replacing Selwyn Lloyd as Chancellor. Selwyn Lloyd had become unpopular as a result of the economic squeeze and pay pause that he had imposed in July 1961. During 1962, however, Powell was to implement the ensuing incomes policy with greater rigour than any other minister, and by taking on the nurses over their pay claim, he was to set the Government against the group of workers who evoked the strongest public sympathy. But while he seemed determined to make an example of the nurses, he was anxious to ensure that the pay review body for doctors and dentists, that was set up in 1962, was not affected by the incomes policy and in early 1963 urged that the Government should accept its recommended rise of 14 per cent.[31]

Trouble over the pay of nurses and midwives had been building up for some time. Although they had received a pay rise of about twelve per cent in 1959 – their biggest award since the creation of the NHS – they had soon felt at a renewed disadvantage to teachers, who also received a big pay increase.

The following summer, the nurses sought a ten per cent rise, but in December 1960 received an increase of only five per cent. By the spring of 1961, their dissatisfaction over pay was intensified by a growing sense that nurses were slipping behind other groups, notably NHS administrative staff, teachers and social workers. Moreover, nursing had become more skilled, but numbers had fallen and many trainees were leaving, leading to bed closures and greater reliance on immigrant, part-time and unqualified staff. As a result, the nurses revived their demand for a full revaluation of salaries, and made a claim that amounted to an average increase of 33 per cent. But by the time that their claim was formally submitted in August 1961, the Chancellor had imposed his pay pause.

Negotiations were not ruled out during the pay pause, and these began on the nurses' pay claim between the management and staff sides in the bureaucratic and slow Whitley Council system. During the autumn, however, Fraser, the permanent secretary at the Ministry, sought, with Powell's backing, to stiffen the management's resolve. Moreover, Powell would neither allow the management side to respond to the claim nor discuss a package with the Treasury until he was fully satisfied about the alleged decline in recruitment and increase in wastage among nurses. Powell was to continue to maintain that he 'was staring at two facts'. In the first place, 'there was an undoubted misuse of trained nurses for traditional tasks' – he always treasured the reply of a matron, who, when asked what she would do with more nurses, replied, 'more polishing'. Secondly, 'the standard of nurses being recruited was steadily rising, which means that at current pay nursing was more competitive with alternative employments'. Yet these claims were fiercely disputed at the time, not least by Tory MPs.[32]

Powell took a tougher line on nurses' pay than either his officials or his fellow ministers wanted. Indeed, he sought to encourage a more rigid application of incomes policy than the Cabinet had envisaged. Initially, he was inclined to accept his officials' advice and recommend to his colleagues either a revaluation of nurses' salaries, leading to an average rise of eleven per cent, or an increase on the basis of the existing salary structure of five per cent. The Treasury had indicated informally its readiness to accept an increase of eight per cent. On 2 January 1962, however, Powell informed the Treasury that he proposed an increase of only 2.5 to three per cent. This was in line with the Government's approach following the pay pause – in February, Selwyn Lloyd formally announced a figure of 2–2.5 per cent as the guideline for the average increase in wages and salaries, in keeping with the average annual increase in productivity. Although the Chancellor accepted the need for flexibility on merit in particular cases, Powell applied the guideline rigidly to the nurses.[33]

Powell tried to force the rest of the Government into the same strait-jacket. He emphasized to other ministers in the Cabinet committee on wage negotiations that it would put the management side in the nurses' negotiations in an impossible position if the Government were not clearly seen to be following a policy of holding increases in wages and salaries down to this level

(2.5 per cent) in all sectors within their control. Powell's colleagues sought to persuade him to adopt a more flexible position, insisting that claims should be decided on their merits, but since Powell had argued that 2.5 per cent was the right figure for nurses, he was allowed to proceed on that basis.[34]

The offer of 2.5 per cent was formally made on 13 February. Long before the formal rejection exactly a month later, it was clear that ministers were heading for a major confrontation with the nurses. The effect was to make an already deeply unpopular Government even less popular, with immediate and dramatic results. The day before the nurses' formal rejection of 2.5 per cent, Powell came under intense pressure during Health questions in the Commons. On the same evening, the Royal College of Nursing and the Royal College of Midwives held large public meetings to put their case. On the day of the rejection itself, 13 March, the Conservative majority in the Blackpool North by-election fell by nearly 16,000 to a wafer-thin 973. But the biggest shock came the following day when a 15,000 Conservative majority was overturned in the Orpington by-election and replaced by an 8,000 majority for the Liberal candidate, Eric Lubbock. Powell was one of the first Tories to show his astonishment, as he was appearing on a televised discussion when the result was declared.[35]

Powell was unshaken in his commitment to a tough stand on incomes policy by the Government's disastrous showing in the by-elections. By chance, a few days later, on Monday 19 March, Powell was guest speaker at Macleod's policy group, the Chairman's Committee, of which Peter Goldman, the hapless Tory candidate at Orpington, was a member in his capacity as a policy adviser. After the main discussion on social policy, led by Powell, the group heard Goldman's explanation of the Tory defeat. A verbatim note of the meeting provides a fascinating insight into Powell's thinking, and the reaction of party workers to his unflinching stand. According to this note, Powell offered a provocative defence of incomes policy:

[I] really do think that what we are doing and rightly doing on pay must be making a real impression on current by-elections. I am all for the Chancellor's pay policy. I have just antagonized all the nurses in the country, and all those who go to the physiotherapists, and all the doctors and the civil servants throughout the country, and the universities.

His comments proved too much for Dame Peggy Shepherd, a senior party worker, who interjected, 'and it is all the people everyone likes, like the nurses and teachers and postmen, whereas the car workers who seem to be doing well already get more pay'. Powell, however, was unmoved, and was explicit in his view of the Government's stand on public sector pay as an essential element in controlling government spending. '[H]aving settled on this line', he argued, 'we have got to stick to it. [I] believe it is a necessary reinforcement of the financial mechanism, and our only hope is to stick to it until it is seen and proved to be right.' His reasoning cast him in an unlikely role as the champion of incomes policy, and he won support from the centrist Tory, Sir Edward Boyle.[36]

As the pressure on him from Tories seeking a settlement with the nurses intensified, Powell cited the incomes policy itself as the main reason for sticking rigidly to the 2.5 per cent offer. 'Mr Powell took the incomes policy "as read",' reported the minute of his private meeting with Tory MPs on 26 March,

> [and] as being the main reason why nurses' salaries had to be contained within $2\frac{1}{2}$ per cent in 1962. Unless the Government played its part in applying the incomes policy in the public sector it had no chance of success.

Powell acknowledged that he had advised the management side in the negotiations accordingly. But his intransigence failed to allay the anxieties of Tory back-benchers, including Dame Irene Ward, the Tyneside MP, who had previously been a supporter of Powell's. Dame Irene, however, had been closely involved in the health service in the north-east, represented the physiotherapists and was active on the council of the Royal College of Nurses. She told Powell that his figures on recruitment 'did not bear inspection in the hospitals themselves' – a criticism that was repeated by others. But her call, also echoed by others, for Powell to apply the Government's own acceptance that claims had to be considered on their merits, merely prompted him to retort that 'merit cannot be divorced from economic realities'.[37]

Powell's unconvincing performance, resulting in sharp criticisms from his own back-benchers, was a dress rehearsal for the following evening's debate in the Commons. During this twelve-hour confrontation, that lasted until breakfast time on Wednesday 28 March, Powell was subjected to heavy and prolonged attack. He would not yield an inch, and was still convinced that the nurses would settle for 2.5 per cent even after a further debate in the Commons on 13 April, accompanied by a mass lobby of parliament. Such was the anger among the demonstrators that Powell, on the advice of the police and his parliamentary private secretary, Martin Maddan, had to avoid the Central Lobby and abandon his plans to travel home by underground, for fear of being attacked at Westminster station. Disdainfully spurning Maddan's suggestion that he should take a taxi, Powell left the Palace of Westminster through the House of Lords and, despite the pouring rain, put up his umbrella and began walking home to South Eaton Place. He had not gone far, when he heard the booming voice of a big Irish male nurse: 'If I could get my hands on that bastard Powell, I'd wring his neck.'[38]

Evidence of the massive political damage being caused by Powell's stand against the nurses was confirmed in an NOP opinion survey in Orpington, conducted after the by-election. During April, Powell was still resisting any suggestion that the nurses' dispute should be allowed to go to arbitration, but by the end of the month, Macleod, the party chairman, had become convinced that the Government's position was unsustainable if they were to recover their support before the next election. In a private note to Macmillan, Macleod wrote of the unpopularity of the pay policy among their supporters, adding 'that the issue of nurses' pay has done us an immense amount of harm. It is really very difficult to project the image that "Conservatives Care" in the face of this.' Macleod urged the Prime Minister that 'we must try to get off the hook as far as nurses and perhaps university teachers are concerned'.[39]

On 2 May, Powell was still seeking to reassure the Prime Minister that the nurses' campaign would fade and they would accept 2.5 per cent. Only a day after Powell's reassurance, however, the Conservatives suffered heavy defeats in the local elections, losing 800 seats. Ministers finally lost patience with Powell's inflexibility. During the following week, in the Cabinet committee on wage negotiations and in the full Cabinet, they pressed Powell to be more flexible. Their new, conciliatory approach was first aired publicly the following Monday, 8 May, when Lord Hailsham, then Minister of Science, acknowledged that the nurses 'had been persistently undervalued and would be better valued in the future'. He also added that the 2.5 per cent 'guiding light' had never been intended as a rigid or permanent form of wage control. At the end of the week, the dockers won a nine per cent pay rise from the shipping companies.[40]

Yet Powell's reluctance to make the necessary concessions lengthened the process of reaching a final settlement and antagonized the nurses even further. He told the Cabinet that the nurses would settle for only a minor improvement in the original offer, and proposed an immediate interim increase of 2.5 per cent, with a promise of a joint 'study' into their grading structure, to be followed by a further staged increase, if this proved necessary. This was the basis of the offer that he made during the Commons debate on nurses' pay on 14 May, but his announcement was so guarded that it had no impact. Winding up the debate, however, Sir Edward Boyle, the Financial Secretary, confirmed that if the nurses took their claim to arbitration, the Government would be bound by the findings of the Industrial Court, even if the final award was above 2.5 per cent.[41]

The Tory press turned on Powell. The incomes policy was savaged in editorials in *The Times* and the *Daily Telegraph*, and the latter was even provoked into complaining that the Government were 'making the whole burden of its pay policy fall on its own relatively underpaid employees'. The propaganda battle peaked over the weekend of 18–20 May, as the nurses held a rally at the Albert Hall. Powell, in a speech at Chipping Sodbury, admitted failures in the Government's pay policy, especially the 'open defiance' of the dockers' award, but claimed that there had been many solid successes.[42]

The Government were fighting a losing battle, but Powell failed to realize it. On 4 June, he told ministers that a settlement costing £10 million would satisfy the nurses. Again, he was proved wrong as the nurses rejected an offer of 2.5 per cent plus staged increases up to the £10 million ceiling. On 13 June, Powell minuted the Prime Minister that the nurses were likely to seek arbitration, which they finally did in July. In early September, they won an increase of 7.5 per cent, backdated to April – half a per cent below the figure that the Treasury would have accepted at the start of the year. In addition, there were to be immediate discussions on grading structures. These talks on grading, however, caused more trouble as Powell insisted that any further increase should be limited to 3.5 per cent. Recruitment was again in his mind. He told Tory MPs in December 1962 that the hospitals had had no difficulty in recruiting nurses and midwives during the year up to September 1962, despite the long-running pay dispute – 'a cynic might observe that a touch of unemployment stimulates the sense of vocation', Powell added caustically. But the nurses again sought arbitration and were awarded a further rise of 6.5 per cent from July 1963.[43]

Powell felt that his usefulness as Minister of Health had finished by the summer of 1962. Possibly this feeling was intensified because it coincided with arbitration of the nurses' pay claim and his defeat at the end of a bitter battle, but in his own mind it was the result of a politician's limited life-span as the head of a department. He made this discovery after he had been little more than two years at the Ministry of Health, when, to his shock,

> a new Parliamentary Secretary asked me to explain certain terms I was using that he found unintelligible. I realized I had absorbed the departmental jargon to the extent of being unconscious that it *was* jargon. When a minister begins to think like his officials and understands before they explain, his work in that office is done; he is losing the power to see the issues in a political light from the outside, which alone is what he is there for.

Moreover, from July 1962, Powell was distracted from his work at Health by his membership of the Cabinet. 'The mere extraction', he later wrote, 'from the working week of a minister, of five hours in conclave, plus time to read the Cabinet papers, is no small interruption to the smooth flow of administration and application of the ministerial mind.' This interruption was accentuated by the overriding priority of the Cabinet's claims'; the nature of 'the fascinating but mostly insoluble problems that engage a Cabinet's attention'; and 'the endlessly varied interplay of a score of personalities'.[44]

A departmental minister is fortunate if he or she can achieve one great reform, and Powell had achieved this landmark in January 1962 when he put in place his forward-looking plan to modernize Britain's hospitals. This points to the most interesting aspect of his time at Health, namely that his reformist zeal was directed into long-term planning, rather than towards introducing a more market-oriented NHS. His acceptance that, at the time, the modernization of the hospital service had to take overriding priority is to his credit. He gave an insight into his reasoning in the private paper that he prepared in March 1962 for Macleod's policy group. As far as the NHS was concerned,

> I would not contend that medical care and treatment are better or more

widespread under it than they would have been if it had not been invented and other systems developed. The balance of argument is rather to the contrary.

To this extent, Powell expressed himself in agreement with recent critiques by free-market writers. 'Where I part company', he went on to explain, 'is with their assumption that one can restore or breed those alternative systems now by some simple device, such as allowing people to "contract out" of the Health Service'. He found it 'impossible' to imagine how the growth of private treatment 'could be more than very limited; and the more the Health Service, and especially the hospital service, improves, the less the incentive will be.' This was the line that he reiterated to the policy group, as the verbatim note reveals. '[I] don't myself feel that the structure of the NHS is in any way ripe for reconsideration', he argued,

> and [I] don't see the time when it will be. So for the time being, the only thing is the business-like improvement of efficiency of it, tightening of the organization, and strengthening of the structure.[45]

But cutting across Powell's pragmatic realism as Minister of Health was his continuing preoccupation with government spending – that made him behave at timcs as though he were still at the Treasury – and his lack of political judgement. His maladroit handling of the nurses' dispute had confirmed the views of his critics more than a year earlier, when the *Observer* had referred to their saying,

> how extraordinary it is that a man who could have risen to somewhere near the top as a proconsul, staff officer, civil servant, or academic should have chosen politics, the one career which seemed certain to defeat him. For the outstanding thing about Powell has been that he is not a politician, which means, quite honourably, a compromiser.

Yet despite Powell's evident weaknesses as a politician, Macmillan had seen fit to promote him to his Cabinet.[46]

12

A Difficult Horse

Alec, you know perfectly well that if I were to give you a different answer
now I'd have to go home and turn all the mirrors round. I could never look
at myself in the face again.

    Enoch Powell's explanation to the Earl of Home of his refusal to serve
in his administration, 19 October 1963.

'Aristides' at the Cabinet table

On Monday 28 May 1962, although he was not yet a member of the Cabinet,
Powell was summoned to attend a Cabinet meeting in his capacity as one of
the ministers most closely involved in implementing the Government's pay
policy. It was an unusual occasion. Whereas Cabinet meetings are mostly
preoccupied with the immediate business of government, on this occasion the
Prime Minister delivered a philosophical and strategic exposition on the
difficulty of maintaining the four objectives pursued by successive post-war
governments – full employment, stable prices, a strong pound and sustained
economic expansion. Unusually, Macmillan's lengthy talk was recorded. The
verbatim transcript reveals that his conclusions for Conservative strategy were
diametrically opposed to Powell's beliefs in monetarism and a reduced role for
the state, other than in health and education.[1]

Only the previous autumn, Powell had asserted that it was 'doubtful how far
Governments can or do, influence and control economic activity and growth
itself' – an explicit rejection of the Keynesian assumption, held by the
Government of which he remained a member, on which post-war economic
policy was based. Yet the Prime Minister, in his May 1962 talk to the Cabinet,
rejected any return to earlier restrictionist policies, specifically mentioning the
seven per cent Bank Rate of September 1957 as an admission of failure and a
recipe for 'stop and go'. In addition, he ruled out the idea of having a
permanently higher level of unemployment, because 'then you would abandon
growth'.[2]

Instead, Macmillan advocated precisely the policies that Powell most
strongly opposed – reflation of the economy; sustained economic expansion

(he appeared to have in mind the NEDC's 'ambitious' growth target of four per cent a year); and the introduction of some form of permanent incomes policy for the public *and* private sectors (though Macmillan accepted that in the immediate future the existing pay curbs had to be relaxed). Moreover, in return for the acceptance of a permanent pay policy, the Prime Minister envisaged a 'new approach', in which the state would use its power to remove distinctions in industry between wage-earners and salary-earners; to curb monopoly power in favour of the consumer; and to spend more on 'the things we know are necessary – the housing, the slums, the universities, the schools would follow'.

Despite Powell's subsequent condemnation of Macmillan as a cynic, the difference between them was one of conflicting political moralities. Macmillan believed that 'some accepted plan' of the kind that he outlined to his ministers was essential 'if we are to obtain the four objectives [of post-war policy] which is the purpose of it all'. Accordingly, anybody who was against an incomes policy should be denounced – one type of critic was to be condemned as 'an anarchist, in favour of a sort of nineteenth-century liberalism or free-for-all and the devil take the hindmost'. There was no doubting that Macmillan had in mind those, like Powell, who preferred allowing market forces free rein in the private sector rather than introducing a pay policy.[3]

Almost twenty years later, Powell mockingly recalled how Macmillan 'had entertained his Cabinet, instead of going through the agenda, with the reading of an essay he claimed to have composed over the weekend'. Powell dismissed even the most moderate reforms that derived from the Prime Minister's paper, such as contracts of employment and redundancy payments, as 'socialist measures'. Moreover, these reforms had been seen by Macmillan 'entirely in the spirit of the Middle Way, as the *quid pro quo* to the workers for co-operating in an inflation-free planned economy'. And in a biting reference to the Prime Minister's ruthless sacking of a third of his Cabinet – 'the night of the long knives' – that followed in little more than six weeks after Macmillan's exposition, Powell added: 'I still relish recalling how the heads which were to roll not long after nodded like cuckoo-clocks in sycophantic approval'. In all, Macmillan sacked seven of his Cabinet, including the Chancellor, Selwyn Lloyd, in an attempt to give his Government a younger image. The main beneficiaries of the purge were Maudling, who by becoming Chancellor at the age of forty-five was the first member of the 'Class of '50' to hold one of the great offices of state, and Boyle, who became Education Secretary at thirty-eight.[4]

Powell was another beneficiary. Despite his deep antipathy towards Macmillan, and his intense opposition to the new strategy that he had heard him set out, Powell none the less joined the Cabinet on 13 July 1962, a month after his fiftieth birthday. 'I remember the grim amusement', he later recalled, 'with which I took my place at the new Cabinet table and noted the absence of those seven heads who had nodded assent to the PM before they fell off altogether.' Powell's promotion was intended by Macmillan as further proof that a new generation of Tories had come to the fore, with fresh ideas for the future. It was recognition of Powell's performance at Health – despite his intransigence over nurses' pay – notably the launch of the Hospital Plan, and reflected the department's increased importance as the Tories emphasized their commitment to the welfare state. 'He is perhaps most known for his dour political integrity and courage', observed William Rees-Mogg of Powell's entering the Cabinet, 'but he is another example of the promotion of sheer intellectual ability.' By retaining Powell at Health, however, Macmillan kept him away from the senior posts and also from economic policy where he might sabotage the new strategy – likewise, Thorneycroft's promotion to Defence prevented him from interfering in economic policy.[5]

Macmillan privately referred to Powell as 'the fanatic' and, during the Hola Camp affair, likened him to a 'fakir'. He also deprecatingly nicknamed the former Professor of Greek, 'Aristides', after the Athenian statesman who was surnamed 'The Just' and was never wrong. Powell, for his part, regarded Macmillan as an 'actor-manager', who had the 'cynicism of a born political tactician'. But he also acknowledged the applicability to his former leader of the dictum of Julian Amery, Macmillan's son-in-law, that 'good jockeys ride difficult horses'. In Powell's view, Macmillan avoided the mistake of recruiting a Cabinet all of one opinion, and overcame his natural dislike of Powell sufficiently to put him in his Cabinet.[6]

Yet the relationship in Cabinet between the Prime Minister and his Minister of Health remained uneasy. Powell was later to reflect that although conversation in the Cabinet is 'influenced by the knowledge that we all have to hang together', none the less 'it's like having a debate with Henry VIII ... I was conscious that he [Macmillan] had the axe down by his chair'. Yet Macmillan appeared to find Powell's presence even more disconcerting. 'Powell looks at me in Cabinet like Savonarola eyeing one of the more disreputable popes,' Macmillan remarked. Eventually, the Prime Minister could bear it no longer. On one occasion, Lord Home, the then Foreign Secretary, arrived for a Cabinet meeting to find that,

> the PM was changing the places round and I said to the Cabinet Secretary, 'Has one of us died in the night?' And he said, 'Oh no. The PM can't have Enoch's accusing eye looking at him straight across the table any more.' And poor Enoch was put away down the left where Harold couldn't see him.[7]

Collectively responsible

In the event, Powell appears not to have been such a difficult horse after all. The Cabinet conclusions show him intervening only twice on matters other than health during his sixteen months at the Cabinet table – on housing and planning policy. Although ministers are rarely identified by name in the official summary of their discussion, a more outspoken critic would have submitted a greater number of papers to Cabinet, and, as a result, been mentioned more in the conclusions. Indeed, his only minuted strong objection to Government policy concerned the proposals in May 1963 to set up a Housing Corporation in order to encourage a housing society movement, since it ran 'counter to the normal machinery of supply and demand'. He was overruled, except on the compulsory powers for the Corporation, where other ministers feared the impact on owner-occupiers.[8]

On the potentially divisive issue of non-white immigration, the new Commonwealth Immigrants' Act had only come into effect less than a fortnight before Powell was promoted to the Cabinet and its effectiveness would not be apparent for some time. Powell's position on economic policy seemed more problematic. For more than a year, he remained a member of a Cabinet whose Prime Minister and Chancellor indulged in a repetition of the reflationary policies of 1958–59 that he had roundly condemned from the back benches. Indeed, about the only difference between the two great reflations was that on the latter occasion, the Tories were also committed to economic planning and a permanent incomes policy – both of which were anathema to Powell's market economics, though as Minister of Health Powell had taken up planning and incomes policy with such zeal that he might have been mistaken for a convert. During the latter half of 1962 and early 1963, the Government pursued the classic Keynesian policy of stimulating demand in the economy with an array of measures, including easier monetary and credit policies, a cut in purchase tax, and increases in private and public investment. After unemployment had reached a post-war record high of 873,000 (3.9 per cent) in February 1962, Maudling delivered the main boost in his 1963 budget by announcing tax cuts of £460 million in a full year and special assistance to the high-unemployment regions. The intention of the budget and its effect on production were much as they had been in 1959, but neither Powell nor Thorneycroft resigned. Not only was Keynesian-style reflation completely contrary to Powell's thinking, but he had previously opposed the abolition of Schedule A tax on housing, and he was unsympathetic, to put it mildly, to a regional policy. Every politician has to trim at some point if he or she is to gain advancement, but by any standards Powell's acquiescence in the Macmillan Government's second great reflation represented a massive compromise. It is not entirely fanciful to suppose that Powell's subsequent bitter expressions of contempt for Macmillan were, in part, reactions to his own subordination of conscience.[9]

Yet there appears to be an even greater contradiction in Powell's membership of the Government that, in July 1961, took the historic decision to apply for membership of the European Economic Community (EEC). A decade earlier, Powell had abstained rather than back the party's pro-European stance on British participation in the European Coal and Steel Community (ECSC) – the embryonic EEC. In April 1961, in a speech to the Royal Society of St George, while a minister in Macmillan's administration, he gave free rein to the romantic nationalism that had superseded his imperialism. His paean of praise to the unique qualities of English nationhood seemed inappropriate to a country that was about to seek a new role in Europe, especially since he asserted that 'our generation is like one which comes home again from years of distant wandering [to] discover affinities with earlier generations of English, generations before the "expansion of England", who felt no country but this to be their own'. This romanticizing was to give an emotional flavour to his later utterances on Europe, after he had emerged at the end of the 1960s as the most senior Tory opponent of British membership of the EEC.[10]

Yet in the early 1960s there was no inconsistency in Powell's views on Europe and his membership of Macmillan's Government: at the time, he was in favour of joining the EEC. Powell's attempt in later life, as an implacable opponent of European integration, to explain his support for British membership of the EEC during 1960–63 is not wholly convincing. 'I only later came to see that the European Community was a political and not an economic structure,' he argued in 1993, explaining that 'my mistake in the early 1960s, which I only recovered and repented of in the late 1960s, was failure to understand the political intent, was failure to understand that it was in a sense a renunciation of a balance of power as the basis of British policy.'[11]

As regards the EEC's political purpose, Powell recalled that he judged the application for EEC membership entirely in economic terms: 'I said to myself, "that's going for free trade. I'm in favour of free trade. That's going for an increase in the volume of trade. I'm in favour of the increases in the volume of trade".' At the same time, as Minister of Health he was pre-occupied with his plans for the health service, and thought, 'I've got to get on with the hospital plan and the health and welfare plan'. Moreover, Powell was not yet a member of the Cabinet. 'Had I actually been in the Cabinet my focus would have been different', he suggested, while admitting 'though I can't say that I would yet have perceived in 1962 the essentially political thrust of the European Community.'[12]

Powell, however, was mistaken on the economic facts. Britain, a member of the European Free Trade Association (EFTA), or the 'seven' as it was commonly known, had tried to find an accommodation between EFTA and the EEC. But little progress had been made because the EEC was a protectionist customs union whose members sheltered behind a tariff wall. As such, the EEC was clearly the antithesis of 'free trade' – except, of course, between its six members. As to Powell's claim to have been unaware of the EEC's political purpose, in 1950 the opponents of British membership of the ECSC – of which he was one – had identified the threat to British sovereignty as one of their main objections. The EEC was a development of the ECSC, and the 1957 Treaty of Rome (the EEC's written constitution) was explicit in its political objective. Indeed, in 1960, an exhaustive Whitehall study for the Cabinet on British membership counselled that 'joining means taking far-reaching decisions' and involved political action: 'we must show ourselves prepared to join with the Six in their institutional arrangements, and in any development towards closer political integration.'[13]

Moreover, by the end of 1960, Macmillan was committed to British entry into the EEC as much on political grounds as for economic reasons. Whitehall's study on joining the EEC had suggested that the economic arguments were balanced, but the strategic argument was strongly in favour – Britain could no longer hope to exercise great influence in the world unless it was part of a wider political entity, represented by the EEC. The idea of a European power-block, allied to the United States, as another pillar of the free world against the perceived Communist threat was important in Macmillan's mind. Implicit in this approach was the notion of a closer, European union. 'We must now accept the fact', Macmillan told the Conservative conference in October 1961, two months after the building of the Berlin Wall,

> that the bleak ideological struggle may last for another generation, perhaps even longer. We cannot retire from this contest, but we cannot wage it alone. It is with this in mind that we have approached the question of Europe and of the Common Market.

Macmillan had no relish for political integration, but feared that Britain's influence would decrease outside the EEC. He hoped that the EEC might become a confederation as opposed to a federation, but this would still have entailed some loss of sovereignty.[14]

Political arguments about Britain's role in the world, and the nature of its relationships with the Commonwealth, Europe and the United States, permeated the Government and the Conservative Party during this period. Powell was no friend of the Commonwealth, and so had nothing in common with many Tory opponents of the EEC at this time, such as Neil Marten, the Tory MP for Banbury. Neither did he have anything in common with the imperialist rearguard, including most notably Lord Beaverbrook, the press baron, who sought to re-kindle the imperial dream in the pages of the *Daily Express*, the *Sunday Express* and the *Evening Standard*. Powell also subsequently attacked, with some justification, the notion that attracted many pro-European Conservatives of Europe as 'the new, the final surrogate for lost Empire', in that it would enable Britain to re-assert itself on the world stage. But in this respect, the older Powell, the latter-day opponent of European integration, tried to have it both ways – on the one hand, arguing that the underlying impulse for EEC membership was evidently political, but, on the other hand, claiming that in the early 1960s he was oblivious to this political motivation. The latter position seems highly implausible, especially for a politician who had long been obsessed with Britain's position in the world.[15]

Again, only in retrospect it would seem, Powell saw the long hand of Uncle Sam at work, pushing a compliant Britain into Europe. One of the reasons that Macmillan was so keen to join the EEC, Powell claimed in 1993, was 'undoubtedly American pressure, which was exerted steadily in favour of our joining the European [Economic] Community, [and] was already at work in the late 1950s and the early 1960s'. In his view, the United States saw the EEC as 'a political-economic counterpart to NATO. They were obsessed with NATO, as they were obsessed with their picture of America leading one half of a divided world.' According to Powell, Britain meekly fell in with American wishes, because 'we believed that America had won the war for us ... so massive was the input of the United States, so impressive was its effort, that we fell into the vulgar and common error of supposing that the Americans won the [Second World] War, and therefore we had to be on the side of America in any further conflict'. In Powell's mind, Britain had 'won the war in 1940. We won it without the United States.'[16]

But Powell's love of hyperbole should not be allowed to obscure historical fact. Apart from the error of supposing that the heroic achievement of standing alone and resisting invasion was tantamount to victory, Powell's assertion that the decision to enter the EEC was dictated by Washington is a gross over-simplification. Certainly, Macmillan's mind was much influenced by America's calculation that power in Europe increasingly resided in the EEC and her wish, in consequence, to see Britain as a member. This reality was bound to weigh heavily with any Prime Minister. But the decision on EEC membership involved many complex judgements. Powell also asserted that EEC membership marked 'the decisive abandonment of that on which the independence of the United Kingdom has always rested, the balance of power in Europe, or the balance of power in the world.' But his admonitions about the supposedly supine acceptance of American strategy sit uneasily, to say the least, with his own readiness to enter, and to remain in, Macmillan's Government as Britain became increasingly dependent on the US nuclear deterrent. Powell accepted office only months after the abandonment of the British surface-to-surface missile, Blue Streak, and its replacement by the American alternative, the ill-fated Skybolt. He also remained a minister when, in the autumn of 1960, London and Washington agreed on the stationing of US submarines, armed with Polaris missiles, at Holy Loch, on the Clyde. And he remained in the Cabinet at the end of 1962, when Macmillan negotiated the replacement of Skybolt by Polaris.[17]

Powell's rationalization of his pro-EEC attitude in the Macmillan administration in terms of his ignorance of the political aspects does not hold water, even though discussion in the Government focused on the economic aspects after the decision in principle to apply had been taken in July 1961. Whitehall concentrated on the economic issues because they had to be resolved immediately, whereas the political ones lay in the future. But in the parliamentary debate on membership in early August 1961, Walker-Smith, Powell's predecessor at Health, and Lord Salisbury, the former leader of the Government in the Lords, both warned from the Conservative benches of the pretence that the EEC was purely economic. Moreover, in October 1962, when Hugh Gaitskell, the Leader of the Opposition, finally came down against membership, he made the political issue his rallying cry, protesting that it would mean 'the end of a thousand years of history'. It seems inconceivable in these circumstances that Powell, who had already shown a close interest in questions of parliamentary sovereignty and the constitution, could have been unaware of the EEC's political aspects.[18]

In the event, President de Gaulle's veto of Britain's entry into the EEC in January 1963 relegated Europe to the lower reaches of the domestic political agenda. But its effect on the Government and the Conservative Party was traumatic. The 'Grand Design', on which Macmillan had pinned so many hopes, was shattered. 'He hadn't been given the magic counter that he had been looking for. It had been struck from his hand,' Powell later observed. Indeed Powell was impressed by the extent to which Macleod, then Party Chairman and Leader of the House, 'regarded de Gaulle's brush off as disastrous to Macmillan' and thought he was 'disintegrating'.[19]

Detailed policy work, however, had been under way in the party for some time, and in early 1962 Powell had been the first minister whom Macleod invited to address his new policy group, the Chairman's Committee. Although Powell responded to Macleod's request to 'introduce a discussion on the long-term thinking in your field with particular reference to the Election manifesto', by submitting a six-page hand-written paper on the whole field of social policy, his prescription fell far short of being radical. 'There is an inherent dilemma in the construction of a Conservative election policy for 1963–64', he began. 'On the one hand, the record of our past achievement and the pejorative comparison of Socialist achievement and policies have become boring to the point of irrelevance.' An increasing number of voters had no recollection of a Labour Government. 'What we need, more than ever before', he urged, 'is the momentum and attraction of bold and new policies.' On the other hand, however, 'the longer our continuous period of office extends, the harder it becomes suddenly to propound such policies: the question "Why have you only just thought of this?" becomes increasingly embarrassing.'[20]

Moreover, Powell warned that this dilemma was 'most oppressive in the field of the social services'. The welfare state was still geared to the conditions of the 1930s, but however much Powell regretted the lack of radicalism since 1951, he saw the dangers in radical reform at this late stage, since 'the remoulding of a system, unlike piecemeal addition to it, involves *minuses* as well as *plusses*: and present benefits to be removed are not welcome ingredients of an Election policy, however many new benefits to be conferred in future are adumbrated'. Powell could see no scope for radical reform in the health service, and argued that 'anything about health in the manifesto must be very undynamic'. The area where he saw scope for 'a new and bold policy' was the one that he had first identified before 1959 and that straddled 'social security, health and welfare, and housing: a comprehensive policy for the old'.[21]

In particular, Powell proposed increasing the purchasing power of the old, and again he suggested a guaranteed minimum income, as he had before the 1959 election. He envisaged 'a really substantial means-tested pension for the old (over 70s?) divorced from National Assistance'. The cost of this proposal would require an additional charge unless economies were made, for example, by raising the retirement age; by merging the existing state pension over 70 in the new pension and subjecting it to a means test below 70; by freezing state benefits at sums actuarially earned; or by reductions in other social policy budgets. Although a rise in their basic money income was a necessary condition for helping the elderly – housing needs, for example, were unlikely to be fully met until the elderly were 'in the market' – Powell argued that it was not, in itself, sufficient. Local social services and geriatric care in hospitals were integral to any comprehensive policy – as Powell demonstrated in September 1962 by announcing the strengthening of local authorities' powers to improve standards in privately-run residential homes and mental nursing homes, and the phasing out of old work-houses as geriatric wards.[22]

Curiously, Powell failed to address in his paper the major problem of his proposal for a guaranteed minimum income in old age – the disincentive to saving. His oversight is remarkable in view of the priority that he attached to saving, especially as a means of self-reliance. But what encouragement would there be for people to save for their retirement if the state guaranteed them a reasonable means-tested income in old age, as Powell proposed? His ambitious ideas prompted a mixed reaction from Macleod's policy group, especially his notion of a means-tested pension. In early 1963, following a further note on the subject from Powell, Macleod established a small sub-committee (consisting of himself, Powell, Sir Keith Joseph and Lord Balniel) to examine the practicalities. Ministers considered the proposal during their day-long strategy meeting at Chequers in late April, but Powell introduced the session on social policy and the discussion became over-technical.[23]

By this time, however, Labour had lifted Powell's idea of a minimum income in old age and included it in their plans on social security. The Tories further discussed the scheme in July, at Macmillan's steering committee on policy, when Macleod presented detailed proposals and it was agreed that the cost and practical implications needed further examination. In early October, Labour's emphasis on their plans for pensions at their annual conference prompted Macleod to write to Powell that, 'Scarborough makes your policy on the minimum income in old age not only desirable but essential.' Within little more than a fortnight, however, Powell and Macleod were no longer ministers. The idea had lost its two strongest advocates in Whitehall. Powell's plan was considered in drafting the 1964 Conservative manifesto, but was finally rejected on political, social and practical grounds. It was left to Labour to pledge a minimum income in old age in their 1964 manifesto. The promise, however, was unrealized.[24]

Sea-green incorruptible

In early June 1963, when it seemed that the Government had put de Gaulle's veto behind them and were beginning to focus on winning the next election, they suffered another hammer blow with the resignation of John Profumo, the War Secretary. Profumo admitted that he had lied to the Commons in March when he had denied any impropriety with Christine Keeler, a call-girl, who had also been a lover of Captain Yevgeny Ivanov, a naval attaché at the Soviet Embassy. With the Conservative Party in a state of panic, Macmillan would almost certainly have been brought down by one more ministerial resignation, whether through some further scandal, or over his handling of the Profumo case.[25]

For a few days, Powell seemed to hold the Government's fate in his hands, as a series of well-informed reports was planted in the press suggesting that he was considering resigning over Macmillan's handling of the case. These reports gained credibility because Powell, especially after his Hola Camp speech, seemed well-suited to act as the Cabinet's constitutional and moral guardian. It was at this time that Powell was depicted in the press as the 'sea-green incorruptible' – the phrase coined by Carlyle to describe Robespierre, the sternest and most unforgiving of the French revolutionaries. The source of the press reports, however, was not Powell, but Nigel Birch, his former colleague at the Treasury and fellow resigner in 1958. The embittered Birch, who unlike Powell and Thorneycroft still languished on the back benches, had a deep *animus* against Macmillan. He saw in Powell the means to destroy the Prime Minister. He reckoned that Powell's resignation would cause many back-benchers to abstain when the Commons debated the Profumo case on 17 June, thus forcing Macmillan to resign in much the same way that Chamberlain had had to quit in 1940 after his Government's majority had been massively reduced in the Norway debate.[26]

The Government's handling of the Profumo case and its coverage in the press were deeply affected by the Vassall case of the previous autumn. Unfounded rumours in the press about John Vassall, an Admiralty official and homosexual who was convicted of spying for the Russians, and his relationship with a minister had led Macmillan to require the resignation of Tam Galbraith, the Scottish Office minister who had previously served at the Admiralty. The Government's relations with the press were further poisoned when two journalists were imprisoned for refusing to disclose their sources in the Vassall case. In addition, sensational revelations during the Duchess of Argyll's divorce case had put people in a mood to believe anything. After the Profumo affair became known, wild rumours about ministers, judges and other eminent figures titillated a public that simultaneously indulged in one of its periodic fits of morality.

Speculation about Powell's intentions became intense immediately after the Cabinet's first discussion of the Profumo case on Wednesday 12 June at Admiralty House, off Whitehall – Number 10 was still being renovated. Powell's forbidding, hawk-like appearance, as he hung on every word uttered during the Cabinet's discussions, was vividly recaptured many years later by the then Solicitor-General, Sir Peter (later Lord) Rawlinson. 'When I was called to speak by the Prime Minister,' Rawlinson recalled, 'I looked down the long table. I remember looking straight into the intense eyes set in the white face of the Minister of Health as he leaned forward the better to hear. They never shifted while I spoke'.[27]

The Cabinet's inquest, in which Powell and others sought to satisfy themselves as to security and the Prime Minister's role, established that Macmillan had been unaware that the Cabinet Secretary had warned the War Secretary in August 1961 about Dr Stephen Ward's connection with the Soviet Embassy – it had been through Ward that Profumo had met Keeler. After the rumours of a scandal had finally been brought to his attention, Macmillan had relied on the strenuous assurances that Profumo had given to the Chief Whip and law officers – but believing a colleague's untruths was hardly a resigning matter. Of greater concern was the vulnerability of the five ministers who had quizzed Profumo during the night before his fateful Commons denial and discussed with him the text of his personal statement in which he lied.[28]

Powell's role, and Macmillan's handling of him, can be gleaned from the diary of Harold Evans, the Prime Minister's press secretary at the time – the Cabinet conclusions, now released under the 30-year rule, only summarize the discussion and few ministers are identified by name. 'Enoch Powell made his points,' Evans recorded,

but seemed to find the explanations acceptable and did not press the matter to an issue. To make quite sure the Prime Minister, in effect, made him stand up and be counted by saying that, of course, if the judgement of the five Ministers were to be challenged there would be no option but for him (the Prime Minister) to resign.

The Cabinet discussion was to be continued the next day, but Powell and Brooke, the Home Secretary, stayed on for a word with Lord Dilhorne, the Lord Chancellor, whose inquiry had flushed out Profumo. Their late departure through the throng of cameramen and reporters in the courtyard outside appeared to add substance to the *Evening Standard*'s claim that Powell was 'now at the stage of considering not whether to resign but when to do so', in order to force a 'major reconstruction of the entire Tory hierarchy'.[29]

Powell's every move came under intense scrutiny. Reporters followed him to Wolverhampton, besieged him at his constituency office and at Merridale Road, and returned with him on the overnight train. Powell would say nothing, and even declined to deny the rumours of his impending resignation 'off the record', as other ministers had done. He was under intense pressure to resign not only from Birch, but from several friends, including Martin Maddan, his parliamentary private secretary. After Thursday's Cabinet meeting, Powell was again besieged by the reporters as he laid the foundation stone for a new Centre for the Jewish Blind in north-east London. Turning to the accompanying gaggle, he expressed his hope that they would continue to show the same level of interest in the disabled. Finally, on Saturday the 15th, Powell ended the speculation by exonerating Macmillan during a speech at a Conservative fête in the Norfolk town of Narborough. 'I will speak out here and now,' he told the pack of reporters who had been tipped off by his agent. With reference to the Profumo case, Powell stated that he was

> convinced that from the beginning to the end of the affair, and in every aspect of it, the personal honour and integrity of the Prime Minister, Harold Macmillan, are absolutely unsullied. I look to be in my place to support him.

As reporters rushed for the 'phones, Powell moved to his main theme – the 'supreme issue' of the free society versus the socialist state.[30]

Macmillan and his Government survived Monday's Commons debate, despite a withering assault by Birch, who concluded by quoting Browning's poem, *The Lost Leader*, ending with the line, 'Never glad confident morning again'. None the less, the Government's majority in the vote fell by nearly thirty, and there followed weeks of feverish speculation about Macmillan's future and who should lead the Tories into the next election. Powell was never a serious contender to replace Macmillan. A public opinion poll in June in the *Daily Express* showed him in fifth place with only 3 per cent. But he won praise from a surprising quarter in view of his earlier membership of the Suez Group, as the Earl of Avon (formerly Sir Anthony Eden), the former prime minister, revealed to Lord Beaverbrook the following month. 'Among the candidates', Avon wrote, 'I prefer Quintin [Hailsham] for courage and robustness and Enoch Powell for his flame of faith. But the second has not sufficient experience and following.'[31]

During the long summer recess, Macmillan fretted over his position and what he should say about his future when he addressed the Tory faithful in the leader's rally at the end of the party conference at Blackpool in October. By the evening of Monday 7 October, bolstered by support within his Cabinet, Macmillan had decided to soldier on, but during the night he was taken ill with prostate trouble. He managed to chair Tuesday morning's Cabinet meeting, but was in obvious discomfort and at noon he cut short the official business and told ministers that there had to be a decision about his leadership and that he would announce it at Blackpool. He then left the room to allow his bewildered ministers to discuss the matter freely. What happened next was to have a crucial bearing on events and on Powell's behaviour over the following eleven days.[32]

Because of the unease caused by Macmillan's obvious ill-health, Dilhorne stated that in the event of the Prime Minister's being unable to continue, he would be available to help in any Cabinet discussion on a successor. Home then intervened to say that since he was in no circumstances a candidate, he would also be ready to assist. Almost all the Cabinet then agreed to back Macmillan if he decided to lead the party at the next election. Only Powell, as he would later put it, 'had the bad manners' to disagree, since he thought that the party would lose under Macmillan's leadership. Powell's sole voice of dissent produced a reaction round the Cabinet table akin to that in one of

Bateman's cartoons on social gaffes, in which a person's naïve comment reduces everybody else to open-mouthed shock.[33]

That evening, after most ministers had arrived in Blackpool, the news broke that Macmillan would have to undergo surgery. From that moment, the leadership became virtually the only topic of conversation at the conference and the next two days' debates – including Powell's speech on the opening morning – became a sideshow. On Thursday afternoon, Home arrived hot-foot from seeing the Prime Minister in hospital and, in his capacity as that year's President of the National Union (the voluntary wing of the party, whose conference it was), at the end of the day's final debate read out Macmillan's statement that he would resign – a statement that his private secretary, Tim Bligh, told Butler had been due to the pressure of Home, Redmayne and Oliver Poole, the joint party chairman. In his statement, Macmillan had expressed his 'hope that it will soon be possible for the customary processes of consultation to be carried on within the party about its future leadership'. But his determination to ensure that the 'customary processes' reached what he regarded as the right conclusion, thereby enabling him, in effect, to nominate his successor, was to lead Powell to accuse him of having acted unconstitutionally.[34]

Outside the 'magic circle'

Powell backed Butler for the leadership. As early as the previous January, following the failure to enter the EEC, he had told a senior Cabinet colleague that Butler should replace Macmillan, although this had prompted a sceptical reaction. The strength of his commitment to Butler, however, appears puzzling, since Butler would never have embraced Powell's free-market or monetarist views, although as Chancellor he had wanted to float sterling. But Powell's preference is one example of his subordinating his market economics to his Tory politics. By 1963, he was 'utterly convinced that the whole development of the Conservative Party and the Conservative Government was moving towards its representation by Rab Butler'. Secondly, despite their differences on economic policy, Powell, the 'Church and Queen Tory', saw a kindred spirit in Butler, who was 'supremely at that moment' the person 'to represent the truly Tory element in modern Conservatism'. Powell's faith in Butler's destiny, however, blinded him to the forces that were mobilized against Butler and the qualities in the man that were to prevent him seizing the Tory crown.[35]

Macmillan's handling of the Tory succession represented a change of mind. Two years earlier, when Butler privately told Macmillan that he wanted to avoid any repetition of their competition for the leadership in 1957, Macmillan had responded that if he resigned as Prime Minister, 'he would not nominate his successor. He had told the Queen to consult her friends Alec Home and the like' – an ironic comment in the light of events during October 1963. Moreover, Macmillan added that Butler 'would have a far better chance of succeeding him if the issue lay with the crown before the election, than if the choice were to be left to a Party Meeting after the Election when we had lost'. A year later, however, Macmillan told Butler that Home was 'the only Minister now who could displace me'. Although he added that Home 'did not wish to be Prime Minister and leave the Lords', Macmillan none the less thought that 'Alec had some special genius, probably from his Lambton mother'.[36]

Following Home's dramatic announcement of Macmillan's resignation at Blackpool, the Tory conference came to resemble an American presidential convention. Speeches were treated as beauty contests between the contenders, while the smoke-filled rooms were to be found at the sea-front Imperial Hotel where ministers and other senior Tories lobbied and sounded out opinion. This was not Powell's natural habitat, but with Macleod and Boyle, he helped stave off moves within the Cabinet on Wednesday evening to prevent Butler's standing in for Macmillan and addressing the traditional leader's rally after the conference proper had finished. Powell told friends of his backing for Butler, and conferred with him in his room – if they could weather the tumult of the conference, the succession would be settled in the calmer atmosphere of London. But they reckoned without the manipulative role played by Macmillan and his inner counsel – 'the Magic Circle', as Macleod famously dubbed them in the riveting exposé that he published a few months later in the *Spectator*. 'Macmillan was determined', Macleod alleged, 'that Butler, although incomparably the best qualified of the contenders, should not succeed him.' Powell and Macleod were in close touch during the crisis, and Macleod privately told Butler that Powell was one of three close colleagues with whom he had 'checked every detail' of his subsequent exposé. Amidst the brouhaha caused by Macleod's article, Powell publicly confirmed 'the accuracy of Mr Macleod's narrative on all matters within my knowledge, and I agree with his general assessment of those events'.[37]

Powell, like Macleod, was hoodwinked during the leadership crisis. In particular, Powell failed to appreciate the full implications when he first heard of Home's decision to consult his doctor. Both Viscount Hailsham and the Earl of Home, the Government's two leading ministers in the Lords, had suddenly become eligible as potential prime ministers because of the new Peerage Act that allowed peers to renounce their titles and seek election to the Commons. A late amendment to the original Bill enabled existing peers in the Lords, such as Hailsham and Home, to renounce their titles straightaway instead of having to wait until the current parliament was dissolved – the Government accepted this late change to the Bill in July, only after the immediate pressure on Macmillan to resign had eased. The Bill had been prompted largely through the campaigning of Tony Benn, who was anxious to renounce the Viscountcy that he had inherited from his father and resume his career in the Commons, but the last-minute amendment conveniently provided Macmillan, who no longer feared being replaced immediately, with two options to block Butler. But whereas Hailsham had been a 'reluctant' peer, who had pressed for similar reform years earlier, Home could not be described, by any stretch of the imagination, as sitting reluctantly in the Lords as opposed to the Commons. This difference between the two leading Government peers was to add to the row over Macmillan's succession. The Prime Minister initially backed Hailsham, but quickly deserted him when his candidacy provoked strong reaction and switched to Home. This was the significance in the news of Home's check-up that Powell missed.[38]

In Macmillan's absence, Butler addressed the leader's rally in Blackpool and chaired the Cabinet meeting on the following Tuesday, 15 October. He read to the Cabinet Macmillan's minute setting out the method by which Tory opinion was to be taken – the Cabinet were to be sounded by Dilhorne; MPs and junior ministers by Redmayne; peers by the Lords' whip, Lord St Aldwyn; and party workers by Lord Poole and senior figures in the National Union. This process had, in fact, already begun in Blackpool. Ministers realized that they could do nothing more until it was completed, but questions of the Cabinet's further role and the method by which the Queen was to be advised were left unstated. These constitutional aspects were of deep concern to Powell. While the Cabinet were being informed of Macmillan's plan for sounding party opinion, the Prime Minister was dictating his ruminations on the leadership, that was to form the first draft of the memorandum that he was later to read to the Queen on his resignation. 'Lord Home is clearly a man who represents the old governing class at its best,' he noted in a revealing indication of his own thinking.[39]

Events came to a head more quickly than the Cabinet expected. Macmillan's intention was to prevent their discussing the leadership any further. On the morning of Thursday 17th, Macleod learned that the matter was about to be settled and assumed, wrongly, that a speedy resolution meant that Butler had emerged as the successor. But Maudling, one of the contenders, was concerned that ministers should have a further opportunity to discuss the position. Dilhorne, however, was turning down calls for a Cabinet meeting to review the procedure by which the Queen was to be advised. During the afternoon, Macleod heard from William [later Lord] Rees-Mogg of the *Sunday Times* that 'the decision had been made, and that it was for Home'. Macleod immediately telephoned Maudling and Powell and arranged to meet them as soon as possible at his Chelsea flat. They were later joined by Lord Aldington, Macleod's former deputy at Central Office. The phone calls soon started from the leading political reporters, all with the same story. Maudling made his own inquiries and confirmed that Home, not Butler, was to be recommended to the Queen as the party's preferred choice.[40]

Powell, Macleod and Maudling realized that if, as ministers, they 'were going to make any serious protest against an invitation being extended to Lord Home to form a Government, it was essential that he should know about this at the earliest moment'. Powell and Macleod each decided to speak to him direct. Macleod telephoned Home, but found that he was out, and made an appointment for Powell and himself to see the Foreign Secretary after dinner.

Macleod had a dinner engagement in Westminster, but afterwards called Powell and went round to his house in South Eaton Place. It had been Jennifer Powell's seventh birthday party, and with the balloons still decorating the room the Tory rebels began the 'midnight meeting' that was to become political folklore.[41]

Before Powell and Macleod could contact Home, they were called by Hailsham, who had learned of the intended nomination of Home and who at this stage was saying that it would not do. When Macleod and Powell rang Home, it was apparent that they could not see him without running the gauntlet of the press, who were encamped outside his official residence, 1 Carlton Gardens. Instead, they spoke to him on the phone separately, each telling him that he was an unsuitable candidate – unlike Hailsham, he was not a reluctant peer, and it was unacceptable that the Tories were proposing to admit that, in the modern day and age, they could not find a leader among their 363 members in the Commons. Maudling and Aldington arrived at the Powells, as did Frederick [later Lord] Erroll, the President of the Board of Trade and Maudling's closest ally in the Cabinet. There were at least three other ministerial conclaves that night, but the South Eaton Place gathering was discovered when Henry Fairlie, the journalist, rang Maudling's home and was given a number that he traced as Powell's. Derek Marks of the *Daily Express* acted on a hunch, went to Belgravia to investigate, and was rewarded with his scoop.[42]

Powell and his colleagues at South Eaton Place began to feel more optimistic, as it was established that not only were Hailsham and Maudling opposed to Home, but they 'believed Butler to be the right and obvious successor and would be happy and ready to serve under him'. It meant that most of the Cabinet were against Home and prompted Lord Aldington to inform the Palace of the opposition to Home. Similar warnings were made to the Palace by supporters of Butler and Hailsham. But Powell and his colleagues were made aware of the determination of Macmillan and his close advisers to nominate Home, when the Chief Whip, Redmayne, arrived, having had a lift from Home's by one of the Foreign Secretary's strongest backers, Selwyn Lloyd. It had been Redmayne who, during a conversation with a journalist, had uttered the cryptic comment, 'Don't forget Goschen' – a warning to any potential rebel of Lord Randolph Churchill's error in offering his resignation as Chancellor to Lord Salisbury, who promptly called his bluff, appointed Goschen to the Exchequer and consigned Churchill to the wilderness.[43]

Redmayne, however, could make no impression on Powell and the others. According to the Chief Whip, Home had the strongest backing among Tory MPs and junior ministers. This seemed odd, since in the summer Maudling had been the most popular choice among MPs, but Redmayne and the chairman of the 1922 Committee, John Morrison (later Lord Margadale) were strong Home supporters and the whips had pressed Home's name on MPs. Powell was almost certainly right in believing that had Butler become leader, there was no question but that the party would have rallied to him. Powell and his colleagues finally asked Redmayne 'to report to the Prime Minister the fact of the understanding which had arisen between Butler, Maudling and Hailsham. He promised to do this.' This again raises the question of the advice finally given to the Queen. Macleod, Maudling and Powell each 'spoke to Butler himself, told him what had been agreed, and assured him of our support'. When Powell told him that 'things were stacked his way and passed on to him, with their permission, the assurances of those who would serve under him, he actually said, "This is very important. The Prime Minister must hear of this".' In Powell's view, Butler was typically assuming that Macmillan would play fair.[44]

Powell's and Macleod's conclusion that Butler had the support of most of the Cabinet contradicted Dilhorne's soundings, on which Macmillan's choice of Home was largely based. Dilhorne correctly identified Powell among Butler's supporters, and had noted Powell's strong objection to Hailsham ('on no account Quintin'). But his finding that ten ministers favoured Home, against four for Maudling and three for Butler, was inaccurate – Dilhorne had even listed Macleod and Boyle as Home supporters, which was inconceivable. When Powell was first shown the detailed figures many years later, he initially regarded them as a forgery but then suggested that Dilhorne 'did not hear what was being said'. Although Powell was unaware of the detailed findings at the time, the suggestion that Home had the backing of the Cabinet was so obviously wrong that he discounted the other soundings of party opinion.[45]

Powell put on the record ten years later, in his review of Macmillan's memoirs, that by the morning of Friday 18th, seven ministers had 'declared, to Mr Butler and to one another that they did not consider Lord Home should be Prime Minister, that they would serve under Mr Butler, and that they would not serve under Lord Home unless Mr Butler had previously agreed to do so'. The seven were: Macleod, Maudling, Powell, Erroll, Hailsham, Boyd-Carpenter and Boyle. With Butler, this made eight ministers opposed to Home and in favour of Butler, without taking account of others who were not prepared to make a stand but had privately opted for Butler. 'So much', Powell dismissively commented, 'for Macmillan's alleged "general impression" from the selection of Cabinet ministers (including Macleod, Maudling and Hailsham themselves!) whom he had summoned to the hospital on October 15 and 16, that "if Lord Home would undertake the task of PM the whole Cabinet would cheerfully unite under him".'[46]

In Powell's view, the critical time for Butler was between 3.00 a.m. on Friday 18th, after Powell had phoned him, and 10 o'clock that morning. Butler agonized over his decision, but finally lacked the mettle to seize the Tory crown from Home's grasp. Powell later spoke of having handed Butler 'a loaded revolver and told him that all he had to do was pull the trigger'. Home could not have formed an administration without Butler and a majority of the Cabinet were willing to serve under Butler. Butler could have refused to serve Home, but he had not wanted to use the revolver if it would make a noise or hurt anyone. Powell privately attributed Butler's failure to pride – he was unwilling to be Prime Minister as second choice – and a streak of weakness, that was curious in a senior politician.[47]

By 9.30 a.m. on the Friday, Macmillan had tendered his resignation in a letter to the Queen. He and Home knew, however, that the other contenders had agreed to support Butler. This meant, in Powell's words, that 'a Butler government enjoying general acceptance was available by the time Macmillan's resignation reached the Queen'. According to Macmillan, Home 'felt like withdrawing', and had to be 'urged not to do so'. The Queen visited Macmillan at 11.15 a.m., and heard him read the memorandum that, in Macleod's words, 'purported to be not the advice of one man, but the collective view of a party'. At 12.15 p.m., the Queen asked Home to the Palace, and followed earlier precedent by asking him first to consult his colleagues and see whether he could form a government before formally appointing him Prime Minister. Home shrewdly hosted his consultations at Number 10.[48]

Powell later graphically recalled his meeting with Home at Number 10 on the Friday afternoon, before Home had 'formally accepted the Queen's commission':

Now that is the moment [at] which a Cabinet minister actually has a personal opportunity to take part in deciding who shall or shall not be Prime Minister, when he is able to say, 'No, I'm sorry but I wouldn't accept office under you', or to say, 'Yes, I'd love it, I'd want it on any terms'. That is the moment when the responsibility of taking part in making a Prime Minister lands with a Cabinet minister. And I exercised that ... by saying, to Alec Home, 'You know I like you very much but you oughtn't to be Prime Minister. Rab ought to be Prime Minister, he's the man who ought to be Prime Minister. So if you ask me, would I serve under you, no, my answer has to be no.'[49]

All the efforts of Powell, Macleod and their allies to wrest the premiership for Butler finally collapsed on Saturday morning when their candidate agreed to serve under Home. But any hopes that Home harboured that all Butler's supporters would follow suit were shattered by Powell and Macleod. Powell remembered returning to Number 10 on Saturday afternoon, the 19th. When Home put to him the question that he had put hypothetically the day before, Powell gave the memorable reply quoted at the head of this chapter. Home said that he understood.[50]

Recriminations

'There is little sympathy for Iain or Enoch', Paul Channon, Butler's parliamentary private secretary, told his boss, 'but tremendous respect and sympathy for you.' In the recriminations that followed their refusal to serve,

Powell and Macleod were accused of inverted snobbery for having opposed the choice of an aristocrat as Prime Minister and of jockeying for the succession, on the assumption that the Tories would lose the next election. Home was stung by their refusal to serve, and repeated both accusations in his memoirs. As to the first charge, Powell was appalled to discover inverted snobbery in his reaction to Home's appointment, and equally appalled to discover a lack of such snobbery in other people's. His constituency association had been primarily concerned that the leadership should be settled, whoever was appointed, and small shopkeepers to whom he had spoken in Wolverhampton were not at all dismayed by the spectacle of the fourteenth Earl of Home having become Prime Minister. Yet he had detected inverted snobbery among some people, which suggested that his and Macleod's qualms about an aristocrat leading the modern Tory Party were not entirely misplaced.[51]

On the second count of jockeying for the succession after an election defeat, instead of rallying to the party, Powell was less heavily criticized than Macleod. The view among Tory MPs in the smoking room was that Macleod, whose radical policy in Africa had offended traditionalists, was scheming and 'getting off the boat', whereas Powell was an eccentric former professor, possessed of an erratic brilliance and liable to act entirely by his own lights. Macleod was devious, but Powell was dotty.[52]

Powell would certainly have been 'totally miserable' had he behaved otherwise. The 'privilege' of being able 'to look oneself in the face' was 'an important means to living at peace with oneself, and to living at peace with the world – not to be ashamed.' And Powell 'would have been ashamed to have denied my true opinions at that moment ... simply in order to cling onto office'. He also thought that he would have given Home 'the same answer even if he'd offered me Foreign Secretary', although the idea of rejecting such a great office prompted more soul-searching:

> Now how do I know that? I don't know that. I can't know that. I can only say, 'I believe I would have done.' I hope I would have done it, I feel sure I would have done it.[53]

But this was not the end of the matter. Macmillan's guileful conduct of the Tory succession had again stirred the 'Country' Tory in Powell. His complaint against Macmillan went much further than the question of whether Butler or Home was better qualified. Ten years later, when reviewing his former leader's memoirs, Powell alleged that Macmillan had acted unconstitutionally. In particular, he claimed that Macmillan had effectively designated his successor while still in office and thus deprived the Queen of the exercise of her principal prerogative – appointing the Prime Minister. Powell charged that Macmillan had 'publicly, with the authority of the Prime Minister in office, carried out a process designed to produce the answer, so that the Queen then would be obliged both to ask his advice and to take or seek no other.' Macmillan revealed in his memoirs that when he had first broached the subject of his resignation some weeks before, the Queen had felt 'the great importance of maintaining the prerogative intact. After all, if she asked someone to form a government and he failed, what harm was done?' To which Powell retorted, 'Just so. What Macmillan did was deliberately (and, in retrospect, conclusively) to destroy the very prerogative which his Sovereign had thought of great importance to maintain'.[54]

But Powell's charge does not stick. The soundings of Conservative Party opinion were not unconstitutional, even though they may have been undermined by bias and incompetence. The key point is that the procedure for appointing a prime minister is governed by convention. In 1963 this was upheld. Powell was confused and mistaken on the constitutional position. Further to his charge that Macmillan had acted 'with the authority of the Prime Minister in office', Powell dismissed as 'an uncomprehending quibble' the fact that 'Macmillan had resigned at 9.30 a.m. on Friday, 18 October, and the Queen asked his advice at 11 a.m.'. In one sense Powell was right, but not in the way that he meant. In 1957, the Queen had given Eden, as the retiring Prime Minister, an opportunity to express his opinion on his successor *before* he had formally tendered his resignation. In precedent, therefore, there would have been nothing against Macmillan's giving his advice before he had resigned. Later, Powell was confused on the timing of events, and in 1980 attacked Macmillan's 'theatrical coup of sending for his Sovereign and tendering advice to her on the succession before resigning instead of waiting to be asked, if at all, afterwards'. Powell was mistaken on the facts, but in precedent it made no difference whether Macmillan's advice was sought before or after his resignation.[55]

The Queen was at liberty to seek other advice, however persuasively Macmillan had sought to suggest that his evidence was conclusive. The precedent of 1957, when Eden had indicated his preference for Butler, also established that Her Majesty was not bound by the advice of a retiring prime minister. Since the Palace had been alerted to the serious opposition to Home that existed in the Cabinet, Powell's wrath might have been better targeted at the failure of the Queen's advisers to persuade her of the need for wider consultation. The real failing, however, lay with Butler.[56]

Powell was also wrong on another constitutional point. In 1976, he criticized Lord Home for having thought that a Cabinet meeting could have been summoned after Macmillan's resignation, and before he had kissed hands as Prime Minister, in order to allow Home to withdraw his earlier statement that he was not a contender for the leadership. According to Powell, once Macmillan's resignation had been accepted by the Queen, 'neither Lord Home (either before or after receiving her commission) nor anyone else could bring it together again for any purpose'. But this is not the case. On the death or resignation of a Prime Minister, other Ministers do not automatically cease to hold their offices. They continue to be paid as Cabinet ministers under the Ministerial and Other Salaries Act and remain entitled to exercise their statutory powers.[57]

This fact is also significant for another reason. It raises the question of whether Butler, who chaired the Cabinet during Macmillan's illness, would have been within his powers in calling a Cabinet meeting after Macmillan's resignation on the Friday morning in order to consider the leadership. Indeed, it has been suggested – though obviously not by Powell – that Butler's summoning the Cabinet would have forestalled the Queen's invitation to Home to see if he could form an administration. These matters raise complex constitutional questions, and the present author therefore consulted the Cabinet Secretary, Sir Robin Butler, and Lord Charteris, formerly the Queen's private secretary. Sir Robin, who was advised by First Parliamentary Counsel, believes that Rab Butler could have called a meeting of his Cabinet colleagues without the Queen's commission, and that if they had met to discuss government business, 'it would seem proper and appropriate for the usual machinery for Cabinet meetings to be used'. But it would have been a totally different matter if the ministers had met to discuss the leadership. In Sir Robin's view, 'a meeting to discuss party business, including the question of who might succeed as leader of the party, would not naturally be regarded as a Cabinet meeting merely because those attending were members of the outgoing Cabinet'. Even if Rab Butler had summoned a meeting of ministers after Macmillan's resignation, however, would it have forestalled the Queen's invitation to Home? Sir Robin concludes that it could not have done, 'since the Queen is not bound to take formal advice from her Ministers on this matter'. Lord Charteris is more forthright. In his view, it would have been 'wholly unacceptable', from the point of view of 'custom and common-sense' for Butler to have summoned a meeting of Cabinet ministers while the Queen was visiting Macmillan and subsequently sending for Home. Indeed, it would have been 'an act of disloyalty'. Any notion that Rab Butler, of all people, would have considered committing an act that might have been construed as disloyal, is quite out of the question.[58]

Despite Powell's complaints that the constitution was violated in October 1963, precedent *was* followed. The Queen took the precaution of first asking Home to see if he could form an administration rather than kissing hands immediately. This was in line with the exercise of her prerogative. From what she had said to Macmillan, she would not have regarded it as a problem if Home had reported that he was unable to form an administration. Indeed, it was this procedure which gave Butler his opportunity to become Prime Minister, as Powell acknowledged, when he could have quite properly refused to serve Home. Only after Home had established that he could form an administration that would command a majority in the Commons did the Queen formally appoint him Prime Minister.

There is an element of humbug in Powell's adopting the role of constitutional guardian. He and the rest of Butler's supporters wanted to create a situation in which the Queen's only practical option would have been to ask Butler to form an administration. There was nothing unconstitutional in their actions. But neither was there in Macmillan's, however much Macleod and Powell objected to some of his methods. The Butler camp failed because their principal let them down, not because of any constitutional violation.

Yet in Powell's view, Macmillan was guilty of having 'conclusively' destroyed the Queen's prerogative in appointing the prime minister. This, again, is quite wrong. He appears to have had in mind the abandonment by the Conservative Party of the discredited 'customary processes' in 1965 and their replacement by formal rules for electing a new leader. The introduction of leadership elections by the Conservatives has not destroyed the royal prerogative in appointing a prime minister – quite the contrary. As Vernon Bogdanor has pointed out, George VI's private secretary, Sir Alan Lascelles, had written to the Cabinet Secretary as early as 1947 that, 'a clear advance indication by the members of the party in power as to the man [sic] they want to be their leader is, it seems to me, a help to wise ruling by the Sovereign rather than a derogation of the Sovereign's power'. And as Peter Hennessy has shown, the prerogative of appointing a prime minister remains an important feature of the constitution that survives and might well be brought into play in the event of an election that leaves no party with an overall majority in the Commons.[59]

Powell's refusal to serve Home was his third, and final, refusal to serve in a Conservative Government. Neither he nor anybody else could have dreamt for a moment that when he walked from the Cabinet room on Tuesday 15 October 1963, it was to be the last occasion that he would do so as a minister. He was aged only fifty-one and was barely a third of the way through his parliamentary career. It was strangely appropriate, in view of their association since the late 1940s, that his last Cabinet meeting should have been chaired by Butler, the would-be Prime Minister whom he most wanted to serve.

Whereas Macleod was extremely unhappy at having returned to the back benches, Powell had the compensation of experiencing again the feeling of 'coming home to mother'. 'The circumstances in which I ceased to be a Cabinet Minister in 1963', he recalled almost twenty-five years later, 'gave me a freedom of expression and a freedom of exploration at a very important stage, and that enabled me to exploit and explore the public speech as an instrument of political persuasion.' By taking advantage of this opportunity, Powell was to have a dramatic impact on British politics.[60]

13

Powellism

I have no intention of going out of politics. I would have to be carried out feet first. I live and die a politician.

> Enoch Powell, rejecting any idea that, having left office, he might quit politics, Bromley, 25 October 1963.

Discovering a new weapon

Powell's experience after his refusal to serve in Douglas-Home's Government in October 1963 was in marked contrast to the position in which he found himself after his resignation from the Treasury in January 1958. On the earlier occasion, as Powell acknowledged, he, Birch and Thorneycroft had been isolated and even unpopular figures in the party, but during the winter of 1963–64 he claimed that he was positively embarrassed by protestations of friendship. This was not to deny, however, the anger and dismay that was felt in the party at his and Macleod's refusal to serve. Three constituencies cancelled Powell's speaking engagements in the immediate aftermath, although his speech on the Friday after his departure from the front bench went ahead, and, by coincidence, happened to be in Bromley – Macmillan's constituency. But even where Powell's invitations were cancelled, other Tories, including the candidates and agents, apologized for the attitude that their people had taken towards him. He had also received offers of help and advice from party officials in Central Office. A Gallup poll had shown approval for his decision not to serve Douglas-Home by 38 to 25 per cent, and in November, he was elected chairman of the Tory back bench education committee.[1]

The sympathy for Powell reflected the underlying difference between 1958 and 1963 in the party's prospects and in his standing. Not only had the controversy surrounding the selection of Douglas-Home as Macmillan's successor created an unease within Central Office and the parliamentary party, but in addition, there was a widespread expectation that after a dozen continuous years in power the Tories would lose the next election, due by the autumn of 1964 at the latest. This sense of unease was compounded by the difficulty that Tories and other politicians were having in establishing what

Douglas-Home stood for. Powell believed that this was largely because the new Prime Minister had not been in the Commons during the preceding decade – the party would have felt more secure with Hailsham or Butler, both of whom were known quantities.

Many Tories, among them Powell, were already looking ahead to what might follow in Opposition. Those who talked with him at the time were struck that he did not appear unduly pessimistic at the prospect. The impression that he did not much care whether or not the Tories won the next election was confirmed by his view that he had felt for more than a year that the country wanted socialism and the Conservative Government had seemed determined to give it to them; and that, as in 1945, it might do the party some good to suffer a spell out of office. Indeed, Powell even went so far as to speculate that October 1963 and not the date of the forthcoming election would loom as the Conservatives' second 1945.[2]

In this frame of mind, Powell saw the necessity to re-think the purpose of the Conservative Party after October 1963 as being as unavoidable as it had been in the 1940s. He was not alone in seeing the urgent need to revitalize the party. Several years earlier, he had given some thought to the demands on any party when it is in Opposition. In an article written for the journal, *Political Quarterly*, shortly before the 1959 election, he had reviewed Labour's performance since they lost office in 1951. In a comment that was to have a bearing on his views about his own party's future, Powell had argued that an Opposition

> must have a categorical imperative: 'Do this, and this alone, if you would be saved'. There must be a great, simple, central theme, branching into all fields and subjects of debate, but in itself easily grasped, which runs through the words and actions of a successful Opposition.[3]

Powell's return to the back benches, and the greater freedom of expression that it brought, now enabled him to begin developing the 'great, simple, central theme' of the Conservative Party, even before they formally went into Opposition. From the autumn of 1963, Powell could speak as a former Cabinet minister, and as one who, despite his refusal to serve Douglas-Home, was likely in the future to become a senior figure in the party. Moreover, taking the first steps to open up the debate on the party's future was more likely to enhance his personal prospects in the long term than damage them.

None the less, Powell saw that he had to choose his ground carefully in launching the debate on the party's future ahead of a general election. This was evident from his reaction to the decision by Macleod, who had also refused to serve Douglas-Home, to accept an offer less than a fortnight later to edit the political and literary weekly magazine, the *Spectator* – a move that caused something of a sensation in Fleet Street. Powell thought Macleod's decision mistaken. This was significant, since Powell himself was an active freelance journalist and broadcaster whenever he was out of office, but he appreciated the crucial distinction between the role of freelance, on the one hand, and that of editor on the other. Instead of being able to select on which issues, and when, to nail his colours to the mast, Macleod would be obliged, as editor, to express an opinion on different issues virtually every week. In this respect at least, Powell was the cannier of the two men. There was never any prospect of Powell's taking up the tongue-in-cheek invitation from *Private Eye* to become their editor, on the same £5,000 salary that Macleod had accepted. Like Macleod, Powell's salary had fallen from £5,000 as a minister to £1,750 as an MP. The following February, however, he supplemented his parliamentary salary by accepting a less risky invitation than an editorship – a directorship with the National Discount Company.[4]

Whatever misgivings Powell had about Macleod's editorship, he attached great importance at this stage of his career to their bond, that stretched back for almost eighteen years and that had been strengthened by their having backed Butler and their refusal to serve Home. Powell defined his own Toryism in terms of his agreement with, and difference to, Macleod, and in the process mapped out the main features of what Macleod was later to dub, 'Powellism'. Powell saw much in their shared assumptions that could inform and inspire a new-look, post-1963 Conservative Party. He and Macleod were, above all, post-imperial in their outlook. Powell was convinced that if he had been involved in colonial matters, he would have been in complete agreement with Macleod's policy. He also thought that they were agreed in wanting to give a peculiarly Tory twist to the idea of the welfare state. Moreover, ever since their days in the One Nation group in the 1950–51 parliament, they had believed that the new Conservative Party had been able to influence and to draw upon a new segment of the middle classes – Powell saw himself as being more lower-middle class than Macleod, who was a doctor's son and had been brought up in a market-town. Perhaps most important in Powell's mind, he and Macleod, and other like-minded Tories, felt strongly and self-consciously that the Conservatives were a national party.

But it was the difference between the two men on economic and social policy that threw Powell's thinking into sharp relief. Powell regarded Macleod's instincts as being more political, in the sense that he was apt to be concerned whether a particular policy was acceptable to the party and the voters, whereas Powell admitted to being something of an ideologue. In essence, Powell saw himself as a High Tory who believed in liberal economics, and acknowledged that this was a peculiar position. He was a 'Church and Queen Tory' who accepted Burke's evolutionary view of society, while he also believed in competitive capitalism mainly because it was in the nature of the beast (i.e. mankind). These beliefs of Powell's explain his view that by 1963 it was in the long-term interest of the Conservatives to distinguish themselves more clearly from Labour on ideological grounds. In particular, he wanted the party to become committed to competitive capitalism, although he realized that this was unlikely to happen in the immediate future.[5]

Yet Powell had grave doubts during 1963–64 about the Government's controversial decision to abolish resale price maintenance. This was ironic, since the protagonist of this liberalizing reform was none other than the then President of the Board of Trade, Heath, whom Powell was to come to regard as the arch-interventionist. Powell, however, thought that it appeared an isolated and almost gratuitous act, since it was not accompanied by any other similarly liberal economic measures. In addition, he appreciated the political fact that thousands of small shopkeepers, and the people to whom they talked, were extremely unhappy about it. For these reasons, it undermined the troops' faith in the generals: Tories in the constituencies could not imagine why the Government were behaving in this way.[6]

None the less, Powell was determined to shift the Conservatives as far as he could towards his vision of a post-imperial, nationally-minded, High Tory and economically liberal, party. These four aspects comprised the compass points of 'Powellism'. But Powell still had to find a way of putting 'Powellism' on the Tory agenda. As a first prerequisite, he had to continue to command attention in the media and in the party. This, however, was bound to become more difficult, since his news value as a former Cabinet minister would wane the longer he remained on the back benches. But at the end of January 1964, he stumbled on the answer.

On 17 January, Macleod had given the most dramatic demonstration in modern times of a former Cabinet minister's ability to capture the headlines by publishing his sensational exposé of what had happened behind the scenes during the previous October's Tory leadership crisis. Such was the depth of hostility that was unleashed towards Macleod after he had caricatured the Tory leadership as the 'Magic Circle', that he thought it had ended his political career. Powell, however, disagreed. He not only confirmed publicly Macleod's version of events, but privately was vehement in denying any suggestion that the whole party had turned on Macleod. In his view, Macleod's critics were vocal, but his many friends were silent. And although Powell was to keep his counsel on the leadership crisis for almost ten years, he was convinced that Macleod had gained in strength and stature.[7]

Less than a fortnight after Macleod's headline-grabbing revelations, Powell created a fresh furore in a speech that he came to regard as a turning-point in his career. Although his speech to the National Liberal Forum in Caxton Hall, Westminster, on Monday 28 January, lacked the sensationalism of Macleod's exposé, he emulated Macleod by the uncompromising savagery of his language, as he derided the Government's attempt to restrain pay and prices as 'hocus pocus'. This policy had been pursued by successive Conservative Governments since the mid-1950s, but Powell's particular target was the National Economic Development Council (NEDC), that comprised representatives of the Government, employers and unions. The NEDC had been created by Macmillan in 1961, and was seen as having a crucial role to play in achieving economic expansion without inflation – assisted by the National Incomes Commission, that had been set up in 1962. In Powell's view, however, such interventionism inevitably led deep into the jungle of detailed control. 'Wages, profits, prices', he declared, 'are determined, always have been determined, and always will be determined, until we go communist, by the market – by supply and demand working through the market.'[8]

Such an outspoken attack on a central plank of the Government's economic policy by a former minister was bound to attract attention, but this speech was to assume enormous significance for Powell. His reasons were two-fold. Some six years later, he was to identify 28 January 1964 as the exact date when the divergence started between him and Sir Edward Heath. Although Powell had long been committed to *laissez-faire* economics, and Heath was not to become Tory leader until 1965, this speech was the launch of Powell's campaign to convert the Tories to competitive capitalism.

Yet the form of the speech's delivery was, if anything, even more important to Powell than its content. It was on this occasion that, quite by accident, he first hit upon the device of handing out the entire text of his speech. Previously, he had assumed that it was pointless to give the media the full text, as this would receive less publicity than if he were to provide brief, edited highlights – what are now called 'sound-bites'. But as he discovered, much to his surprise, providing the entire text beforehand had the opposite effect. It was a lesson that he was never to forget: for him, at least, the massive presentation of an argument was a weapon. Moreover, it taught him that he could combine political speech-making and the literary impulse that had previously inspired his poetry.[9]

This impulse was revived by his liberation from office and his excitement at having a mission in defining and expounding a new Toryism, and he could now channel it into his new method of speech-making. As he later commented, in a classical allusion, 'the egerian stream was forcing itself up again'. In a speech to the parliamentary press gallery in February 1964, he told his audience of political journalists and politicians that he intended to continue spelling out his brand of Toryism – quoting Martin Luther, he declared, 'God help me, I can do no other!'[10]

This new weapon in Powell's hand was tantamount, in his view, to a new medium. His speeches were now more fully reported, and in addition, he believed that his new technique had an impact on his audiences because they were not just hearing another platform speech, but were being treated to something that combined the tension of the platform speech with the rigour of a treatise. 'The Powell image, seen in fine focus, as his audience appreciated,' remarked the *Express and Star* of his speech to the parliamentary press gallery, 'is one of dynamic force, complete mastery of his subject and innate honesty of purpose'. Powell's ability to create this impression in his speech-making became his trademark and was to bring him some spectacular coups. On occasion, however, his treatise could seem arcane and his language convoluted, with the result that his audience were sometimes left with the impression of having heard something profound with little idea of what it meant – a failure, by any standards, in a political speech.[11]

Powell exploited this new weapon in a series of critical speeches principally

devoted to the errors of economic intervention of one form or another –
incomes policy, planning, regional policy – over the months before the 1964
election. He was careful to focus his critique of Tory policy mainly on
economic policy, and otherwise exercised extreme caution. On three successive
mornings at the start of April, however, *The Times* gave prominence on its
editorial page to a series of articles that amounted to a treatise on modern
Conservatism and argued for a new, more radical approach. The articles were
anonymous, and were signed simply, 'A Conservative'. Other suspects
included Sir William Haley, then editor of *The Times* and Michael Oakeshott,
the political philosopher – as Alan Watkins, the political columnist, has
recalled, a hapless lobby correspondent misheard the latter's name, and came
up with Sir Hendrie Oakshott, a little known Tory MP. Nicholas Tomalin,
the journalist, put the articles through a computer and came up with the name
of Enoch Powell, while Watkins guessed their authorship from Powell's
distinctive style. But Powell was the prime suspect principally because the
arguments that the author presented on foreign policy, defence and social and
economic policy, had – in the vernacular of the detective novel – his
fingerprints all over them. But when he was interviewed by Sir Robin Day on
BBC's *Panorama*, he refused either to confirm or to deny authorship – a
refusal that he insisted on maintaining, albeit with wry amusement, some
thirty years later.[12]

Those who best knew his politics were in little doubt that Powell was the
author. Macleod had heard him expound identical arguments over a period of
eighteen years in the parliamentary secretariat, at the One Nation group (that
they now rejoined as back-benchers) and to party policy groups. Writing
under his pen-name of 'Quoodle' in the *Spectator*, Macleod had been provoked
by criticism of the articles by Lord Dilhorne, the Lord Chancellor, who had
been one of the 'Magic Circle' in October 1963 and who had now
'pontificated' that whoever had written the articles could not claim to be 'a
Conservative'. Macleod retorted that he had not previously been aware that
the Lord Chancellor was also 'keeper of the membership roll for the Tory
Party', and continued,

> Nor if one studies his [Dilhorne's] contributions to the practice or
> philosophy of the party and compares them (say) with Mr Enoch Powell are
> the Lord Chancellor's claims exactly overwhelming.

In a further pointer, Macleod found 'the anonymity of the articles oddly out of
character'. The fact that he also admitted to detesting the author's views on
the Commonwealth and planning also pointed to the strongest areas of
disagreement between him and Powell. But Macleod valued Powell's
contribution to Tory debate, and as he commented of the author of the
articles, 'unlike the Lord Chancellor I would defend to the death his right to
put them forward and to proclaim himself a Conservative'. John Biffen, who
had been elected to the Commons in 1961 and during the mid-1960s became

an acolyte of Powell's, comments that 'if the same method of textual analysis that Powell used to apply to classical texts were to be applied to those articles, I'm sure that it would reveal Powell as the author'.[13]

The trio of articles in *The Times* was shot through with the distinctive imprint of emergent 'Powellism', both in language and content. The historical résumé of the party since 1945 dismissed as 'myth' the notion that the centrist policies devised under Butler's aegis explained the party's return to popularity by the late 1940s, and instead stressed that 'people wanted to be rid of the apparatus of war and socialism which seemed to be cramping their lives and holding Britain back'. Similarly, although the One Nation group's first book was said to have given the party 'a good conscience about the social services', emphasis was placed on the fact that they later 'took over the campaign for the denationalization of road transport and the "freeing" of British Railways which looked like faltering'. Macmillan was paid a back-handed compliment for his 'superb gamesmanship', and the departure of Thorneycroft in 1958 was said to have 'marked the assertion of that expansionist policy which Macmillan was determined to pursue at home, to limits that would have been reckless in anyone not living with the promptings of Roy Harrod and the memories of the 1930s'.[14]

The diagnosis and policy prescriptions similarly reflected Powell's thinking at the time. 'The Commonwealth has become a gigantic farce', while Britain's world-wide defence commitments could only be explained historically. Instead, Britain was 'a European power'. The adoption of 'a new defence policy and a non-Commonwealth policy' demanded a shift in foreign policy, not towards 'little England', but to a new role as a European power that would wield influence because it 'could no longer even be caricatured as a colonial power'. 'Has the Conservative Party of today', the author wondered, 'the courage and the candour to base patriotism on reality, not her [England's] dreams?' In the final article, Powell's nostrums in policy group discussions of a guaranteed minimum income in old age and the abolition of housing subsidy were paraded, while state education and the NHS were defined as being compatible with the party's philosophy. As to economic policy, Powell's attacks on the Government were amplified in the assertion that, 'the Party's strength and dynamism depends on belief in the efficiency of capitalism. Contradictory policies here undermine the very basis of its claim to govern.' Interventionism was denounced, whether in the form of regional policy, or 'the gradual approach to planning of growth by NEDC and of incomes by NIC', as representing 'a shift of policy as definite as it is recent'. 'The difficulty is', concluded the article, in a clarion call for the Conservatives to embrace competitive capitalism,

> to reconcile it with the convictions of a party which bases itself, and must base itself, on the belief that economic ends are best achieved by the mechanism of competitive enterprise. The dilemma has to be resolved, and to be seen to be resolved. It can only be resolved one way.[15]

On the day of publication of this last article in *The Times*, Powell reiterated his critique of regional policy in a speech in Glasgow. As he noted, unemployment in Scotland was twice the national average (4.5 per cent against 2 per cent nationally), but he none the less attacked any attempt by the state to bring work to its people, and attacked the Government's policy of 'inducing or cajoling particular firms and industries to establish themselves in places which they would not otherwise have chosen'. The critical editorials in *The Times* and the *Daily Telegraph* on the following day were a barometer of the unease in Tory ranks at Powell's campaign. Wilson, the Labour leader, mocked that it was not unusual for a party to probe deeply into its philosophy after an election defeat; but the Tories had started the argument *before* the defeat.[16]

The thrust of Powell's argument on economic policy, namely that the Tories must stand for competitive capitalism or stand for nothing, was most effectively countered in the *Spectator* immediately after the articles in *The Times* by Ian Gilmour, the Tory MP who had been elected in 1962 and who owned the weekly magazine. As Gilmour observed, it had been the Liberals, and not the Tories, who had been the champions of capitalism in the nineteenth century. 'For the Conservative Party', he wrote, 'which refused to espouse capitalism when she was at her classical and enticing best, to fall in love with her in 1964 would be sheer necrophilia.' Gilmour suggested that 'the mechanism of competitive enterprise, the market, is Mr Powell's Supreme Being'. A more petulant sign of Tory irritation with Powell surfaced later in April, when Quintin Hogg (formerly Lord Hailsham) took the opportunity of a visit to Scotland to denounce Powell's criticisms of regional policy. Hogg recalled his own special, ministerial responsibility for the north-east – Powell had been in the Cabinet at the time – and suggested that Powell, 'if he will forgive me', seemed to be becoming 'a sort of Mao Tse-tung of Toryism'.[17]

Powell's reiteration of his attack on regional policy in the *Sunday Telegraph* on 3 May was less interesting than his recognition that some Tories were worried about the electoral impact of his crusade. '"But", it may be said, "be this all as it may, is it not exceedingly tactless to breathe a word of it before a General Election?"' In a reply that Powell found 'compelling', he revealed his belief in the primacy of ideology over party by writing that,

If more 'Tory freedom' is the right answer to this problem [of regional unemployment], as the Conservative Party has proved it to be the right answer to so many other problems, then one would not be justified in keeping silence now.[18]

Accordingly, he continued his one-man crusade. In June, in the *Spectator*, he put forward his argument for selectivity in the social services and repeated his criticisms of family allowance, pensions and housing subsidy – a familiar litany to those who had served with him before 1963 on ministerial committees and policy groups. Powell's distinctive view struck many others as novel, and he was invited to put his case on the welfare state to a much larger audience during a televised debate with Professor Peter Townsend on ITV's flagship current affairs programme, *This Week*. In September, he contributed an essay extolling the virtues of competitive enterprise to *The Rebirth of Britain*, a rejoinder by the IEA, the free-market think tank, to 'Suicide of a Nation', a special edition of *Encounter* in July 1963, in which eighteen authors had diagnosed Britain's ills and concluded that there was need for greater overall direction of the economy and greater uniformity in education.[19]

Powell's language was as provocative as his content. All the while, he sought to stir up debate and repeatedly threw down the gauntlet to his fellow Tories. 'Does it matter?' he had asked about his thoughts on the social services. 'Why wake up these quiescent dogs – the pension dog is pretty wide awake, actually! – when the Conservative Party is well known to be a pragmatic party and doesn't bother about principles or theories?' Similarly, when he turned to the problem of the trade unions, he cruelly highlighted the difficulty for the Conservatives, reminding his fellow Tories that they had built up trade union law but were now attacking monopoly power and restrictive practices in industry. 'It is no use thinking', he warned, 'that if we pull the blankets up over our heads, this question will somehow just go away and not bother us any more.' It was not the kind of argument that the party wanted to hear when the Tories badly needed to win as many as possible of the eight million or so trade unionists' votes. The 1964 election, however, was to highlight another issue that had already begun to loom in Powell's mind and to which he was eventually to apply his new weapon of speech-making with devastating effect – immigration.[20]

Shock-waves from the Black Country

'There's no point beating about the bush over the prospects here,' Ernest Prince, political correspondent of the *Express and Star*, reported after only a week of the October 1964 election campaign in Wolverhampton South-West, 'it looks like "Enoch for ever".' But although the result was a foregone conclusion, Prince enlivened his assessment by revealing the candidates' views on the campaign. 'The biggest issue locally?' Prince asked,

> Immigration say two of them, Mr Powell and Mr Lloyd [Liberal] ... For years now – since the late 'fifties, in fact – discussions with people, whether about education, housing, pensions, employment or other things, always comes round to this topic, says Mr Powell.

Prince noted that Wolverhampton had felt the impact of immigration early, and that about ten per cent of the town's population were now immigrants.[21]

At the start of the campaign, Powell had mentioned immigration in his election address for the first time. It was the only specific issue that was accorded a separate heading. 'I must, before concluding', Powell told his electors,

> refer to one matter which is of special interest to Wolverhampton. This is immigration. In my view it was essential, for the sake not only of our own people but of the immigrants themselves, to introduce control over the numbers allowed in. The Labour Party opposed this in principle and has obstructed and voted against it on every occasion. I am convinced that strict control must continue if we are to avoid the evils of a 'colour question' in this country, for ourselves and for our children.

Yet his statement was unexceptional, in that he was repeating party policy.[22]

Powell had stood apart from the enormous pressure that built up among some Tory candidates in the West Midlands to demand increased immigration control and to 'run' the issue in the election campaign. In Smethwick, immigration became an explosive election issue. In this constituency on the western outskirts of Birmingham, the birth-place of Powell's paternal grandfather, and represented in the Commons by the liberal-minded Shadow Foreign Secretary, Patrick Gordon Walker, the Conservatives had won seats at every local election since 1959 and gained control of the council in 1964. Local feeling against immigrants was the main cause of this extraordinary swing to the Conservatives, against the national and regional trend. The Tory candidate, Peter Griffiths, had fought the seat in 1959 and was active in local government and had spearheaded the overthrow of the Labour council. In the spring of 1964, the town had been plastered with stickers bearing the slogan, 'If you want a nigger neighbour, vote Labour' (Griffiths and the Tories denied responsibility). On 24 September, only two days before Powell wrote his election address, the *Express and Star* reported that stickers with the slogan, 'Vote Labour for More Nigger-type Neighbours!' had appeared in Wolverhampton. Renée Short, Labour's candidate in Wolverhampton North-East condemned the stickers as 'fascist tactics', but Powell cautiously commented that he had 'not seen nor heard of these'.[23]

Without having campaigned publicly on the issue, Powell had supported control of Commonwealth immigration for some years before its introduction, and as a minister had been actively involved in the discussions that led to the imposition of curbs on the numbers of Commonwealth immigrants. In the autumn of 1964, he still stood by the 1962 Act. But his regret that control had not been introduced sooner, and his belief in the need for continued tight control had been reflected in the second of the anonymously written articles that had appeared in *The Times* in April. 'For Britain', Powell's *alter ego* had written of the Commonwealth,

> the absurdities it imposes on our laws and thought have already done more harm than enough. To have our laws so far out of relation with realities was

the cause of the massive coloured immigration in the last decade which has inflicted social and political damage that will take decades to obliterate.[24]

This theme was developed by Powell in June, in a review for the *Sunday Times* of W.H. Hutt's book on racial discrimination in South Africa, *The Economics of the Colour Bar*. Addressing 'the live issue of immigration and coloured immigration in the United Kingdom', he justified the control of Commonwealth immigration on the grounds that 'the United Kingdom and the Commonwealth do not constitute one community'. Within a community, the free movement of labour was 'excellent', but between communities it had to be controlled.[25]

In a speech to the Royal Society of St George, Powell had stressed that unlike other empires that had assimilated their colonies, the continuity of England's 'existence was unbroken when the looser connections which had linked her with distant continents and strange races fell away'. Powell had referred to 'England', as opposed to Britain, because he regarded the English kingship as the unifying force of the nation – 'English it is, for all the leeks and thistles and shamrocks, the Stuarts and the Hanoverians, for all the titles grafted upon it here and everywhere, "her other realms and territories".' But the most revealing aspect of Powell's speech had been his mystic nationalism. He explained the uniqueness of 'the unbroken life of the English nation over a thousand years', as having been 'the product of a specific set of circumstances like those which in biology are supposed to start a new line of evolution'. He spoke of the 'deepest instinct of the Englishman – how the word instinct keeps forcing itself in again and again!' And he eulogized 'this continuous life of a united people in its island home spring', as having been the source of 'all that is peculiar in the gifts and the achievements of the English nation, its laws, its literature, its freedom, its self-discipline'. Powell's perspective can, perhaps, best be described as 'English exceptionalism'. But in lauding the unique continuity and homogeneity of England and the English, he was bound to regard the integration of immigrants as being immensely difficult, if not virtually impossible.[26]

None the less, Powell still believed in 1964 that it was just possible for immigrants to be integrated into British society. As he argued in his review for the *Sunday Times*,

> the immigrants who have come already, or who are admitted in the future, *are* part of the community. Their most rapid and effective integration is in the interest of all. Anything which tends to create a separate market for the labour and abilities of the immigrants prejudices the general interest as well as that of the immigrants themselves.

Powell put his faith in the free, undiscriminating play of market forces as the motor of integration. 'Money is colour-blind', he asserted, 'and economic forces will help the work of integration which must be done if a homogeneous

(Left) Ellen and Albert Powell with young John Enoch ('Jack') at home in Stechford, Birmingham, 1913.

(Left) The scholarship boy.

(Below) The scholar-poet, sketched by his artist friend, H. Andrew Freeth.

(Left) A.E. Housman, the poet and Cambridge Professor of Latin, who in his seventies imbued Powell with a fierce intellectual self-reliance.

(*Above*) Brigadier Powell in 1947, the Tory back-room boy and would-be MP.

(*Above right*) 'B', Barbara Kennedy, Powell's first love, in 1949.

(*Right*) The recently married Enoch and Pamela Powell celebrate the Coronation, June 1953.

(*Left*) With Angus Maude (left) and Sir Edward Boyle (right), attending the 1954 summer school at which Powell, the one-time imperialist, left 'no shred of Empire'.

The Financial Secretary dispatches Treasury business from his Wolverhampton home during the September 1957 crisis.

The Minister of Health hops into a photo-opportunity with his family, January 1962.

(Above) Rab Butler (left) and Harold Macmillan (right), respectively Tory hero and Whig villain in the Powellite pantheon.

(Right) New blood in the Cabinet, July 1962, with (left to right) Viscount Hailsham, Christopher Soames and Iain Macleod.

(Right) An inscrutable Powell leaves the Cabinet inquest into the Profumo scandal, June 1963.

(Facing page) The Powells sift through a fraction of the letters that deluged their London home, after the 'River Tiber' speech.

(Above) A one-off Tory leadership contender but frequent tube passenger, July 1965.

(Right) Picnicking at Beeston Castle, Cheshire, with Susan, twelve, Jennifer, nine, Pamela and an au pair (at left), spring 1966

Powell demands a halt to immigration and says the nation is heaping up its own funeral pyre

RACE BILL 'A MATCH ON GUNPOWDER'

'Like the Roman, I seem to see the River Tiber foaming with much blood'

Powell rockets into the headlines and out of the Shadow Cabinet, April 1968.

RACE SPEECH UPROAR

Why did Powell do it?

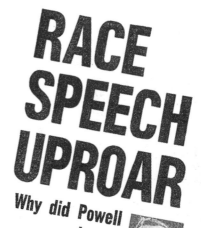

Powell's 'River Tiber' speech and his sacking get the workers on the street - *(right)* Smithfield porters march to the Commons, while supporters *(below)* rally in Wolverhampton.

Heath acts against rebel

Powell sacked for race speech

Comment
Don't split the nation

SIR HEATH has acted with dismaying speed in dismissing Mr. Enoch Powell from the Shadow Cabinet for his Wolverhampton speech about the dangers of coloured immigration...

Olympic bar on South Africa

SMITHFIELD SAYS A GEORGE CROSS FOR ENOCH

THOUSANDS BACK POWELL WITH STRIKES

24 Tory MPs rebel in vote on race Bill

BY MIRROR REPORTERS

THOUSANDS of British workers demonstrated their support of Mr. Enoch Powell's immigration yesterday . . . and produced the strange spectacle of London dockers marching to Parliament to express their support for a Tory politician.

Thousands of workers ranged themselves behind Mr. Powell, either by walk-outs yesterday or by threatening token stoppages for today.

(Above) Powell among his own people, at a time when his meetings were often picketed by demonstrators (right).

(Right) The man who had entered politics to keep India in the Empire wins a certain kind of fame in Bombay with his call for assisted repatriation.

(Left) The Powells spread the word, Wolverhampton, June 1970.

(Below) Attacking the 'enemy within' and helping make Edward Heath Prime Minister, Birmingham, June 1970.

(Above) The Tory orator backs Labour and helps defeat Heath, Birmingham, February 1974.

(Right) Saying 'No' to the European Community with Labour's Barbara Castle during the 1975 referendum.

(Left) Canvassing in his new
Ulster constituency, October 1974.

(Below) The gospel according
to Enoch.

(Left) Enoch and Pamela, who jointly
weathered the vicissitudes of Powell's
explosive political career.

(Right) Powell
and the habitat
that he relished
for thirty-seven
years.

community, local and national, is to be restored.' This comment helps explain his antagonism to race relations legislation, since viewed in these terms, it constitutes another form of intervention.[27]

During the 1964 election, Powell maintained his cautious approach. He was fastidious during elections in supporting local Tory candidates, but he had no involvement in the campaign at Smethwick because his planned visit was cancelled, apparently because a double-booking had made it inconvenient for Griffiths. According to the *Express and Star*, it was 'widely assumed that Mr Powell, who is extremely hostile to bringing race into politics, was thought an embarrassment', but Powell hotly denied this interpretation to Paul Foot.[28]

Shock-waves from Smethwick, however, were felt throughout the West Midlands. On 10 October, the *Express and Star* published articles on the issue by Powell, for the Tories, John Stonehouse, a candidate in nearby Walsall, for Labour, and by Jo Grimond, the Liberal leader. Powell reaffirmed his integrationist approach, while emphasizing his tough line on control. Referring to his immigrant constituents, Powell wrote that he

> was not only glad to serve them exactly as I would anyone else, but I have set and always will set my face like flint against making any difference between one citizen of this country and another on grounds of his origin.

The Tories and the overwhelming majority of people, he was certain, were at one in wanting

> to see the coloured immigrants no less integrated into the life and society of what is now their homeland than any other group, such as the Jewish community or the thousands of Poles in Britain today. No other prospect is tolerable.
>
> It will be no quick or easy thing to assimilate the million West Indians, Indians and Pakistanis now in Britain, especially as they are, and will surely tend for a long time to continue, concentrated in particular regions such as the Black Country ... Not merely years but generations will pass before this large and sudden influx has been fully assimilated into the society of this country.[29]

Achieving integration, according to Powell, depended on 'one condition', namely continued, tight control of immigration. The 1962 Act was the minimum, but the numbers admitted, he felt, were 'still considerably higher than can be sustained over the years'. In 1963, 50,000 had been admitted. 'Surely no one can imagine that, with a million already here, this country is capable of assimilating a further million coloured immigrants every twenty years.' This would constitute five per cent of the population before the end of the century. But he acknowledged that the dependants of immigrants already here had the right to enter Britain. 'As there is an inescapable obligation of humanity to permit the wives and young children of immigrants already here to join them,' he wrote, 'it follows that the rate of all other new admissions must be reduced further still.' In short, he would grant fewer vouchers to Commonwealth citizens wishing to come and work in Britain. His article was reprinted in the *Sunday Express*, but it sparked little interest.[30]

Smethwick and immigration dramatically forced their way into the national headlines when the election results were declared. In a spectacular upset, Griffiths bucked the overall swing to Labour and defeated Gordon Walker, who was about to become Foreign Secretary. Powell was contemptuous of Gordon Walker, declaring that he was 'not a martyr, he is much more like a humbug'. It was 'humbug', he explained, to have voted against the Commonwealth Immigrants Bill 'and to change one's position during an election campaign after finding that sentiment was not what one had supposed' – Gordon Walker had proclaimed at Smethwick that 'this is a British country with British standards of behaviour. The British must come first.'[31]

Surveying the political landscape after the election for the *Sunday Telegraph*, Powell repeated his view that,

> It is not colour prejudice or racial intolerance to say that only if substantial further addition to our immigrant population is now prevented, will it be possible properly to assimilate the immigrants already here, which in turn is the only way to avoid the evils of a colour question.

In his view, 'a politician who says these things – in the Black Country or elsewhere – does no more than his duty'. He confessed himself 'shocked by the sounds of self-righteous unction which arose after the defeat of Gordon Walker at Smethwick.'[32]

The following day, the *Express and Star* reported that Powell 'made it clear that he was not supporting or defending Alderman Griffiths, but was supporting and defending his own line'. Sensing Tory embarrassment over Griffiths, Harold Wilson, in his first speech in the House of Commons as Prime Minister, denounced Griffiths as a 'parliamentary leper'. But both front benches were anxiously looking over their shoulder at the support that Griffiths had received in an industrial seat. After October 1964, Powell was well placed to ensure that the Tory leadership took greater notice of the strong feelings on immigration in his West Midlands homeland.[33]

Free-market revivalist

The October 1964 election confirmed Powell's personal hold on Wolverhampton South-West. He restricted the swing to Labour to a fraction under one per cent, against an average national swing of 3.5 per cent to Labour, and won 57.4 per cent of the vote. Ernest Prince, writing in the *Express and Star*, listed the ingredients of Powell's success as being that,

> he's an Enoch, son of an Enoch and grandson of an Enoch; that he is Black

Country and loves the Black Country – the no-nonsense attitude of its people is very much to his own instincts. The constituency is entirely congenial to himself and to what he stands for in politics.[34]

During the campaign, Powell had continued his crusade for market economics, attacking Labour's plans to provide cheap land and houses as 'fraudulent', and welcoming the accusation of a Tory 'free-for-all' in the economy by proclaiming that 'we want free and even more competitive enterprise'. He took care, however, not to go out on too much of a limb when seeking his electors' support. Writing in his election address of the 'cause for pride' in the country's prosperity since 1951, the champion of market economics and lower state spending chose to illustrate this material success by emphasizing that the country was able 'to finish ten new schools every week and to begin building a new hospital, or rebuilding an old one, every ten days', while the retirement pension had been increased 'no fewer than five times in twelve years'. Neither was there even a hint of anti-EEC populism. On the contrary, Powell put his name to European economic integration. 'The fault is not ours', he declared, 'if the economic unity with Britain which most of Europe desired has not yet been achieved. It will come.' Moreover, although he was later to emerge as a critic of nuclear deterrence, he offered his electors a ringing endorsement of Britain's nuclear arsenal. 'In the worldwide conflict between freedom and communism,' he asserted, 'the fact that Britain is able to maintain her position as a nuclear power gives us a special influence.'[35]

Powell was almost proved wrong in his working assumption since October 1963 that the Conservatives were heading for a spell in Opposition. They achieved a significant recovery from their low-point of 1963, so that Labour's overall majority in the Commons was only four. Yet the closeness of the final result obscures the calamitous collapse in the Tory share of the vote – down by 6 percentage points (a loss of almost 1,750,000 votes) since 1959. The fact that the Tories suffered the biggest drop in support of any single party since their last débâcle in 1945 puts in perspective the argument that had Macleod and Powell not refused to serve in Douglas-Home's Cabinet, the Tories would have won. However, this argument begs the question of why they refused to serve in the first place. The Tory defeat, and Douglas-Home's poor showing against Wilson, vindicated their judgement that he was not the right man to lead a modern party. The Tories would almost certainly have fared better at the 1964 election under another leader – Macmillan was disappointed at his favoured successor's failure to 'impress himself on Parlt. [sic] or people enough for a PM', and by the end of his life, felt that it would have been better for the party after all if Butler had been his successor, 'then we could have won the election in '64 ... though we would have lost the next one'.[36]

In the unlikely event of a Tory victory in 1964, the prospects for Powell and Macleod had seemed extremely bleak. Douglas-Home would have owed them no favours, and, in one way or another, they had angered many other Tories in their year on the back benches. A prolonged exile from office seemed their likely fate. But whereas the deep personal and political animosity that existed between Douglas-Home and Macleod would almost certainly have condemned the latter to a dismal future, Douglas-Home had planned, if the Tories were returned, to invite Powell to join his Cabinet as Minister of Education. Powell had chaired the party's back bench committee on the subject during 1963–64, and, as with the NHS, supported state provision. In 1964 the Tories were still defending Butler's tripartite system of secondary schooling against Labour's plans to replace it by comprehensives. One can only conjecture what impact the teachers' son and scholarship boy from Birmingham might have had on state education in the 1960s. As it was, instead of busying himself with running a new ministry on his return to London after the election, Powell re-borrowed the book that he had had to return to the House of Commons at the dissolution – *The Memoirs of an Ex-Minister*, written by the Earl of Malmesbury in 1884.[37]

The Conservatives were shaken by their defeat. Although Douglas-Home felt that they could have won if Powell and Macleod had 'pulled their weight', he realized that he had to take immediate action to strengthen his team, and asked them to return to the front bench – Powell as Shadow Minister of Transport, Macleod as Shadow Spokesman on Steel. Although Macleod hoped, mistakenly as it happened, that Labour's steel nationalization plans would catapult him into the political limelight, these relatively junior posts reflected the feeling that Powell and Macleod had not been as supportive as they might have been. Neither man had any trouble agreeing to serve the leader whom they had refused to serve as Prime Minister only twelve months earlier, although this was less of a puzzle in Powell's case than in Macleod's. 'Neither policies nor personal antipathies were involved,' Powell explained of his earlier refusal to serve Douglas-Home. On Wednesday 28 October 1964, Powell made his way during the afternoon to the Leader of the Opposition's office at the House of Commons to attend the first meeting of the newly appointed 'Leader's Consultative Committee' – in common parlance, the Tory Shadow Cabinet.[38]

But Powell and Macleod were able to extract a price for their acceptance of posts on the front bench. As Powell later revealed, they had 'agreed that we would not rejoin the Shadow Cabinet unless we had a liberty not restricted to our assigned subject'. Douglas-Home acceded, since he was in little position to decline, and anyway was fairly relaxed, in the Churchillian tradition, about shadow spokesmen expressing their views on different subjects. This was ideal for Powell, who was determined, now that the Tories were finally in Opposition, to step up the debate that he had already begun on the party's future. His license to speak publicly on subjects other than transport was not always to prove welcome, however, to his Shadow Cabinet colleagues.[39]

Powell marked his Commons return to the front bench on 4 November by provoking uproar from the Labour benches. In an allusion to Labour's election slogan, he noted that 'the first fruits of the attempt to "Go with Labour" are to hold up the modernization of Britain's railways'. Powell was referring to

Labour's shelving of the controversial Beeching Plan, as a result of which many branch lines had been axed as uneconomic. But he had already shown his readiness to ruffle Tory feathers the day before in the *Financial Times*, when he attacked Labour for having responded to the balance of payments deficit and pressure on sterling by imposing an import surcharge and providing tax reliefs on exports. In addition to berating Labour, he had taken the opportunity to renew his attack on a fixed exchange rate and to argue for letting the pound float. This attack was out of step with Conservative policy; appeared to add substance to Labour's claim that they were reaping an economic whirlwind sown by Maudling's dash for growth; and undermined the Tory argument that Labour's inept handling of the economy during their first weeks in office had weakened sterling.[40]

This tactic of ostensibly attacking the Labour Government while rebuking the economic policies that the Tories had adopted in office characterized Powell's approach. On 13 November, at Trinity College, Dublin, he spoke on more general themes, again puncturing the myth of empire, and in addition asserting that the notion of Victorian Britain as the 'workshop of the world' was an equally damaging myth that fuelled the peculiarly British preoccupation with relative economic decline. Indeed, Powell's attack on interventionist policies as a reflection of the mood of national self-abasement and defeatism that he detected among decision-makers and opinion-formers was to give his free market crusade a potent, patriotic twist. In Powell's mind, there was no contradiction between, on the one hand, letting market forces rip, and, on the other hand, either his Tory reverence for traditional institutions or his nationalism: indeed, a restoration of market forces offered the only sure route to national revival. It was a simplistic approach to political economy, but since Powell failed to see any contradiction his treatise-like speeches on the virtues of market forces were often imbued with a revivalist and nationalistic passion.[41]

During the autumn of 1965, Powell furthered his crusade for market economics in a spate of speeches and articles. On 28 November in Birmingham, he savaged Labour's increase in the Bank rate and adoption of an incomes policy – the fact that the Conservatives had pursued an incomes policy did not prevent him describing it as 'a narcotic'. This speech triggered a row when the Shadow Cabinet next met. Macleod had proposed as part of a general review of the party's approach in Opposition, the need for greater co-ordination of the line to be taken on various subjects. As the official minute noted, 'discussion centred on Mr Powell's speech on incomes policy as an example. There was some difference of opinion, Mr Hogg and Mr Powell favouring greater freedom, while the majority of the committee favoured greater co-ordination' – it was ironic in view of later events, that Hogg should have sided with Powell.[42]

Douglas-Home took no immediate action, and Powell was undeterred. On 4 December in Liverpool, he revived his criticism of collective bargaining by trade unions. On the 11th in Batley, he suggested the denationalization of post office services, beginning with telephones. On the 17th *The Times* published his critique of the failure by successive governments to defeat inflation. In a second article the following day, Powell delivered a root and branch critique of incomes policy. Also on the 18th, in Wolverhampton, he attacked 'the Socialists and the economic planners', arguing that they were 'the Ptolemaics and the flat-earthers of the modern world. They have not moved on beyond capitalism: they have moved back before it.'[43]

In January 1965, after Labour's Secretary of State for Economic Affairs, George Brown, had sent letters to businessmen asking them why they had raised their prices, Powell commented that the only correct reply was 'mind your own business'. People should not provide the Government with information unless they were under a legal obligation. In the following month's issue of the *Director*, he stirred further controversy by attacking the whole idea of industry cooperating with government through representative bodies and spokesmen – the basis of Macmillan's NEDC. 'In the last few years', he explained,

> the fashion has been strongly anti-capitalist. Everybody who was anybody has been talking about things like economic growth, regional development, planned economy. The whole atmosphere has been charged with the assumptions of state control and direction. So when a government sends for the representatives of industry and commerce and requires their cooperation in the name of these familiar and hallowed notions, they are hard put to know how to refuse or argue.

And in a classical allusion, that Powell was to use in a more emotive context, he added: 'the enemy is within already, and has only to open the gates to let in the main body.'[44]

Powell's combative attitude provoked a furore from Labour MPs, and even caused trouble in his Wolverhampton Tory stronghold. The chairman of Merridale ward in his constituency association, Mr W.E. Gibbs, resigned mainly as a result of Powell's support for 'an unfettered free economy', and told the *Express and Star* that 'Mr Powell is way off the beam', and was 'not doing the party in the country or in Wolverhampton any good at all' – the conditions that existed in Disraeli's time could not be applied today. The Labour-controlled local council, however, seemed determined to prove that Powell was lucky in his choice of opponents. Following the *Director* article, they voted to delete the words 'with gratitude' from a resolution accepting Powell's gift to the town of a pair of silver candlesticks to mark his fifteen years as an MP. The councillors' action was derided as 'churlish', 'loutish' and 'boorish' by the columnist, 'Cassandra', in the pro-Labour *Daily Mirror*. When Powell withdrew his gift – at least until the Tories won control of the council – the *Daily Mail, Daily Sketch* and the pre-Murdoch *Sun* thought he was justified, while the *Daily Mirror* felt that he had behaved 'in the same petty way'.[45]

At Westminster, the coincidence in late January of the death of Sir Winston

Churchill, the memorial service to Lord Woolton, the post-war Tory chairman, and the announcement of Rab Butler's retirement from politics, symbolized a sea-change that was taking place in the Conservative Party. This change was to offer the prospect of a more radical Toryism, though whether Powell could harness it to his purpose was another matter. Many of the old-style paternalist 'knights of the shire', who had long provided the traditionalist core of the parliamentary party, had stepped down at the 1964 election. In their place came a different breed of politician, mainly from the professions, many of whom had been active in Tory politics at university and the Bow Group. They included Geoffrey Howe, Patrick Jenkin, Terence Higgins and Jock Bruce-Gardyne, and in 1966, John Nott. They were, in the main, liberal on economic and social issues, and Powell's championing of liberal economics had already struck a chord with them before they entered the House – as it also had with Nicholas Ridley, who had been elected in 1959, and John Biffen. Powell demonstrated his liberal conscience on certain non-economic issues by voting against capital punishment in December 1964 and January 1965, and also in May 1965 by supporting Leo Abse's attempt to legalize homosexuality between consenting male adults.

Butler's retirement, however, prompted a reshuffle in the Shadow Cabinet in February 1965 that in the long run was to do Powell no good. Maudling was granted his request to replace Butler as Shadow Foreign Secretary, while remaining deputy chairman of the Shadow Cabinet, but the main beneficiary was Heath, who besides opposing George Brown at the newly-created Department of Economic Affairs was already heading the overhaul of party policy. In addition, Heath now took over Maudling's former duties as Shadow Chancellor, a promotion that would give him a golden opportunity to improve his standing in the party by leading the Tory attack when the Labour Chancellor, James Callaghan, presented his first full budget in the spring.

Powell, who remained Shadow Transport spokesman, continued his free-market campaign during the first half of 1965 in a further series of speeches and articles. He also pressed his arguments in the Shadow Cabinet, intervening in a discussion on 15 February on the party's response to the Government's plan to establish a royal commission on trade unions and employers' organizations, to urge that the party should be 'more fundamental' than was being proposed and should 'decide on such problems as the closed shop and other matters affecting the freedom of the individual, and the justification of the combinations of labour or employers'. Two days later, Powell queried whether or not the Tories were opposed to the principle of the Overseas Development and Service Bill, but Macleod retorted that they were committed to the principle of overseas help in the main part of the Bill. The following week, Powell's radicalism on pensions led to a clash with Sir Keith Joseph, then Shadow Social Security spokesman, and Margaret Thatcher, Shadow National Insurance Minister. Powell's proposals, including the replacement of the state flat-rate retirement pension by a guaranteed minimum income, were opposed by Joseph, Thatcher and also Boyd-Carpenter, who stressed the importance of the basic state pension in an inflationary age, and argued that for many people it comprised a very large part of their income. During a broadcast interview in the spring, Powell even proposed extending his idea of a state guaranteed minimum income to the unemployed, as well as to the old.[46]

Although Heath was likely to feel less bound than the former Chancellor, Maudling, by the economic policies pursued towards the end of the Conservative's period in office, Powell none the less clashed with him on taxation and incomes policy. When Callaghan introduced capital gains tax in his first full budget, Heath, as Shadow Chancellor, and Powell outlined their disagreement on how the party should respond in separate papers to the Shadow Cabinet. Heath argued that although Tory Chancellors had rejected a general tax on capital gains, the party's long-term aim should be the encouragement of increased real earnings, and therefore a moderate capital gains tax could be worthwhile if it enabled people to keep more of their earnings and also removed any sense of injustice. This pragmatic approach was backed by Maudling.[47]

Powell, however, countered that the Tories should oppose the tax in principle, regardless of whatever form it took and at whatever rate it was introduced. He argued that 'it was no business of any Opposition to approve new taxes', but he felt 'strongly in any case that a capital gains tax was an inherent nonsense'. On the latter point, Powell had argued in his brief note that there were three, 'and only three', causes of capital appreciation, namely, inflation; investment of income; and a change in relative supply and demand. In each case, taxation was unjustified. Powell's arguments were not accepted by his colleagues. Joseph, for example, saw merit in a moderate capital gains tax if it enabled a reduction in surtax and the highest tax levels. It was finally agreed the following week that it would be difficult to oppose the tax in principle, but the party should probably vote against it on practical grounds. But it was unlikely that the Tories would abolish it.[48]

Nowhere was the conflict between Powell's self-confessed ideological approach on the economy and the pragmatism of Heath more evident than on the issue of incomes policy. Powell's attacks on incomes policy seemed to be directed as much at his front bench colleagues as they were at the Government, and this division threatened to undermine Tory criticisms of the Government and their efforts to convince voters that they had a credible, alternative strategy. The Shadow Cabinet devoted their meeting on 13 April to trying to find an agreed position on incomes policy. Powell circulated his article from The Times of the previous December, in which he had presented nine reasons why incomes policies could not work. Opening the discussion, he argued that the Government's incomes policy 'was doomed and there was no point flogging it further, but we should decide what line we took when it broke down completely'. In the meantime, there were two erroneous views that the Tories 'were in danger of taking up and which should be avoided', namely, 'that an incomes policy had a useful educational exercise'; and 'that an incomes policy was not practical, but that if it were practical it would be a wonderful thing'.

This was too much for Heath, who dismissed Powell's argument as an oversimplification. He claimed that the incomes policies pursued by Tory Chancellors had achieved something – a point endorsed by Selwyn Lloyd, whose intervention served as a further reminder, if any were needed, of Powell's part in enforcing the pay pause and 2.5 per cent guideline a couple of years earlier. The Shadow Cabinet were wary of openly attacking Labour's incomes policy since it had some degree of sympathy from the public. For this reason, it was felt that the cry of failure should come from the Tory back benches rather than the front bench. Above all, shadow ministers were anxious to paper over the cracks on incomes policy, and felt that they should concentrate on developing a positive economic policy.[49]

Policy towards Europe presented a less pressing, but no less awkward, problem for the Tories. On this issue, however, there was nothing to indicate that Powell disagreed with the party policy, which remained in favour of British membership of the EEC. Neither could he have been unaware of the political implications of British entry, since these were discussed by the Shadow Cabinet on 30 March 1965. Shadow ministers appreciated that, by 1968, the Common Market would 'be a political and military as well as an economic grouping'. As a result, the issue would be 'one of joining an already existing organization on its own terms'. They also accepted that 'we would have to sign the Treaty of Rome when it came to the point'.[50]

The impression that Powell was an enthusiast for European unity was reinforced shortly after the Shadow Cabinet discussion with the publication of *One Europe* by the One Nation group of MPs, whom Powell had re-joined the previous year. Powell and four other members of the group (Heath, Joseph, Macleod and Maudling) did not sign the pamphlet as members of the Shadow Cabinet, because it did not represent official party policy. But it was edited by Nicholas Ridley, who was then a fervent advocate of British membership of a united Europe and was one of Powell's strongest supporters. According to Andrew Roth, who is a reliable source on these matters, Powell wrote about a quarter of the pamphlet. *One Europe* freely acknowledged that 'European unity implies the full economic, military and political union of the free states of Europe', and was even prepared to countenance the pooling of the British and French nuclear deterrents. The One Nation group recognized that in Britain there had 'always been resistance to the idea of participating in a European political union', but argued that it

> was inevitable, if we join an economic or military Community, to participate to the extent that that requires; indeed, we have lost much sovereignty – in monetary, defence and foreign policy matters – by joining such organizations as IMF, GATT, NATO and UNO. European unification is taking place step by step, and each step requires that extra political step.[51]

Although the group advised against any prior commitment on whether Europe should become 'an association of sovereign states ("l'Europe des Patries") or a closer knit political whole like the United States', they argued that 'Britain should not be frightened of political union'. The tone of *One Europe* was, by recent standards, federalist – Labour were criticized for insisting on Britain's freedom to pursue an independent foreign policy and plan its own economy as conditions of EEC membership. Even if Powell was less enthusiastic than some members of the One Nation group about European unification, it is difficult to imagine how he could have been ignorant of the EEC's political dimension.[52]

Tory hawk on immigration

The replacement in February 1965 of the liberal Shadow Home Secretary, Sir Edward Boyle, by Peter Thorneycroft, one of Powell's closest political friends, reflected a toughening of Tory policy on immigration that was encouraged by Powell. With the strong likelihood of an early election as Wilson sought to increase Labour's parliamentary majority, pressure had grown on the Tory leadership in the wake of Smethwick to take a strong anti-immigration line. This was resisted in the Shadow Cabinet by Boyle and Macleod, the latter arguing that the electoral evidence on the issue was mixed, since Norman Pannell's vigorous campaign for immigration control in the last parliament had not prevented him losing his seat in Liverpool, and some anti-immigration candidates in the West Midlands had not fared as well as Griffiths.[53]

Powell, however, had learned from an impeccable source that the new Labour Government would not lift immigration controls and might even apply them more restrictively. His source was George Thomas (later Viscount Tonypandy), who was then a junior minister at the Home Office, and whom Powell happened to meet in January 1965 when they travelled to Nuneaton to support their parties' candidates in the by-election (Frank Cousins, the trade union leader whom Wilson had appointed to the Government, was standing for Labour). During the train journey, Thomas and Powell discussed immigration. On his return to London, Powell saw Maudling and Redmayne, the Chief Whip, and told them of his own concern about immigration and of what he had learned from Thomas. The three men drafted a policy statement on the subject for Douglas-Home, but it was no surprise that the Shadow Cabinet were split when they discussed the draft on 1 February and again on Tuesday 2nd. It was left to Sandys, the Shadow Colonial and Commonwealth Secretary, and Selwyn Lloyd, who was to chair the party's policy group on immigration, to prepare a final draft.[54]

Douglas-Home, speaking at Hampstead on 3 February, echoed Powell's emphasis on preventing an increase in the numbers already settled in Britain, notably by including the number of dependants in the total number allowed in; a clamp-down on evasion; and a Government scheme to assist immigrants who wanted to return home – this latter proposal marked the adoption of voluntary repatriation as Conservative policy. Powell immediately endorsed this shift, reacting to the announcement by Labour's Home Secretary, Sir Frank Soskice, of new steps to prevent the alleged evasion of immigration controls, by reiterating the three main proposals that he had helped draft in Douglas-Home's speech. 'I have had examples here in Wolverhampton', Powell commented on the idea of voluntary repatriation, 'of immigrants who have come to me and whom we would have been glad to help back home.'[55]

But hopes that Douglas-Home's speech might settle the row in the Tory Party were immediately dashed by Cyril Osborne, the long-time anti-immigration campaigner, who put down a Commons motion calling for a ban on all future immigration except for those whose parents or grandparents were born in Britain. On 1 March, after Thorneycroft, the new Shadow Home Secretary in place of Boyle, had persuaded Osborne to moderate his motion by calling for 'periodic and precise limits' on immigration, Douglas-Home and other front-benchers, including Heath and Powell, voted for the motion. Four days later, Thorneycroft, in his first major speech as Shadow Home Secretary, supported a call at the Conservative Central Council for the cessation of mass immigration, by proposing specific measures to tighten controls, including steps to locate and return illegal immigrants.[56]

Fears that the party risked being split on the issue were addressed during a lengthy Shadow Cabinet discussion on immigration on 9 March. Many Tories favoured tighter control but, as Thorneycroft warned, others were insistent on better treatment of immigrants. Although he accepted that immigration control would have to be tightened up and the numbers very much reduced, Thorneycroft strongly opposed the idea of a moratorium, 'and anything in the way of a coloured labour force doing menial tasks or coloured bachelor communities must be avoided'. Although he doubted that full integration was possible, it must be carefully studied for all possibilities of success, 'and should always be talked about at the same time as stricter control'. He also urged that the response to the Government's proposed race relations legislation should, if possible, be kept non-partisan – when the Government's modest Race Relations Bill was subsequently published, Thorneycroft felt that 'he could hold 99 per cent of the party on this Bill and persuade them to take a line that would be supported by the immigrants themselves'. Thorneycroft's formula for trying to preserve some semblance of party unity was always to talk about integration and control together. 'Politically', the minute of the Shadow Cabinet's meeting concluded,

> we must not have so tough a policy on immigration that we offended the middle vote, and while strengthening control we must also make a political appeal to the immigrants themselves. It was most important for members of the Leader's Committee Shadow Cabinet to make balanced and reasonable statements on the subject.[57]

Powell, however, was about to resume the battle that he had waged within

Government in 1961, when he had wanted a much more drastic measure of control than was subsequently adopted in the 1962 Act. His intervention followed new developments in Wolverhampton. On 22 March, the leader of the Conservative group on the council and chairman of Powell's constituency association, Peter Farmer, asked the chairman of the council's Health Committee about the coloured birth rate. Farmer's question had been prompted by a report by the Medical Officer for Health in Wolverhampton, Dr J.F. Galloway, that in 1963 Commonwealth immigrants had 'produced 22.7 per cent of all births and accounted for 30.4 per cent of hospital confinements'. Farmer was dissatisfied with the answer to his question, and began pressing the issue. The *Daily Telegraph* reported on 19 April that Farmer and other Tory councillors intended to draw Powell's attention 'to the implications of the Galloway report'. On 30 April, the *Birmingham Post* reported Farmer's comment that 'places like Wolverhampton with high immigrant birth rates, could find themselves with white minorities within a quarter of a century'.[58]

That same morning, Powell was one of three Tory MPs who represented constituencies with comparatively large numbers of immigrants to attend a meeting of the party's policy group on immigration – the other two were Sir Edward Boyle (Birmingham, Handsworth) and Arthur Tiley (Bradford West). The strength of feeling about immigration was evident from the comments of the liberal-minded Boyle, who said that it had given him more trouble than any other single issue. Many of his constituents had never forgiven the Conservatives for not acting sooner in introducing controls, although the 1962 Act had not reduced the numbers coming in as had been expected. There was also strong feeling that 'the native born children were being hindered in schools by the coloured ones and Sir Edward felt that there should never be more than 30 per cent or 40 per cent of the latter per class'. Tiley, like Powell, had referred to immigration in his election address, and felt that 'the tap should be turned off but a trickle of dependants should be allowed'. But Powell went even further.

Powell's comments to the policy group reveal his thinking at a crucial moment. His main concern was that (in the words of the minute), 'unless something further was done the centre of cities such as Wolverhampton would in effect become coloured ghettoes and act as a sump'. Reporting that about ten per cent of the population was coloured and lived in the older property in the centre of the city, he noted that in some cases, due to slum clearance, 'immigrants had been given council houses and on these estates they were acceptable, as it was felt they would not alter the basic character of the estate or that it would become a ghetto'. About 60 per cent of the immigrants were West Indian, and the rest were Indian and Pakistani. Powell felt that the Indians would become 'completely integrated' and a substantial minority of the others would spread out as their standards rose, but 'the rest would always remain hewers of wood and drawers of water' – whereas Jamaicans had come to his surgery, Indians had served on his ward committees. As regards the schools, in some classes 'more than 50 per cent of the pupils were coloured'.

But Powell felt that if there was to be a flashpoint, 'it would come over maternity beds, not schools, for in Wolverhampton five years ago half the number of beds were occupied by immigrants.'

Powell's response was to advocate an uncompromising, radical, policy for controlling Commonwealth immigration. In his view, 'the time had come for the virtual termination of net immigration. This was the absolute *first* priority – both from the point of view of immigrants and the local population.' In an example of the extreme language that he would later use in public, Powell spoke of 'a widespread fear of this growing threat and unless this fear was removed nothing else was of use'. It was also clear that he had been influenced by the figures on birth-rates. 'Our own people', as the minute has him arguing, 'would continue to be alarmed unless we could reassure them that the flow of new wage earners would cease – for there was the growth rate of those already here to be considered as well.'

Powell therefore revived his call for a new citizenship law by urging that 'the same rules should apply for Commonwealth citizens as for those of foreign countries, i.e. they should only come in on an alien basis'. This proposal marked a shift in Powell's position from the line he had taken during the 1964 election, since the Aliens Act of 1919 that covered immigration from non-Commonwealth countries had not allowed the 'right' of an immigrant to bring in any of his or her family – dependants were sometimes allowed in, but this was a matter of discretion and they were as much subject to the immigration controls as the original immigrant.

Equally significant was Powell's strong advocacy of 'net emigration' in order to reduce immigrant numbers. He proposed that

> we should also open the door in the reverse direction and encourage a backward flow: there should be no net increase of immigrants even if it was economically desirable for them to come to this country.

Powell's reasoning was that 'we would not be able to get away with net immigration with public opinion as it now was'. He told the policy group of his belief that 'there were many immigrants, who found life a misery in this country and would be only too glad to return home', and added that 'we should finance the return passages'. Moreover, he argued that most immigrants hoped to obtain an honoured position in the community. 'What *they* feared most', he claimed, 'was that they might be swamped by fresh arrivals. They feared that this would lead to real discrimination against them.'[59]

It was one matter to press for a change of approach in the privacy of a party policy discussion, but quite another, as Powell was soon to do, to make the demands in public and jump the gun a couple of months before the policy review was due to be completed. At the start of May, Councillor Farmer commented after meeting Powell that 'the Conservatives will press strongly that the Government should tighten up the control on immigration'. Less than a fortnight later, Powell addressed Conservative women in his constituency and called for the change of policy that he had proposed to the policy group. His speech was triggered by a report that in the second full year since the introduction of the 1962 controls, the total number of immigrants from all Commonwealth countries had risen from 66,000 to 75,499.[60]

'It is almost inconceivable that this can be permitted to continue', he declared – in the next 20 years, it would mean an increase of 1.5 million in addition to the million immigrants already in Britain and their natural increase. Powell accused the Government of 'fiddling with irrelevancies about the ownership of steel', while 'an urgent necessity that can only be met by a change of the law remains unattended'. Spelling out his demand that Commonwealth immigrants be treated the same as aliens, Powell argued that,

> It is wholly absurd that while entry of aliens whether from France or China is controlled and policed with the utmost efficiency and permission to work and, even more, to settle is granted only with the greatest care and circumspection, Commonwealth immigrants still stream in with little surveillance and an absolute right to bring or fetch an unlimited number of dependants ... These immigrants from the Commonwealth should be subject to the same considerations, controls and conditions as people from anywhere else.

Powell's speech received considerable publicity. 'POWELL'S SEND THEM HOME PLAN', read the main headline in the *Daily Mail* in a reference to his emphasis on repatriation, while the *Daily Telegraph* noted the hardening in Powell's position by reporting that he had 'rejected economic arguments for Commonwealth labour and spoke of the "appalling consequences of having allowed our nationality law to be put out of step with facts for years too long"'.[61]

Powell's renewed demand for a change in the citizenship law, however, was rejected by the party policy group. Instead, the group proposed tightening control by introducing screening, including a health check in the country of origin, followed by conditional entry for a preliminary three years, subject to reporting to the immigration authorities. In addition, there was to be assistance for repatriation, with the objective, as the group's chairman, Selwyn Lloyd put it, of 'one in – one out'. It was in this latter respect that the group most closely approximated to Powell's wishes.[62]

During his meeting with the policy group in April, Powell had made two further comments that are especially significant in view of his subsequent, outspoken anti-immigration campaign. Referring to the scale of immigration up to 1965, Powell believed that it 'was miraculous that we had got as far as we had without a major clash'. In addition, he spoke of a 'lightning conductor theory', by which he meant that 'those MPs who in any way supported local pressure against the immigrants, immediately became the focus of an anti-immigrant feeling, whether they liked it or not'. This, he suggested, had happened to Griffiths. In which case, Powell can have been under no illusion when he launched his outspoken attacks on mass immigration and race relations legislation later in the 1960s that he, too, would become a 'lightning conductor'.[63]

Leaving his visiting card

However much Douglas-Home's qualities might have fitted him for the role of Prime Minister, they were ill-suited for the hurly-burly of Opposition. But with the prospect of an imminent election, the Tories had had little choice since the autumn of 1964 except to soldier on with him as leader. In late March 1965, however, the Tory defeat in the Roxburgh, Selkirk and Peebles by-election by the 26-year-old Liberal candidate, David Steel, led to fresh speculation about the Tory leadership. Douglas-Home broached the question of the leadership to the Shadow Cabinet on 31 March and sought 'their unanimous and wholehearted support'. In the ensuing discussion, Thorney-croft suggested that Douglas-Home should submit himself to a vote of the parliamentary party as the only way of clearing dissension among the back-benchers, but Powell countered that 'there was a danger of getting over-excited about the whole situation – time would do its work'. It was a striking display of loyalty by a man who, less than eighteen months earlier, had refused to serve in Douglas-Home's Cabinet – though like Macleod, Powell had nothing to gain from an early leadership election in which Maudling and Heath were likely to fare best.[64]

Time, however, was not on Douglas-Home's side. Three months later, he claimed there would be no Tory leadership election that year, only for Wilson to announce on the same day (26 June) that he had no intention of calling an election during 1965. The Prime Minister's statement provided the Conservatives with an opportunity to replace Douglas-Home and make their new leader known to the public ahead of an election campaign. Douglas-Home none the less intended to reaffirm his intention of leading the party into the next election during the leader's annual address to the 1922 Committee on 22 July. But a disappointing opinion poll, further demands in the Tory press for him to step down and another poor performance at the despatch box, finally convinced him that he could no longer continue as leader. He informed the Shadow Cabinet of his decision to resign on the afternoon of Thursday 22 July, before telling the 1922 Committee.[65]

The Conservative Party would have to choose a new leader in Opposition for the first time for more than fifty years, since Arthur Balfour's resignation in 1911, and for the first time by its new electoral procedure. Immediately after Douglas-Home's statement, Macleod made it known that he would not stand for the leadership – his soundings with his advisers had indicated that he might receive about 40 votes, perhaps up to 45, but far fewer than either Heath or Maudling. The leadership election looked like being a two-horse race, but 'as midnight approached', *The Times* reported, 'a new wave of popularity seemed to be bearing Mr Enoch Powell towards a candidature.' Powell had no comment to make, and after it had become known that he had been nominated as a candidate he declined at first to confirm his acceptance of the nomination. But Powell had decided to stand in order to establish a future claim. He was letting the party know that he wanted, one day, to lead it. 'I was leaving my visiting card,' as he later told Macleod.[66]

By chance, only the previous week, before the question of a leadership contest had arisen, Macleod had been prompted by the publication of *A Nation Not Afraid*, a collection of Powell's speeches and writing edited by John Wood, to write a profile of his long-time colleague and rival in the *Spectator*. 'Enoch Powell has the finest mind in the House of Commons,' he wrote, 'the best trained, and the most exciting.' As to what Macleod termed the 'attitude of mind which can be called "Powellism"', he suggested that,

> Powellism is not wholly or even mainly a right-wing creed: by those rather absurd touchstones that 'progressives' delight to use – abolition of corporal and capital punishment, implementation of the Wolfenden Report, the humanizing of penal and mental health reform – Powell is a progressive. Typically, Powell declines to be typed. He does not fit into any political slot. He is just Enoch Powell.

Macleod enjoyed pointing out that Powell had not been as consistent in his politics as *A Nation Not Afraid* implied, quoting Emerson's dictum that 'a foolish consistency is the hobgoblin of little minds'. But in a crushing and subsequently much-quoted gibe about Powell's ideological approach and excess of logic, he wrote, 'I am a fellow-traveller, but sometimes I leave Powell's train a few stations down the line, before it reaches, and sometimes crashes into, the terminal buffers.' As to their differences on economic policy, Macleod noted that 'no one could be further away than Powell from the philosophy of Keynes. It is, indeed, one of the main reasons why Powell is always challenging and stimulating to listen to or to read.' But Macleod did 'not believe that in an affluent society the laws of supply and demand are as inexorable as Powell holds them to be' – he was wont, off the record, to describe Powell's economic dogmatism as 'Enochery'. In particular, he could not share Powell's view of labour as being, for all practical purposes, a commodity, and unlike Powell he believed in regional policy. None the less, Macleod concluded his profile-cum-review by suggesting that,

> In the rethinking of policy that is now being pursued in the Tory Party, Powellism gains converts every day. Much of our programme when the general election comes will be based on the ideas in this book. As long as we are wise enough not to swallow it all, Powell's medicine will do us a power of good.[67]

Despite the generous suggestion by Macleod that 'Powellism' was gaining converts every day, the same could not be said of Powell's candidature for the leadership. The anger and puzzlement at the news that Powell had entered the contest went beyond the natural irritation in the Heath and Maudling camps. Some senior back-benchers were reported to be 'unable to conceal their anger and dismay' with Powell. His action was attacked as 'an act of sheer mischief', since some older Tory MPs had sought to ensure that candidates with no chance of winning would not stand. Powell was also dismissed as the candidate for 'Goldwaterism' – an unflattering comparison with the extreme right-wing views associated with Senator Barry Goldwater, the Republican candidate in the 1964 American presidential election. As to Powell's effect on the outcome, *The Times* noted that his 'speeches and writings have begun to have a potent influence on youngish, technocratic Tories', including the 1964 intake. For this reason, it was suggested that Powell might 'draw off some votes from Mr Heath, especially Midland votes'. On the other hand, 'if only because it is easy for Mr Powell's message to be slightly misunderstood by the Tory right wing as a reassertion of what might be called classical Conservatism, Mr Maudling could lose support'. The *Express and Star*, however, made a more hard-headed assessment of Powell's impact, reporting that he was expected to receive between 15 and 25 votes.[68]

As Powell was a rank outsider, his support was eroded by the feeling among some MPs that backing him was a wasted vote, especially since Powell's canvassing was virtually non-existent. Heath was able to attract many of the younger Tories who might have voted for Powell's liberal economics. 'Mr Heath may not believe in *laissez-faire*,' Alan Watkins, the political columnist, noted, 'but he is much nearer to Mr Powell than Mr Maudling is.' After the contest, the *Spectator* commented that 'the division between the supporters of Heath and Maudling was in part at least between the younger and the older members of the Conservative Party, between those who wanted to live dangerously and those who wanted a quieter life.' When the votes were announced at 2.15 p.m. on Tuesday 27 July, Heath had won 150 votes, Maudling 133 and Powell only fifteen. Although Heath had won an overall majority, he was short of the required 15 per cent margin of the votes cast over the runner-up. But no second ballot was needed as Maudling stood down within a matter of hours and Powell, as *The Times* reported, 'also took little time to consult with his backers before he formally announced that he would not want to break another lance with Mr Heath'.[69]

Only nine of Powell's supporters have been positively identified – Nicholas Ridley (his observer at the ballot), Edith Pitt and Bernard Braine (his junior ministers at Health), John Vaughan-Morgan (a member of One Nation since the 1950s), John Hay (an associate on housing policy), Harry d'Avigdor-Goldsmid (MP for Walsall), Tam Galbraith, and, from the younger generation, John Biffen and Michael Alison. It is also thought that Powell won support from members who supported tough immigration control – Peter Griffiths, Harold Gurden, Sir Cyril Osborne and Henry Kerby. Among the liberal-minded members of the new intake, Geoffrey Howe had been inclined to vote for Powell, and said as much to Michael Alison, who was thinking of backing Heath. But the upshot of their discussion, as they only discovered later, was that Alison switched to Powell and Howe transferred to Heath.[70]

Powell's poor showing confirmed that his decision to stand had been a misjudgement. He was, as Biffen later recalled, 'devastatingly self-contained', and made no effort to cultivate support among the younger intake of MPs, instead preferring to work in the Commons library, where he wrote many of his speeches. But instead of concentrating on this new political weapon and continuing to build support gradually for his new, radical brand of Toryism, Powell had entered an electoral battle on weak ground. He was bound to lose, and his derisory vote was a serious setback for his longer-term objective. 'Powellism', as Watkins observed, had been destroyed as 'a newsworthy headline-making creed.' No longer could 'Powell's speeches be written up as if they represent the views of any significant group within the Conservative Party'. Powell's vote had almost certainly under-represented the sympathy for his views within the party, especially on economic policy. For the time being, however, Heath was in a strong position. The new Tory leader was more likely than Maudling to attract those who favoured liberal economic policies, while the result of the leadership contest suggested that, in the last resort, he could always call Powell's bluff.[71]

Temperamentally, Powell would never have allowed such a setback to deter him. But it helped that he was fulfilled in his life outside politics. He had a deep hinterland in the classics, history, literature and the scriptures. During the mid-1960s, he and Hailsham used to sit together on the Opposition front bench, capping Greek quotations. Hailsham was always the originator, and used to write his quotation on a piece of paper and pass it to Powell, who would then reply with an apposite quotation that surpassed Hailsham's effort. 'He never failed to beat me on my ground,' Hailsham has recalled. 'He remembered the rarest of things. He had it instantly available. It was always exactly to the point.' Powell demonstrated an extraordinary range of subject-matter and knowledge in his book reviews and broadcast journalism, whenever he was not beset by the need to work on ministerial boxes. Each evening he used to read to Pam in bed before they went to sleep.[72]

Powell's rediscovery of his religious faith had much to do with his sense of being at one with himself. He observed the Sabbath, to the extent of keeping it free from politics if he possibly could, and almost invariably attended church. If the Powells were spending their weekend in London, he preferred to worship at St Peter's, Eaton Square, rather than his own parish church of St Michael's, Chester Square, because he considered the latter to be too 'low' in its Anglicanism. He would sometimes preach – while he was Minister of Health, he had been guest preacher at the Sunday service at a Butlin's holiday camp.

Powell was a happy man, who, as Macleod explained, 'rejoices in his family'. Family holidays during his daughters' summer vacations and picnics on Sundays between February and November were fixed points in the

Powells' calendar. Although Powell had stopped fox-hunting when he married, Michael Strachan's influence lived on for many years, since he continued riding into his sixties, and the Powells' daughters learned to ride. Strachan, however, had less impact on Powell's behaviour behind a steering wheel, since his driving remained idiosyncratic. On the Monday following Powell's refusal to serve Home in October 1963, the *Express and Star* reported that he had been involved in two collisions, on the first occasion hitting the bumper of a parked car, and four hours later colliding with a following photographer's car on Putney Bridge. One fellow MP, who was given a lift by Powell from the Midlands to London, was immensely relieved when they finally arrived in one piece, only to be told by Powell: 'All the way from Birmingham to London, and never legally overtaken once!' After this experience, any offer of a lift by Powell was politely declined. At elections, Pam used to act as his driver as he toured his constituency in a Landrover, canvassing support and delivering impromptu speeches.[73]

Among the Powells' favourite holiday locations were fishing villages. In September 1964, they spent a fortnight at a small hotel in Port-na-Blagh, in County Donegal, Ireland, where ten-year-old Susan was able to go riding, and seven-year-old Jennifer proved so skilful with a fishing rod that her daily catch supplied the family's needs, and on some days, the other guests'. The following year, they spent two weeks at Pornis, on the west coast of France, one of their favourite holiday areas. Indeed, France was to become a regular destination, as Powell once commented, 'because God spends his holidays there'. In later life, the Powells used to explore a different region of the country each year. Powell's enjoyment was enhanced by taking one of the novels of Emile Zola with him, 'because when in France, one should read French', and Zola gives 'a vivid description of French society under the Second Empire' – a particular favourite was *La Débâcle*, because of its description of the Franco-Prussian war.[74]

If the Powells were spending the weekend in Wolverhampton, they might be accompanied on their family picnic by Clem Jones, then editor of the *Express and Star*, and his wife and sons – Pam, Marjorie Jones and the children would sometimes swap between cars during the day's outing. Jones and Powell had discovered their common interest in history and literature not long after Powell's adoption in Wolverhampton, when Jones was writing a regular column about the surrounding countryside and local history and Powell took him to task, in a friendly way, over some of his comments. They found that not only had they both read George Borrow, but they had also walked the route of Borrow's journey through mid-Wales. Housman and Doctor Johnson were among other shared literary tastes – the Joneses and the Powells were sometimes guests at the annual Johnson Society supper in nearby Lichfield, the doctor's Staffordshire birthplace. In 1961, the *Express and Star* reported Powell's witty parody of the poet, Rupert Brooke, at the Staffordshire Society's annual dinner in London, when he substituted the names of Black

Country towns such as Bilston, Darlaston, and Tipton for Brooke's Grant-chester and other Cambridgeshire haunts.[75]

Country picnics were often combined with a visit to a historic building, and Powell was especially fond of looking round a village church. He would give expert talks on the building's architecture and history. If a printed guide was available to visitors, Powell was quick to detect any mistakes and rural vicars were sometimes astonished to receive a letter correcting an error of which they had previously been unaware. Although he was protective of his family's privacy, he was not entirely beyond succumbing to a good photo-opportunity, especially if it showed him in a different light from his forbidding public image. As Minister of Health, he had been snapped hopping through Belgravia on a pogo-stick as his family looked on, and in the spring of 1966, an *Observer* profile gave a rare glimpse of Powell, the relaxed and happy family man. 'Picnicking with his family near the Welsh border,' reported Colin Cross,

> Mr Enoch Powell poured claret into a plastic mug. He sipped at it, then stretched himself on the grass. 'I can't understand', he said, 'why people keep describing me as austere. I enjoy life – that's part of what Toryism is about – enjoyment.'

Powell romped with his daughters, Susan, aged twelve, and nine-year-old Jennifer, but the didactic personality was never far below the surface. Their destination was Beeston Castle, near Chester, and as he led his daughters round, he was soon 'lecturing them on its construction. He said the castle was obsolete almost as soon as it was finished, a characteristic of military weapons still.'[76]

One of the photographs of the Powells' picnic at Beeston showed Powell laughing uproariously. But even on such an informal and relaxed occasion, he wore a collar and tie. However hard he might try, Powell was never able to shed his image of being a very buttoned-up English gentleman. Yet Colin Cross achieved an important insight into Powell's personality. Without explicitly mentioning Powell's well-publicized difficulties with Heath, Cross none the less asked Powell about his situation. In reply, Powell 'laughed and laughed. "Unalloyed enjoyment", he said, "and vigorous activity".' As Macleod had written a year earlier, although Powell was a happy man, he was also restless. This restlessness was to contribute to Powell's increasing sense of frustration with his party leader during the next two years.[77]

14

Divergence

You are trying to provide people with words and ideas which will fit their predicament better than the words and ideas which they are using at the moment. This is, to me, what politics is about.

Enoch Powell, expressing his belief in the 'educational' purpose of politics, 1968.

Powell and Heath

Although parliament was about to rise for the 1965 summer recess, Heath chose his new front bench team immediately after his election as leader, in order to give them time to acquaint themselves with their new duties well in advance of October's party conference. Heath's major reconstruction of the Shadow Cabinet was seen as being adroit and imaginative. Maudling was appointed to the new post of deputy leader, Macleod became Shadow Chancellor, and Douglas-Home took over as Shadow Foreign Secretary Powell was appointed Shadow Defence Minister, but only after he had satisfied himself in a discussion with Heath that they saw eye-to-eye. Defence was one area on which Powell thought he would not be in disagreement with Heath, and when Heath asked him which of the positions that were available he would prefer, he had replied, 'Defence'.[1]

Heath readily agreed, and could not have given Powell 'greater satisfaction'. Powell, the former Brigadier, was in his element. His love of the subject was evident to his closest political friends, including John Biffen who used to find him engrossed in military maps that showed the line of battle, or de-briefing Tory MPs on their return from overseas visits. One of these MPs was Neil Marten, whose belief in the Commonwealth and Britain's overseas commitments, especially in the Persian Gulf, ran counter to Powell's views, but whose knowledge Powell respected. But in the Commons, Powell was given a difficult time by his opposite number on the Government front bench, Denis Healey, the Defence Secretary, whose longstanding expertise in international relations and knowledge of the debates and personalities enabled him to exploit Powell's questioning of a broadly bipartisan defence policy.[2]

The appointment of Powell to the Shadow Defence portfolio seemed consistent with his vision of a new, modernizing Tory Party. It is possible to see in Powell's and Heath's shared view of Britain's role as a European power and Heath's readiness, as the *Economist* put it, 'to be tough with national illusions', the reasons why Powell thought that they agreed on defence. But whether the party would accept Powell's radicalism remained a moot point. The previous year, 'A Conservative' had argued in *The Times* that Britain's commitments in Asia and the Middle East could be explained 'only by a fixed determination to remain blind to the true facts of Britain's altered power and role in the world'. As the *Economist* noted on Powell's appointment, 'Mr Heath must know that Mr Powell has harshly realistic views about Britain's role overseas ... This may be a sign that the Government could find itself outflanked in the defence cuts business.' But Heath seems to have assumed that Powell's radicalism could be squared with the strong defence lobby in the Tory Party through the 'overlord' role on overseas affairs that he had assigned to his predecessor, Douglas-Home. Heath could hardly have dropped Powell at this stage, and although Powell indicated that he intended to continue making speeches on other issues, Heath had at least kept him away from either economic policy or home affairs, where his trenchant views would have created deep divisions in the party.[3]

In the light of the subsequent explosive hostility between Heath and Powell, it would be easy to assume that their relationship at this stage was already beset by mutual dislike and distrust. This would be wrong. Although Heath had been closely associated with Macmillan, he was never one of the 'grouse-moor' set, and he and Powell had some things in common. They were both from lower middle-class families, had attended state schools, won scholarships to Oxford and Cambridge respectively, had a good war, entered the House in 1950 and become founder-members of the One Nation group. Moreover, both men saw the 1950s as locust years when the Tories had missed an opportunity to increase efficiency, make Britain more competitive and recover some sense of national pride. They both wanted the Tories to make good this wasted opportunity when they returned to power by using their period in Opposition to make the Conservative Party a force for change.

Powell and Heath had never had reason to work as close colleagues before 1963, and they did not know each other well when Heath became leader. But Powell quite liked Heath, and was keen to get to know him better. This led to an amusing incident when Heath was invited to dinner at South Eaton Place. The Powells' daughters, Susan and Jennifer, used to hand round snacks before dinner and introduce the guests to their pet hamsters. On this occasion, the guests were in the back-garden and, as Jennifer recalls, Heath 'did not like having a hamster running all over him, but the hamster liked him and the hamster sat on his lap and washed his little face'. Heath was the only guest who was paid what was, for a hamster, a great compliment. The Powells 'subsequently realized it was a momentary lapse of judgement by the hamster, but we didn't hold it against him'.[4]

But the political relationship between Powell and Heath was bedevilled by their very different view of politics. This was not simply a matter of differences in policy, or even whether one man was more idealistic than the other, since they both had a strong vision of Britain's future. Their conflicting ideals and policy ideas were later to create an unbridgeable gulf between them. But at the root of the trouble was their fundamentally different assumptions about their role as politicians, and what they wanted to achieve in politics. Powell regarded politics primarily as being 'educational', in the sense that it was about ideas and changing people's minds, as he told Julian Critchley in 1968 in the words quoted at the head of this chapter. Heath, by contrast, saw politics in terms of finding practical answers to real problems, and implementing these solutions in government.[5]

Nowhere was this distinction between Powell and Heath as politicians more evident than in the wholesale review of Conservative Party policy that Heath master-minded. It is as difficult to imagine Heath's confessing to a nostalgic hallucination in his mind's eye of 'Her Majesty's ships' still sweeping the oceans of the world, that Powell depicted in the summer of 1965, as it is impossible to envisage Powell setting up the myriad of detailed policy groups that Heath created between 1965 and 1970. Powell respected Heath as a brilliantly capable administrator, but thought that he suffered from the delusion that if all the right, expert advice was assembled and put together, it would produce the right answer. In fact, Powell chaired one of the first post-1964 policy groups, that examined the local rates, but otherwise played very little part in the formal structure of policy groups. His group's main recommendation was that the rates should be on capital values instead of hypothetical rental values (a precursor, in principle, of the council tax).[6]

Although a Defence Policy Group had been established in early 1965, it was not resurrected by Powell, who preferred to work through his regular meetings with his junior defence spokesmen and elected officers of the Tory back bench defence committee. He always arrived for their meetings, usually held on Wednesdays at 9.45 a.m., well prepared with the points that he wished to raise and his marked passages in *Hansard* to hand. He also used to have draft parliamentary questions and possible supplementaries ready to hand out to his team for discussion. He was a good leader – creating a sense of teamwork by making a personal mention in a speech, a private note or a quiet word of encouragement. Powell reviewed what he regarded as the two most important aspects of Britain's defence needs through two study groups – one on landward defence, the other on maritime defence. Philip Goodhart, Rear-Admiral Morgan Giles, James Ramsden and Major Patrick Wall were among the MPs most closely involved in interviewing witnesses and discussing the issues. Powell prepared papers based on their work, and an additional paper on 'The Shape of Our Future Armed Services', shortly after he left the Shadow Cabinet in 1968.[7]

Powell regarded the Shadow Cabinet discussion on trade union reform as providing a classic example of Heath's approach. None of the policy groups was as thoroughgoing in its work as the group on industrial relations law, that finally produced a massively detailed report, but when the Shadow Cabinet eventually came to discuss the subject, Hogg and Powell sought to raise 'some matters of fundamental theoretical significance' on which they felt the party needed to be clear before deciding how to legislate. 'I remember vividly the anger which Ted Heath showed at this interruption,' Powell later recalled. While acknowledging that he was 'not naturally fair to Ted Heath because our personalities are not entirely consonant', Powell explained that Heath

> always seemed to me a person who had a natural detestation for an idea. If you showed him an idea he would immediately become angry and go red in the face. The notion that the ideas and theories underlying industrial law should be considered and discussed, if necessary, philosophically, was deeply repugnant to him. He felt that here was something on which work had been done, experts had been assembled, opinions had been put together; here was a report for publication based upon it all and that ought not to be upset.

This meeting was also recalled by Robert Carr, who had been one of the three chairmen of the industrial relations group since its formation in 1965, and who observed that after three years' consultation, it would have been 'devastating to be sent back to base'.[8]

This mutual incomprehension between Powell and Heath extended to the role of tradition in British politics. Powell, to whom tradition was integral to a sense of national identity, was always surprised by Heath's matter-of-fact attitude. Their difference was illustrated by their sharp clash in Shadow Cabinet over a proposal to abolish an ancient parliamentary custom that involved Black Rod. Until the rule was changed in 1967, this senior official in the Lords was liable to arrive in mid-debate in the Commons and interrupt proceedings in order to summon MPs to hear the Royal Assent to Bills. Powell, who was completing his history of the medieval House of Lords, was appalled when the reform was first mooted:

> I remember bursting out and saying, 'But, Ted, we can't do this ... Do you realize that the formula which is used ... is that which was used in 1306 when Edward I was ill at the time of a parliament of Carlisle, and it was probably two hundred years old at that time. You simply cannot destroy a thing like that.' And Ted flushed with anger. He said, 'This is exactly the sort of thing that does us so much harm. People simply do not understand that mumbo-jumbo.'[9]

Yet Powell's first major divergence from Heath was to stem from the complete renunciation that he had made some years earlier of Britain's imperial past, but to which many still clung. In challenging the combination of tradition and wishful thinking that caused Britain to retain military commitments in far-flung corners of the globe, he was to offer Heath the chance to outflank the Labour Government and transform the country into a European power. Heath would have been saved a great deal of trouble if he had seized this opportunity.

Heath misses an opportunity

Immediately after his appointment as Shadow Defence Secretary in August 1965, Powell spent a fortnight's family holiday on the west coast of France. In September, his continuing fascination with old churches and their history led to the publication in *History Today*, and subsequently in the *Express and Star*, of his article, 'Riddle of a King's Tomb', in which he argued that a tomb in the parish church at King's Langley in Hertfordshire had been designed to hold the remains of Richard II. But all the while, in addition to fulfilling his speaking engagements, he was thinking through Britain's defence policy, in preparation for his speech to the Conservative conference at Brighton in October. The conclusions that he reached ran counter to the policy that had been pursued by the Conservative Government until 1964 and subsequently continued by the new Labour Government. Indeed, his radicalism on the key questions of the day – east of Suez and nuclear deterrence – gave the Conservative Party's defence spokesman more in common with Labour's left-wing than with the bulk of opinion on either his own benches or the Government front bench.[10]

The new Labour Government had accepted their Tory predecessors' view that Britain's forces overseas made an important contribution to international security. Wilson saw the Commonwealth as a going concern and regarded it as an important source of trade and investment opportunities, and in addition was concerned to maintain close Anglo-American relations. Britain could not therefore afford to relinquish its world role. Labour's 1965 Defence White Paper even suggested that the scale of Britain's commitment in Germany might be reduced in size in view of the lessened Soviet threat, and that the resources thus saved could be used to increase British forces east of Suez, i.e. in Asia, the Far East and the Persian Gulf. This approach was echoed in the Conservative policy document, *Putting Britain Right Ahead*, that was published for the October 1965 party conference at Brighton, which stated that the 'immediate threats to peace are now in the East'. After referring to the danger posed to southern Asia by communist China, the Tory document added:

> Now that the position in Europe has been stabilized by collective action, we must aim at building up and safeguarding the independence of these countries. Present circumstances require that our military presence there continues.[11]

There had been an intimation in September of Powell's concern not to be constrained by the existing consensus when the Shadow Cabinet considered the draft of *Putting Britain Right Ahead*. His query as to whether the document committed every Shadow Minister or was the basis for further discussion at the conference, put the new Shadow Cabinet on the spot. Their response was a classic fudge; although the foreword should make it clear that it was 'not the last word, it would inevitably be taken by the public as a fairly firm commitment'. But at the last meeting of the Shadow Cabinet before Brighton, Powell told his colleagues that he proposed to keep within the line of the document, although he would stress that we should not become too dependent on foreign defence equipment in the context of European aircraft production. He also cleared his speech with Douglas-Home and Christopher (later Lord) Soames, his fellow front bench spokesmen on overseas affairs.[12]

None the less, Powell's conference speech was to spark an enormous row, although its implications were not immediately understood. Indeed, he received a rapturous reception for his *tour de force*, impressing the party faithful by the kind of performance that was becoming his hallmark, as he established a basic premise and then developed his argument, step by logical step. It was, in fact, the first time since the 1950s that Powell had 'had the opportunity to address this conference on any subject more important than the supply of wigs and teeth to foreigners under the NHS'. It was also a proud moment for him, 'because to carry the responsibility, although it is only for the present "shadow" responsibility, for the defence of this country is the fulfilment of an almost lifelong ambition'.

The motion being debated had referred to 'the defence of our national interest'. The basic premise from which Powell derived his view of Britain's defence strategy followed in his statement that 'the United Kingdom is a European power'. It followed, therefore, that 'an alliance which can successfully defend Western Europe against attack from the East – the only present direction from which danger is apprehended – is central to our defence policy'. But when Powell stressed the importance of 'an alliance', he failed to refer specifically to the North Atlantic Treaty Organization (NATO). Indeed, Powell determinedly eschewed any mention of NATO or the United States throughout his speech. These omissions were exceptional in a major statement of policy by the Conservative Party's defence spokesman, since the Atlantic Alliance was generally accepted as being the bulwark of Britain's defence. But Powell believed that British policy had long been subordinated to American interests.[13]

Instead, Powell put much greater emphasis on Britain's role as a European power, and he appeared to be ready to contemplate British membership of some new European defence organization of the kind then being quite widely canvassed. The One Nation group's *One Europe* pamphlet the previous April had proposed European military unity. In June, Soames had suggested to the Shadow Cabinet that the European members of NATO should commit some of their conventional and nuclear forces to a European defence organization, that would also be an integral part of NATO. And the party's foreign affairs policy group had argued that the greater economic and political independence of a more united Europe should extend to greater military independence. Although he was not explicit at Brighton, Powell saw British membership of the existing West European Union as the main focus of Britain's defence effort as a European power. But he made one crucial proviso about British involvement in any European defence organization, namely that

> no commitment be entered into which would irrevocably deny us all possibility of independent action, to deter an enemy or to maintain our own existence, however unforeseen the circumstances may now be in which that might be necessary.[14]

Whereas the Conservative policy document and Labour's White Paper had identified the main threat to world peace as lying *in* the East, Powell's contention was that British policy should concentrate on the threat to the United Kingdom *from* the East. It followed that the 'forces and material' for defending Europe should 'have an overriding claim on the resources which we can devote to our defence'. Moreover, he devoted a substantial section of his speech to demolishing two of the main arguments for Britain's commitments 'east of Suez'. In rebutting the claim that trade and access to raw materials required a military presence, Powell pointed out that Britain's competitors had outstripped its performance without any such presence. And this former imperialist, who used to despair of the party's defeatism on the Empire, now counselled the Tory faithful that, in the post-imperial world, 'a military presence has more than once proved rather an obstacle than a safeguard to the development of trade, and hindered instead of promoting that recognition of mutual material interest which is the only sure basis of all trade'.

Powell gave the notion that Britain had a role in containing the Communist threat outside Europe similarly short shrift. He was somewhat dismissive of the threat of communism as such, since it was an abstract theory, 'and you do not shoot theories with bullets'. Instead, the threat came from the Russian and Chinese empires, 'both which we apprehend might threaten Europe and thus ourselves by commanding the adjacent continents of Asia and Africa'. He emphasized that 'two great propositions' had to be weighed 'with the utmost candour'. In the first place, assuming that Western military power could limit Russian and Chinese influence in Africa and Asia, 'we should still have to measure the practical effect of British military effort against the size of the resources it demands and the consequences of diverting them from other pressing uses'. Secondly, the eventual limits of Russian and Chinese advance in Asia and Africa 'will be fixed by a balance of forces which itself will be Asiatic and African'. And, in addition, 'we have to reckon with the harsh fact that the attainment of this eventual equilibrium of forces may at some point be delayed rather than hastened by Western military presence'.[15]

As with Powell's crusade over the previous two years to convert the Tories to liberal economics, his comments were directed as much at his own party as they were at Labour. 'These are the great issues in Europe and in the world which any defence policy must weigh,' he declared. 'The service required of us in peace', he concluded, 'is the deepest insight, the clearest and most unprejudiced thinking, and the most resolute decision that the minds of men with a common purpose can achieve.' Powell won his standing ovation for his eloquence, but Sir Robin Day, who was reporting the conference for the BBC, overheard a Tory activist comment in the bar afterwards, 'It will be very interesting to see what Enoch actually said. It was a very good speech but it had some serious undertones.'[16]

In Powell's interview with Day, he denied the charge of inconsistency between the questions that he had raised and the policy document's support for a British role east of Suez. In his view, it was all a matter of timing and detail. But his speech had sown confusion and created an open split in the party. Aidan Crawley, a Tory back-bencher, former Labour MP and defender of Commonwealth links, called for Powell's resignation. Heath put it about discreetly that Powell's approach was definitely not Conservative policy. Douglas-Home did the same, though only in response to queries. Labour's Defence Secretary, Denis Healey, teased the Tories over their disarray, and the press were hot on the scent of disunity. In the *Spectator*, Alan Watkins noted that Powell had 'asserted the complete opposite' to the position on Britain's world role outlined in the policy document. 'Here we have an apparent disagreement between Mr Powell and Mr Heath which in due course will have to be cleared up.' To the intense discomfort of the Tory leadership, as the minutes of the Shadow Cabinet make clear, all this 'was having a disturbing effect on our American allies and on our Commonwealth and other friends' east of Suez.[17]

Yet the issue was not at this stage primarily a clash between Powell and Heath. The real dispute lay between, on the one hand, those like Powell who recognized the damaging economic and financial burden imposed by Britain's defence commitments and, on the other hand, those like most of the Tory foreign affairs and defence establishment, who believed that Britain had to honour its commitments east of Suez at practically any cost. Significantly, the *Spectator*, then being edited by the new Shadow Chancellor, Macleod (who had every reason to be concerned at defence costs), strongly backed Powell's speech. 'Mr Enoch Powell has offered the Government a great opportunity which one hopes it will have the courage to take,' the magazine's editorial declared. After his Brighton speech, 'the Government defence review could come out tomorrow advocating eventual British withdrawal from all overseas bases and the Opposition could only applaud.' The question was whether Heath would also back Powell's radical line and dish Labour, or would bow to the powerful and strong Tory defence lobby.[18]

Heath was forced to devote the first meeting of his Shadow Cabinet after the conference to the east of Suez issue. Powell asserted that

our continued commitment to the remnants of the old system of bases and world wide involvement made us less effective than we could be and had forced us to contract out prematurely from the technological race. Our long term policy should be designed to make it easier when we got back into power to exercise greater freedom in the redeployment of our resources and our effort by deciding what the options really were and which we should go for.

Soames, on the other hand, 'felt strongly that some presence east of Suez, and in particular in the Far East, would remain a necessary part of our policy for the foreseeable future and that through it we could continue to exert an influence on American policy'.[19]

The verbatim note of the discussion that followed in the Shadow Cabinet's overseas sub-committee shows that Heath had some sympathy for Powell's position, but it also demonstrates that the formidable strength of the Tory foreign policy and defence establishment effectively blocked any change in policy. As Soames observed, the 'crunch' between him and Powell came over whether there should still be a British presence east of Suez after the end of the present confrontation. But Powell feared that the Tories risked finding themselves with 'the Far East tail, however important, wagging the whole of the dog ... I simply don't want our long-term commitments to be such that they would influence our immediate defence expenditure.' At this Sandys, who took the most hawkish line, interjected that he had been in Washington, 'and they are very concerned about Enoch, and say that if it means we are going to get out it will affect our relationship'. Heath, however, countered the criticism of Powell by pointing out that the present rate of defence expenditure could not continue, because the economy could not stand it.[20]

The meeting ceased to be a discussion, but became a matter of Powell versus the rest, with Heath trying to hold the ring. The verbatim note captures the flavour:

> *Powell* – but we must not let our commitments out there [east of Suez] dictate our whole defence expenditure, which at the moment it does.
> *Chorus* – but it is bound to, because there *is* a military presence out there. It is just a fact of life.

And when Heath tried to move the discussion on to managing the divisions in the party, the 'chorus' again struck up:

> Powell wants us not to commit ourselves to a presence in the Far East after disengagement in Malaysia which would be of a size to influence our whole defence effort. But we must have a military presence all over the place in order to keep our influence in the world.

In Heath's view, Britain had no influence in the world as long as the economy was in its present state, but the Americans kept bailing Britain out every few months so that it would stay in the Far East. American documents since released, show that in September 1965, the British and American Governments had reached a secret agreement whereby the US would provide financial help, contingent on no British devaluation and no British withdrawal from east of Suez.[21]

Despite Heath's evident sympathy for Powell's concern about defence costs, the Tory defence and foreign affairs lobby won the day. The party remained committed east of Suez up to and after their return to office in 1970. As an immediate step after his comments at Brighton, Powell was required to make a speech to clarify the position, and also to address a special joint meeting of the party's back bench foreign affairs and defence committees (as the relevant shadow spokesman, he chaired the defence committee). For a while, his public endorsement of existing overseas commitments calmed matters, but his known doubts about Britain's role, while the party remained firmly committed east of Suez, was a recurrent source of tension.[22]

Heath had got the worst of all worlds, since the Tories were divided and also still saddled with an unrealistic policy. He had grasped the economic impossibility of Britain's maintaining such an extensive military role, but had failed to make this realization the basis of Tory policy. As a result, he was unable to reap the political benefit as the Labour Government were forced by financial problems to announce a succession of retreats and cutbacks – in 1966 from Aden; in 1967 from Singapore and Malaysia; and in 1969 from the Far East and the Persian Gulf. The announcement in early 1966 of the withdrawal from Aden and the cancellation of an aircraft carrier threatened to expose Tory divisions when a general election was imminent. This crisis prompted lengthy discussion in the Shadow Cabinet and its overseas committee, in which Powell's colleagues insisted that he should state that the Tories would honour their commitments and would build the carrier.[23]

But any hopes among the Tories that they had avoided embarrassment on defence during the 1966 election campaign were dashed as a result of another speech of Powell's. This incident also had a deeper significance for relations between Powell and Heath because it involved a misunderstanding between them. Powell's version is that he was contacted by Central Office and told of a firm rumour that Britain was being pressed by the Americans to send a contingent of troops to Vietnam. He was encouraged to speak out on the subject, and was assured that it was Heath's wish that he should do so. Accordingly, in Falkirk, only five days before polling, he challenged Wilson to confirm or deny whether there was any such plan afoot. But his anti-Americanism gave his comments an added spice, as he claimed that Britain's being 'in pawn' to Washington denied it an independent foreign policy. 'Under the Labour Government in the last eighteen months,' Powell declared, 'Britain has behaved, perfectly clearly and perfectly recognizably, as an American satellite'. Healey immediately countered by mocking the 'anti-American rigmarole' from Powell and calling on Heath to sack him – during the mid-1960s, there was, according to Wilson's biographer, Ben Pimlott, enormous pressure from the Americans, with support in the Foreign Office and the Treasury, for British troops to be sent to Vietnam, but Wilson steadfastly resisted the idea. A statement by Central Office, that 'Mr Powell was speaking on his own behalf', signified Heath's disowning of his defence spokesman. Powell's opposition to United States involvement in Vietnam was to put him at odds with Heath, who had returned from a tour of the Far East at the end of 1965 convinced not only that it was in the West's vital interest that the Americans should win, but that inevitably they would.[24]

Moreover, Heath's commitment to a continuing British military presence east of Suez appeared to grow stronger rather than weaker. Powell, however, was not a lone voice within the parliamentary party. He had some support within the Tory back bench defence committee for developing a more mobile, maritime force in place of expensive overseas land bases. There was also some agreement from younger Tory MPs elected in the 1960s with his position that Britain's defence strategy had to be re-examined on the basis of a more realistic view of what could be afforded. This internal party debate was largely conducted in the relative privacy of the party's back bench foreign affairs and defence committees, but it flared into the open again (as it had in 1965), following another speech of Powell's, at Aislaby on 24 June 1967.[25]

Prompted by Britain's determination to eschew involvement in the Arab-Israeli conflict and the Nigerian civil war – both in areas of 'traditional British influence' – Powell argued that such events 'could be a blessing in disguise'. In Powell's view, they had vindicated his argument that military commitments overseas were pointless and potentially damaging – he forswore to mention his speech at Brighton in 1965, but 'I told you so' was implicit in his message. In the Middle East conflict, not only had the much-vaunted British military presence in the Mediterranean and the Persian Gulf been 'powerless to protect our interests either in oil or sterling', but, even worse, 'it became obvious that it was just because we *were* physically present in the area that our oil and our reserves were in danger, when other people's were not'. In Nigeria, Britain had, rightly in Powell's view, avoided any involvement.

Although Powell's specific criticism was levelled against the Labour Government and the press for perpetuating the 'make-believe' that Britain had somehow played a part in 'having stopped the bloodshed', it was again clear that he had his own party's position in his sights. 'Self-knowledge, the old precept of the oracle: "know thyself", is as needful for nations as for men,' he contended in another of his classical allusions, before declaring that 'too often British politicians have been the most pertinacious in using the language of delusion'. Yet one of the most striking features of this speech was its populist appeal. Powell adopted the role of the politician apart, the man who appreciated the same realities and truths that were perceived by 'ordinary people' (his phrase), whereas other politicians 'might almost seem to be engaged in a conspiracy to fasten Britain's delusions more firmly upon her'.

As Powell became increasingly out of step with the official party line even on defence, the area of policy where he had expected Heath's support, he began to appeal over the heads of his fellow politicians to the British people, and was claiming to speak for them. This was not an attempt on Powell's part to step outside party politics, for he appreciated that in British politics, parties were indispensable. But he had detected a growing disillusion with politics and politicians, and wanted to harness it in his crusade to convert the Tories to a more radical policy, and to build a new radical consensus in the country:

I do not think that the mass of our people, who hear and watch these goings on, like a show on the stage, are much longer in a mood to be amused. They are not deceived. They know the difference between make-believe and the real world. How much longer are they to be practised upon by politicians who treat them like children, to be put to bed happy with a fairy tale? How much longer are we to be held back from exerting our real character, our real effort, and our real resources in that world where all the rest are already living. It is time to be up.[26]

Three days later, Powell again had to defend his comments at another joint meeting of the Tory back bench foreign affairs and defence committees. The majority of MPs who spoke felt that his speech contradicted party policy. But a contingent from the defence committee, including Major Patrick Wall and Rear-Admiral Morgan Giles, voiced their support for switching from land bases to more mobile, maritime forces. Gilmour, an ally of Heath and Macleod, thought that Powell's comments about the Middle East were almost demonstrably true, while the young economic liberals, Ridley, Biffen and Bruce-Gardyne weighed in to support Powell's view that Britain should concentrate on defending itself against an external threat. In reply, Powell doggedly maintained that his speech had been consistent with party policy, but more interesting was his continued emphasis on Britain's role as a European power despite de Gaulle's making clear the previous month his continued opposition to British entry into the EEC – indeed, Powell attributed Britain's difficulty in joining the EEC to its overseas commitments:

British claims of this kind were relevant to the views which were taken of us in Europe, particularly in France. It was impudent to invite them to share in overseas commitments which had brought Britain herself disastrous loss.

The joint meeting, however, failed to resolve the conflict at the heart of Tory defence policy, since Douglas-Home summed up by re-stating the case for the British presence in the Middle East and in Singapore. The Tories could unite in attacking Labour's arbitrary cuts in defence, but they were unable to resolve the same dilemma that was causing Labour such problems, namely, on the one hand, continuing to act as a world power, and, on the other, acknowledging Britain's reduced circumstances. Remaining a world power, however, entailed not only possessing a military presence outside

Europe, but also belonging to the nuclear club. And on the question of the nuclear deterrent, Powell was again at odds with party policy.[27]

Nuclear heretic

'I never believed in the nuclear deterrent,' Powell declared in 1993, explaining that, 'I've always regarded the nuclear deterrent as a piece of logical nonsense.' The theory of nuclear deterrence never convinced Powell,

> because there is an inherent contradiction which is very obvious. The nature of the weapon and its consequences to all concerned, especially where the weapon is held by more than one party, are so immense that the notion that it can be used as a card in a game, as a tool at a certain stage in a [conflict], has always to me self-evidently had something contradictory about it.

He is as dismissive of the co-called intermediate, or tactical, nuclear weapons that were deployed in Europe as he was of the strategic nuclear panoply, arguing that 'as soon as a weapon becomes decisive in the sense of being utterly intolerable, it has passed into the realm of the nuclear absurdity'. In consequence, he was unawed by the possession of nuclear weapons, but thought that they had caused the British seriously to underestimate the residual power of their Atlantic position. His anti-nuclear views were inextricably linked with his anti-Americanism. They set him apart from many on the Tory right, especially Margaret Thatcher and her followers, and, as was the case with certain of his other views, led to his finding closest accord with the Labour left.[28]

Despite his long-standing scepticism towards the nuclear deterrent, Powell remained a minister in the Macmillan Government in 1957 when Sandys's Defence White Paper made the deterrent the cornerstone of British defence policy. 'When an absurdity is convenient', he later suggested, 'its absurdity is very easily overlooked.' What could have been more convenient in the 1950s than to say,

> 'Well, after all it's absurd to have these [conventional] weapons when a war nowadays will only last two, or was it to be five, days?' So it was highly convenient, and I remember because I was a Treasury Minister at the time, in 1957, how the nuclear deterrent was a pivot upon which it became possible to scale down over a relatively short period the proportion of the British national product which was invested in defence. It was highly convenient. And once a convenience has been adopted – advertised, advocated, clasped to the bosom – then it's a very brave or a very strange politician indeed, a kind of Keith Joseph as it were, who having been in office will say, do you know, that was always nonsense, it was very convenient at the time, but I'm telling you, it was nonsense.[29]

As Shadow Defence Secretary, Powell was actively seeking to wean the Tories away from their dependence on nuclear weapons. Had it not been for the furore caused by his comments on east of Suez in his 1965 conference speech, more might have been made of his intriguing reference to the nuclear deterrent. Indeed, Powell confessed during his interview with Sir Robin Day that, in his view, the most significant point in his speech had been his argument 'as to whether we are justified in assuming, and basing all our defence for major war, upon the assumption that any major war will be terminated very shortly by the use of a strategic nuclear weapon'.[30]

Powell had opened his remarks about nuclear weapons in his 1965 Conservative conference speech by arguing that, for the foreseeable future, 'our right to control the use of our own strategic nuclear weapon must be retained to the limit of our ability'. He also dismissed 'as the merest casuistry' any suggestion that the independence of Britain's nuclear deterrent was compromised by its purchase 'from another nation', as he chose to refer to the United States. 'With a weapon so catastrophic', he proclaimed, 'it is possession and the right to use which count.' But Powell's use of the phrase, 'to the limit of our ability', signified an important qualification, since the nuclear weapon had not fulfilled its promise as a cheap alternative to conventional weapons. His careful choice of words, while not contradicting existing policy, implied the possibility that, at some point, the cost of retaining the nuclear deterrent might become prohibitive.

His concern that the defence strategy adopted in 1957 had put too many eggs in the nuclear basket at the expense of conventional defence was evident when he speculated that war might be waged in Europe without the strategic nuclear weapon being invoked almost instantly. 'But any British Government might shudder', he commented, 'before the responsibility of resting the safety and the existence of this nation on the blind assumption that no such war which could endanger them would ever happen.' Powell had gone as far as he dare at the Tory conference to question Britain's reliance on the nuclear deterrent.[31]

Much of what Powell had left unsaid about the nuclear deterrent from the party platform at Brighton, he was happier to elaborate during a broadcast on BBC Radio's Third Programme the following February. He was replying to earlier talks by the former Defence Correspondent of *The Times* and then Foreign Office minister, Lord Chalfont, who had spoken of the need 'to devise a system of international politics from which war and the threat of war have been eliminated'. Powell's talk amounted to a systematic demolition of the theory of nuclear deterrence. Pointing out that during the twenty years since the atomic bombs fell on Japan, the world had suffered a variety of conflicts and wars, Powell argued that it was 'increasingly difficult to sustain with any conviction certain propositions' that had been held over the same period, namely: that the possession of nuclear weapons meant 'that there could be no war which was not total, that is, nuclear'; that it was the American and British nuclear arsenal that prevented the Soviet Union from engulfing western

Europe; and that the possession of nuclear weapons by the United States and by Russia prevented any attempt by one hegemony to encroach upon the other.[32]

As Powell noted, NATO's official thinking had replaced the notion of the 'trip-wire' that would automatically set off nuclear war, in favour of 'the less grotesque idea of substantial forces which have to be driven in before nuclear escalation is deliberately set in train'. This led him to the more contentious suggestion that it had simply been the risk of war with the United States and Britain that had enabled the Alliance to halt Russian penetration of western Europe in 1949–50, implying that it had not been the nuclear deterrent. He was to repeat this claim that the Soviets had not been deterred from attacking western Europe by the West's possession of nuclear weapons on subsequent occasions.[33]

In retrospect, Powell suggested that it was not difficult to see why the nuclear weapon had failed to keep the peace. Resort to nuclear warfare between major nuclear powers would spell near-destruction for both. A nation could lose or forfeit or risk a great deal before a point was reached anywhere near to complete destruction. This applied even more to a nation's allies, and is still more the case where a nation's remote or peripheral interests were concerned. 'It follows' Powell argued,

> that those remote or peripheral interests can be forcibly disturbed – indeed more, that very great inroads can be made into a nuclear nation's allies or even a nuclear nation's own integrity – before the time comes when the balance tips over in favour of the choice of near-destruction. This is why very big operations of war and violent disturbances of the balance of power can and do and will take place, even when the interests of major nuclear powers are at stake.[34]

Powell was not explicit in this talk about his anxieties concerning the dominant position of the United States in NATO, but his dislike of this situation was the kernel of his opposition to Britain's relying for its defence on NATO – a strategy largely dependent on America's readiness to use its nuclear weapons to protect western Europe. At the time of Powell's broadcast, there was concern in the Shadow Cabinet about the future of NATO, especially as de Gaulle was threatening to give it notice to quit its Paris headquarters. Yet Powell had drafted such a brief note on the subject that there were fears in the Research Department that if his paper were circulated to the Shadow Cabinet it would be greeted with 'a hoot of laughter'. Eventually, Powell's one-and-a-half-side paper was accompanied by a five-page factual appendix. This incident is as much testimony to his underlying hostility towards NATO as to his economy of language.[35]

Although Powell revealed in his Third Programme broadcast his scepticism concerning the usefulness of Britain's independent deterrent, he was not explicit about the full extent of his misgivings. 'It is possible', he suggested, 'though only just possible', to imagine nuclear self-defence becoming acceptable to a nation that is regarded by the major nuclear powers as 'peripheral' to their interests. The desire of countries other than the super-powers to possess nuclear weapons stemmed from their feeling that, 'one day', as Powell put it,

> that moment might come for us when the risk of doing a Samson act and pulling down the temple on our own heads by nuclear assault on an enemy about to destroy us, might be our only safety in a world where other powers, however friendly, were unwilling to commit *hara-kiri* for the sake of our beautiful eyes.

As a result of nuclear weapons, Powell concluded, 'a further octave has been added to the scale of human conflict, without however eliminating any that existed before'. It followed, although he did not spell it out in his talk, that Britain should devote considerable resources to conventional defence. In the light of his comments as Shadow Defence Secretary, it is not entirely fanciful to imagine circumstances in which Powell, had he become Defence Secretary in a Tory Government, would have argued for abandoning the nuclear deterrent on the grounds of cost in favour of strengthening Britain's conventional land and maritime forces.[36]

Powell's conviction that Britain's conventional forces needed strengthening and his views on the nuclear deterrent alarmed his colleagues during the Shadow Cabinet's discussion of defence policy in early 1967. He argued that 'so long as the nuclear threat could be used in international relations, he felt Britain should stay in "the nuclear business"'. It was particularly difficult in Opposition, however, to see what form this would take – at this stage, he was not ruling out the possibility of something more substantial than the existing Polaris system. But Powell's rather loose comment about Britain keeping in with the thinking on the ABM (the strategic anti-ballistic missile system) prompted concern from others. At a subsequent meeting, he had to clarify his remarks on this point, and on several others.[37]

Powell also made clear his profound concern at the baleful effect on Britain's conventional defences of depending on American protection. 'The assumption that America would act', Powell argued, 'had had a numbing effect on British maritime defence thinking. He had reluctantly come to the conclusion that we had fallen too far behind, and that for the safety of this country our maritime forces should be built up.' As regards the defence of Europe, he

> did not personally believe in the present theology that any outbreak of fighting in Europe would quickly escalate into nuclear fighting, since he found it impossible to believe that any country would in every case risk what was tantamount to suicide for the sake of another country's national status or frontiers.

In discounting the Defence Secretary's assumption that a conventional war in Europe would last only seven days instead of thirty before nuclear escalation, Powell suggested that the ratio in conventional forces between the Soviet Union and western Europe of three-to-one, 'could be changed by juggling order of battle assessments', and maintained that Europe and Britain were

> surely capable of fighting a successful defence against Russia with conventional forces. The British Army would in future be essentially a European Army, and would therefore have a wholly new role. He felt it should, with reserves, be built up to fulfil this role as a European defence force.

Powell also had to clarify this latter point, subsequently suggesting that 'he had not intended to deny that a European war could escalate into a nuclear war', but that he felt it was 'necessary to work on the assumption that a "conventional" war in Europe could continue for a long time'.[38]

Maudling, the deputy leader, was plainly perturbed at the underlying anti-Americanism and cost implications of Powell's thesis and countered it from the standpoint of the prevailing bi-partisan approach on defence policy. As Maudling argued, Powell's approach 'carried the inherent danger of dividing the forces of the free world – the European forces dealing with the defence of Europe, and America dealing with the rest of the world'. Moreover, 'a re-building of the Navy on the scale Mr Powell envisaged, together with a large conventional force and a nuclear deterrent would be an impossible financial burden on this country'.[39]

Powell, however, was not prepared to drop quietly his questioning of the nuclear deterrent. On the contrary, on 6 March 1967, only a month or so after the Shadow Cabinet's discussion, he openly questioned the bipartisan consensus on the 'nuclear assumption' when he spoke from the Opposition front bench during the Commons debate on the Government's Defence White Paper. He again accepted that nuclear weapons were 'a probable and valid deterrent to nuclear war', but attacked the notion that there could never again be conventional war on the Continent of Europe or the waters around it. He contended that neither the French nor the British in 1940, nor even the Poles in 1939, would have used nuclear weapons if they and the Germans had possessed them, because whatever lay ahead would have seemed preferable to destroying their own countries. Powell omitted to consider whether their possession of nuclear weapons might have deterred Hitler from attacking in the first place because of the risk, however small, that they might be used.

In reply to Healey's question as to whether he was arguing that Britain 'should prepare itself to fight and win a purely conventional war in Europe', Powell replied that, in the event of an attack by the Soviets and their Warsaw Pact allies, Britain should have the ability 'to oppose to it, with our allies, such forces as might have a rational prospect of eventual victory'. He envisaged Britain having 'an army in being', by which he meant an army equal in armament, training and philosophy to any other in Europe, and of such dimensions and structure, and supported by such reserves, as to be able, and to be seen to be able, to play an important and continuing part in Continental warfare; a part which would make it the cement and fulcrum of the indispensable alliance.

But before this 'new concept of what the Army is about' could be given effect, 'an underlying prior decision' had to be taken first, namely the question of 'whether we intend to be able to defend ourselves at all, in the rational, human sense of the term'. In saying this, Powell served notice to his own party that he had no intention of ceasing his criticism of nuclear deterrence. It was 'vital', he declared,

> that the issue of nuclear assumption, which denies alike the possibility, the desirability and the necessity of rational defence, should be fought through to a finish. On the rightness of our answer may hang not only the future of the British Army, but the existence of the nation.[40]

Heath's tolerance of Powell's repeated assaults on 'the nuclear assumption' finally snapped some months later, when Heath vetoed the publication of Powell's proposed CPC pamphlet on the defence of Europe – though it was left to Sir Michael Fraser, Deputy Chairman of the Conservative Party, and former Director of the Conservative Research Department, to tell Powell that it would not do. Powell's draft had caused consternation in the Conservative Research Department, where it was minuted that if some of Powell's statements were 'allowed to appear in a document written by the Chief Opposition Spokesman on Defence', they 'could do serious damage to the Party's interests'. Under the heading of 'The Nuclear Veto', Powell had apparently cited the Berlin blockade and the Cuban missile crisis in support of his assertion that during the past twenty years nations could not be shown to have behaved otherwise than they might have done if the nuclear warheads had not existed. But Guy Hadley of the Research Department's Foreign Affairs section countered that the facts were precisely the reverse. In both crises, the Soviets drew back from a final showdown because it became quite clear this would have meant a nuclear war – indeed, the Cuban crisis arose because the Soviets were installing nuclear missiles aimed at the United States.[41]

Similarly, Powell's argument that the presence of American and European armies on the Continent demonstrated that Europe did not believe that Washington's nuclear deterrent protected them against invasion, was held to be contrary to the facts. Conventional forces were maintained in West Germany and Berlin, Hadley argued, because the Europeans were not prepared to leave an undefended vacuum that would have invited Soviet military and subversive penetration with little risk of provoking a nuclear riposte. As to Powell's reiterating that the 'nuclear veto' was either wholly incredible or improbable, because countries would always prefer defeat or surrender to nuclear annihilation, the temptation to start a war without fear of nuclear retaliation would be very much greater. Hadley felt that Powell's remarks implied that a British nuclear deterrent was superfluous, and should be scrapped.[42]

Heath's veto, however, only temporarily silenced Powell. In February 1968, in an article that he wrote for the *Journal of the Royal United Services Institute*, Powell repeated the arguments against nuclear deterrence that had so alarmed the Research Department when he had expressed them in his draft pamphlet. In the same month, he seized on re-assessments by the US Defense Department of Soviet military strength as vindication of his approach. He told the Shadow Cabinet that this downward revision of the estimate of the Soviet land and air threat in Europe, 'and the evidence of a considerable build-up of Soviet maritime strength, meant a change of emphasis in Western defence thinking away from the assumption that any large-scale hostilities would inevitably escalate into nuclear war after a matter of days, and towards long-term "conventional" land fighting and, particularly, maritime warfare'. The resulting shift from nuclear to conventional defence forces within NATO was in line with Conservative defence policy. Douglas-Home, the Shadow Foreign Secretary, however, was less sanguine and thought that Britain would still have to be ready to resort to the nuclear weapon, since it could not match Soviet 'conventional' maritime strength. Powell maintained, not very convincingly, in reply to questions, that accepting the re-assessment would not necessarily mean 'an enormous build-up of our defence forces'.[43]

But as far as Powell was concerned, the US Defense Department's re-assessment had provided proof that he had been right all along. 'The nuclear mushroom cloud which has hung over national defence policy for two decades', he triumphantly told the Conservative Central Council on 15 March, 'is at last rising into the stratosphere and dispersing.' In short, the prevailing assumptions about nuclear deterrence had been 'torn up'. A conventional, or at any rate a non-nuclear, war at sea and a conventional, non-nuclear war in Europe, were now seen as being distinct possibilities. British defence policy had to be revised accordingly, on the lines that he had proposed.[44]

Yet Powell had read too much into the US Defense Department's re-assessments and had overstated his case. The possible risk of nuclear conflict had not disappeared from Europe, or from anywhere else, to anything like the extent that Powell appeared to imagine. It is impossible to see how Heath could have resolved the increasingly open conflict between, on the one hand, Powell's anti-American and anti-nuclear views on defence and, on the other hand, the Conservatives' commitment to the nuclear deterrent and NATO. Indeed, Powell visited Washington only once as Shadow Defence Spokesman – in the autumn of 1967 – after he had held the position for more than two years. He combined his trip with seminars at the Harvard Center for International Affairs, and, in Chicago and Los Angeles, for the free-market Mont Pelerin Society; in addition, a 'confrontation' was arranged with

Professor J.K. Galbraith, the Keynesian economist. But Heath did not have to resolve the conflict, because in April 1968, a month after the speech to the Conservative Central Council, Powell was sacked from the Shadow Cabinet over his provocative comments on immigration and race relations. In Government after 1970, the Conservatives continued Britain's bipartisan defence policy.[45]

Not a team player

On several occasions between 1965 and 1968, Powell's iconoclastic approach as Shadow Defence Secretary stretched almost to breaking point the bounds of what it was reasonable for him to say while remaining a member of the Shadow Cabinet. But his performance as Defence Spokesman was only one aspect of the challenging, provocative role that he believed was essential in Opposition if the Conservatives were to avoid repeating what he saw as the follies of the Macmillan years when they next returned to office. In an unabated flow of speeches and articles, he continued the one-man crusade that he had launched in 1963 to wrench the party away from the interventionist consensus of the early 1960s.

As early as November 1965, Angus Maude, a long-time political friend of Powell's and a front bench Tory spokesman on Commonwealth affairs, warned, in the wake of the furore over Powell's east of Suez comments at the previous month's Tory conference, that '"Powellism" is approaching some kind of crisis, as was ultimately inevitable.' In Maude's view, however, this crisis stemmed from the party's urgent need to 'come to terms with Powellism, and without much delay'. Maude argued that Powellism, contrary to the impression given in the edited collection of speeches and writings, *A Nation Not Afraid*, was 'not as monolithic as all that, and much of it is debatable'. Although he welcomed Powell's practical criticisms of state planning, Maude queried some of his theorizing, notably on environmental planning and regional policy, and thought that Powell had said too little on the state's role in social policy. But Powell, he argued, was 'doing more than simply purport to tell us what are the right answers to our problems. He is performing the invaluable function of suggesting what are the right questions.' Maude, however, was certainly no great fan of Heath's, and like Powell, had every interest in opening up the debate on party policy.[46]

Powell's unerring tendency to expose contradictions and highlight inconsistencies ran directly counter to Heath's approach. Heath was by background a party manager, having spent eight years in the whips' office, and, as leader of a party that was disoriented at finding itself in Opposition, he was inclined to see party unity as the wherewithal to regaining office. Indeed, when Maude claimed in January 1966, also in the *Spectator*, that the voters saw the Tories as a 'meaningless irrelevance', he was eventually forced to resign from the front bench. His departure was seen as a warning shot by Heath across Powell's bows.[47]

In a speech in Birmingham on 21 November 1965, Powell returned to the issue of immigration by renewing his demand for a change in the citizenship law. The Tory leadership had managed to play down the issue at October's party conference, largely because Labour, despite having attacked the 1962 Commonwealth Immigrants Act, had in August 1965 severely tightened control of primary immigration by reducing to only 8,500 the number of work vouchers that were to be issued under the legislation. Labour's restrictive measure had disturbed Tory liberals, but Powell was concerned that 'even after the August controls were enforced there was an inflow of over 10,000 from the West Indies and the Indian sub-continent alone in August and September'. He regarded this rate of inflow as 'still far too high', and argued that it would 'not be got right until admission for aliens and Commonwealth immigrants is on the same basis'. But his call for voluntary repatriation was in line with party policy. Although his speech received little national publicity, it was specifically attacked by the Labour MPs, Roy Hattersley and Norman Buchan.[48]

Yet the first major disagreement with Powell in Shadow Cabinet after Heath became leader, apart from Powell's comments on east of Suez at the party conference, occurred in January 1966 over incomes policy. This issue was extremely awkward for the Conservatives. In Government, they had adopted an incomes policy and were in a difficult position to attack Labour as they followed suit. The Tories were also divided on whether they should commit themselves to such a policy when they next returned to Government. Although neither Heath, nor Macleod, the Shadow Chancellor, were dogmatic on the matter, and there had been no mention of it in *Putting Britain Right Ahead*, Powell's repeated attacks on incomes policy since November 1964 had annoyed Maudling, the former Chancellor and deputy leader. In the New Year of 1966, Maudling, who was deeply concerned that abandoning incomes policy would create mass unemployment, publicly dissociated himself from Powell's argument that incomes should be left to the self-regulating mechanism of the labour market. In a speech at Wellingborough, he argued that since trade unions existed and would continue to exist, there could be no free market in labour. Neither could labour costs be kept down simply by deflation. He therefore advocated an incomes policy applied to all forms of income. Powell flatly contradicted this argument the following week when he addressed the Manchester Statistical Society. He contemptuously dismissed as 'superstition' the belief that the unions comprised 'an autonomous force in the economy, capable of obliterating other influences – such as government action – on the level of demand'. 'Trade unionism', he declared, 'though it may be and probably is relevant to economic inefficiency, is irrelevant to inflation and the balance of payments.'[49]

Before Heath could attempt to bridge this gulf between Powell and Maudling, Labour's resounding success at the Hull North by-election meant that the next general election was now imminent. This prospect ensured that party unity was the overriding consideration when the Shadow Cabinet tackled the issue of incomes policy on 31 January. As a result, it needs the Tory equivalent of a Kremlinologist to detect that there had ever been any conflict between Powell and Maudling. According to the minute of the meeting, 'Mr Macleod said that the public impression at the moment was, he thought wrongly, that there was a wide area of disagreement between members of the Shadow Cabinet on incomes policy.' And so it continues.[50]

But any prize for understatement must be awarded to Powell, who is recorded as having said that 'the apparent disagreement was mainly a semantic problem'. He also agreed with Macleod's outline of policy. None the less, there was a warning of possible future trouble in his reiteration that

> no Government should attempt to control or to act on individual prices or wages, because it was not possible to know how much each individual case should be allowed to increase in relation to other cases or to keep within the national growth rate.

Powell went on to suggest that 'employers' decisions depended on the level of recruitment they needed to attract, and as Minister of Health, for example, acting on nurses' pay, this had been the criterion he had used'. In saying this, he only served to remind his colleagues of his unfortunate involvement in the last Conservative Government's incomes policy. His notion that a Minister could act in the same way as a private employer was contradicted by Boyle, who pointed out that a Minister had to act in accordance with Government policy. Powell was isolated. 'All other members of the Committee agreed with the policy as set out in Mr Maudling's speech at Wellingborough and as outlined by Mr Macleod,' the minute concluded. Moreover, it was agreed that the two institutions that Powell most abhorred should continue – the Prices and Incomes Board, though with a modified role, and the National Economic Development Council (popularly known as 'Neddie'), with its subsidiaries. These conclusions ran counter to the free-market case that Powell had been expounding the length and breadth of the country since leaving the Government.[51]

Around this time, during a party at the Powells' Belgravia home, Pamela Powell tried, on her husband's behalf, to intercede with Heath and reassure him of Powell's intentions. But the moment was lost when a newspaper editor arrived. None the less, the peace in the Tory camp looked set to hold during the 1966 election. When Heath sought at his first press conference to exploit the divisions in the Labour Cabinet on incomes policy, he was inevitably asked about Powell's position. His reply was a model of tolerance, as he pointed out that an Opposition had not the same responsibilities as the Government, and was able to engage in a period of re-thinking. And Heath said of Powell: 'He has done considerable good for the Tory Party by the provocative attitude he has taken in Opposition on a number of subjects.'[52]

On the Friday before polling, Powell devoted an entire speech to immigration, but he adhered to party policy and stressed the importance of integration. 'I am for my part resolutely determined', he said of the immigrants who had already made Britain their home, 'that they shall, as far as is humanly possible, have the same rights and the same treatment, as anyone else'. But 'all our efforts at integration', he argued, 'will be overwhelmed and swept away if the tide of new immigrants continues to flow in.' He repeated Conservative policy that 'the rate of admission must be further and greatly reduced', carefully adding that 'for my own part and speaking as one who has represented one of the areas most directly affected, I believe there would be no small benefit in a period of years during which the inflow and the outflow roughly balanced'. None the less, as the Institute of Race Relations Newsletter noted of Powell's comments, 'while advocating even stricter control, he did not attempt to whip up popular support on the subject'.[53]

The next day, however, in Falkirk, Powell made his ill-fated intervention on Vietnam. Heath's heavy-handed rebuttal, in contrast to his earlier diplomatic comments about Powell, meant that by polling day their relationship had been further soured. The Tories suffered a heavy defeat, their worst since 1945, as Labour won a majority of 96 seats in the Commons. Powell's majority in Wolverhampton South-West fell to 6,585, with a swing to Labour of 3.9 per cent since 1964, slightly above the national average of 3.5 per cent, but in line with the average across the West Midlands. Although Heath was not held responsible for the defeat and salvaged some credibility with an effective final broadcast, he was none the less denied the authority that only victory can bestow upon a party leader.[54]

Within less than a week of the Tories' defeat, Powell served notice that, in his view, there was no longer any excuse for the Conservative Party's avoiding a fundamental re-assessment of its philosophy and purpose. Speaking to the City of London Young Conservatives on 6 April, Powell reiterated that a break from office had its advantages, and listed four main areas where he thought the Young Conservatives could make their greatest contribution to the re-examination of party policy – trade union law; the nationalized industries; taxation; and immigration and overseas aid. In his call for a policy of denationalization, Powell spoke of the need for the adherents of capitalist free enterprise to

> liberate themselves from the ratchet of nationalization which seems always to advance and never retreat. If a ratchet there is to be, let us reverse it and make it work the other way round.

The need to 'reverse the ratchet effect' was to become the clarion call of Sir Keith Joseph in his campaign for free-market economics and monetarism in the mid-1970s. Moreover, in calling for reviewing the nationalized industries 'in their entirety', Powell included 'even the telegraph (subsequently discovered to include the telephone) which (I regret to say) a Conservative Government was persuaded to nationalize one hundred years ago'. Some sixteen years later, it was to be the decision by the Thatcher Government to sell off British Telecom that led the Tories to stumble on 'privatization' as a major policy.[55]

Yet Powell's call for a substantial re-think in 1966 was a clear repudiation of Heath's approach, and was worded in such a way that it was bound to give offence to the leader. The Tory manifesto had been entitled *Action not Words*, and epitomized Heath's belief that the Conservatives should show that they were ready to act decisively with practical proposals, and not seem pre-occupied by general ideas that meant little to the public. But the upshot was, as Macleod pointed out privately to Heath, that *Action not Words* had contained no fewer than 131 specific promises. Powell now delivered a public insult. 'The levers of power have been removed from our reach or even our remote control', he acknowledged, adding that, ' "Words not Action" describes with precision the role of the Conservative Party as this new phase opens in its and the nation's political life.'[56]

In part, Powell's message simply reflected the adage that the Opposition's duty is to oppose. 'Some of our words will be harsh, fierce, destructive words, aimed in defiance and contempt at men and policies we detest', he declared. Yet again, however, his real message was directed at his own party. 'But there will be other and very different words', he suggested,

of discussion, debate, dialectic, of speculation and exploration, in which we are free to range far into the future and to disinter the past. We have liberty to question and to propose, without fearing the jealous scrutiny for pedantic consistency to which the words of a party in office or on the brink of it are forever of necessity obnoxious.

This statement in itself would have led to the storm signals being raised in the leader's office. 'There are implications here', *The Times* observed, 'that Mr Heath suspects to be dangerous when they are set in the context of Mr Powell's freelancing record.'[57]

Three days later Powell caused further trouble by issuing a public statement condemning the Government's decision to use the Royal Navy to enforce the blockade of the African port of Beira – the Government's apparent intention being to cut off oil supplies to Southern Rhodesia, where the unilateral declaration of independence by Ian Smith's white minority Government the previous autumn had led to the imposition of international sanctions against the rebel regime. Powell's main point was that the Beira patrol was futile since the Rhodesians would continue to get all the oil they needed through South Africa. And since Wilson was on the record as having stated that the Navy would not be used to enforce the blockade, Powell did not regard his statement as making policy. None the less, it appeared to be a thinly-veiled attack on sanctions, which was an exceptionally sensitive issue since the Conservatives had split three ways on it in the Commons the previous December. Moreover, he had not issued his statement through Central Office, and had acted without prior group consultation or discussion with the deputy leader, Maudling, who was in charge of affairs while Heath was on holiday. His action was reported to have made Maudling, the most mild-mannered and relaxed of men, 'really cross'.

It was little surprise that Powell was summoned to see Heath on the latter's return, before the leader announced his changes to the Shadow Cabinet for the new parliament. 'Mr Powell called to task by Mr Heath: need to follow party line', read the headline in *The Times*, above a report by its Political Correspondent that reflected a briefing from the Heath camp. Powell's advocacy of a free play of ideas, it was reported, was contrary to the view taken by Heath, who

> will tell Mr Powell that he believes politics to be about responsible and practicable ideas to which the party leadership, the Shadow Cabinet, have committed themselves after careful study of interrelationships and conse-quences ... He [Heath] holds that individual and capricious policy tangents do more to confuse the party rank and file and the electorate generally than to damage the Government. He remembers, too, that on several occasions since he has become defence spokesman, Mr Powell has created embarrass-ment for his colleagues in the Shadow Cabinet.

But the report also acknowledged that Heath would 'not be able to forget that there are few Conservative leaders today who think so deeply and originally on politics as Mr Powell, or who have such a growing following in the Conservative Party'.[58]

The Heathite press briefing after Heath and Powell had talked at Heath's apartment at the Albany on Friday 15 April suggested that, in the words of the *Sunday Times*, Powell 'will accept the general Shadow Cabinet rule – that he issues statements only on his specific responsibility, and then generally after consultation with the Leader, and that any speeches he makes on other matters will be by arrangement with the colleague most concerned'. There is, however, no such formal rule, and the general understanding has been that a member of the Shadow Cabinet should at least consult the relevant Shadow Minister if what he or she plans to say on a colleague's subject might be controversial. This point was to assume special significance two years later. The most percipient comment on the affair was made, not surprisingly, by the *Express and Star*. '"Toe the line or take your cards" was the ultimatum Mr Heath was reported to have delivered to Mr Powell,' noted the Wolverhampton paper, but observed knowingly: 'And Mr Powell, so we are told, meekly shuffled into line.'[59]

Heath, however, had achieved his purpose. Although there was never any prospect that Powell would fall silent, or abandon his ideological crusade, Heath had set his terms for Powell's continued membership of the Shadow Cabinet. All trace of Douglas-Home's dispensation in 1964, that had enabled Powell to speak out on virtually any subject, had finally been expunged. When Heath reconstructed his Shadow Cabinet a few days later, his retention of

Powell as Defence Spokesman showed that he thought Powell would be more trouble on the back benches than if he remained on the front bench. But Heath had prepared the ground to justify sacking Powell if his maverick tendencies began to cause too much trouble.

In practice, a rigid enforcement of party policy is impractical after a heavy election defeat and Powell was bound to enjoy a certain amount of leeway. Heath's wish to keep him in the Shadow Cabinet suggested that, as long as Powell did not rock the boat too much, he would be tolerated. Moreover, few Shadow Ministers could rival Powell's ability as a scourge of Labour policies or were as popular on the Tory speech-making circuit. As regards economic policy, it is hard to detect any change in Powell's speeches during the two years following the 1966 election. He preached his familiar theme, fiercely criticizing Labour for their assault on the right of individuals and companies to go about their business as they thought fit, arguing that only by allowing people and businesses to pursue their own interests could the country prosper. And always, underlying his advocacy of free-market economics was the sub-text, that was addressed to his own party – namely, the need to avoid any return to Macmillan-style interventionism.

Before the end of April 1966, Powell renewed his attack on the creation of a '"New Model Army" of [the] gentlemen who know best', namely the businessmen and industrialists who 'staff an ever-growing multitude, a multitude which presently no man will be able to number, of committees, councils and bodies of every kind: big Neddies and little Neddies, development councils and planning councils, promotion committees and reorganization committees'. Similar speeches followed on different aspects of Labour's interventionism, but no Tory spokesman was going to be sacked (or so it seemed) for his sub-text while he was ostensibly attacking a Labour Government. Moreover, Powell was prepared to amend the text of a speech if requested to do so – he revised his October 1966 Tory conference speech at the behest of Douglas-Home, who was concerned at the interpretation that might be placed on a particular passage in the light of the east of Suez controversy.[60]

The awkwardness of the *modus vivendi* between Powell and Heath was illustrated by an incident that occurred in the early summer of 1966, when Heath made a gaffe during his visit to the United States. At his press conference in Washington on 3 June, Heath was asked if Powell was now 'under wraps, and would he stay there?' Heath replied: 'Yes to both questions – at least he was when I left, and I think he has talked about nothing since but milk and the Co-ops.' It was an offensive remark, that suggested his self-satisfaction at having cut Powell down to size. It seems unlikely that Heath would have been so unguarded in Britain, where he would have been more immediately conscious of the damage that such a comment might cause, but to have spoken in this way in America about Powell, who was so antipathetic to the United States, could only serve to add insult to injury. This incident made little difference to Powell's determination to continue his free-market crusade, but it gave a further cause for resentment.[61]

Labour's resort to a statutory prices and incomes policy for two years from the summer of 1966 ensured that the Conservatives were continually dogged by their divisions on the issue during the remainder of their period in Opposition. In November 1966, Powell debated prices and incomes policy at the Cambridge Union with Richard Crossman, the Labour Minister. Crossman felt confident that his carefully prepared argument would win the day, and 'had dug out all the statements Powell himself had made when he was a member of the Macmillan Government and had spoken strongly in favour of an incomes policy'. Powell, however, 'without the faintest hesitation turned his audience against an incomes policy', and won a standing ovation. Although Powell's bravura performance had made the Labour minister 'grind his teeth a little', Crossman none the less offered Powell a lift back to London. Crossman noted in his diary that Powell was running a campaign up and down the country against Heath and the prices and incomes policy, and he asked Powell what he thought Heath would have made of his speech. 'Oh, it's Reggie Maudling who's the problem', Powell replied, 'and Reggie is so busy with his business affairs that he's hardly ever with us. If it wasn't for him I think Macleod would go along with us.' But this impression is not borne out by the party's papers or the recollection of other Shadow Ministers at the time. Powell also regarded Heath's speech at Carshalton in July 1967 as endorsing his denunciation of prices and incomes policy, but it was not seen in this light by other Shadow Ministers. Heath's speech was, in fact, an attempt to explain the party's equivocal position.[62]

The debate over incomes policy came to a head in the party in early 1968, and was discussed by the Shadow Cabinet on 7 and 13 March. Macleod and Carr, the Shadow Employment Secretary, recommended softening the party's opposition to every aspect of pay policy, since they wanted to avoid the Tories' being blamed for encouraging pay awards that eroded the competitive advantage that had been achieved as a result of the pound's devaluation the previous November. Shadow Ministers rehearsed much the same arguments that they had used shortly before the 1966 election. Macleod was convinced that although the Conservatives had to oppose a compulsory wages policy, they would be ill-advised to deny themselves any form of incomes policy in Government. Powell never rated the Shadow Chancellor as an economist. 'You really ought to take an interest in economics,' Powell used to tell him. In their October 1968 policy document, *Make Life Better*', and their 1970 manifesto, the Tories were to reject a *compulsory* wages policy, but as Macleod made clear at the 1968 Conservative conference, they believed that the Government still had to have a wages policy of some form, in the public sector and in influencing 'key wage negotiations'. Powell, however, had long attacked 'voluntary' pay policies before Labour opted for statutory control, and Macleod's formula would have been a continuing source of conflict had Powell remained in the Shadow Cabinet during the Tories' final two years in Opposition.[63]

But it was not simply a matter of Powell's stance on specific policies that set him apart. It is impossible to imagine any other senior Tory front-bencher of this period making the comment that Powell uttered at a private luncheon with parliamentary lobby correspondents. 'Often when I am kneeling down in church,' he remarked, 'I think to myself how much we should thank God, the Holy Ghost, for the gift of capitalism.' In view of this comment, it was less surprising that in March 1968, Powell should have argued against economic intervention in a Cambridge Union debate with the leading Keynesian economist, J.K. Galbraith.[64]

February and March 1968 were a fractious time for the Tories. In addition to the debate over incomes policy, Powell's seizing on the US Defense Department's report to revive his questioning of nuclear deterrence only served to emphasize his iconoclastic approach to politics at an inopportune moment, for the potentially explosive issues of immigration and race relations had forced their way back to the top of the political agenda. Moreover, Powell had played his part in stirring the controversy. It was to lead to the final break between Powell and his leader.[65]

As a self-appointed irritant and spur to fresh thinking, Powell was unconvincing when, recalling his period in Heath's Shadow Cabinet many years later, he adopted an air of injured innocence at the suggestion that he might have irritated Heath or his former Shadow Cabinet colleagues. 'I remember more than once in those years', he later commented, 'going to see Willie Whitelaw', the then Chief Whip', who would be 'tearing his hair'. According to Powell, their conversations on these occasions went as follows:

'What's the matter, Willie?'
'Well, Enoch, it's this speech that you're making on Saturday. Ted's frightfully upset about it.'
'Well that's all right, Willie, tell me what's upsetting him, and I'll change it.'

This impression Powell gives of his readiness always to amend any speech is all very well, but it is reminiscent of the protestations of a barrack-room lawyer that he never meant to cause anybody any trouble. It is, in itself, an admission by Powell that he had to be kept in line from time to time. And it ignores the wearing effect on his leader and other front-benchers of always having to keep an eye on the fine print of what he might be about to say.[66]

15

'The River Tiber'

As I look ahead, I am filled with foreboding. Like the Roman, I seem to see 'the River Tiber foaming with much blood'.

Enoch Powell, speaking about immigration and race relations, Birmingham, 20 April 1968.

Preparing for a reaction

Powell may have been right, in retrospect, in believing that without the unique dynamite of the issue of immigration in April 1968, he would have been able to continue in Heath's Shadow Cabinet until the 1970 election. But by the early months of 1968, he had become deeply frustrated. He was irritated by Heath's pursuit of consensus and by his leader's complaint that he alienated the party's friends in industry, whereas Powell never thought of such people as the Conservatives' friends. Powell looked back fondly to the Conservatives' last period in Opposition in the late-1940s, when he remembered free enterprise rushing to support the Tories. By contrast, he felt that Labour's failure in the late 1960s was regarded as being administrative, not doctrinaire. The Conservatives were merely seen as an alternative Government that would provide better administration.

Powell felt that debate in the party had been muted by both the habit of Government acquired during the thirteen years in office before 1964, and, from the latter part of 1967, by the party's growing lead in the opinion polls. He sensed that the leadership were becoming more concerned about what they would do in office and were correspondingly hesitant to consider radical alternatives. In particular, he was annoyed that although the Government's incomes policy was a nonsense and was not working, some of the Shadow Cabinet were saying that, if they were catapulted into office, they would have to continue the policy temporarily. The Tories' success was discouraging new thought, and the fresh impact of any new points they had made had failed. Powell was a disappointed man. Although his sense of being the only Powellite reflected a self-deprecating wit, he certainly feared that Powellism was on the wane.[1]

It was in this frame of mind that Powell addressed the issue of immigration during the latter part of 1967 and early 1968. Having urged control of Commonwealth immigration as a minister before the Tory Government introduced the first curbs in the autumn of 1961, he had emerged as a Tory hawk on the issue after the Conservatives left office. Although Powell identified immigration as one of the four issues on which Conservative policy needed re-examination after the 1966 election, it was almost a year before he made his next major intervention by further developing his claim that the increasing size of the immigrant population, including children who were born in Britain, would inevitably pose a severe threat in the future.[2]

Powell's exaggerated imagery and the starkness of his warning in a prominent, leader-page contribution in the *Daily Telegraph* on 16 February 1967, ostensibly reviewing a major study of immigration in Birmingham, Sparkbrook, were precursors of his much more explosive intervention a year later. During the dozen years before 1966, he wrote, 'entire areas' of Wolverhampton had been 'transformed by the substitution of a wholly or predominantly coloured population for the previous native inhabitants, as completely as other areas were transformed by the bulldozer'. Looking back, he confessed to his 'astonishment that this event, which altered the appearance and life of a town and had shattering effects on the lives of many families and persons, could take place with virtually no physical manifestations of antipathy'. And with the memory of the wartime blitz on the industrial West Midlands only a quarter of a century earlier still fresh in many minds, Powell continued,

> Acts of an enemy, bombs from the sky, they could understand; but now, for reasons quite inexplicable, they might be driven from their homes and their property deprived of value by an invasion which the Government apparently approved and their fellow-citizens – elsewhere – viewed with complacency. Those were the years when a 'For Sale' notice going up in a street struck terror into all its inhabitants.

In an adroit reminder of his qualifications to write about this issue as a Tory MP, Powell added, in a reference to his home in Merridale Road: 'I know; for I live within the proverbial stone's throw of streets which "went black".'[3]

Powell was again showing, as he had in 1965, that he was the only senior politician who was prepared to voice the undoubtedly deep resentment that existed among urban lower-middle and working-class whites that their communities had been changed without their having any say. But at the same time, by talking in such extreme terms of bulldozers, shattered lives, bombs, invasion and terror, he was giving respectability to language and views that were likely to foster prejudice. At the very least, the fact that a Privy Counsellor, former Professor of Greek and ex-Brigadier, who was seen as the soul of integrity, readily resorted to such hyperbole, was unlikely to encourage rational debate about immigration. Neither was it likely to make it any easier for immigrants to integrate into the community, as Powell had said he hoped would happen.

Powell's article is important for two reasons. In the first place, it made clear that he no longer believed that full integration was possible. Secondly, he developed his argument on numbers and the concentration of immigrant populations in certain areas that had become the key to his thinking on immigration. He rehearsed his earlier attempts to explain to his constituents the freedom of entry enjoyed by Commonwealth citizens and his efforts to persuade his fellow ministers to 'make our law like that of every other country on earth, in recognizing the difference between its own people and the rest'. Lamenting that 'to subsequent generations it will seem incredible that this was not done until almost a million Commonwealth immigrants had entered', he noted that despite the 1962 controls and their tightening in 1965, the flow of immigrants had continued at around 50,000 a year. 'In any one year this rate of inflow is imperceptible', he accepted, 'but 50,000 a year would still mean additional net immigration from these countries of $1\frac{3}{4}$ million by the end of the century.'

Moreover, Powell argued that the significance of these figures was reinforced by two other factors, both of which he acknowledged were 'conjectural'. In the first place, although the Registrar General had estimated that the United Kingdom would have *nil* net immigration by 1975, Powell drew attention to how the balance was calculated – 120,000 'UK citizens' were expected to leave Britain and would be replaced by 60,000 from the Commonwealth and 60,000 from Ireland and foreign countries. Secondly, there was natural increase. 'One estimate', he noted, 'is that by the end of the century it will have been sufficient to raise the total coloured population to about $3\frac{1}{2}$ millions, or five per cent of the population.'

It was the concentration of the immigrant population in certain areas, however, that preoccupied Powell. He accepted that long before the total reached five per cent, 'a proportion will have filtered into the general population, mingled with it in occupation, residence, habits and inter-marriage'. But he feared that the rest, 'numerically perhaps much the greater part, will be in larger or smaller colonies, in certain areas and cities, more separated than now in habits, occupation and way of life'. It was for these 'self-perpetuating' colonies and 'the problems thereby entailed on our descendants, that they will curse the improvident years, now gone, when we could have avoided it all'. If net immigration were virtually terminated, he thought that voluntary repatriation might achieve a small but significant net emigration. In turn, this might help the dispersal of the immigrants and their children who remained. But he was pessimistic. 'The best I dare hope', he suggested, 'is that by the end of the century we shall be left not with a growing and more menacing phenomenon but with fixed and almost traditional "foreign" areas in certain towns and cities, which will remain as the lasting monuments of a moment of national aberration.'

Notwithstanding his doom-laden warning, Powell sensed, as he wrote in early 1967, that there was 'a feeling of stabilization', and that immigration had 'disappeared below the surface of public consciousness'. The feeling in Wolverhampton was that 'the first phase, the sudden impact of Commonwealth immigration, is over'. None the less, he made a startling prediction. 'I am going to prophesy', he declared, in oracular vein, 'that there will be subsequent phases, when the problem will resume its place in public concern and in a more intractable form, when it can no longer be dealt with simply by turning the inlet tap down or off.' Within a matter of months, events in East Africa were to trigger a new influx, causing immigration to 'resume its place in public concern' and provoking Powell to champion a fierce reaction against the liberal thinking that increasingly held sway in policy-making on immigration and race.[4]

This period, during 1966 and 1967, is commonly referred to as 'the liberal hour', since the liberal-minded Roy Jenkins had replaced the cautious Soskice at the Home Office. Jenkins had appointed as his special adviser the liberal lawyer, Anthony Lester, who had been involved in the American civil rights movement, and installed Mark Bonham-Carter, another liberal, as head of the Race Relations Board. They were setting the pace in policy-making, and on 24 April 1967, the Shadow Home Secretary, Quintin Hogg (later Lord Hailsham), informed the Shadow Cabinet that, following the publication of several recent reports on race relations, the Government were likely to extend the existing legislation against racial discrimination to cover employment and housing. Since Powell could not attend the Shadow Cabinet's scheduled discussion of the subject the following week, he intervened to counsel (in the words of the minute) that,

> we should not assume that the present liberality of outlook and the disappearance of the racial feeling that had welled up for instance at Smethwick would last for ever. He felt that these emotional attitudes went in waves, and that there could be a recrudescence of the 'Smethwick' attitude, particularly when people became aware of the prediction of 3 million coloured people in Britain by the year 2000. The present net intake of non-European Commonwealth immigrants was 50,000 a year, which seemed an excessively high figure. It was this intake, more than breeding by past immigrants, that was putting up the total prediction figure; but the breeding aspect would always be exaggerated and blamed.[5]

Powell's last comment about exaggeration and blame with regard to 'breeding by past immigrants' sits oddly with his own references since 1965 to the significance of 'natural increase'. But his general view was endorsed by the leading Tory liberal, Sir Edward Boyle, who agreed that 'the climate of opinion could easily change'. Boyle, who also represented an area in the West Midlands where many immigrants had settled, 'was receiving a great many forceful letters from constituents who resented coloured immigrants', but he added that he was also hearing 'from immigrants who could not get their families into the country, or felt that they were badly treated in other ways'. He judged that 'feeling was as strong as ever, though the press were not at present pushing it'. In the ensuing Shadow Cabinet discussion, Heath was keen to give a liberal lead to the party. He wanted the Tories to take credit for the fact that the conciliation arrangements now in force on race relations had resulted from Conservative policy. It was not too soon after the 1965 Act, in Heath's view, to talk about further legislation.[6]

Jenkins announced his plan for a new Race Relations Bill in June, but there were signs of a reaction in the public mood, especially following renewed race riots in America. Powell was in the vanguard of the reaction, reiterating his demand for curbing the immigration by dependants in an article for the *Sunday Express* on 9 July 1967 under the headline, 'CAN WE *AFFORD* TO LET OUR RACE PROBLEM EXPLODE? Two months later, following a speech in Gloucester in which he had not mentioned immigration, he replied to a question on the issue afterwards by calling for 'no addition to the Commonwealth immigrants still coming in at an annual intake of 50,000', and stressed the need to provide 'an outgoing for those not fitting in, or fitting in less well, in what is called, in sociologists' jargon, "the host country"'. And he declared that, 'the British people have been told that they must deny that there is any difference between those who belong to this country and "those others". If you persist in asserting what is an undeniable truth, you will be hounded and pilloried as a racialist.'[7]

Powell had thrown down the gauntlet to the liberals on race. But the eruption of a crisis in one of Britain's former East African colonies and the ensuing political storm was about to provide him with a golden opportunity to pursue his counter-attack against the liberal policy-makers, and to exploit their failure to build up public support. In consequence, all his frustrations with Heath's leadership were also to come to a head.

Rift over the Kenyan Asians

In 1967, Jomo Kenyatta's Government in Kenya passed a law that required all non-Kenyan citizens to apply for work permits. This measure was part of a policy of 'Kenyanization', and only people who were considered essential for the economy would be allowed to stay. Europeans and Asians began to leave in increasing numbers. Already, six thousand Asians who held United Kingdom passports issued by the United Kingdom Government, and as such were not subject to existing British immigration controls, had entered Britain in 1965 and another six thousand had done so in 1966. After the change in Kenyan law, 1,500 Asians entered in August 1967 alone, and 2,661 in September. Britain faced a new wave of non-white immigration. On 18 October, in a speech at Deal, in Kent, Powell called for controls to be imposed on Kenyan Asians. He was stepping out of line with Tory policy, and was to open a breach with his long-time colleague, Iain Macleod, that was never closed before Macleod's death in 1970.[8]

Powell's comments stole attention from the first day of that year's Conservative conference at Brighton. The Tory leadership were angered, and they let it be known in off-the-record briefings that they were 'alarmed at the charge that they would like to discriminate on purely racial grounds in favour of Europeans as against Asiatics'. But Powell's demand was popular with many Tory activists. Duncan Sandys, the former Colonial and Commonwealth Secretary, who had overseen the final steps towards Kenyan independence and (as the official papers for the period show) was fully aware of Britain's obligation to the Kenyan Asians, was campaigning to keep them out and was cheered at Brighton when he declared that the aim of party policy should be to preserve the British character of Britain.[9]

Powell alleged at Deal that the Kenyan Asians only enjoyed the right to come to Britain as a result of an 'unforeseen loophole', or, as he put it later, 'a draughtsman's oversight', in the 1962 Commonwealth Immigrants Act. He was right that when this measure was passed by Parliament while Kenya was still a colony, the large-scale immigration of Kenyan Asians into Britain was neither foreseen nor desired. Butler, the then Home Secretary, told the Commons in November 1961 when he introduced the Commonwealth Immigrants Bill, that the clause concerning the inhabitants of colonies who held passports issued by the United Kingdom Government would exempt from control and guarantee unrestricted entry to 'persons who in common parlance belong to the United Kingdom', a euphemism for whites. But those citizens who held passports issued by the Governor of a colony were not exempt. The main reason was to control the immigration of West Indians, because at the time of the Act much of the West Indies were still colonies. While Kenya was still a colony, Asians there had passports issued by the Governor and, in 1962, came under the Commonwealth Immigrants Act.[10]

In his speech at Deal, Powell sought to explain the changes in citizenship law that occurred on Kenyan independence in December 1963 as follows:

Parliament enacted that anybody who then became a citizen of Kenya automatically ceased to be a citizen of the United Kingdom and Colonies. However, the Kenya Government defined their own citizens and did so in such a way as to exclude hundreds and thousands of Asiatics and others who were living there. Until that moment these people had been eligible for passports issued by the Governor of Kenya and were therefore, in the same position as other Commonwealth citizens who, under the definitions of the 1962 Act, did not belong to Britain. After that time, however, they became eligible for passports issued by our High Commissioner in Nairobi, which are regarded as United Kingdom passports by the British Government. Thus by a decision of the Kenya legislature defining a Kenyan citizen, hundreds and thousands of people in Kenya who had not belonged to the United Kingdom and never dreamt that they did, started to belong to it just like you and me ...

By December 1963, of course, Powell was no longer a member of the Government and could not be held responsible. But Kenyan independence and the associated provisions on citizenship followed the pattern that had been set in Britain's other East African territories – Tanganyika, that became independent in December 1961 and Uganda in October 1962. The official papers for the period confirm that many of the key decisions on the citizenship of East African Asians were taken while Powell was a minister (from July 1962 until October 1963 he was in the Cabinet). Moreover, he was a member of the Cabinet committee that prepared the 1961 Commonwealth Immigrants Bill, which was enacted in 1962.

Powell told his audience at Deal that the 1962 Commonwealth Immigrants Act defined, under three headings, those people who 'belonged' to the United Kingdom and who therefore were exempt from the immigration controls that were imposed on citizens of other independent Commonwealth countries. The first two categories included those born in the United Kingdom or who held a current UK passport, issued in the UK or the Republic of Ireland. 'It is the third category', Powell argued, 'that has raised problems which must now be dealt with urgently.' This third category exempted from control those citizens of the UK and Colonies who held a current UK passport issued by a UK High Commissioner in an independent Commonwealth country.[11]

There were, however, good reasons for this provision. In some colonies, especially in East and Central Africa – Kenya, Tanganyika (later Tanzania), Uganda, Nyasaland (Malawi), and Northern and Southern Rhodesia (Zambia and Zimbabwe) – there were many white settlers who were concerned that they should retain UK and Colonies citizenship and continue to be exempt from the new British immigration controls *after* independence. The British Government accepted that the settlers' right of entry into Britain should be upheld. They did so, partly because many of the settlers were white and were of British descent or origin, and also because such a guarantee would encourage them to stay in newly independent countries. Uppermost in ministers' and MPs' minds was the example of the Congo, where the precipitate Belgian withdrawal in 1960 had resulted in chaos and violence, triggering a panic-stricken exodus of European settlers. As long as the white settlers in British East and Central Africa knew that they could obtain a UK passport, it was hoped that they would not rush to leave as soon as colonial rule ended.[12]

It was partly because of this wish to exempt white settlers from the new immigration controls, and also because of a concern not to weaken the ties between the United Kingdom and its colonies, that the Cabinet Committee on Commonwealth Migrants had ruled out Powell's plan in the spring of 1961 to carve out a new United Kingdom Citizenship from the existing citizenship of the United Kingdom and Colonies. The need to provide an exemption for UK passport holders in East and Central Africa *was* a consideration in the minds of ministers and officials when they prepared Britain's first controls on Commonwealth immigration. The 1962 Act accordingly exempted people who, as citizens of the UK and Colonies, held UK passports issued by the United Kingdom Government. These passports were routinely issued in independent Commonwealth countries by UK High Commissioners. This normal facility would be essential after independence in East and Central Africa if white settlers were to continue to be exempted from immigration control.[13]

But there were two further complications in East Africa. In the first place, in addition to the white settlers, there were large numbers of Asians who predominated in the business and professional sectors and had been encouraged to migrate to Africa by previous British Governments. As the Government did not want to state publicly that the purpose of the 1962 Act was to control non-white immigration into Britain, it was politically impossible for the Government to exempt from immigration control white settlers without also exempting Asians, many of whom were citizens of the UK and Colonies and (unless they opted for citizenship of the independent East African countries) would be equally eligible for UK passports issued by High Commissioners after independence. The only way in which the new immigration controls could have been applied to the Asians, but not to white settlers, would have been through a blatant colour bar. Ministers, however, had been at pains to impose immigration controls that were not explicitly racialist. Such a distinction between white and non-white holders of passports issued by the UK Government outside the UK would have exposed as a pretence the claim that they were introducing non-racial controls that applied to the entire Commonwealth. As the Commons debates during 1961–62 demonstrate, a more avowedly racialist measure at that time would have split the Tory Party, and quite possibly, would not have been passed by Parliament. It would also have created a furore in the Commonwealth and brought international obloquy.[14]

Secondly, in East Africa, there was a problem over citizenship, which meant that many Asians did not automatically become citizens of the independent East African states. It is in this respect that Powell's account of Kenyan independence is, perhaps, most misleading. In the negotiations on Tanganyikan independence during 1960–61, the British Government accepted the demand by the African nationalist leader in Tanganyika, Julius Nyerere, that only people who had a parent born in the territory could automatically become citizens of the new country on independence. This qualification included all African Tanganyikans, but excluded many others (notably Asians) who lived in the territory. Those who were excluded would remain citizens of the UK and Colonies, or British protected persons, unless, within a period of two years after independence in December 1961, they elected to become citizens of Tanganyika.[15]

These provisions on citizenship were included in the new Constitution introduced by the British Government. The terms of Tanganyikan independence were debated in the House of Commons – following the usual procedure, independence was conferred by an Act of Parliament and by an Order in

Council containing the Constitution. Despite the British Government's efforts, Tanganyika's provisions on citizenship set the pattern for Uganda and for Kenya. Their terms for independence were also debated in the Commons, and the Constitutions, agreed by the British Government, were included in Orders in Council.[16]

Before Tanganyikan independence, the British Government had appeared to assume that most East African Asians would opt for citizenship of the newly independent countries. Ministers on the Commonwealth Migrants Committee (including Powell) were aware in early 1961 that a small number of Asian immigrants into Britain had originally come from East Africa, but expected that the problem would cease after independence. Even when it became clear immediately after independence that many Asians were choosing not to become Tanganyikan citizens, it was still assumed that most of them would not want to come to Britain. The Colonial Office's fortnightly briefing from Dar-es-Salaam, on 23 December 1961, reported that 'a steady flow (sometimes amounting almost to a flood) of applications' had been received by the British Passport Office since its opening on the 12th. The majority of applicants were Asians domiciled in Tanganyika 'who showed little inclination to apply for registration as Tanganyikan citizens'. They were exercising their right as citizens of the United Kingdom and Colonies to obtain United Kingdom passports issued by the High Commissioner before the 1962 Commonwealth Immigrants Act became law, and while the Bill that eventually became the Act was still being debated by Parliament. It is therefore misleading of Powell to suggest that the right of East African Asians to obtain UK High Commissioner passports was an unforeseen consequence of, or loophole in, the 1962 Act.[17]

Developments in Tanganyika had implications for Kenya. A senior Colonial Office official noted that the news from Dar-es-Salaam of Asians applying for United Kingdom passports was 'interesting re-nationality in Kenya. It looks as though the stock African and Asian politicians' line is likely in practice to leave the UK with a good many phony British subjects claiming her protection.' For those who seek a conspiracy theory, the official's reaction might suggest a Whitehall plot – ministers and MPs should have been alerted to developments in Dar-es-Salaam while they could still amend the Immigration Bill. But it is likely that Maudling (Colonial Secretary) and Sandys (Commonwealth Relations Secretary) either saw this briefing, or were advised of what was happening by their officials (Sandys was notoriously keen on knowing every detail). In any case, events in Tanganyika were not a state secret. The Government had accepted responsibility for those who did not opt for Tanganyikan citizenship, even if the obligation was accepted reluctantly and the Asians might be regarded as 'phony British subjects'. But it was not thought that these people would want to come to Britain in large numbers – hence the official's reference to their 'claiming her protection'.[18]

This assumption is confirmed by the official briefing for the Kenya constitutional conference in London from 14 February to 6 April 1962 – while the 1962 immigration controls were still before parliament. Referring to the right of people born in Kenya to opt for Kenyan citizenship, the draft brief noted that there were 'many in this category, e.g. among the Asian community and perhaps among the European community also, who would find difficulty in making a home elsewhere'. And the brief continued:

> From our point of view, the more persons that acquire Kenyan citizenship, the fewer there will be for whom we shall be responsible after independence and whose interests we shall then be under a duty to protect. If there were any large body of such persons who were still citizens of the United Kingdom and Colonies and not Kenyan citizens and who yet had no real connection with the United Kingdom, we might be seriously embarrassed in our relations with the new Kenya Government.

It was accepted that the British Government had a duty to protect people who retained citizenship of the United Kingdom and Colonies, but it was clearly assumed as late as 1962 that most of those who had no real connection with the United Kingdom would not come to Britain. The concern was the possible conflict after independence between, on the one hand, the UK High Commissioner's duty to afford UK passport holders his protection and, on the other hand, Britain's relations with the Kenyan Government.[19]

Powell, however, contrived in 1971 to develop a more sinister theory of events following a speech during the passage of the Heath Government's Immigration Bill by Monty Woodhouse, who had been a junior minister at the Home Office at the time of Kenyan independence. Powell alleged that there had been a conspiracy of deliberate concealment, and wrote of 'an aura of guilt [that] has hung around what started as a simple oversight of drafting'. But again, he continued to overlook salient facts. According to Powell, Woodhouse had disclosed that by 1963 ministers were aware that Asians might emigrate to Britain after independence:

> when Kenyan independence was in the offing, the Home Office had warned 'the Government of the day' of the consequences of the definition in the 1962 [Commonwealth Immigrants] Act, and that they must therefore choose between (a) legislating to amend the 1962 Act, (b) withholding passports from Kenyan United Kingdom and Commonwealth citizens after independence, or (c) shutting their eyes and hoping for the best.

But Powell failed to point out the crucial fact that Woodhouse had contradicted Powell's view that the Kenyan Asian immigrants were exploiting an 'unforeseen loophole'. 'I recognize', Woodhouse told MPs,

> that there was no explicit, openly expressed, public commitment, but the meaning of the nationality clauses in the Kenya Independence Act and its successors was entirely clear. It was understood at the time by the Home Office, it was communicated by the Home Office to other Departments and

the decision embodied in the Act was taken by the Government of the day with their eyes open.[20]

Fortunately, the official papers are now available for 1963. They confirm Woodhouse's recollection. On 30 October, less than a fortnight after Powell had left ministerial office and shortly before Kenyan independence, the then Home Secretary, Henry Brooke, circulated a memorandum entitled, 'Position of Asians in Kenya' to the Commonwealth Immigration Committee. Those present at the subsequent ministerial meeting that discussed Brooke's paper included Sandys and, incidentally, the junior minister at Pensions and National Insurance, Margaret Thatcher. Brooke explained that there were two categories of Asians, numbering about 150,000, who would, on Kenya's independence, retain citizenship of the UK and Colonies – similar groups in Tanganyika and Uganda numbered about 100,000. It was doubtful whether many of them would take up Kenyan citizenship. There was no tradition of Asian immigration into Britain from East Africa, but Brooke counselled that some of the Asians were starting to think that they might need to come here sooner or later, and, if they did decide to immigrate, they would be entitled to do so without restriction.[21]

Although Brooke's warning of the prospect of increased non-white immigration shows that the earlier assumption about East African Asians not wanting to come to Britain had been wrong, he felt that the Government had to honour its obligations. Brooke, who was anything but a liberal Home Secretary, explained that:

> Since, in spite of our efforts, none of the Governments in East Africa has been prepared to consider granting citizenship of their countries automatically on independence to these Asians, there has been no alternative but for us to agree that they should retain their United Kingdom citizenship. To withdraw that citizenship immediately on independence or after a stated interval would render these Asians stateless.

It was an object of British policy not to increase statelessness, and would have been contrary to the spirit of the 1961 UN Convention on the Reduction of Statelessness. 'It would be out of the question to withdraw their United Kingdom citizenship, so making them stateless,' Brooke told the committee.[22]

There was an additional reason. It was 'equally out of the question', Brooke emphasized, not to accord normal passport facilities to United Kingdom citizens of Asian origin, with the object of rendering them subject to our immigration control. 'Such action would be, and would be seen to be', the Home Secretary declared, 'a discrimination based on racial origin, and would be tantamount to a denial to these persons of one of the basic rights of a citizen, namely to enter the country of which he is a citizen.' None of Brooke's colleagues, including Sandys, is minuted as having demurred at this uncompromising reaffirmation of Britain's obligation to the East African

Asians. It is an intriguing thought that if Powell had not refused to serve in Douglas-Home's Cabinet only a couple of weeks earlier, he might have attended this meeting and had a say over a decision that was subsequently to have such an impact on his life.[23]

If Sandys had felt that the obligation to the Kenyan Asians should not have been honoured, he should have taken the matter to the full Cabinet. He chose not to do so, but four years later spoke emotively of the Kenyan Asians having been given a 'privileged back-door entry' into the United Kingdom. Powell contemptuously observed that the ministers concerned, 'decided to stay mum and hope for the best', while omitting to say whether he thought that the Government in 1963 should have rendered many people stateless or imposed a colour bar. Woodhouse recaptured rather better the attitude of ministers when they decided to honour Britain's obligation to UK passport holders, by emphasizing to MPs that, 'the then Government made that choice, to my certain knowledge, deliberately – not by default, not by mistake – and [that] they did so after the choice had been explicitly put forward, explained and discussed'.[24]

Brooke's paper in 1963 and Woodhouse's recollection in 1971 confirm the correctness of the interventions made in February 1968, at the height of the Kenyan Asian crisis, by Macleod, who had served as Colonial Secretary until 1961, and by Maudling, his successor, who served until July 1962. Referring to the British Government's obligation to the Kenyan Asians, Macleod declared: 'We did it. We meant to do it. And in any event we had no other choice.' Maudling stated, 'When they [the Kenyan Asians] were given these rights, it was our intention that they should be able to come to this country when they wanted to do so. We knew it at the time. They knew it, and in many cases they have acted and taken decisions on this knowledge.'[25]

It is also clear that Powell misconstrued the position when he claimed that, 'no trace of any undertaking having been given in respect of Kenya High Commissioner passport holders has ever been produced'. In March 1971, Maudling explained to Powell that, as Sandys had said, no specific pledge had been given to the Kenyan Asians. 'But none was necessary since, as the Government in 1963 were aware, one of the effects of the Kenya Independence Act would be to make the Asians in Kenya, who did not acquire local citizenship on independence and so remained citizens of the United Kingdom and Colonies, eligible for the issue of United Kingdom passports, and so exempt from control under the Commonwealth Immigrants Act, 1962.' Powell subsequently tried to argue that Maudling's phrase, 'as the Government in 1963 were aware', was immensely significant, because it showed that until then they had been unaware of the effect of the 1962 Act. But the real significance of 1963 is that, although it was recognized that some Kenyan Asians were likely to come to Britain, ministers none the less reaffirmed their obligation to them.[26]

Two years later, in July 1965, when the Labour Government were considering stricter immigration rules, the then Home Secretary, Sir Frank

Soskice, submitted a Cabinet paper on the exemption of an estimated quarter of a million or so East African Asians from existing controls. 'At first these people showed no tendency to migrate to the United Kingdom,' Soskice noted, echoing the earlier assumption, but added that reports from the immigration staff at London Airport since December 1964 indicated that they were arriving at an annual rate of at least 5,000'. He personally felt that 'legislation depriving them of their existing rights and status as citizens of the United Kingdom and Colonies would be difficult to justify'. But if the Cabinet felt that such legislation was unavoidable, 'the necessary studies should begin at once before the rate of arrivals increases substantially, as it is perhaps in the nature of things likely that it will'. But according to Crossman, the Cabinet's instruction to its Commonwealth Immigration Committee to study the problem and make recommendations was 'completely disregarded'. It was not until two years later, in October 1967, when the problem had suddenly become acute that Soskice's successor, Jenkins, presented his proposals on the matter to the Cabinet Home Affairs Committee.[27]

In February 1968, when Powell was asked by Sir Robin Day about the Kenyan Asians who were coming into Britain 'outside the immigration control', he was prepared to acknowledge that,

> as a result of a combination between a provision in the 1962 Common-wealth Immigrants Act and a provision in the relevant Kenya and other legislation, passports issued after independence by the High Commissioner are regarded as United Kingdom passports. Now I think *it's impossible to say that this possibility wasn't envisaged at the time when both laws were passed, but what certainly was not anticipated or taken account of was the large and sudden influx which might result from it.* [present author's emphasis]

This statement was one of the most accurate that Powell made on the subject. He was right that the Government had not anticipated that Asian UK passport holders would eventually come to Britain in such large numbers. But it is a very different matter to allege, as he did in 1971, that there had been deliberate concealment.[28]

In 1994, reviewing the present author's biography of Macleod, Powell acknowledged that the need to avoid 'statelessness' had been a factor in the crisis over the Kenyan Asians. Referring to the 'mutual misunderstanding' that existed between him and Macleod, he wrote: 'Thus did the equation of "statelessness" with lack of unconditional admission to the United Kingdom, become the cause of Macleod's attributing to me opinions and attitudes which he had good reason to know I did not hold, as one who had enthusiastically supported his African policies as Colonial Secretary.' Macleod saw the problem from the perspective of the Colonial Office and as a believer in multi-racialism, whereas Powell viewed it from Wolverhampton and as a believer in the importance of race to national identity. It was Powell's increasing stridency on immigration during the winter and spring of 1967–68 and Macleod's reaction to it that were to make their rift unbridgeable.[29]

Upping the ante

Shortly after his outspoken warning at Deal in October 1967 about the Kenyan Asians coming to Britain, Powell and his wife left for a fortnight's visit to the United States. He experienced the same feeling of remoteness 'from everything that ultimately mattered, from all that gave one birth', that he had felt in Australia thirty years earlier. Pamela Powell, however, had looked forward to their visit because she had happy memories of New York from twenty-one years earlier when she had worked for the military staff at the United Nations. But New York had been transformed since her departure, and she and her husband were deeply disturbed at the racial tension that they found there and in other American cities. 'Integration of races of totally disparate origins and culture is one of the great myths of our time,' Powell told the American journalist, Frank Melville, after his return to London. 'It has never worked throughout history. The United States lost its only real opportunity of solving its racial problem when it failed after the Civil War to partition the old Confederacy into a "South Africa" and a "Liberia".'[30]

Because of his American visit, Powell missed the Shadow Cabinet meeting on 13 November at which Hogg, the Shadow Home Secretary, consulted his colleagues about a speech on immigration that he intended to make in the Commons in which he would reiterate the need for strict control and 'equality of treatment for everyone once they were in the country', and express his support for extending the law against discrimination in housing. Having read the recent reports on race relations, Hogg 'had come reluctantly to the conclusion that legislation would be necessary to prevent the formation of coloured "ghettos"' – though his colleagues recommended that he should avoid using the word 'ghetto'. But despite accepting this slightly more liberal stance on race relations, the Shadow Cabinet were also concerned at the entry of large numbers of Kenyan Asians into Britain, and at the lack of any reliable estimate of the total involved. The most striking aspect, however, was the report by Sir Edward Boyle 'on the strong feelings in Birmingham', that he thought would be 'greatly increased by the knowledge that there were thousands of statutory dependants who could still come here' – on this more general point, he 'wondered if there were not a case for a deadline after which a voucher-holder's dependants would lose the right of admission'.[31]

Two days later, Sandys raised the matter of the Kenyan Asians in the Commons debate, but was rebuffed by Jenkins and got no support from the Opposition front bench. Indeed, Hogg explicitly sought a bipartisan approach, and decried any attempt to use 'disagreeable racial overtones' in order to exploit 'what is potentially an emotionally charged atmosphere'. And in marked contrast to Powell's position, Hogg played down the long-term significance of numbers. As we now know, however, during the autumn,

Jenkins commissioned work in the Home Office on contingency legislation to control the flow of Asian immigrants from Kenya – the measure that his predecessor, Soskice, had been instructed to put in hand by the Cabinet in July 1965. Jenkins put the problem to the Home Affairs Committee of the Cabinet before Wilson moved him to the Treasury, in the post-devaluation switch with Callaghan, but nothing more was done about it until the following February.[32]

Powell, fresh from his return across the Atlantic, soon found that there was a greater response to his comments on immigration than on any other subject. On 19 November, he addressed a packed meeting of 800 Hampshire and Dorset Tories at Bournemouth, and when questioned afterwards about the continued growth in the immigrant population, he suggested that 'this is the American proportion', and re-stated the party's policy on tougher control and voluntary repatriation. Almost three weeks later, on 8 December, he spoke to his constituency association's annual general meeting of the 'folly which has already introduced into this country approximately one million immigrants from the Commonwealth'. Citing the 50,000 immigrants, most of them young people aged under sixteen, who were still coming in every year, he called for a drastic curtailment on the entry of dependants. According to the *Express and Star*, he also remarked that under the present law, it was 'possible for very large numbers of Asians and others under peculiar legal circumstances to enter the country'. Yet probably the most significant statement in Powell's December speech came in yet another of his comments that seemed to be directed at Heath and Hogg as much as at anybody else. 'No amount of misrepresentation, abuse or unpopularity', he declared, 'is going to prevent the Tory party, my colleagues and myself from voicing the dictates of commonsense and reason.'[33]

Events were soon to give Powell new cause to speak out on immigration, though his colleagues were to doubt that he was guided by the 'dictates of commonsense and reason'. In January 1968, the numbers of Kenyan Asians entering Britain increased again, to 2,294, after a reduction during the autumn. On Sunday 4 February, the *Sunday Telegraph* published Sandys's comment that the minority safeguards on Kenyan independence were never intended to provide 'a privileged backdoor entry into the UK'. At the Shadow Cabinet on the following Wednesday, Heath raised the matter of the large number of immigrants from Kenya arriving in Britain. Macleod proposed that Heath should write to Wilson on the subject, but Heath suggested further discussion of the issue on Monday 12th.[34]

But before the Shadow Cabinet next met, Powell delivered what the *Express and Star* described as 'a straight from the shoulder speech', in which he 'talked bluntly about the immigration problem'. Speaking on Friday 9 February, at a Conservative dinner in Walsall, only six miles to the east of Wolverhampton, he identified with those urban whites who resented the change in their communities, and captured their sense of powerlessness and of being neglected by the national, political elite. 'There is a sense of hopelessness and helplessness which comes over persons who are trapped or imprisoned', he declared, 'when all their efforts to attract attention and assistance bring no response. This is the kind of feeling which you in Walsall and we in Wolverhampton are experiencing in the face of the continued flow of immigration into our towns.' Explaining that 'we are of course in a minority', since perhaps fewer than sixty constituencies were affected out of the total of 600, he commented that 'the rest know little or nothing and, we might sometimes be tempted to feel, care little or nothing'. Powell then made a claim that was to stir much controversy. 'Only this week,' he revealed, 'a colleague of mine in the House of Commons was dumbfounded when I told him of a constituent whose little daughter was now the only white child in her class at school.' The *Express and Star* tried to confirm his claim about the white girl, but was unable to find any school where such a situation was permanent. Powell felt that he was vindicated when the chairman of the town's Education Committee, Councillor Walter Hughes, was reported to have confirmed that there was a school with only one white child in her class, but the councillor finally accepted that this had only come about on one day because of illness and absenteeism among the white minority. Yet if Powell had kept to the fact that at West Park Infants school in Wolverhampton 82 per cent of the pupils were the children of immigrants, he would have avoided controversy over the facts – whether or not one agreed with his conclusions.[35]

The controversy over the speech was fuelled by Powell's choice of words and vivid imagery as much as by the content. The MP to whom he had told the story about the white girl, he reported, had looked at him 'as if I were a Member of Parliament for Central Africa, who had suddenly dropped from the sky'. And he added that, 'so far as most people in the British Isles are concerned, you and I might as well be living in central Africa for all they know about our circumstances'. Powell again spoke of the Kenyan Asians, this time claiming that 'some 200,000 Indians in Kenya alone' enjoyed absolute right of entry into Britain – the Government had estimated a total of 167,000 Asians, though it also reckoned that a further 203,000 people elsewhere had a similar right. He also appeared to mock Hogg. During the 1964 election, Hogg had memorably and unwisely suggested that voters who supported Labour were 'stark, staring bonkers'. Powell now noted that other countries who expelled their illegal immigrants, 'must think that, to use a famous phrase, we are "stark, staring bonkers" to offer all illegal entrants a prize for breaking the law, by promising that if they slip through they can stay here for keeps'. Whatever had been Powell's purpose in choosing these words, his speech was bound to increase the pressure on Hogg over the Kenyan Asians.[36]

Powell's Walsall speech attracted great publicity and much comment over the weekend. Significantly, he won support from the *Express and Star*, whose editor, J. Clement Jones, was liberal-minded on race. 'He expressed what has been on many people's minds in towns and cities where an influx of immigrants has caused social unrest that tends to find an outlet in bitter racialism,' the paper's editorial commented:

Neither Wolverhampton nor Walsall is able to provide proper education for all children of statutory school age because of the continued rush of immigrant families into the area.

Mr Powell will, no doubt, be falsely accused of racialism. Yet he is speaking not only for white people but for coloured people already settled here and being herded into ghettoes and forced to take menial jobs.

Nationally, Powell won strong support in the *Daily Sketch* and the *Sunday Express*, whose readerships included the kind of conservative-minded working-class and lower-middle class people to whom Powell most naturally appealed. But he was subjected to vehement criticism by the *Sunday Times*, whose savage editorial was entitled, 'Powell on Prejudice'.[37]

When the Shadow Cabinet gathered on Monday 12th to discuss the Kenyan Asians, Hogg and Macleod voiced their distress at the language and tone of Powell's speech. Powell sought to defend himself, but was interrupted by Heath who begged him not to repeat it all again. The reaction to his speech should have made Powell aware of the extreme sensitivity of this issue. But his comments had also demonstrated the enormous interest and publicity that could be aroused on immigration. Powell received 800 letters, and claimed that only two had been against what he had said and that many immigrants had written to support his call for tougher controls. Many people wrote, including traditional Labour supporters in the Midlands, to say that at last somebody had been prepared to say what they had been thinking. 'Mr Powell warned', the *Express and Star* reported, 'that if there was something 99 per cent wanted to say and wanted to hear said, and if their own representatives would not say it for them, they would find a different and much less pleasant person to say it instead.' This latter comment was to become Powell's dictum.[38]

On Thursday 22nd, James Callaghan, Jenkins's successor at the Home Office, told the Commons that the Government would introduce emergency legislation to extend the 1962 Act to cover United Kingdom passport holders not connected by birth or descent with the United Kingdom. This provision would remove from Kenyan and other Asians who were exempt from the 1962 Act their right of entry to Britain, although Callaghan admitted that an undertaking had existed. Hogg gave the Opposition's assent, but on the same afternoon, journalists and MPs were busily reading Macleod's open letter to Sandys in the latest edition of the *Spectator*. In addition to rejecting Sandys's version of the Conservative Government's undertaking, Macleod took a very different line from Powell's on the significance of the numbers involved. Macleod reckoned that about 120,000 Asians had not acquired Kenyan citizenship, but believed that 'nothing like all these people will come and they are in the main prosperous and hardworking'. Exceptionally among senior politicians, he argued publicly that the exodus of the Kenyan Asians was 'being speeded by the fear that we will break our word on which they have relied'. Moreover, he recognized the concern felt in the Walsalls and the Wolverhamptons at the number of immigrants entering the country, and offered a rational *quid pro quo*. Britain had no comparable obligation to the 61,000 immigrants, including 53,000 dependants, who had been admitted from the rest of the Commonwealth during 1967, and although he 'would dislike it, that flow could be checked or even stopped while we try to achieve with Kenya a reasonably phased Africanization'.[39]

When the Shadow Cabinet gave their general support to the Government's legislation bringing the Kenyan Asians within British immigration control, Macleod stated that he would have to vote against the Bill. Boyle and Carr only voted in favour on the understanding that the Opposition would not vote against the new race relations legislation that the Government had promised. The new Commonwealth Immigrants Bill passed through all its stages in the Commons in two days. The debate was enlivened by an attack on Powell by Andrew Faulds, the Labour MP for Smethwick who had defeated Griffiths in the 1966 election, and who speaks in the Commons with the dramatic effect and volume that befit his profession as an actor. Having denounced Sandys, Faulds declared that Powell

> worries me even more, because one can only guess at the agonies of mind that impel this knight of the sad countenance, the childhood traumas that must have caused his animadversion to any social generosity. Perhaps it is a case of too severe anal training in youth, but it is unfortunate that the people of this country should have to suffer from it.[40]

Even right-wing Tories, such as Frederic Harris and Sir Harry Legge-Bourke, were deeply unhappy that the undertaking given to the Asian holders of British passports was being broken. Not only Macleod but also every other former Colonial Office minister in both Houses, except Sandys, opposed the Bill. The fifteen Conservative rebels in the Commons were drawn from all wings of the party, not only liberals on race like Macleod and the young MP for Tavistock, Michael Heseltine. Thirty-five Labour MPs and twelve Liberals also voted against, as did eighty peers in the Lords. Yet the new controls on the Kenyan Asians were nullified before they even came into effect when Callaghan admitted that if those with British citizenship were expelled from Kenya and had nowhere else to go, he would admit them. The following autumn, the Government conceded that their estimates of the numbers likely to enter Britain had been exaggerated.[41]

The Labour Cabinet Minister, Richard Crossman, himself a West Midlands MP, defended the new immigration controls to the liberal-minded guests at a London dinner party by arguing that Labour's bipartisan approach since 1964 had 'taken the poison out of politics', and had brought 'the social problem in the Midlands under control by severely limiting the incoming stream of immigrants and taking trouble in the schools'. Crossman claimed that the annual intake of immigrants was at about the maximum of 50,000, but 'if that were doubled the whole of the good work we'd done in the last three years would break down and Powellism would become the philosophy of the

Birmingham area. We were right to stop that. We were right to keep a bipartisan policy.'[42]

Yet Powell had attacked the liberal consensus of the late 1960s at its weakest point, and partly as a result, the bipartisan policy on immigration had shifted markedly in his direction. The tension between him and Heath was never far below the surface, and at times burst through for all to see. Powell was provoked during an interview with Nicholas Tomalin, into expressing an overweening confidence about his ability to be outspoken and build support in the party while continuing in Heath's Shadow Cabinet. When Tomalin suggested that, like Muggeridge, Powell deliberately attacked fashionable views for the sake of publicity, Powell dismissed the comparison but added:

I deliberately include at least one startling assertion in every speech in order to attract enough attention to give me a power base within the Conservative Party. Provided I keep this going, Ted Heath can never sack me from the Shadow Cabinet. But I never assert anything so extreme that I could not put it into practice in office – allowing of course for the inevitable compromise of office.

It was a reckless comment that questioned Heath's authority.[43]

Launching a rocket

In early April 1968, Callaghan, the Home Secretary, finally introduced Jenkins's long-promised Race Relations Bill in an effort to placate Labour ministers and MPs who had been uneasy about imposing immigration controls on the Kenyan Asians. In doing so, he unwittingly provided the catalyst that was to transform the simmering tension between Heath and Powell into open conflict. The Shadow Cabinet faced a dilemma at their meeting on Wednesday 10 April in deciding how to respond to Labour's proposals for extending the law against racial discrimination to employment and housing. In particular, they had to decide how to vote in the lobbies on the Bill's second reading when the party was deeply divided on the issue. There was little time for further back bench consultation, since parliament was about to rise for the Easter recess and the Bill's second reading was due to be debated on Tuesday 23 April, the day after the House returned.[44]

Heath opened the discussion, saying that although the Bill itself appeared to have many flaws, he thought some legal machinery would be necessary to help raise the standards of coloured immigrants in this country. Hogg explained that he had come to the conclusion that some such legislation was necessary, but was critical of certain aspects of the Bill and suggested various amendments. He also pointed out that many back-benchers were hostile to the Bill. Maudling endorsed Hogg's assessment, and suggested that the best approach on second reading might be to table a reasoned amendment (this enables an Opposition to vote against the Government while explaining their reasons for opposing a specific proposal before the House). The main concern in the discussion that followed was whether voting against the Bill at second reading would be misinterpreted as racist. Powell, according to Hogg, 'with a face like a sphinx, remained silent throughout the debate'. According to Peter Walker, then Shadow Minister of Housing and Local Government, before concluding the discussion, Heath 'went all the way round the table asking if there was any additional comment. Enoch, sitting next to me, said he had no comment.' It was clear that Macleod, Boyle, Carr and Joseph would all prefer not to vote against the Bill. The Shadow Cabinet finally agreed to move a reasoned amendment to the Bill, and to have a two-line whip, in effect, telling Tory MPs that they should be present to support the party in the vote, but that this instruction was likely to be enforced less stringently than a three-line whip.[45]

Because of the recess, however, the Shadow Cabinet had to act straight away if they were to table the reasoned amendment in time for the debate. Maudling chaired a small sub-committee that included Hogg, Macleod and Powell, to agree a form of words that might preserve party unity. Boyle and Carr, whose support for the controls on Kenyan Asians had been conditional on the Tories' not opposing the Race Relations Bill, joined Joseph in reserving their position until they saw the wording. A final decision about the vote on the second reading was to be taken later. The wording of the reasoned amendment represented a compromise between the warring wings of the Tory Party, and read as follows:

This House, reaffirming its condemnation of racial discrimination and accepting the need for steps designed to improve the situation, nevertheless declines to give a Second Reading to a Bill which, on balance, will not in its practical application contribute to the achievement of racial harmony.

Hogg was under the impression that Powell had 'acquiesced in what had been agreed', but to make certain, Hogg said to him as they left the room, 'I hope I explained it fairly.' Hogg was reassured by Powell's reply: 'You could not have put it more fairly.' 'At no stage', Hogg recalled, 'did he indicate that he differed, still less that he contemplated a speech of his own.' Powell's colleagues were relieved that, with his acceptance, the party had successfully negotiated a compromise.[46]

The Shadow Cabinet were not due to consider the matter again until their next meeting, immediately after the Easter recess, on Monday 22 April, the eve of the second reading debate. In the meantime, Powell had a long-standing engagement to address the annual general meeting of the West Midlands Area Conservative Political Centre (CPC) in Birmingham, on Saturday 20th. The Powells spent Easter week at Merridale Road, and their daughters went horse riding near Albrighton. While they were in Wolverhampton, Pamela typed her husband's speech for Saturday's CPC meeting. The Powells have since denied that either of them had any idea that this speech would create the sensation it did. This is undoubtedly true – the furore that was caused is without parallel in Britain since the Second World War. None the less, Powell was well aware of the strong response that his speech on immigration in Walsall two months earlier had evoked. Moreover, it has not previously been known that a day or so before his Birmingham meeting, he told an acquaintance that he was about to make a speech, 'that would go up like a rocket and would stay up'.[47]

This latter comment suggests, at the very least, that Powell suspected that what he was planning to say in Birmingham would have an even greater impact than his Walsall speech. In turn, it raises a further query over his failure to advise his front bench colleagues beforehand, and specifically the Shadow Home Secretary, Hogg, of his speech – this matter will be considered more fully below. Had Powell sent an embargoed copy of his text to Conservative Central Office for distribution to the media, there is little doubt that Heath's office would have been alerted to Powell's planned comments. But because he was addressing a meeting in his own area, Powell followed his practice of sending his text to the party's area office a day or so in advance, but not to Smith Square in London – one copy, however, was to be forwarded to the Press Association in London for the national press. The *Express and Star* had fully reported his Walsall speech, and now received four advance copies of his new speech, presumably to ensure that it would not be spiked.[48]

The key to the immediate impact of Powell's Birmingham speech, however, was the realization by television, radio and press editors when they read the text that it merited headline coverage. The only forewarning that the head of the press department at Central Office in London, Gerald O'Brien, had of Powell's speech came, quite by accident, on the morning that it was due to be delivered. When O'Brien, who was on holiday in Oxford, telephoned the editor of the *News of the World* to check the arrangements for an article by Heath on race relations for the following morning's edition, he was warned that the Tory leader's comments were almost certain to be overshadowed by 'a shaker of a speech' that Powell was giving that afternoon.[49]

Powell was returning not only to his native city, but to his old schoolboy stamping ground, to deliver his speech, since the CPC meeting was being held at the Midland Hotel in New Street, close by the station, in the very heart of Birmingham. It seems appropriate that the speech that was to change his life, and for which he will always be remembered, was made a stone's throw from where he had attended King Edward's School – though the school had long since left the city centre. At one level, this fact might appear to be no more than one of those curious coincidences in life, just another quirk of fate. But there is little doubt that although Powell was fully aware that he was addressing, through the media, a much wider, national audience, he spoke as he did because he was on his home ground and was among his own people – as he had been at Walsall, two months earlier.

When Powell rose to speak at 2.30 p.m. on Saturday 20th, the chairman of the meeting, Reginald Eyre, the Tory MP for the Birmingham suburb of Hall Green, realized that something newsworthy was about to happen. As the

Conservative Political Centre is the party's organization for political education, its speakers rarely attract major media interest, and on this occasion, as on most others, the television cameras had not been invited. But as Eyre looked out at the audience of about eighty-five West Midlands Tories, he noticed that the television crews had arrived to film Powell's speech. Soon after Powell began, Eyre detected a stirring in the audience. 'They knew that a major politician was giving voice to their long-held fears,' Eyre was to recall.[50]

Powell's Birmingham speech is a classic example of the method of speech-making that he had developed since January 1964. He had found that combining an academic-style treatise with the tension of a platform performance had a powerful effect. He had made immigration one of his main themes, and had come to perceive a long-term, though unspecified, threat being caused by the numbers of immigrants, their concentration and their predicted future growth. He was also conscious of the strong response that his comments on the issue elicited, especially at Walsall, where he had adopted the role of spokesman for urban whites and dignified their sense of resentment towards a remote political elite. At Birmingham, he conjured up an extra-ordinarily heady mix, that was part-treatise, part-speech, part-anecdote and part-prophecy. Probably no other politician could have played, in a single speech, the roles of philosopher, politician, street-corner gossip and classical prophet. The effect was to be devastating.

'The supreme function of statesmanship', Powell began in the nature of a philosophical treatise, 'is to provide against preventable evils.' The use of the word 'evil' by a religious man like Powell was, in itself, indicative of the strength of his feeling on the issue, and his opening remarks suggest that he had some sense of the controversy that the rest of his speech would spark. Immediately, he outlined a defence for the politician who sought to lift people's eyes beyond the present and address future problems. Because of human nature, he asserted, 'people are disposed to mistake predicting troubles for causing troubles and even for desiring troubles: "if only", they love to think, "if only people wouldn't talk about it, it probably wouldn't happen".' In Powell's view, however, he had a duty to speak out, whatever the consequences were for him, since 'the discussion of future grave, but with effort now, avoidable evils is the most unpopular and at the same time the most necessary occupation for the politician. Those who knowingly shirk it, deserve, and not infrequently receive, the curses of those who come after.' This latter injunction echoed many others that he had directed at his own party as much as at Labour.

Powell then related the first of his shocking anecdotes, and he explicitly anticipated the howls of protest that it would provoke. A 'middle-aged quite ordinary working man' in his constituency had told Powell that he would not be satisfied until he and his children and their families had all settled overseas. 'In this country in fifteen or twenty years time', the constituent had remarked by way of explanation, 'the black man will have the whip hand over the white man.' At this point, Powell declared, 'I can already hear the chorus of execration. How dare I say such a horrible thing? How dare I stir up trouble and inflame feelings by repeating such a conversation?' In reply to these rhetorical questions, Powell answered, 'I do not have the right not to do so.' As MP for his constituent, Powell argued that he did not 'have the right to shrug my shoulders and think about something else'. Moreover, he again claimed to speak for vast numbers of urban whites as he generalized from the particular instance of his constituent's remark. 'What he is saying', Powell proclaimed, 'thousands and hundreds of thousands are saying and thinking – not throughout Great Britain, but in the areas that are already undergoing the total transformation to which there is no parallel in a thousand years of English history.'

The speech continued with Powell's now familiar emphasis on the projected growth of the immigrant population (he now suggested a total of five to seven million by the year 2000). And again, he reiterated that the 'simple and rational' answers to the problem were 'by stopping, or virtually stopping further inflow, and by promoting maximum outflow'. Both remedies, he noted, were part of official Conservative policy, although Powell put much greater store by repatriation than the party leadership. In part, this was because of his preoccupation with the numbers of dependants entering the country. 'Those whom the gods wish to destroy, they first make mad', he declared, in a characteristic, classical allusion that lent his speeches their special sense of impending doom. And he continued, in one of the passages that was filmed by the television cameras, with an analogy that appeared to suggest that there was little prospect of the majority of the descendants of immigrants ever becoming British:

> We must be mad, literally mad as a nation to be permitting the annual inflow of some 50,000 dependants, who are for the most part the material of the future growth of the immigrant-descended population. It is like watching a nation building its own funeral pyre.

An irrational mysticism informed Powell's sense of nationhood and nationality. But if he had been more rational on these subjects, he might have recognized that it would not be as difficult as he imagined for non-white descendants of immigrants to see themselves, and to be seen by others, as British.

Race relations was to be the subject of debate in the Commons the following Tuesday, and Powell repeated the Conservative commitment to equality of treatment for citizens within Britain. He even endorsed Heath's statement that the Tories would have 'no first-class citizens' and 'second-class citizens'. But there was a sting in the tail. Those who demanded legislation 'against discrimination', Powell contended, 'had got it exactly and diametrically wrong'. He turned the liberal consensus on its head. In another emotive passage that was captured by the cameras, he again took up the cudgels for the urban whites, by declaring that:

> The discrimination and the deprivation, the sense of alarm and of resentment, lies not with the immigrant population but with those among whom they have come and are still coming. This is why to enact legislation of the kind before Parliament at this moment is to risk throwing a match on to gunpowder.

Powell added the gratuitous insult that 'the kindest thing that can be said about those who propose and support it is that they know not what they do'. Heath, Hogg, Boyle, Carr and Joseph in the Shadow Cabinet were all inclined, in varying degrees, to support further legislation on race relations, while not necessarily going quite as far as Labour intended.

But the most explosive section of Powell's speech occurred when he dealt with the grievances of urban whites in areas where immigrants were concentrated. 'For reasons which they could not understand', he argued, 'and in pursuance of a decision by default, on which they were never consulted, they found themselves made strangers in their own country.' He recited the litany of resentments over maternity beds, schools, housing and employment, and he even claimed that 'they began to hear, as time went by, more and more voices which told them that they were now the unwanted'. In addition, the new race relations law, 'which cannot, and is not intended, to operate to protect them or redress their grievances, is to be enacted to give the stranger, the disgruntled and the *agent provocateur* the power to pillory them for their private actions'.

Having created an image of a beleaguered and persecuted minority, Powell reported that many of his correspondents after his Walsall speech had omitted their addresses because they believed that it was dangerous to have committed to paper their agreement with the comments that he had made as an MP, 'and that they would risk either penalties or reprisals if they were known to have done so'. He then read from a letter that he had received from a woman in Northumberland 'about something which is happening at this moment in my own constituency'. As Powell put it, he was allowing 'just one of those hundreds of people to speak for me'.

The letter related the distressing plight of an elderly widow in Wolverhampton, who was the only white resident left in her street. By far its most controversial passage, that Powell read out, claimed that the elderly widow

> is afraid to go out. Windows are broken. She finds excreta pushed through her letterbox. When she goes to the shops, she is followed by children, charming, wide-grinning piccaninnies. They cannot speak English, but one word they know. 'Racialist', they chant. When the new Race Relations Bill is passed, this woman is convinced she will go to prison. And is she so wrong? I begin to wonder.

These allegations, quoted from a letter by a woman, hundreds of miles away, who was relating them at second hand, was to fuel a furious controversy.

According to Powell, the real danger of the Race Relations Bill stemmed from changes in the immigrant community. 'Integration', for him, summed up the delusion suffered by those who were, as he put it, 'wilfully or otherwise blind to realities'. Integration was difficult enough for the early immigrants, but to imagine that 'a great and growing majority of immigrants and their descendants' had any thought of becoming integrated into British society was, he claimed, a 'ludicrous misconception, and a dangerous one to boot'. And as he·had done at Walsall, he again referred to the campaign among the Sikh community to maintain their customs in Britain, citing the attack on such 'communalism' by the then Labour Minister and Walsall MP, John Stonehouse.

Against this background, Powell maintained that the new Bill was 'the very pabulum' that 'these dangerous and divisive elements' would need to flourish. 'Here is the means', he said in a fantastic claim about Labour's legislation,

of showing that the immigrant communities can organize to consolidate their members, to agitate and campaign against their fellow-citizens, and to overawe and dominate the rest with legal weapons which the ignorant and the ill-informed have provided.

It was at this point that he made the classical allusion to Virgil's *Aeneid* that is quoted at the head of this chapter, and that prompted the headlines about 'rivers of blood' – though this section of the speech was not filmed. 'That tragic and intractable phenomenon which we watch with horror on the other side of the Atlantic,' he concluded, in another reminder of America's racial problem,

is coming upon us here by our own volition and our own neglect. Indeed, it has all but come. In numerical terms, it will be of American proportions long before the end of the century. Only resolute and urgent action will avert it now. Whether there will be the public will to demand and obtain that action, I do not know. All I know is that to see, and not to speak, would be the great betrayal.[51]

Powell stayed for questions, but had to leave after a short while to record a BBC television news interview. As he departed, the audience rose, in keeping with normal convention, and applauded, but there was no standing ovation as has sometimes been suggested. Indeed, the reception for his *tour de force* was remarkably low-key in view of the consequences that rapidly began to flow from it, but such is the decorous conduct of Conservative Political Centre meetings and its members. The reaction in the wider world, however, was to be momentous.

Into orbit

The impact of Powell's speech was immediate from the moment when the first filmed extracts were broadcast on the early evening BBC and ITN news bulletins. Hogg, who was staying with friends in the Lake District, had returned from fell-walking late on Saturday afternoon to be greeted by their younger son who asked whether he had heard about Powell's speech, and suggested he should watch the news. To his 'horror', Hogg 'heard and saw as the main item Enoch's warning about the Tiber "foaming with much blood". To say that I was outraged would be an understatement'. Hogg telephoned Willie Whitelaw, the Chief Whip, who happened to live locally, to alert him to the fact that Powell had made 'a rather odd speech' and to ask him to watch the next bulletin. Whitelaw was 'distressed' by what he saw, since he had hoped that the compromise on the reasoned amendment would maintain party unity.[52]

Immediately they heard of Powell's speech, other Shadow Ministers urgently conferred with Heath and Whitelaw by telephone. Whitelaw was in no doubt following conversations with Macleod, Boyle and Carr that 'the whole shooting match' would quit unless Powell went. Hogg was also planning to confront Powell at the next Shadow Cabinet meeting and present his colleagues with a choice: unless Powell's speech was publicly condemned by them, Hogg would have to resign and, almost certainly, end his public life. But Whitelaw, who returned to London and spent most of Sunday with Heath, found that the Tory leader was more affronted than anybody.[53]

Powell's speech was the lead story in every Sunday newspaper, and a large part of BBC Radio's Sunday lunch-time programme, *The World This Weekend*, was devoted to him. During the course of the day, Heath spoke with the rest of the Shadow Cabinet, including one of its most junior members, the Shadow Minister of Power, Magaret Thatcher, who had been appointed the previous year. 'I have come to the conclusion that Enoch must go,' he told Thatcher, who recalls his comment as 'more statement than enquiry'. A decade later, having ousted Heath as party leader, she was to talk of people feeling 'swamped by people with a different culture'. From what she has now revealed of her feelings about Powell's comments in 1968, her subsequent remark was unsurprising. Although she regarded his speech as 'strong meat', she none the less 'strongly sympathized with the gravamen of his argument about the scale of New Commonwealth immigrants into Britain. I too thought this threatened not just public order but also the way of life of some communities'. Immigration was linked with other aspects of the 1960s that she disliked, since these communities were 'already beginning to be demoralized by insensitive housing policies, Social Security dependence and the onset of the "permissive society"'. She was 'quite convinced that, however selective quotations from his speech may have sounded, Enoch was no racist'.[54]

In response to Heath's suggestion that Powell had to go, Thatcher thought 'that it was better to let things cool down for the present rather than heighten the crisis'. She wanted to 'just wait and read the whole speech and just think about it for a few days'. The debate on the Race Relations Bill, however, was to be held two days later, and the sensational reaction to the speech precluded this option. Heath was adamant. 'No, no. He absolutely must go,' he told Thatcher, 'and most people think he must go.' She later learned that several members of the Shadow Cabinet would have resigned if Powell had not gone, but none the less continues to insist that 'it was a conclusion jumped to far too rapidly, if you looked at the logic and reason in his speech'. Yet Hogg told his colleagues that he would not have been able to remain in the Shadow Cabinet if Powell had continued to be a member. At the very least, the Tories would have lost the Shadow Chancellor (Macleod) and Shadow Home Secretary (Hogg), and their chief spokesmen on Employment (Carr) and Education (Boyle). The speech was widely seen as a challenge to the authority of Heath and his Shadow Cabinet, and also to the liberal consensus on immigration and race, that had already taken a battering over the Kenyan Asians. It is difficult to see what else Heath could have done to avert a catastrophic split in his Shadow Cabinet other than to sack Powell.[55]

The Powells had, as usual when they spent the weekend in Wolverhampton, attended St Peter's Church for morning service. As they left, they were confronted by a large number of reporters and photographers. Powell agreed to be interviewed for *The World This Weekend* and ITN news. On the radio, he repeated the defence he had given in his speech about his duty to speak 'about the deep fears, the resentments and anxieties for the future which I know exist'. Asked by ITN whether or not the speech had been cleared with Heath, he said, 'No, one doesn't. It was a speech entirely on the lines that he had set out ... I was speaking the official line.'[56]

Late on Sunday evening, Heath spoke with Powell. Since the Powells had no telephone at their Merridale Road home, the constituency agent had to be contacted, and it was at his house that Powell heard what Heath had to say. Heath told Powell that he was sacked from the Shadow Cabinet because he considered his speech 'to have been racialist in tone and liable to exacerbate racial tensions'. Powell returned home and told Pamela. The Powells decided that it would be better to deal with the crisis in London, and immediately got their daughters up, drove to their Belgravia home, and arrived there in the early hours of Monday morning.[57]

As the Powells headed south, news editors were hurriedly recasting their front pages in response to the 10.30 p.m. press statement by Heath that he had sacked Powell. After a few hours' sleep, Powell wrote to Heath, complaining at Heath's attempt to 'stigmatize my speech at Birmingham as "racialist" when you surely must realize that it was nothing of the kind'. Powell was prepared to say that he expected Heath to become Prime Minister, and that he would 'be an outstandingly able Prime Minister, perhaps even a great one'. But a glimpse of his intense frustration with Heath surfaced when he added that there was 'one cause of anxiety'. 'It is the impression you often give', Powell wrote, 'of playing down and even unsaying the policies and views which you hold and believe to be right, for fear of clamour from some sections of the press or public.'[58]

Powell's speech and his sacking, however, had unleashed a clamour from the press and the public that is without parallel in Britain – certainly, nothing like it has been seen in the fifty years or so since the Second World War. Monday morning's newspapers brought a flood of condemnation, most notably in *The Times*, whose editorial was entitled, 'An Evil Speech'. Powell's speech was described as 'disgraceful', 'racialist' and 'shameful'. 'The language, the innuendoes, the constant appeals to self-pity, the anecdotes', the editor argued, 'all combine to make a deliberate appeal to racial hatred. This is the first time that a serious British politician has appealed to racial hatred, in this direct way, in our postwar history.' In its news and features section, *The Times* reported reactions to the Birmingham speech under the headline, MOSLEY SPEECHES RECALLED, leading with a quote from the former Tory MP Humphry Berkeley comparing Powell to the fascist leader, Sir Oswald Mosley. Of 45 editorials in local and national newspapers surveyed by Douglas Schoen for his study on Powell's popular support, 28 were unfavourable, ten had mixed reactions and only seven were favourable – though the combined circulation of the two national papers that were supportive, the *Daily Express* and the *News of the World* at ten million nearly matched the total circulations (11.3 million) of the seven that were unfavourable. In the regions, the *Glasgow Herald*, *Birmingham Evening Mail* and *Liverpool Daily Post* had the same mixed reaction as the *Daily Telegraph* and the *Daily Sketch*.[59]

In Powell's Black Country base, however, the *Express and Star*, that had supported his Walsall speech, now turned against him. If Powell, it argued, had 'contented himself with expressing in moderate language the very serious misgivings that many people of the West Midlands have about the conditions which now exist in this area, his speech would have been justified'. The paper also accepted that 'many people in this country have suffered from declining property values following social changes in a neighbourhood when coloured immigrants have arrived', and contended that the new Race Relations Bill was likely, 'as Mr Powell says, to increase this trend and with apparent injustice to the people of this country'. None the less, its editorial concluded that Powell 'was unnecessarily extravagant in his language. It is always possible to damage a cause by overstatement and this in our opinion is what Mr Powell has done.'[60]

Newspaper editors found that they were caught in the role of piggy in the middle, between, on the one hand, the anti-Powell views of the majority of the political elite, and on the other hand, the pro-Powell sentiments of the majority of people. Several opinion polls conducted during the month or so after Powell's speech and his sacking found that between 67 and 82 per cent agreed with what he had said about immigrants; and that between 61 and 73 per cent disagreed with Heath's sacking him. The *Express and Star* overcame the dilemma by clearing the leader page and the page facing of all but the leader and devoting them entirely to readers' letters on the issue – the proportion received was approximately 5,000 for Powell, and 300 against. The letters of support for Powell included petitions from local factories, with many saying that his speech was that of a realist, not a racist, and that he was doing his job as an MP in expressing the views of his constituents. His speech encouraged people with similar thoughts about immigration to those that Powell had expressed to voice them openly – at the town's Rotary Club, chapel-going, worthy, local citizens were commenting that 'if Enoch's said it, it must be right'. But the race issue was overshadowed by anger at Heath's sacking their local MP from the Tory front bench – of 35,000 readers who took part in a post-card poll organized by the *Express and Star* on whether or not Heath was right to sack Powell, only 372 thought that Heath had been right. 'Sack Heath not Powell', was a frequent response. At the end of the week two groups of marchers met head on outside the paper's offices – one protesting at the anti-Powell editorial line, the other complaining that the *Express and Star* was a racist paper to have given space to Powell's policies.[61]

From Monday morning, the Powells were besieged by the media who were encamped outside their Belgravia home. The police were also there to offer protection against any violence. Shopping was impossible for the Powells, and they had to rely on neighbours handing baskets over the back-garden fence. Susan and Jennifer used to go out by climbing over a neighbour's wall into the Mews at the back, and after a few days, the girls left to stay with friends. On Tuesday morning, sackfuls of mail began to arrive – some 23,000 letters in all. The next day, another 50,000 letters arrived. The Post Office had to provide a van solely for Powell's mail. During the next ten days, he received about 700 telegrams and over 100,000 letters, many carrying more than one signature. Only 800 or so were in disagreement. Enoch and Pamela Powell went through some of the letters again for the first time in twenty-seven years with Michael Cockerell, for his television profile in 1995. Powell read from one of them: 'Thank God I've found someone that has spoken for the white people of England. Did we go through the day and the night terror of doodlebugs, incendiary bombs and bombing so that these hoards of black locusts might come here and buy the homes we've known for years and make our lives unbearable?'[62]

Powell's postbag was surveyed by Diana Spearman, who analysed a random sample of over 3,500 letters. The editor of *New Society*, in which her findings were published, pointed out that Spearman had been a member of the Conservative Research Department for twelve years, and might have added that she was a strong supporter of the free-market views that Powell espoused and had known him for many years. None the less, her findings are an important insight into the nature of Powell's support. As far as she could see from the paper, address and style, the writers 'came from every social class and every part of the country'. Only a relatively small number (71) were blatantly racialist, although others were concerned solely with complaints about immigrants (66); or were worried about the strain on the social services (204) and the burden on taxes and rates (52). Just over ten per cent (361) were 'ugly or vicious'. Much the largest number (1,128) feared that continued immigration was a threat to British culture and traditions. The tone reflected the numerical analysis, as none of them, except for the blatantly racialist letters, showed what Spearman considered to be rancour towards non-whites already in Britain and there was no wish for expulsion – though Spearman conceded that 'the words foreign or black or coloured invasion are freely used', and there was 'a sense of being overwhelmed by an unforeseen, unplanned event'. But her most interesting discovery was that 'most of the letters that went beyond a simple message of congratulation included phrases like "at last an honest MP", "the only man who has spoken for us", "a man who puts country before party"'. She considered adding a category: 'alienation', to describe a distrust of the political parties or the 'establishment'. 'The letters reflect the feeling', she noted, 'that *they* by their actions have produced problems for *us*, which do not in any way affect *them* and which they are not doing anything to help us solve. *Their* idea is to tell *us* what we must and must not do.'[63]

Sackfuls of mail also arrived for Heath. As Jim (later Lord) Prior, who was then Heath's parliamentary private secretary, has recalled, 'ninety-nine per cent of it backed Powell. But I wonder if Powell really knows or understands to this day the filth he collected to his side. A number of letters were so vilely written that it was offensive for the girls in Ted's office to read them: others carried their message by including excrement.' The Conservative Party Archive has retained many of the letters sent to Central Office after Powell's sacking. The file of letters supporting Heath is thin, but another seven full files contain letters supporting Powell. Some read like caricatures – one from Tonbridge is addressed, 'Dear Colonel Heath', is dated 'St George's Day', and tells Heath that 'your action over Brigadier Enoch Powell's speech is probably the most serious you have inflicted on the Conservative cause since you became the Party's leader'. But another file is full of petitions from Wolverhampton and the Black Country, many from local factories and offices, and signed by trade unionists.[64]

Working-class support for Powell erupted in public demonstrations in Wolverhampton and London on Tuesday 23rd, the day of the debate on the Race Relations Bill. In Wolverhampton, men from the Wolverhampton and Dudley Breweries company led a 50-strong march on the Town Hall, chanting 'Ted out, Enoch in' and carrying broom-handled banners declaring: 'Support Enoch, the man who speaks the truth'; 'Enoch is right', and 'Back him, not sack him'. They were joined by workers from other factories, who cheered as a branch official of the Transport and General Workers' Union posted a 250-signature petition to Heath. About a thousand men at Norton Villiers engine manufacturers stopped work early in support of Powell.[65]

In London, over four thousand London dockers stopped work in support of Powell, and about 800 of them marched on Westminster, as did a group of Smithfield meat porters. 'It just happened,' one of the four dockers who organized the march recalled. He thought Powell had talked 'a lot of sense' and told some of his mates, 'and before you could blink everybody was agreeing with everybody else'. The fact that the dockers had just accepted heavy redundancies may have been a factor. The reaction at Smithfield was equally spontaneous, but was exploited by Big Dan Harmston, a member of the Union Movement and a supporter of Mosley. 'There was a mood about the place,' Harmston told Martin Walker, 'if that day I'd said, "Pick up your cleavers and knives and decapitate Heath and Wilson", they'd have done it. They really would – but they wouldn't have done it the next week. It was just that mood of the moment – like storming the Bastille, I suppose.' The dockers and porters said that their protest was not racialist, but the Kenyan High Commissioner was booed when he arrived at St Stephen's entrance to the Commons, and Ian Mikardo, the Labour MP who represented an East End seat, was called a 'Japanese Jew' by one of the protesters.[66]

The sight of a political demonstration by working men in support of Powell appalled many liberal-minded people, especially on the left. At a TUC reception that evening, Frank Cousins, the leader of the Transport and General Workers' Union and former minister, tried to tell Barbara Castle, then Employment Secretary, that people were disillusioned with politicians, to which she retorted that politicians were disillusioned with his dockers. 'This is the first time in recent history', she rebuked him, 'that anyone has been able to get them out on the streets on a political matter.' Richard Briginshaw, leader of a print union, 'said openly that Enoch Powell had a lot of right on his side', causing Castle to reflect in her diary that, 'the lid is off the box with a vengeance'.[67]

Although the policy director of Britain's recently formed National Front, A.K. Chesterton, was exaggerating when he claimed that, 'what Mr Powell has said does not vary in any way from our view', the National Front was given a boost by Powell's speech. 'Before Powell spoke', Robert Taylor, National Front organizer in Sheffield recalled, 'we were getting only cranks and perverts. After his speeches we started to attract, in a secret sort of way, the right-wing members of Tory organizations.' The National Front marched in Huddersfield in support of what Powell had said and signed up eight people as members that afternoon. But as Martin Walker has pointed out, 'confirmation that there was a great deal of submerged racialism in British society did not automatically mean that there was a corresponding potential for natural NF recruits'. The National Front also had to guard against the erosion of its members to the Powellite wing of the Conservative Party.[68]

Members of Britain's non-white communities suffered mental and, in some cases physical, pain, following Powell's speech. 'I was one of those "wide-eyed, grinning piccaninnies" that he saw fit to quote in a letter, and that was hurtful,' Paul Boateng, the Labour MP, who was then a schoolboy, has recalled. 'For the first time in the country of my birth and the country of which I'm proud to say I belong,' Boateng added, 'I was shouted at and spat at and abused in the street for the first time ever, the day after that.' Powell's reaction to Boateng's experience was to suggest that 'it only revealed the underlying tension'. When confronted on television by other members of ethnic minorities who had been frightened by his speech, Powell has seemed genuinely surprised, as though he had had no idea that his comments might have had such an effect on them.[69]

Powell's speech appears to have had an immediate impact on public support for the Government's Race Relations Bill. In mid-April, before his speech, Gallup found that 42 per cent approved the Bill against 29 per cent who disapproved, but by the end of the month the percentage who approved had slumped to 30 per cent whereas 46 per cent disapproved. But Powell's former colleagues on the front bench regarded his method of achieving such a dramatic turn-around in public opinion against the Government's proposals to have been quite unacceptable. During the second reading debate on the Bill in the Commons on Tuesday 23rd, Powell, who had taken his place on the back benches and was seated on the third row, heard Hogg turn the tables on him and gain revenge for Powell's use at Walsall of the phrase, 'stark, staring bonkers'. If, as Powell had commented in his Birmingham speech, the Bill risked 'throwing a match on to gunpowder', Hogg pointedly suggested that 'it might be thought a little careless to go about with a lighted cigarette in one's mouth, flicking ash all over the place'.[70]

Powell was shocked to discover that he was shunned by virtually the entire Shadow Cabinet. His long-time colleague, Macleod, was deeply shaken by Powell's speech and the unpleasantness, and in some cases, sheer viciousness, of the mail that poured in supporting Powell. 'Enoch's gone mad and hates the blacks,' he told young Tory friends, but his anger was real. 'Iain never forgave him,' Patrick Jenkin, one of Macleod's junior front bench team, has recalled. 'You lift the stones,' Macleod said of Powell's speech, 'but you have no idea of how nasty some of the things underneath them are.' Powell was bitter at Macleod's treatment of him. 'His dealings with me', Powell later recalled, were 'those of one's dealings with a pariah. There was nothing in it for him to be in any way associated with me.' Powell was especially resentful because Macleod 'knew what I said was not motivated by what is crudely called racialism, but he behaved as if he did not so know'. There is some evidence that Macleod made an attempt to see if a rapprochement might be possible, but Powell has no recollection of it. At the time of the 1969 Conservative conference, the political journalist, Keith Kyle, recalls Macleod telling him that he (Macleod) had been worried at Powell's increasing isolation in the Conservative Party, and had hoped to persuade Powell to work with the Conservatives. According to Macleod, he and his wife, Eve, arranged to spend a weekend with the Powells, but he came away feeling that Powell was mad. The gulf between these two former colleagues was unbridgeable.[71]

Powell's support, such as it was in the parliamentary party, was weakened by his speech. The Powellites among Tory MPs and candidates suffered a decline in quality, since the younger economic liberals, like Geoffrey Howe, who felt that the Birmingham speech 'set us apart', distanced themselves from his views on race. Talented Tories like Biffen and Maude continued to back him, but he was now more dependent on a motley collection, who included the anti-immigration campaigner, Harold Gurden, the extreme *laissez-faire* right-winger, Ronald Bell, and the maverick, Sir Gerald Nabarro. At the 1922 Committee meeting on 25 April, Nabarro demanded that, in view of Powell's sacking, Boyle should also be dismissed from the Shadow Cabinet for having failed to back the party line at the end of the debate on the Race Relations Bill, but he was routed. It is doubtful if all 45 Tory MPs who eventually voted against the third reading of the Race Relations Bill would have backed Powell in a leadership contest with Heath, since David Wood of *The Times* reckoned that only seventeen of them were hard-core, right-wing opponents of the legislation.[72]

Thatcher regarded Powell's departure as a 'tragedy', although she thought that his subsequent 'preaching in the wilderness' had some advantage for those 'of us on the right in the Shadow Cabinet and Cabinet', since 'he shifted the balance of the political argument to the right'. None the less, as she recognizes, 'the very fact that Enoch advanced all his positions as part of a coherent whole made it more difficult to express agreement with one or two of them. For example, the arguments against prices and incomes policies, intervention and corporatism might have been better received if they had not been associated with Enoch's views about immigration.' Powell himself realized that his influence on economic policy had been reduced.[73]

Although Powell's views were shared by many local Tories, most activists remained loyal to Heath. A number of constituency associations passed resolutions condemning Heath's action, and in the May 1968 local elections, some Tory candidates in Southall, Orpington and Lambeth put out literature saying, 'We back Powell, don't you?' One 25-year-old Tory hopeful in Lambeth, who was fighting his first election campaign as a Tory candidate in the London borough elections, was John Major. Although Major was standing in Lambeth's Ferndale ward, an area of high immigration, where Powell's speech evoked strong support among white, working-class voters, he refused to follow a vocal minority of Tories in Vauxhall who took up the Powellite crusade. After his election in the landslide victory that saw the Tories capture Lambeth council after forty years of Labour control, Major had no truck with the minority of Powellite councillors and, along with other Tories, ensured their isolation.[74]

Powell's speech had sent up a rocket, as he had intended, but he had not foreseen that he would be sent into orbit with it – highly visible, but excluded from the front bench by his sacking from the Shadow Cabinet. He found himself in the paradoxical position of being a pariah at Westminster while becoming a national figure. Gallup's monthly political index found that in March 1968 only one per cent had identified Powell as their choice for Tory leader should Heath resign, behind Maudling with 20 per cent and Douglas-Home with ten per cent, but after the Birmingham speech Powell had become the most popular alternative leader with 24 per cent.[75]

Powell's life and that of his family, was totally transformed. Some politicians no longer attended their dinner parties. Powell was now instantly recognized wherever he went in Britain, and was greeted either by adulation or hatred. The constituency home became a target for attacks. Family holidays always had to be taken abroad. Powell led a weird existence as he travelled the country and preached his message, spending hours alone each week on long journeys, interspersed by rowdy, and sometimes violent, receptions when he reached his destination. His speech and sacking coincided with the student unrest of the late 1960s, and he became a target for demonstrations.[76]

Following Powell's Walsall speech in February 1968, there had been a bomb threat at Essex University where he was due to address the University's Conservative Association, and although there was no bomb, a violent demonstration by students was to set the pattern after the Birmingham speech. When an invitation to him to speak at Birmingham University in June was withdrawn on grounds of fear for his safety, he claimed that the real reason had been disagreement with his opinions – he was able to visit the university a few days later. At High Wycombe in June he was interrupted by cries of 'Fascist!' and his speech ended amidst uproar – he suggested that the trouble had been caused to create a false impression in the press. Swastikas were daubed on his constituency party's offices. In July, he was mobbed by students. An edition of *Any Questions* had to be switched from its planned venue at the Pressed Steel Sports Club at Cowley, near Oxford, to BBC Broadcasting House, when the club's committee members heard of Powell's presence on the panel and feared a student demonstration. Demonstrators greeted him at Gillingham in September, and at Exeter, in October, he was forced to abandon his meeting after fifteen minutes as fighting broke out between rival student groups. 'Thank you ladies and gentlemen', Powell shouted above the jeering, 'for your intelligent reception and for your demonstration of the academic principle of free speech.' There were more student demonstrations against him at Bath and Cardiff in November, and following a further speech on immigration policemen had to guard the Powells' home in South Eaton Place as demonstrators gave the Nazi salute and hung a swastika on the railings outside (he had earlier met a deputation organized by the Young Communist League). In December, Powell's planned visit to his old school, King Edward's, that had moved since his time there to Edgbaston, near the university campus, was cancelled for fear of disruption by student demonstrators. In the same month, Powell walked out of a meeting at the Wolverhampton College of Technology after constant interruptions and uproar.[77]

None of these demonstrations was likely to discourage Powell from continuing to speak out on immigration: quite the reverse. They were only likely to confirm him in the rightness of his views and strengthen his determination to keep expressing them. Moreover, although he accepted that his Birmingham speech and his sacking had reduced his effectiveness with the party leadership, he felt that they had enhanced it among the party as a whole. But some idea of the strain that the controversy that Powell's speeches attracted can be gleaned from the comments of his younger daughter, Jennifer, who became a student at Cambridge during the mid-1970s. 'Inside me I used to feel quite sick', she has admitted, 'when I knew that he was going to be speaking about immigration, because I just hated what I knew I would read in the papers and the headlines, and what I might see on television. It would make my stomach churn.'[78]

'Stick to the Latin'

Pamela Powell has said of life with her husband that a bomb exploded every five years or so, but April 1968 was incomparably the biggest explosion of them all. Yet the overriding impression from Powell's subsequent comments about the speech that changed the entire course of his life, is of his denial of responsibility for having lit the fuse. Regret, never a word that sprang readily to Powell's lips, was virtually banished from his discussion of the speech and all that flowed from it. Apology was simply unnecessary.

Powell's distancing himself from the whole event may reflect more than a convenient rationalization for his grave misjudgement in using such provocative language. He seemed genuinely to feel that the speech and the events surrounding it were, in a curious way, separate from him or external to him. In part, this denial, or distancing, may be a reaction to the severe shock he felt at being sacked and treated as a pariah. Although he was buoyed up by the enormous public support for him, even this phenomenon emphasized that his world had been turned upside down. He was a man whose determination and talent had led him to achieve much of what he wanted in life. Now, almost overnight he seemed to be entirely at the mercy of forces beyond his control. Perhaps the fact that his predicament was his own doing was too painful to admit.

Looking back at his Birmingham speech, Powell sometimes talked of having been a passenger, as though he was carried along by events. It is as though the issue of immigration found him, rather than *vice versa*, and – so he has argued – as the estimates of the immigrant population increased he was startled into increasingly talking about the subject. He likened himself to a man who had found a small, unexploded bomb and discovered, to his horror, not only that it was nuclear but also that nobody believed him. As to the 'River Tiber' speech, he referred to it as 'the earthquake', and on other occasions spoke of having felt like a man who was walking down a street when a tile fell from a roof, hit him on the head and temporarily stunned him.[79]

After the immediate hubbub over the Birmingham speech had receded, one of Powell's closest political friends, John Biffen, called on him at South Eaton Place to see how he was feeling and to offer moral support. Having first to assure Pam of his identity before she would open the door, Biffen went up to the small first-floor study, where he found Powell preoccupied in a search among his classical reference books. 'I can't find the Roman,' was Powell's comment. Biffen was initially puzzled, but then realized that Powell's main concern was that he might have misquoted Virgil's *Aeneid*. Powell had, indeed, been mistaken in referring to 'the Roman', when it is the Sybil, in one of her prophecies, who sees the Tiber 'foaming with much blood'. He could be forgiven for having identified himself, however inadvertently, with 'the Roman', since Virgil describes the Sybil as storming wildly in her cave before chanting 'her dread enigmas' and 'wrapping the truth in darkness'.[80]

Almost the only regret to which Powell ever confessed having about his Birmingham speech concerned one detail. 'If I had a regret', he admitted in Channel 4's 1987 profile, 'it was that I didn't quote Virgil in Latin, but then I didn't want to appear pedantic, so I took the Latin out and put in a translation.' But it was not his confusing the Sybil for 'the Roman' that he had in mind. 'I probably ought to have stuck to the Latin,' he added. 'That's a good motto in life: "stick to the Latin".' When Nick Ross, who interviewed him, suggested that his speech would still have been taken as warning of 'rivers of blood', Powell disagreed. 'Nobody would have troubled to translate it,' he argued. 'They would have said: "That's a Latin quote of some sort".' His cynicism as a classicist whose subject had been neglected is understandable, but such was the explosiveness of his speech that any Latin phrase would have been immediately translated and analysed.

Yet Powell's regret that he did not 'stick to the Latin' has been his only suggestion that he might have phrased his speech differently. He always maintained afterwards, despite his comment beforehand about sending up a rocket, that he 'never intended to blow the top off everything', and that his sole purpose was to explain the Opposition's decision to vote against the Government's Race Relations Bill the following Tuesday. 'That this was going to change my life and in some ways the course of British politics wasn't in my mind,' he later claimed,

> and I'm not absolutely certain that if some celestial finger had tapped me on the shoulder while I was drafting the speech of the 20 April and said, 'You know the following will be the consequences', that I wouldn't have said, 'Well no, what I'm really doing is to write a speech to explain the vote which we're giving next week, and if there is anything which I can alter or put differently and which would serve that purpose better then I would.'

The only error of judgement that Powell has admitted to was his assumption that the Shadow Cabinet's decision to vote against the Race Relations Bill signified that the Tory leadership shared his views:

> It's true that I was delighted, relieved that the Conservative Party had decided to vote against the second reading of that Bill, and indeed I believed, mistakenly, that that in a sense committed them to all that I believed they needed to be committed to, for the good of the country and for the future of the country.

For Powell, the decision to vote against the Race Relations Bill marked another step by the leadership in his direction. Already, he had seen them move from opposing tougher controls on the Kenyan Asians to supporting the Government's emergency legislation at the end of February. Now, despite all the misgivings of liberals in the Shadow Cabinet, and Heath's and Hogg's evident reluctance, the Shadow Cabinet had decided – notwithstanding the reasoned amendment – to oppose the Race Relations Bill.

Although Powell sensed that on immigration, at least, he was in the ascendant, he would have been aware from the Shadow Cabinet discussions that, after the second reading debate, Heath and Hogg might be prepared to accept parts of the Race Relations Bill, especially on employment and housing, at the committee stage. It was even possible that they might commit the party to voting in favour of an amended Bill on third reading. When Powell referred before his Birmingham speech to sending up a rocket that would stay up, he appears to have envisaged giving another strong warning to his party leadership that they should not think they could relax after the following Tuesday's vote and adopt a more liberal attitude. If this was indeed his thinking, it would explain his apparent insensitivity to the concern that had been expressed in the Shadow Cabinet at his Walsall speech in early February. From Powell's point of view, this speech had been a great success. His outspokenness had evoked strong support in the country, and within three weeks the Government and Opposition front benches had done a *volte face* on the Kenyan Asians. Powell's Birmingham speech was designed to stir the same public response, and to ensure that the leadership did not waver from their increasingly Powellite position. Walsall had shown him that shock tactics won him publicity and public support, and a similar response to his Birmingham speech would ensure that his point was made only days before the main debate on the Race Relations Bill.

According to Powell, there was no need to circulate a draft of his speech beforehand to either Heath or Hogg. He was only doing his job: 'as a member of the Shadow Cabinet in the Black Country [and Birmingham], I was making a speech which would give the background reasons to the decision which my colleagues and I had taken' to vote against the Race Relations Bill the following week. Moreover, 'I'd been one of those who had helped to draft the reasoned amendment on which we were going to vote'. On the day before he made his speech, he had shown the text to the Conservative area agent for the West Midlands, who apparently thought that it would be useful in explaining the Opposition's vote.[81]

The charge that he should have circulated his speech stung Powell. When he next made a major speech on immigration, at Eastbourne in November 1968, he fiercely denied the allegations that he 'was somehow guilty of a breach of discipline or of disloyalty, either to my colleagues generally or to the party's spokesman on Home Affairs, Hogg, in particular, in speaking as I did. There is no substance in this charge.' He explained that,

No rule or convention forbids front-benchers to advocate or defend, even before parliamentary debate, the line which the leadership of the Party has publicly decided to take. There is none which requires them before doing so to consult or even inform their colleagues. Such speeches are continually made and indeed expected. It is, of course, different if they intend to recommend a divergent policy; but this it was not suggested I had done.

It was to the 'tone' of his speech that objection was taken. Powell accepted that 'tone' was a matter of personal taste, 'and a leader is entitled to be guided by his own taste in the choice of his colleagues'. And, he concluded,

> What is matter of fact and not of opinion, is that neither in making the speech, nor in any of the circumstances attendant upon it, did I neglect or break any of the rules or conventions which govern honourable behaviour between colleagues.[82]

Powell's interpretation of those 'rules or conventions' as they applied to his Birmingham speech differs from that of his former colleagues. 'I felt that as Chief Whip,' Whitelaw later made clear, Powell 'should have told me about it in advance, particularly as I had always had good and courteous relations with him.' Whitelaw 'was totally outraged' when he discovered that Powell had told neither Heath nor Hogg, and wrote in his memoirs: 'Frankly, I knew than that I could never bring myself fully to trust him again.' Hogg later observed that 'even in Shadow Cabinets', he had regarded it as his 'duty' to circulate his public speeches through Central Office and, in case he spoke on a subject within the responsibilities of another colleague, to make sure that what he planned to say was known in advance. 'No one had ever told me about this, but I had always regarded it as an obvious corollary of the essential collegiality of Cabinet and Shadow Cabinet decisions.'[83]

Moreover, Powell's colleagues regarded his speech as being, in Hailsham's words, 'plainly inconsistent with the decision' that had been taken at the previous meeting of the Shadow Cabinet. In terms of the specific proposals in his speech, Powell had not gone beyond party policy. But the thrust and tenor of the speech was highly provocative, and it was for its 'racialist' tone that he was sacked. Powell, however, saw another reason for Heath's dismissing him from the Shadow Cabinet. 'He was frightened out of his wits', not by what Powell had said, but 'by the outcry. I had said the same thing over and over again in previous speeches. But he was alarmed by the outcry, and sensing danger, ran for cover.' Powell has also claimed that it is impossible for any politician to predict the impact of a speech, and many politicians have had the experience of making the same speech many times before anyone takes notice.[84]

But Powell had not 'said the same thing over and over again in previous speeches' on immigration and race that he said at Birmingham. This latter speech was more explicit in its language, and he had not previously quoted such extreme comments about the situation in his constituency. In Powell's view, however, people were frightened, and it is a legitimate activity of an MP to express the fears and anxieties of those whom he represents. But an MP also has an obvious duty not to repeat any stories, or views, simply because they have been expressed by his constituents, or purport to represent what is happening in his or her constituency, without any regard to their effect on everybody whom he or she represents.[85]

The most shocking story that Powell quoted in his speech was the allegation by a correspondent who wrote to him from Northumberland that an elderly widow, the only white person left in her street in Wolverhampton, had had excrement pushed through her letter-box and had suffered terrible abuse by immigrants and their children. The *Express and Star*, a reputable regional newspaper, staffed by professional journalists who knew the town well, made every attempt to identify the woman concerned, examining the electoral register to determine in which street she might live and conducting exhaustive enquiries. They could not find her. Neither did the journalists and researchers who descended on the town from the national media.[86]

During this period, the *Express and Star* used to receive letters that reflected an extremely strong anti-immigrant mythology, but that were obviously orchestrated because of their similar phraseology and line of argument – the perpetrators were based in several working men's clubs in the area, although the letters obviously carried other addresses. This led some journalists who investigated the story of the elderly white widow to surmise that it might have emanated originally from such a source and subsequently been relayed to Powell, either mischievously, or in good faith, by his Northumberland correspondent. A large number of racialist anecdotes were in circulation, as Ann Dummett, a community relations worker in Oxford, noted. She had been told a similar anecdote – the old lady was said to live in London, but otherwise 'almost every circumstantial detail was the same'.[87]

Powell was pressed about his repeating the story in his speech during an electrifying television confrontation with Sir David Frost in January 1969. When Frost suggested to Powell that he had a duty to put more than quotation marks round it, and to check the story to make sure that it was true, Powell replied that he had 'verified the source from which I had that information', and added that he had not 'the slightest doubt that it is true as it is typical'. As Frost pointed out, verifying the source was a different matter to checking the story, and neither was it correct to suggest that the incident was 'typical'. 'But do you really disbelieve', Powell retorted,

> that in the areas where the immigrant population is taking over – and I use that word quite neutrally – one street, one area, after another, do you doubt that over and over and over again, experiences like these are suffered by women exactly like that person? If you don't, then go and ask the police. Go and make enquiries. You don't even need to do that. Read the Milner Holland Report of – what? four or five years ago – on housing in London,

and you will find case after case similar, similar in its details, similar even in the excreta, to the one which I quoted, listed in that official report.

As Sir David relates in his memoirs, he subsequently checked the 1965 Milner Holland Report (the Report of the Committee on Housing in Greater London), and found that the report emphasized that 'bad behaviour was not a racial matter'. Moreover, Frost found that the report contained 47 cases of bad behaviour, 'and only six described bad behaviour by coloured immigrants towards white residents. Six out of 47. It was another documented example of Powell being "creative" with the facts.'[88]

Not surprisingly, Powell's repeating in his speech the story of the white widow and the claim that immigrants would have the 'whiphand' prompted accusations not only that the tone of his speech had been 'racialist', as Heath had said, but that Powell was himself a racialist. When he was asked whether he was a racialist in an interview for the *Birmingham Post* a fortnight after his speech in the city, he replied,

What I would take racialist to mean is a person who believes in the inherent inferiority of one race of mankind to another, and who acts and speaks in that belief. So the answer to the question of whether I am a racialist is 'No' – unless, perhaps, in reverse. I regard many of the peoples in India as being superior in many respects – intellectually for example, and in other respects – to Europeans. Perhaps that is over-correcting.

Some twenty years later, Nick Ross suggested to Powell that a test used by psychologists when measuring prejudice was to ask people whether they would be happy to marry somebody who was black, or would they have been happy for their daughter to marry somebody who was black. Powell replied that he had said 'that if there were inter-marriage on a large scale, the dangers which I foresaw and foresee would be very much less'. He also claimed that

so far as I can judge from the behaviour towards me of what are now called black people, who frequently meet me in public, there is not only no resentment but there is far reaching comprehension, because nothing is commoner than for them to come up to me and say, 'You're Mr Powell ... May I shake your hand, it's an honour to meet you. Well, thank you for what you're doing.'

Close friends relate that he always took immense pleasure in dining at Indian restaurants, and would invariably talk happily with staff in their own tongue. Of course, a person can get on with people of different races while harbouring racialist attitudes, but Powell is not a racialist in the crude sense of the term.[89]

Powell has denied that his conviction that the prospective size and distribution of the non-white, ethnic population cannot 'prove otherwise than destructive of this nation' was racialist. 'The basis of my conviction is neither genetic or eugenic', he claimed: 'it is not racial because I can never discover what "race" means and I have never arranged my fellow men on a scale of merit according to their origins.' But the line between Powell's nationalism and what is generally regarded as racialism at times seems extremely fine. In 1995, he was challenged by Michael Cockerell, who suggested that the language which he had quoted in his Birmingham speech was inflammatory and could be used by people who were racialists against non-whites. Powell has tended to rebut any such suggestion by arguing that his speech did not give racialists any ammunition that they did not already possess, or that if he had not expressed the sentiments that he had, people might have turned to extremist organizations – arguments which miss the point that no other senior, front bench politician had previously dignified anti-immigrant comments by repeating them from a public platform. But in reply to Cockerell's query, Powell retorted, 'What's wrong with racism? Racism is the basis of a nationality.' He continued by elaborating that, 'nations are, upon the whole, united by identity with one another, the self-identification of our citizens, and that's normally due to similarities which are regarded as racial differences.'[90]

The qualifying phrase in Powell's latter comment has to be noted: 'similarities which are regarded as racial differences'. For him, it is a matter of numbers and a question of national identity. He accepted that an individual, 'however remote and strange his background and origins', could choose and achieve the self-identification which is the touchstone of belonging to a nation, but suggested that this same process was somehow impossible when millions of people were involved. His projections of the future size of the non-white population fuelled further controversy. Powell repeated the Registrar General's estimate of 3.5 million Commonwealth immigrants and their descendants by 1985, although the Government had revised this downwards several months before he spoke to 2.5 million. Powell extrapolated his own forecast for the immigrant and immigrant-descended population of between five and seven million by 2000, 'approximately one tenth of the whole population'. By 1996, the official figures were over three million non-whites, or more than one twentieth of the total population.[91]

In Powell's view, differences of tradition and culture are so strong between people of different nationalities, that when large numbers of immigrants (whether Pakistani or West Indian, German or Russian) live together in communities where such differences are perpetuated, they can never identify themselves as being members of the host nation or be regarded as being such by the host nation. Powell suggested in November 1968 that the problems that would be caused by the introduction of a large bloc of Germans or Russians into a few areas of Britain 'would be as serious – and in some respects more serious – than could follow from the introduction of a similar number of West Indians or Pakistanis'.[92]

The nationality that a person feels 'is the nation that he'll fight for, or play cricket for'. Yet on this rough and ready test, many of the first West Indians who settled in Britain in the late 1940s and early 1950s were unequivocally

British – as members of the West Indian Ex-servicemen's and Ex-service-women's Association in Clapham testify. They might fail Lord Tebbit's trivial 'cricket test', but many of them are former members of Britain's armed services who fought for Britain in the Second World War, briefly went back to Jamaica, and when they subsequently returned regarded themselves not as immigrants, but as British. Yet even when confronted by Paul Boateng's statement of his Britishness, Powell maintained that, 'it's not impossible but it's difficult', for a non-white person to be British.[93]

Powell's Birmingham speech was also more explosive than anything that he had previously said because of his lurid warning of violence. He dispelled any notion that his reference to 'the River Tiber foaming with much blood' was purely metaphorical later in 1968 when he told listeners to BBC Radio's *Any Questions* that, 'if there is a large and increasing concentration of unassimilated immigrants in certain areas in the country, tolerance will break down and there will be violence, that is the danger which I foresee, unless we take steps to ensure that the numbers do not increase, as is foreseeable, and that the concentration does not continue.' Moreover, his vision of Britain's future came to envisage the threat not merely of racial violence – a problem that is serious enough – but of civil war and the destruction of the British nation. When asked in 1987 whether he had any concern for, or understanding of, the fears of non-whites as well as those of whites, he replied: 'There is a concern for a country which is threatened with civil war,' and asserted that 'we are moving towards it as we see the consequences of the application of our democratic system to the population which is changing in the way it is bound to change, given its age structure.'[94]

Powell could not say exactly how, or when, such a civil war would start, but believed that such a conflict would be 'not wholly, but essentially' between non-whites and whites. When Nick Ross pressed him on this threat in the 1987 Channel 4 profile, Powell was characteristically delphic:

> *Powell*: The people who think they are the people of this country will be fighting for their country.
> *Ross*: I'm not sure that I understand that. Surely many black people regard themselves as genuinely British.
> *Powell*: People fight for power, people fight for domination.
> *Ross*: And this will be a battle for domination?
> *Powell*: And they try to resist it.
> *Ross*: What do you think the outcome will be?
> *Powell*: Appalling.

In Powell's view, the only means of averting this fantastic threat was by preventing large concentrations of immigrants and their descendants becoming established. This meant, as he argued at Birmingham, limiting the size of the non-white population by 'stopping, or virtually stopping further inflow, and by promoting the maximum outflow' – policies that were, as he put it, 'part of the official policy of the Conservative Party'. Powell put great emphasis on repatriation, but as the journalist and traditionalist Tory writer, T.E Utley, could see in 1968, such an approach was deeply flawed. 'Suppose they decline to go home,' Utley queried of those immigrants who had entered with work vouchers, 'are they to be deported? Or are they to be allowed to remain only on condition that they accept continued separation from their families?' As Utley noted, Powell's words at Birmingham suggested the latter, 'but a certain amount of ambiguity is allowed to remain'.[95]

In putting so much emphasis on voluntary repatriation, Powell was proposing a solution that, if it had ever been pursued with the vigour that he demanded, was likely to exacerbate race relations. Moreover, it was extremely unlikely to produce the dramatic impact on the size of the non-white population that he envisaged. A more realistic approach – and the one that was adopted to varying degrees by both main parties – was to control the level of immigration while seeking to improve race relations. But Powell regarded race relations legislation not as part of the remedy, but as part of the problem. Even as relatively a modest piece of legislation as the 1965 Race Relations Act, that had been introduced by the Labour Government but that reflected Tory policy at the time, was seen as 'a fatal error'. Powell deplored 'the fact that the law of this country has been not merely able but obliged to see colour'. He thought it would exacerbate racial tensions, not calm them. In attacking Labour's 1968 Race Relations Bill – the immediate trigger of his Birmingham speech – he assumed that anti-discrimination laws automatically created 'a privileged or special class'. But not only was this assertion an absurd caricature of anti-discrimination legislation, he omitted to point out that the Bill's purpose was to prevent racial discrimination in housing and jobs. Yet it was such discrimination that was helping to create the concentrations of non-whites in certain areas that he chillingly depicted as such a dire threat.[96]

Perhaps the most revealing insight into Powell's alarmist talk of a nation 'busily heaping up its own funeral pyre' is that it can be traced to his abandonment, in 1954, of the imperialism that had first brought him into politics, and its replacement by a romantic, English nationalism. In that year's lecture to the Conservative Political Centre summer school, he had argued that the collapse of the British Empire had been inevitable all along (although he had not spotted it until then), because of the incompatibility of parliamentary government with imperial rule. Moreover, the Empire's demise had been hastened, he claimed, by the existence of colonies, 'with large populations unconnected in origin with the United Kingdom and potentially antipathetic to it by tradition or colour'.[97]

To Powell's mind, large-scale immigration from Britain's former non-European colonies posed a similarly mortal threat to parliamentary politics and, as a result, to the British nation. He argued that the basis of his opposition to large-scale immigration was 'political':

It is the belief that self-identification of each part with the whole is the one essential pre-condition of being a parliamentary nation, and that the massive shift in the composition of the population of the inner metropolis and of major towns and cities of England will produce, not fortuitously or avoidably, but by the sheer inevitabilities of human nature in society, ever increasing and more dangerous alienation.

His reasoning was that parliamentary democracy works when people are prepared to accept being overruled by other people, but they only accept being overruled by others whom they regard as being the same as themselves – Labour supporters in Yorkshire are prepared to accept a Conservative Government, because they regard non-Labour voters as essentially the same as themselves and hope that enough of them will change their minds at the next election to elect Labour. But because of the concentration of large numbers of non-white immigrants and their descendants in certain towns and cities, they were likely to remain separate from the body politic and elect their own representatives. If, as a result, he explained in 1987,

we are to have a parliament of which the members are elected on the basis of unchangeable characteristics, it will be an entirely different parliament from a parliament elected on the basis that people can change their minds and change their party and change their allegiance, on which depends our acceptance of the parliamentary system. Once you apply the parliamentary system to an electorate which is divided by unchangeable characteristics, visible and unchangeable characteristics, then you'll destroy the system.

Powell saw this threat arising if neither of the main parties could command an overall majority in the Commons, while a minority group of racially elected MPs, held the balance of power.[98]

Yet in making his dire predictions, Powell assumed that large numbers of non-whites would not see themselves as, or be accepted as, British, and would not vote for, or be represented by, the existing parties. In addition, he assumed that sufficient numbers of such alienated non-whites would rally behind the same candidate in their constituencies – though many are from different communities and diverse backgrounds. He also had to assume that, if elected, such racially elected MPs would form a distinctive bloc. Yet even if all these eventualities were to come about, any group that represented a small minority of the total population would have to compromise in order to exercise influence. It might amount to a new development in British politics, but it does not suggest the demise of either parliamentary government or the British nation.

Indeed, to hear Powell talk about immigration or to read his speeches on the subject, one could be forgiven for imagining that the entry of several million immigrants into the country had been a peculiarly British phenomenon, explicable in terms of Britain's supposedly unique folly in enacting the 1948 British Nationality Act and seeking to perpetuate the illusion of Empire through the creation of the Commonwealth. These events have been central to Powell's politics, and they feature prominently in his nationalistic mythology about British politics, but they overlook the entry of millions of immigrants into other European countries during the same period. By the late 1980s West Germany had a foreign population of 4.5 million (7.3 per cent of the total population), France 3.7 million (6.8 per cent), and the Netherlands 0.6 million (4.2 per cent). The cause was the same throughout western Europe – a huge demand for labour, generated by rapid economic growth. This European-wide phenomenon points to the greatest irony of all in Powell's views on immigration. For Powell was the leading exponent of market forces and free trade, and yet in respect of the free movement of labour he advocated the strictest possible state control.[99]

The best defence that can be mounted for Powell's speech is that it provided a release for the resentment that had built up as a result of immigration, and that had been festering beneath the surface until he spoke out. The extraordinary eruption of public support for him and what he said cannot be gainsaid. The 1950s and 1960s had brought tremendous changes in some urban working-class and lower-middle-class communities, with virtually no attempt by politicians to consult those who were affected, or to explain what was happening. The immigration of non-whites, was, for many people, an all too obvious touchstone of all the changes about which they felt neglected and impotent. But Powell's speech was more likely to reinforce than release such feelings.

Above all, Powell's speech revealed a serious lack of judgement. In personal terms, it had led to his being sacked from the Shadow Cabinet – an outcome that he had not intended. More seriously, as a leading figure of a major party who was highly regarded for his intellect and integrity, he had bestowed respectability on the most extreme language and anti-immigrant sentiments. In doing so, he provoked an enormous demonstration of public support, but at the price of losing the means to influence immigration policy at ministerial level. As he knew, without party in Britain, it is impossible to achieve office; and without office it is impossible to achieve anything practical. At that stage, however, he had not given up all hope that he might yet, in certain circumstances, return to the centre-stage. But any hope of his restoration to the front bench depended on the outcome of the next election. A victory for Heath, as looked highly probable in 1968, would seal Powell's fate.

16

Shaking the Tree

In short, Mr Powell is seen by his lieutenants as the latter-day Joe Chamberlain in the Tory Party, the boy from 'Brum' who, though he is unlikely ever to lead his party, will change its orientation and nature by driving it into a Gaullist radicalism rather than on to the right.
David Wood, *The Times*, 15 July 1968.

Cast as Radical Joe, the boy from 'Brum'

'From that moment onwards', Powell said of his April 1968 sacking from the Conservative Shadow Cabinet,

> it was virtually certain that I would not occupy a government office. Now, a politician, and a politician in full possession of his political effectiveness, in full command of his constituency base, is a different person when, in speaking and acting, he is conscious that he is not dicing with ministerial office. This, after all, is the principal inhibition under which most politicians in and out of office labour – the effect of what they say then upon their possible future in terms of office. After 1968, that potentiality, I soon recognized, did not exist.

Powell made this comment in 1987, and it is no doubt an accurate reflection of his memory. But in the light of what we now know, it is easy to forget that in 1968 his future was highly uncertain, at least till the next general election, that might not be called until early 1971. In the meantime, it seemed that Powell and 'Powellism' might yet exert enormous influence on the Conservative Party and perhaps more generally, since there was a widespread feeling that the main parties had failed to remedy Britain's economic problems and were not satisfying their supporters.[1]

Powell had been rocketed to national prominence by his 'River Tiber' speech, and his sacking had transformed him into the focus of opposition in the Conservative Party to Heath's leadership, especially among party activists and lower-middle and working-class Tory supporters. 'Mr Powell is the first

Conservative politician since Stanley Baldwin who seems to make a significant impact on the minds of the working classes,' suggested the anonymous author of a series of articles in *The Times* on 'The Crisis of the Parties'. In contrast, Heath had not appealed to Tory instincts, and had failed to publicize Tory policies effectively and to establish his authority as leader. 'Sacking Enoch was another cross for Ted to bear,' Jim Prior, one of Heath's closest aides at the time has recalled:

> Never a popular figure, [Heath] was now doubly unpopular. There was plenty of support in the constituencies for the right wing's anti-black position. The impression was created that [Heath] was not a strong man like Enoch, who knew the truth, was prepared to say it and would act upon it.

The tension between Heath and Powell was palpable. 'Ted had a very difficult, very unpleasant time with the party for some months,' Prior noted. Although the Conservatives enjoyed a commanding lead in the opinion polls of about 20 percentage points during 1968 and most of 1969, and chalked up impressive victories at by-elections and local elections, Heath constantly looked over his shoulder at Powell, while Powell could not believe that the huge Tory lead was true.[2]

Powell's dilemma of how to react after his sacking was more apparent than real, whatever implications were drawn from hypothetical computations of the next election. On the one hand, a Conservative victory might consign Powell to the back benches for the duration of a Heath Government. He was fifty-six years old in June 1968, and a Tory Government elected in early 1971 might last until 1976, by which time he would be approaching sixty-four and would have been in exile for nearly eight years. On the other hand, if Heath were to lead the Conservatives to a second election defeat he would be removed as leader and Powell would almost certainly return to the front bench. But this eventuality would also result in more than a decade of continuous Labour rule. Another highly conditional scenario sketched in *The Times* envisaged the Tories winning by an overwhelming majority because Powell had ensured that immigration was an issue, and 'those who vote for Powell must vote Conservative'. In these circumstances, the new intake of Tory MPs, many of whom would never have expected to be elected, would feel indebted to Powell. Whereas the Tory left would be increasingly hard-pressed in the new parliament, Powell's influence would grow.[3]

Powell was bound to keep his hand in the game. He had to continue his crusade to shift the Conservatives, and the country, towards his radical Toryism, or 'Powellism'. At the same time, however, the majority of Conservatives had no wish for another leadership struggle, and in the event of such a contest, there was not even a remote possibility that Powell would be chosen. He had to avoid any direct, personal challenge to Heath, although only a fortnight after his sacking he told the *Birmingham Post* that 'there is no politician who is not ambitious, it is the definition of the animal'. Later in May, he was more circumspect when he replied to a question about Heath's leadership that 'in all human probability' Heath would be the next prime minister. 'I will try to help him get there so far as it rests with me and I shall support him before he gets there and afterwards.'[4]

Powell increasingly felt that the country was approaching a psychological turning-point. He sensed that people wanted to break out of a whole set of problems and were coming round to the idea of radical change, as opposed merely to choosing which of the parties would run the existing system better. On this assessment, differentiating the Conservative Party's position more clearly from the one taken by Labour and moving away from the conventional notion of the centre-ground of politics, would be advantageous to the Tories. Although Heath wanted large-scale change, Powell did not believe that he shared his own sense that although an historical era had closed, it was still hanging over the country and people had not escaped from it. Heath thought administratively and not historically: he thought about 'policies' in the plural, and not about 'policy' in the sense of a strategy. Powell thought his Birmingham speech was relevant in this context. He felt that it had suddenly crystallized feelings of national identity and hope, and sensed that people wanted this same message to be brought to other issues.[5]

Among those who wanted Powell to extend his message in other directions were the small band of Powellites in the Commons. Typically, they abhorred the label 'right' and preferred 'radical'. The 'essence of Powellism', according to one such Powellite was encapsulated by the political journalist, David Wood, in July 1968, as being 'its frankly Gaullist emphasis on national independence and its marking out of political ground in which a realistic patriotism can flourish again'. Powell, however, differed from some on the Tory right who saw Europe as a substitute for Empire. 'For his back bench converts, Mr Powell offers, as Mr Heath and his colleagues have not yet succeeded in offering, a Tory ideology spanning modern politics to replace the chaos of expediencies in which Mr Macmillan left the Tory Party.' He allowed his followers 'a sense of escaping from the squirrel cage of economics', and gave them 'a faith as well as statistics'. In the comment that is quoted at the head of this chapter, Wood concluded that Powell's followers saw him as a latter-day Joe Chamberlain, who might never become the leader but who had the cross-party appeal to refashion the modern Tory Party and reshape British politics.[6]

The comparison with Chamberlain, however, confirmed the worst fears of Powell's enemies. The nineteenth-century Birmingham political boss had split the Liberals over Ireland in 1886 and denied his old party power for almost twenty years, and had then split the Tories over tariff reform in the early 1900s, with equally disastrous results. In modern times, the most divisive issue for both major parties has been Britain's relations with Europe. Among the Shadow Cabinet, the former Tory leader and Shadow Foreign Secretary, Sir Alec Douglas-Home, was prescient about Powell's likely strategy. 'Within weeks of Enoch's sacking,' Prior has recalled, 'Alec Home was betting that it would not be long, probably only a matter of months, before Enoch came out against British entry into the Common Market.'[7]

During the summer of 1968, Powell was kept in the public eye by the demonstrations that accompanied him, or were threatened, rather than because of the content of his speeches. In May, at Chippenham, he reiterated his monetarist view of inflation. In June, on Waterloo Day, at Weybridge, he issued a Gaullist-style call for greater national self-confidence – and even stressed the need to recognize Britain's shared interests with France. Later on the same day, any idea that he might try to woo support on the traditional right of the party was discounted at the weekly meeting of the Tory back bench Foreign Affairs committee, when he not only declared that Britain should not sign a proposed nuclear non-proliferation treaty, but also advertised his anti-nuclear views. Only two months after having served as Tory Defence spokesman, Powell roundly declared that the nuclear guarantee was absurd, since no country was going to commit suicide in its own defence, still less in defence of other countries. The following week, his anti-imperialism was again on show at the same committee. During a discussion on Portugal's remaining African colonies, he queried whether a new regime in Lisbon would continue to impoverish a potentially rich country by continuing to pour out resources in retaining a so-called empire.[8]

In July, he was unrepentant about his Birmingham speech on ITV's *This Week* programme, but he made no contribution to the debate on the third reading of the Race Relations Bill. In the vote, however, when it was no longer procedurally possible for the Tories to disguise their disunity by tabling a reasoned amendment, he was among 45 Tories who forced a division and voted against, instead of accepting the leadership's decision to abstain. Amidst the controversy that now surrounded Powell wherever he went, his academic, and massive, history of *The House of Lords in the Middle Ages*, co-authored with Keith Wallis, was finally published, some twenty years after he had first begun working on it.[9]

But the events of the summer were mere skirmishing. October's Conservative conference at Blackpool would offer the first real test since the Birmingham speech of Heath's leadership and of Powell's standing in the party. A month beforehand, Heath implicitly acknowledged the popularity of Powell's demand for tougher curbs on immigration by stealing his clothes. On 2 September in York, Heath announced that a Conservative Government would remove the remaining privileges of would-be Commonwealth immigrants who wanted to enter Britain by classifying them all as aliens – a policy that Powell had advocated before the first controls were introduced on Commonwealth immigration in 1962. In addition, there would be further curbs on the right of dependants to join heads of family already in Britain. Heath also confirmed that the Conservatives would offer assisted repatriation to those who wanted it.[10]

Whereas it was in Heath's interest to try and dish Powell on immigration and exploit the popular support that Powell had attracted for the Conservatives, it was in Powell's interest to exploit the opportunity that his national standing had brought him to widen support for his other views. Opinion poll evidence in the summer of 1968 found that Powell's huge popularity in the summer had been single-issue based. Although voters had a general sense after his Birmingham speech that Powell was on the right of the Tory Party, he received little support for his economic views. Indeed, it seemed possible that many of his supporters did not know of his views on issues besides immigration. During September, Powell began sketching out what amounted to an alternative programme to the policies being offered by either the Conservative or the Labour parties – on industrial policy, for example, he went much further than the cautious party line in calling for radical denationalization, including even the loss-making publicly-owned industries.[11]

Significantly, as the main British parties struggled to come to terms with the rise of nationalism in Scotland and Wales, and the insistent demand for civil rights in Northern Ireland, Powell addressed the theme of 'national identity'. The idea of increased autonomy for the Scots and the Welsh was attracting support on the Government and Opposition front benches, but in a speech at Prestatyn, Powell dismissed any such proposal as being incompatible with the United Kingdom's existence as a single nation – either Scotland and Wales should become independent, or they should remain members on the same conditions as other regions. But the most intriguing aspect of his absolutist opposition to devolution was his rejection of Ulster's Stormont Parliament as proof that autonomy need not lead automatically to independence. Indeed, Ulster self-government had resulted from Ulster Unionism. Ulster, he argued, had 'accepted only with reluctance' the autonomy that emerged during 'the tangled process' of Irish independence in the early 1920s, and ever since then, 'the motivation of Ulster has remained not nationalist, not separatist, but the opposite'. From the early 1970s, Powell was to take a closer interest in Northern Ireland's position within the United Kingdom.[12]

At the 1968 Labour Party conference, Wilson sought to exploit Powell's image as an extremist by speaking as if Powell, and not Heath, were the Tory leader, and denigrating Powellism as a virus that had infected the Conservative Party at every level of its organization. How to handle Powell was a major headache for the Tory leadership, as Macleod, his former close colleague and the then Shadow Chancellor, admitted by acknowledging the 'hope that Mr Powell will go away, but he will not'. In a speech shortly before the Tory conference, that criticized Powell's 'ivory tower' economics, Macleod indicated the leadership's plan to head off any Powellite challenge by portraying Powell as an extremist and his nostrums as impractical. It was the first attack by a senior front-bencher on Powell on any issue other than his views on race since the Birmingham speech. In a further, thinly veiled attack on Powell on the eve of the conference, Macleod warned that 'this is the year of the hothead and the demagogue and the pedlar of panaceas'. Nineteen sixty-eight had already brought the assassinations of Martin Luther King and Robert Kennedy, and also the demagoguery of Governor Wallace, in the United States – in an apparently well-informed comment, *The Times* explained that 'Mr Macleod no doubt included Mr Enoch Powell among the pedlars of panaceas'. Likewise, Maudling warned against pushing Tory policies 'deliberately to extremes that would in practice be unrealistic'.[13]

Powell had to play his hand carefully. 'One of the problems has been to disentangle the arguments about policy from the implied personal challenge to Mr Heath', observed the political commentator, Ian Trethowan. 'Mr Powell has insisted that he has meant no such challenge, but it was a bit ingenuous to imagine that his activities would not be so interpreted.' By requesting to speak in the debate on immigration and race relations at the October conference, Powell chose an issue on which he could have little quarrel with Tory policy after Heath's York speech. He also avoided testing his support on other issues where his reception was likely to be less tumultuous. Yet his long-awaited confrontation with the Tory leadership provided the dramatic highlight of the conference.[14]

'Delighted shivers rippled round the hall as Mr Powell came down like a wolf on the fold from his retreat high in one of the conference galleries,' reported *The Times*. His arrival at the microphone was greeted with prolonged booing, stamping, cheering and clapping. 'We deceive ourselves if we imagine, whatever steps are taken to limit future immigration,' he told a packed hall, 'that this country will still not be facing a prospect which is unacceptable.' Assisted repatriation was the answer, and to those who said that this was impossible, he replied, 'Whatever the true interests of our country call for is always possible.' His five-minute speech was punctuated by loud applause and set the conference alight. As he returned to his place, he received cheering and stamping, while many activists gave him a standing ovation. But Hogg, who replied to the debate, had the measure of Powell. Addressing him directly at the end of his speech, Hogg identified the central flaw in Powell's approach: while delivering apocalyptic warnings on the impact of a sizeable non-white population in the future, his suggested remedy of repatriation was unlikely to make a significant difference. Hogg concluded by referring to his and Powell's common education in classics, and reminded Powell of the Greek dictum, 'Meden Agan' – 'do not become an extremist. Moderation in all things'. Hogg's speech angered Powell's wife, Pam, who can be seen in the television recording expressing her fury to her husband. Hogg won a standing ovation from three-quarters of his audience for his impassioned plea for moderation. Although the conference had come close to tearing itself apart and Hogg had not landed a knock-out punch, he had won on points and Heath emerged from the conference in a stronger position to rebuff any Powellite challenge.[15]

Powell, however, contrived to steal some of the headlines from Heath's success at Blackpool by unveiling his radical, alternative budget when he addressed a political rally in neighbouring Morecambe, the evening after his confrontation with Hogg. His plan to halve the standard rate of income tax from 8s/3d (41.5p in present money) in the pound to 4s/3d (21.5p), and to abolish capital gains tax and selective employment tax, without taking a penny from defence or the social services, would be funded by abolishing all investment grants, all assistance to development areas, all grants and subsidies to farmers, all overseas aid, as well as all housing subsidies, and also by eliminating losses in the nationalized industries (though the mines and railways were left aside) and denationalizing (or privatizing) the profit-makers. But not even Thatcher in her heyday, despite her commitment to cutting government spending, lowering taxes and (from 1983) wholesale privatization, was able to deliver Powell's budget (the standard rate was already down to 33p when she entered Number 10). Although by the mid-1990s the standard rate of income tax had been reduced to a level close to the one that Powell suggested and higher rates had been slashed, this achievement had taken the Thatcher and Major Governments over fifteen years and was only done by massively increasing taxes on spending.[16]

Powell's alternative budget reinforced the leadership's message that he was a useful goad but a dangerous guide. As the *Spectator* had observed on the day of his Morecambe speech, Powell's 'principal techniques are the two standbys of publicists throughout the ages: exaggeration and over-simplification'. But in its front-page editorial entitled, 'The trouble with Enoch', the *Spectator*, that was then edited by Nigel (later Lord) Lawson, the future Conservative Chancellor, argued that the Conservative Party needed to move in the direction of Powell's English nationalism and free market economics. In his Birmingham speech, Powell's ploys as a publicist had been carried to 'regrettable lengths', as they had in his calls for rejection of any form of regional policy and total denationalization, and in his demolition of nuclear deterrence (Powell argued this latter case in the same edition). It was also accepted that the party hierarchy had 'found him an almost impossible person to work with', and his criticisms of colleagues did not inspire affection.

Above all, the *Spectator* argued, the Tory leadership distrusted Powell, 'because they believe he has no interest in the Conservative Party winning the next election'. Certainly, Powell was the 'only prominent Tory who actively enjoys opposition', and he was 'more concerned with where the Conservative Party stands than with who wins the next election'. But according to the paper, it did not follow that 'he is attempting to emulate Disraeli, who effectively wrested the Tory leadership from Peel only by splitting the Conservative Party so badly that it spent eighteen of the next twenty-two years in the wilderness'. The Tories needed to differentiate their policies from those of Labour, and despite its caveats about Powell, the *Spectator* argued that 'the directions in which he is trying to get policy to move are, on the whole, the right ones. To reject Powellism in every shape and form, to react against whatever Mr Powell happens to put forward, would be as foolish as to accept it lock, stock and denationalized barrel.' Over the next eighteen months, Heath was to differentiate Conservative policy more clearly, but any faint prospect of a rapprochement with Powell rapidly receded. To friend and foe alike, Powell increasingly appeared to be more of a Chamberlain than a Disraeli.[17]

From pariah to parliamentary champion

Powell's opposition to immigration remained the basis of his national appeal, and at Eastbourne on 16 November 1968, just over a month after his confrontation with Hogg, he delivered his most strident speech yet on the subject. In addition to defending his actions over his Birmingham speech, he unashamedly took on the role of tribune of the people by warning of a 'deep and dangerous gulf' that he claimed was developing in Britain between

> the overwhelming majority of people throughout the country on the one side and, on the other side a tiny minority, with almost a monopoly hold upon the channels of communication, who seem determined not to know the facts and not to face the realities and who will resort to any device or extremity to blind both themselves and others.

Powell once again quoted from a letter that he had received alleging intimidatory behaviour by immigrants, but although on this occasion he identified his correspondent (a general practitioner), an allegation that an 84-year-old white woman had been harassed by her immigrant landlord failed to satisfy the press. Even the *News of the World*, a supporter of Powell's politics, reacted with the headline, 'THIS WON'T DO ENOCH!' The West Indian family concerned denied the charge, and the *People* reported that the old lady's daughter said that they had helped her mother.[18]

Powell predicted a minimum immigrant population of 4.5 million by the year 2000, or six per cent of the total population, and claimed that this would create several Washington DCs in Britain. 'The West Indian or Asian does not, by being born in England, become an Englishman,' he declared. 'In law he becomes a United Kingdom citizen by birth; in fact he is a West Indian or an Asian still.' To avert the 'impending disaster', he renewed his demand for 'large-scale voluntary, but organized, financed and subsidized repatriation', and suggested that a special Ministry of Repatriation should be set up. And in language redolent of far right publications, Powell warned against 'reproducing in "England's green and pleasant land" the haunting tragedy of the United States'.[19]

If anything, the reaction of the press, his fellow politicians and religious figures showed even more outrage than after Birmingham. Heath condemned the speech as 'character assassination of one racial group', and added: 'that way lies tyranny'. But the charge against Powell that seemed to affect him most deeply emanated from the Church, and suggested that his views on immigration were implicitly condemned in the reference in Chapter 25 of St Matthew's Gospel concerning the duty to welcome strangers. Over a year later, Powell's apparent attack on the idea of giving extra Government help to areas of high immigration provoked Heath, who is also a religious man, into denouncing it as 'an example of man's inhumanity to man, which is absolutely intolerable in a Christian society'. This in turn angered Powell, who felt that

Heath had misrepresented him. Heath, however, insisted that he had carefully read Powell's speech. An attempt by Whitelaw to mediate between the two men foundered. Shortly after his Eastbourne speech, Powell participated in a BBC radio dialogue on 'Christianity and Immigration', in which he rejected the Archbishop of Canterbury's criticism that his views were a 'counsel of despair', and dismissed the notion that an immigration policy could be deduced from the commands and truths of Christianity, that were 'unfulfillable to men in this world'. More dialogues with churchmen and others followed over the coming months, including a notable encounter with Trevor Huddleston, the then Bishop of Stepney, after he had condemned Powell's comments on immigration in Wolverhampton in June 1969 as 'evil'. Huddleston was plainly exasperated by Powell's idiosyncratic interpretation of Christianity and his refusal to accept that it had any relevance for public policy. Powell was later to apply his technique as a textual critic in order to establish the precise meaning of the Gospel and this was eventually to result in the publication of his interpretation of the St Matthew gospel – a version that was to provoke renewed controversy.[20]

In the secular world, the impact of Powell's campaign on immigration policy was further demonstrated in January 1969, when Heath journeyed to Walsall, where, almost a year earlier, Powell had first boosted the emotive content in his speeches on immigration. As Powell sat grim-faced with other Midland Tory MPs on the platform, he heard Heath reaffirm the commitment to equality of treatment for those immigrants already in the country. But Heath also demanded that the Labour Government should introduce tough new controls by August that year. Reiterating that a Tory Government would treat Commonwealth immigrants like aliens, he declared that they 'will only be allowed in for a specific job in a specific place for a specific time'. Heath's speech was greeted enthusiastically by local Tories, one of whom asked to thunderous applause, 'May I say how delighted we are that Mr Heath appears to have adopted many of the views expressed by Mr Enoch Powell?'[21]

The dramatic political effect of Powell's campaign was borne out by the Conservative Party's private polling in early 1969. The party's survey of issues circulated to Heath and his inner group of senior Shadow Ministers and advisers in the spring, showed that by early 1969, 'controlling immigration' emerged not only as the fourth 'most important issue facing the country', but also, more significantly, that it was mentioned by a larger proportion (41 per cent) of people than any other issue when they were asked on which issues they saw much difference between the parties – 'keeping taxation down' was the only other topic on which more than a third of people saw much of a difference. Moreover, 'controlling immigration' was rated as the third most important factor in influencing people to vote Conservative, and was only exceeded in importance by 'keeping the cost of living down' and 'keeping taxation down.' Yet when the last survey had been conducted in February 1968, the pollsters had not even bothered to ask people for their views on immigration.[22]

There had been a postcript, however, to the furore over Powell's Eastbourne speech that demonstrated, and further deepened, the gulf between Powell and the leadership. Heath's Party Chairman, Anthony (later Lord) Barber, had been stung by criticism that Central Office had distributed copies of the Eastbourne speech – party surveillance of speeches by back-benchers had been more a theory than a practice, and many speeches had been issued that were not in accord with party policy. After Eastbourne, however, Barber was anxious to avoid any further accusations of acting as Powell's handmaiden. Three weeks later, when he saw the text of Powell's speech to his Wolverhampton constituency annual general meeting, in which Powell flatly contradicted Tory policy towards the illegal, white minority regime of Ian Smith in Southern Rhodesia, Barber judged that copies should not be distributed by Central Office.[23]

Rhodesia was an immensely sensitive issue for the Tories. Although Powell was anything but a die-hard on African majority rule, he opposed the imposition of economic sanctions on Rhodesia and, in this latest speech, argued that a negotiated settlement was impossible. 'The independence of Rhodesia is something stronger than law,' he declared. 'To recognize fact is neither shame nor dishonour.' Douglas-Home, whom Barber had consulted about Powell's speech, had sought to construct a fragile truce by proposing that a future Conservative Government would seek a negotiated settlement, and had already advised Powell against taking the line that he adopted in his speech. Barber vetoed distribution of Powell's speech on the implausible grounds that it was likely to prejudice the success of future negotiations. But Barber's over-reaction smacked of censorship and an aversion to any new ideas. Powell correctly thought that the refusal by Central Office to put out his speech helped him.[24]

In the country, Powell's high-profile stance on immigration had mass appeal, but it had led to his being reviled by many Labour and Liberal politicians and activists. Their deep antipathy towards him was to create new difficulties and tensions as Powell took up issues that cut across party lines. This problem was first highlighted only three days after Powell had delivered his controversial Eastbourne speech, when he spoke during the second reading debate on the Parliament No. 2 Bill, that fulfilled Labour's 1966 election promise to reform the House of Lords. The 'unholy alliance', as Macleod described it, between, on one side of the Commons, Powell and other traditionalists, and, on the other side, Michael Foot and other Labour rebels, who opposed the Bill, in many ways resembled the old Country party that had previously cut across Whig and Tory divisions. Powell never seemed happier than when he was playing the role of a Country Tory taking on the Court Party. Although his presence threatened to impair the effectiveness of a new-style Country coalition on this issue, his contribution to the debates on the Bill and the key role that he played in defeating it were to establish his reputation as a parliamentarian.[25]

The planned reform of the Lords had followed all-party talks. It had the hallmarks of a cosy deal between the front benches, in which the upper House would become largely the tool of party patronage – a classic Court Party approach. Indeed, Dick Crossman, the main author of the reforms, confided somewhat ruefully in his diary after the first day's debate on the Government's White Paper, that 'back-benchers have a point when they feel that we on the front bench are creating a better hole for ourselves'. The initial all-party proposals had provoked fierce debate in the Shadow Cabinet in December 1967 and January 1968. Although Powell was still a member of the Shadow Cabinet at the time, and would undoubtedly have been among those who voiced their strong concern, he is not specifically identified in the minutes as having done so. The main proposal was to create a two-tier second chamber: hereditary peers would be allowed to continue to sit in the Lords, but voting would be limited to 230 'voting peers', who would also receive a salary. These were to be divided into 105 Government peers, 80 for the main Opposition party, 15 for the other Opposition party (i.e. the Liberals), and about 30 cross-benchers with no party affiliation. The power to delay Commons legislation would be further curtailed to six months.[26]

The Commons debate on House of Lords reform was opened for the Government by Crossman, followed by Maudling for the Opposition, whose unenthusiastic backing reflected the deep misgivings felt by Tories at a measure that would remove their perennial majority in the Lords. Macleod, who was to speak first from the Tory front bench on the following day, was even more sceptical – 'he knew a dog's breakfast when he saw one', as Powell later reflected. But since the Government had a majority of about 90 and had the support of the Opposition, however lukewarm, it was widely assumed that the reform would be enacted, even if peers in the existing House of Lords were to resist. But the moment that the front bench speeches were concluded, the strength of back bench opposition became clear. Sir Dingle Foot, who had recently resigned as Labour's Solicitor-General, and elder brother of Michael, launched a scathing attack in which he argued that the reforms would produce a 'House of Lackeys'.[27]

As a senior privy counsellor, Powell spoke first from the Opposition back benches. Confessing that he found himself in 'unwonted and far-reaching concurrence' with Sir Dingle's speech, Powell began by assuming, for the sake of argument, that reform was needed. If that were the case, though he personally disagreed, the existing system could be replaced only by election or nomination. Election of a second chamber made sense in a federal constitution, but not for Britain. 'However the mode of election was rigged, we would never escape from this dilemma: how can the same electorate be represented in two ways so that the two sets of representatives can conflict and disagree with one another?' But the plan for a nominated House of Lords was flawed:

At one and the same time the proposals seek to secure a built-in government majority and also to make it possible for the upper House to disagree with this House, vote against it, throw out the Government's proposals and get away with that ... Upon that inherent dilemma this scheme is bound to perish.

Crossman's attempt to incorporate into his plan the existing independent-mindedness of the Lords by creating 30 cross-benchers was derided as a 'grand absurdity', since these nominees were to be

> appointed on the basis that they are neither fish, fowl, nor good red herring, upon the very basis that they have no strong views of principle on the way in which the country ought to be governed; upon the promise that they will fluctuate from case to case, from question to question, and not seek to decide in the light of any such general principles as bind us respectively together in this lower House.

Powell was against any substantial reform of the Lords. Accepting that it might be said that there was no case for the existing House of Lords, he argued: 'Our reply to such questions can only be: "It has long been so, and it works".'

Powell's speech had been an impressive performance, but his offering himself as an ally to the Labour abolitionists in their campaign to defeat the proposals caused immediate consternation. Powell was followed by Willie Hamilton, one of Labour's most ardent abolitionists, who admitted that he agreed with Powell in rejecting 'this consensus ragbag ... if on no other', although he chided Powell for not making more speeches on other subjects in the House rather than to audiences elsewhere – a remark that prompted Andrew Faulds to shout at Powell: 'He has not the courage. He is too much of a coward!' There was further uproar when Hamilton expressed the discomfort that many Labour rebels felt at the prospect of allying with Powell on this issue, by disclosing that some of his colleagues had hesitated to go into the lobby to vote against the Bill, 'lest it be soiled by the presence of the Right Hon. Gentleman [Enoch Powell]'. The Deputy Speaker required Hamilton to withdraw the phrase. 'I was simply stating the fact,' Hamilton commented, and added, as Powell sat opposite, 'he can make of that what he likes.'[28]

The attacks by Powell and Hamilton during the first day's debate had perturbed Crossman, who felt that their speeches were 'ribald and dangerous, with Powell fanatically proving the case that no change could be made, [and] Hamilton fanatically proving the case that the whole House of Lords must be abolished'. At the end of the second day's debate, the 'unholy alliance' of traditionalists and abolitionists secured an impressive 161 votes, but the front benches mustered 272. The odds still favoured the reform's enactment, but because major constitutional change was proposed, the committee stage was to be taken on the floor of the House. As a result, any MP who opposed the measure would be able to join the campaign against it. Moreover, Crossman was unlikely to win Tory support for a guillotine motion to curtail debate. This provided a golden opportunity for the 'unholy alliance'.[29]

A pattern was set on 12 February 1969, the first of the ten days over which the committee stage was stretched. After a series of points of order were raised, delaying the start of the committee stage for half an hour, Robert Sheldon, the Labour MP, moved an amendment to bar hereditary peers from the Lords and spent 45 minutes explaining his reasons. Powell then spoke against Sheldon's amendment, and, in the didactic manner that befitted the co-author of the recently published major study of *The House of Lords in the Middle Ages*, argued that it was wrong to describe the Lords as 'hereditary'. Instead, it was better described as being 'prescriptive', or prescribed by custom: 'the fact that the elder son succeeds arises from the convention ... of primogeniture'. In Powell's view,

> The value of that prescriptive institution is that it provides a second Chamber constituted on a principle basically distinct from that of this House, a principle which does not enable it seriously to defy the wishes of this House, but which also enables it on many questions to take a different point of view from this House. It can often be a point of view which reflects just as well and importantly what is being felt and thought in the country, and deserves to be taken into account by the legislature.[30]

This pattern was continued as the two sets of opponents tabled their own delaying or wrecking amendments, and the other side joined in the ensuing debate. The chamber presented a curious scene, as there were often only a dozen or so MPs in the Chamber, although many others were at hand whenever a vote was called. Powell would be in his place on the back bench above the gangway, surrounded by his reference books, with John Boyd-Carpenter and half a dozen or so other traditionalists. On the Government benches, Michael Foot sat on the front bench below the gangway, with Sheldon behind, surrounded by his reference books, and half a dozen or so other rebels. There were another couple on each front bench. Little liaison was needed between the two camps, but limited coordination about tellers for any vote and day-to-day business was conducted by Boyd-Carpenter on the Tory side and Labour's Robert Sheldon. Neither Powell nor Foot had any need to be involved, and Powell's non-involvement helped some Labour MPs overcome their doubts sufficiently to vote in the same lobby as Powell – a practice that was to become much more common than anyone ever expected after 1970.[31]

Frustrated by a week of delay, the Government's patience with the opponents of the Bill snapped. After the Attorney-General had been savaged by Powell over his attempt to explain why the principles of the Bill, as stated in its preamble, had not been included in the body of the Bill, James Callaghan, the then Home Secretary, referred to 'frivolous opposition'. Powell sprang to his feet. It was a classic confrontation between front bench and back bench, or Court and Country. Powell did not know which MPs the Home Secretary had in mind in referring to frivolous opposition. Those who have sat through this debate, as he has not, will be aware that the vast majority of speeches have been very far from frivolous and have gone to the heart of about the most serious matter, the constitution of Parliament, that the House of Comons could possibly debate.

Later on the same day, Powell backed Hamilton's amendment to scrap the proposal for non-voting peers. Deriding the proposal as a 'sweetener' to existing peers to secure their agreement to the Bill, he castigated them for their readiness 'to sell out valuable elements of our constitution':

As long as it is 'O.K.' for them, they are prepared to swallow the consequences for the future and the inherent absurdities and obscenities of the scheme. '*Après moi le deluge* – it is a good aristocratic rule. Over and over again, it has been the common people, the people represented in this House, who have shown the truest appreciation and valuation of the prescriptive parts of our Constitution.

This was not the language of a right-wing Conservative. Neither was it the talk of a populist. It was the authentic voice of a Country Tory.[32]

In the spring, the Cabinet finally decided to cut their losses and abandon House of Lords reform. The Prime Minister announced the Government's climbdown in a statement to the Commons immediately before the Budget debate, on 17 April. As Wilson hurried through his humiliating statement, Powell called out: 'Eat it slower!' That evening, addressing the annual dinner of the Primrose League, the Tory organization dedicated to Disraeli's memory, Powell could not resist the temptation to poke fun at his front bench adversary and to rake over the ashes of his own sacking from the Shadow Cabinet. 'My good friend and colleague, Quintin Hogg', he began, and with even heavier irony referred to a pamphlet that Hogg had published, 'with that freedom of personal expression our party traditionally allows to its front bench spokesmen'. Powell delighted in pointing out that the publication of Hogg's argument that parliament had virtually become an elective dictatorship, 'where debate has dwindled to a ritual', had coincided with the back bench victory over the front bench plan to reform the House of Lords.

Although the Government had won every vote on the Bill to reform the Lords by majorities of two to one, Powell claimed that a relatively small number of MPs had been able to force the abandonment of the plan because they spoke for the general feeling of the Commons. 'I believe that Members on all sides have felt a lightening of spirit at this proof that, in a matter which affected its own position in the constitution, the House of Commons could and would assert itself and get its way.' Powell's comments were made a month after he had given the first indication of his next great cause – opposition to British membership of the European Economic Community.[33]

Coming out against Europe

Although his speech went largely unnoticed, Powell first indicated his conversion from supporting to opposing British membership of the European Economic Community on 21 March 1969, when he addressed Conservative women at Clacton. Despite the lack of attention that his change of mind received, Powell regarded the occasion as significant because he had voiced a stronger warning about EEC membership than any other politician of equal standing had expressed since both main parties had become committed to Britain's entry. Despite his refusal as a new MP in 1950 to support the Tory leadership on British participation in the European Coal and Steel Community, he had supported the application to join its successor, the EEC, as a Minister in Macmillan's Government. In 1965, he had helped Nicholas Ridley produce a pamphlet urging closer European unity.[34]

In his 1966 election address, Powell had made clear his continued support for British membership of the EEC. The Conservatives, he claimed, were '*determined* to get rid of the barriers between this country and its natural market in Western Europe', and he attributed Europe's prosperity to its 'freedom, opportunity and incentives', in contrast to Labour's Britain. While he served in Heath's Shadow Cabinet, Powell remained what is commonly known as a 'good European'. Indeed, in November 1966, in his capacity as Conservative Defence Spokesman, he criticized the Labour Government's threatened withdrawal of British troops from Germany as a move that would be felt

> as a deliberate turning of our back on Europe. All the suspicions that Britain is not serious in her concern for participation in Europe would be reinforced. All our professions of anxiety to enter the Common Market would be discounted.[35]

Powell clearly regarded Britain's military commitment on the Continent as being essential to the success of its European policy. In February 1967, he told the Shadow Cabinet that he would deplore the disappearance of the British Army of the Rhine (BAOR) 'on political and on military grounds'. Although he considered that BAOR's disappearance was ultimately inevitable, he argued that 'this island country had a need which did not exist for the continental countries, to give continuing proof to Europe that we were involved in European problems'. The coincidence, in May, of Wilson's declaration of the Government's intention to seek British entry into the EEC with the announcement of the withdrawal of a brigade of troops and a squadron of aircraft from the Continent, drew fierce condemnation from Powell. 'So at the very moment when Britain declares she wants to become part and parcel of Western Europe, economically and more than economically,' Powell declared, 'she tells her allies on the Continent that in order to save £5 million in

European currency she is going to bring forces "home" (as it is called).' And he continued,

> If a thing is worth doing at all, it is worth doing well. If an enterprise is undertaken at all, it must be undertaken whole-heartedly. It is deeply to be regretted that the announcement of our application to join the Common Market was accompanied by such a demonstration of our unconcern for the feelings, the opinions and the solidarity of our continental allies.[36]

Powell voted with the rest of the Shadow Cabinet in support of the Labour Government's application to join the EEC. Later during the same month, he reiterated the importance that he attached to Britain's military presence on the Continent, and suggested that BAOR's 'strange name' conveyed 'in an instinctive, uncomplicated way a popular recognition that somehow Britain henceforward belongs with Western Europe'. With the failure of Labour's 1967 application, Europe faded from the political agenda, but after Powell's sacking from the front bench Tory opponents of British membership urged him to take up their cause – Douglas-Home expected him to come out against the EEC within months.[37]

Opposing British membership of the EEC, or Common Market as it was usually called, had obvious appeal for a politician who, by 1969, had been crusading for five years to orientate his party towards a radical, nationalist Toryism that would reshape post-war politics and attract strong popular support. Although the Labour and Conservative leaderships favoured British membership, public opinion appeared to be against the EEC. Powell was certainly aware of the division between front bench thinking and public opinion on the Common Market. Although he seemed to think that it was unlikely that he would make a similar impact on another issue to the one that he had made on immigration, it sometimes seemed that he felt Europe might prove the exception.[38]

Powell's specific point at Clacton had been that Britain's second application to join the EEC, that had been left on the table since 1967, was fast becoming 'an absurdity and a humiliation' and should be withdrawn. But as with his speeches on immigration, his real message was to be found in the emotive language and forceful imagery that he deployed, as much as in the content of his comments. As a consequence of the country's suffering a series of 'humiliations' in recent years – Suez, the elimination from Empire, the double veto on its entry into the EEC – 'a mood somewhere between dejection and desperation' had been engendered. In his view, it had become all the more necessary 'for Britain to stand back, as it were, and take a fresh look at "Europe and all that", without prejudice or passion, but also with "no holds barred"'.[39]

Arguing that people should not be prevented from talking candidly about their own country (implying to his audience that there were curbs on free speech in Britain), Powell declared, in a parody of the Southern Rhodesian regime: 'Let me start with a unilateral declaration of independence.' Britain had no need 'to be tied up with anybody', and was 'no more drowning than these islands are sinkable.' 'So let us have none of the eleventh-hour stuff, please: no jumping to conclusions and saying "if it is not this it has to be that. If it is not Europe it must be America or the Commonwealth or something or other".' There was no evidence that, if Britain would only manage her economy and currency on rational lines, she could not go on by herself, and go on successfully, for years to come. Moreover, the Common Market was not stationary. General de Gaulle was prepared to accept that the community might be 'changed into a looser form of free trade area', and 'a "Europe of nations", of sovereign nations, is the only Europe to which Britain, so long as she herself remains a nation, could belong.'[40]

It was not until the following September when Powell made a similar speech at Smethwick, but also claimed to detect a more questioning mood towards the Common Market, that his new anti-EEC stance attracted much attention. His conversion on Europe was highly significant for the Conservatives, since the pro-Commonwealth Tories who had formed the bulk of the party's anti-EEC wing were now reinforced by nationalists, who had previously been prepared to accept EEC entry. In mid-July, an anti-EEC early day motion on the Commons Order Paper included ten Tory MPs, who, like Powell, had voted for entry in 1967. Over the years, the nationalist opponents of European integration have steadily superseded the old pro-Commonwealth group to become the dominant force among so-called Tory 'Euro-sceptics'.[41]

By coming out against the EEC, Powell had taken up another issue that resonated with many Tory activists and there was every prospect of a repetition of the previous year's 'High Noon' showdown at October's Conservative conference, but this time on Europe. Indeed, at Preston, only days before the Tories gathered in Brighton, Powell had declared: 'Whip that application back from the table in Brussels – it will barely be noticed amongst the wrangles and the quarrels of that ramshackle organization, the Common Market.' Reports that a group of businessmen were ready to offer Powell financial backing if he challenged Heath for the Tory leadership added to the tension, but Powell dismissed such speculation. Some measure of Powell's support was evidenced in the Tory conference debate on immigration, when the party's policy – notwithstanding Heath's tougher line at Walsall earlier in the year – was backed by only 1,349 votes to 954. But to the relief of the party managers at Brighton, Powell chose instead to intervene in the economic debate by arguing the case for letting the pound float – an issue that, by comparison with the others that he had taken up, was bound to seem arcane to most of the party faithful.[42]

Powell had long advocated a floating exchange rate as the lynch-pin of his alternative, free-market economic policy. He had been elated in September when the D-mark was suddenly allowed to float, since this represented the first crack in the Bretton Woods system of fixed exchange rates that had held sway for a quarter of a century. 'It's happened, it's happened, it's happened,' an exultant Powell proclaimed at a National Liberal Club dinner, on 30 September. 'Without so much as a by-your-leave to anybody, let alone to the other members of that wonderful, indivisible, glorious political unity, the European Common Market – "splash!" The German went overboard, protesting he did not mean to do it at all but could not help it.' Powell appealed to his fellow countrymen:

Come on, let's all join Fritz in the water. Like those Magnificent Men in the Flying Machines, 'We'll go up tiddley-om-pom, we'll go down tiddley-om-pom'; but the main thing is: we'll float. The long nightmare of deficits and surpluses on the balance of payments, of repression and controls and 'squeezes' and all that nonsense, will be over at last. Our nation will turn again to face the world and tell the facts about itself and its money – 'Supply and demand', the Germans called it; did you hear? We shall have the truth and daylight to do our work by.[43]

In the immediate aftermath of the floating of the D-mark, the temptation for Powell to press his free-market economics on the Tory leadership was too strong to resist. Arguing that the recurrent financial crises that afflicted the British economy went back 'far before the advent of Harold Wilson', Powell told the Tories that:

If we are to offer our countrymen an end to all that, there must be some decisive change, not only from the policies since 1964 but from policies before 1964. It is not enough to promise that we will try to do better than last time. We have to show why, and how, it is going to be quite different from last time.

In particular, Powell proposed, 'we have to do what we were on the verge of doing after 1951 but unhappily did not. We have to set the rate for the pound free to behave like any other price and keep supply and demand in balance'.[44]

Within three years of the floating of the D-mark in September 1969, a Conservative Government was left with no alternative except to let the pound float following the collapse of the Bretton Woods system. But Powell's attack at Brighton on previous Tory Governments and his call for the party to abandon every aspect of intervention enabled Macleod to win the political argument by claiming that Powell's approach was 'a Whig rather than a Tory doctrine'. 'Everything has its price,' the Shadow Chancellor pointed out, would mean no regional policy: 'it is an excellent policy for the strong, but we are concerned also with the weak.'[45]

In the summer of 1969, Powell felt that Conservative economic policy had moved in his direction on denationalization, prices and incomes and taxation. He detected a sharper edge to Tory arguments on the economy and less hesitation in condemning socialism. But Heath and his Shadow Cabinet colleagues had engaged in a change of tone as opposed to any change of substance, and their attempts to differentiate their approach from Labour's had not heralded any great shift in policy – as Macleod's speech in October 1969 demonstrated. Indeed, Powell was right to be sceptical in early February 1970 that the Shadow Cabinet's gathering at Selsdon had marked a shift towards *laissez-faire* economics and a tougher approach on law and order and immigration – speculation had been fuelled by Heath's ill-prepared briefing of the press and Wilson's lampooning of 'Selsdon Man'.[46]

Powell's defeat at Brighton illustrated the difficulty he faced in trying to build support while pressing a combination of policies, each with equally unqualified conviction, but each of which antagonized different groups of potential allies or supporters. His stance on immigration had already weakened his support among economic liberals who had previously sympathized with his free-market economics, as the liberal-minded economics commentator, Samuel Brittan, noted in his review of *Freedom and Reality*, a collection of Powell's speeches that was published in early 1969. Although Brittan applauded the attacks on some aspects of conventional wisdom, he judged that Powell 'seems to have read no economics'. As a result, although Powell sometimes went to the heart of a problem more sharply than many professionals, 'a great deal else is oversimplified and dangerously open to attack'. Yet the greatest problem with Powell was his polarization of debate among Tories. He had 'attracted to his banner the anti-blacks, hangers, floggers, censors and the martinets, who support him despite rather than because of, many of his actual beliefs'. In response, 'many of the younger and more liberal Conservatives have become so preoccupied with fighting "Powellism" that they believe – quite under-standably – that they must rally round the official leadership, which is given a clear run on issues such as economic policy, overseas defence or Vietnam'. In addition, the Tory leadership had become 'even more obdurate on those issues where Mr Powell speaks for enlightenment'. Indeed, Powell's adding the EEC to his list of political anathemas further distanced from him socially liberal Tories like Geoffrey Howe. As Brittan observed, Powell's 'economic liberalism is allied uneasily with an attachment to the nation-state as the absolute political value'.[47]

Yet Powell's nationalistic anti-EEC line potentially had great appeal to a public that was evidently sceptical, if not downright hostile, to the policy of British membership then being pursued by both front benches. On the one hand, Powell's approach might win support among traditional working-class Labour supporters who tended to identify the Common Market with higher prices and raised the prospect of his campaigning in alliance with anti-EEC Labour politicians. But on the other hand, although his anti-immigration stance also appealed to traditional Labour voters, it repelled Labour politicians – it was one thing for them to vote with Powell in order to defeat reform of the House of Lords, but it was quite another matter to share a public platform with him. Above all, however, Powell's belief in competition and market forces stood as a major obstacle to his winning working-class support at a time when the majority of voters were working-class, the unions were powerful and the merest suggestion of increased unemployment was politically damaging. No matter how much Powell might argue that successive Governments, and not the unions, had been to blame for inflation, his critique of collective bargaining and his monetarist prescriptions were anathemas to the Labour movement and its millions of supporters.

Powell, however, did not help his cause when he made his first speech in the Commons against membership of the EEC on 25 February 1970. Speaking on the second day of the two-day debate on the question of British entry, he began by mocking the supposed economic benefits of belonging to a large domestic market – although he had supported Macmillan's and Wilson's attempts to take Britain into the EEC on economic grounds. But as he had already made clear at the Tory back bench Foreign Affairs committee the previous week, his real objection now was political rather than economic:

> All pretence is now aside. All the words with which we amused ourselves two or three years ago, eight or ten years ago – I confess that I also amused myself along with the rest – that this was really an economic matter, a matter of trade and that the rest was pure theorizing – 'a few European theorists, perhaps, but we pragmatic British take no notice of that' – that is all stripped aside. The question we are deciding is whether we can and will enter into a political unit that deals with all the major matters of political life affecting the daily lives of all the people in this country, under a Government sustained by a European-elected Parliament.

In order to rationalize his own late conversion, Powell spoke as though the political objectives agreed by the original six member-states, and written into the 1957 Treaty of Rome, had only recently been revealed. He ignored the fact that the Government of which he had been a member had applied for membership of the EEC for avowedly political reasons as well as economic ones.

Instead, Powell rehearsed the nationalistic argument that he had taken up in reaction to his abandonment of imperialism some fifteen years earlier, in the mid-'50s. For much the same reason that he had argued that the collapse of the British Empire had been inevitable, he now argued against European unity. In essence, parliamentary government was only feasible when the electorate was homogeneous.

> Now, an electorate which sustains a true Parliament has to be an homogeneous electorate. By that I mean every part of the electorate has consciously to say, 'We are part of the whole: we accept the majority of the verdict as expressed at the poll', and then, somewhat curiously, as reflected in the composition of this House. That is why this Parliament works. That is why this Parliament is our pride and our guardian, because it rests on an electorate which, with vanishing exceptions, is in that sense homogeneous, in that it is prepared to accept the verdict of the majority, because it feels

that it is the majority of themselves. The question posed to us is: can we now, or in the next ten years, or in the foreseeable or imaginable future, believe that the people of this country would regard themselves as so much part of an electorate comprising 200 or 250 million other electors that they would accept the majority view on taxation, on social policy, on development, on all matters which are crucial to our political life? I have to confess that I do not believe such an attitude of mind is foreseeable.

Powell, of course, was exaggerating the prospect of Britain's being ruled by a federal European Parliament, especially in the light of the 'Luxembourg compromise' in 1966, when de Gaulle finally ended the French boycott of EEC institutions in return for an agreement that the national veto would continue to hold sway on matters that any member-state regarded as being of overriding national importance.

But by this stage in his speech, Powell was moving towards an evocation of nationalist myth, and was not applying his intellect to contemporary reality. Although he was able to dismiss George Brown's intervention that the 300 million inhabitants of an enlarged EEC would be *white* – a clumsy allusion to Powell's opposition to Commonwealth immigration – Powell lost his fellow MPs as he attacked any idea that Britain's national survival should be decided by others. For the joint pooling of sovereignty in the NATO Alliance had been the basis of British defence policy for more than twenty years by 1970. Yet Powell now argued against membership of the EEC – an economic, non-military organization – on the grounds that if we had been part of a unified command in 1940, British forces would have been quickly destroyed. In his view, the 'acid test' of people's sense of a common identity was 'whether we identify ourselves as part of that whole just as surely as Coventry and Bristol regarded themselves as part of the United Kingdom in 1940'. But Powell's invoking the national myth of 'standing alone' struck those MPs who had lived through, and, in some cases, fought in, the Second World War as absurdly anachronistic. 'The atmosphere of the House changed at once', noted Andrew Alexander, parliamentary sketch-writer for the *Daily Telegraph*. 'Tory MPs shook their heads, Labour MPs jeered. It was as if a fine timepiece had suddenly struck thirteen'.[48]

In his campaign for a radical, nationalist Toryism, Powell 'was shaking the tree, but the fruit would not drop'. This analogy by Powell's close colleague, John Biffen, appropriately echoes Powell's idiosyncratic and impatient treatment of the fruit tree in his Wolverhampton back-garden. The next general election, however, due sometime in 1970 or early 1971, would offer Powell an opportunity to have his say on matters that he regarded as important and to stamp his impression on the political debate. It was with this purpose in mind that, during the early autumn of 1969, he planned his personal election campaign – there was never any prospect that Heath would permit Powell to be involved officially in the party's national campaign. Indeed, following their clash over Powell's comments about assistance to immigrant areas, Heath had stated publicly that he had no intention of bringing Powell back into the Shadow Cabinet. Yet however much he may have wished it to be otherwise, Heath simply could not rid himself of Powell during the 1970 election campaign. Indeed, at times, it seemed that Powell was the main issue. Paradoxically, however, Powell's shaking of the tree was to help the fruit drop into Heath's lap.[49]

Powellite campaign

Powell made an immediate impact on the June 1970 election by timing the publication of his election address in Wolverhampton to capture the attention of the Sunday newspapers during the first weekend of the campaign. His warning that Britain faced 'three great dangers, at least as great as any she has faced before' – immigration, the Common Market and the socialist state – immediately differentiated his position from Heath's. Echoing the dire predictions that he had been issuing since 1968, Powell regarded 'Commonwealth immigration and its consequences' as being the greatest threat, and it was no accident that he placed the Common Market second, before the socialist state. As he later reflected on the 1970 election, 'the whole question of the New Commonwealth population and the question of British membership of the EEC were planted by me quite deliberately as the subjects which overrode in their importance all others'.[50]

Powell's election address encapsulated the Powellite programme as it stood by 1970 and was designed to focus attention on the themes that would follow in his campaign speeches. But whereas his post-1963 crusade to convert the Conservative Party to a radical Toryism had initially emphasized free-market economics in reaction to Macmillan's interventionism, he now highlighted the nationalist appeal, that had become more prominent on immigration from 1965 and on the EEC from 1969. During the year preceding the election, he estimated that for every three speeches that he made on the economy, he made one on other subjects, but many of his speeches were delivered to Tory audiences, for whom his economic arguments had great resonance. At the election, however, immigration and the EEC were the two subjects on which Powell's cross-party appeal among working-class Labour voters was likely to be strongest.

There has been much speculation about Powell's motives at the 1970 election. Was he trying to gain the credit in the event of a Conservative victory? Or was he assuming that the Tories would lose, and was therefore preparing his ground to launch a post-election bid for the Tory leadership? Powell, in common with almost every opinion pollster, political commentator, Labour politician and also many Tories, thought that the Conservatives were heading for defeat – although Powell's wife, Pam, expected a Tory victory. But he had long been suspicious of the large Tory lead in the opinion polls during 1968–69, and seemed as willing as Wilson to believe in Labour's recovery in the spring of 1970, as evidenced by May's municipal election results and the turn around in the polls. The general assumption that a Labour victory was a foregone conclusion contributed to a lacklustre campaign by the main parties, and fuelled increased interest in what was likely to happen to the Tory Party after defeat. In turn, this led the media to turn their spotlight on Powell – the Press Association assigned one reporter each to Wilson and Heath, and two to Powell.[51]

Besides reflecting the widely held expectation that the most interesting political story of the summer was likely to occur inside the Tory Party *after* the election, the attention that Powell attracted was a reflection of his transformation since his Birmingham speech and subsequent sacking into a devil figure for the left and a folk hero of the right. At his meeting in Smethwick on June 3, some forty 'skinheads' formed a bodyguard for their hero and declared that they would guard him throughout his thirty campaign meetings in the West Midlands. These supporters belonged to a white working-class youth cult, that stressed violence and had been heavily politicized by far right groups. Powell's speaking engagements in the West Midlands marginal seats had been arranged with the area's Tory agent six months before the election. In marked contrast to the low-key, highly managed and lifeless campaigns being run by Wilson and Heath, Powell's meetings were dramatic occasions, at which his impassioned performances excited a powerfully emotional response among his packed audiences.[52]

The Powell 'phenomenon', as it had evolved by 1970, was witnessed by Michael Pinto-Duschinsky, co-author of the 1970 Nuffield election study, who jotted down his immediate impressions. He was struck by the elegance of Powell's wording, the brilliance of his style, the fierce logic with which his speech was constructed and the fire with which it was delivered. Powell's delivery was 'nasal, deliberate, fluent'. His head protruded as he spoke, and he used his hands as a battering ram to hammer home his argument. The speech was a 'logical, theological, revivalist' mixture. The 'whole phenomenon' was totally different from that associated with any other Tory back bench MP. In Powell's grasp of facts, in the logical structure of his speeches, in his elegance, in his sheer virtuosity, Pinto-Duschinsky judged that he was 'surely far ahead of any British statesman or any one in America', adding that, 'many of his words were reasonable in themselves. It is the emotional environment and the whole context of his speeches that makes it evident that something more extreme is going on than plain words might imply.'[53]

The extraordinary response that Powell evoked and the media interest that he generated were also a reflection of the disillusion with the leaderships of the main parties by the late 1960s. As a result, he towered over his fellow Tories as the most popular alternative to Heath, despite having been condemned to exile on the back benches for two years, and not having held a senior front bench position. Heath came under strong pressure during the campaign from his colleagues and many Tory candidates and supporters to dissociate himself from Powell, but instead he merely sought to play down Powell's importance. The Tory leader's attempt to ignore Powell, however, was flawed, because of the publicity that Powell attracted and the questions that kept being raised about him at the daily press conferences. Indeed, with the opinion polls continuing to show a Labour lead during the campaign, the main concern of Lord Carrington, Willie Whitelaw and Heath's senior advisers became a matter of damage limitation, and how to prevent Powell challenging successfully for the leadership – by the last weekend of the campaign, the likelihood that Whitelaw would be chosen as Heath's successor was being advanced in the press.[54]

In truth, Powell never stood a chance of becoming Tory leader, as his closest lieutenants recognized. The leader was selected neither on the basis of a national popularity poll, nor by a poll of Tory activists, but instead was elected by Tory MPs, and there was no realistic prospect that the parliamentary party of the late 1960s or early 1970s would choose Powell. The media attention that was lavished on him and the emotional support that he attracted at his meetings in 1970 makes it easy to forget that in reality he had been sidelined by his party. His future role, and the extent of any influence that he might wield in the party, would only become apparent when the outcome of the election was known and had been fully assessed. But though he was sidelined, he was not silenced. His best strategy – indeed, virtually his only practical option – was to try to put his stamp on the election and to keep playing his distinctive tune. If he succeeded, his resonance with the voters, notwithstanding the Tory defeat, might help to shift the political debate in his direction. It was a tall order in a party-dominated political system, but Heath's apparently certain defeat and the popular notion that Powell was the alternative Tory leader gave him the opportunity to attract more publicity during a general election than any other individual back bench politician in modern times.[55]

Powell's election address was a masterpiece in the art of differentiating his position from that of Heath's, while remaining in the Conservative fold. Predictably, on immigration, Powell repeated his argument on numbers, and gave added bite to his claim that the true size of the immigrant population was being deliberately concealed, by asserting that 'it is nearer two million than the $1\frac{1}{4}$ million which the Government allege, and it is rising rapidly'. Arguing that, in time, a quarter or more of Wolverhampton and other inner cities would be 'coloured', he warned that such an increase 'carries a threat of division, violence and bloodshed of American dimensions, and adds a powerful weapon to the armoury of anarchy'. Capturing the sense of impotence and resentment among white working- and lower-middle class voters at the various upheavals that had transformed the old urban communities, of which immigration was one of the most visible changes, Powell repeated the charge that 'the British people have never been properly informed, let alone consulted'. And with his familiar chilling tone, he proposed three remedies 'before it is too late'.

The first of Powell's proposed measures went beyond official party policy, as defined in the Tory manifesto. 'Halt immigration now', Powell urged, explaining that this meant 'ending automatic entry for wives and children'. It was a far cry from his earlier insistence that it would be inhuman to split families. As regards his other two proposals, he was able to append the endorsement, 'To this the Conservative Party is committed'. In both cases, the party had moved in his direction. The Tories were now committed to a reform of citizenship law that 'distinguishes between those who belong to Britain and the rest of the world', and also supported assisted, voluntary repatriation. But on this latter proposal there was a marked difference in emphasis. Whereas Powell implied a vigorous pursuit of such a policy by claiming that 'the signs are that the scope is large if we act promptly', the Tory manifesto was anxious to caution that 'we will not tolerate any attempt to harass or to compel [Commonwealth immigrants] to go against their will'.

Yet the sharpest contrast between Powell's programme and the Tory manifesto was on the question of British entry into the EEC. Powell was correct in writing that 'the Conservative Party is not yet committed to Britain entering the Common Market' – the manifesto stated that the party's 'sole commitment is to negotiate; no more, no less'. But whereas he argued that he would do his 'utmost' to make sure that the Tories never became committed to British membership, the Conservative manifesto declared that 'if we can negotiate the right terms, we believe that it would be in the long term interest of the British people' for Britain to join the EEC. The party's reasoning was couched almost entirely in terms of the economic benefits that were claimed for EEC membership, but Powell countered by urging 'freer and wider trade all round' and by endorsing the continuation of Britain's existing defence alliances. And although the Tory manifesto omitted any mention of Britain's becoming involved in closer European unity, Powell warned that:

> the Community is designed to be a political unit, with common internal and external policies: the same tax-system, the same laws, the same economic policies, the same currency, the same treaties. All this means a single government, and therefore a common parliament based on one electorate. For my part I do not believe the British people should consent to be a minority in a European electorate. I do not want to see this country give its political independence away.

Powell's unequivocal statement was to remain the corner-stone of his politics for the remainder of his life.

It was striking that the politician who had long campaigned for free-market economics and non-interventionism now placed socialism as the 'third great danger' that faced Britain, and not the first. Since the Conservative manifesto echoed the leadership's recent rhetoric in favour of lower taxation and more competition, and also ruled out any repetition of Labour's compulsory wage control, Powell's characteristically forthright economic argument seemed unproblematic. Yet even here, there was a sense that Powell was putting Heath on probation. He argued that only a Conservative Government that put into effect a list of free-market nostrums would 'lift from the people of this country the fear of a future without freedom and without pride' – in other words, the election of the Conservatives was a necessary condition, but it was not a sufficient one unless they pursued free-market policies. Implicit in Powell's phraseology was a suggestion that it was yet to be seen whether Heath would be a latter-day Macmillan, or would make a clean, non-interventionist break with the past.[56]

Powell's chances of highlighting immigration and the EEC as major issues were remote as long as the Labour and Tory leaderships remained firm in their determination to focus the national debate on the economy. His cross-party appeal presented risks not only to Heath in the event of the expected Tory defeat, but also to Wilson, as was confirmed when the Labour leader's campaign committee issued a directive that Powell was not to be made an issue in the campaign. To Wilson's fury, however, Tony Benn, the then Minister of Technology, went against the Labour game-plan at the outset of the campaign and, as a result, helped Powell make immigration an issue. Although Benn vehemently opposed Powell's views on the subject, he felt strongly that politicians should address issues that were of deep concern to the public. In March 1970, he had vigorously denounced Powell's approach on the race issue, without naming Powell, in a speech at Huddersfield. After Powell had stressed immigration in his election address, Benn decided not to let the matter rest, but instead prepared a violent attack on racialism and argued that Heath was merely a cover for Powell, who had become the real power in the Tory Party. In the passage that he drafted for his speech on Wednesday 3 June, and that was issued to the press by Transport House, then Labour's headquarters, Benn attacked Powell's approach as being 'evil'; condemned Central Office for distributing 'filthy and obscene racist propaganda'; and included the sensational charge that: 'The flag of racialism which has been hoisted in Wolverhampton is beginning to look like the one that fluttered over Dachau and Belsen'. Told of Benn's comments by a television reporter at his meeting in Smethwick, Powell snatched the microphone and replied: 'All that I will say is that for myself, in 1939 I voluntarily returned from Australia to this country, to serve as a private soldier against Germany and Nazism. I am the same man today.'[57]

Benn's 'Belsen speech', in his own words, 'exploded across the election'. The fond hopes entertained by party campaign managers that immigration and race, on which both parties were divided, might be kept out of the election, were instantly shattered. The television news bulletins broadcast Benn's comments, and the next day's newspapers led with the story. Cartoons featured Benn fanning the flames of Powellism, or putting a match to the touchpaper of the Powell rocket. Heath, who had sacked Powell in 1968 for extreme language, demanded that Wilson should dismiss Benn from the Government and repudiate his speech. Although Wilson ordered Benn to keep off the racial question, Powell and Powellism were now major election issues in their own right. There were even demands that the reporting of Powell's campaign should be censored. In one incident, George Gale, the political columnist, had begun his report for the *Evening Standard* on Powell's meeting of 3 June with the words, 'A moment of dignity has arrived in this election'. The National Union of Journalists' chapel at the *Standard* tried to 'black' the copy, on the grounds that a person with Powell's views should not be given friendly coverage, but the editor, Charles Wintour, stood firm. Benn, for his part, afterwards regretted having made such a personal attack on Powell. As he told his biographer, Jad Adams, 'I realized as soon as I'd said it because I've known Enoch very well and I didn't want to be very personal and I think I did go over the top with "Dachau and Belsen".' But he did not regret having tackled Powell 'on the question because his influence has been wholly pernicious'.[58]

During the second week of the campaign, as he had long planned, Powell made the first of four speeches that were designed to attract major attention during the final six days of the campaign. The subject of his speech, delivered on Thursday 11 June, a week before polling day, was immigration. Powell rehearsed his familiar arguments, but one comment in particular captured the media's attention. During the previous year, Powell had been engaged in a debate over the size of the immigrant population, and he now claimed that the latest facts and figures showed that his offence had been *under*statement and not exaggeration, as his opponents had alleged. 'On this subject', he declared, 'so vital to their future, the people of this country have been misled, cruelly and persistently, till one begins to wonder if the Foreign Office was the only department of state into which enemies of this country were infiltrated.'[59]

There was, however, rich irony in Powell's allegation against Government officials. Powell had referred specifically to the publication of figures by the Registrar-General in March 1970, and argued that they had shown that the true figure for immigrant births was much higher than had previously been estimated. These figures and their presentation had, in fact, provoked fierce debate within the Government during the previous year, but this had been because Richard Crossman and Professor Nicholas Kaldor, one of Wilson's economics advisers, believed that the Registrar-General and his assistant wanted to provide statistical ammunition to support Powell. Where Powell alleged enemy infiltration, Crossman and Kaldor suspected Powellism, or worse. Indeed, in August 1969, Crossman had forbidden the Registrar-General to publish some immigration statistics in the form that he desired because Crossman thought the figures would help Powell's case. In 1970, the particular point at issue concerned the assumption made about the future rate of immigrant births. When these figures had been published in March, Powell had argued that the official estimate of a non-white population of 2.5 million by 1985 had to be revised drastically upwards. But the Runnymede Trust, a respected, independent organization on race relations, shared the Government's view that the revised birth-rate figures gave no cause for alarm because the future birth-rate of immigrants would slow and there was no reason to revise upwards the estimated size of the non-white population.[60]

The morning after Powell's June 1970 attack against Government officials, Heath issued a special statement repudiating the allegation and distancing the party from Powell's views on immigration. Inevitably, Powell's position became the only live issue at the daily press conference. Heath could not entirely disown Powell, since he was an official Tory candidate, but his discomfort was evident as he tried, unsuccessfully to change the subject. Heath had wanted to keep attention focused on the economy, but Powell had again become a major issue.[61]

On the evening of Friday 12th, Heath's advisers received the advance text of Powell's next major speech, that he was to deliver on Saturday, at the same time as they heard that the latest opinion poll put Labour 12.4 points ahead. Douglas Hurd, then Heath's political secretary, noted of Powell, that 'he seemed determined that we should lose, and lose badly. It was a dramatic and unsettling moment.' During Saturday morning, Heath's closest confidants discussed how they should handle Powell's latest speech. They were convinced that Powell had calculated that the election was lost and was now launching his bid for the leadership. Heath told Prior, 'if we are to go down, we will at least do so honourably and with our flags flying'. The former Prime Minister, Harold Macmillan, passed on his advice that Powell's actions should be treated as a matter for the parliamentary party after the election. In Birmingham meanwhile, Powell, at his own request, met a representative of the Conservative whips' office. He declared that he 'had a shot ready for firing', and intimated that he would support the election of a Conservative Government before the end of the campaign.[62]

Although the Sunday newspapers made gloomy reading for the Tory leadership, the Powellite spectre that had hovered over them was about to vanish. Speaking in the Northfield district of Birmingham, a stone's throw from King's Norton where he was brought up, Powell had portrayed with spine-chilling relish the threat that the country faced from an enemy that he claimed was already within its walls. He had in mind not only a tiny minority of extremists, such as student demonstrators and terrorists, whom, he argued, were subverting the state and its institutions through disorder and violence; he also pointed the finger more widely at all those who were assisting the enemy to win the battle in the moral sphere. In a remarkable passage, he appeared to detect a conspiracy to suppress and undermine the views of the majority, while only the conventional wisdom of liberals was allowed to be expressed on matters such as race relations, student representation, overseas aid, civil rights in Northern Ireland, and so on. His speech pandered to the prejudices of those who felt that they had been ignored and marginalized by rapid social change and Britain's relative decline during the 1960s. Later on Saturday the 13th, however, the Tory leadership were encouraged by the news that the next Gallup poll showed the Labour lead down to one per cent, and also by the positive response that they were receiving in the constituencies.[63]

Heath was finally able to move the spotlight from Powell at Monday morning's Tory press conference and concentrate on attacking Labour's economic record. That evening in Tamworth, Powell delivered the third of his four speeches that were designed to make an impact on voters' minds. On this occasion, he reiterated his outright opposition to British membership of the Common Market because of the long-term objective to transform the EEC into a single state, with a common currency and a common parliament. But in retrospect, the most interesting aspect of Powell's speech was his rejection of any suggestion that 'the parliamentary system itself should be short-circuited, and the people offered the direct opportunity to say Yes or No by referendum'. His opposition to a referendum could not have been clearer. 'I am no supporter of a referendum, least of all on this sort of subject,' he declared. He mentioned two reasons, 'out of many'. In the first place, a referendum would lead to 'irresponsible government', since ministers would deny responsibility for any consequences that flowed from a referendum in which the people had rejected their advice. Secondly, only close and continuous debate in parliament and the country during the course of negotiations for British entry could ensure that the terms that were accepted were such as to satisfy opinion – though Powell, as he made clear, opposed entry on any terms. Instead, Powell urged that voters should insist that their candidates 'come clean' on the EEC. 'This is the right way for public opinion on such a subject to find expression,' he urged. 'And let no one say that Members are mere lobby-fodder, and that a Government will get its way, no matter', he argued, citing the Government's recent defeat over reform of the House of Lords. 'I would not care to put much money on entry to the Common Market coming about if a substantial minority of Members of the Government side were pledged to oppose it,' he declared, optimistically. Moreover, Powell noted that 'the maximum ventilation of the whole issue is something to which the Conservative Party is committed', and he quoted Heath as having said that 'the greatest possible mistake would be for the British people to go into this without themselves realizing the full implications'. In effect, Powell was putting a future Tory Government on notice to allow full and free debate on the issue. This was later to become the source of Powell's main complaint against Heath's handling of British entry into the EEC.[64]

Finally, on his fifty-eighth birthday and speaking in his constituency, Powell delivered his promised message to the voters, urging them to elect a Conservative Government. But his endorsement of the Conservatives could not be construed as a message of loyalty to Heath. Instead, his speech was couched in terms of a national figure who had been wronged by his party and who had no hope of gaining office if the Tories won, but who, none the less, was magnanimously delivering his followers to the party's cause. 'This election is not about me, not about Enoch Powell, not about any other named variety,' he declared. 'If a socialist majority is returned on Thursday,' he warned, 'then before another three or four years are over, the ownership and control of the state will have been extended, by one means or another, over the greater part of British industry and business.' His message to the voters was kept till the end. Asserting that the election would decide whether Britain's freedom survived, he concluded: 'You dare not entrust it to any Government but a Conservative Government'.[65]

The Enoch effect

Although Powell had voted by post, he was undeterred by the rain and arrived at 7 a.m. on Thursday, 18 June, at one of the polling stations in Wolverhampton South-West to greet the first voters. By ten o'clock, when he went with Pam as she cast her vote, there was brilliant sunshine. As he toured Wolverhampton, where he was a familiar figure in his dark suit, he was greeted by shouts of 'Enoch!' and the hooting of car horns. But while the strength of feeling was clear, the direction of the sentiments expressed was not always obvious. In Penn ward, many of the pictures of Powell had been given black faces with the aid of a spray. After lunch, he and Pam visited his committee rooms and, according to *The Times*, encouraged his workers with the news that the latest opinion poll was giving the Conservatives a one per cent lead over Labour.[66]

This report of a slender Conservative lead briefly raised the prospect of Heath becoming Prime Minister with only a wafer-thin majority and of Powell wielding great influence in the new parliament from his customary position on the back benches, in the middle of the third bench above the gangway. But the opinion poll was, like any other, only a snapshot, and had probably detected a late swing to the Tories that still had some way to run. When the votes were finally counted, the Conservatives' lead was 3.4 per cent.[67]

Although Powell's result was one of the earliest to be declared, shortly after 11.30 p.m., the signs of a sizeable swing from Labour and shock victory for the Tories were already apparent. Just after 11 p.m., Tory Guildford and Cheltenham, and Labour Salford, had all pointed to a swing of around five per cent to the Tories. At 11.30 p.m., Powell's neighbouring Labour MP in Wolverhampton North-East, Renée Short, learned that her majority had been slashed from 8,102 to under 2,000, as a result of a swing to the Tories that exceeded nine per cent. At 11.42 p.m., television viewers saw Powell speaking after his declaration, as the on-screen sub-title informed them that, 'Enoch Powell holds Wolverhampton South-West' – in fact, he had won his biggest ever majority in the seat, with a swing from Labour of ten per cent (the seventh highest in the election).

Initial impressions as the results flooded in suggested that Wolverhampton was the epicentre of a seismic political shock that had defied all predictions. There was also a huge surge of support for the Tories in neighbouring Bilston and Cannock – Labour only held the former seat after a recount, and in the latter, Jennie Lee, Nye Bevan's widow, was defeated in a swing to the Tories of eleven per cent. Wilson reckoned that Benn's attack on Powell had cost Labour five seats. According to David Wood in Friday morning's late edition of *The Times*, Renée Short's result 'suggested that the working-class constituencies in some parts of the Midlands might be breaking away from Labour on special issues'.[68]

Powell was guarded. In response to the suggestion during the televised election coverage by Jo Grimond, the Liberal leader, that Powellism appeared to have had some effect, Powell quipped that 'Powellism is not yet in the Oxford dictionary and I would not want to comment on what it might mean'. He refused to be drawn on whether his success in Wolverhampton was a vindication of his policies. 'I cannot say that,' he remarked, 'even after studying the results of the whole country, since it is not possible to attribute specific causes to electoral movements, local and general.' His comment reflected his long-held view on the impenetrability of voting behaviour, but when asked whether he had helped the Conservative cause during the election, he replied, 'I would like to think so.' Although he felt that people 'would see this as one part of a whole picture rather than that I had something to do with a Tory victory', he had 'noticed that during the last few days I have been seen to help my party more than to hinder it'.[69]

By the weekend, however, the view that Powell had played a major part in the Conservative triumph was being played down. Political pundits and psephologists (academic students of elections) argued that Powell's impact had been exaggerated, and the victory was widely seen as Heath's. 'On the evidence one should revise one's views of the influence of Mr Powell on the campaign,' opined *The Times*. 'It does not seem likely that he had a very large effect one way or the other on the surprisingly large and broadly uniform swing to the Conservatives.' The psephologists Richard Rose and David Butler discounted Powell's impact, and pointed to the uniformity of the swing to the Conservatives throughout the country. Despite the very large swings to the Tories in five or six seats in and around Wolverhampton, the pro-Tory swing in the West Midlands as a whole was only slightly above (by 0.3 per cent) the national average – some seats in the region had experienced hardly any swing to the Conservatives. The notion that Powell's impact had been minimal was reinforced by Nicholas Deakin and Jenny Bourne in their study for the Institute of Race Relations, and by Michael Steed, who analysed the results for the Nuffield study of the election and concluded that there was no variation in the swing to the Tories, whether or not their candidate was a Powellite. 'Mr Powell certainly cannot claim to have won the election for Mr Heath,' Butler concluded. 'No individual can.'[70]

It was also argued that in some seats, Labour had gained from the immigration issue, since the heavily pro-Labour sympathies of non-white immigrants produced a discernible counter-swing to Labour. In the constituencies ranking highest in the numbers of non-white immigrants, the swing to the Conservatives was actually one per cent less than the national average. This enabled Labour to hold several London marginals, such as Baron's Court, and the Tory candidate in Eton and Slough, Nigel Lawson, thought that Powell helped him lose. Much the same point was made by Steed, though he noted that white electors were unwilling to vote for a non-white candidate –

Labour lost Wandsworth Clapham, 'on a swing which was enormous by South London standards almost certainly because their candidate, Dr Pitt, was black'.[71]

These studies, however, almost certainly underestimate Powell's impact on the 1970 election. In effect, they lose sight of the wood for the trees. Immigration was an important issue and Powell demonstrably made an impact on the campaign. Moreover, as Steed acknowledged, the *constituency* statistics cannot be used to test whether or not Powell brought votes to the Conservatives *nationally*. Subsequent studies, however, analysed other sources, and they show that Powell had a decisive influence.[72]

Powell's impact during the campaign is indisputable. As the Nuffield election study reported, he received an extraordinary share of the election coverage in the national press (20 per cent in *The Times*, 17 in the *Daily Sketch*, 16 in the *Daily Express*, 14 in the *Sun*, 13 in the *Daily Mail*), at times equalling or outdoing each of the three major party leaders. 'In this respect', Douglas Schoen has noted, 'it was a virtual four-party election, except perhaps in the eyes of the furiously anti-Powell *Guardian* and *Daily Mirror*.' During the campaign, Powell also received hundreds of supportive letters each day. Moreover, three of the major polling organizations – Harris, Gallup and NOP – concluded in their post-election analyses that Powell had influenced a substantial number of voters.[73]

NOP's evidence is the fullest and most persuasive, since they compared people's voting intentions during the campaign with how they finally voted. They found that 42 per cent said Powell had an influence, and that 60 per cent of this group admitted to having been influenced by him. Among the intending and actual Tory voters who mentioned him, 47 per cent were encouraged to vote Conservative, while only 6–7 per cent were discouraged. Among potential and actual Labour voters, about 20 per cent were influenced towards the Tories by Powell. But his influence was greatest among non-voters, 65 per cent of whom admitted to having been influenced by him, seven out of eight in a pro-Tory direction. This suggests that Powell's impact might have been greatest in cross-pressuring traditional Labour supporters into abstaining. The findings of the other pollsters also indicate that Powell had an impact. Harris reckoned that Benn made the biggest mistake of the campaign by attacking Powell, since immigration was almost the only issue on which the Tories had a better poll rating than Labour. Moreover, Powell came across better on television than almost any other politician, and had strongest appeal with working-class voters who had recently returned to Labour – 55 per cent obtained favourable impressions of him on television, as opposed to 25 per cent who had a bad impression. Likewise, Gallup found that 23 per cent of their sample said that his speeches had made them more inclined to vote Tory, against only 11 per cent saying they were less inclined. There was also a strong belief (50 per cent to 10 per cent) that Powell's speeches had helped and not hindered the Tories. Another polling organization, MORI, found in a later study that voters who said that Powell best represented their views showed three times more straight conversions from Labour to the Conservative between 1966 and 1970 than did the non-Powellite voters.[74]

The pollsters' findings are compelling, but a further indication of Powell's impact became available with the publication in 1975 of the second edition of the major study, *Political Change in Britain*, by David Butler and Donald Stokes. Their updated study showed that whereas in 1964 and 1966 voters had seen little difference between the parties on the issue of immigration, during 1969 and 1970 the electorate came to associate tough anti-immigration policies with the Conservatives. Donley T. Studlar and Douglas Schoen, two American academics who have studied this matter independently, both conclude that Powell was responsible for this change of perception, since his speeches between 1968 and 1970 gave the Tories a national reputation as the party that was most strongly opposed to non-white immigration. 'Most of the electorate had heard of Powell,' Studlar noted, 'knew generally what his proposals on immigration were and were closer in their own positions to Powell than to the actual positions of the Labour and Conservative parties'. Powell had not created the antipathy towards immigrants in Britain, but he had channelled this hostility into votes for the Conservatives. Butler and Stokes found that in 1970, 75 per cent of the electorate knew of Powell's position on immigration – an astonishingly high proportion to express their awareness of an individual politician's views. Moreover, 78 per cent said that they were glad that Powell had spoken out during the 1970 campaign.[75]

Although Butler and Stokes were cautious on the impact of immigration on the 1970 election, further analysis of their survey data supports the view that Powell made a strong impact. Schoen and R.W. Johnson confirmed MORI's conclusions, since they found that non-Tory Powellite voters were three times as likely to switch to the Conservatives as were anti-Powellites. Even racial liberals who were Powellite on other issues were ten per cent more likely than anti-Powellites to swing to the Tories. But Powell's views on immigration had the greatest impact. His popular support was based primarily upon his position on this subject, and his impact was strongest on the working-class, in the Midlands and the North, and on people aged over 45. By articulating the feelings of the public, he drew an otherwise politically disparate group of people to his support. Studlar concluded that the Tories profited substantially from the heightened perception of their being tougher than Labour on immigration, and was in no doubt that this was attributable to Powell. He calculated that the gain to the Tories from their advantage on immigration was equivalent to a national swing from Labour since 1966 of 1.3 per cent. In another study, W.L. Miller estimated that the Tory lead on immigration was worth a swing of about 1.5 per cent.[76]

It is, of course, debatable whether the impact of a single issue or an individual politician on an election result can be measured as precisely as these studies suggest. In one sense, it hardly matters, since the polling evidence all points to the same conclusion – that largely because of Powell, immigration had a very strong impact on the outcome in 1970. But if the precise calculations of this impact are correct, the Conservatives' advantage on immigration made the difference between victory and defeat. The national swing of 4.7 per cent to the Conservatives since the 1966 election enabled them to capture 77 seats from Labour and to win an overall majority of 30 seats in the Commons. If, however, the national swing to the Conservatives had been 3.6 per cent, or only 1.1 per cent less, the Labour Government would have stayed in office with a few seats' lead over the Tories. According to the detailed studies, if voters had continued to perceive little difference between the parties on immigration, the swing to the Conservatives would only have been between 3.2 and 3.4 per cent. As a result, Wilson would have remained in Downing Street and Heath's days as Tory leader would have been numbered.[77]

It is impossible to say whether Powell would have succeeded Heath as Tory leader in these circumstances. Without the clash over immigration, Powell might have remained in the Shadow Cabinet until the election, although the issues of Lords reform and EEC membership might have served as flashpoints for his increasing frustration with Heath's leadership. On the one hand, as a Shadow Minister he might have been able to appeal to a wider range of opinion in the party while offering an alternative, distinctive view of Toryism. On the other hand, without his campaign against immigration, he would not have become a national figure. But his arch-rival Heath, would not have survived as leader and Powell would have stood to gain from Tory politics becoming, in Powell's phrase, 'fluid again'.

Powell's impact on the 1970 election was extraordinary. Paradoxically, however, he was the victim of his own success. The return of a Conservative Government in June 1970 with a comfortable majority in the Commons of 30 seats was a political disaster for him. As Powell later reflected on the 1970 election, 'it sealed my exile'.[78]

17

Rebel With A Cause

I'm a Tory, full stop. People say, 'Mr Powell, you said you were born a Tory, you are a Tory, and you will die a Tory, and yet you said, "vote Labour"'. There is no contradiction. Many Labour Members are quite good Tories.

Enoch Powell on being a Tory and voting Labour, 1987.

'A voice rather than a leader'

Despite Powell's role in the Conservatives' 1970 election triumph, he suffered the galling experience of seeing Heath being given virtually all the credit for the victory. Moreover, the new Prime Minister's authority over the party was enormously strengthened. Powell's prospects were bleak. No matter how effectively he had expressed public feeling on immigration and harnessed it to the Tory cause, the realities of parliamentary and party politics now reasserted themselves. Heath's triumph had dashed any hopes of an early return for Powell to the front bench. Indeed, it appeared finally to have ruled out any remaining possibility that he might ever again hold office, an eventuality that he was to acknowledge publicly in the following October. As long as Heath remained in Downing Street, Powell's route to the front bench was blocked. The new Government's 30-seat majority seemed to guarantee Heath's tenure of Number 10 until late 1974 or early 1975. A second election victory for Heath would seal Powell's fate. But even if the Conservatives lost, and Powell was to find himself restored to the front bench, they would not, in all probability, return to office until 1978 at the earliest, by which time he would be sixty-six and it would be fifteen years since he had last served as a minister.[1]

In addition, support for Powell in the parliamentary party was limited and uncohesive. Seventy years earlier, Joseph Chamberlain had wielded influence as leader of the Unionist Party, with his own party organization, electoral domain in the West Midlands and bloc of loyal MPs. Powell had no comparable power base. After the 1970 election, *The Times* reckoned that he spoke for no more than 30 Tory MPs, while a survey of the 101 newly elected Conservative MPs in the *Sunday Times* suggested that although 35 agreed with

Powell on the need for tougher measures on immigration, they did not necessarily admire him – though equally, some moderates on race held 'a warm regard for Powell'. Similarly mixed views were held in the country: an opinion poll by ORC found 78 per cent of voters agreeing that Powell had 'great courage and sincerity' (11 per cent disagreed), but 63 per cent disagreed that he should be leader (19 per cent agreed).[2]

There was, however, a ray of hope for Powell on the issue of Europe. Assuming that negotiations with the EEC made satisfactory progress, he was bound to come into confrontation with Heath on the question of British membership. Encouragingly for Powell, the *Sunday Times* reckoned that Europe was 'the issue that might give Powell real sway with the new men'. Their survey of the recent intake found that 'the ardent Marketeer, once a Tory almost by definition is now extremely rare'. Although two-thirds of new Tory MPs backed entry 'on good terms', emphasis was put on the latter qualification. Moreover, 'there was much more evidence of passion on the issue among the anti-Marketeers'. In addition to sixteen anti-EEC newcomers, who included the little-known 'N. Tebbit (Epping)', another fourteen were said to need a lot of persuasion (some favoured a referendum before entry). 'Should Mr Heath's instincts tempt him to force the issue against public opinion,' Lewis Chester suggested, 'Powell would find a base for opposition within the House since, apart from the new men, 29 old members are tied with the anti-Common Market League.'[3]

But Powell was his own worst enemy. He had waged a crusade for his radical, and increasingly nationalist, Toryism since refusing to serve Heath's predecessor in 1963, with the aim of ensuring that the Conservatives would not adopt Macmillanite policies when they next returned to office. Now that a new Conservative Government had been formed, he found himself on the back benches. But instead of trying to organize and build support, Powell behaved as though it was sufficient for him to continue delivering treatise-like speeches and, meanwhile, to watch, hawk-like, for Heath to deviate towards Macmillanite policies. In November 1970, as the new Parliament resumed in earnest after the long summer recess, Powell told television viewers that the Prime Minister was afraid of him. 'He generally seems to exhibit the symptoms of fear. It seems to be the only thing which really rationalizes his behaviour where I am concerned.' It was an ill-judged and insulting comment, however much Powell believed it to be the case.[4]

Even after events began to move in his direction and he was in open rebellion against the Heath administration, he still made no attempt to build an anti-Heathite party. Powell's 'intellectual austerity', in John Biffen's phrase, set him apart from most politicians. Although this quality attracted a small band of loyalist MPs it was not going to win the wider support and secure the necessary leverage that was needed if Powellism was to capture the Tory Party and transform British politics. But Powell was not a political boss in the Chamberlain tradition, neither was he even a factional leader in the Aneurin Bevan mould, although he possessed the pedigree for such a role, as Richard

Rose noted at the time: 'he is of senior ministerial stature, articulate, able to exploit the press and broadcasting media, and in disagreement with the party leadership on many major issues, both foreign and domestic'. But without organized followers, Rose tellingly observed, 'Powell is a voice rather than a leader.'[5]

By any standards, however, Powell was some voice. During the seven years before Heath entered office, Powell had developed an alternative and distinctive form of Toryism. While the party remained in Opposition and during the early stages of the Heath Government, support for Powellism among Tory MPs was limited by a combination of self-interested career calculation and also by the fact that those who sympathized with Powell on one issue disagreed on others – for example, some economic liberals were antagonized by his stridency on immigration. But as the Heath Government began increasingly to rouse back bench opposition, through a combination of radical reform, policy U-turns and the Prime Minister's insensitivity to his MPs, Powell's advocacy of an alternative view served as a unifying focus of dissent. Between 1970 and 1974, as Philip Norton has convincingly demonstrated, Powell used the floor of the Commons, its standing committees and Tory back bench party meetings as the forum for articulating his alternative Toryism. His effectiveness was captured in an acute observation by Alan Watkins in March 1971, when he wrote of an attack on the Government's Northern Ireland policy in which, 'with his usual percipience, his eye for a sub-editor's phrase, his talent for mischief-making, Mr Enoch Powell seized on the question of the no-go areas before anyone else did'.[6]

The extent of Powell's rebelliousness during the 1970–74 parliament is astonishing. He again resembled an eighteenth-century back bench Country Tory, who seemed set on finding grounds to oppose his front bench Court counterparts whenever possible. Powell voted against the Conservative Government in 115 divisions – more often than any other Tory dissenter. According to Norton's painstaking calculation, Powell was joined by one or more Conservative MPs in 109 divisions and entered the Opposition lobby on only six occasions on his own. His advocacy of an alternative view fuelled the extraordinary amount of Tory back bench dissent, championing a set of attitudes that had a certain Country Tory appeal against the managerial pragmatism increasingly pursued by the Heathite Court. As Julian Critchley, the anti-Powellite Tory MP, wryly noted in 1973, Powell acted as 'a magnet for the disaffected … a comfort to those like he who advocate simplistic solutions to complex problems'.[7]

Powell's unrivalled ability to exert a magnetic pull in the country on the Tory faithful and disillusioned voters alike made him a lurking menace for Heath's party managers at Central Office. At times during the Heath administration, Powell's threat was latent and he seemed an isolated figure. But he always remained a big beast of the political jungle who was roaming loose and who might, if suddenly provoked, go on the rampage, tear apart the

Tory camp, trample their crops and kill the livestock. His ability to appeal over the heads of the party leaders directly to voters of all persuasions, his reluctance to dirty his hands in organizing a faction and the sense that he sometimes gave of believing that he was a man of destiny, were to elicit increasingly frequent comparisons with the recently retired French President, General de Gaulle.

Yet it was a reflection of Powell's isolation from the mainstream of party politics, as well as of his cross-party appeal in the country, that the allusion came to be commonly made to his waiting on a call from the nation in its hour of need – in the same way that de Gaulle had been summoned from his retreat in Colombey-les-deux-Eglises to settle the French constitutional crisis in 1958. 'Wolverhampton-les-deux-Eglises' became a satirical commonplace that conveyed a sense of Powell's detached predicament and his idiosyncratic approach. Powell had helped to reinforce this impression by his decision not to attend October's Conservative conference at Blackpool, that became a victory rally for Heath, although as late as the end of July he had suggested that it would be necessary to await the conference before being able to judge what had happened in the 1970 election – one implication being that the conference would show that the Tory triumph had been a result of the enthusiasm generated in the constituencies by Powell rather than by Heath. The Powells planned a cruise instead of going to the conference, but although they called it off because of a dock strike they stayed away from Blackpool.[8]

The Gaullist analogy was further encouraged by Powell, less than a month after he had failed to turn up at Blackpool, in his eulogistic review for the *Spectator* of the first volume of the General's memoirs. In an echo of his attack on the media during June's election campaign, Powell noted de Gaulle's ability, despite the opposition of 'virtually the whole press, as well as other organs of public opinion ... to appeal successfully over their heads direct to the listeners and viewers'. And in strong echoes of his views on Britain, Powell highlighted that the psychological renewal of France could not begin until the French had 'put their own imperial and colonial past behind them', following de Gaulle's decisive action on Algeria. Moreover, he lauded de Gaulle's rejection of the 'nuclear hypothesis' that America's strategic umbrella afforded protection to western Europe. But it was his conclusion that pointed to the strongest common denominator of Gaullism and Powellism. 'De Gaulle's ultimate assertion,' Powell noted approvingly,

> was first, last and always the nation. In a Europe and a Western world which was trying to pretend the nation away, the replacement of the nation in the centre of politics and diplomacy worked like a spell. As de Gaulle expresses it in one passage: 'the action of a France which does not avoid or conceal the fact of being France arouses the attention of the peoples of the Third World'. But it was not only in the Third World. From Moscow to New York, from Bonn to Montreal, the other nations discovered that they

were vulnerable to a head of state who asserted this simple but sovereign fact. It was, de Gaulle believed, what he was there to do: *Moi suis-je là pour autre chose?*

As Powell implied, he himself was a Gaullist figure in that by trying to restore the nation to the centre of Tory, and British, politics, he was doing what he believed he was there to do. But he was not in a Gaullist situation, and instead was working in a political system that demanded the mobilization and organization of support in parliament and in the country.[9]

Lonely dissident

The terrible shock felt at the sudden death of Iain Macleod in July 1970, only a month after his appointment as Chancellor, seemed to cause Powell to lose his judgement. While others paid tribute, Powell tactlessly dredged up their final rift. 'I am sad to think', Powell commented, 'that when Iain Macleod and I entered the House of Commons together twenty years ago, no two members of our generation were closer, politically or personally; when he left it, no two were further apart.' Macleod's death also threw Heath off balance, and in the reshuffle occasioned by the need to appoint a new Chancellor, Powell saw the new Prime Minister's first mistake. Heath moved Barber to the Treasury and gave his job of handling the negotiations on British entry to the European Economic Community to Rippon, who had originally been put in charge at Technology. Heath's error, to Powell's mind, came in his choice of John Davies, the former Director-General of the Confederation of British Industry, who had only been elected to the Commons for the first time just over a month earlier, as the new Minister of Technology. As Powell realized, this appointment was bound to offend many Tory MPs who had expected office. Davies also epitomized the professional spokesman for business whom Powell detested, and was by instinct an interventionist. As Alan Watkins shrewdly observed, Davies's appointment suggested that behind Heath's free enterprise rhetoric, a retreat to orthodox, i.e. interventionist, industrial policy was on the cards. In Powell's view, the choice of Davies would hasten Heath's nemesis.[10]

Within six months, Powell was in dispute with the front bench on the issue of Government intervention, but his first public disagreement with Heath after the 1970 election concerned the threat from terrorism that Powell had highlighted in his 'enemy within' speech during the election campaign. On 30 September, Powell fiercely attacked the Government's decision to free Leila Khaled, who had been arrested at Heathrow several weeks earlier, after a failed attempt by members of the Palestinian Front for the Liberation of Palestine to hijack an Israeli airliner. Khaled's release, and that of six Palestinian terrorists held by Switzerland and West Germany, followed the PFLP's release of the remaining hostages whom they had seized in several other hijacks and had threatened to kill. Powell, however, condemned the Government's decision to 'interfere with the course of law' as an unconstitutional act. 'Like all breaches of the rule of law,' he argued, 'it is not only wrong in itself but fraught with grave consequences for the future.'[11]

Yet Powell's censure failed to take into account the Government's difficult legal position. Heath had to play a careful hand because of legal advice by the Attorney-General, Sir Peter Rawlinson, that unless the hijacking could be shown to have been committed over British soil, there would be no case against Khaled under British law – a prosecution seemed unlikely to succeed, since the captain had reported that the hijacking occurred 'south of Clacton'. As the case against Khaled was almost certainly unsustainable, the most that the Government could have done was to deport her. But the Palestinians were unaware of this, and Heath called their bluff by insisting that only when all the hostages were safe would Khaled be released. This was part of the deal finally brokered through Egypt's President Nasser. There was no interference with the law in Britain, and the hostages had been saved. None the less, as far as Powell was concerned, Heath had revealed the vulnerable side of his personality.[12]

It was not many months before Powell detected further evidence of Heath's vulnerability to pressure, but he remained a lone voice of public dissent. On 4 February 1971, less than eight months after the Conservatives had returned to office pledged to disengage the state from industry, they announced their remarkable decision to nationalize Rolls-Royce Aero Engines. Rolls-Royce was one of Britain's most prestigious companies whose name was synonymous with free enterprise, but it was in serious difficulty because of the disastrous miscalculation of a contract to supply engines for the American Lockheed RB 211 airbus. The Labour Government had provided £20 million of support through the Industrial Reorganization Corporation – an action that had prompted Powell in his June 1970 election address to include Rolls-Royce in the list of industries he cited to support his claim that 'under Labour state ownership has spread'. When the Conservatives granted a further sum of £42 million in public funds only five months later, Powell abstained in the Commons vote on 23 November 1970. His abstention was, in fact, his second revolt against the Heath Government, but it was a more significant portent than his vote against the renewal of the Rhodesian sanctions order on 9 November, since this was something of an annual ritual.[13]

Within two months, the Tories' extra financial aid to Rolls Royce had proved insufficient, but the company was an important supplier to the Ministry of Defence and was nationalized. Powell, however, was scathing in the Commons emergency debate on this Tory nationalization, arguing that the Government had cast doubt and discredit upon the belief in capitalism and private enterprise. As he understood the Conservative Party's principles, if Rolls-Royce failed to make a profit, so much the worse for them. Yet the nationalization of Rolls-Royce was easily presented as a special case. Even Powell abstained instead of voting against the Government, and fervent economic liberals on the Tory back benches, including Biffen, Richard Body and Jock Bruce-Gardyne, who were later to join Powell in opposing Heath's economic policies, voted with the front bench. None the less, the division lobby rang with gibes from disquieted Tories, and Heath's claim to offer a break with the fixing and fudging of his predecessors in Number 10 was badly dented.[14]

Only a week after his dissent on the Tory nationalization, Powell appeared to go out even further on a limb in a fresh outburst on immigration. As always with Powell, the timing of his speech was chosen for maximum effect. He had not made a major speech on the subject since the election campaign, eight months earlier, but within the next month MPs were to debate the main item of legislation in the opening, 1970–71, session of the new parliament – the Tory Immigration Bill. Powell increased pressure on the Conservative Home Secretary, Reggie Maudling, to stiffen the curbs on immigration and to include provision for a major scheme of assisted repatriation as an urgent priority.

In his speech on 15 February, Powell renewed his allegations that both the size of the immigrant population and its rate of growth had been underestimated. As a result, he claimed, the non-white population would be at least four million by 1985, representing seven per cent of the total population (the official figure by 1996 was over three million, or almost six per cent). Echoing his apocalyptic 'River Tiber' warning of the consequences of large non-white populations in the inner cities, he declared that 'the explosive which will blow us asunder is there and the fuse is burning, but the fuse is shorter than had been supposed'. As the only hope of averting disaster, he urged that immigration from the New Commonwealth 'must cease and cease now', and that a massive programme of voluntary repatriation should be introduced. Yet as the immediate furore over Powell's speech died down, it seemed that he had misjudged the political mood. Heath again dissociated himself from Powell's comments, and found support in the popular press. The *Daily Sketch*, whose readership of working-class Tories included natural Powellites, attacked his views on repatriation as 'blindly, dangerously wrong', while the *Sun*, in a front-page editorial, argued that he was more dangerous than the immigrants. Even in his Wolverhampton base, the *Express and Star* believed that Powell's repeated 'solution' of massive, voluntary repatriation, coupled with his emotive language, 'can only lead to a further setback in community relations. That such a repatriation plan could solve Britain's problems is a delusion. That a voluntary scheme, even on a limited level could work, is also a delusion'. Moreover, the Black Country paper feared that 'the introduction of repatriation could lead to harassment and persecution of immigrant families to return home'.[15]

Powell would have been justified in claiming much of the credit for the Government's new Immigration Bill, since the legislation tightened immigration control principally by treating Commonwealth citizens the same as aliens, and included provision for voluntary repatriation. Even Powell's sympathizers hoped that he would now end his anti-immigration campaign. 'A POWEL-LITE TRIUMPH', was the headline judgement of the *Spectator* on 6 March. Claiming that the Bill was 'a great vindication for Mr Enoch Powell', the Tory-inclined paper hoped that 'he, and everyone else, will come to regard it as a culmination, and as an end', since it provided 'an excellent opportunity' for the removal of race and immigration from politics. 'We suggest that everyone seize that opportunity, not excluding Mr Powell.'[16]

Any such hope, however, was dashed when Powell was called to speak first from the Tory back benches in the Bill's second reading debate on 8 March, and immediately dismissed the notion that the legislation would achieve 'finality'. He lamented the failure to tackle the problem of defining United Kingdom citizenship head on – although he did not reveal that he had urged the creation of a new United Kingdom citizenship as long ago as 1961. The 1971 Immigration Bill, however, continued in the same vein as its predecessors. Instead of reforming the citizenship law, it legislated by exception. In an attempt to define who 'belonged to' the United Kingdom, the 'patrial' provision excluded from immigration control anybody who had a grandparent born in the United Kingdom. Powell was heavily critical of this 'patrial' provision, arguing that it was anomalous and untenable. He pointed out that many Australians who felt bound by 'affection and loyalty' to Britain did not have a grandparent born in the United Kingdom, and would be denied the right of entry to Britain that was now extended to some of their compatriots. And he noted that the tens of thousands of Anglo-Indians, many of whom were employed on Indian railways, would qualify as 'patrials' with the right of entry. Moreover, he argued that the 'patrial' definition would be seen as racial, and recalled the phrase used in Nazi Germany, *Grossmutter nicht in Ordnung* ('grandmother not in order'), meaning that if there was one grandparent who was Jewish, a person would be subject to the discrimination and persecution imposed upon that race.

In addition, Powell criticized the fact that although the Bill removed from future immigrants the right to bring in dependants, it none the less continued to allow existing immigrants already in the country to bring in their wives and children up to the age of sixteen. For this reason, Powell argued that the Bill would not achieve the drastic reduction in immigration that he had advocated. He also condemned Maudling's statement that 'repatriation in practice cannot be on a substantial scale', but welcomed the Bill's provision for repatriation, with the caveat that there should be no limit on the availability of assistance for any immigrant who voluntarily applied for it.[17]

Despite Powell's severe criticism of the Bill, and his warning over the Government's limited concept of repatriation, he none the less voted with the front bench at the end of the second reading debate. The battle, however, was by no means over. He sparred with Maudling over the Government's responsibility to the Kenyan Asians (see above, pp. 334–6), and served on the standing committee on the Bill, where he was depicted by the journalist, Sally Vincent,

> sitting like some deadly catalyst in unearthly contemplation while the drift of his philosophy flows back and forth on the lips of others. He is still and silent as a lizard. For an eternity he holds himself bolt upright, hands clasped together on the back of his head. Let your eyes slide away for a split second and – bingo! – he is slumped right down in his seat, arms hugging knees to bosom, but equally still, frozen in a kind of cataleptic tension.

Powell scored a significant victory during the committee stage. In an unholy alliance with the liberal-minded Tory MP, Sir George Sinclair, and Opposition MPs, Powell succeeded in deleting the proposed 'patrial' clause. Instead of trying to restore the clause, ministers conceded defeat and replaced it, to Powell's satisfaction, with a new formula that restricted the right of patriality to anybody who had British nationality status at the time of their birth. But he emphasized his dissatisfaction with the Government's new controls on 2 May with another dire prediction, on this occasion warning that there would be 'fighting' between white people and immigrants in fifteen years time. Powell had succeeded in taking credit for the introduction of tougher immigration controls, while retaining his status as the focus of discontent on the issue in the country.[18]

Powell sought to link the issues of immigration and Europe in January 1971, when addressing a Young Unionists Rally in Londonderry – Ulster was to become a regular feature of his speaking itinerary. In this speech, he explained that he could not understand how a nation that was in the throes of rescuing its identity from the 'delusions and deceits of a vanished empire and a vanished Commonwealth, can at the same time undertake to merge that identity again in half the Continent of Europe'. But in April, his accusation against the Prime Minister of having 'misled' the electorate over entry into the EEC was unlikely to win Tory waverers to the anti-EEC cause. Powell's charge against Heath provoked Rippon, who was leading the official negotiations on British entry, to recall Powell's earlier support for the EEC. Emphasizing Powell's isolation by dismissing him as 'poor old Mr Powell', Rippon declared: 'People may change their minds, but they should be humble about it.' Powell, however, was unabashed and in May took the credit for the 1970 Conservative election victory. Speaking in Wolverhampton at a celebration of his twenty-first year as MP, he claimed that 'without what was done and said here and from here a year ago Edward Heath would not be Prime Minister of England'. Many Conservatives knew that this was so, he argued, but he understood the reasons for the party's reticence on this subject. As has been shown, there is compelling evidence for Powell's boast, but his comments about the party's reticence in acknowledging his role were unlikely to win new friends in the party.[19]

Battle over Europe

Rippon's irritation with Powell reflected the fact that while Rippon was doggedly pursuing the Government's negotiations in Brussels, Powell had taken his campaign against British entry into the EEC to the European mainland. During the first half of 1971, Powell spoke in Frankfurt, Turin and Lyons in the language of his audiences, and at The Hague in English. But in May, Heath achieved an historic breakthrough in Paris, when de Gaulle's successor as French President, Georges Pompidou, having been reassured of the British Prime Minister's European credentials and seeing the benefit of Britain's becoming a net contributor to the EEC budget, lifted the French veto. The roadblock that had barred British entry for eight years had been removed, and entry terms were quickly agreed – though at a price. The scene was set for the anticipated head-to-head confrontation in Britain between Heath and Powell.[20]

Although the 1970 Conservative manifesto had committed a future Tory Government 'to negotiate, no more, no less', British membership of the EEC had long been Heath's overriding political ambition and was the corner-stone of his administration's policies. The manifesto put the onus for deciding on British membership on parliament, but Heath appeared to acknowledge the need to convince a sceptical public by stating that: 'Nor would it be in the interests of the Community that its enlargement should take place except with the full-hearted consent of parliaments and peoples of the new member countries.' But although referenda were to be held on EEC membership in the other three applicant countries (Ireland, Denmark and Norway), there appeared to be no prospect of one in Britain. Powell, like many other opponents of British entry, was against the idea as being at odds with parliamentary government.[21]

Despite having to face an inbuilt majority in the Commons in favour of British entry, Powell was not downcast that the battle over British membership of the EEC was to be fought in parliament. Only two years earlier, a determined minority of Tory and Labour rebels had thwarted their front benches over the proposed reform of the upper House, and it seemed likely that the Bill required to bring about the constitutional revolution of British entry into the EEC would provide even greater opportunity for delay and obstruction than had the legislation to reform the Lords. Initially, there were encouraging signs for Powell. The Government's majority by 1971 was below 30, and was easily exceeded by the 44 Tory MPs who had signed an early day motion in 1970 opposing British entry. The postponement of a parliamentary vote on the principle of British entry, from the summer of 1971 until after the party conference season, was a measure of the Conservative party managers' nervousness. Powell, however, was misled by the back bench triumph in 1969 over a measure that had only lukewarm front bench support into underestimating the lengths to which Heath and his supporters and pro-EEC allies in other parties were prepared to go in order to secure British membership of the EEC. Part of Powell's problem was that he never regarded Heath as possessing the Whiggish cynicism and deviousness of Macmillan (though Heath had been Macmillan's Chief Whip), although he was fully aware of the strength of Heath's European commitment and of his efficiency in achieving his goals.[22]

The public's apparent hostility to the EEC was too powerful a counter for any anti-EEC campaigner to ignore, even if, as in Powell's case, he was opposed to a referendum. Powell envisaged public opinion as a powerful means of exerting pressure on MPs, but he totally misjudged public opinion. In June 1971, the persistence of a year-long large majority in the polls against British entry led Powell to liken the British people to a heavy sleeper who had been roused at last by an insistent alarm bell:

> In these last months and weeks a national instinct and resolution has stirred and visibly grown and taken shape and strength, until the onlooker is tempted to think or say: 'Perhaps, after all, they are the same nation which so many times before has risen late, but not too late, to assert itself in the face of the world.'

Powell, however, failed to appreciate that most voters, to the extent that they thought about British entry into the EEC, tended to link it with higher prices. His concern at the EEC's threat to Britain's national sovereignty failed to resonate with many people. But they were ready to follow the advice of their party leaders because they saw the question of British entry as a foreign policy matter more than a domestic one.[23]

Within a month, Powell's claim to have detected a stirring of national resolution against the EEC was shown to be completely misplaced. During July 1971, the pro-EEC campaign launched by the Government and Conservative Party propaganda machines yielded immediate dividends. The mass distribution of the White Paper on Britain's negotiations with the EEC led to a dramatic surge in popular support for entry, even though public opinion swung generally against the Government – a revival of hostility towards the EEC during late 1971 reflected the Government's unpopularity. But crucially, in terms of the debate within the Conservative Party, EEC entry became more popular with declared Conservative voters, who had been hostile in the 1960s – a balance of 54:34 against entry in February was transformed to 68:19 in favour by late July. Over 2,000 senior party activists enthusiastically backed Heath at a special meeting of the Central Council, and 800,000 copies of a shortened version of the White Paper were mailed to Tory members. The majority of Tory MPs also rallied strongly behind Heath now that the party was on the brink of achieving a major British objective of more than a decade's standing. The overwhelmingly pro-EEC stance of most national newspapers, the pro-EEC bias of broadcasters and the European Movement's well-funded campaign for British entry, all helped reinforce the Conservatives' decisive shift in favour of entry.[24]

The pro-EEC propaganda campaign swamped Powell's series of speeches against British entry between July and October 1971. His prediction in September that Britain would never join the EEC was brushed aside. By October's party conference at Brighton, the swing in favour of British membership among Conservatives in the country was reflected in the 69 constituency motions supporting entry, against only four motions that were totally opposed. In an impassioned plea to the conference to oppose British entry, Powell defiantly declared:

I do not believe that this nation, which has maintained its independence for a thousand years, will now submit to see it merged or lost; nor did I become a member of our sovereign parliament in order to consent to that sovereignty being abated or transferred. Come what may, I cannot and I will not.

The implications of his last sentence were only to become fully apparent in 1974. Yet he was unable to change the basic arithmetic – at the end of the debate Heath took the highly unusual step for a Tory leader of calling for a ballot in order to demonstrate the party's overwhelming support for British entry (representatives voted in favour by 2,474 to 324).[25]

In referring to 'a thousand years' of British independence, Powell had closely echoed the phrase used at Brighton in 1962 by Gaitskell, the then Labour leader, when he had committed the Labour Opposition to oppose British membership of the EEC. Powell had been a minister in Macmillan's Government at the time, and, as such, had been on the opposite side of the European debate. But in 1971 his hopes of preventing British entry had been raised by the shift of opinion that was occurring within the Labour Party now that they were in Opposition. Indeed, at Labour's October conference, also at Brighton, Wilson had signalled the Opposition's intention to fight the Government over the Bill on British entry that would follow the forthcoming vote on principle: 'I cannot imagine a single Labour member who, faced with this legislation, will not be in the lobbies against the government.'[26]

Powell was the only national figure among the anti-EEC Tories, but despite the intellectual force and passion of his speeches on Europe he was of limited value in winning support where it now counted most, in the Commons. The long-standing anti-EEC Tory campaigner, Neil Marten, was more clubbable than Powell and he undertook the task of cultivating potential anti-EEC dissidents on the Tory benches. The scale of the problem that faced Powell and his fellow anti-EEC campaigners was apparent soon after parliament resumed in the autumn. Heath acted on the advice of his Chief Whip, Francis Pym, in allowing a free vote to Conservative MPs at the end of the historic debate in late October on the principle of British entry. Pym had received intimations that by allowing a free vote on the Government benches, pro-EEC Labour MPs would be prepared to defy the Opposition's three-line whip and support the Government. This tactic succeeded handsomely, though it fuelled some of the angriest scenes in the Commons for decades when the result of the division was declared. MPs voted by 356 to 244 votes, a majority of 112, in favour of British membership. Labour's 69 pro-EEC rebels more than cancelled out the 39 anti-EEC Tories (including six Ulster Unionists), who trooped through the Opposition lobby – two Tories also abstained. In scenes reminiscent of the passionate debates over Munich in 1938 or Suez in 1956, Jenkins was called a 'fascist bastard' by another Labour MP, while Powell was provoked to call out to a minister who was leaving after the division, 'It won't do! It won't do!'[27]

Despite their crushing defeat, Powell and other anti-EEC campaigners still entertained hopes of blocking the legislation that was required to give effect to British entry. It was widely assumed that the constitutional upheaval created by bringing British institutions and law into line with the EEC would require a massive Bill – possibly amounting to as many as one thousand clauses. The parliamentary draftsman, however, boiled down the necessary provisions in the European Communities Bill to a mere twelve clauses. It was a severe blow to the anti-EEC campaign. 'The simplicity of the Bill overwhelmed all who saw it,' Powell later recalled. 'I think the Government was as delighted with it as the opposition was horrified by it.'[28]

None the less, Powell remained hopeful, since the Labour Opposition were now committed to vote against it and therefore only a dozen or so Tory dissidents might be sufficient to defeat the Bill. Powell was one of four Tory anti-EEC rebels who rose to oppose the Bill on second reading in mid-February 1972. The significance that he attached to this debate was evident from his opening comments. 'We are approaching this question for the first time as a practical one', he told MPs. 'Never till now has the House of Commons had placed before it proposed legislation on which it must take a definite view and on which it must envisage as a practical issue what it will mean for this country if we accede to the Community'. According to Powell, the Bill manifested some of the major consequences of British membership of the EEC: parliament would lose its legislative supremacy; the Commons would lose its control over taxation and expenditure, on which its ability to control the executive rested; and the independence of Britain's judiciary would be surrendered. Those 'essential sacrifices of sovereignty' were evident upon the face of the Bill. In addition, Powell argued, the Bill implicitly strengthened the executive vis-à-vis the Commons.

In the tradition of the best debaters in the Commons, Powell met the arguments of his opponents head on. As to the suggestion that joining the EEC involved a loss of sovereignty over only a few areas and the Bill was therefore not very important, Powell countered that the Prime Minister and all the greatest advocates of British membership had argued for entry on the grounds 'not that the effect will be minimal but that this is intended to lead progressively to the political unification of Western Europe. That has been said candidly, frankly, over and over again.' And as to the argument that the elected Government – and therefore the Commons – would be able to control

Community law and Community powers, Powell contended that in future ministers would tell MPs that they had to accept decisions reached in the EEC's Council of Ministers, because otherwise Britain would be in breach of the Treaty of Rome. The power of the Commons, and of the electorate, depended on their ability to reverse decisions, yet this power would be lost inside the EEC. 'What meaning has the right of the electorate to send Members here,' Powell queried, 'unless, so far as legislation and administration can bring it about, what has been done in the past can, if the electors decide, be reversed?' Although Powell had made a telling argument on sovereignty, he failed to acknowledge that Britain, like any other member-state, would retain the power of veto on matters of national interest – a power that had been established for national Governments by de Gaulle.

A more immediate tactical problem for Powell was how to counter the Government's majority in the Commons. He sought to maximize the effect on MPs of the rather shallow public scepticism towards the EEC by reminding them of Heath's words about needing the 'full-hearted consent' of parliament and people. Nobody could seriously claim, he argued, that the people had given their full-hearted consent. Neither would the anticipated narrow Commons majority for the Bill meet the Prime Minister's conditions. Powell's final, moving plea to MPs reflected his own passionate attachment to the House of Commons as the embodiment of the British nation, its history and traditions:

> For this House, lacking the necessary authority either out-of-doors or indoors, legislatively to give away the independence and sovereignty of this House now and for the future is an unthinkable act. Even if there were not those outside to whom we have to render account, the very stones of this place would cry out against such a thing.[29]

During his speech, Powell repeated an accusation that he had made a few days earlier and that was to become the basis of his subsequent claim that Heath had forced Britain into the EEC. 'In order to secure a narrow majority tonight,' Powell said of the Government, 'they have brought to bear upon hon. Members of different views, despite my right hon. Friend's [Heath's] assurance that they would have an absolute right to vote as they so decided on this question, every available form of pressure.' Heath had, in fact, allowed a free vote on the principle of entry, but no Government could afford to allow a free vote on a major Bill, especially since the Opposition were committed to vote against. Accordingly, the Conservative whips' office had responded with their customary ruthlessness and coarseness, identifying three groups of Tory MPs – 'the robusts' were staunchly pro-EEC, and were ticked with a blue pencil; 'the wets' were less certain in their views; and 'the shits' were against entry and were ticked with a brown pencil. Powell was regarded as too much of an out-and-out 'shit' by the whips for them to try and prevent him opposing the Bill, but pressure was brought to bear on 'wets' and the more pliable 'shits' and the number of dissenters was gradually whittled down. Powell alleged that Ulster Unionist MPs, who had mostly voted against entry in October, had been told that the Government would refuse to support Northern Ireland if they failed to support the Government on the Common Market. An Ulster Unionist MP, however, suggested that the main pressure originated with their rank and file, who feared that Heath's defeat would again place their destiny in the hands of Wilson and a Labour Government.[30]

But the threat of 'de-selection' of anti-EEC Tory MPs by their constituency parties was real – a fate that the leading anti-EEC Tory, Neil Marten, averted only by issuing his own threat to resign, force a by-election and stand as an independent. In addition, Heath issued a spine-chilling threat to Tory dissidents by declaring the vote a matter of confidence. In other words, if the Government were defeated, Heath would resign and call a general election. It was virtually certain that a Government that called an election in such circumstances would be defeated. Powell was scornful of those would-be rebels who succumbed to this threat, since he did not believe that any Prime Minister would surrender power voluntarily, especially one who had occupied Number 10 for little more than eighteen months. But he recognized that there had been a 'more intensive brainwashing operation on the potential dissenters than any Prime Minister, reverting to his previous character as Chief Whip, has ever carried out'. Although no attempt was made to 'soften up' Powell, he has recalled that 'those who went into Ted Heath's room in the week before the second reading came out looking more like ghosts than men'. Of the nine doubters who were taken to see Heath, four responded to his appeals and a fifth would-be rebel also subsequently supported the Government.[31]

At the end of the debate, Powell and fourteen other Tories voted with the Opposition, and another five abstained. Although Labour's pro-EEC MPs all voted with the Opposition, the Government none the less won a majority of eight. The vote would have been even closer had not Wilson been so partisan that he prompted three would-be Tory rebels to support the Government (two had intended to abstain, and one to vote against). As Philip Norton has pointed out, it was the first occasion since the Second World War that a group of Conservative MPs had entered an Opposition lobby against a Conservative Government on a vote of confidence. In the graphic phrase of John Biffen, Powell's strongest Tory ally in the battle against the Bill, the second reading was the high-water mark of dissent.[32]

Powell was probably the only Tory dissident who was prepared to bring down the Government on the second or third reading of the European Communities Bill. But as the Bill was concerned with a major constitutional reform, its committee stage had to be held on the floor of the House, and this appeared to give the anti-EEC Tories a strong chance to defeat the Government on amendments to the Bill. Powell, Biffen and Marten met regularly to discuss tactics, and the Government whips faced the daunting task of maintaining a majority given the likely opposition of between five and twenty Tory dissidents.

At this point, Powell had another change of mind when he decided to support the call for a referendum on British membership of the EEC, even though one of his main reasons for opposing the EEC was its threat to parliamentary government in Britain. His conversion became apparent in his support for an amendment, proposed by Neil Marten, that would require a consultative referendum to be held before Britain could enter the EEC. This proposal was to have a profound effect on British politics. Labour's Shadow Cabinet had rejected Tony Benn's call for a referendum on 15 March, but the following day President Pompidou announced that the French would hold a referendum on EEC enlargement. At the same time, there was much talk about holding a plebiscite in Northern Ireland on the Province's future – such an initiative was formally announced by the Government on 24 March. On 22 March, Benn, as Labour Party chairman, persuaded the party's National Executive Committee to support a referendum on the EEC. A week later, the Labour Shadow Cabinet discussed whether or not to support Marten's amendment when it was debated after the Easter recess – it was also expected that Powell would support the amendment. On 29 March, the Shadow Cabinet reversed their earlier decision and recommended a whipped vote of the Labour Party to follow Marten and Powell into the lobby. It was this *volte-face* by Labour that prompted Roy Jenkins to resign as Deputy Leader and leave the front bench, with George Thomson and Harold Lever.[33]

Labour's decision to back a referendum marked a spectacular triumph for the anti-EEC lobby. Even if they were defeated in the Commons vote on Marten's amendment, there was now every prospect that at the next election Labour would propose a referendum, thereby giving the voters a choice on the issue of British membership. Judging from the tone of a speech that Powell delivered in Staffordshire on 8 April – and that he circulated privately, not through Conservative Central Office – he appeared already to be thinking of a future election battle with Heath on the EEC instead of the imminent debate in the Commons. Arguing that it was an insult to the intelligence of the British public for the Government to pretend that parliament had given full-hearted consent to British membership of the EEC, his strong language was likely only to deepen the division in the Conservative Party, instead of appealing to Tory doubters. He alleged that the Government were so conscious 'of not having even the bare consent of the House of Commons that no device of political pressure and thuggery has been omitted to constrain Conservative MPs to vote on this issue against their opinion and conscience – a fine commentary on the meaning of full-hearted'. And Powell warned Heath that if he took Britain into Europe he would 'go down to history bearing with him the indelible brand of broken faith and trust betrayed'.

The speech was one of Powell's more emotive efforts and, according to *The Times*, 'some Conservative MPs could scarcely contain their wrath'. One or two Tory back-benchers urged Powell's immediate expulsion from the party, while others suspected that this was what Powell most desired. 'He'd love to play Becket to Heath's Henry II', one MP remarked. Since, however, it was unlikely that Powell's rift with Heath could ever be mended, the party managers had no intention of withdrawing the whip from Powell as they would eventually be faced with having to field an official Conservative candidate in Wolverhampton South-West in the certain knowledge that Powell would be elected. This was a significant decision. Withdrawing the whip might well have acted as the impetus that Powell needed for him and his lieutenants to start organizing a party within a party. Powell was later to regard his failure to organize in this way as having been a mistake.[34]

During the debate on Marten's amendment on 18 April, Powell made clear his preference for another amendment, moved by Labour's Peter Shore, that would require a general election (as opposed to a referendum) to be held before British membership of the EEC could come into effect. Explaining that he was no friend of a referendum, Powell told MPs that he found it hard to reconcile a referendum, even on a matter of this unique character, with responsible parliamentary government as it was known in this country. None the less, he argued, MPs 'owed it to our constituents and to the House of Commons itself to place on record tonight that that consent, that authority, is not in our hands. Each of the amendments does it in its own way, and for each for that reason I shall record my vote.' As he sat down, his words were cheered by Labour MPs. Powell was the only Conservative to support Shore's amendment, that was defeated by a majority of 29 votes. Powell was among 22 Tories who joined 209 Labour MPs in supporting Marten's call for a referendum, but the Government won a majority of 49 votes.[35]

By May, so little progress had been made in committee that the Government were forced to introduce a 'guillotine' motion, limiting the remaining time for debating the Bill. The Government won this crucial division by only eleven votes, with the support of the Liberals. At times, the Government majority fell as low as five. In fact, Powell and his allies never stood a chance of carrying a single amendment because Labour's pro-EEC MPs always made sure that a sufficient number of them abstained in order to guarantee the Bill's passage. The Bill finally received its third reading in July 1972, with Powell again voting against. In all, Powell voted against the European Communities Bill and related motions on 80 separate occasions, more than any other Tory rebel (Biffen voted against in 78 divisions, and Marten in 69).[36]

Powell could never forgive Heath for having forced the European Communities Bill through the Commons. In view of Heath's past as a chief whip, Powell should have realized that every ploy known to the whips' office would be used in order to overcome the anti-EEC minority of MPs. However much Powell abhorred the methods that were used, an experienced politician who distrusted government and its officials should not have been so surprised. He had to try and rationalize how such an unmitigated disaster could possibly have happened. In his speech to the parliamentary press gallery in May 1972, he was scathing about the readiness of his fellow MPs to think only of themselves when they were persuaded or pressurized into voting away the centuries-old powers of the House of Commons. Having developed an idealized view of the Commons, Powell was deeply disappointed when other MPs demonstrably failed to share his ideal.[37]

It was equally difficult for Powell to appreciate how the Conservative Party, that had always represented the evolutionary and organic Tory approach to politics, could have supported such a profound constitutional and political upheaval. He predicted dire consequences for the Conservatives and their leader as a result. He believed that his fellow Conservatives had succumbed to a fashionable theory that Britain had to belong to something big. The Empire had gone, and there was a feeling that it had to be replaced by something else – Europe seemed the obvious alternative. Powell had a point, especially given the assumption among some pro-EEC enthusiasts that the EEC was the route by which Britain would again be able to become a world power, but he seemed equally guilty of mythologizing Britain's past as a guide to future strategy in his belief that his country's greatness and invincibility stemmed from its always having stood apart.[38]

The attitude of the British people had been equally disillusioning for Powell. 'I don't think that people understood,' he later suggested as being the reason why they had neither cared nor taken any notice of the European Communities Bill. He explained this apathy in terms of the deferential trait that Walter Bagehot, the Victorian student of British society and politics, had detected in the English (four-fifths of the British population are English). In Powell's view, there was something very deep in the English character that rendered it less than respectable to disagree with those who occupy the seats of power. None the less, he believed that the English always react eventually, and although they react only slowly and reluctantly, he sought some solace in the fact that they had, hitherto, always reacted successfully. In his conversion to supporting a referendum, Powell now pinned his hopes for reversing British entry into the EEC on the people.[39]

Battle on all fronts

While the battle over Europe was being fought in the Commons during the early months of 1972, Heath's mounting problems on the economy had prompted speculation that Powell's prospects might yet improve. In February, the Government's attempt at pay restraint in the public sector was shattered by the 17 per cent rise in miners' pay following the Wilberforce enquiry (the miners had been offered seven per cent). Powell reacted by repeating his view that, in the long run, nationalization was intolerable in a free society, and argued that the miners had achieved an 'unconditional surrender' from the Coal Board, which meant its bankers, the Government. As 'Crossbencher' in the *Sunday Express* observed, 'suddenly the sensitive nostrils of Mr Powell can detect on the political wind a most enticing odour'. Noting that Powell remembered how Heath had 'cracked' over Leila Khaled in 1970, 'Crossbencher' added, 'the question Enoch is asking himself now is: "Just how many times does Ted have to crack before I am back in with a chance?"' And in early March, when the Government reversed its policy of refusing to support 'lame duck' industries by providing £35 million of aid to the Upper Clyde Shipbuilders, the *Spectator* reported a conversation between Powell and his political friends, during which Powell was said to have commented on Heath's chances at the next election:

'Even I can't carry him a second time.'
Enoch then thought for a moment, realizing that he may have suggested too much fallibility in himself.
'At least', he added, 'I can't guarantee to carry him.'[40]

By the summer of 1972, however, Powell was isolated. He and his small band of anti-EEC Tories had been routed in the battle over the European Communities Bill. He was increasingly at odds with the Government on a range of issues, and his fierce criticisms of Heath had limited his support on the back benches and among Conservatives in the country. In April, Powell's attacks prompted Lord Carrington, the newly appointed Party Chairman, to minute senior Tory officials that no press hand-out from Powell that was in any way doubtful should be issued by Central Office without having been cleared by Jim Prior, his deputy chairman, or Carrington himself. As a result, Central Office refused to distribute a speech of Powell's on the Common Market and another on Northern Ireland.[41]

In June, the *Economist* seemed justified in writing off Powell as a 'dead duck'. Ironically, Powell's apparent demise coincided with the Government's decision, after great speculative pressure, to let the pound float against other currencies – Powell welcomed this event as an exception to the rule that one should never say 'I told you so'. But a side effect of floating the pound was to muffle one of the warning signals of inflation during 1972–73, just when it was most needed. Previously, increased inflation had triggered a sterling crisis, but that immediate restraint had now been removed. Moreover, the fall in the value of the pound by nine per cent during the first six months after the float increased import prices when inflation was already becoming a problem.[42]

By this time, Nicholas Ridley, who had long been an ally of Powell's, had left the Government in protest at Heath's introduction of the interventionist 1972 Industry Bill, that was designed to increase Government support for industry. Like other friends of Powell's, Ridley was concerned at the prospect of Powell's leaving the party over British membership of the EEC, and set up the Economic Dining Club, with the object of trying to anchor Powell in the Conservative Party. Consisting of twelve economically liberal MPs, the group met once a month. Their first meeting was held at a club in Mayfair, where they stayed talking so late that they found themselves locked in. Ridley never forgot the sight of Powell climbing down the drainpipe, wearing his black overcoat and homburg hat. Later in the year, Powell was also accidentally locked in a cemetery that he had wanted to see while visiting the Glasgow constituency of the anti-EEC Tory, Teddy Taylor. Their only escape was to climb the gate. When Powell reached the top, he looked back at Taylor, grinned, and said, 'Can you imagine the pleasure of the press if they could print a picture of this with the caption, "Enoch Powell climbing out of a graveyard?"'[43]

Powell, however, would require incomparably greater political agility if he was to extricate himself from his predicament in the Conservative Party. His opposition to EEC membership was fundamental, and there was no question that he might become reconciled to Heath's policy after Britain formally joined in January 1973. He seemed to have little alternative except either to leave the party, or to win the party over to his side, but this latter course would involve challenging the leadership. Suddenly, however, an event occurred that was to enable him to demonstrate that he remained a potent force within the Conservative Party. At the start of August 1972, the Ugandan dictator, Idi Amin, announced the expulsion of Asians from his country. During the run-up to October's Conservative conference, the Ugandan Asians' crisis rekindled the fierce controversy that had raged over the Kenyan Asians over four years earlier, and that had first helped bring Powell to national prominence.

The Government responded to Amin's action by stating that Britain had a 'special obligation' to those Ugandan Asians who were United Kingdom and Colonies passport holders. There were reckoned to be around 50,000 Ugandan Asians, and the prospect of a new wave of immigration prompted Powell to counter immediately that there was no obligation to the Ugandan Asians and they should be subject to the controls imposed by the 1968 Commonwealth Immigrants Act. In September, he recalled Heath's comments before the 1970 election that immigrants would only be allowed into Britain for a specific job, in a specific place, for a specific time. When the Attorney-General, Sir Peter Rawlinson, stated that Britain had a legal obligation to Ugandan Asians who held British passports, Powell accused him of having 'prostituted' his office. Powell, in turn, was rebuked by his old adversary, Lord Hailsham, the Lord Chancellor. But Powell retorted that Hailsham was deceiving people. And to add insult to injury, Powell said of Sir Alec Douglas-Home, the Foreign Secretary, who had sought to explain the position in a televised broadcast, that he 'was never quite sure what Sir Alec understands or doesn't understand'. Moreover, Powell contended that the Ugandan Asians held 'spoof passports' – a reference to the circumstances in which they, like Asians in Tanganyika and Kenya, had been able to obtain United Kingdom and Colonies passports after independence from the British High Commissioner.[44]

On the eve of the Blackpool Tory conference, the impending confrontation between Heath and Powell was billed as 'a battle for the soul of the party'. The right-wing of the party were busily stoking up trouble for Heath. As resignations and resolutions of protest were received in Conservative Party offices throughout the country, the Western Area reported that 'many of those writing and telephoning agents are known to be (a) anti Common Market, (b) members of the Monday Club, (c) pro-Enoch Powell'. In the ballot among representatives to debate a motion on a subject that was not already on the conference agenda, the Tory right orchestrated the highest such vote since the Second World War for a motion on immigration. This motion had been submitted by Hackney South and Shoreditch Conservatives, and, in itself, presented no threat to the leadership. But the stakes were raised on the eve of conference when Harvey Proctor, the original proposer, announced that he had waived his right to speak in favour of his association's president – Enoch Powell. It had been assumed that Powell would intervene, but by proposing the motion he would set the tone of the debate and would be able to speak for ten minutes instead of only five.[45]

Powell opened the immigration debate, as *The Times* reported, 'in the familiar tones of impending doom that are his hallmark', but his speech was more moderate than was anticipated. Even so, he argued that 'the Government's precipitate acceptance of an unqualified duty to admit these Asians' had sparked a reaction from one end of Britain to the other, because of the 'massive immigration' that had already taken place. He again warned of the dangers of large concentrations of New Commonwealth immigrants in urban areas, and repeated his exaggerated predictions of the total number of non-whites with an admonition: 'Those who four years ago derided forecasts of 3 million or 4 million in the 1980s and of 5 million or more at the end of the century are now silent and, I hope, ashamed.' Moreover, he suggested that the party's immigration policy had won the 1970 election victory, since the promises substantially to end immigration and to offer help to all those immigrants who wanted to return home, 'may well have attracted those few additional votes that gave us our narrow majority'. In one of his sharpest barbs at the Tory front bench, he was severely critical of the numbers of immigrants still entering and the 'cynical' failure to keep the promise to assist all who wish to return home. Powell was heard in silence, but as he returned to his seat there were cheers and boos, and he received a standing ovation from about 200 representatives.[46]

Much of the debate that followed concentrated on Powell and his attacks on the party leadership. It was, in the words of the *Economist*, 'one of the most emotional, and at times ugliest, debates ever seen at a Tory gathering'. Powell sat throughout 'with lips tightly clamped, expressionless except for the occasional shake of the head or the slight hint of a scorn-filled smile barely hissing out beneath his pencil-thin moustache'. His criticisms were powerfully rejected by Robert Carr, who had succeeded Maudling at the Home Office in July, and who was given a standing ovation by most representatives, led by a grateful Heath. The Young Conservatives' amendment congratulating the Government on accepting its obligations to the Ugandan Asians was carried, after a ballot, by 1,721 votes to 736. Powell had carried about 30 per cent of the conference, and although the debate was hailed as a triumph for Heath, Powell had not been routed as the leadership had hoped.[47]

Moreover, when the Commons returned in the autumn, Powell helped to inflict a significant back bench defeat on the Government. The Tory revolt was triggered by the stirring of old loyalties to the white Commonwealth and the revival of anti-EEC sentiment following the publication of new immigration rules on 23 October. These rules were to be introduced from January 1973, and were designed to give effect to parts of the 1971 Immigration Act and to govern the entry of EEC nationals after British membership in the New Year. But many Tory back-benchers objected to the rules as discriminating in favour of aliens over Commonwealth citizens – EEC nationals were to be allowed to enter Britain to take or seek employment on the production of a valid passport or national insurance card, whereas non-patrial Commonwealth citizens could only enter, initially for a maximum period of twelve months, for a particular job with a particular employer. The rules provoked protests from Tory MPs to Home Office ministers and the whips, accompanied by a vigorous campaign in the *Daily Express*.[48]

Powell's objections stemmed from his opposition to British membership of the EEC. He was one of many Tory MPs who strongly criticized the rules at a meeting of the party's back bench home affairs committee, attended by 120 MPs and Robert Carr, the Home Secretary. Two days later, on Wednesday 22 November, Powell was also one of six back-benchers who attacked the rules during the Commons debate. The Government had expected to win the vote, but the speeches of Carr and Douglas-Home received a hostile reception from their own benches. As the *Economist* reported:

> By the time that Sir Alec sat down and the division bells sounded it was clear that the Government had lost. A great block of Tories sat firmly in their seats as their colleagues trooped off to vote, and another seven led by a buoyant Mr Powell, walked into the Opposition lobby.

Forty-nine other Tories abstained, and the Government were defeated by a majority of 35 votes. Among the 56 Tory dissenters, there was a strong correlation between voting against the new rules and having opposed EEC entry in 1971 and also being opposed to sanctions against Southern Rhodesia. The division was a watershed, as Norton has pointed out, since it was the first occasion since the Second World War on which a Government had suffered such a major defeat despite having imposed a three-line whip. Heath's refusal to resign established the precedent that only the loss of a confidence vote automatically results in the Government's resignation.[49]

Powell sought to press home his advantage on immigration, and during December he echoed his much earlier proposal for a separate United Kingdom citizenship by calling for a new code of nationality to provide the Government with a permanent legal distinction between Commonwealth and United Kingdom citizens. He also questioned the right of Pakistani citizens to vote in Britain following Pakistan's departure from the Commonwealth. But Powell had less reason to be in buoyant mood in January 1973, when the Government responded to the defeat over the statement on immigration rules by incorporating in the revised rules the 'patrial' provision that he and other rebels had managed to delete from the original Immigration Bill in 1971. Powell abstained but the Government won the division by 283 votes to 240.[50]

The Ugandan Asians' crisis had again brought Powell to public attention and shown his popularity amongst the Tory rank and file and with voters. An ORC poll in October found that although 60 per cent felt that he had stirred up racial feeling, 40 per cent said that he was the only politician they admired and 39 per cent thought that the Conservatives would be better off with him as Prime Minister. In December, an NOP poll showed that Powell was seen as 'the MP who best understood the problems facing the country' by 29 per cent, whereas only 18 per cent nominated Wilson, 14 per cent Thorpe and 12 per cent Heath. Powell was also chosen by listeners to BBC Radio's *World at One* programme as their 'Man of the Year' with twice as many votes as Heath. But the fact remained that Powell was unable to overcome the paradox of his position. His campaign on immigration continued to polarize debate and reduced his appeal to a wider cross-section of Tory MPs, who were, after all, the crucial audience in terms of challenging the leadership or even changing policy during the 1970–74 parliament. Moreover, as William (later Lord) Deedes, the then chairman of the all-party select committee on Race Relations and Immigration, counselled the Government Chief Whip in November 1972, the unintended consequence of Powell's activities had been

> to pre-empt and sterilize a large portion of ground on which sensible Tories and other opinion formers ought to be entering certain reservations and cautions about immigration generally. Because they instinctively shy off this ground, so heavily occupied by Enoch, there is a vacuum sensed and resented by very many in our party. Thus Enoch has indirectly and perhaps unwittingly widened the gap between government and governed in this matter.

Although Powell's extreme tone attracted publicity and elicited strong public approval, it repelled decision-makers and opinion-formers whose support was essential in achieving effective immigration control. In this respect, his impact was counter-productive.[51]

Powell's isolation was increased by his fierce condemnation of Heath's U-turn on economic policy during 1972, especially on prices and incomes policy. In reaction to the rise in unemployment in early 1972 to one million – a total that had been regarded as unthinkable since 1945 – and in an attempt to stimulate industry in readiness to compete in the larger EEC market, the 1972 spring budget reflated the economy and raised the target for economic growth to five per cent a year. At the same time, with wages rising at around ten per cent a year and prices increasing only slightly less rapidly, there were renewed calls for a prices and incomes policy. It was more than eight years since Powell had begun his campaign against Macmillanite policies, and in June he repeated his total opposition to any new effort to control wages and prices. '"Do we really", one groans aloud, "have to go through all that once more? It is bad enough to have seen the X film once; but is it necessary to stay in our seats through another, and yet another performance?"[52]

Heath, however, had in mind something more ambitious than an old-style prices and incomes policy. He envisaged developing the tripartite approach that Macmillan had initiated in the National Economic Development Council, and planned far-reaching discussions between the Government, industry and the trade unions on managing the economy, and especially the vexed issue of maintaining full employment and stable prices. But this corporatist vision ran counter to everything that Powell had been advocating. The Government's plans were repeatedly bedevilled by the conflict with the unions over the 1971 Industrial Relations Act, but the day after Heath announced the beginning of tripartite talks on 26 September, Powell – in a speech not released by Central Office – again argued that a prices and incomes policy would be positively harmful.[53]

At the start of November 1972, Heath's tripartite talks collapsed. On the 6th, the Prime Minister jettisoned his 1970 manifesto pledge not to introduce a compulsory pay policy and told MPs that the Government were imposing a statutory 90-day freeze on pay and prices. Powell, who was the first Tory back-bencher to be called after Heath's statement in the Commons, was scathing:

> Does my right Hon. Friend know that it is fatal for any Government, party or person to seek to govern in direct opposition to the principles on which they were entrusted with the right to govern? In introducing a compulsory control on wages and prices, in contravention of the deepest commitments of this party, has my right hon. Friend taken leave of his senses?

But Powell's invective won him little support – the idiosyncratic Tory MP, Robin Maxwell-Hyslop, was a lone voice at the 1922 Committee when he called for Heath's resignation. As Powell's fellow economic liberals, Biffen and Bruce-Gardyne, later acknowledged, by November the bulk of the parliamentary party were ready for some action by the Government, and were delighted when action was taken.[54]

Powell and his closest allies could offer only token resistance during the second reading of the Counter-Inflation (Temporary Provisions) Bill. Powell, Biffen and Bruce-Gardyne were the only Tories to abstain instead of voting against an Opposition amendment to reject the Bill. Powell was the only Tory to vote against the Bill on both second and third readings – four Tories abstained on the former occasion and only two on the latter. There was, however, a sign of some back bench resistance in November's election of Nicholas Ridley as chairman of the Conservative back bench finance committee. About 20 to 30 Tory back-benchers generally attended the committee's weekly meetings, and invariably included the party's beleaguered band of about a dozen economic liberals. In December 1972, the Conservatives suffered a shock defeat in the Sutton and Cheam by-election, but as Biffen discovered, Powell was more shocked that Labour had failed to win the Hillingdon, Uxbridge, by-election from the Tories on the same day.[55]

The introduction of the second stage of the Government's prices and incomes policy in January 1973 initially seemed likely to stir stronger opposition. After the Chancellor, Anthony Barber, attended a packed meeting of the back bench finance committee on the 23rd, it was reported that Powell might be joined by between twelve and fifteen rebels in the lobbies. Six days later, during the second reading debate on the new Counter-Inflation Bill, Powell delivered a withering attack. Powell's theoretical objections reflected the monetarist approach that he had sought to pursue as a Treasury minister. A prices and incomes policy was futile, he argued, because inflation 'can occur only when the supply of money, the total of monetary demand, is rising faster than the supply of goods and services'. His theorizing was much more relevant in the early 1970s than it had been in the late 1950s. By 1973, Britain was in the middle of an enormous boom in bank lending, that had been unleashed following the Bank of England's reform of bank credit in the autumn of 1971, which had reduced its control over credit creation and the stock of money. Between 1963 and 1972, bank lending had grown at a little over 12 per cent a year, but in 1972 it rose by 37 per cent and was to soar by another 43 per cent in 1973. The money supply increased accordingly. Sir Alec Cairncross, the former economic adviser to the Government during the latter years of the Macmillan administration, has observed that, 'whatever the contribution of changes in the stock of money to inflation in other years, their contribution in 1972 and 1973 is beyond dispute'.

But in January 1973, Powell saw the main culprit as the Chancellor for having reflated the economy over the previous eighteen months in a futile attempt to boost output. Inevitably, Powell claimed, this had fuelled inflation. And since inflation was unpopular, ministers had to be seen to be doing something about it. The Government's fight against inflation was a 'sham', and the Bill was merely intended to resolve, 'at any rate for the time being, an otherwise intolerable dilemma between the necessity to inflate and the necessity to be seen to be doing something about inflation'. Powell found it 'difficult to understand how those who argued, as we did in the last Parliament against something essentially indistinguishable from this Bill, who denounced it in principle and forswore anything of the sort when they presented themselves to the electorate, can support it now'.[56]

Yet despite earlier predictions of a more sizeable revolt against the Bill, only Powell entered the Opposition lobby to support Labour's amendment against the policy and also to oppose the second reading. He was unable even to attract any support in Conservative abstentions, although his sympathizers, Biffen and Ridley, managed to secure their appointment to the Bill's standing committee by voting with the Government. In committee, these two Powellites succeeded in defeating the Government by passing an amendment to reduce the duration of the policy's initial application from three years to twelve months. But the weakness of Powell and his fellow economic liberals was demonstrated when only thirteen Tory dissenters resisted the Government's reversal of this defeat at report stage – Powell and four others voted against, while another eight abstained.

Powell and his allies, however, won stronger support on the Tory back benches for their calls to cut government spending. Although the Chancellor received a warm reception at his traditional meeting with the Tory back bench finance committee immediately after delivering his March 1973 budget, Ian Aitken reported in the *Guardian* that 'Mr Powell and his allies can be expected to return to their attack on the yawning gap between public expenditure and taxation.' Later in the month, Biffen's call for increased direct taxation was echoed by Powell (Ridley called for higher indirect taxation). In May, the Chancellor announced what was to be a first instalment of spending cuts, in order to counter the overheating of the economy. Some months later, Barber was to launch a furious attack on Powell, but by then the dispute between Heath's Government and Powell had more to do with electoral calculation than with economic policy.[57]

End-game with the Conservatives

During the early 1970s, Powell was deeply embroiled in another battle with the Heath Government, and again was one of only a small band of dissenters. At issue was the future of Northern Ireland, a corner of the United Kingdom that had long been neglected by successive British Governments, but that by 1972 was teetering on the brink of civil war. Powell viewed the conflict from the perspective of a United Kingdom nationalist – or, in terms of the debate over relations between the United Kingdom and the Republic of Ireland, as a unionist. Although questions of nationhood and national identity had been at the root of the bitter division over Irish Home Rule that shaped British politics for thirty years after 1886, they had largely lain dormant since Lloyd George negotiated independence for the 26 southern Irish counties and created a devolved parliament and government in six of the counties of Ulster. For decades the British thought the Irish question had been settled. At Westminster, Ulster's Unionist MPs took the Conservative whip and, to all intents and purposes, were counted as Tory MPs. But Dublin never abandoned the aspiration of reunification, while Northern Ireland's Government at Stormont, in east Belfast, became synonymous with Protestant domination over the Catholic minority.

The violent eruption of the conflict over minority civil rights in Northern Ireland, followed by Wilson's decision in 1969 to send in British troops, forced the Irish question back onto the political agenda at Westminster. 'The Troubles', as the increasingly bloody conflict became known, claimed thirteen lives in 1969, and twenty-five in 1970. In a dramatic escalation of the violence, 173 civilians and soldiers were murdered in Northern Ireland in 1971, and 467 in 1972. There was a real risk of all-out civil war in Northern Ireland, with

Britain and the Republic of Ireland being dragged in on opposite sides. And there was a fear that, in addition to sporadic terrorist atrocities spreading to the mainland, sectarian bloodshed might also spread to cities such as Glasgow and Liverpool with their traditional rivalry between Catholics and Protestants.

Northern Ireland was a potentially explosive issue, in every sense of the term. For a politician in Powell's predicament after the 1970 election, who had to be ready to take some risks if he was to force his way back onto the front bench, Ulster offered a gambler's throw. Initially, the Heath Government let the situation in Northern Ireland drift, but as matters went from bad to worse during 1971 the Prime Minister devoted an increasing amount of time to the problem. Yet there was every possibility that all his efforts would fail, and Ulster would again come to dominate British politics. In the event of such a dire outcome, Powell might stand to gain if he were able to offer an alternative approach.

Powell, however, has maintained that Northern Ireland was an issue that found him, rather than *vice versa*. Exceptionally for a British politician of his generation, he attached overriding importance to nationhood and national identity. He was making speeches on Ulster from the late 1960s, and had developed a distinctive approach and mapped out its main elements before the 1970 election. Moreover, anybody who became closely involved in the debate in Northern Ireland as 'the Troubles' escalated was liable to risk his or her personal safety, and Powell was fearless in this regard.

Powell regarded Heath's policy on Northern Ireland as another instance of his failings as Prime Minister. Powell's call for the integration of Ulster into the United Kingdom was likely to appeal to instinctive Tory sentiment and to those who yearned for a straightforward answer. As such, it readily became another facet of Powellism. But it reflected a simplistic view of a deep-seated problem, and was rejected by Heath, and later, by Thatcher. Whereas Powell saw the different treatment of Northern Ireland as being at the root of the trouble, Conservative Prime Ministers sought policies that reflected the difference between politics in Northern Ireland and on the British mainland.[58]

In September 1968, in the course of his attack on the idea of Scottish and Welsh devolution, Powell had referred to the strong desire of the majority in Ulster to remain within the union of the United Kingdom and Northern Ireland. His implied criticism of the Stormont model in this speech, however, suggested that he did not share the attachment of many Ulster Unionists to the large degree of autonomy that the Province had enjoyed for almost fifty years. In April 1970, during a debate on Northern Ireland in the Commons, he challenged the widely held view that the conflict in the Province stemmed from fifty years of Unionist domination. Instead, he identified one source of the problem as being a worldwide trend towards 'violence for violence sake' – Powell himself had been the target of student demonstrations. In Northern Ireland, this was combined with another factor: 'The violence which seeks to promote the aspiration for the absorption of the six counties of Northern Ireland into the Republic. That violence feeds upon the prospect of that aspiration being achieved.' Powell put forward three proposals for bringing peace to Northern Ireland: membership of the six counties as part of the United Kingdom was not to be treated as negotiable; greater administrative, economic and political amalgamation between the six counties and the rest of the United Kingdom; and citizens of the Republic of Ireland should no longer enjoy any special privileged status when they came to reside in Britain, but were to be treated the same as other aliens. Powell's unionism was integrationist. His approach was designed both to remove any sense that Northern Ireland was politically separate from Britain and that Britain's relations with the Republic were, in some way, special.[59]

In his 'enemy within' speech during the 1970 election, Powell spoke of the '"civil rights" nonsense', and dismissed any idea that in Ulster 'the deliberate destruction by fire and riot of areas of ordinary property is due to the dissatisfaction over allocation of council houses and opportunities for employment'. In early 1971, he undertook his first speaking tour in the Province, and at Londonderry on 13 January, explained his brand of unionism. Stormont, that had come to symbolize the Unionist domination of the Province, was dismissed as a form of government 'that half denies the fact that the six counties are an integral part of the United Kingdom'. Again, he attacked the rights enjoyed by Irish citizens in the United Kingdom. In his view, such factors were 'a standing invitation to violence to try to drive home the wedge these ambiguities represent'.[60]

This uncompromising espousal of the unionist cause by a senior British politician had a marked effect in Northern Ireland, where the majority community felt increasingly beleaguered and feared that they would be deserted by London. A parallel was sometimes drawn, albeit jokingly at first, between Powell and the Unionist hero, Sir Edward Carson, who had fought the Unionist cause at Westminster in the early twentieth century. As James Molyneaux, the former leader of the Ulster Unionist Party, told Anne Colville,

> Enoch was making an impact in the late '60s, he was coming to meetings and he got people to say, playfully at the beginning, that he should be offered an Ulster seat and represent the Province in the role of Carson. That in a way was said facetiously because at the time it didn't seem remotely likely that he was ever going to need an Ulster constituency.

By the summer of 1971, the bond between Powell and the Unionists was strengthening. Following a speech in Banbridge, he had been driven to Aldergrove Airport by an official of the Down, South, Unionist Association. As they waited for Powell's flight, the Unionist asked Powell whether he would give more time to Ulster, perhaps in a more tangible form. 'If I get the call,' came the immediate reply, 'I will not ignore it.' And with that, Powell headed for the check-in desk. He was later to stand as a Unionist in Down,

South, though the specific cause of his break with the Conservatives was not Ulster.[61]

The irreconcilable disagreement between Powell and Heath over Ulster first became fully evident in the autumn of 1971. Six months earlier, Powell had severely criticized the Government's apparent acceptance in Northern Ireland of 'no go' areas – Irish republican strongholds that were not patrolled by the police or army. In September, addressing a Unionist rally in Omagh, County Tyrone, he explicitly attacked Heath's policy. Powell's integrationist belief was clear from the start. 'It is remarkable', he commented,

> that there should appear to be anything remarkable in a Conservative Member of Parliament from Staffordshire addressing a meeting of his political colleagues in County Tyrone, any more than that he should do so at Dover or at Inverness. In so far as it may appear remarkable, that is perhaps an indication of what ails Northern Ireland and of the remedy of that ailment.

But the gist of his speech was clear from his implicit warning that Northern Ireland was the victim of British appeasement. Recalling Neville Chamberlain's notorious description of Czechoslovakia at the time of the Munich Agreement in 1938, as 'a far-away country of which we know nothing', Powell claimed that the British public were now being invited to view Ulster in the same light.[62]

Powell's particular target was a recent meeting between Heath and the Taoiseach (Prime Minister) of the Republic of Ireland, Jack Lynch. 'British politics and the British character are profoundly insular, and one of the effects of our insularity is an amazing innocence', he suggested, and the British Government had been guilty of 'stupefying innocence' in expecting 'the assistance of the Irish Republic in ending terrorism and disorder in Ulster'. In Powell's view, improved Anglo-Irish cooperation was damaging because of the impression it gave about Britain's lack of commitment to Ulster:

> When the British Government is seen taking counsel about peace and security in a part of the United Kingdom with the prime minister of the very country which is dedicated to the annexation of that part and cannot fail to approve the objects and consequences of the disorder, what must people think? I will tell you. They think: 'Oho, so the British are wobbling and preparing to get out; else why would they be parleying with the residual beneficiary of their embarrassments?' That may be mistaken. I trust it is. But can you blame anyone, friend or foe, who draws that conclusion?

At this stage, Powell derived no immediate political advantage in Britain from his stand on Ulster. The public though appalled by the violence was, for the most part, politically uninterested. Most Tory MPs were content to follow the Government line. Labour were moving in the opposite direction to Powell – in November 1971, Wilson proposed a fifteen-point programme that held out the prospect of Irish unity. In one respect, however, there was an immediate benefit for Powell in fighting the unionist corner, since he could encourage the Ulster Unionists in their inclination to reinforce the anti-EEC coalition at Westminster.

Powell's speech to Ulster Unionists in Omagh was made in the interval between the publication of the White Paper on British entry and the crucial debates on British membership at the Conservative conference and in the Commons. At that stage, the eight Ulster Unionist MPs in the 1970–74 parliament were still counted as Conservatives, and if they were all to oppose British entry, Heath's majority would be dented. In a clear appeal to Unionist MPs to support the anti-EEC campaign, Powell warned that although 'the debate about Britain and the Common Market has largely passed Northern Ireland by', it none the less concerned Northern Ireland 'more literally vitally than any other part of the United Kingdom'. Since the advocacy of British entry was 'openly and avowedly based upon the progressive political unification of the participating countries', Powell warned bluntly that:

I do not see how any Unionist Member of Parliament representing an Ulster seat can vote for British entry. A vote for British entry is a vote for the political unification of Ulster with the Republic, and only a dangerously innocent or dangerously subtle politician would quibble that it means association with the Republic without dissociation from the United Kingdom. For Ulster unification with the Republic is dissociation from the United Kingdom: that is what unionism in Northern Ireland has been about. A vote for Europe is a vote against Ulster.

In the event, the majority of Ulster Unionist MPs opposed British entry. Although some were criticized by anti-EEC Tories for failing to attend regularly, four Unionists voted against the European Communities Bill and related motions in ten or more divisions – Molyneaux did so on 46 occasions. Although Unionist opposition failed to prevent British membership, it was to have a crucial bearing on Powell's future career.[63]

After Powell and the anti-EEC Unionists had made common cause against the European Communities Bill, their bond was further strengthened. In March 1972, when Brian Faulkner's Northern Ireland Government resisted losing responsibility for law and order, Heath imposed direct rule from Westminster. Molyneaux, the most actively anti-EEC Unionist, has vividly recalled a meeting he had at the Commons with Powell, who told him that:

You and I know that a Member cannot exist in this place unless you have a cause for which to fight. We have lost one such cause, namely that of the Common Market. The second one is Ulster. We have lost the one; the other remains. All I want to say to you is that if you feel at any time I can be of any assistance to you, do let me know.[64]

Powell allied with the Unionists in opposing direct rule. Although he had been a critic of Stormont and had advocated the integration of the Province within the United Kingdom, he argued during the Commons debate on the Bill to abolish Stormont that, 'direct rule is the opposite to parliamentary unification'. Indeed, he told MPs that the Government's proposals marked, 'in a special and unique way, the separateness of the six counties from the rest of the United Kingdom and not their unity with it'. In the first place, the Bill was renewable every year and therefore carried within itself the seeds of disunion. Secondly, because of its devolved government, Northern Ireland had fewer seats at Westminster in relation to its population than any other part of the United Kingdom. With the demise of Stormont, the Province was seriously under-represented. In Powell's view, instead of bringing an end to the terrorist violence, the Bill abolishing Stormont would only encourage it. The effect, Powell contended, 'will be for people to say, "You see, violence is succeeding. It is paying off. Another stage has been gained."' Powell was one of nine Conservatives who joined the eight Ulster Unionists in voting against the Bill – an estimated 33 Tories also abstained.[65]

Ending Northern Ireland's under-representation at Westminster became Powell's objective, as he made clear to a Unionist rally at Newtownards in County Down in May 1972. In this instance, he had taken up a campaign that won wider appeal. When he repeated his call for more seats for Ulster at a meeting of Tory MPs the following November, he was supported by the liberal-minded former Tory Home Secretary, Reggie Maudling, who thought that 'the acceptance of sovereignty as residing at Westminster meant that there was an unanswerable argument for Ulster to have equal representation with the rest of the United Kingdom'.[66]

Direct rule and the appointment of a British Secretary of State (Willie Whitelaw was the first) in place of Stormont, stretched to breaking-point the historic link between Ulster Unionists and the Conservative Party. In June 1972, a new Conservative back bench committee was established specifically on Northern Ireland – two Ulster Unionists were among its five officers. Powell was an infrequent attender, but he told Tory MPs that the Government's assurances on the union (between Britain and Northern Ireland) were not to be believed because the Government were not committed to the union. 'We must take one side or the other,' Powell is minuted as having stated, 'in this case the majority side.' Fittingly, Powell's uncompromising declaration had been made on 12 July – the date on which the anniversary of the Battle of the Boyne is celebrated. The following week, he was involved in fierce exchanges in the Commons with Whitelaw over the latter's 'secret' meeting with leading members of the Provisional IRA.[67]

The 'majority side' in Northern Ireland, however, were deeply shaken by the abolition of Stormont and were increasingly divided. Unionist politics descended into factionalism, feuding and, among the loyalist paramilitaries and their allies, threats to take the law into their own hands. In August 1972, Powell was invited to chair a conference of the extremist Loyalist Association of Workers, but declined – as did Faulkner and Ian Paisley. Instead, Powell made a speech at Ballymena reiterating his call for the integration of Northern Ireland into the United Kingdom. Six weeks later, he repeated the argument in Belfast, but he then said little about Northern Ireland for almost six months. Powell's attacks on Heath over Northern Ireland were cited in the *Spectator* as another reason for his shrinking support on the Tory back benches.[68]

During the autumn of 1972, Heath and Whitelaw went against everything that Powell had advocated by launching a new initiative that was designed to broker a compromise between the majority and minority communities in Northern Ireland. Whereas Powell favoured integration, they proposed the election of a new Northern Ireland assembly and the appointment of a new devolved government. Whereas he backed the unionist majority, they proposed elections by the single transferable vote (as opposed to the Westminster system of 'first past the post') and a government in which power would be shared between representatives of the majority and minority. And whereas Powell wanted no truck with the Republic, they proposed that there should be an 'Irish dimension' to the government of Northern Ireland.[69]

In the Commons debate in March 1973 on the Government's White Paper, Powell condemned power-sharing as a built-in contradiction and absurdity. He was one of fifteen MPs who supported an Ulster Unionist amendment and one of only seven MPs to vote against the White Paper. In April, during the committee stage of the Bill to establish the Northern Ireland Assembly, he was one of only a handful of Tory MPs to vote against the Government in two of the three revolts on the Bill. The main Unionist opposition, however, was reserved for May's Northern Ireland Constitution Bill. Powell joined the Unionists in opposing the Bill at second reading, and again at third reading. On 3 July, Powell repeated what had been a common experience during the debate on the European Communities Bill, by again entering the division lobby with Labour MPs to support an official Opposition amendment. On this occasion, Labour's amendment would have deleted the provision for another border poll within ten years (a border poll in March 1973 had been boycotted by the SDLP and most republicans). In the vote, the Government's majority fell to only six.[70]

A month or so before his return to the Opposition division lobby, Powell had given a couple of indications of his impending break with the Conservatives. In late May, his disagreements with the Government on immigration, the EEC and prices and incomes policy led him to decline to support the Conservative candidate in the West Bromwich by-election. He had, in fact, given an intimation of his likely split from the Conservatives on the issue of Europe in a speech to Yarmouth Conservatives the previous October. Although he had not asked Conservative Central Office to circulate this speech, Chris Patten, then special adviser to the party chairman, none the less drew it to the attention of Lord Carrington and noted that the last paragraph was presumably meant to be ominous. In his speech, Powell strongly condemned the Government's acceptance of the EEC's plan for 'economic and monetary union' by 1980. His last, ominous, paragraph alleged that the compact between the Government and parliament and the electorate had been ruptured. And he concluded:

> There is another compact, less explicit but more solemn, which has been broken. It is the compact which above all the Conservative Party exists to uphold: the compact between the past, the present and the future. That compact, too, has not been honoured. What we have to ask ourselves is whether any British party and government, least of all a Conservative Government and the Conservative Party, can do this and survive. Upon our answer to that question depends what we must individually do and say in the coming months.[71]

The threat in the last sentence of Powell's Yarmouth speech remained unclear, but speaking in Stockport on 8 June 1973, he was more explicit. He began in the manner of an academic treatise on politics, but his analysis packed an explosive punch. 'It has often been observed in a democracy', Powell began, 'that opposing parties tend for the most part to move closer together, because their outer wings have no alternative refuge ... while the supposed floating vote lies in the middle, and each party aims at detaching from its opponents that portion of the spectrum which is nearest itself'. This was the 'normal condition', but, Powell continued,

> The political earthquakes which alter the physical geography of politics for a long period afterwards can only occur when this rule is suspended; that is to say, when the outer wing of one party finds that some single object, which for the time being seems to it more important than all the rest, is procurable not from its political allies and comrades but from its enemies.

In case his audience were unaware of the scale of upheaval that Powell envisaged, he reminded them that 'the historic and endlessly instructive case in point is the great split in the Liberal Party in 1886'. It was an apposite example. Not only was the key actor Joseph Chamberlain, with whom Powell was often compared, but the cause on which the Liberals' radical wing split from their party was their unionist opposition to Irish Home Rule. 'Sooner than consent to the dismemberment of the United Kingdom,' Powell noted, emphasizing the enormity of their action,

> Chamberlain and his friends were prepared to vote with their lifelong enemies, the Tories, and to place and establish them in office for the sake of that one overriding object. Twenty years of Conservative government were

the result; and the Conservative Party, which apart from Lord Beacons-field's six-year administration, had hardly known office since the repeal of the Corn Laws, became and remained the preponderant vehicle of British government from that day to this.

Powell left nobody in any doubt that he saw membership of the EEC as the modern-day equivalent of Irish Home Rule, with, potentially, the capacity to cause an even bigger political earthquake. Britain, he argued, had 'not as yet had the opportunity to express a national opinion upon the potentially biggest event in its political history'. The question of the EEC had been 'anxiously withheld' at the 1970 election. But it would be very different if at the next election, whenever it was held, 'the two main parties offered the electorate a choice'. In that event, Powell suggested, the election would become a referendum on British membership of the EEC, and he warned that:

There is one respect in which such a conjunction would be more explosive than the historical parallel of Chamberlain and the Liberal Unionists. I intend no imputation against any person or party when I say that the mental association of patriotism and the Tory Party is strong and persistent. It is perilous to any party in the state for the appeal of country to conflict with the appeal of party. To the Conservative Party it is a conflict which could be mortal.

He had no need to remind his audience in the summer of 1973 that the voters were likely to be given a choice on the EEC at the next election. In Opposition, the Labour Party had adopted a policy of re-negotiating Britain's terms and – partly in response to Neil Marten's initiative – making entry dependent on the assent of the British electorate, either through an election or a referendum.

In Powell's contention, the EEC's aim of 'economic and monetary union' by 1980 effectively meant the establishment of a unitary European state within the lifetime of one parliament. There was, however, 'one event, one hurdle to be cleared, one barrier across the way – a general election'. Powell's purpose was 'to assert that a choice, and that of the most fundamental nature, is still to be made; and to warn that no one ought to hope that it can be burked'. And he declared:

Yet I would not conceal, even if I could, where my own counsel lies. Independence, the freedom of a self-governing nation, is in my estimation the highest political good, for which any disadvantage, if need be, and any sacrifice, are a cheap price. It is worth living for; it is worth fighting for; and it is worth dying for.[72]

Powell's message was clear, although its full implication was not as widely appreciated at the time as it should have been – the officers of his constituency association, for example, were to be astounded by his subsequent actions. But his Stockport speech left room for little doubt that unless there was a dramatic change in the respective positions of the Government and the Opposition on the overriding question of British membership of the EEC, he could not, in all conscience, stand as an official Conservative candidate at the next election; he would have to support the Labour Party. Indeed, two days later during a radio interview, Powell declared that he would rather live under a Labour Government for the rest of his life if it meant that the ideals of parliamentary sovereignty over the country's affairs were preserved.[73]

In June 1973, Powell made sure that one man understood his position, and knew that he was likely to endorse Labour at the next election – this man was Harold Wilson, the Leader of the Opposition. Powell's liaison with Wilson from mid-1973, while he was still taking the Conservative whip, represented a lethal threat to the Conservative Party. It was to culminate at the next election in an orchestrated campaign to do the Conservatives maximum damage. Yet the story of this most explosive, unholy alliance between the self-confessed High Tory and the Labour leader has the air of Ealing comedy about it rather than Machiavellian conspiracy. The meetings between Powell and Wilson always took place in the mid-afternoon in the gentlemen's lavatory in the Ayes' lobby of the House of Commons. 'Our contacts were incidental rather than by assignment,' Powell told Wilson's biographer, Ben Pimlott. 'There were half a dozen meetings with Wilson in the loo'. During these meetings, Powell gave signals 'which would not have been understood by Wilson other than as indications that I wanted the Labour Party to win the election'.[74]

The seriousness of the threat that Powell might pose to the Conservatives' hopes of re-election was underlined by the surge in support for the Liberals in the opinion polls and at by-elections since 1972. The outcome of the next election would depend on whether or not Heath could win back the support of disaffected Tories, and opinion research revealed that Liberal supporters were strongly Powellite – in the absence of an alternative, they were treating the Liberal Party as a vehicle for demonstrating their dissatisfaction with the Government. Interviewed in October 1973, Powell dismissed the Liberals as 'a sort of political James Bond' – people seemed to think that it could do impossible things – but he thought that as its supporters returned to the two-party system at the general election, Labour would benefit rather than the Tories. Although Powell did not say as much, if he were to urge people to vote Labour in a nationalistic rejection of the EEC, his popular appeal, especially among the urban lower-middle and working-class, gave him the potential to unleash a political earthquake of the same seismic proportions as Chamberlain's in 1886.[75]

There was, however, one crucial difference between Chamberlain and Powell. Whereas Chamberlain, when he split from the Liberals, led a group of 79 MPs after the 1886 election that followed his defeat of Gladstone's Home Rule Bill, Powell had eschewed organizing his own faction or group on the Conservative back benches. In retrospect, he believed that his failure to do so had been a deliberate decision to avoid entrapping others in a position that he saw would probably result in their political isolation. This explanation, however, smacks of *post-hoc* rationalization. A more plausible reason is that Powell knew that any hint of deliberately promoting factionalism or organizing a party within a party would have compromised his image as a man who was fighting on ideas, not personal ambition. It was one matter to dissent from the leadership's view, even as often as Powell had during the 1970–74 parliament, but the vast majority of Tories would have regarded it as quite another matter to organize a party within a party.

None the less, Powell came to regard his failure to organize an anti-EEC group as a big mistake, because when the election came he could see no justification or point in standing as a lone anti-Common Market Conservative. If, however, there had been a dozen or so Conservatives standing on the same anti-EEC platform, and promising to take every opportunity in the Commons to help extricate Britain from the EEC, he felt that it would have been reasonable for him to stand and seek people's votes. In short, Powell's failure to organize a party within a party led inexorably to his decision not to stand as a Conservative candidate when the next election was called.[76]

By the autumn of 1973, Powell was in a peculiar political predicament. On the one hand, as he had indicated four months earlier, it was possible that he might not stand at the next election – certainly not as a Conservative candidate. On the other hand, he represented a potentially lethal threat to the Conservatives – a point he underlined during October's Conservative conference at Blackpool, by plugging his latest collection of speeches that had, as its title, a neat summary of official Labour Party policy, *The Common Market: Renegotiate or Come Out.*

Others besides Wilson were sensitive to Powell's predicament. The Ulster Unionist Party had split over the Government's plans for a power-sharing assembly in Northern Ireland. Whereas Brian Faulkner accepted the proposals, Harry West, a former Stormont Unionist MP, now led the anti-assembly Unionists, who included at least four Unionist MPs at Westminster. Faulkner and his supporters were convinced that Powell was approached on the possibility of his leading the Ulster Unionists when he visited Ulster in September at the invitation of James Molyneaux, the anti-Faulknerite MP. Following a speech at Portrush on 18 September, Powell was asked by one of the audience whether he would accept the Unionist leadership. Powell 'smiled rather wryly', according to James Laird, an officer of the Londonderry Unionists, before replying, in the form of a pointed historical analogy with William of Orange in 1688, that 'William had waited before crossing to England to make sure that the people who were begging him to go there represented all the English population'. This was greeted with tumultuous applause. Harry West apparently approached Powell during the 1973 Conservative conference at Blackpool. But if West suggested that his anti-assembly Unionists needed a leader, it was not taken seriously by Powell, who stated publicly that he 'had no knowledge of any such matter'.[77]

At the conference, Powell spoke in the debate on the economy, and repeated

his well-rehearsed argument for controlling the money supply and balancing
the budget. It was, by his standards, an unexceptional speech. But in reply, the
Chancellor, Anthony Barber, echoed Heath's attack on Powell after the
Stockport speech as 'a bitter and backward-looking man', by denouncing
Powell as having evinced 'all the moral conceit and intellectual arrogance that
are the hallmarks of the fanatic'. Indeed, so intemperate were Barber's
comments that there was much speculation over his motives, and some Tories
feared that his outburst would lose votes. By the end of October, however,
Terence Lancaster, political editor of the *Daily Mirror*, had reason to suggest
that Barber's intention was a 'pre-emptive strike'. 'If Mr Powell comes out
against Mr Heath at the election,' Lancaster noted, 'Mr Barber wants those
phrases about fanaticism and intellectual arrogance to be remembered by the
Tory activists.' As Lancaster added, 'they may have stuck already', since the
latest Gallup poll showed that 37 per cent of Tory supporters thought that
Powell was not an asset to the party, against 32 per cent saying that he was.
'Round One, I would say, to the brutal Barber,' Lancaster concluded. Nobody
realized that the contest between Powell and Heath was about to reach its
climax.[78]

Double knock-out

Although Barber's outburst in October 1973 had fuelled speculation about a
showdown with Powell at the next election, such an eventuality seemed
unlikely to occur until the following autumn at the earliest, and the Prime
Minister could delay calling an election if he wished until the summer of 1975.
On the eve of the 1973 Tory conference, however, two events had occurred
that were to precipitate the final confrontation between Powell and Heath
much sooner than was expected. On 6 October, the Jewish festival of Yom
Kippur, Egyptian tanks crossed the Suez Canal and invaded Israel. Two days
later, the Heath Government published proposals for Stage Three of their
prices and incomes policy. The interplay between, on the one hand, the Arab
countries' use of oil embargoes and price rises to pressurize Israel's western
backers, and on the other hand, the miners' determination to return to the top
of the wages league, was to plunge the country into crisis during the winter of
1973–74. Britain was not yet a major oil producer and depended for about
two-thirds of its supplies on the Middle East, while its power stations were
heavily dependent on coal. The Government's maladroit response was to
speed the dramatic dénouement of Powell's feud with Heath.

By mid-November, it was clear that Heath's ploy in framing Stage Three to
avert another pay dispute with the miners had failed. The miners rejected an
offer of 13 per cent, and on 12 November began an overtime ban in pursuit of
a 40 per cent pay claim. The Government were desperate to avoid a repetition
of their climb-down to the miners in 1972. Faced with a cut in oil supplies,
strikes by electricity power engineers and reduced coal stocks, the Government declared a state of emergency – in particular, street lighting was

curtailed, floodlighting banned and television programmes were stopped at 10.30 p.m. Heath sought to justify Stage Three of his prices and incomes policy by arguing that the Government had been given responsibility by parliament for controlling inflation by imposing a limit on wage increases. This was too much for Powell, who held Heath responsible for having subborned the Commons into surrendering parliament's independence to the EEC. Provoked beyond endurance, Powell said of the Prime Minister that 'one cannot but entertain fears for the mental and emotional stability of a head of government to whom such language can appear rational'.[79]

Powell later explained his extraordinary attack by suggesting that Heath's comments had been such an inversion of political reality that he must have become mentally unbalanced, as he was an essentially honest man. Powell's accusation stirred fresh controversy over his continuing to receive the Conservative whip. The Tory Party managers, however, again declined to make him a martyr, and Heath scored a point in the Commons by referring to Powell as 'my right hon ... [pause] Friend' – the Prime Minister's apparent search for the right word to describe Powell prompted laughter from Tories and appreciative nods from Labour MPs.[80]

The probable result of Powell's campaign was shrewdly examined by David Wood, whose weekly column in the *The Times* on 3 December, was entitled, 'Mr Powell's destiny with doom'. For the first time since Churchill's campaign against Baldwin and Neville Chamberlain in the 1930s, Wood noted, 'a Conservative politician of front-rank abilities is set on a sustained, embittered and personalized strategy of destroying his party leadership'. The notion that Powell had done no more than stay true to party principles and was concerned, above all, to bring Heath back to the straight and narrow path, was dismissed contemptuously with a curt, 'that will not do'. As with Joe Chamberlain, Powell had to 'find or form a party that suits him better,' or, as with Churchill, 'in a time of crisis, his party must bring him to the leadership'. Otherwise, Powell was 'on a path to destruction, and it cannot be that he chooses deliberate self destruction'. Powell remained a lonely figure in the Commons, but among Tory activists he attracted economic liberals and the right-wing Monday Club, while 'in the country he lives in the limelight amid the multitude, making better use of the hustings, radio and television than any other politician of his day'. Within three months, Powell was to demonstrate why the Tory leadership was right to be apprehensive of his popular appeal and talent for publicity. But in the process, he was to fulfil the prophecy in the headline to Wood's column.[81]

While the mounting industrial and economic crisis engulfed the Government, Heath sought to give substance to the Anglo-Irish dimension of his initiative in Northern Ireland. Although Powell fundamentally disagreed with the Government's approach, he none the less kept his counsel when Heath and his new Secretary of State for Northern Ireland, Francis Pym, held talks at Sunningdale with a new Taoiseach, Liam Cosgrave, and members of Faulkner's putative power-sharing executive. The Sunningdale agreement proposed creating a Council of Ireland with representatives from both sides of the border, and was an attempt to find a compromise between conflicting demands. Although the Republic accepted that 'the factual position' of Northern Ireland within the United Kingdom could not be changed except by a decision of a majority of the people of Northern Ireland, Unionists saw the Council of Ireland as the thin end of the wedge towards a united Ireland. Indeed, Faulkner was repudiated by many of his fellow Unionists within a few days of the new executive taking over on 1 January, and Heath was soon inadvertently to give the Unionists an opportunity to wreak their revenge upon him at Westminster.[82]

Powell was later dismissive of Heath's efforts. 'It was very typical of Ted Heath', he was to observe, 'that he thought he achieved something by dragooning people at Sunningdale into accepting something that they not only didn't mean, but which those upon whom they depended – the electors upon whom they depended – couldn't possibly mean.' Heath's 1973 power-sharing constitution for Northern Ireland, Powell suggested, was obviously a house of cards, because responsible government cannot be run by people with opposite beliefs. Similarly, the Council of Ireland was obviously going to be seen in Northern Ireland as meaning reunification. Powell felt that only someone as intensely bureaucratic and allergic to human emotions as Heath could have failed to see this, while the eventual demise of the power-sharing executive, brought down by Unionist opposition to the Council of Ireland, typified the political disasters that Heath caused by disregarding the most important things about human beings. In Powell's view, nobody else made Heath as angry as an Ulster Unionist: that people were prepared to be bombed and shot in order to belong to a particular nation was not only beyond Heath's comprehension, he alleged, but even made Heath sick. Powell's scorn for Heath revealed the depth of the gulf that had developed between them.[83]

It was not Northern Ireland, however, but the growing clamour among Conservatives for an election that was to provoke a fresh outburst from Powell. In mid-December, ministers imposed a three-day week on industry in order to save electricity. The possibility of a 'snap' election if the crisis worsened was already being discussed in Downing Street and at Conservative headquarters in Smith Square, and the idea surfaced in well-informed articles in *The Times*. These reports brought to a head the speculation about Powell's intentions that had rumbled on for months in his constituency and at Westminster, since his speech in Stockport the previous June. Powell's original plan had been to tell his local party of his intentions during the spring of 1974, well in advance of an autumn 1974 or spring 1975 election. But he was now urged by senior officers of his Wolverhampton constituency to take the opportunity of the association's annual general meeting on 14 December to say what he would do if an election were called in the next few months. Although the officers had the impression that Powell would do so, when he was asked about his intentions at the meeting he declined to answer what he regarded as a hypothetical question. Criticism of Powell was voiced at the meeting by the association's vice-chairman, Peter Wesson, who announced his resignation and urged him to 'turn aside from the flames of martyrdom. I beg you desist from your obduracy'. Wesson echoed the resentment felt towards Powell's anti-EEC stance among Tories in Tettenhall, a suburb that had been added to the constituency in a recent re-drawing of boundaries and whose inhabitants included middle-ranking managers of national companies. Although there was no show of strength against Powell at the meeting and he received a standing ovation at the end of the meeting with only about a dozen of the 90 people in the hall not standing up, his behaviour worried a number of his friends. 'I got the impression he wasn't with us', one long-time friend observed, adding that he 'wasn't himself'.[84]

In the Commons, rumours of an early election triggered anxious discussions among Powell's small band of close supporters in the Commons, including Biffen and Ridley, as to what Powell might do. Their fears that he might stand down were also exacerbated by his refusal to state his intentions and his 'being evidently in a state of considerable distress'. But immediately before the Commons rose for the Christmas recess, the Chancellor's emergency budget offered a ray of hope. In an effort to dampen inflation, Barber announced major expenditure cuts and a credit squeeze to reinforce the earlier increase in the minimum lending rate (a variant of the old bank rate) to 13 per cent. When Powell offered his support for Barber's measures, cheers and jeers appeared to come in equal volume from both sides of the House. Soon afterwards, speaking in his constituency, Powell pledged his loyalty to the Conservative Party and endorsed the December budget.[85]

Over the Christmas break, the economy was dealt a further severe blow as the oil-producer countries again doubled the price of oil, to $11.63 (a quadrupling in price in a period of only three months). But the deepening crisis only served to whet the appetite for an early election at all levels of the Conservative Party. A mixture of opportunism (the opinion polls had moved in the Tories' favour) and a desire to stand up to the miners with a fresh mandate fuelled intense speculation that Heath was considering a poll on 31 January or 7 February. Powell, however, denounced a snap election as 'an act of total immorality', since the Government had painted themselves into a corner and would have to make a generous settlement with the miners after such an election.[86]

Powell had every reason to oppose a snap election on grounds of self-interest. He had not yet told his constituency association of his intentions, and an election early in 1974 would destroy any faint hope that the Conservatives might revise their pro-EEC policy before the next election. Moreover, there was every prospect that Heath would win an early election on the issue of 'who governs?' with the result that any hope of renegotiation on the EEC, as Labour were promising, would be lost. A Conservative victory in a snap election was certainly anticipated by most Labour MPs. When the Prime Minister let pass the deadline for calling an election on 7 February, the Leader of the House, Jim Prior, told Heath that 'all the Labour Members were coming up to me in the tea room to tell me that we have let them off the hook. They're throwing their hats in the air.' Other MPs told Powell that his attack on the idea of a snap election had headed Heath off an early poll. In fact, senior Tory ministers were deeply split on whether there should be an election or not and Heath had still not made up his mind. The 'hawks', Carrington and Prior, were pressing for an early poll, while the doves, Whitelaw and Carr, were counselling Heath against – as Whitelaw was only too aware, an early election threatened to disrupt the fragile political initiatives in Northern Ireland.[87]

By early February, however, the miners had voted 81 per cent in favour of an all-out strike, starting on the 11th. On the 6th, Prior told a press gallery lunch that 'the miners have had their ballot, perhaps we ought to have ours'. In the Commons, Powell was involved in a final clash with the Chancellor, who had attacked him so vehemently at Blackpool the previous autumn. Barber had got into difficulty trying to explain whether the oil price rise was inflationary or deflationary. Denis Healey, Nicholas Ridley and Enoch Powell rose to intervene. As Barber struggled on, Julian Critchley recalls that Powell, who was sitting next to him on the back benches, 'again half rose to his feet and with a sweep of his arms, cried loudly, "imbecility, imbecility", (his Black Country intonation was very obvious) in the general direction of the Government front bench'. Critchley caught sight of a Government whip, Spencer le Marchant, a large man, bearing down on Powell, 'presumably to sort him out'. 'Hurriedly, Enoch's neighbours grasped at his coat and hissed at him to sit down. Happily he did so just in time. It was to be Enoch's last appearance in the House as a Conservative'.[88]

On Thursday 7 February, Heath called an election for three weeks' time. Powell immediately wrote to his constituency chairman, George Wilkes, explaining that he regarded the election as being 'essentially fraudulent', would not seek re-election for Wolverhampton South-West as the Conservative candidate, and had 'no intention of standing otherwise'. Powell also sent a copy of his letter to his agent, Robin Pollard, at the association's offices, and gave another copy to the press, embargoed for midnight. Although his letters to Wolverhampton arrived within hours, the press embargo was broken and many of his local Tory Party officers and members were shattered to learn of Powell's decision not to stand from radio and television news bulletins on the evening of the 7th. They were bitterly disappointed that, despite having worked closely with him, in some cases since his adoption almost twenty-five years earlier, Powell had neither told them beforehand of his intentions, nor explained his reasons in person – he later wrote personally to thank his associates, but the anger at his action lingered. Indeed, the resentment felt in Wolverhampton was exacerbated by an even bigger blow that Powell was to deliver against the Conservative cause before polling day.[89]

As the campaign began, Powell maintained his public silence – one exception was a non-political engagement to preach at St Peter's, Eaton Square on Sunday 17th, when his subject was the feeding of the five thousand.

Reports of a previously commissioned profile by Powell of de Gaulle prompted renewed suggestions that he was hoping for the call if Heath was defeated. 'Enoch looks good now, alone and out of the domestic squabbles', one of his parliamentary friends told the *Sunday Times*, 'but if Ted gets back with a 100 majority it could be all over for him.' On the other hand, if Heath were to lose, or even to win but make a mess of the job, Powell could still be an alternative leader: 'he's waiting for a call from the people'. In Ulster, some anti-Sunningdale Unionists still hoped that Powell might be ready to assume the mantle of Carson, rather than de Gaulle.[90]

Privately, however, Powell was putting a different plan into action. On the day that the election was called, 7 February, he let Wilson know what he had in mind. Powell was risking his political career, but Wilson was also sensitive to the danger of any contact with Powell, whose views on market economics and immigration were anathema to many Labour MPs and activists. Their liaison during the election was therefore conducted indirectly through Andrew Alexander, a journalist who was sympathetic to Powell, and Joe Haines, the Labour leader's press secretary. 'My messages to Wilson during the campaign amounted to saying, "I am proposing to intervene at such and such a stage on such and such a day and will be prepared to modify my remarks to suit your own tactics"', Powell later confessed to Ben Pimlott. 'Wilson and Haines did their best to present me with a clear run for my speeches on the Saturday [23 February] and Monday [the 25th]. Such was the nature of the alliance.'[91]

Powell was taking the biggest risk of his career. Coming out publicly for Labour was almost certain to condemn him to the political wilderness. Barring some extraordinary, unforeseen upheaval inside the Conservative Party, he was burning his bridges with the party for which he had worked and that he had represented since returning from India at the start of 1946. With his views, there was no question of him finding refuge in the Labour Party. Moreover, there was no guarantee that Wilson would deliver on Labour's pledge to renegotiate better terms and to put the outcome to the people. Listening to Labour's anti-EEC rhetoric, there seemed little prospect that a Labour Government would be able to reach agreement on terms that they could recommend to the voters. But although there was a risk that Wilson might renege, the return of a Labour Government would at least offer an opportunity to reopen the debate on the EEC, whereas Heath's re-election would finally settle the matter. But Powell's refusing to stand as a Conservative would not, in itself, make sufficient impact to help elect a Labour Government. He therefore had to intervene actively in the campaign and throw the gambler's dice.

There was an additional reason for Powell's decision to speak out. As long ago as 1972, he had suspected that he would not stand for election to a parliament that had lost its sovereignty on Britain's entry into the EEC. By mid-1973, he was indicating his readiness to support Labour, although the precise details of how he intended to do this remained unclear. But Heath's calling a snap election muddied the water. Powell's specific reason for refusing to stand as a Conservative in February 1974 was not Europe, but his denunciation of the Government's prices and incomes policy and Heath's decision to go to the country over the miners' strike. As a result, the overriding issue on which Powell disagreed with Heath, namely British membership of the EEC, had been lost in the controversy over the holding of an election.[92]

Among the organizations that pressed Powell to speak out during the election was the anti-EEC 'Get Britain Out' campaign. On Wednesday 20th, it was announced that Powell would address two rallies organized by the campaign – on Saturday 23rd in Birmingham, and on Monday 25th in Shipley, Yorkshire. The timing of Powell's rallies, on the last weekend and at the start of the final week, and their location in venues that maximized his appeal in Midland and Northern marginal seats, carried the Powell hallmark. Although the Conservative Party chairman, Lord Carrington, exerted considerable pressure to keep him off BBC's *Panorama* on the final Monday before polling, Powell was interviewed for Thames Television's *Today* on the final Tuesday of campaigning in what amounted to an 'eve of poll' appeal that attracted great publicity. Powell never uttered the words 'vote Labour' in February 1974, but his meaning could not have been clearer.[93]

Powell's two rallies were electrifying, emotionally-charged occasions. When he arrived at the Birmingham Bull Ring Centre to make his first speech of the campaign, he was greeted by a cheering crowd of about 1,500. Hundreds of people stood and chanted, 'Enoch, Enoch', inside the hall. Powell was vitriolic about Heath. 'The whole story of Britain and the Common Market to date has been one long epic of deception,' he claimed. He derided Heath for having committed Britain to full 'economic and monetary union by 1980', which, Powell argued, would deprive the British Parliament of being able to decide its own laws and taxes. Alluding to the bitter controversies over the Government's legislation on housing and industrial relations, Powell commented of Heath that,

> This is the party leader who, on the basis of a few defaulting councillors at Clay Cross and some foolish utterances by a union official is heard accusing his political opponents of lacking respect for Parliament and the law. It is a savage irony, and not the less so for being unconscious, that these taunts come from the first Prime Minister in 300 years who entertained, let alone executed, the intention of depriving Parliament of its sole right to make the laws and impose the taxes of this country.

Asked if Heath should be taken to the Tower and tried for offences against the state, Powell replied: 'Do not ask judges, tipstaffs and police to do what you should do for yourself at the ballot box next Thursday.'[94]

The next morning's headlines were unequivocal about Powell's advice. As the *Sunday Times* declared, 'Powell message is Vote Labour'. The Conservatives were furious, and Powell's former constituency loyalists in Wolverhampton were 'devastated'. The Tory leadership, however, hoped that his intervention had come too late to help Labour and would finally discredit him with Conservatives. They decided to react more in sorrow than anger, and Heath commented that he was 'rather sad' that Powell 'should find himself in such company'.[95]

At Shipley on Monday 25th, although he again failed to utter the phrase 'vote Labour', he none the less explicitly endorsed Labour's position on the EEC. Repeating his warning that the voters would not have another chance to speak on British membership of the EEC, he declared that in order to take this last opportunity:

It means giving a majority in the next House of Commons to the party which is committed to fundamental renegotiation of the treaty of Brussels and to submitting to the British people thereafter for their final Yea or Nay, the outcome of that renegotiation, succeed or fail, so that the question will remain and be seen to remain – where it ought to be – firmly in the hands of the electorate as a whole.

By way of a personal testament, Powell explained that he was born and would die a Tory, but he had 'never yet heard that it was any part of the faith of a Tory' to take the institutions, liberties, laws and customs that had evolved over centuries in this country and merge them with those of eight other nations into a new-made, artificial state.

The test of a political debater is his or her ability to respond to heckling, and it was a heckler who triggered the dramatic climax of Powell's February 1974 campaign. Powell was meeting the claim that Labour could not be trusted to keep their pledges on the EEC, or as Powell put it, 'to use the more elegant expression, "Wilson will rat on his undertakings"'. As he continued with another attack on Heath by pointing out that there were 'a lot of people about, whom it behoves to be very cautious in accusing their political opponents of past or prospective U-turns', he was interrupted by a cry of 'Judas!' For a split second he hesitated. But pointing his finger in the direction of his accuser and turning his stare on him, Powell retorted, 'Judas was paid! I am making a sacrifice.'[96]

Although he revealed on television the following evening that he had already cast his postal vote for Labour, he told friends that the door had closed on his political career. He anticipated that Heath would win a majority of about sixty seats – the opinion polls, the bookmakers and most commentators expected Heath to stay in Number 10 with a comfortable majority, although during the final week, the Tories began to fear that increasing Liberal support might lead to a hung parliament. After the polls closed on the evening of Thursday 28 February, Powell retired to bed at his Belgravia home at his usual time of 11 p.m. instead of staying up with others to watch the results. The next morning, he had a great surprise:

> Having risen at my usual time of seven, going down, tiptoeing down and seeing the paper slanting through the letter-box, and reading the words, 'Heath's gamble ...' 'Heath's gamble'? I thought. '*Gamble*'? So I pulled it through and it fell out on the mat. 'Heath's Gamble Fails'. So I took it up with me to the bathroom and I sang the Te Deum.[97]

Elated though he was at the news of Heath's defeat, Powell would not be returning to the parliamentary ring when the new House of Commons met. The feud between him and Heath had ended in a double knock-out. Yet the uncertainty over Powell's future was matched by the political uncertainty at Westminster. For the first time in 45 years, a general election had yielded an indecisive result. The Conservatives had pipped Labour nationally by only 226,000 votes out of more than 31 million, winning 37.8 per cent of the vote to Labour's 37.1. But crucially, Labour had squeezed ahead of the Tories in the Commons by four seats, emerging as the largest single party with 301 MPs to the Tories' 297. It therefore seemed that Heath would resign. Powell made no public comment until the Saturday after polling, when he declared that 'the one clear good to come out of this election has been that the issue of the Common Market has been decisively kept open'. But since neither party had an overall majority, Heath remained in Downing Street over the weekend of 2–3 March and sought a deal with the Liberals, who had won fourteen seats. It was only after this had failed that Heath finally resigned, and on the evening of Monday 4th, Wilson became leader of a minority Labour administration.[98]

An important factor in Heath's demise had been the Conservatives' loss of the automatic support of the Ulster Unionists at Westminster. If Heath had been able to rely on the eight Ulstermen who had taken the Conservative whip at the start of the 1970 parliament, he would have remained leader of the largest single party. But his policies in Northern Ireland had cost him dear, and among the 23 minority party MPs in the new House of Commons, eleven were anti-Sunningdale Unionists. In the new and uncertain situation that prevailed at Westminster, this disaffected group were soon to make fresh contact with Powell.

But what of Powell's impact? Although he later tended to dismiss the idea that it is possible to ascertain the effect of a single event, issue or politician on an election, he expressed a different view on the weekend following Labour's return to office. He was appearing on BBC Radio's *Any Questions*, when Norman St John Stevas, the Tory MP who was also on the panel suggested that Powell would not view the prospect of another election quite so calmly if he had just fought an election, as Stevas had. 'I did and won it', was Powell's immediate riposte. The programme's final question was to prompt a second comment by Powell that made headline news the following day. When the panel were asked if they had any unfulfilled ambitions, Powell replied, 'I have the unfulfilled ambition, but not an ignoble one, of leading the Tory Party.' At this, Stevas remarked, 'there are worse things than an electoral defeat, I see!'[99]

As had happened in June 1970, Powell made a significant, and possibly, decisive impact on the February 1974 election. Heath had been the unintended beneficiary on the first occasion, but less than four years later Powell wreaked his revenge. 'I put him in and I took him out,' Powell was wont to observe pithily in later years. It also seemed that, as in 1970, Powell's impact – as he intended – was strongest during the final week of the campaign. The opinion polls indicate that again there was a late swing from the Government. But was this due to Powell? There is evidence to suggest that any contribution by Powell to the pro-Labour swing was achieved during, rather than before, the campaign, but other events intervened in the final stages, as they had in 1970 – notably in 1974, the disclosure of figures by the official Pay Board, exactly a week before polling day, appearing to suggest that the miners were not as well paid as ministers had claimed; and on the last Tuesday, maladroit comments about the 1971 Tory Industrial Relations Act from the Director-General of the CBI, Sir Campbell Adamson.[100]

Although Powell's support was smaller in February 1974 than it had been in 1970, or even in 1973, he none the less retained substantial support: three weeks before the poll, fifteen per cent of respondents told MORI that he best represented their views – a staggering response for somebody who had been on the back benches for almost six years. Even more remarkable, 56 per cent of voters could spontaneously mention speeches by Powell. Although he was not standing as a candidate, he none the less attracted front-page coverage on no fewer than five of the twenty-one days of the campaign. He also stole the television news headlines with his condemnation of the election on 7 February and his Birmingham speech on 23 February. And as Martin Harrison found from an analysis of TV and radio broadcasts, 'Powell was heard and seen more in the last few days of the campaign than anyone but the party leaders.'[101]

Moreover, none of the late set-backs for the Government can explain the political earthquake that undermined Tory support in Powell's native West Midlands, and that had its epicentre in his former base, Wolverhampton South-West. Whereas the national swing from the Conservatives to Labour between 1970 and 1974 was about one per cent, the regional swing in the West Midlands was 3.9 per cent. As Britain's main manufacturing base, voters in the region possibly resented the three-day week more than others in different areas, but the pattern of the swing within the region tells a different story. In the West Midlands conurbation, the swing to Labour since 1970 was 5.8 per cent and in the Black Country was 7.5 per cent, compared with 2–3 per cent in urban seats elsewhere. In the six seats in Wolverhampton, Dudley and neighbouring South-West Staffordshire, the swing to Labour averaged 10 per cent. In Wolverhampton South-West the swing to Labour was 16.7 per cent, and would have been about 20 per cent if the strongly Conservative Tettenhall had not been brought within the constituency since 1970. It is difficult to imagine what else could have produced such a markedly above average swing to Labour in Powell's native West Midlands, other than 'the Enoch effect'.[102]

It has been suggested that Powell's impact on the West Midlands had no effect on the result, because no seats changed hands in the region. This is quite wrong. The confusion stems from the redrawing of constituency boundaries between 1970 and 1974. As a result, although 307 seats remained the same, or underwent only minor change, 328 seats underwent major change and were no longer directly comparable with 1970. Many seats in the West Midlands were substantially altered. In his post-election analysis, David Butler adjusted the election results for boundary changes and calculated that nationally, Labour gained 20 seats net over what they would have won if the new boundaries had been in force in 1970. As to the West Midlands, Butler reckoned that 'no fewer than eight of those gains were in this Powell territory. If Mr Powell had held his peace last weekend Mr Heath would have been very much nearer to a working majority today.' On another calculation, five West Midlands seats changed hands. But in such a close contest, even this was sufficient to deny Heath the all-important prize in British elections of emerging as leader of the largest single party in the Commons.[103]

In the Nuffield study of the February 1974 election, Michael Steed, who had originally dismissed Powell's impact in 1970, was again dismissive of his effect on the result. But Steed now suggested that Powell's influence had weakened since the last election, and that the return of Labour voters to their traditional party allegiance helped explain the marked swing back to Labour in the Black Country. On Steed's 1974 analysis, the large swing to Labour in and around Powell's old seat was 'a remarkable tribute to the influence of Enoch Powell in 1970' – a conclusion that sits oddly with Steed's view in 1970. But the opinion poll and survey data suggest that Powell again exerted a significant impact in February 1974, as R.W. Johnson and Douglas Schoen countered. Further confirmation of Powell's impact in the West Midlands is provided by an opinion poll by Marplan in Birmingham Perry Barr – a week before Powell's speech in Birmingham backing Labour, the Tories had a lead of 13 per centage points, but afterwards Labour had a two point lead. In addition, NOP found that whereas six per cent of all respondents said that Powell made them more likely to vote Labour, the figure for West Midlands respondents was eight per cent.[104]

Although Powell's impact appears to have been less marked nationally, other campaign polls suggested a 2:1 movement in favour of Labour among those who admitted that Powell's withdrawal from the election influenced their vote. No less than 49 per cent of Labour candidates in marginal seats thought Powell's intervention helped them, and only two per cent thought he had done them damage. An 'Enoch effect' was also evident in data from the panel of voters who were questioned for the major study of voting behaviour by Butler and Stokes. Overall, the panel swung by 0.9 per cent to Labour – virtually the same as the national swing. But whereas those members of the panel who were identified in 1974 as anti-Powellites showed a 2.3 per cent swing *to the Tories*, the Powellites showed a swing of 4.6 per cent to Labour. In his detailed study, Schoen emphasizes that no matter how the 1974 Powellites voted in 1970, they were much more likely in 1974 to move towards, or remain, Labour voters than anti-Powellites were. Indeed, if only anti-Powellites had voted in February 1974, the Tories would have won a majority of 100–150 seats. But Powell helped encourage a massive defection among 1970 Conservative voters, since 'no less than 35 per cent of this group who were pro-Powell in February 1974 deserted their party'. Only about half of these Tory Powellites went as far as to vote Labour, and Powell probably helped swell the third-party vote (there were strong overlaps between Powellite sympathies and voting Liberal and for other third parties, especially the Scottish Nationalist Party). It was, of course, the strong third-party showing that denied either main party an overall majority in the Commons.[105]

It is appropriate that the outcome of the February 1974 election had all the makings of Greek tragedy as far as Powell, the former classical scholar, is concerned. He had helped prevent the re-election of the man whom he held responsible for the loss of Britain's independence as a self-governing nation, but at the cost of condemning himself to the political wilderness. There was some consolation, in that had the election produced a decisive result for either party, Powell's decision to end his political career would, as Richard Ritchie has suggested, probably have been final. The stalemate of February, however, made another election inevitable within a very short period. Yet Powell had committed what many Conservatives regarded as the ultimate betrayal by encouraging people to vote Labour, and the door was probably slammed shut on his hopes of reviving his career on the Conservative benches. Neither was there even a remote possibility of his becoming a Labour MP. In the event, Powell's allies among the Ulster Unionists were to throw him a lifeline.

None the less, after February 1974 Powell was exiled from mainstream British politics. And this is where the element of Greek tragedy is strongest. For the end of cheap world energy not only contributed to the downfall of the Heath Government, but also heralded the end in the West generally of the *belle époque* – the quarter of a century from the late 1940s until the mid-'70s of rapid growth, full employment, relatively low inflation, increased government spending and generous welfare policies. In its place, dearer fuel brought slow growth, unemployment and an anti-inflationary emphasis on cutting government spending, especially welfare. The expansionary, Keynesian era finally gave way to balanced budgets and a monetarist revival – albeit often honoured more in the breach than the observance. The one British politician who had long castigated the supposed follies of the *belle époque* had been Enoch Powell. Yet at the moment when the tide of political economy had turned strongly in his favour, he was marooned. Even when he returned to the swim, he was trapped in the eddies and whirlpools of Ulster, never to return to the mainstream.

18

'Like the Song of the Birds Before Dawn'

It's a compulsive song. Like the song of the birds before dawn. Something tells them the dawn is coming, and they just have to sing. They don't cause the dawn to come, though maybe they are under the illusion that they cause it to come. Many politicians have had the corresponding illusion. I hope I don't have that. But at any rate I sing my song, and if the dawn comes, well, so much the better, but I sing the song about what I see and what I feel.

Enoch Powell on his life in politics, 1987.

Orange card

Winter's turning to spring in 1974 was a time of having to cope with the unfamiliar. Powell had to adjust to life without Westminster and Wolverhampton, the twin pillars of his political existence for a quarter of a century. He told the leading Ulster Unionist, Harry West, that he felt 'like a man without his right arm'. But with the imminent prospect of another election, Powell's actions and intentions continued to attract close interest. Life was almost as disorienting for those who were returned to the new House of Commons. Wilson had to grapple with the crisis bequeathed him by Heath while learning to run the first minority administration since Ramsay MacDonald's. Labour, however, at least held the initiative as the party in office. The Conservatives' predicament was much worse. They knew that there would soon be another election, but they also knew that at a time of national crisis they might face massive defeat if they were to precipitate an election by doing as some of their more bull-headed MPs and supporters urged – allying with other parties to bring down the new Government. On the other hand, failing to attack Labour at every turn was bound to cause irritation within a demoralized party. The Tory leadership's resolution of his tactical dilemma during the spring was to have an important bearing on Powell's future.[1]

Yet the group who were in the most unfamiliar territory in the 1974 parliament were Ulster's eleven Unionist MPs. Unlike their predecessors, who had taken the Conservative whip for decades until direct rule, they were members of the United Ulster Unionist Council (UUUC), or Ulster Coalition, that had been formed to fight the Sunningdale agreement – the UUUC included anti-Faulkner Ulster Unionists led by Harry West; Ian Paisley's Democratic Unionist Party; and William Craig's Vanguard Unionists. The UUUC's 51 per cent share of the vote in Northern Ireland reflected the strength of opposition to Sunningdale amongst the unionist majority, and enabled them to win every Ulster seat except one – the twelfth seat was won by the Social Democratic and Labour Party's Gerry Fitt. During the weekend after the election, Heath had explored the possibility of a deal with some of the Unionists and reportedly offered seven of them the Conservative whip, to no avail. The UUUC's electoral coup and the hung parliament brought them potentially considerable influence. But how should they use it? In April, the three UUUC leaders decided that they should approach Powell, whose credentials as a parliamentarian and as a unionist were unquestioned.[2]

They also had another motive. The leader of the Ulster Unionists in the previous parliament, Captain Lawrence Orr, had been re-elected for Down South, although he rarely visited the Province. Indeed, it was already known to the leadership of the UUUC – West, Craig and Paisley – and to Powell, that, for personal reasons, Orr would not stand at the next election and had suggested Powell as a suitable replacement. Within a matter of weeks after the February election, West, Craig and Paisley called on Powell at his Belgravia home in order to check on his availability. According to one account, the Unionists told Powell: 'Look, we've got power in our hands, but most of us are new to this and we don't know how to use it. Will you come and help us?' Powell could not see any grounds for refusing, even if he had been disposed to decline such an offer.[3]

But certain matters had yet to be resolved. The political outlook in both Britain and Northern Ireland was highly uncertain, and so too was Powell's position. In mid-April, his address to a Unionist rally in the Ulster Hall, Belfast, prompted speculation that he might stand for an Ulster seat. His attack on the power-sharing executive as 'a dummy, a wreck, a waterlogged hulk', and his rallying cry to Unionists to use their new power to win full representation at Westminster won a standing ovation. But his speech also demonstrated that his views on Northern Ireland continued to set him apart from the majority of Unionists, who remained strongly in favour of devolution. The previous September, he had told Unionists in Londonderry that the mould of Stormont was 'broken and like it or not cannot be put together', and he now repeated his commitment to the integration of the Province into the United Kingdom – the antithesis of devolution. In doing so, he revealed how deeply his approach was rooted in his romantic nationalism. 'I believe in magic,' he confessed to UUUC supporters, 'in the magic of a free parliament of a united nation'. Moreover, he reasserted that,

> Ulster cannot share in that unity except by sharing, without qualification or diminution, in the undivided sovereignty of that Parliament. Hitherto the people of Northern Ireland have been provincial in nothing but their

politics. Now their politics too, through the transformation that the general election brought about, must cease to be provincial.[4]

A week later, Powell repeated his integrationist call at the UUUC's conference at Portrush, County Antrim. But no sooner had he left the conference hall, than representatives agreed to a policy statement that totally repudiated Powell's approach and advocated a Northern Ireland regional parliament within a federal United Kingdom. Not only had the UUUC rejected his integrationist plea for the Province, they were now totally at odds with his emphasis on the continuing 'undivided sovereignty' of the United Kingdom parliament. Indeed, in early May, Powell was to repeat his view that the issue of devolution had brought the United Kingdom to the brink of a great divide. If Powell was to stand in Ulster at the next election, he looked like being as much out of step with his new party as he had ever been with the Conservatives. There was, however, one mitigating fact. The Unionists were opposed to British membership of the EEC. For Powell, this consideration outweighed all others.[5]

Many of Powell's friends and supporters in Britain, however, were appalled at the political danger that he would run by being sucked into the 'Northern Ireland quagmire' and 'graveyard of many a national reputation'. To British metropolitan eyes, the notion that Ulster politics were dominated by 'bloodthirsty extremists' was further confirmed in May by the loyalist Ulster Workers' strike after the power-sharing executive had won a vote in the Northern Ireland assembly in favour of Sunningdale, and by the slaughter of thirty people in the Republic by car bombs (the cars had earlier been hi-jacked in Protestant areas of Belfast). On 18 May, the day after the bombings, Powell delivered a scheduled speech to the Conservative Trident Group in London, that was presented as an olive branch from Powell to Heath and the Conservative Party. Indeed, 'the cleverly mounted advance publicity', as David Wood described it in *The Times*, created the impression that Powell had grown weary of life in the wilderness and, with the humility of a big man, wished to be taken back into the Conservative fold. Past differences had been removed, and the time had come for reunion.[6]

Powell may have judged that, with an autumn election looking increasingly likely, it was the right time to make a conciliatory gesture. Many Conservatives longed for an end to the ideological differences that had divided the party. Those who sympathized with Powell's economic policies wanted to see Powell return, and included, according to Ronald Butt in *The Sunday Times*, 'one or two in the Shadow Cabinet' – Sir Geoffrey Howe had long been an economic liberal, while Sir Keith Joseph and Margaret Thatcher were undergoing their conversion to monetarism. Yet any idea that Powell's speech offered a basis for 'reconciliation' was sheer fantasy. In the first place, there was no question of Heath and his closest colleagues in the Shadow Cabinet going back on all that they had done in office. Secondly, the Tory leadership realized that people had no desire for further confrontation and, as a result, were moving towards a strategy that was mapped out at the start of May in *The Times* by Ian Gilmour, the new chairman of the Conservative Research Department. Since voters plainly opposed the madcap socialism that a re-elected Labour Government would offer, Gilmour urged that after the radicalism of 1970–74 the Tories should now offer a spell of moderate government in the national interest. This call to consensus was echoed by Heath on 10 May, and the seeds were sown for the Tories' campaign of 'national unity' at the next election.[7]

In this context, there was no prospect of Powell's being welcomed back to the Conservative fold, especially since his supposed olive branch admitted to no change of opinion on his part. He made the assumption that conciliation was only possible, as Ronald Butt noted, 'because events have moved in such a way as to justify his own policies' – notably since the prospect of European economic and monetary union had receded. 'He is not asking to rejoin Mr Heath and the Conservative Party,' commented David Wood; 'he is asking the Conservative Party to join him, and in so doing seek the destruction of Mr Heath as party leader.'[8]

It was widely suspected that Powell, who was sixty-two years old in June, realized that the next election would be his last opportunity to return to the Commons and was advertising his availability to Tory constituency associations. Yet the attempts to have him adopted as a Conservative candidate were initiated by his supporters, and not by Powell. In one instance, Sir Harry d'Avigdor Goldsmid, the former Tory MP for Walsall South, contacted Jim Salt, the Tory agent at Aldridge-Brownhills and told him that if Salt wanted Powell to fight the seat, Sir Harry could get him. Salt, however, was a forthright character and replied that he had no wish to have Powell in the seat after his behaviour at the February election. The party officers at Aldridge-Brownhills shared Salt's view. Attempts to have Powell selected in Derbyshire and in Batley and Morley, in Yorkshire, were also rejected.[9]

None the less, the prospect of Powell's adoption was causing deep anxiety in Central Office, although, on Powell's admission, he was no longer subscribing to the party and therefore was not in receipt of the 'Candidates' List', that advises would-be candidates of constituency vacancies. In early July, the new chairman, Whitelaw, counselled Heath on how he might respond publicly if Powell were selected and adopted virtually overnight. Whitelaw was strongly opposed to giving Powell formal endorsement. But refusing to endorse him on the grounds of his support for Labour in the February election ran the risk, if the local party were obdurate, of having to run an official candidate against Powell. Another option was neither to approve nor oppose him. Powell later revealed that between March and August 1974, he received 'approaches of various kinds' in about 'a score of constituencies'. But he also stressed that 'in every case' he had 'made it clear to those who approached me that I could not accept nomination as a Conservative candidate. If my name was considered anywhere, it was without my knowledge or against my advice'.[10]

Indeed, in early July Powell effectively signalled an end to the speculation about his possible return as a Conservative candidate when he indicated his support for Labour's approach to the EEC – in Heath's office, William Waldegrave suspected that Powell's speech had made the situation slightly easier. By this time, events had moved fast in Northern Ireland. Faulkner's power-sharing executive collapsed on 28 May, and a few days later, Powell told Unionists in Ulster that he had warned parliament in 1973 that the Heath-Robinson Constitution would prove unworkable. During his visit, he further delighted Unionists by taking up demands that were close to their hearts – he supported the re-introduction of the 'B specials' (the special constabulary set up in 1920 to counter the IRA were a potent symbol for unionists but were distrusted in the minority community and had been disbanded in 1969); and he also called for the rejuvenation of the Royal Ulster Constabulary.[11]

Moreover, Powell removed the main stumbling block to joining the UUUC's ranks by making a significant concession on devolution. While repeating his integrationist call for Ulster's full representation at Westminster, he accepted that such a reform 'no more prejudges or prejudices future arrangements which may be thought best for its administration than it does for Wales or Scotland'. At the end of August, in a speech in County Armagh, he suggested that Northern Ireland should be entitled to any form of devolution that might be introduced in Britain.[12]

Powell's Armagh speech marked his first public indication that he was interested in standing for an Ulster seat, and on the same evening the Ulster Unionists in Down, South, received his note applying to become their candidate. The following day, Saturday 31 August, the sitting Unionist MP, Lawrence Orr, formally announced his decision not to stand at the next election and indicated that he wanted Powell to be adopted in his place. Two other applications had been received during the previous week, but were withdrawn before Powell put his name forward. Powell's selection was unanimous, and was confirmed at a meeting at the Orange Hall at Dromore, near Banbridge, County Down on 3 September. Powell, who had stayed in London rather than return for his selection, put an integrationist gloss on his joining the Unionists by commenting that he would be 'pressing for what the official policy of the Ulster Unionist Party has to say and the first part of that is the full and fair representation of Ulster at Westminster'.

The ambivalence that was to characterize the Unionists' attitude towards Powell was evident from the start. Many were pleased that a national figure, with his skills as a communicator and speechmaker, had taken up their cause. Powell's style in Northern Ireland, as Robert Fisk observed, was 'to project other people rather than himself', and his audiences liked him for it. 'The Protestants have risen to their feet when Mr Powell took the platform, not because he adopted the techniques of Mr Craig and Mr Paisley, offering himself as another Carson to lead the fearful from the valley of Republicanism – but because he only claimed to be an interpreter, making the Protestants heroes instead of himself.' The magic worked time and again. Even when giving Unionists an unpalatable warning that Stormont would never return,

'Mr Powell, his eyes flicking from one side to the other and his finger wagging demonstratively, told his audience that they would win their fight to stay British and to the man they rose and cheered him again and again.' This impression was shared by the Unionist leader, Harry West, who later recalled that on many occasions, 'Powell's great oratory overawed people and they found themselves agreeing with him when in fact he had entirely dismissed party policy.'[13]

None the less, Powell's impressive style in Northern Ireland could not entirely soothe Unionist sensitivities. After all, he was an Englishman who wanted to return to the Commons and yet had no prospect of fighting a British seat – the 'Wolverhampton Wanderer' as Paisley was wont to call him. Suspicions that Powell was merely using Ulster for his own ends were fuelled by speculation that he was seeking to emulate Lord Randolph Churchill in the 1880s, who had played the 'Orange card' in his bid for power. Some commentators suspected that Powell, after he had returned to Westminster, might seek to lead the disgruntled Tory right; others suspected that he would make an early bid for the Unionist leadership.[14]

There were also doubts about Powell's motives because he had fallen out so badly with the Unionists' traditional Tory allies and many Unionists were deeply suspicious of Labour's sympathy for a united Ireland. Moreover, Powell was out of step with many Unionists not only on devolution, but also in opposing regional and industrial aid. Orr's endorsement of Powell drew only cautious approval from William Craig, the Vanguard leader, who stressed that although he was amenable to having Powell in the UUUC's team, he did not want him as leader. The loyalist paramilitary Ulster Defence Association, that was closely aligned with Craig, was openly critical, suggesting that Powell would be as much use to the Province as the member for Land's End or John o'Groats. Indeed, after Powell's adoption, the UDA held a secret meeting with him on 20 September, the day that the 1974 parliament was dissolved, before agreeing to support his candidature. It is remarkable that Powell, who vilified others whenever he sensed that they condoned or encouraged violence, had any truck with a paramilitary organization.[15]

Yet despite all the speculation about Powell's motives for moving to Ulster, his election in Down, South, was by no means guaranteed. Orr's majority in February had been 5,602, and he had received 52 per cent of the vote against the SDLP's 43 per cent (a republican candidate had also stood). By September the strains within the UUUC had fuelled rumours that Paisley might field a Democratic Unionist (DUP) candidate in Down, South, in which case the Unionist vote would be split. In the event, there was no challenge from either the DUP or from Faulkner, the moderate Unionist leader who lived in the area and who had had to stomach Powell's attacks on power-sharing. Faulkner's supporters, however, were said to have run a whispering campaign against Powell by alleging that he had ousted Orr. As a newcomer, Powell was vulnerable to such a charge, especially since he had had no time to become acquainted with his new constituency and its people.[16]

Whereas Wolverhampton South-West had been a comparatively compact urban and residential constituency, Down, South, had no natural centre and stretched across 900 square miles from Belfast's south-western rural hinterland to the dramatically scenic Mountains of Mourne, and beyond to the Province's southern coastline. In south Staffordshire, Powell had represented about 60,000 voters; his new electorate numbered above 90,000. Powell pored over maps of his far-flung constituency and launched himself into the second 1974 election with the same enthusiasm and military-style planning that he had shown in Wolverhampton. As Caroline Moorehead observed, 'the machine-like precision of his campaigns clashed with the rather happy-go-lucky approach of his followers'. Again, Pam Powell took an active role in campaigning.[17]

In a constituency that was divided roughly fifty-fifty on sectarian lines, Powell's reception varied from warm and welcoming to downright hostile. His energetic campaign included door-to-door canvassing in Protestant and mixed areas – he was reported to be on the IRA's 'list', and was advised for security reasons not to canvass in republican areas. In numerous speeches, Powell stressed those parts of the UUUC manifesto calling for fair parliamentary representation for Ulster; the same policing and administrative arrangements as the rest of the United Kingdom; and again he praised the old 'B specials'. As in Wolverhampton, he also made it clear that, if elected, he would serve all his constituents equally, but he did not endear himself to nationalists by giving the impression in an interview for RTE that he thought that the aspiration of the nationalist minority community had to die because it was impossible for the same territory to belong to two nations and there had to be total victory for the wishes of the majority.[18]

The convincing show of unity at a Belfast UUUC rally seemed to paper over any cracks between West, Paisley, Craig and Powell, when all four men were greeted with equal enthusiasm. But Powell soon revived tensions among the Unionists. Although West, who was leader of the anti-assembly Unionists, had requested him not to endorse Labour, Powell none the less travelled to Manchester a week before polling day to repeat his advice of February that people should vote Labour. But whereas the EEC remained the overriding national issue as far as Powell was concerned, many Unionists were much more perturbed that Labour would seek a united Ireland. Moreover, Powell's mockery of Heath and the Conservatives for their vague appeal to national unity worried Unionists who hoped for a *modus vivendi* with the Tories after the election. These Unionist anxieties were exacerbated when Powell appeared to criticize the Unionist plan to revitalize Ulster's shipyards with state subsidies that would bring extra jobs for the Protestant working class.[19]

As a result of Powell's adoption for Down, South, and the extra interest that his status as a controversial, national figure generated, his constituency was one of the few Ulster seats where the turn-out increased since February. Towards the end of the count, Powell and his wife, Pam, looked grim and worried on television as they waited for the result. In the event, Powell won

2,600 more votes than Orr, but the Unionist share of the vote fell slightly to 50.8 per cent, giving Powell only a 3,567 majority (5.4 per cent) over the SDLP. But having won the seat, Powell devoted himself to trying to make a marginal seat safer, as he had in Wolverhampton. In his first seat, he had taken a flat and then, after his marriage, had bought a house (the Powells were soon to sell their old home in Merridale Road). Now, the Powells bought a constituency home, in Loughbrickland, that happened be on the route taken by King William's troops when they marched from Belfast to the Boyne in 1690 – Powell was soon familiarizing himself with the architecture and history of County Down as passionately as he had done in the West Midlands.[20]

Because the February election had failed to yield an overall winner, Powell was able to return to the Commons within ten months. The February and October 1974 elections represented only the second occasion in the twentieth century when two elections were held during the same year, and the interval between them was the shortest for almost ninety years, since the elections of November 1885 and July 1886 – the latter election having been precipitated by Joseph Chamberlain's resignation over Irish Home Rule. Yet Powell was to have mixed feelings about becoming an MP again after the 1970–74 parliament and Britain's membership of the EEC. 'I've sometimes wondered', he confessed after his parliamentary career eventually ended,

> whether I shouldn't have stuck to my decision that the last independent parliament of the United Kingdom should be the last parliament to which I would belong. For if you belong to a parliament and seek to belong to a parliament which has surrendered the supreme rights over its own people to an external body, then you are tarred with the brush.[21]

Isolation

After his return to the Commons in October 1974, Powell was to serve as an MP for almost thirteen more years. Yet he was now largely isolated from British politics as he became embroiled in the factional battles of Ulster Unionism and no longer enjoyed the security of the political stronghold that he had built in Wolverhampton South-West. Indeed, Powell was nothing like the threat to the Conservatives in October that he had been at the previous two elections. Writing in *The Times* towards the end of the campaign, he had pointed to conflicts of conscience that were stretching party loyalties to breaking point. But his ability to bring about a political re-alignment in Britain was seriously weakened by his involvement in Ulster. As the authors of the Nuffield election study noted of the Tories' treatment of Powell's threat at the second 1974 election: 'he just needed keeping an eye on in case, like the San Andreas fault in San Francisco, he caused an earthquake'. He never did, and after the election he quickly grew out of touch with national politics, even though the new era of dearer energy, higher inflation and mass unemployment was to give a great impetus to the monetarist, economic counter-revolution that he had long since championed.[22]

Much though Powell's admirers on the Tory right hoped that he might return to the Conservative fold, they were to be frustrated by his attitude as much as by the implacable opposition of other Conservatives. Powell maintained an obdurate, almost perversely defiant, stance, as he waited for the party to rejoin him. On Sir Keith Joseph's much-heralded call in early September for the Tories to abandon compulsory prices and incomes policies and instead curb inflation through control of the money supply, Powell commented acidly: 'I have heard of death-bed repentance, but it would perhaps be more appropriate to refer to post-mortem repentance.' Neither could he resist noting that Joseph was merely repeating the arguments that Powell, himself, had advanced much earlier. After the Tories' two election defeats within a year, Powell dismissed the Conservatives as a 'hollow shell of a party' and, to add insult to injury, condemned as an instance of modern political corruption the behaviour of those Tory MPs who had changed from backing Heath to calling for him to go since the election. On the issues that Powell now regarded as being of overriding importance – Europe and Northern Ireland – he was to be deeply disappointed by Governments of both main parties after 1974. Only for a brief period in the late 1970s, when the Labour Government lost their overall majority in the Commons, was Powell able to wield any effective influence on Northern Ireland.[23]

Although Powell believed that Governments cannot legislate against reality and emphasized the importance of national identity, he seemed to assume that if Ulster were integrated within the United Kingdom and any prospect of Irish unification removed, Irish nationalism among the minority community would die and terrorist violence would fade away. Yet this theory flew in the face of reality in Ulster, where two communities were divided by their commitment, down the centuries, to conflicting national identities and political traditions. As a result, Powell's impact on his new party at Westminster was increasingly baleful from the late 1970s, and the Unionists were marginalized as London and Dublin sought to resolve the impasse in Northern Ireland. But whereas other senior back-benchers and ex-Ministers in his predicament by the 1980s might have retired, perhaps to take up directorships and write their memoirs, Powell remained a compulsive politician and controversialist.

Yet when the results of the October 1974 election were first declared, Powell had reason to feel reasonably optimistic. The Labour Government had been re-elected, which he had wanted because of their commitment to renegotiate with the European Economic Community, notwithstanding a significant softening of the Government's position during the summer. But because Heath and the Conservatives had fared better than expected, Labour had won an overall majority of only four seats. In consequence, the Ulster Unionists and other minority parties were likely to be listened to more carefully, especially as such a wafer-thin majority would probably not last the length of a five-year parliament and Labour would again have to depend on the smaller parties to remain in office.

There was also a chance that Powell might emerge as the new leader of the Ulster Unionists at Westminster, following the defeat of Harry West at Fermanagh and South Tyrone. West had been leader of the anti-Sunningdale members of the Ulster Unionist Party – sometimes known as the 'Official' Unionists to distinguish them from Faulkner's pro-Sunningdale party. With six MPs, including Powell, the 'Official' Unionists were the largest group among the ten United Ulster Unionist Council MPs in the new parliament, and their leader would effectively become UUUC leader in the Commons. West's eventual successor, James Molyneaux, a quietly spoken and unassuming man, wanted Powell to take over. He was willing to assume the leadership at Westminster, but West, and the other two leaders of the UUUC, Paisley of the Democratic Unionists (DUP) and Craig of Vanguard, vetoed Powell because of the strong resentment that would be stirred among Unionist activists. Indeed, evidence of the anti-Powell feeling surfaced shortly after the election, when it was suggested that Powell had yet to understand 'the complexities of Ulster politics'.[24]

While Molyneaux became leader of the Unionists at Westminster, West continued as their leader in Ulster. Powell became Unionist spokesman on the Treasury and financial matters, and the EEC. By keeping to his brief he avoided giving offence to his fellow Unionists. They respected Powell's knowledge of parliamentary procedure and tactics, and under his tutorship the Unionists became more effective in the Commons. From the start, Molyneaux and Powell developed an especially close working relationship. Indeed, Molyneaux's lack of presence; his wooden delivery; and his known preference for Powell as leader; all prompted the suggestion that Molyneaux was 'Enoch's poodle'. The new Unionist leader at Westminster seemed in awe of Powell. Their relationship was vividly characterized by Jim Prior, who served as Northern Ireland Secretary in the early 1980s, as being that of 'a rabbit transfixed by a stoat'. Prior felt that Molyneaux 'always sounded very integrationist in the Commons as he spoke with Enoch at his side. But once he had got off the London-Belfast air shuttle and was back on Ulster soil, he sounded much more devolutionist.' During Prior's talks with the parties at Stormont during 1981–82, that preceded the establishment of a new Northern Ireland assembly, Molyneaux was often accompanied by another Unionist MP, the late Harold McCusker, and other senior party figures, but not by Powell.[25]

In the months that followed the October 1974 election, however, the imminent prospect of a leadership challenge in the Conservative Party preoccupied the media. Powell was Heath's strongest political enemy, and had done more than any other Tory to bring him down. Yet Powell was now out of the running for the Tory crown, and was reduced to the role of jaundiced observer, as Margaret Thatcher, whom he derided for having remained in Heath's Cabinet, emerged as Heath's challenger in the first ballot on 4

February 1975. Although she almost certainly won the support of economic liberals and others on the right who had previously supported Powell, her victory on the first ballot owed more to the fact that MPs wanted to be rid of Heath and vote for alternative candidates on the second ballot – a desire skilfully manipulated by Thatcher's campaign manager, Airey Neave, who suggested to some MPs on the eve of the first ballot that Heath looked set for an outright win. As a result, Thatcher won the first ballot, and was then unstoppable. There was no great ideological conversion among Tory MPs to monetarism, Powellism, or any other '-ism'. Powell himself was under no illusion about Thatcher's triumph. 'She didn't rise to power,' he later commented. 'She was opposite the spot on the roulette wheel at the right time, and didn't funk it.'[26]

There was no prospect of Powell's return to the Conservative ranks, despite hopes raised among Powellite sympathizers by the election of a new leader, and the belief held by a significant number of Tory MPs that 'he alone has it in him to swing between a million and two million votes to the Conservatives'. Thatcher told interviewers after her election that Powell would not join the Tory front bench. Powell responded somewhat tartly that she was right: 'In the first place I am not a member of the Conservative Party and secondly, until the Conservative Party has worked its passage a very long way, it will not be rejoining me.' Within weeks of her election as Tory leader, he attacked her for having decided as Education Secretary that no figures should be collected of immigrant children in schools.[27]

Barely a month after Heath's demise as Tory leader, Powell's hope that Britain might also leave the EEC was dealt a mortal blow when EEC heads of state reached agreement on renegotiated terms for Britain at their Dublin summit in March 1975. A year earlier, such an outcome had appeared improbable after Wilson had appointed James Callaghan as Foreign Secretary. In Opposition, Callaghan had seemed to be against British membership and he began by lecturing his European counterparts on the impact of the EEC on the British housewife. But Callaghan soon changed his tune – a deeply disappointed Powell reckoned that he was 'turned by the Foreign Office within a month'. More probably, Callaghan's shift reflected the disappearance of economic and monetary union from the EEC's immediate agenda, and the replacement of Willy Brandt as West German Chancellor by Helmut Schmidt, who was closer to Britain's Atlanticist approach on defence and was sceptical about political union. By the summer of 1974, Labour were talking about negotiating better terms under the existing treaties, rather than challenging the major issues of sovereignty and the non-acceptability of the Common Agricultural Policy. After the October election, the negotiations were speeded up, and in April 1975, Wilson secured the backing of his Cabinet for the new terms by sixteen to seven. The improvement in Britain's terms was modest, but it enabled Wilson to achieve his real objective, namely to prevent Labour from being torn apart over the EEC. Although most of the Labour Party and some of the Cabinet opposed the new terms, the Labour Government's endorsement ensured that the leadership of the three main parties recommended their acceptance. A 'Yes' vote to British membership in June's referendum became a foregone conclusion.[28]

The 'No' campaign showed passion, but it lacked the funds and the polish of the pro-EEC lobby. Neither could the 'No' campaigners overcome their main handicap of having their leading spokesmen drawn from the extreme wings of the political spectrum. Powell and Tony Benn were their best communicators, but they also produced negative responses among large numbers of voters. The 'No' campaigners were 'a motley crew', as Powell acknowledged: 'after all, all sorts and conditions of men can resent the destruction of their own country's independence'. But as Powell also suspected, even the most discerning elector must have been confused to see Powell and Benn on the same side. Persuading other anti-EEC campaigners to share a platform with Powell, who was still treated as a pariah because of his 'River Tiber' speech, was also a problem for the 'No' campaigners, but before the poll, most of their leading spokesmen had shared a platform with him. His call for people to vote Labour at both 1974 elections – at meetings organized by 'Get Britain Out' – had helped matters, and during the year before the referendum, Powell had addressed anti-EEC meetings with the trade union leaders, Clive Jenkins and Jack Jones, the Labour MP, George Wigg, and some Tory MPs. Benn, however, refused to share a platform with Powell and other Conservatives.[29]

Powell must take a large share of responsibility for the biggest weakness in the 'No' campaign, namely their failure to win Conservative votes. About 40 per cent of voters were Conservative supporters, and, as the authors of the Nuffield study of the referendum note, 'the anti-Market appeal to patriotism and sovereignty should have struck a chord with many of them'. Yet Conservatives overwhelmingly supported a 'Yes' vote. Although the new Conservative leader was nothing like as strongly committed to the European ideal as her successor, she none the less urged people to vote 'Yes'. Powell was the only 'No' campaigner who might have appealed to Tory voters and persuaded a significant number to go against the party leadership. But as far as the vast majority of Conservatives were concerned, he had betrayed their party at the last two elections and had deserted them for Ulster. Powell's departure and the demoralization of his followers made it easier for Conservative constituency associations to take up the EEC cause with enthusiasm. The irony of Powell's position was captured by Philip Goodhart, the former Tory MP and advocate of a referendum. 'When Enoch Powell first urged his supporters to vote Labour, he made a substantial contribution towards the Labour victory that made a referendum possible,' Goodhart noted; 'at the same time his defection made a "Yes" vote more likely when the referendum came.'[30]

Even so, some 'Yes' campaigners feared that Powell was the one man who, if he produced a performance to match his 'River Tiber' speech, could transform the contest. But Powell never delivered, and made only six speeches during the campaign. Some observers sensed that his old fire was lacking, but he attracted most attention on the 'No' side after Benn – though the BBC failed to report Powell's speech at Bournemouth early in the campaign on the grounds of having to accord equal time to both sides. Powell argued that he had detected a new and sinister argument being advanced by some 'Yes' campaigners, that the EEC was a means of defeating socialism in Britain, but he singled out his former party for sharpest criticism by warning that:

> As I watch and listen to the voices that are raised to persuade electors to surrender their own birthright because they fear their fellow subjects, I think I discern ahead the shape of a Conservative Party that is the party of a class, and not of a nation – and thus doomed to extinction.

His gloomy, class-conscious admonition might have come from the pages of the *Morning Star*, the communist newspaper. By re-opening old wounds with the Tories, Powell's likely impact was to turn off Conservative voters whom he should have been wooing.[31]

Yet in the final week of the campaign, Powell displayed a lighter, but none the less mischievous, touch, and brought much-needed wit to the debate. In the *News of the World* on the final Sunday before polling, Powell drew an analogy with backing horses and characterized the pro-EEC lobby as touts who were saying that the Common Market was too complicated for people to understand and were telling them:

> 'You must take the advice of the people who know best – the Conservative Party; the big industrialists; the CBI; the National Farmers' Union; above all, Ted Heath. Take their tip. Do what they tell you. Vote to stay in.' So let's look at the record of these people who 'know best' who can tell you what will be good for Britain, not just this year or next year but for generations to come. We discover that these are the very people who have always been wrong. Not one horse they have tipped has ever won.

Two days later, in what the authors of the Nuffield referendum study described as 'the most brilliant of all the main press conferences', Powell entertained the journalists with 'a bravura blend of doom and humour'. Powell exposed the contradictions in Thatcher's position, and said of Heath: 'I would dearly have liked to be friends but ... [pause] like everyone else, I found it impossible.' Powell delivered his final campaign speech in Sidcup – Heath's constituency.[32]

The resounding 64.5 per cent 'Yes' vote on 5 June was a shattering blow for Powell. Although there was some opinion poll evidence that he had helped keep a significant number of 'No' voters loyal to his cause, even Northern Ireland, where the Unionists (though not Craig) had urged a 'No' vote, opted to stay in. As Powell later revealed, the referendum was the second occasion on which he had felt ashamed of his country – the first had been when Britain appeased Hitler in the 1930s. Even after the result, he continued to substitute hyperbole for reason, while claiming that the verdict was not final:

> Never again, by the necessity of an axiom, will an Englishman live for his country or die for his country: the country for which people live and die was obsolete and we have abolished it. Or not quite yet. No, not yet. The Referendum is not a 'verdict' after which the prisoner is hanged forthwith. It is no more than provisional ... This will be so as long as one Parliament can alter or undo whatever that or any other Parliament has done. Hence those golden words in the Government's Referendum pamphlet: 'Our continued membership will depend on the continuing assent of Parliament.'[33]

Powell had never been an enthusiatic supporter of a referendum, but had regarded it as being preferable in a situation where voters were denied a clear choice on the EEC at a general election. Indeed, he explained the result partly as the voters having treated it as an opportunity to register their dislike of the Labour Party, and partly as a reflection of English deference in being ready to take the advice of those in government. The fact remains that he had been gullible in taking at face value Wilson's commitment to renegotiate and put the outcome to the people, instead of seeing it for what it was – a ploy to preserve Labour unity. But he had no alternative, because he had become so isolated in the Conservative Party by 1973–74 and seemed to have no prospect of challenging the leadership successfully. Powell's only remaining hope of obtaining Britain's withdrawal from the EEC had been to defeat his party. But although Powell had helped bring down the Conservative Government in 1974, the 1975 referendum turned to dust in his hands. It marked the end of his impact on national politics. He was now more isolated than ever.

Disunity

The 1975 referendum campaign coincided with the start of a turbulent phase in Unionist politics, in which Powell's opposition to devolution for the Province was a prominent factor. For the next couple of years, the strains and stresses among the Unionists were all too evident just as the erosion of Labour's majority in the Commons promised to give them greater influence at Westminster than at any other period in modern times. Yet Powell deserves much of the credit for winning a significant prize for Ulster. It was to be his last concrete, political act.

Powell set out his demands for the Province in a speech at Hollywood, County Down on 9 January 1975. He was alert to the Labour Government's plan for a Constitutional Convention in Northern Ireland in order to seek new agreement following the collapse of power-sharing, and also to their promise to introduce devolution in Scotland and Wales. In a balancing act between his belief in the integration of Northern Ireland into the United Kingdom and the

Unionist commitment to devolution in Northern Ireland, Powell reiterated that Ulster must remain an integral part of the United Kingdom and have full representation. In addition, he argued that Ulstermen should have the same right as every other citizen of the United Kingdom to democratic local government. These integrationist demands were coupled with a nod towards devolution by stating that 'we intend to share fully in whatever forms of devolution to regions are consistent with full representation in parliament'. Yet his scepticism of devolution was evident in other speeches. In April at Downpatrick, he warned that devolution might weaken the union, and queried why, if Ulster was part of the United Kingdom, was a Constitutional Convention needed?[34]

A new crisis within the Unionist coalition was triggered by the election of the Constitutional Convention on 1 May. The United Ulster Unionist Council won 47 of the 78 seats, well ahead of the second largest party, the nationalist Social Democratic and Labour Party, with only 17 seats, but there was an impasse because the British Government would only restore devolution, as most Unionists wanted, on condition that there was cross-community support. There seemed to be no prospect of any such agreement, since the UUUC were staunchly opposed to the SDLP's demands, namely the return of power-sharing and the Council of Ireland. Suddenly, however, William Craig, the Vanguard Unionist leader, suggested to his fellow Unionists that they should enter a voluntary coalition with the SDLP, arguing that there had been coalition governments at Westminster during both World Wars and in the 1930s. But at a UUUC meeting in June to discuss tactics, Powell opposed Craig and denounced any plan that involved power-sharing. Although Craig had been under the impression that he had Paisley's support, Paisley now came out against him. Craig was left completely isolated. He resigned his place in the UUUC leadership in September and his Vanguard Party eventually broke up. It was widely believed that most of his supporters swelled the ranks of Paisley's Democratic Unionist Party, though Powell doubted this – at Westminster, Craig and the Rev. Robert Bradford, were to join the Ulster Unionist Party, while a third Vanguard MP, John Dunlop, became an Independent.[35]

In early July, exactly a month after his defeat in the EEC referendum, Powell fuelled the controversy within the Unionist movement by comments that demonstrated how sharply his idea of unionism differed from that of many Ulster Unionists. Possibly his success in denouncing Craig encouraged him in this forthright expression of his views. It would also have been in character for Powell to react to his disappointment over the EEC by taking up his other great cause – Northern Ireland's union with Britain – with renewed vigour. Whether or not he was making his bid for the UUUC leadership, as some suspected, is unclear: after the referendum débâcle he was marginalized in British politics and becoming leader of the Unionist coalition offered a route back to the national stage. But even if Powell was merely seeking to stake out his own ground, his effort was counter-productive, since he offended the Unionist hierarchy while fuelling suspicions of a leadership bid.

Powell's main offence when he spoke at Kilkeel, County Down, on 5 July 1975 was to deliver a thinly veiled attack on what many Ulster Unionists regarded as the basis of their tradition. As an Englishman, he needed to take special care of Unionist sensitivities in Ulster, but on this occasion he insisted on the classic English, High Tory doctrine as being the only true Unionism. According to Powell:

> What, however, no person who calls himself a Unionist can do without contradiction is to place limits or conditions upon his obedience to the Crown in Parliament. He cannot say, 'if Parliament makes laws I don't like, I will not obey them'. He cannot say, 'unless parliament amends the present law in the way I want, I will go off and declare myself independent'.

In addition, Powell's call for Unionists to unite under a single leader at Westminster and Ulster appeared to betoken his own leadership ambition. 'Only one thing can deny us success, and so deny to this Province the peace and progress it is entitled to,' Powell declared; 'that thing is division, diversity of ourselves, discordancy of voices, infirmity of tactics, uncertainty of strategy, the political ailments of a house divided that cannot stand.'[36]

But, in much the same way as he had done with his fellow Conservatives, Powell was telling Unionists that they were the ones who were out of step, and not him. Whereas his statement of total obedience to the supremacy of parliament was unexceptional to an English High Tory, it stirred deep misgivings among Unionists. Powell had exposed the gulf between his Toryism and the radical, Covenanter strand in Ulster Unionism. Almost 300 years earlier, Ulster's Protestants had rebelled against the English state because James II had attempted to enforce Catholicism as the state religion. They had transferred their loyalty to William of Orange on condition that their liberty was protected. Ever since, their continuing loyalty to the state has been conditional on their Protestant religion and the union with Britain being protected. Their annual commemorations of the Siege of Derry in 1689 and the Battle of the Boyne in 1690 are expressions of solidarity and reaffirm their readiness to defend their tradition. If they have felt under threat, they have felt justified in defying the state, as they demonstrated over Irish Home Rule, with encouragement from Lord Randolph Churchill and Bonar Law.[37]

As a High Tory, Powell rejected any idea that loyalty to the Crown in Parliament could be less than total. But the logical conclusion of Powell's High Tory argument was that the Unionists should accept whatever form of government Westminster might decide to impose on Ulster, including power-sharing (though Powell rejected any suggestion that parliament had the right to expel them from the Union). Paisley dismissed Powell's comments as utter nonsense, and suggested that Powell, as an Englishman, had failed to understand what loyalism meant to true Unionists:

Mr Powell's loyalty was to the Government, and Parliament at Westminster, but to traditional Unionists, this has never been the case. We hold no allegiance whatsoever to the Wilsons and Heaths of this world.

In Powell's view, however, the logical conclusion of this conditional view of loyalty to the British state was that Ulster would either become independent, or would become part of a federal Ireland, with certain constitutional guarantees. Yet neither of these options was politically realistic.[38]

Three weeks after his comments on the need to obey the Crown in Parliament, Powell further outraged Unionist opinion. In a speech at Ballyhill, County Antrim, he attacked the Constitutional Convention and declared that, 'the proposition that it is for the people of Northern Ireland to decide the government of Northern Ireland is the most anti-Unionist proposition that could be devised'. But many Ulster Unionists were uneasy at putting their future entirely in the hands of an institution in which they had only ten out of 635 MPs. They wanted to determine Ulster's future in a body where they enjoyed a majority, such as they had at Stormont, or in the Convention. Harry West, leader of the UUUC in Ulster, suggested that Powell had not been in Ulster long enough to understand grassroots Unionist opinion. The Unionists' Chief Whip in the Convention, Austin Ardill, declared that Powell's speech was a 'betrayal' of his fellow Unionists.[39]

By September 1975, Powell was trimming as he blamed the press for misrepresenting him as a 'total integrationist'. In speeches in Belfast and Banbridge, he reiterated his support for the UUUC's Portrush Declaration, that advocated devolved government for Ulster within the framework of a federal United Kingdom. But the struggle between the integrationists and the devolutionists in the Unionist movement was about to become intertwined with the debate on devolution in Britain. Many Unionists saw new hope for the return of devolved government in Northern Ireland with the publication in January 1976 of the Labour Government's plans for devolution in Scotland and Wales. After all, if devolution was suitable in Scotland and Wales, on what grounds could it be denied in Northern Ireland? Powell, however, was determined to prevent the United Kingdom's ever possessing a federal framework. In November 1975, he warned that he regarded devolution, or a federal United Kingdom, as 'constitutional nonsense'. In the Commons the following January, he left no room for any doubt that he would oppose devolution with the same determination that he had opposed entry into the EEC:

But that this House by its own actions, by its own self-deceptions, should set in frame a course of constitutional action which must lead to the conversion of this country into something totally different and unrecognizable or to the destruction of the unity of whatever this realm is to be, the unity brought to a focus in this House, I say 'No' to that, whether that sovereignty be seen from inside or from outside. That at any rate is the conviction in which I have lived. It is a conviction for which I tore apart the limbs of my whole political life. It is a conviction from which I will not depart.[40]

Powell's uncompromising commitment to the English doctrine of parliamentary sovereignty provoked further anger among Unionists in the spring of 1976. In March, the British Government finally dissolved the Convention after the UUUC's call for devolved government failed to win support from the nationalist SDLP. The Unionists now faced the bitter prospect of indefinite direct rule from Westminster. Powell, however, infuriated many of his colleagues by making a speech in Belfast in which he seemed positively to welcome direct rule, since Northern Ireland would be 'governed as a part of the Union'. In addition, he renewed his integrationist demands that Northern Ireland should be given full representation at Westminster and the same form of local government as the rest of the United Kingdom enjoyed. Amidst reports that some members of Powell's own constituency association were eager to deselect him before the next election, Powell claimed in April that the UUUC no longer existed, because of the divisions that had emerged following the dissolution of the Convention. Moreover, he argued that not only should direct rule be accepted, but the union was more secure than it had been since 1968. Such statements prompted reports that Craig and Paisley were planning to put up another candidate against Powell, or to persuade his party to drop him.[41]

Speculation about Powell's future as an Ulster MP was also fuelled by events at Westminster, where the position of the Unionists was becoming more important to the main parties. Callaghan had succeeded Wilson as Prime Minister in April 1976, but Labour's majority in the Commons was eroding, and as a result the influence of the minority parties was increasing. Powell delightedly claimed that Ulster's MPs were now an integral part of the Commons, and 'are no longer a contingent of half-strangers who come from outside to complain or acquiesce'. Moreover, his prized goal of equal representation for Northern Ireland was within reach. As he told Unionists at Portadown in May, the Government had at last abandoned their refusal to consider 'fair and equal representation of this Province' at Westminster.[42]

But the Unionists' new influence was also attracting close interest from the Opposition. Some Conservatives were anxious to discover whether talk of Powell's unpopularity in the Province might make possible the renewal of their old alliance with the Unionists. Shortly before Down, South, Unionists met to discuss Powell's renomination, their President, Colonel Brush, was contacted by Airey Neave, the head of Margaret Thatcher's private office and Shadow Northern Ireland Secretary; John Peyton, the Shadow Leader of the House; and John Biggs-Davison, a staunchly unionist back-bencher. Peyton revealed that he had told Brush that it was 'tragic' that Tories and Unionists could not again unite to defeat a socialist Government. Brush gained the impression that none of these senior Conservatives would have felt regret if

Powell was not re-selected. In the event, Powell's constituency association stood by him. Although Thatcher strongly opposed devolution, Powell still refused to give the Tories any succour. In November 1976, in a speech that he was barred from making to a meeting of Young Conservatives, he attacked Labour's devolution proposals, but insisted that there was nothing in the interests of the United Kingdom, or of Ulster, that required the replacement of the Labour Government by the Conservatives.[43]

Callaghan's struggle during 1977–79 to cling to office after Labour had lost their overall majority in the Commons was to give Powell his opportunity to extract a key concession from the Government. But Powell saw that if the Unionists were to exert any influence on the Government, they needed to maintain maximum unity. In September 1976, he was fulsome in his praise of Paisley's role as a 'cooperative and cordial' member of the Unionist team, but later in the autumn, the Government's devolution Bill was to put a new strain on Unionist cooperation. Powell, with a glance over his shoulder at the devolutionists, argued that the *form* of devolution being offered to Scotland and Wales would weaken the unity of the United Kingdom, and 'without a strong and sovereign United Kingdom, sovereign internally and externally, Ulster Unionism is meaningless and doomed'. But the real test of Unionist unity came the following month, when the ten Unionists had to decide the line for the second reading debate of the Bill to grant devolution to Scotland and Wales. They responded by drafting an amendment in which they expressed their opposition to the Government's proposals, 'so long as Northern Ireland, an integral part of the United Kingdom, is denied a fair and just representation in this parliament and remains deprived of any devolved or local administration above the level of district councils'. It was masterly draftsmanship that carried all the hallmarks of Powell's skills as a parliamentary tactician and incorporated the three main Unionist demands – equal representation at Westminster; devolution; and the restoration of full local government. In the event, eight of the ten UUUC MPs opposed the Devolution Bill.[44]

The Unionists' opportunity to extract a bargain from the Government was not long delayed. In February 1977, the Government were defeated when they tried to end the delaying tactics being used against the Devolution Bill, and the Bill was lost. On Friday 18 March, the Opposition tabled a motion of 'no confidence'. Labour's total voting strength was now 310, eight short of an overall majority, and defeat for the Government on the confidence vote, scheduled for Wednesday 23rd, would lead to a general election. During several days of frantic negotiating, Callaghan sought to ensure that the minority parties did not support the Opposition. Roy Mason, who had succeeded Merlyn Rees as Northern Ireland Secretary the previous autumn, and Michael Foot, the Leader of the House, were appointed to mediate with the Unionists. Foot and Powell had been allies against both the reform of the House of Lords and the EEC, and had developed mutual respect for each other as parliamentarians (when Powell had declined to sign the new register of Members' interests in 1975, Foot, as Leader of the House, had taken a tolerant view).[45]

By Monday, the Liberal leader, David Steel, had agreed to meet Callaghan ahead of a meeting of Liberal MPs, and Molyneaux agreed to an exploratory discussion – though he would be bringing Powell with him. Notwithstanding the Government's vulnerable position, Molyneaux and Powell had a more difficult hand to play than Steel. Whereas the thirteen Liberal MPs were largely united, and Steel could promise their presence in the Government lobby, the most that the Unionists could offer was half a dozen abstentions. Secondly, Molyneaux, as leader of the UUP at Westminster, had to heed the views of the devolutionists in Ulster – indeed, Harry West voiced majority Unionist opinion when he told Molyneaux to accept nothing less than devolution. In the event, the Unionists made three demands, in line with their amendment to the Devolution Bill – equal representation at Westminster; the restoration of local government; and a devolved administration for the Province.

The talks between the Government and the minority parties continued until the Wednesday morning. The outcome is mainly remembered in Britain for the Lib-Lab pact, by which the Liberals agreed to support the Government in return for regular policy consultation with ministers; direct elections to the European Parliament; the re-introduction of devolution proposals for Scotland and Wales; and various other measures. Yet Molyneaux and Powell were to achieve a significant concession for Ulster. They won an unconditional offer from Callaghan to refer their demand for equal representation at Westminster, as was normal practice on such matters, to an all-party conference chaired by the Speaker of the House of Commons. The Prime Minister made this offer irrespective of whether or not the Unionists supported the Government in the confidence vote. As to the second demand, Molyneaux and Powell understood that the Prime Minister was prepared to consider the restoration of local government. Callaghan, however, was to claim that he had warned them that he would pay close attention to the wishes of the minority, nationalist community. Powell suspected that the offer was killed the moment that the Foreign Office and Northern Ireland Office – his *bêtes-noires* – heard of what Callaghan had been prepared to concede. Finally, Callaghan ruled out the third demand for devolution in Northern Ireland. The Prime Minister's failure to concede this demand was to provoke anger in the Unionist community. When the vote came at the end of the confidence debate on 23 March 1977 only three Unionists abstained, including Powell. Molyneaux, however, joined the majority of his party in the Opposition lobby with the Conservatives. The Labour Government won by 322 votes to 298, a majority of 24.[46]

For Powell, achieving the objective of equal representation for Ulster represented a great coup. He had done more than any other Unionist MP to persuade the Government's parliamentary managers of the justice of this demand. It was to be his final, concrete achievement in politics. He watched like a hawk to ensure that, following the Speaker's conference, the necessary Bill was introduced to increase the number of Ulster MPs from twelve to seventeen and that it received the Royal Assent before Labour finally left office. The five extra Ulster seats were first contested at the June 1983 election. After Powell had left the Commons, he expressed his pleasure that Ulster MPs were playing a fuller part in the House of Commons than had ever happened in the days of Stormont, and that the nationalist SDLP MPs had become, as he put it, part of the party system of the United Kingdom.[47]

But in 1977, many Ulster Unionists, especially at the grassroots level, had expected their leaders to win devolution instead of equal representation at Westminster. Their expectation of what Molyneaux and Powell could have obtained may have been unrealistic, but this did not prevent them protesting furiously at the deal. Bitter anger was expressed at the three abstentionists. Indeed, this anger appeared to boil over in what seemed to be an attempt on Powell's life. Three weeks after the Commons vote, three pounds of gelignite were found by the army in an Orange Hall at Lisburn the morning after Powell had spoken there. An outlawed loyalist paramilitary group, the Ulster Freedom Fighters, was suspected of having planted the explosive – it was reported that Powell was on a loyalist death list. But some of Powell's supporters believed that the incident stemmed from the bitter feud within the UUUC coalition over the Commons vote. Although Molyneaux avoided naming the Democratic Unionists, he claimed that members of a certain party had been waging a sinister campaign against Powell and other colleagues. Paisley issued a swift denial, and told his detractors to provide proof for their allegations, or shut up. But there were renewed moves during this period to put up another Unionist against Powell, or even to have him deselected.[48]

The feud between Powell and Paisley came to a head almost immediately afterwards. The mercurial Paisley, frustrated by the failure to extract a return to devolution from the Government, now proposed ending direct rule by resorting to the same tactics of a workers' strike that had ended power-sharing in 1974. The 1974 strike had entered Unionist folklore, and although it represented a defiance of parliament, Powell has argued that it had succeeded because people could see that the power-sharing constitution would not work. He has even justified what was a political strike by suggesting that the 1973 Northern Ireland Constitution Act had been conditional – it was not a binding law of the land, like a road traffic act or finance act, but had only provided a framework for an experiment that any fool could see was foredoomed. Powell, however, drew the line at Paisley's proposal for a strike in 1977, by condemning it as unconstitutional and as an act of 'criminal irresponsibility perpetrated against the Province by a small knot of men'. As he predicted, the stoppage collapsed in dismal failure. Paisley's support for the strike led to the final break-up of the UUUC coalition, and the DUP and the UUP finally went their separate ways.[49]

While Molyneaux was now leader of the largest Unionist group at Westminster, Powell played a dual role as its star parliamentarian (as he demonstrated in the debate on direct elections for the European Assembly) and as the UUP's chief parliamentary strategist. Powell was to display his exceptional parliamentary skill as he pressed for the other main integrationist objective of allowing Northern Ireland again to share the same degree of local government that existed in the rest of the United Kingdom. In a brilliant ploy, Powell seized the unlikely occasion of a debate on an amendment to the Finance Bill to reduce income tax in order to protest at the Government's refusal to allow Ulster parity with Britain in local government. Powell's tactical skill culminated in a publicity coup when the Ulster Unionist votes helped inflict a defeat on the Government.[50]

Powell, however, ran into serious trouble with the Ulster Unionist Party in Northern Ireland by pressing his integrationist campaign for stronger local authorities as opposed to devolution. He felt that the devolution debates during 1976–78 had helped persuade his fellow Ulster Unionists of the difficulties of any return to devolution in Northern Ireland, but events in the spring of 1979 suggested otherwise. With a general election imminent, Powell called on voters in Northern Ireland to send a united Unionist team to Westminster. But having stressed the importance of unity, he told a meeting at Desert, County Down, that local democracy 'rather than a devolved government is the course that ought to be pursued'. But his argument was immediately countered by Harry West, the UUP leader in Ulster, who stated that Powell's speech should not be taken to mean that the Ulster Unionist MPs might support the Labour Government a second time in a 'no confidence' vote for something less than a fully devolved government in Northern Ireland. West's comments were a severe rebuke for Powell and a warning to him to toe the party line.[51]

Within days of West's contretemps with Powell, another 'no confidence' motion was tabled by the Conservatives. The Government were now in a much weaker position. Labour had lost three more by-elections, and the Liberals had ended their pact in the expectation of an imminent election. Following Callaghan's fateful decision not to call an election in October 1978, the Government's pay policy had collapsed in the chaos of the 'winter of discontent' and Labour's claim to handle the unions had lost all credibility. The final straw came on 1 March, when the referendum on devolution for Scotland resulted in a vote in favour of a Scottish assembly, but failed to clear the necessary hurdle of gaining at least 40 per cent of the total electorate. As a result, the embittered Scottish Nationalists were determined to bring down the Government.

As ministers again struggled to cobble together deals that might stave off defeat, Powell was inclined to ensure Labour's survival in office despite the rebuke from the UUP leader in Ulster. In his view, the Unionists' interests were best served by perpetuating the hung parliament, and not by hastening the election of a Conservative Government led by Margaret Thatcher – the Tories were enjoying huge leads in the opinion polls. None the less, Molyneaux and Powell had to have something to show for their support, if their argument about being better off with a minority Labour Government was to mean anything. At the time, alternative proposals for supplying gas to Northern Ireland by pipeline were under discussion – one plan was to lay a pipeline from Dublin; the other was to provide the supply from Britain. But the Unionists' demand that the latter plan should be adopted was vetoed by Callaghan.[52]

'Watching Callaghan in that last eighteen months,' Powell later recalled, 'I couldn't help saying to myself, "There's a man who's fed up."' In Powell's view, if Callaghan 'hadn't been fed up he wouldn't have lost the vote of confidence ... He could certainly for a ha'porth of tar or a whiff of gas have had the two or three votes which were necessary'. In the event, eight of the UUP's ten MPs, including Powell, supported the Opposition. The Government lost the 'no confidence' vote on 28 March 1979 by 310 votes to 311. Callaghan was immediately granted a dissolution. On 3 May, the Conservatives returned to office with a comfortable majority of 43 seats. In Down, South, the threatened challenge from the DUP, following Powell's controversial comments on devolution, was removed at the last moment, when their putative candidate, Cecil Harvey, decided not to split the Unionist vote. Powell increased his majority to 8,221, although his share of the vote remained at 50 per cent. But in the Province as a whole, the UUP suffered at the hands of the DUP. Powell was now one of only five UUP MPs, while Paisley's DUP won three seats, and independent Unionists another two (the remaining two Ulster seats were won by a nationalist and an independent republican).[53]

The new Prime Minister, Margaret Thatcher, was determined to follow the monetarist and free-market policies that Powell had spent much of his career as a Conservative before 1974 espousing. Moreover, she had declared herself as a committed Unionist. Yet he had sought to prevent her entering Number 10. As Powell had feared, the 1979 election destroyed the Unionists' power to exert decisive influence at Westminster.

Powell and Thatcher

In 1977, Powell published a biographical essay on Joseph Chamberlain, the Radical-turned-Unionist politician with whom he was often being compared, especially after 1974 when he had stood down as a Conservative candidate and told people to vote Labour. There had been a suggestion that Powell might write a life of Disraeli, and when Powell proposed Chamberlain instead, the publisher had asked, 'Who's he?' But Powell had an unsurprising motive in view of his own experience: he wanted to study the turning-point in the career of a prominent politician, and see whether there was anything in his earlier life that visibly led to it. Whereas a previous, massive, biography of Chamberlain by J.L. Garvin and Leo Amery had concentrated heavily on the years 1901–06, when Chamberlain took up tariff reform, or protectionism, Powell 'deliberately shifted the point of balance' by placing 'the pivotal year 1886' at the centre of his study. In 1886, Chamberlain had resigned from the Cabinet over

Gladstone's plan for Irish Home Rule and, with his fellow Unionists, abandoned the Liberal Party to form an alliance with the Conservatives.[54]

In the event, Powell found that the more he investigated Chamberlain's philosophy and psychology, the less attractive he found the man. Despite this, Powell's insight into Chamberlain's feelings as he abandoned the Liberals to support the Conservatives, was acute and clearly reflected his own similarly searing experience. 'As the door closed behind him,' Powell wrote of Chamberlain's departure from the Cabinet in March 1886,

> he turned his back upon all that his political life had been for twenty years, over ten of them in parliament. His face, and he knew it, was towards his political opponents, opponents whom he had denounced and detested, but whom he could not now help but place and maintain in power. It was the watershed of his life. Henceforward its currents would all flow in the opposite direction and find their way to an ocean undreamed of.[55]

Yet in much the same way that Powell had placed the pivotal period in Chamberlain's life earlier than his conversion against free trade in 1901, the pivotal period in Powell's life occurred some years before his conversion against British membership of the EEC. The defining political experience for Powell had been the years of the Macmillan Government between 1957 and 1963. His reaction against Macmillan's Keynesian and interventionist policies first set him on the road to 'Powellism' and triggered his disagreements with Heath – although without the subsequent explosions over immigration and Europe, their divergence on economic policy probably would not have culminated in the final rupture. But the yardstick against which Powell had judged Heath's leadership was a mirror-image of Macmillan's approach – the further that the Conservatives kept from the 'middle way', the better it would be for all concerned in Powell's view.

On this Powellite test, Heath had proved to be a disappointment. After voicing free-market rhetoric in the last year or so before the 1970 election, in Government he resurrected Macmillanite policies with a vengeance. But whether Sir Keith Joseph's anguished renunciation of past Keynesian misdemeanours and interventionist follies, or Margaret Thatcher's espousal of market forces, monetarism and cuts in government spending, would herald a genuine departure from Macmillanite Conservatism in office remained to be seen. The new Tory leadership came to regard the January 1958 Treasury resignations of Thorneycroft, Birch and Powell as the turning-point in post-war Britain when the Conservatives had strayed from true Conservative principles – a conviction symbolized by Thatcher's appointment of Lord Thorneycroft as her first party chairman. But the main intellectual inspiration for Joseph and Thatcher was the economic liberals associated with the Centre for Policy Studies (CPS), the new 'think tank' that they set up with Geoffrey Howe to counter the Conservative Research Department, and also the Institute of Economic Affairs (IEA). In addition, academics and journalists were influenced during the 1970s by a new wave of free-market and monetarist thinking from Professor Milton Friedman and his colleagues at the University of Chicago. After earlier false dawns, Powell reserved judgement when Thatcher entered Number 10 in May 1979. As he had previously pointed out, she had remained in Heath's Cabinet for its duration. Her Shadow Cabinet had remained heavily Heathite; the manifesto on which she was elected in 1979 was less radical than Heath's in 1970; and in her first Cabinet, Heathites outnumbered economic liberals (though the latter were in control of the main economic departments).

An incident had occurred while the Conservatives were still in Opposition that Powell regarded as an illuminating insight into Thatcher's politics. On 30 January 1978, during a televised interview for Granada's *World In Action*, Thatcher identified herself with those who felt that immigration was too high and sympathized with those who felt 'really rather afraid that this country might be rather swamped by people with a different culture'. Immigration had again become a live political issue from the mid-1970s, and the National Front were seen as an increasing threat. Powell had also attracted fresh publicity when he seized on an admission by the Home Office in November 1975 that the net intake from the New Commonwealth in 1973 had been not 17,000, as originally stated, but 86,000. Powell exploited the error by echoing his 1968 speech about 'a nation busily engaged in heaping up its own funeral pyre', and claiming that even in his 'gloomiest forebodings' he had never thought that 'eight years later we should still be heaping that funeral pyre not just at the same rate but twice as fast'. In fact, once allowance was made for the fluctuating number of British passport holders expelled from East Africa with nowhere else to go but Britain, the statistics indicated a tendency for the numbers given permission to settle permanently in Britain to decline. But Powell also claimed to detect a conspiracy in the Home Office, alleging that 'a considerable ring' of officials had attempted to cover up the error, despite an assurance by the Home Secretary, Roy (later Lord) Jenkins, that the error had been a clerical one and that officials had not behaved discreditably.[56]

A few months later, Powell achieved an even more spectacular publicity coup when he was sent anonymously a report by an official in the Foreign Office, Mr D.F. Hawley, that contradicted Home Office claims about immigration from India and Pakistan. Powell created a sensation by revealing the contents of this document during the Commons debate on immigration in May 1976. The Hawley report challenged the Home Office assumption 'that the immigration problem in the sub-continent is finite and that we are in the last stages of clearing up a backlog of "entitled" dependants'. The report also suggested that previous Home Office estimates of the number of dependants entitled to come to Britain were far too low; that there was a substantial illegal immigrants' industry in India helping migrants come to Britain; and that arrangements in India were too generous for intending migrants. Under considerable pressure, Jenkins appointed Lord Franks to head an inquiry into the feasibility and usefulness of a register of dependants. The following

February, the Government rejected the idea of a register, but tightened the immigration rules by preventing men being accepted for settlement through marriages of convenience.[57]

Although the Conservatives had already toughened their policy on immigration before Thatcher spoke of people feeling 'rather swamped', her televised comments led to a further toughening and put the Government on the defensive. When Powell first heard her say that people were feeling 'rather swamped', he thought that she shared his understanding of the problem and assumed that her deliberate use of such an expression meant that she had definite plans. But the new proposals subsequently announced by the Shadow Home Secretary, Willie (later Viscount) Whitelaw, fell short of Powell's continued demands for a halt to immigration and assisted repatriation. Despite Powell's disappointment, however, he found Thatcher's choice of the word 'swamped' and its non-repetition afterwards instructive. In Powell's view, she had revealed her trait of allowing her sympathy with the instincts and expressions of the man in the street to lead her into making statements and using vocabulary with implications that she was not prepared to follow through. The incident had shown that Thatcher's practical-minded determination to become Prime Minister ultimately overruled her instincts. Implicit in Powell's insight is an awareness of why she became Prime Minister instead of him.[58]

At the 1979 election, the Conservatives concentrated on holding their lead in the opinion polls and did not emphasize immigration – though during a radio phone-in Thatcher stood by her comment about people feeling 'rather swamped'. But Powell was marginalized in the national campaign as neither Europe nor Ulster, the two subjects that he regarded as being of overriding importance, became major issues, and there was little difference on them between the main parties. Having supported Labour on the EEC at both 1974 elections, Powell put a plague on both Labour and the Tories for their pro-EEC stance, and told people to vote for the candidate in their constituency who was most strongly opposed to the EEC.[59]

On Ulster, however, Powell's hopes had been raised that a Conservative Government would reverse the policy of Conservative and Labour Governments since 1973 by integrating the Province with the rest of the United Kingdom instead of seeking an early return to devolved government. The 1979 Conservative manifesto stated that 'in the absence of devolved government', a Conservative Government would 'seek to establish one or more elected regional councils with a wide range of powers over local services'. In effect, the Tories were promising to restore to Northern Ireland democratic control of local government matters – the policy that Powell had made his priority after achieving equal representation for Ulster at Westminster. But Thatcher's failure to follow this approach after 1979, provoked Powell into developing conspiracy theories. These became sub-themes to a grander theory that reflected his deep-seated anti-Americanism and his detestation at what he saw as British subservience to the United States since the Second World War, and especially since Suez.

Officials in the Northern Ireland Office were treated by Powell with the same deep suspicion and hostility that he had previously reserved for their counterparts in the Foreign and Home Offices. Cries of betrayal and treachery have long been a common feature of the Unionist tradition in Ulster, but why did Powell develop this attitude towards officials when, as a minister, he had enjoyed cordial, courteous and trusting relationships with civil servants? Could he have believed that the denizens of Whitehall had changed so profoundly within twenty years? The explanation is that his views on immigration, Europe and Ulster were rooted in his deep sense of nationhood and national identity. Almost by definition, anybody who disagreed with him was acting against the true national interest, was being disloyal, or was betraying his or her fellow countrymen.

Romantic nationalism combined, as it is in Powell's case, with intellectual arrogance produces a heady mix. Powell was so utterly convinced of the veracity of his own views that anybody who disagreed risked being dismissed as either a knave or a fool. Politicians, churchmen, journalists, soldiers and some civil servants might fall into either category – in September 1979, he argued that the aiders and abetters of IRA terrorism were not the 'godfathers' skulking in the back parlours of the Ardoyne or the Falls Road, but included many people of public esteem, such as the Archbishop of Canterbury, Dr Coggan, Bishop Cahal Daly, and others among 'the thoughtless, the woolly-minded, the men and women of so-called "goodwill", the open-mouthed and empty headed in all walks of life'.[60]

But in developing his theory, Powell had to contend with the fact that senior Foreign Office officials are, for the most part, intelligent. They must therefore be knaves. Any cock-ups must be conspiracies. The Northern Ireland Civil Service and the Northern Ireland Office were allies to the Foreign Office, whether as dupes or collaborators. As *The Times* observed when commenting on Powell's more lurid suggestions, 'conspiracy theories are an attractive weapon for politicians to deploy'. It is easy to beguile an audience into drawing inferences from truths and half-truths, skilfully arranged into a sinister pattern and given speculative embroidery. Governments are reluctant to give any credence to the claims by responding, and are further constrained by official secrecy and collective responsibility. 'The theorist sees only confirmation of his suspicions in the resulting silence.'[61]

In Powell's contention, British policy on Northern Ireland was dictated by the United States. 'Now it's true that Britain too is unscrupulous', Powell argued,

> but America's perception of its interests is so embracing and its methods are so penetrative that the unscrupulousness of the United States is, I think, very dangerous. And it's dangerous where it perverts what a self-governing country would otherwise be doing. And that is what I think American

influence has done in the last twenty years in the attitudes of the United Kingdom towards the part of itself which is Northern Ireland.

Powell believed that a united Ireland was an axiom of American strategy, in the same way that it had been an axiom of British strategy in the nineteenth century to secure the Suez Canal as the link between England and India. According to Powell, in return for unification, Dublin would renounce its neutrality and join the North Atlantic Treaty Organization (NATO). As a result the United States would finally have secured their eastern approaches.[62]

Every fact and event in Northern Ireland had to fit this axiom. All roads led to Washington, with occasional detours to Brussels, Dublin and the Vatican. Thatcher's almost symbiotic relationship with President Reagan after 1980 served to confirm Powell's worst fears. 'I don't think one can underestimate the importance of the American input into the actions of Her Majesty's Government,' he caustically observed in 1987, 'particularly where as in the last eight years the Prime Minister has been a person so prone to American interpretation and to American vocabulary.' Thatcher's failure in 1983 to dissuade the Americans from invading Grenada and her readiness in 1986 to sanction the use of British bases for the American air strike against Libya, are widely seen as instances of her servility to Reagan.[63]

But whether Powell likes it or not, any American President is bound to take a close interest in Ireland. The large American-Irish community in the United States has strong sympathy for the nationalist cause and wields great influence in Congress and the White House. The searing experience of mass starvation and emigration during the 1840s' Irish potato famine is etched deep in their folk memory. Some Irish-Americans have been susceptible to republican propaganda about alleged British oppression in Northern Ireland, and have been a source of funds for the IRA. The response of British Governments, especially since the 1980s, has been to counter nationalist and republican propaganda in the United States, and to try and demonstrate that the majority of people in Northern Ireland wish to remain British. This latter fact is now recognized in Washington and Dublin. For Powell, however, it seemed that virtually any contact with the Americans was further proof of British subservience.[64]

Before the 1979 election, the principal architect of the Conservative policy that had raised Powell's integrationist hopes had been Airey Neave, one of Thatcher's closest confidants and the Shadow Northern Ireland Secretary. But on Friday 30 March, just two days after the Conservative triumph in the 'no confidence' vote and following the Shadow Cabinet's morning meeting to finalize the manifesto, Neave had been murdered when a bomb attached beneath his car exploded as he left the House of Commons car park. Powell commented cryptically that he was sure that, 'Airey Neave would have wished nothing better than to share the same end as so many of his innocent fellow citizens for whom the House of Commons is responsible.'[65]

Responsibility for Neave's assassination was claimed by the Irish National

Liberation Army (INLA), the military wing of the Irish Republican Socialist Party, but Powell became convinced that the murder fitted in with his theory about American strategy. Powell first alleged American involvement in a major assassination in 1984, when he was asked by a CND supporter about a possible connection between Lord Mountbatten's murder in Ireland in 1979 and Mountbatten's strongly anti-nuclear views. He replied to the effect that 'the Mountbatten murder was a very high level "job" not unconnected with the nuclear strategy of the United States'. But Mountbatten had been killed by the IRA, and Powell's allegation was considered so preposterous that it prompted little reaction. Two years later, however, Powell appeared to allege that the Americans were responsible for Neave's murder, an extremely grave charge that he made in the incongruous setting of a rally of the Federation of Conservative Students in Birmingham. He sought to explain Neave's murder in the context of the alleged plan to create a united Ireland within NATO. This plan had supposedly begun twenty years earlier, and involved the British Foreign Office, British intelligence and the United States, especially the Central Intelligence Agency (CIA). The first aim had been to remove the stumbling block of the Unionist Government at Stormont. He argued that MI6 and its friends 'proved equal to the job', but the Americans became alarmed when they realized before the 1979 election that Thatcher and Neave were not going 'to play ball'. According to Powell, 'the roadblock was cleared by eliminating Airey Neave on the verge of his taking office as Secretary of State for Northern Ireland and events were moved along the timetable path'.[66]

Powell failed to provide the supporting evidence that might reasonably have been expected, especially from a senior politician. When he was pressed in 1987 to say whether he had evidence for his claim that the CIA had used the IRA, or whether it was an assumption, he referred to revelations about American involvement elsewhere and asserted that, 'no doubt if I had told people what had been happening in Central America and in Iran, they would have equally asked for evidence before that evidence started to become available'.[67]

Powell's allegation about Neave's murder is dismissed by the writer, Martin Dillon, in his definitive study of terrorism in Northern Ireland, *The Dirty War*. Not only does Dillon contend that 'there is no evidence whatsoever to link the CIA or any other official body with Neave's death', he demonstrates convincingly the reasons why, during 1978–79, INLA 'selected a major British politician for assassination and how their decision bore no relation to Powell's theory that his death was part of a "dirty tricks" policy to further a British-American conspiracy'. An INLA source stated that Neave was not killed because he posed a threat, but because he 'represented oppression'. In Dillon's view, the assassination was as much a 'callous stunt' to bring INLA to prominence as it was a politically motivated act.[68]

Whether Neave would have fulfilled Powell's hopes and sought to integrate Northern Ireland with the rest of the United Kingdom will never be known. But Thatcher has since made clear that she fundamentally disagreed with

Powell's call for full integration combined with a tough security policy. As she explains in her memoirs, she 'did not believe that security could be disentangled from other wider political issues'. Secondly, she utterly rejects Powell's thesis that devolution for Northern Ireland was a stepping stone to Irish unity. 'I never saw devolved government and an assembly for Northern Ireland as weakening, but rather strengthening the Union. Like Stormont before it, it would provide a clear alternative focus to Dublin – without undermining the sovereignty of the Westminster Parliament.' There was never any question of Thatcher abandoning the guarantee given by successive British Governments since 1972 that Northern Ireland would remain a part of the United Kingdom so long as the majority of its people wished.[69]

Following the assassination of Mountbatten and the slaughter of eighteen British soldiers at Warrenpoint (in Powell's constituency) during the August 1979 bank holiday, Thatcher was convinced of the need for further efforts on the political and security fronts in Northern Ireland. Powell, however, took a sinister view of her initiative. In November, the Northern Ireland Secretary, Sir Humphrey Atkins (later Lord Spelthorne), who had been Chief Whip in Opposition, announced plans for an all-party conference to discuss a range of options, including full executive and legislative devolution (with the exception of security matters). At first, the nationalist SDLP refused to join the talks because there had been no mention of an Irish dimension, but Atkins's concession to allow discussion on this point provoked the Ulster Unionist Party to boycott the talks. Powell led the UUP's offensive against the plan, dismissing it as 'a green edged constitutional set-up like that of 1973, which had to be forced upon the Province and which the Government visibly hoped would promote the euthanasia of the Union'. Moreover, the all-party conference was a trap laid by the British Foreign Office, 'that nest of vipers, that nursery of traitors', in order to appease politicians in the United States and the European Community, whose objective was a united Ireland.[70]

The division between the UUP's integrationist wing, exemplified by Powell, and the party's devolutionist wing was exacerbated by the Atkins initiative. Harry West, the former leader, criticized Molyneaux, his successor, for failing to take part in Atkins's talks. Indeed, West regarded the boycott as the UUP's biggest political mistake. 'When the talks began,' he argued, 'we found that one of the alternatives which was on offer, was a majority government, with safeguards for the minority. That was exactly what we had been looking for in the [1975] Convention.'[71]

At Westminster, Powell's repeated claims to detect conspiracies undermined his credibility, except among a small group of Tory MPs who agreed that simple nostrums offered the means for willing away the Irish problem. Probably no other senior British politician had stronger unionist instincts than Thatcher, but during 1980 she saw the need to work more closely with the Republic, and held talks with the then Taoiseach, Charles Haughey. Their discussions instigated joint Anglo-Irish studies by officials to examine the 'totality of relationships within these islands'. This exercise aroused deep suspicion among Ulster Unionists. But during 1981, divisions in Northern Ireland intensified and violence again began to escalate as a number of IRA prisoners went on hunger strike in their effort to win political status, culminating in ten deaths. Harry West's defeat by Bobby Sands, the IRA hunger striker, at the Fermanagh and South Tyrone by-election in April not only signalled the end of West's political career, but demonstrated the potent impact of martyrdom.

In response to the political initiatives that followed the collapse of the hunger strike, Powell fully expounded his grand theory of British subservience to American strategists in Northern Ireland. In November 1981, Thatcher and the new Taoiseach, Dr Garret FitzGerald, agreed to establish a joint Anglo-Irish Intergovernmental Council that, as Thatcher has since noted, 'really continued the existing ministerial and official contacts under a new name'. For Powell, however, the agreement meant that, 'in return for an undelivered and unspecific promise of cooperation against the IRA, Britain undertook to instigate a process which would lead to the absorption of Ulster into an All-Ireland state'. The new Anglo-Irish institution was 'the key which opens the lock' to Irish unity, and 'the great prize to crown the achievement will be the entry of that state to NATO, this filling the gravest of all gaps in the United States strategy for Europe and the Atlantic'. Powell's suspicions had been fuelled by President Reagan's expression of support for the Anglo-Irish process. Powell claimed to have confidential evidence to support his allegation that there was a plot to set up an all-Ireland state, but when questioned about his allegation, he said he could not reveal his source of information on grounds of confidentiality. But his claims, he insisted, 'stand up without evidence because the construction is the only one which fits all the facts'.[72]

During 1982, Atkins's successor as Northern Ireland Secretary, Jim Prior, launched another initiative by the British Government. Thatcher had insisted on toning down Prior's proposed references to the Irish dimension in his White Paper, and was not happy at his plan to set up a devolved assembly and hand over executive responsibility on a step-by-step basis ('rolling' devolution). Ian Gow, her parliamentary private secretary, was implacably opposed (he was later to resign from the Government when Thatcher signed the Anglo-Irish Agreement), and as Prior recalls, 'was seen to be conferring with the right wing of the party and tipping the wink to the Official Unionists that the Prime Minister was not in favour of it'.[73]

It was during these debates that Powell claimed to have evidence to support his theory of a secret plan to unify Ireland. His attention had been drawn to a statement about Northern Ireland that was made in 1979 in *Daily Notes*, a briefing service for Conservative candidates provided at elections by the Conservative Research Department. But he read too much into a warning in the edition of 25 April, that the next Conservative Government would come under considerable pressure to establish 'another "power-sharing" government in the Province, which could pave the way for a federal constitution linking Ulster to the Irish Republic' – the parties in Dublin and nationalists in Ulster had drawn up their plans, while the Irish–American community were ready for a war of words. Powell claimed that in the light of events since 1979,

> Whoever wrote those notes knew perfectly well what was in preparation, for no more accurate a description of what was to follow in the subsequent three years could have been penned and certainly would not have been inserted where it was inserted except upon the basis of reliable knowledge which has since been verified.

But the Tory official concerned, Alistair Cooke, had merely described the pressures that the Conservatives would face from nationalists. Although nationalists hoped that power-sharing would be a step towards eventual Irish unity, Thatcher and her ministers regarded devolution and cooperation with the Republic as posing no threat to the Union whatsoever. Cooke was angered at the inference that might be drawn from Powell's remarks that he (Cooke) had, in some way, been party to a conspiracy to end the Union. Anybody who knows Cooke realizes the absurdity of such a suggestion.[74]

But Powell had another much more dramatic trick up his sleeve. He revealed to MPs a note of an interview early in 1981 between an academic researcher, Geoffrey Sloan, and a young official in the Northern Ireland Office, Clive Abbott – the note also covered a second interview in October 1981. 'We had to tell them it was just not on,' Abbott had supposedly commented of the Conservatives' plan in 1979 to restore local government in Northern Ireland. And Abbott was said to have added that,

> In terms of the future government of Northern Ireland integration is a non-starter for two main reasons. First, we would automatically lose the cooperation we are getting from Haughey over border security. Secondly, we couldn't break certain undertakings we have given to the Irish Government over the constitutional future of Northern Ireland.

Powell quoted other extracts, and pressed for the matter of the undertakings apparently given to the Republic, but not disclosed to ministers or to the Commons, to be resolved immediately.[75]

Powell had named an official and made grave allegations against him without giving notice beforehand to the responsible minister. Labour's Northern Ireland spokesman, Don Concannon, condemned Powell's action as 'character assassination at its worst', and as having 'the political equality of pulling the trigger of an Armalite at a British soldier in a back street in Northern Ireland'. David McKittrick and Ed Moloney, experienced journalists in Northern Ireland, were suspicious of the allegations. Not only were there absurd errors of fact in the comments attributed to Abbott, but as McKittrick, who often spoke with officials, noted, 'if the document is to be believed, Clive Abbott is the most casually indiscreet civil servant who ever lived'. After an investigation by Sir Robert (later Lord) Armstrong, the then

Cabinet Secretary, on Thatcher's behalf, it was found that Sloan's note was not verbatim (even though it included the words 'Phone rings' as an interruption). Neither had Sloan checked his version of the interview with Abbott, who denied that it represented even a remotely accurate record of his answers. It also emerged that although Abbott had been approached by Sloan about his research subject, Sloan had also worked, unpaid, on research projects for Molyneaux, the UUP leader. Following Armstrong's inquiry, Prior dismissed the allegations as 'unjustified and irresponsible'.[76]

Powell quoted from the alleged transcript in Northern Ireland three months later. His only regret, as he commented in 1993, was that he 'did not do more to reveal even further the Government's duplicity and Northern Ireland Office and Foreign Office intrigue. It made me ashamed that I did not ask sufficiently searching questions years before, to have arrived at the same conclusion.' Yet Powell's persistence in peddling conspiracy theories reduced their shock value and detracted from his general argument. His actions served to emphasize, not minimize, his isolation at Westminster.[77]

To Powell's mind, however, events in Britain in the early 1980s encouraged him to stick to his guns. After all, his predictions since 1968 of racial strife had been dismissed out of hand by *bien-pensant* politicians of all parties and other public figures, and led to his being treated as a pariah. Yet during 1981, riots erupted in Britain's inner-cities, most seriously in Brixton, in south London, and in Liverpool's Toxteth district. The searing images of the 1980s' riots have remained etched in people's minds, especially those of the large numbers who recall the close-knit lower-middle and working-class communities of their childhood and youth, before they and most of their relatives moved to the suburbs and new towns. The riots crystallized the unease at the changes that had overtaken inner-city Britain for a host of economic and social reasons. The impact of large-scale immigration is the most visible sign of these changes, and prompts many people to respond spontaneously to the mention of Powell's name by saying, 'Enoch was right, wasn't he?'[78]

Powell unequivocally placed the blame for the riots on mass immigration from the new Commonwealth. His speech in the Commons debate on the disorders in July 1981 was continually interrupted by angry Labour MPs, as he argued that in many inner cities new Commonwealth inhabitants comprised up to one half of the population. Over the next generation, he claimed, the size of that population would double or treble, and this inexorable increase would create a conflict that neither side desired. MPs were regaled with the discredited standby of assisted repatriation – his suggestion that the new socialist Government in France were considering something similar made little impact, since it was irrelevant to the many non-whites who were British-born. But it was Powell's other madcap suggestion that provoked the greatest anger, when he argued that the Government should tell people in the inner-cities what the future composition of the population would be, and should go before them and say: 'That is the future which we believe you can and must accept, and we believe that it is a future in which there will not be, need not be, conflict, ungovernability and civil war in our streets.' Dame Judith Hart, the Labour MP, told Powell that his speech was an evil incitement to violence, while Andrew Faulds shouted 'bloody rubbish' at him, and other MPs yelled, 'cattle trucks' and 'gas chambers'.[79]

But again, the facts did not accord with Powell's theory. The reasons for the rioting were more complex than his explanation could allow. As the Home Secretary, Willie Whitelaw, emphasized, the rioting was not a single, simple phenomenon. Both whites and non-whites were involved in the disturbances at various times and in different places, while the cause varied from place to place. Whitelaw's assessment was commended by the Shadow Home Secretary, Roy Hattersley. Powell's problem was that while he was still fighting the battles of the 1950s and 1960s over immigration control, the world had moved on.[80]

The major, underlying factor in the inner-city riots was not racial conflict but the massive and rapid increase in unemployment. The jobless total was soaring towards three million during 1981 as a result of the deepest recession since the Second World War. Urban areas took the full brunt of the slump as around $1\frac{1}{2}$ million jobs disappeared in manufacturing during 1980 and 1981 alone – this sudden haemorrhaging followed a loss of two million manufacturing jobs over the previous fourteen years. The economic heart had been ripped out of industrial areas the length and breadth of Britain. It was in an effort to reverse this process that Michael Heseltine, the then Environment Secretary, headed a task-force on Merseyside that became the precursor of a variety of inner-city initiatives. In addition, ministers sanctioned extra spending on a new Youth Training Scheme.[81]

In the wake of the riots, when the calls on Thatcher to abandon her monetarist experiment were at their loudest and most shrill, Powell emerged among the few who urged her not to respond to yet another peak in post-war unemployment by reflating the economy. In July 1981, the Chancellor of the Exchequer, Sir Geoffrey Howe, had been supported in Cabinet only by Thatcher, Joseph and his Treasury colleague, Sir Leon Brittan, when he demanded a £5,000 million cut in projected spending – a revolt that led the Prime Minister to reach for the axe at the side of her chair and reshuffle her Cabinet. Powell's intervention during October's censure debate on the economy prompted Frank Johnson, in his parliamentary sketch for *The Times*, to observe wryly that, 'in a departure from tradition, he (in effect) supported the Government'.[82]

Powell spoke immediately after Thatcher, and outshone her in his clinical dissection of the calls by the Labour leader, Michael Foot, for massive reflation. This was acknowledged by Foot, when he asked Powell, 'since the right hon. Gentleman has put the Government's case so much better than the Government have put it, will he tell us ... how heavy will be the unemployment that we shall have to tolerate in order to carry out his policies?' Powell was too much of an old campaigner to be drawn, but pointed out that for the first time since the War, Britain had a favourable balance of payments surplus with three million unemployed. The country was having to face major readjustment as a result of a massive turn round in the pattern of production, not least because of North Sea Oil. Returning to earlier, failed policies was no answer. 'We deceive those who are affected if we pretend otherwise to them.' But as Sir Alec Cairncross has demonstrated, the main cause of the slump in manufacturing and the massive destruction of jobs was the Government's use of 'very tight money' to fight inflation – a reflection of the monetarist views that Powell had long expounded. The regime of extremely high interest rates and a strong pound dealt a crippling blow to export industries. In fact, when Powell made his speech in the autumn of 1981, the Government were beginning to put greater emphasis on the exchange rate and interest rates as opposed to the money supply alone.[83]

Yet it was Thatcher's response to an urgent, international crisis the following year that drew the strongest praise from Powell. On Friday 2 April 1982, the Argentinians seized the Falkland Islands, a British colony off the south-eastern tip of Latin America. The Prime Minister sanctioned the preparation of a naval task force to recapture the islands, but many doubted the Government's will. The scar of Suez had never fully healed. Thatcher was extremely vulnerable. As she recalls, during the highly charged Commons emergency debate the following day, Powell 'looked directly across the Chamber at me', and evoking her soubriquet as the 'Iron Lady' because of her anti-Soviet views, 'declared sepulchrally',

> there was no reason to suppose that the right hon. Lady did not welcome and, indeed, take pride in that description. In the next week or two this House, the nation and the right hon. Lady herself will learn of what metal she is made.[84]

The Foreign Secretary, Lord Carrington, resigned, and it was virtually certain that Thatcher would have to go if the task force were to fail. After all, her Government had discussed plans on the future of the Falklands but had failed to resolve the matter, and by withdrawing the naval patrol ship, HMS *Endurance*, as part of a cost-cutting exercise, had given a signal that encouraged the Argentinian junta to invade. Powell's view of Thatcher's reaction is intriguing:

> If I'm asked whether any of Mrs Thatcher's recent predecessors would have done what she did in April 1982, I'm afraid I'd have to say 'No'. They were after all gentlemen. And they were gentlemen who perfectly well knew that all the papers had been across their desk which spelt out clearly enough – and she's not unintelligent – how the Falklands was going to be handled, and they would simply not have had a woman's shamelessness in changing their minds to say, 'Well, that was yesterday; this is today, and out you go.'

By Powell's standards, this was a rare compliment. Indeed, in talking about his mother's determined personality, he commented that she was not a gentleman; and that unlike his father, neither was he.[85]

Whereas Powell had seen Suez as an impractical attempt to maintain a lost imperial role, he saw the Falklands in an entirely different light. As Shadow Defence Secretary in the 1960s, he had defined the Falklands as occupying a strategic position in the Atlantic Ocean. But the eventual repossession of the Falklands also symbolized something much deeper, because he shared 'the overwhelming instinct of the British people'. Britain had been threatened at sea, its 'vital element', but had won and found a new self-recognition. For Powell, this 'striking moment' of realization occurred during the Falklands victory parade:

There was this huge crowd spreading out into all the streets radiating from the Mansion House, and one band came down and started to play Rule Britannia, and the entire crowd, right as far as one could see or hear, took it up. That was what it was about. And England had known itself, it had recognized itself. The England which tolerated the British Nationality Act of 1948, the England which thought it could reoccupy the Suez canal, was an England which had not recognized itself.[86]

Yet Powell's partial presentation of the Falklands war reflected nationalist myth rather than reality. 'Britain fought a war on its own, and Britain won it', he crowed. 'Moreover, the war was one which the United States obviously did not want it to fight.' In fact, the Americans were in a quandary as conflict loomed between their main supporter in Latin America and their closest NATO ally. Although it took the Reagan administration all April to come out in favour of Britain, behind the scenes the Pentagon backed Britain from the start. During the conflict, the Anglophile Defense Secretary, Caspar Weinberger, helped to ensure that Britain received ammunition, equipment, aviation fuel and 200 Sidewinder air-to-air missiles. And most significant of all, Britain received vital military intelligence from intercepted signals and from an American surveillance satellite that was specially moved from its orbit over Russia. The repossession of the Falklands *was* a triumph for the British forces, who retrieved the errors made by politicians and officials, but American help was crucial.[87]

Powell's sentiments echoed Thatcher's claim immediately after the Falklands war that Britain had 'ceased to be a nation in retreat'. He had observed the Prime Minister at close hand during the two-month crisis, since she offered the party leaders confidential briefings on a privy counsellor basis – Molyneaux waived his right to attend, and nominated Powell in his place; the spring and early summer of 1982 was thus the last occasion on which Powell had any direct input into Government. He felt that Thatcher had sensed instinctively what the public and her party felt at the time of the Falklands invasion, and knew how she had to respond. Indeed, during the crisis, the Conservatives briefly became the kind of nationalist party that he had sought to create through the political realignment that he had hoped 'Powellism' might bring. Thatcher's alertness to the tangle of emotions at the time of national identity, indignation, pride and self-assertion, enabled her to tap strong support among all classes that had eluded the Tories for decades.[88]

Yet Powell also saw in Thatcher a couple of striking similarities with her (and his) arch-rival, Sir Edward Heath. Like Heath, Thatcher was never what might be termed an ideas person – Powell even used to wonder sometimes whether she had fully understood monetarism, and his back bench allies used to suggest that he might give her a seminar on the subject. But whereas ideas made Heath angry, Thatcher simply treated them with a complete lack of interest. She was, in Powell's view, a stranger to philosophic doubt – there was never any danger of her being an Arthur Balfour, the intellectual Tory leader of the early 1900s, or of pondering the paradoxes of life and politics like a Macmillan. Moreover, Thatcher, like Heath, worked up a brief with identical pride in the sheer, technical accomplishment of the task. Whereas most other politicians might look for a joke or some telling line, Thatcher and Heath used to gather all the statistics and insist on reading them out at the despatch box, as though this was always sufficient answer to any question.[89]

Despite Thatcher's similarities with Heath, Powell was prepared, in his post-Falklands euphoria, to award Thatcher the fulsome plaudits that he had never been able to give Heath for her conduct of the Falklands campaign and an economic policy based on sound money. The ghost of Suez had finally been exorcized. 'The contrast between Port Stanley and Port Said is not all in the moral category. In 1956 the United States had only to threaten to lend us no money, and it had us fawning like a whipped cur,' Powell declared. Yet as he acknowledged, growth was much slower in 1982 than in 1956, while unemployment and inflation were much worse. The crucial difference, however, was that Britain had 'discovered that our fears of 25 years ago were dupes'. Exchange rate crises no longer occurred because the pound was allowed to float, and Thatcher's Chancellor, Sir Geoffrey Howe, had removed exchange controls – Powell had told Howe that he envied him the opportunity to take such action. In addition, Britain had both a trade surplus and ample energy resources. 'Independence, indeed, is the key word,' Powell proclaimed. Yet Thatcher was to take steps during Powell's final years in parliament that he felt crucially undermined British independence on the two causes on which he felt most passionately – relations with Europe, and Ulster's union with the rest of the United Kingdom.[90]

Powell versus Thatcher

The June 1983 election was the first occasion on which Northern Ireland gained equal representation with the rest of the United Kingdom. Yet Powell, who had done more than anybody to ensure this, was almost not re-elected. In the boundary changes caused by the creation of five extra seats in the Province, Powell's old constituency of Down, South, was reduced by about a quarter, and in addition he faced a challenge from the Democratic Unionist, Cecil Harvey, who was a local sub-postmaster and staunch Orangeman. Powell, however, remained defiantly optimistic, and repeated Queen Victoria's dictum at the time of the Boer War: 'In this household the possibility of defeat does not exist.' Yet in the 1983–87 parliament, that was to be Powell's last, he was to suffer some major defeats.[91]

Since he had stood down in Wolverhampton nine years earlier, intervening in the national election had become something of a ritual for Powell. In June 1983, he maintained his habit of being unhelpful to the Conservatives. On this occasion, he chose a new subject on which to embarrass them as he attacked the Government's reliance on nuclear deterrence – an issue on which he had long disagreed with Conservative policy and that was now attracting attention because of the stationing of American cruise missiles in the United Kingdom. Powell echoed an anti-nuclear sentiment at the time by arguing that trading missiles with the Soviets after a nuclear attack would simply lead to 'the extinction of our race'. Two days later, he argued that people were right to mistrust the promise that the use of American nuclear weapons based in Britain would be subject to joint decision by the two Governments. Before polling day, he also came close to advising people to vote Labour in order to obtain Britain's withdrawal from the EEC.[92]

Following his earlier eulogy of the Thatcher Government on the Falklands and the economy, Powell's apparent preference for a Labour Government was astonishing. Labour's manifesto was its most socialist programme in recent times. On the economy, it contained the shibboleths that Powell had fought since first entering politics. But he was attracted by the anti-EEC and anti-nuclear sympathies of his old political ally, Michael Foot, who had become Leader of the Opposition, and Powell was not one for maintaining a diplomatic silence. Powell's comments, however, were utterly irrelevant to the national result, as Thatcher won a landslide majority of 144 seats – the largest of any party since 1945.

In South Down, Powell won by a whisker, with a majority of only 548 votes over the nationalist SDLP candidate, Eddie McGrady. Despite Powell's close call, the Ulster Unionists fared much better than in 1979, more than doubling their total of MPs by winning eleven of the seventeen seats (Paisley's DUP again won three; an independent unionist won one seat, as did the SDLP; and Sinn Fein's Gerry Adams unseated Gerry Fitt). Indeed, the Ulster Unionists had reason to feel that things were going well at Westminster, as the integrationist strategy advocated by Molyneaux and Powell seemed to be succeeding with the gradual integration of Northern Ireland within the United Kingdom. Moreover, Powell's undoubted parliamentary skill and the following that he continued to enjoy among a small group of Tories who also included some of Thatcher's confidants and soulmates – notably Ian Gow – led Unionists to believe that they were in a much stronger position than was the case. Respect for Powell was mistaken for influence, as Arthur Aughey has pointed out in his study of Unionism in the 1980s. The Unionists were to be bitterly disillusioned.[93]

In Northern Ireland, the British Government's hopes for a return to devolved government had been stalled by the SDLP's abstention from the elected assembly. But there was no prospect of a new initiative while the New Ireland Forum, that had been convened in the Republic, continued their discussions on a possible political settlement for the island of Ireland. The Unionists boycotted the Forum, and the final report, published in 1984, reflected nationalist thinking. But in November that year, Unionist spirits soared following the Chequers summit between Thatcher and FitzGerald. A month earlier, the Prime Minister had narrowly escaped assassination in the IRA bomb attack during the Conservative conference. At Chequers, she reasserted her unionist instincts by declaring that each one of the Forum's 'options' for Ireland – unification, confederation, and joint authority – was 'out'.[94]

Thatcher's stout denunciation of nationalist nostrums seemed to lull Powell and many other Unionists into a false sense of security. In March 1985, he reassured his constituents that he and his fellow Unionist MPs had recently detected a 'lightening of the sky', that he believed was not a false dawn. The Prime Minister would be taking full charge of Northern Ireland policy, and this would rule out any further deals on Ulster by the Foreign Office and Northern Ireland Office. Indeed, Powell had also been encouraged that new defence technology and the development of an 'over-the-horizon' radar system could strip the Republic of its strategic importance to Britain and the United States. So long as defence surveillance had been limited by the horizon, the Republic's position in the Atlantic had been vital. But if that limitation was removed, the effect could be a trump card for Northern Ireland. It was, he declared, 'chill news' for FitzGerald, Haughey, the IRA and Sinn Fein; 'the days when they basked in the sunshine of British and American official countenance will have gone by. The writing is upon the wall.'[95]

During the first half of 1985, Powell's attention was focused on his private member's bill to prevent a human embryo created by *in vitro* (test tube) fertilization being used as the subject of experiment. Powell's rationale for his Unborn Children (Protection) Bill was based on neither scientific argument nor religious scruples, but on his instinctive reaction to the report of the Warnock Committee on 'Human Fertilization and Embryology', that had appeared the previous summer. The Warnock Report included a majority recommendation to allow experiments on *in vitro* embryos to be permitted until the embryo is fourteen days old. But when Powell first read the report, he

had a sense of revulsion and repugnance, deep and instinctive, towards the proposition that a thing, however it may be defined, of which the sole purpose or object is that it may be a human life, should be subjected to experiment to its destruction for the purpose of the acquisition of knowledge.

He argued that experimentation was an affront to the dignity of man. As to the objection of those who argued that medical research into *in vitro* embryos was crucial in overcoming many genetic disorders, he asked MPs to exercise a choice, 'and to decide that nevertheless the moral, human and social cost of that information being obtained in a way that outrages the instincts of so many is too great a price to pay'.[96]

The Government had wanted more time for consultation on the sensitive issues raised by Warnock, but Powell jumped the gun. 'Not for the first time,' as Margaret Jay noted, 'Enoch Powell has highlighted a divisive populist issue. This time it seems to be one where the "moral majority" scents an important victory over the liberal pragmatists.' Powell won a large majority on second reading and was given an easy passage in committee. Although his Bill had no bearing on abortion (he had, however, opposed David Steel's Bill to liberalize abortion in 1967), the anti-abortion lobby mobilized in his support. Public opinion was muddled, but Patrick Steptoe, the pioneer in test-tube babies, claimed that he could never have achieved success if Powell's rules had been on the statute book. Other scientists argued that embryo research was vital in helping to prevent the abnormalities that led to 20,000 severely handicapped children being born in Britain each year. In the event, Powell's Bill failed because its opponents used parliamentary procedure to prevent further debate. He was left complaining that his opponents had been taken in by commercial interests and protesting – in an echo of his allegations on immigration and Ulster – that the full evidence submitted to the Warnock Committee had been suppressed.[97]

Powell, however, soon had a much bigger battle on his hands. Following Thatcher's crushing dismissal of any weakening of British sovereignty over Northern Ireland at the November 1984 Chequers summit, it had been widely assumed that there was little prospect of anything concrete emerging from talks between the British and Irish Governments. But in the summer, speculation grew that a joint Anglo-Irish body would be created, giving the Republic an input into the administration of the Province. Powell's anger at such an idea revived his fears of betrayal by the British Government at the behest of American strategists. Speaking at Kilkeel in August, he argued that the suggested agreement with the Republic was 'as treacherous as it is stupid', and that no other part of the United Kingdom would accept such a 'monstrous absurdity'. He decried the role of the Thatcher Government as being the equivalent of 'sprinkling petrol in a wing of their own house and setting fire to it'.[98]

Powell and Molyneaux spent late-night sessions mulling over what the British and Irish Governments might agree. Molyneaux was asked by a minister in Thatcher's Cabinet if he and Powell wished to request a briefing on a privy council basis. The offer was declined, on the grounds that, once briefed, they would be muzzled by the privy counsellor's oath and unable to reveal a word of what they had been told to their anxious colleagues.[99]

Powell was specially angry at the proposed new Anglo-Irish Agreement. Many had assumed that he had the confidence of the Prime Minister and that she would never sign a deal giving Dublin a role in the running of the Province. But this belief had been exposed as a myth, and his stock among Unionists had fallen. In the Commons on the eve of the Agreement's signing in November, Powell launched a damning attack on Thatcher. 'Does the Prime Minister understand – if she does not understand, she soon will – that the penalty for treachery is to fall into public contempt?' Thatcher replied icily: 'I think he will understand that I find his remarks deeply offensive.' He was later to claim that she had been 'bombed into submission' by the IRA.[100]

The Anglo-Irish Agreement included a major concession by the Republic, since it affirmed that any change in the status of Northern Ireland would only come about with the consent of a majority of its people and recognized that their present wish was for no such change. But Unionists were outraged that the Agreement allowed the Republic to put forward proposals on a wide range of matters affecting Northern Ireland, even though there was no derogation of British sovereignty and FitzGerald accepted that any matters devolved in future to Northern Ireland would be removed from the new Anglo-Irish arrangements. The Unionists faced a tactical dilemma, however, in judging their response. It was imperative that they remained united, but there were divisions on how far the protest should go, and Powell was again seen as being reluctant to toe the party line.[101]

Molyneaux and Paisley jointly called on UUP and DUP members to shun ministers at every level of public life and demanded a referendum in Northern Ireland on the Agreement. If the Government were to refuse this latter demand, Unionist MPs would, in effect, hold their own referendum by resigning their seats and standing for re-election. This plan, however, caused deep division among Unionist MPs. The leaders also wanted a great show of public unity at a mass rally in Belfast on the Saturday before the Commons debated the Agreement. Powell, however, failed to attend, and as a result did not join the fourteen other Unionist MPs on the platform in signing a public declaration promising to resign their Westminster seats on 1 January 1986. His absence was noticed by a section of the huge crowd, who chanted, 'Where is Powell, where is Powell?'[102]

Although Powell had excused himself on the grounds that the rally had been organized too late for him to change his existing engagements, the speculation about his motives overshadowed the impact of the rally. His fellow Unionists were furious, and suspected that he did not want to resign his seat and risk a by-election because of his tiny majority. For a while, Molyneaux was in the embarrassing position of not knowing whether Powell would join in the Unionists' collective resignation of their seats. Powell then wrote to Molyneaux in what Julian Haviland described as 'characteristically elliptical language', to explain that an MP's decision to resign was a matter of personal responsibility that could not be shared, but if Molyneaux were to intimate that it would help him if Powell resigned his seat with a view to re-contesting it, he would be 'disposed to do so'. After Powell's eventual compliance with the tactic, he held his seat in the January 1986 by-elections although his neighbour in Newry and Armagh, Jim Nicholson, lost to the nationalist SDLP. But Powell's failure to fulfil to the letter the Unionist boycott of Westminster caused further consternation within Unionist ranks.[103]

There was no doubting Powell's detestation of the Anglo-Irish Agreement, but arguing against it posed a particular problem for him. However much he might oppose giving the Republic a say in the affairs of part of the United Kingdom, the Agreement had been made by the democratically elected Government of the United Kingdom and was to receive overwhelming approval in the United Kingdom Parliament. Powell had consistently called for the integration of Northern Ireland within the United Kingdom, but he was now having to argue that the people of Northern Ireland were under no obligation to accept an agreement made by the United Kingdom Government and supported by the United Kingdom Parliament. His basic premise, as he later expressed it, was that:

all the people who send representatives to parliament accept the right of a parliament of the United Kingdom to legislate for the whole of the United Kingdom and all parts of it. But they do not give the parliament of the United Kingdom the right to expel them.

This begged the question of whether the Anglo-Irish Agreement amounted to expelling the people of Northern Ireland. In Powell's view, it clearly represented the first step in that direction.[104]

In the Commons debate on the Agreement, he sought to justify Northern Ireland's right not to accept the Agreement on two grounds. In the first place, it imposed upon Northern Ireland, 'a change in the manner of which it is administered by the authority of this House, contrary to the wishes of the majority of the people of that part of the Kingdom'. Taking such an action, he claimed, was 'to strike at the very essence of that compact between the electorate and parliament upon which parliamentary sovereignty depends'. Secondly, he argued that Commons' approval of the Agreement did not amount to a change in the law of the United Kingdom, and therefore placed no obligation on the people of Northern Ireland to accept what was essentially an external contract, or agreement, between two Prime Ministers. 'We are again straining beyond its moral limit the authority of this House when we demand that by a resolution of the House we shall have the power to impose the will of the Government upon a portion of this country differentially from the rest.' Yet the basic conundrum remained that Powell, the integrationist, was seeking to justify the right of a part of the United Kingdom not to accept an action by the United Kingdom Government.[105]

Such was Powell's shock that Thatcher had signed the Anglo-Irish

Agreement, that he reserved his most bitter comments for her. 'This has been done because the United States insisted that it should be done', he declared, as he revived his theory about America's strategic axiom. But as a result of her compliance with the United States, Powell chillingly warned the Prime Minister that as she watched,

> with incomprehensible confusion the continued sequence of terrorism, murder and death in Northern Ireland, which this Agreement will not prevent but will maintain and ferment, let her not stand to ask for whom the bell tolls – it tolls for her.

Powell's frustration at the sudden turn of events in Northern Ireland provoked him into making extreme allegations about American involvement, to the evident consternation of his close supporters in the Conservative Party and the Tory press.[106]

Powell's uncompromising commitment to the full integration of Northern Ireland within the United Kingdom injected a large dose of intellectually consistent ideology into Ulster Unionism. But by encouraging the Unionists to set their face against political initiatives in Ulster, it may have had the opposite effect to the one that Powell sought. In his view, integration would guarantee British rights to everybody in Northern Ireland and remove uncertainty over the Province's future. But it was naïve to assume that nationalists and republicans would accept the result. Indeed, it has been suggested that Unionist intransigence was one factor in encouraging the SDLP leader, John Hume, to turn his back on hopes for an internal settlement in Northern Ireland and to attempt 'to build an international constituency to support his party's position'. By opposing any prospect of power-sharing and an Irish dimension, Powell may have contributed to the increased involvement of Dublin and Washington in Ulster's political future.[107]

Thatcher inflicted depressing reverses for Powell during his final two years as an MP not only on Ulster, but also on Europe, his other great cause since the early 1970s. At the European Summit, also at the end of 1985, she agreed to the Single European Act, that in addition to making possible the European single market also increased political unification and paved the way for economic and monetary union. The necessary legislation was rushed through the Commons in a truncated debate during 1986, and although Powell raised objections, there was little organized opposition. Some years later, after the reins of office had been prised from her grip, Thatcher was to rue the Anglo-Irish Agreement and to admit that she had not appreciated the full significance of the Single European Act. But by then it was too late. When she was in office, she had, in Powell's terms, sold the pass.[108]

There was, however, one issue on which the 'Iron Lady' would never recant: her support for nuclear weapons. Powell, by contrast, was a long-standing critic of nuclear deterrence, and had said as much at the 1983 general election. In the closing stages of his political career, Powell was provoked into delivering a withering assault on Thatcher's pro-nuclear argument. In October 1986 during a summit meeting at Reykjavik, the US President, Ronald Reagan, and the Soviet leader, Mikhail Gorbachev, found that they both favoured the elimination of all nuclear weapons. Although the summit collapsed because of their disagreement over American plans to develop the so-called SDI, or Star Wars, system, the fact that the American President had been prepared to contemplate removing the shield of nuclear missiles sent shock-waves through the capitals of Europe. Thatcher was horrified. 'The fact is that nuclear weapons have prevented not only nuclear war but conventional war in Europe for forty years', she told the Lord Mayor's banquet in mid-November. 'That is why we depend and will continue to depend on nuclear weapons for our defence.' A few days later, she made the same case in Washington and won a joint statement that confirmed existing NATO strategy and the American promise to supply Trident missiles for the new generation of the British deterrent.[109]

It was at this moment that Powell spoke out, in flat contradiction to Thatcher. It had not been the nuclear deterrent that had prevented the Soviets from invading western Europe, he proclaimed, but the 'one simple, overwhelming reason' that 'it would have meant a war they couldn't expect to win. Alliance or no alliance the United States would be dragged into it, as in World War One and Two.' He also openly repudiated the idea that Britain's independent nuclear deterrent afforded protection against blackmail. For Powell, Labour's policy offered an opportunity to liberate Britain from an American-dominated alliance that he had always distrusted. The Labour Party, he noted, had resolved to renounce the British 'independent nuclear deterrent' and to require NATO's nuclear deterrent to be no longer based in Britain. 'The Labour Party and – if it listens to the Labour Party – the whole country, will find that they cannot stop there,' he declared. The theory of the nuclear deterrent would have to be re-examined from top to bottom. 'If it goes much else goes with it', he argued. 'We should not be far from a wholesale reappraisal of Britain's defence and foreign policy and of the nature of the Western Alliance itself.'[110]

This opportunity, for which Powell had longed all his political career, prompted his dramatic intervention in the 1987 general election, his last as a candidate. Although he was facing a tough struggle to hold a marginal seat in Northern Ireland, he visited London during the final weekend of the campaign to denounce as a 'myth' the notion that nuclear weapons had kept the peace in Europe for forty years. Western Governments, he argued, had 'ceaselessly inculcated in their subjects until it assumed the status of an axiom and a self-evident truth rather than a paradox and an absurdity'. He described the argument for an independent nuclear deterrent that he had publicly endorsed as Shadow Defence Spokesman twenty years earlier, as 'barmy'. Underpinning Powell's critique of nuclear deterrence was a soldierly, traditionalist ethos. As he was later to explain, 'it has always been the pride of the professional soldier, the pride of mankind – for warfare is one of the supreme activities of mankind

– so to conduct warfare, that the maximum result, political result shall be achievable with the minimum of crime.'[111]

Yet again, this soldierly, nationalist, Tory was to suggest that people should vote Labour. He sensed that the disastrous accident at the Chernobyl nuclear reactor had strengthened

> a growing impulse to escape from the nightmare of peace being dependent upon the contemplation of horrific and mutual carnage. Events have now so developed that this aspiration can at last be rationally, logically and – I dare to add – patriotically seized by the people of the United Kingdom if they will use their votes to do so.

His failure to back the Conservatives was as striking as it had been in 1983 after the Falklands and Thatcher's espousal of monetarism. By 1987, the Conservatives were embarked upon a programme of wholesale privatization – he had long called for radical 'denationalization'. To oppose Heath's interventionism was one thing; to oppose Thatcher seems perverse, unless it is realized that for Powell, economic policy was always subordinate to the overriding consideration of national independence. In 1974, Powell had vehemently denied the accusation of being a Judas. When asked in 1987 whether he was saying that people should vote Labour, he quoted Pontius Pilate: 'What I have written I have written'.

Before polling day in June 1987, Powell anticipated that Thatcher was about to share Heath's fate in 1974 – or worse. 'I have the feeling of 1945,' he commented with fervour during the campaign, referring to an earlier Conservative débâcle. 'Mrs Thatcher has never known losing office as Gladstone did and the need to face changing circumstances and clear new obstacles before returning to power'. But Powell was notoriously bad at forecasting the results of elections. Thatcher's overall majority in the Commons was reduced from its peak in 1983, but remained in three figures. It was Powell who was to suffer his final election defeat.[112]

Life after death

The June 1987 election was Powell's fifth campaign as an Ulster Unionist candidate and his thirteenth in all, stretching back to the Normanton by-election more than forty years earlier. Whereas in 1983 he had faced the threat of the Unionist vote in South Down being split by the intervention of a Paisleyite, there was no such threat in 1987 as the Unionist parties fought on a common manifesto against the Anglo–Irish Agreement. But Powell was at serious risk from the challenge being mounted by a rejuvenated SDLP, whose members had been buoyed by their success in neighbouring Newry and Armagh in the 1986 by-elections and who knew that South Down had a nationalist majority. Previously, Powell's record as a constituency MP, his non-sectarian advocacy of British rights for all, and his status as a national figure had helped him to attract sufficient Catholic support to hold the seat.

The strained looks of Powell and his wife during the count told the story. Finally, after a recount, the SDLP's Eddie McGrady was elected with a slender majority of 731, only slightly larger than Powell's majority in 1983. 'Shadows we are and shadows we pursue,' Powell philosophized after his defeat. It was only days before his seventy-fifth birthday, but he refused to be drawn on whether his defeat marked the end of his political career. Yet his emotional comments to his South Down supporters suggest that he realized that his thirty-seven-year career in the Commons was at an end. Referring to his period as an Ulster MP, he told them: 'For the rest of my life, when I look back on the thirteen years, I shall be filled with affection for the Province and its people, and they and their fortunes will never be out of my heart.'[113]

Within a week of Powell's defeat, a suggestion was made that Thatcher should offer Powell a life peerage, thereby enabling Powell to continue to contribute to parliamentary debate in the House of Lords. In the view of T.E. Utley, the Tory journalist (who had also stood as a Unionist in Ulster), although it was frequently said that Thatcher had changed the course of history, it was Powell who, 'to a very large extent,' had made this possible. A peerage would recognize Thatcher's debt to Powell, since it was clear 'that Mrs Thatcher's philosophy is roughly the same as that of Mr Powell, and that if he had not existed she would not have won'.[114]

Utley, however, hinted at a stumbling block by proposing that Powell might be offered 'even a viscountcy if he will not accept a life peerage'. Implicit in Utley's somewhat cavalier attitude to the peerage was the recollection that almost thirty years earlier, Powell had opposed Macmillan's introduction of life peerages on the principled grounds that it would transform the Lords and the constitution. Utley's suggestion of a viscountcy reflected Thatcher's revival in 1983 of the practice of creating hereditary peerages by offering viscountcies to George Thomas, the former Speaker of the House of Commons, and Willie Whitelaw, her former deputy. The fact that neither Viscount Tonypandy (Thomas) nor Whitelaw had direct male heirs had helped minimize any criticism – and Powell, like Whitelaw, only had daughters. Ian Gow, a strong supporter of Powell's and one of Thatcher's closest confidants (despite his resignation from her Government in protest at the Anglo–Irish Agreement), shared Utley's thinking and was anxious that Powell should continue to speak in parliament. He urged Thatcher to offer Powell a life peerage, and sought to ascertain Powell's response. Gow gathered that Powell would not accept such an offer because of his earlier opposition to the introduction of life peerages. A viscountcy, on the lines suggested by Utley, failed to materialize. Powell would have liked to have been offered the Garter, but neither did that happen.[115]

Powell was desolate after losing South Down, sometimes commenting that he was 'dead'. He missed his constituency and the cut and thrust of political battle. But although he was no longer a combatant, any idea that Powell's public career was at an end was soon dispelled. There was life after death. He was a star turn on the political and literary speaking circuits. His broadcasting work, journalism and reviewing had long been an important means of extending his knowledge, floating ideas and arguing his case. A torrent of articles, reviews, scripts and speeches, now flowed from the small back-room that served as his study, on the first-floor landing of his Belgravia home.

Although a window looks on to the back-garden, Powell's work room is rather claustrophobic. There is just enough space for Powell to sit at his desk and work with a secretary or talk with a journalist – though the present author contrived to film an interview with Powell at his desk. Being taken into his work room gives a strong impression of entering an inner sanctum, with personal mementoes along the mantelpiece and books lining the walls. His collection of books about India fill the blocks of shelves on either side of the window, but his bound volumes of *Hansard* had to be stored elsewhere. He found the 'very incongruity' of the room comforting and reassuring:

> The past years, unchangeable in their familiar shapes and now beyond the reach of effort or regret, observe with kindly tolerance the feverish endeav-ours crammed into the narrow space of the present, with a sort of Housmanic, 'lie down, lie down, young yeoman, the sun moves ever west'. The pokiness of the room, only a pace or two in any direction, is part of the secret of its soothing quality, as if the passion for concentration and self-sufficiency which is part of its occupant found a matching mood in the confined and crowded space. I think I never could be at ease in a room with ample vistas and large acres of wall and carpet.[116]

The notion of writing his political memoirs was dismissed by Powell as being 'like a dog returning to its vomit'. Instead, in addition to his formidable output on an array of political, historical and philosophical subjects, he completed the study of the evolution of the St Matthew Gospel that he had begun in 1974, when he had first thought that his political career was at an end. This work combined his skill as a textual critic of Greek manuscripts with his knowledge of the scriptures, and on its publication was, yet again, to put Powell at the centre of a new controversy. As with so much that mattered to Powell, his mother's influence is evident. He still had the Greek Testament in which, as a girl learning Greek by herself, she followed lessons in the parish church at Newport in Shropshire. At school, his discovery from reading the Greek Testament that the Gospel was 'not true', because the historical and internal evidence would not support the narrative, had contributed to his losing his faith. But ever since his return to religion during 1949–50, he had studied, 'in part consciously, but probably even more below the conscious surface of the mind', certain words and passages and ideas in the Bible. Over the years, his studies informed his preaching, his writing about the scriptures and his religious debates. Two collections of his religious works were published: *No Easy Answers* in 1973 and *Wrestling with the Angel* in 1977. 'We are all prisoners of our personalities', Powell observed in his introduction to the first book, 'and I fear it will be all too evident that for me intellectual effort – the grinding, drilling activity of the mind – is an inescapable and large ingredient in religion, as in so many of the other good things of life.'[117]

Powell's studies had first been given fresh impetus by accusations from the late 1960s that his views on immigration and race were incompatible with his Christian faith. These charges against Powell reflected the notion of the social gospel – the idea that the gospel is relevant to political and social behaviour, that finds strongest expression in the Gospel of St Matthew. This assumption has inspired politicians of all parties, but is totally rejected by Powell. He believes in the resurrection of the body and regards Christianity as being about personal redemption. In his view, the practical world and the religious world are two completely different worlds that lie parallel; people live their two lives simultaneously. This perception leads him to reject the idea that Christianity has any relevance to political action, social organization, business ethics, or any of the other practical choices that people have to make about the way they lead their lives.[118]

According to Powell's idiosyncratic interpretation of the gospel, Christ's simplest and most general injunctions are inherently unrealizable. For example, he contends that to 'love thy neighbour as thyself' – not just to love your neighbour – is commonly misunderstood. 'I am told to do that which no human being can do, which the nature of a human prevents him from doing', Powell asserts; 'namely, loving someone else as himself.' Moreover, according to Powell, 'if we are to draw deductions from this command, then we would say that politically and nationally we ought to treat all human beings alike. Now, no nation on the face of the earth does this.' Indeed, Powell points out that 'the very principle implicit in nationhood, in statehood, seems to me an affront to the injunction to treat all men alike through treating all men "as oneself"'. But Powell regards nationhood and national identity as fundamental to human society, and he therefore concludes that Christ's command has no practical bearing. It does not cause Powell to modify his nationalistic view of the world.[119]

Powell infused his religious debates with the uncompromising and, at times, unforgiving, attitude that he brought to politics. He is dismissive of 'a sugary, romantic, cosy religion, suitable to match the welfare state', and is contemptuous of clergy whom he feels are guilty of indulging in 'amateur politics and amateur economics'. In 1969, he delivered a scathing attack on the Wolverhampton Council of Christian Churches for having sought signatures, in common with other churches, to a Declaration on World Poverty. In Powell's view, the clergy possess 'authority or influence as the keepers and expositors of certain truths and mysteries' on which countless people rely in their personal existence, but 'they profane that authority and prostitute that influence when they put it at the service of fashionable propositions, political and economic, which they are no better placed than other men to understand or judge'. Powell was perturbed because he felt that the Declaration was not an isolated incident. Yet he displayed a doctrinaire vehemence in decrying the Declaration as 'meaningless and absurd' and in castigating the well-intentioned clergy. His forthright insistence that the gospel has no social relevance has invited the counter-charge that his religious views are extremely convenient for his free-market beliefs.[120]

Yet the publication in 1994 of *The Evolution of the Gospel*, Powell's study of the St Matthew Gospel, caused the greatest controversy. His name returned to the headlines because of his claim that Christ did not die on the cross at the hands of the Romans, but was instead stoned to death as a blasphemer by the Jews. This was not the only revision that Powell suggested in his new translation of Matthew's Gospel. As the scholar and critic, Gina Menzies, observed: 'Eliminate the Crucifixion and Resurrection, Jesus's trial before Pilate, the Sermon on the Mount, the anointing of Jesus by an unnamed woman at Bethany, and you have Matthew's Gospel according to Enoch Powell'. In the *Spectator*, the writer on religious matters, Peter Hebblethwaite, judged that Powell's book 'is much more subversive of the Christian message than anything David Jenkins, the sometime Bishop of Durham, has hinted at'. Pressed by Terry Coleman on whether he was a believing Christian, Powell replied cryptically, 'I am an obedient member of the Church of England.'[121]

Powell's book was in three parts: a brief introductory essay, his translation of Matthew, and his commentary. It is his contention that the book known as 'The Gospel according to Matthew' is the primary source for the gospels of Mark and Luke, and that an underlying book hides behind the Greek text of Matthew, that had been added to and amended. Yet Powell's claim runs counter to two hundred years of biblical scholarship, according to which Mark was first written about 65 AD, and Matthew and Luke were written later, relying heavily on Mark. Most controversially of all, Powell suggests that Jesus's stoning for blasphemy by the Jewish authorities was replaced in the Gospel with a 'trial and execution of Jesus by the Romans of the putative king of the Jews', because of a theological conflict between the early gentile and Jewish churches. 'Pilate and the Romans must be exonerated and the blood-guilt accepted by the Jewish people', Powell declares. His reaction to the suggestion that he was reviving the accusation that the Jews murdered Christ was to state: 'Well, I can't help it. What I have read, I have read.'[122]

Christian and Jewish scholars and theologians are dismissive of Powell's theory. Professor Sir Henry Chadwick, one of Britain's foremost historians on the early church, whom Powell consulted, responded that the authority of the Pauline letters, written before the Gospels, is 'far too strong to be withdrawn. The early Christians were quite clear that what had happened was a crucifixion.' Likewise, Dr Tom Wright, the Dean of Lichfield, maintained that the crucifixion 'is one of the most securely attested events in the ancient world'. Powell's claim, based on a hypothetical document that was allegedly suppressed 2,000 years ago, and reached by 'reading the original text without the assistance of other scholars simply beggars belief'.[123]

Challenging conventional wisdom has never given Powell any qualms. This quality was evident in his working method on the Matthew Gospel. As Powell explains, the arguments that he advances 'emerged from a prolonged, repeated, and intensive study of the Greek text of Matthew by the methods of textual and literary criticism'. This is all very well in as far as it goes. Most critics agree that Powell offers some interesting insights – Professor Chadwick acknowledged his formidable scholarship and cited the suggestion that the Gospel text was influenced by early Christian worship. But textual and literary criticism offers only a limited explanation of any text. Powell, however, deliberately discards the 'scholarship of centuries' on the Matthew Gospel, in order 'to clear the mind as far as possible of preconceptions or conclusions arrived at earlier by others'. This is exceptionally arrogant. By turning his back on the evidence of scientific biblical research and neglecting the historical, philosophical and theological aspects of the text, he produces idiosyncratic theories. As Professor Chadwick commented, 'I read his book with wonder, awe and a certain suspension of disbelief.'[124]

Powell accepted that his character had enabled him to 'take isolation very easily'. As he explained,

> Intellectual isolation doesn't frighten me, I haven't got the horror of finding myself alone, at any rate not of finding myself alone intellectually or mentally. This is, I suppose, a counterpart of arrogance. If you are convinced by your own reason, convinced of the validity of your own insights, then the fact that they are not shared – though for a politician or any performer with words, to share with others and to secure from others a reaction, must be the ultimate prize – initially, you are not apt to be disturbed.

Yet Powell's reference to sharing with, and securing a reaction from, others is the key to what being a politician meant to him. 'Politics consists in securing from other people a common insight with that which one holds oneself', he observed, 'and that's why words are so essential to the business of politics.' He sometimes referred to himself as listening for an echo. By this, he meant that he was engaged in a continuing dialectic. Hearing an echo of what he was saying suggested that he was reflecting people's feelings, and indicated that he might also be having some influence.

Influence in politics can also be used to get things done in government. Powell loved nothing more in Government than the speedy despatch of business. But exerting influence in government involves compromises, deals and trade-offs, all of which are as much a necessary part of politics as making speeches. Powell claims that he was always able to do business with his fellow ministers, and accepted trade-offs on day-to-day matters. None the less, he evinces deep suspicion for the practical politics of government. Compromise becomes almost synonymous with corruption:

> You can be corrupted by power. You can say to yourself, or you can allow

others to say to you, 'You know you have splendid ideas. Could you not put those into effect more successfully if you would pretend to go along with and agree with the things with which you disagree?' That is perhaps the deepest corruption in politics.

Powell's attitude helps to explain why, during his thirty-seven years as an MP, he spent only fifteen months in the Cabinet – a period that coincided with Macmillan's reflation of the economy and imposition of pay controls. Powell was haunted by this experience and spent the rest of his career trying to exorcize the ghosts.[125]

Besides the corruption of power, Powell regarded 'the English corruption' as typically being that of 'honours and distinction and status'. But in the 1990s, the growing concern at falling standards in public life, including the financial interests of MPs, led the Prime Minister, John Major, to set up a committee, chaired by Lord Nolan, to investigate the problem. In recommending the independent scrutiny of MPs' interests, the Nolan committee effected something of a political miracle by uniting Powell and Sir Edward Heath. Both men strongly opposed any external regulation of the Commons. In 1975, Powell had refused to sign the register of Members' interests on the grounds that 'a new condition for being a Member of Parliament could only be imposed by statute and cannot be created by a simple resolution in the Chamber'. Powell suspected that by the 1990s, 'the public tend to regard MPs as venal', but introducing new rules was not the way to make it better. 'If "my honourable Friend", or "the honourable Member" is not honourable,' he argued, 'no amount of regulation or supervision will make him so.' In Powell's view, 'there needs to be a change in standards. It is standards that matter – what people think an institution like parliament is about'.[126]

This latter comment goes to the heart of Powell's main political preoccupation. 'My self-imposed business', he said, 'has been telling the English about themselves – who they are and what they are, how they govern themselves and why they govern themselves in that way.' For Powell, how people govern themselves is 'the most important thing about people collectively: they govern themselves in a particular way because they're that sort of people.' Britain has been an evolving parliamentary nation. Its national character and history are inseparable from parliament:

We govern ourselves subject to debate in parliament because we're that sort of people. We're the sort of people who put up with majority decisions taken if necessary by a majority of one, in that sort of assembly, after a debate, provided of course that the procedure has been observed – we're that sort of people.

As he freely confessed, he was obsessive about parliament: 'I have an obsession about being governed by parliament. I have an obsession with the exclusive right to live under laws made by one's own parliament and to pay taxes levied by one's own parliament.'[127]

Powell's obsession continued to dominate his political thinking after he left the Commons. In October 1987, five years since he had entertained high hopes of a revival of national self-awareness and self-assertion in the wake of the Falklands victory, he reflected on his thirty-seven years in parliament and lamented Britain's self-inflicted loss of national independence. His speech to the Salisbury Group, a gathering of intellectuals sympathetic to his 'Church and Queen' Toryism, was vintage Powell – anti-Americanism, distrust of the 'ruling and official classes in Britain', and despair at his fellow MPs and countrymen for allowing their country's destiny to be absorbed into those of the United States and Europe. He was the authentic voice of the old-style Country Tory, suddenly plucked from the eighteenth century when the British doctrine of parliamentary sovereignty took root, and transported into the late twentieth century.[128]

In return for the shelter of the American nuclear shield, so Powell's theory ran, Britain's rulers had accepted the *quid pro quo* of a united Europe and, seeing the final surrogate for the Empire, had thought that they could 'lead Europe' in a 'special relationship' with the United States. The public were in a mood to go along with it: 'Britain, it seemed axiomatic, was no longer an island; Britain, since it could no longer defend itself, was no longer independent. It followed that Britain was no longer a nation.' Finally, in the 1970s, there occurred what 'would have been to me incredible in 1950 and still in 1987 remains incomprehensible'; namely that 'the House of Commons did transfer its powers to an authority outside the realm, and the people of Britain not only did not care but continued to give their support and approval to those who had done this thing'. Political independence and parliamentary self-government were integral to Powell's understanding of his own country. What was he to do? He kept campaigning. In 1988, he was encouraged by Thatcher's renunciation of European political unification in her speech at Bruges, and the following year, another collection of his speeches against European integration was published – *Enoch Powell on 1992*, the date in the title referring to the deadline for the creation of the European single market and the target date for further moves towards a European political union.[129]

In the event, 1992 was to give Powell new cause for hope. The process of ratification of the Maastricht Treaty, that created a new political framework for the European Community, provided a focus for discontent in the member-states. The Danish rejection of Maastricht in their July referendum (subsequently reversed in a second poll) and Britain's humiliating exit from the European exchange rate mechanism in September, fuelled a new mood of Euro-scepticism among British Tories. As the Commons rancorously debated Maastricht, Powell heard increasingly loud echoes.

In June 1992, on his eightieth birthday, Powell was presented with a silver salver by former parliamentary friends and colleagues, inscribed with the words, 'Scholar, Poet, Soldier, Parliamentarian'. If they had wanted to capture his self-designated role since his departure from the Commons, they might have added 'controversialist' and 'Tory sage'. He remained dapper and spry for some years into his eighties, and took special delight in 'observing the evolution' of the grandchildren with which his daughters had endowed him and Pam. Their annual French holidays and his reading of Zola remained a great pleasure. But increased frailty took its toll, and Powell was wont to tell friends that he was not enjoying exploring old age. He came to view death as a hand laid on the shoulder, saying, 'it's all right old chap, you don't have to worry. I'll come and take you away.' He planned his funeral. After a service in the chapel of his regiment, the Royal Warwickshires, he arranged to be buried in full dress brigadier's uniform.[130]

In his biography of Joseph Chamberlain, he asserts that: 'All political lives, unless they are cut off in midstream at a happy juncture, end in failure, because that is the nature of politics and of human affairs'. When he was eighty-three, he was challenged as to whether his political career had ended in failure. 'Mine has ended in failure from one point of view,' he replied:

> without a seat, without office, without apparent achievement. But I've achieved a great deal and I hear my voice coming through in what is said. And I see myself being proved right. What I had to say about immigration, what I had to say about the nation, what I had to say about Europe, was heard and is still echoing.

That Powell's voice stirred an echo is beyond dispute. But many would contest his claim that he is being proved right. Curiously, Powell failed to include his championing of market forces, since this is the area where, for a variety of reasons, the ideas that he advocated in the heyday of Keynesianism became the conventional wisdom during the 1980s – though the results are, to say the least, problematic.[131]

Most politicians, in their assumptions and attitudes, reflect various strands from the stream of historical experience in which they grew up. These strands often derive from the different outlooks and traditions that have shaped their country's political culture. It is not unusual for a politician to reflect strands that originated in political traditions that are quite distinct from the contemporary party to which he or she belongs, and that often appear to be contradictory. At different stages in a political career, in response to events, crises or career opportunities, one strand or another becomes more dominant in a politician's thinking. On occasion, the contradiction may become so great, the crisis so extreme, or the career opportunity so irresistible, that a set of assumptions and attitudes is abandoned.

Powell was no exception to this process. Having entered politics as one of the last of the ardent imperialists, he soon sloughed off the skin of Empire and spent the rest of his career berating his fellow countrymen for their failure to renounce completely the myth of Empire. But he also had an exceptional talent for articulating and expressing his assumptions and attitudes, and making them seem part of a convincing whole in what became known as 'Powellism'. This was possibly because he appeared to take the beliefs and perceptions of a particular nation and epoch as fundamental truths. He was part Country Tory; part believer in the British doctrine of parliamentary sovereignty; part Gladstonian Liberal; part Chamberlainite Unionist; and part Romantic Nationalist. Other strands could undoubtedly be identified at different stages of his career – at the NHS, for example, he was a great state planner.

'Powellism', in its uneasy marrying of liberal economics with a new, post-imperial, nationalism, was a precursor of 'Thatcherism'. Powell kept the flame of economic liberalism burning in the Conservative Party during the years when the leadership subscribed to full employment and a mixed economy. In fashioning a new nationalism with a strong popular appeal, he pointed the way for Thatcher's brand of Conservatism. But the line from Powellism to Thatcherism was not a direct one. Many other events and influences interceded to change the political climate during the 1960s and 1970s before Thatcherism eventually emerged as a broadly recognizable set of attitudes in the early 1980s.

Having fashioned a new radical, nationalist Toryism in the mid-1960s, Powell's spectacular political misjudgement in 1968 condemned him and his ideas to the outer fringes of the Conservative Party. His very success in presenting his ideas as a coherent ideology discouraged economic liberals from arguing their corner for fear of being tainted with the Powellite brush. Debate on immigration within the Conservative Party was similarly blighted, as most moderates and centrists steered clear of the issue. Simultaneously, he polarized debate and locked himself out of the Tory court. A more astute politician would have sought to exercise his influence behind the closed doors, and not end up having to shout from outside. But Powell had made principles of too many policies. Compromise was corruption. The prospect of a new political realignment excited a handful of Young Tory Turks, but scared rigid the traditionalists and career politicians on the Conservative benches.

Thatcher possessed a well-disguised ability as leader to change her policies when it was expedient. After 1963, Powell never had to confront the supreme challenge for a politician of testing his ideas against the responsibility of high office. As the years passed and his distance from office grew ever more remote, the man who had made a name for debunking delusions was increasingly seen to be perpetuating new myths of his own. Powell once recalled that it had been said of Joseph Chamberlain that he always took his hat off to himself when he saw his reflection in the mirror. Powell believed that, metaphorically speaking,

> a politician should never look in the mirror. He should never say to himself, 'Now how am I looking? How do I appear?' Certainly he would be a miserable and an unsuccessful politician if he did. Everyone else will have their view of him, but he must sing his song.

In an age of public relations advisers and spin doctors, Powell's approach is refreshingly ingenuous. He believed in the simple proposition that politicians should give people a tune they could hum. But if he found a song that he liked, he had to sing it, whether or not it was in the party song-book. He was a compulsive singer, like the birds before dawn. It was his political downfall, although the echoes live on.[132]

Notes

CPA refers to files in the Conservative Party Archive at the Bodleian Library, Oxford. PRO refers to files at the Public Record Office, Kew. Details of the books referred to by author and date of publication are provided in the Bibliography. Interviews recorded for television documentaries are signified as follows: *WW* refers to *The Writing on the Wall*, 1985; *PM* refers to *All the Prime Minister's Men*, 1986; *LP* refers to *Enoch, A Life In Politics*, 1987; *TF* refers to *The Thatcher Factor*, 1989 (the above series were produced by Brook Productions for Channel 4 Television); *WB* refers to *What Has Become Of Us*, November – December 1994 (Wide Vision Productions for Channel 4 Television).

CHAPTER 1: A DRIVEN PERSONALITY

1. *Spectator*, 16 July 1965.
2. *LP*.
3. *LP*; T.E. Utley, 1968, pp. 56–7.
4. 'Theory and Practice', in *Philosophy and Politics*, 1990, Cambridge; *Listener*, 28 May 1981; *Observer*, 5 February 1961; *The Times*, 14 April 1994.
5. *Odd Man Out*, BBC 2 Television, 11 November 1995; interviewed by Anne Brown, BBC Radio, 13 April 1986.
6. *Spectator*, 5 February 1994; Raven, 1978.
7. Chamberlain had campaigned for compulsory, free, universal, and non-sectarian education; Mortimer, 1983, p. 49; King Edward VI School, Birmingham, records.
8. *Sunday Telegraph*, 3 September 1995; the present author was told of the raids by his grandparents, who lived in South Yardley, a mile and a half from Stechford.
9. Roth, 1970, p. 10.
10. Interview with Mrs Simpson, former neighbour; Roth, 1970, p. 11; *Observer*, 24 April 1966; *Panorama*, BBC Television, 2 December 1968.
11. Powell, 1973, p. 2; Mortimer, 1983, p. 49.
12. *Panorama*, BBC Television, 2 December 1968; interviewed by Anne Brown, BBC Radio, 13 April 1986; Roth, 1970, pp. 11–12; *Observer*, 24 April 1966.
13. King Edward VI School, Birmingham, records; Roth, 1970, p. 13.
14. Napal, 1975, p. 46.
15. Napal, 1975, p. 43, pp. 48–9; interview with Mrs Simpson, former neighbour.
16. Napal, 1975, pp. 50–1.
17. Interview with Mrs Simpson, former neighbour.

18. *National and English Review*, December 1959; *Spectator*, 18 December 1982; *Books and Bookmen*, 1986.
19. *Sunday Times*, 17 August 1983; *Listener*, 28 May 1981; Powell, 1973, pp. 2–3, 49–50.
20. Powell, *Spectator*, 2 August 1969; Hennessy, 1992, p. xiv; Powell was addressing the Institute of Contemporary British History's summer school at the London School of Economics, July 1991.
21. Roth, 1970, p. 12; *Old Edwardian Gazette*, July 1974, p. 29.
22. *Old Edwardian Gazette*, July 1974, p. 29.
23. King Edward VI School, Birmingham, Blue Books; *Panorama*, BBC Television, 2 December 1968.
24. Interviewed by Anne Brown, BBC Radio, 13 April 1986; Napal, 1975, p. 47. Lyttleton, *Old Edwardian Gazette*, October 1978, p. 34. So strongly did Lyttleton take against the classics, that in later life he played a leading part in removing compulsory Latin from university entrance requirements; *Panorama*, BBC Television, 2 December 1968; Smith wrote of Powell in 1952, cited in Napal, 1975, p. 69.
25. Interviewed by Anne Brown, BBC Radio, 13 April 1986; see also, interview with Terry Coleman, *Guardian*, 15 June 1982; *LP*; Lyttleton, *Old Edwardian Gazette*, October 1978, p. 36; Roth, 1970, p. 15; *Panorama*, BBC Television, 2 December 1968.
26. King Edward VI School, Birmingham, Blue Books; Recollections of Old Edwardians; Roth, 1970, p. 15; Trott, 1992, p. 93.
27. Mortimer, 1983, p. 50; Utley, 1968, p. 47; Trott, 1992, p. 93.
28. *The Times*, 8 July 1960.
29. *Panorama*, BBC Television, 2 December 1968.
30. *Panorama*, BBC Television, 2 December 1968; interviewed by Terry Coleman, *Guardian*, 15 June 1982; Mortimer, 1983, p. 50.
31. Borrow, 1851, John Murray, London – 'lavengro' means 'wordsmith' in Romany, the Indo-European language of the gypsies; 'Sentimental Journey', in *A Second 'Listener' Anthology*, 1970; interviewed by Terry Coleman, *Guardian*, 15 June 1982.
32. Roth, 1970, pp. 17–18.
33. King Edward VI School, Birmingham, Blue Books; Roth, 1970, pp. 16–17.
34. *Old Edwardians Gazette*, July 1974, March 1978.
35. *The Times Higher Education Supplement*, 1 September 1995; King Edward VI School, Birmingham, Blue Books; Michael Cockerell's profile of Powell, *Odd Man Out*, was broadcast on BBC 2 Television, 11 November 1995.
36. Roth, 1970, p. 17.

CHAPTER 2: SCHOLAR-POET

1. 'Enoch Powell at Cambridge', *Snapshots*, 1991, Wild and Fresh Productions / Channel 4 Television; *Panorama*, BBC Television, 2 December 1968.
2. *Panorama*, BBC Television, 2 December 1968.
3. *Panorama*, BBC Television, 2 December 1968.
4. *Panorama*, BBC Television, 2 December 1968; interviewed by Anne Brown, BBC Radio, 13 April 1986; Roth, 1970, p. 18.
5. Michael Cockerell; Strachan, 1949, p. 380; *Sunday Telegraph*, 3 September 1995; Roth, 1970, pp. 19–20.
6. Jebb, 1992, p. 117; the Professorship was named after Benjamin Hall Kennedy, the nineteenth century Cambridge classicist and Old Edwardian; Graves, 1979, pp. 96–7, 164–5, 183, 198–99; Housman, 1921 lecture to the Classical Association, quoted in Graves, 1979, p. 200; *The Times*, 27 September 1962.
7. *The Times*, 27 September 1962.
8. '*Charismatics*', BBC Radio 4, 11 June 1995; *Independent* Magazine.
9. 'Enoch Powell at Cambridge', *Snapshots*, 1991, Wild and Fresh Productions / Channel 4 Television; *Daily Telegraph*, 21 October 1995; '*Charismatics*', BBC Radio 4, 11 June 1995; Graves, 1979, p. 167;

Powell, 'A Personal Recollection of A.E. Housman', *Housman Society Journal*, volume I, summer 1972, pp. 27–9.

10. Powell, 'A Personal Recollection of A.E. Housman', *Housman Society Journal*, volume I, summer 1972, pp. 27–9.

11. 'Enoch Powell at Cambridge', *Snapshots*, 1991, Wild and Fresh Productions / Channel 4 Television; interviewed by Anne Brown, BBC Radio, 13 April 1986; Graves, 1979, p. 208.

12. 'Enoch Powell at Cambridge', *Snapshots*, 1991, Wild and Fresh Productions / Channel 4 Television; '*Charismatics*', BBC Radio 4, 11 June 1995; Cosgrave, 1989, p. 47.

13. Graves, 1979, pp. 205–7, 217; Jebb, 1992, pp. 119–22; *Spectator*, 3 May 1986.

14. *Daily Telegraph*, 21 October 1995; Powell, 1990, p. vii; *Daily Telegraph*, 18 April 1992, reviewing Keith Jebb's study of Housman; Graves, 1979, pp. 106–7.

15. Powell, 1990, pp. vii–viii, 3.

16. Housman, 1939, p. 10; *Sunday Telegraph*, 13 March 1994; '*Charismatics*', BBC Radio 4, 11 June 1995; Powell, 1990, p. viii.

17. Powell, 1990, p. 95; *Odd Man Out*, BBC 2 Television, 11 November 1995; Napal, 1975, p. 121.

18. *Daily Telegraph*, 18 April 1992; Powell, 1990, p. 69.

19. Roth, 1970, p. 20–1.

20. *Listener*, 25 June 1970; *Sue Lawley's Desert Island Discussions*, BBC Radio 4, 1990.

21. *Listener*, 25 June 1970; Nietzsche, *The Will to Power*, section 1067, translated by W. Kaufmann and R.J. Hollingdale, 1968, Viking Books, New York; Roth, 1970, p. 21; for an introduction to Nietzsche, see Stern, 1978, Tanner, 1994; Powell, 1990, p. 5.

22. Nietzsche, quoted in Stern, 1978, p. 81.

23. *Birmingham Post*, 1931, cited in Roth, 1970, pp. 21–2; *The Times*, 9 October 1934; King Edward VI School, Birmingham, Governors' Order Book; the half-day was also granted in recognition of a Yale Fellowship awarded to D.R. Dudley, another Old Edwardian; *The Times*, 20 March 1933; *Guardian*, 5 March 1994.

24. *Panorama*, BBC Television, 2 December 1968.

25. Trinity College Library; *The Times*, 9 October 1934; King Edward VI School, Birmingham, Governors' Order Book; *Panorama*, BBC Television, 2 December 1968; *Daily Telegraph*, 27 March 1993; interviewed by Anne Brown, BBC Radio, 13 April 1986.

26. Powell, 1933, pp. 123–6; Roth, 1970, p. 24.

27. Roth, 1970, p. 24; *Towards 2000*, Radio Clyde, 1977.

28. Roth, 1970, p. 24.

29. Freeth's portraits and etchings can be seen at the National Portrait Gallery.

30. *The Times*, 6 January 1936.

31. Powell, 1990, p. vii; *Sunday Telegraph*, 3 September 1995; Roth, 1970, p. 27; Cosgrave, 1989, p. 53; *Spectator*, 16 April 1983.

32. Interviewed by Anne Brown, BBC Radio, 13 April 1986; Powell, 1990, pp. vii, 46–7.

33. Roth, 1970, p. 27; *The Times*, 4 November 1937.

34. Powell's articles included a number on Herodotus in *Philologische Wochenschrift*; others in *The Classical Quarterly*, including one on 'The archetype of Thucydides' in April 1938; the *Classical Review*; and even 'A palimpsest of St Chrysostom' in the *Journal of Theological Studies*.

35. Powell, 1936; reviewed in *The Times Literary Supplement*, 13 February 1937.

36. 'Enoch Powell at Cambridge', *Snapshots*, 1991, Wild and Fresh Productions / Channel 4 Television; 'The Trinity College Manuscript of Hywel Dda', and 'Floating Sections in the Laws of Howel', in *The Bulletin of the Board of Celtic Studies*, University of Wales, vol. VIII, part II, May 1936, pp. 120–4, and vol. IX, part I, November 1937, pp. 27–34.

37. *The Times*, 21 August 1986.

38. *Listener*, 7 March 1974.

39. See Powell, 1938.

40. Roth, 1970, p. 26.

41. 'Pommy Professor', *Times Educational Supplement*, 28 February 1964; *The Times*, 27 September 1962; Michael Cockerell; Roth, 1970, p. 29; *Panorama*, BBC Television, 2 December 1968.

42. Inaugural lecture, 'Greek in the University', University of Sydney, 7 May 1938; 'Pommy Professor', *The Times Educational Supplement*, 28 February 1964.
43. 'Pommy Professor', *The Times Educational Supplement*, 28 February 1964; Roth, 1970, p. 28; *The Old Edwardians Gazette*, 1938, p. 6.
44. Powell, 1939, preface to *History of Herodotus; Classical Review*, 1939.
45. 'Pommy Professor', *The Times Educational Supplement*, 28 February 1964.
46. Cosgrave, 1989, pp. 54–5; *The Times Higher Education Supplement*, 1 September 1995; Roth 1970, p. 29; *Guardian*, 15 February 1990.
47. Powell, speech at Uppingham School, 1984. Powell admitted to having felt ashamed of his country on two occasions – the first in 1938; the second, in 1975 when the referendum resulted in a vote to stay in the EEC.
48. Powell, 1990, pp. viii, 115.
49. *LP*; Roth, 1970, p. 29; 'Pommy Professor', *The Times Educational Supplement*, 28 February 1964.
50. Powell, 1990, p. viii.

CHAPTER 3: A PURPOSE IN LIFE

1. *LP*; conversation with Sir John Habakkuk, All Soul's College, Oxford, June 1995; *Panorama*, BBC Television, 2 December 1968; Powell, 1990, p. 65.
2. *Panorama*, BBC Television, 2 December 1968.
3. *LP*; interviewed by Anne Brown, BBC Radio, 13 April 1986.
4. Interviewed by Anne Brown, BBC Radio, 13 April 1986; *LP*; *Panorama*, BBC Television, 2 December 1968.
5. 'Pommy Professor', *The Times Educational Supplement*, 28 February 1964; *Panorama*, BBC Television, 2 December 1968; *Observer*, 24 April 1966; *Daily Telegraph*, cited in Cosgrave, 1989, p. 63.
6. *Sunday Telegraph*, 25 March 1995; *The Times*, 30 April 1969; *Evening Standard*, 29 April 1969.
7. Roth, 1970, p. 33.
8. Powell, 1990, p. 127.
9. Powell, inaugural lecture, 'Greek in the University', University of New South Wales, 7 May 1938; Cosgrave, 1989, pp. 66–7.
10. *Sunday Telegraph*, 17 July 1966; Cosgrave, 1989, p. 62.
11. Strachan, 1949, p. 380; Roth, 1970, p. 37.
12. *Sunday Chronicle*, 22 January 1950.
13. Powell, 1990, pp. ix, 149; interviewed by Anne Brown, BBC Radio, 13 April 1986.
14. Roth, 1970, p. 37.
15. *Sunday Chronicle*, 22 January 1950.
16. *Sunday Chronicle*, 22 January 1950; Calvocoressi and Wint, 1972, p. 370.
17. 'Towards 2000', Radio Clyde, 1977.
18. Strachan, 1949, pp. 379–92.
19. 'The Imperfect Dream: A Return Passage to India', *The Times*, 7 May 1983.
20. 'The Imperfect Dream: A Return Passage to India', *The Times*, 7 May 1983.
21. 'The Imperfect Dream: A Return Passage to India', *The Times*, 7 May 1983; *Spectator*, 6 April 1974; 'Pommy Professor', *Times Educational Supplement*, 28 February 1964.
22. *LP*; Powell was unsure of the identity of the politician who made the *apercu*.
23. *LP*.
24. 'The Imperfect Dream: A Return Passage to India', *The Times*, 7 May 1983.
25. 'The Imperfect Dream: A Return Passage to India', *The Times*, 7 May 1983.
26. Quoted in 'The Imperfect Dream: A Return Passage to India', *The Times*, 7 May 1983.
27. 'The Imperfect Dream: A Return Passage to India', *The Times*, 7 May 1983; *Spectator*, 6 April 1974.
28. Daniel, 1986, p. 154; Mason, 1978, p. 196.
29. Mason, 1978, pp. 196–97.
30. Daniel, 1986, pp. 153–4.

31. *Panorama*, BBC Television, 2 December 1968.
32. *WB*; Daniel, 1986, pp. 154–55; 'The Imperfect Dream: A Return Passage to India', *The Times*, 7 May 1983.
33. Powell, 'The Imperfect Dream: A Return Passage to India', *The Times*, 7 May 1983; Mason, 1978, p. 198; cited in Cosgrave, 1989, p. 91.
34. Mason, 1978, p. 198.
35. Mason, 1978, p. 198.

CHAPTER 4: 'MY TIME WILL COME'

1. Powell, 'Theory and Practice', in Hunt, 1990, pp. 1–9.
2. Powell, 'Theory and Practice', in Hunt, 1990, pp. 1–9; *WB*.
3. Powell, 'Theory and Practice', in Hunt, 1990, pp. 1–9; Mason, 1978, pp. 196–8.
4. Conservative Central Office had moved from its large premises at Palace Chambers in 1941 to occupy the smaller Research Department offices in Old Queen Street, Westminster, for the remainder of the war. It was not until the latter part of 1946 that Central Office moved to Abbey House, at numbers 2–8 in nearby Victoria Street; Powell, 'Theory and Practice', in Hunt, 1990, pp. 1–9; Ramsden, 1980, p. 104.
5. Interview with David Clarke about Macleod and Powell.
6. CPA, CRD 2/53/71 (1), Miss Jackson to Miss Wilkins, 7 May 1946; interview with Powell about Macleod; *Spectator*, 16 July 1965; Shepherd, 1994, pp. 42–3.
7. CPA, miscellaneous CRD and CCO files, 1945–50.
8. *Spectator*, 16 July, 1965 (though Powell was not wearing 'hunting pink', as Macleod suggested); Strachan, 1949, p. 392.
9. Strachan, 1949, p. 392.
10. Shepherd, 1994, pp. 45–6; Maudling, 1978, pp. 42–3.
11. CPA, CRD 2/25/1, 3 May 1946.
12. CPA, CRD 2/25/1, 3 May 1946.
13. CPA, CRD 2/25/1, 6 May 1946; 18 May–3 July 1946; CRD 2/23/1, 26 July and 18 October 1946.
14. School of Oriental and African Studies, 30 October 1995; *Hansard*, December 1946, col. 2350; *Spectator*, 13 April 1991.
15. Maudling's Barnet constituency was winnable; Enfield looked less promising for Macleod, but following boundary changes he was adopted in 1948 for the new, safe seat of Enfield West.
16. Bodleian Library, R.A. Butler's papers, RAB 4/1, f.418; f.245, Butler to Powell, 5 February 1947.
17. *Listener*, 13 May 1969; Roth, 1970, p. 52.
18. *Yorkshire Post*, 8 February 1947; Roth, 1970, p. 52.
19. *Yorkshire Post*, 8 February 1947; *The Times*, 13 January 1947; *Yorkshire Post*, 13 January 1947.
20. Hennessy, 1992, p. 235; *LP*.
21. Hennessy, 1992, pp. 233–4.
22. *WB*.
23. Utley, 1968, p. 60; CPA, miscellaneous files, 1945–50; Ramsden, 1980, p. 122, states on the basis of studying the papers that 'the story that he [Powell] sought to persuade the Party of the possibility of a military reconquest of India is wide of the mark'; Cosgrave, 1989, p. 115; *LP*.
24. *Spectator*, 13 September 1968; for Powell's claim, see Cosgrave, 1989, p. 113; *WB*.
25. *LP*.
26. Private information; Michael Cockerell.
27. CPA, CRD 2/53/55 (1); Miss Hodgson to Hopkinson, 12 June 1947.
28. CPA, CRD 2/25/2–6; 2/22/3; 2/23/1; note, 13 May 1947.
29. CPA, CRD 2/37/2, Powell to Head, 13 August 1947; CRD 2/22/3; CRD 2/46/1; Peter Goldman of the Research Department was also responsible for much of the briefing.
30. CPA, CRD 2/37/2, Head to Powell, 30 December 1947; Egremont, 1968, p. 139.
31. CPA, CRD 2/38/22, handwritten note dated 4/1/48; CRD 2/37/2, Powell memorandum, early 1948.

32. *WB.*
33. CPA, CRD 2/53/5; RAB G.20, Clarke to Butler, 13 October 1948.
34. CPA, CCO 4/2/183, Report on Rural Wales, 20 January 1948.
35. CPA, CCO 4/2/183, Report on Rural Wales, 20 January 1948.
36. CPA, CCO 4/2/183, Piersenne to Miss James, 12 March 1948; Report on Industrial Wales, 26 May 1948.
37. CPA, CCO 4/2/183, Report on Industrial Wales, 26 May 1948; Conservative and Unionist Central Office, 1949.
38. CPA, CRD 2/23/6, Powell note, 31 May 1948.
39. CPA, CRD 2/23/6, Powell to Clarke, 31 March 1949; CRD 2/23/24, Powell to Butler, 17 August 1948; CRD 2/23/9, report on housing policy, 8 March 1949.
40. CPA, CRD 2/46/4 and House of Commons debate, 7 July 1948. Many of the Jamaicans who landed at Tilbury were ex-servicemen who had served in Britain during the war. They had been born and brought up as British subjects, and did not regard themselves as 'immigrants' – and London's *Evening Standard* ran the headline, 'Welcome home sons of Empire'; *Hansard*, 7 July 1948, col. 405; Hennessy, 1992, p. 440.
41. CRD 2/46/4: briefings on the British Nationality Bill.
42. *Spectator*, 6 April 1974; *LP.*
43. Lord Roll, discussing Britain's economic performance, ICBH Summer School, July 1995; Conservative and Unionist Central Office, 1949.
44. Interview with Powell about Macleod; Shepherd, 1994, p. 44; Utley, 1968, p. 55.
45. Roth, 1970, p. 56; Campbell, 1993, p. 60.
46. CPA, CCO, 1/7/279, Ledingham to Thomas, 4 October and 23 October 1948.
47. CPA, CCO, 1/7/279, Ledingham to Thomas, 23 October 1948, Thomas to Ledingham, 11 November 1948.
48. Roth, 1970, p. 57; interview with Audrey Rose; CPA, CCO, 1/7/279, Powell to Thomas, 6 December 1948.
49. CPA, CCO, 1/7/279, Stirling to Woolton, 12 December 1948; *Express and Star*, 13 December 1948; *Daily Telegraph*, 15 December 1948; CCO, 1/7/279, Chapman-Walker to Hopkinson, 13 December, Hopkinson to Chapman-Walker, 15 December 1948.
50. Shepherd, 1994, pp. 54–5; CPA, CCO, 1/7/279, Ledingham to Thomas, 20 December 1948; Ledingham to Wightman, 12 February 1949; *WB.*
51. *Express and Star*, 18 December 1948; *Political Quarterly*, April-June 1953, p. 157; *Sunday Sun*, 2 January 1949; *Newcastle Journal*, 2 July 1949.
52. *Newcastle Journal*, 2 July 1949.
53. CPA, CRD, 2/44/4, 23 February 1949.
54. CPA, CRD, 2/53/5, Bremridge to Clarke, Hopkinson, 5 July 1949.
55. CPA, CCO, 1/7/279, August 1949.
56. *Wolverhampton Chronicle*, 27 January 1950.
57. *Listener*, 28 May 1981; Powell, 1973, pp. 3–4.

CHAPTER 5: STRAWS IN THE WIND

1. *WB.*
2. CPA, Powell's election address, February 1950; CCO 1/7/279, August 1949.
3. CPA, Powell's election address February 1950.
4. *WB*; CPA, Powell's election address, February 1950.
5. Shepherd, 1994, p. 57; CPA, Powell's election address, February 1950.
6. CPA, Powell's election address, February 1950.
7. The national swing from Labour to Conservative between 1945 and 1950 was 3.3 per cent. In the Black Country it was 2.7 per cent; *WB*; CPA, CCO, 2/1/6, Lindsay to Ledingham, 1950; the other seats were Bromsgrove and Stroud.
8. Hansard, 16 March 1950, col. 1315.

9. Hansard, 16 March 1950, cols. 1318–9.
10. Lord Hunt, *WB*.
11. Shepherd, 1994, pp. 61–2.
12. Shepherd, 1994, pp. 62–3.
13. Shepherd, 1994, p. 63.
14. *WB*; interview with Lord Carr.
15. *WB*.
16. *WB*; Powell's fellow rebels were Harry Legge-Bourke, Gerald Nabarro, Stephen McAdden, Arthur Vere Harvey and Sir John Mellor.
17. Hansard, 3 July 1950, col. 143.
18. *One Nation*, CPC, 1950, pp. 89–93.
19. *One Nation*, CPC, 1950, p. 16.
20. *One Nation*, CPC, 1950, pp. 27–38.
21. *Express and Star*, 5 October 1950.
22. Interviewed by Anne Brown, BBC Radio, 13 April 1986.
23. *Express and Star*, 5 and 11 January 1949; *Wolverhampton Chronicle*, 27 January 1950.
24. Interviewed by Anne Brown, BBC Radio, 13 April 1986; *Sunday Times*, 5 November 1995; *Daily Mail*, 8 November 1995; *Odd Man Out*, BBC 2 Television, 11 November 1995.
25. Interview with Barbara Hawkins and other contemporaries of Powell's in Wolverhampton; *Sunday Times*, 5 November 1995; *Daily Mail*, 8 November 1995.
26. Interview with Barbara Hawkins; Powell, 1990, p. 158; *Listener*, 28 May 1981.
27. Powell, 1990, p. x; interview with Barbara Hawkins and other contemporaries of Powell's in Wolverhampton; *Sunday Times*, 5 November 1995; *Daily Mail*, 8 November 1995.
28. Interview with Barbara Hawkins and other contemporaries of Powell's in Wolverhampton; *Sunday Times*, 5 November 1995; *Daily Mail*, 8 November 1995.
29. Powell, 1990, p. 173; interview with Barbara Hawkins; *Sunday Times*, 5 November 1995; *Daily Mail*, 8 November 1995; *Odd Man Out*, BBC 2 Television, 11 November 1995.
30. Powell, 'Theory and Practice', in Hunt, 1990, pp. 1–9.
31. Hansard, 19 February 1951, cols. 965–9.
32. *Express and Star*, 11 November 1950; *The Times*, 13 November 1950; *Daily Telegraph*, 14 November 1950; the party papers on the dispute are available at CPA, CCO 1/8/279.
33. CPA, CCO 1/8/279, Ledingham to Watson, 29 January 1951.
34. CPA, CCO 1/8/279, Ledingham to Watson, 29 January 1951.
35. CPA, CCO 1/8/279, memorandum, Graiseley ward to Wolverhampton South-West Conservative association, 18 September 1950; Ledingham to Watson, 29 January 1951.
36. CPA, CCO 1/8/279, Powell to Mills, 16 October; Ledingham to Conservative Central Office, 24 October 1950; Ledingham to Watson, 29 January 1951.
37. CPA, CCO 1/8/279, Ledingham to Watson, 29 January 1951; CCO 1/7/279, Ledingham's note, dated August 1949.
38. CPA, CCO 1/8/279, Thomas to Pierssene, Powell, 15 November 1950; Thomas to Woolton, 20 November 1950.
39. CPA, CCO 1/8/279, Ledingham to Central Office, 17 November 1950.
40. CPA, CCO 1/8/279, Ledingham to Central Office, 17 November; Thomas to Woolton, 13 December; Morrell to Powell 13 December; Thomas to Woolton, 18 December 1950.
41. CPA, CCO 1/8/279, Ledingham to Thomas, 3 January 1951.
42. CPA, CCO 1/8/279, Ledingham to Thomas, 20 January 1951; *Express and Star*, 20 January 1951.
43. CPA, CCO 1/8/279, Ledingham to Thomas, 27 January; Ledingham to Watson, 29 January 1951.
44. CPA, CCO 1/8/279, Ledingham to Central Office, 3 February 1951.
45. CPA, CCO 1/8/279, Ledingham to Central Office, 3 February; Powell to Beattie, 3 February; Ledingham to chief organization officer, 12 February; copy of letter from Bird, 13 February; Powell to Beattie, 25 February 1951.
46. CPA, CCO 1/8/279, May 1951.
47. Shepherd, 1994, pp. 66–7; minutes of the *One Nation* group.
48. *LP*.

49. House of Commons information service; *Hansard*, 9 April 1951, cols. 715–23; 9 July 1951, cols. 149–53; 1 March 1951, cols. 2289–90; *Express and Star*, 2 July 1951.
50. *Hansard*, 5 December 1950, cols. 295–302, 309.
51. CPA, CCO 4/4/324, Garmonsway to Thomas, 17 April; Thomas to Powell, 23 April 1951; Butler, Haverfordwest, 25 May; Powell to Thomas, 28 May 1951; Garmonsway to Thomas, 3 July 1951.
52. Roth, 1970, p. 74; *Hansard*, 14–15 February 1951; 26 April 1951, col. 701; *Express and Star*, 20 and 27 April, 1 May 1951.
53. *Hansard*, 16 April 1951, cols. 1607–9, 1616.
54. *Hansard*, 24 April 1951, col. 312; the Labour Government had taken powers to impose prescription charges in 1949; the 1951 Bill extended this principle; *Hansard*, 24 April 1951, cols. 311–4.
55. *Hansard*, 24 April 1951, col. 314.
56. Rodney Lowe, Institute of Historical Research seminar on Conservative welfare policy, 25 October 1995.
57. Shepherd, 1994, p. 67; *The Social Services: Needs and Means*, CPC, 1952, p. 5; *The Times*, 17 January 1952.
58. *The Social Services: Needs and Means*, CPC, 1952, p. 3.
59. *The Social Services: Needs and Means*, CPC, 1952, pp. 34–5.
60. *The Social Services: Needs and Means*, CPC, 1952, pp. 29–35.
61. *The Listener*, 14 February and 17 April 1952; Powell defined the three philosophies as being distinct from political parties, and wrote of the 'tory' philosophy. I have retained 'Tory', in keeping with normal usage.
62. *The Listener*, 17 April 1952.
63. *The Listener*, 17 April 1952.

CHAPTER 6: FOR QUEEN AND COUNTRY

1. The national swing to the Conservatives was 1.1 per cent (1.7 per cent in the Black Country). Labour polled 13.9 million votes against 13.7 million for the Tories, but the Conservatives won more seats.
2. *Express and Star*, 26 October 1951; Roth, 1970, pp. 82–3; CPA, Powell's election address, October 1951; Cosgrave, 1989, p. 83.
3. Conversations with contemporaries in Wolverhampton.
4. *Odd Man Out*, BBC 2 Television, 11 November 1995; Roth, 1970, p. 86; Shepherd, 1994, p. 44 (Macleod was speaking to the political journalist, Patrick Cosgrave).
5. *Express and Star*, 4 January and 29 March 1960; *Odd Man Out*, BBC 2 Television, 11 November 1995.
6. *Express and Star*, 2 January, 9 July and 21 August 1952, 4 January and 29 March 1960; Roth, 1970, p. 87; CPA, CCO, 1/11/276, constituency report, May 1956.
7. *Express and Star*, 6 December 1950; Roth, 1970, pp. 87–8; *Hansard*, 4 February 1952, col. 727; *Express and Star*, 18 February 1952.
8. CPA, CRD 2/23/10, Powell was elected on 14 November 1951; CRD 2/30/11, Powell attended meetings of the Conservative health committee, chaired by Macleod, about the additional NHS charges that resulted from the economic measures announced by the Chancellor, Rab Butler, on 29 January 1952.
9. *Hansard*, 27 March 1952, col. 856.
10. Shepherd, 1994, p. 77; Powell, interviewed about Macleod; *Hansard*, 27 March 1952.
11. Shepherd, 1994, pp. 73–4; Powell, interviewed about Macleod.
12. Shepherd, 1994, pp. 77–8; *Hansard*, 1 May 1952.
13. Interview with Lord Carr; Roth, 1970, pp. 92–3; Shepherd, 1994, p. 82; Powell, interviewed about Macleod; Roth, p. 93.
14. *Spectator*, 16 July 1965.
15. Roth, 1970, p. 94; CPA, 1922 Committee minute book, 12 June 1952; CRD 2/23/10, meeting of committee, 11 June 1952; ACP(53)21.
16. *Express and Star*, 1 August 1952; Roth, 1970, p. 93.

17. CPA, CCO, 4/4/324, CPO Wales to the Chairman, November 1951, claiming that the *News of the World* had received more letters on this subject than on any other; *Herald of Wales*, 3 November 1951; *Hansard*, 4 February 1952, col. 728.
18. Roth, 1970, p. 97.
19. Conservative Conference, Scarborough, 10 October 1952; *Hansard*, 17 November 1952, cols. 1436–44.
20. CPA, 1922 committee minute book, 11 November 1952; annual elections are held for the posts of chairman, two vice-chairmen, a treasurer, two secretaries and the twelve-strong executive committee; House of Commons information service; *Express and Star*, 6 December 1952, early 1953.
21. *Spectator*, 23 July 1988; Rhodes James, 1986, p. 354.
22. CPA, CRD 2/34/1, minutes of foreign affairs committee; Roth, 1970, p. 100.
23. *Hansard*, 5 December 1951, col. 2455; *Hansard*, 3 March 1953, cols. 239–48.
24. *Hansard*, 3 March 1953, cols. 242–3.
25. *Hansard*, 3 March 1953, cols. 245–6.
26. *Hansard*, 3 March 1953, cols. 246–7.
27. *Hansard*, 3 March 1953, cols. 247–8.
28. *Hansard*, 3 March 1953, col. 248; *New Statesman*, 7 March 1953.
29. *WB*; *LP*.
30. *LP*.
31. *Spectator*, 26 August 1955.
32. Roth, 1970, p. 104; CPA, CRD 2/34/1, meeting of 21 October 1953; *Hansard*, 5 November 1954, cols. 345–7; Amery diaries, 1988, 13–14 December 1953, p. 1064.
33. *Hansard*, 5 November 1954, cols. 348, 403.
34. *Economist*, 21 November and 12 December 1953; *Twentieth Century*, January 1954, pp. 10–21.
35. *Twentieth Century*, January 1954, p. 20; Rhodes James, 1986, pp. 375–84; Healey, *Twentieth Century*, February 1954, pp. 107, 117.
36. CPA, CRD 2/34/1, meeting of 2 December 1953; Powell was co-sponsor of an early day motion in December 1953; he also pressed Eden in the Commons, *Hansard*, 17 December 1953, col. 690; *Truth*, 5 March 1954, p. 299; Neguib was not definitely deposed until the autumn of 1954, Rhodes James, 1986, p. 383; *The Times*, 25 June 1954.
37. *Hansard*, 28 July 1954, cols. 495–7; these appeals were made at a meeting of the Conservative Services committee, 13 July 1954; the Cabinet approved production of a British H-Bomb on 28 July 1954 (the first H-Bomb had been exploded by the Americans in March 1953).
38. *LP*; *WB*; *Spectator*, 26 July 1986 and 31 August 1985; *The Times*, 13 October 1987.
39. CPA, Percy Cohen's unpublished 'History of the Conservative Party'; the lecture is re-printed in *Tradition and Change*, CPC Number 138, December 1954, pp. 41–53.
40. *Tradition and Change*, CPC Number 138, December 1954, pp. 41–2.
41. *Tradition and Change*, CPC Number 138, December 1954, pp. 41–3.
42. *Tradition and Change*, CPC Number 138, December 1954, pp. 44–5, 48–50; South Africa was not explicitly mentioned by Powell, but there is nothing to suggest that he is treating it as anything other than an old-style colony, akin to Australia and Canada, in keeping with prevailing British assumptions.
43. *Tradition and Change*, CPC Number 138, December 1954, pp. 49–50.
44. *Tradition and Change*, CPC Number 138, December 1954, pp. 45–7, 50–1.
45. *Tradition and Change*, CPC Number 138, December 1954, pp. 51–3.
46. *Tradition and Change*, CPC Number 138, December 1954, p. 53; Powell later modified his thesis on the inevitability of the collapse of European imperialism to incorporate wider economic and social change, see *Spectator*, 5 May 1979; *Listener*, 28 May 1981; *Spectator*, 23 July 1988.
47. *Tradition and Change*, CPC Number 138, December 1954, p. 53; Roth, 1970, p. 116; Lord Thorneycroft, *WB*.
48. *Time and Tide*, 9 February 1952.
49. Brittan, 1971, pp. 195–200; Cairncross, 1992, pp. 121–6; *Spectator*, 14 March 1987; Conservative Conference, Brighton, 9 October 1969; Lord Croham, *WB*; Hennessy, 1992, p. 215.
50. *WB*.

51. One Nation Group minutes; *Change Is Our Ally*, CPC, 1954, p. 7; this new book sold a disappointing 5,250 copies in the first month, compared with the 8,500 copies of *One Nation* over the same period, One Nation group minutes, 16 June 1954.
52. *Change Is Our Ally*, CPC, 1954, p. 7; Butler papers, H. 54. f. 32. Fraser to Butler, 1 May 1954.
53. *Change Is Our Ally*, CPC, 1954, pp. 47–55, 78–87, 62.
54. *Change Is Our Ally*, CPC, 1954, pp. 68–77, 96, 69.
55. *Change Is Our Ally*, CPC, 1954, p. 97.
56. Harris, 1972, p. 206; *Hansard*, 1 April 1954, col. 2213; *The Times*, 2 April 1954.
57. CPA, ACP 1/5, Powell to Fraser, 18 July 1954 (Powell should have written 'atheticize', which is derived from Greek and means to set aside, or invalidate); CRD 2/47/3, transcript of 'Straight from Conference', BBC Radio Light Programme, 7 October 1955.
58. *Hansard*, 9 July 1954, cols. 2540–44; *Spectator*, 23 July 1954; *Spectator*, 23 July, 15 October 1954.
59. CPA, ACP 3/2, ACP (53)21, ACP 54(29).
60. CPA, CRD, 2/30/12, minutes of health and social security committee, 5 May 1954.
61. *Hansard*, 16 November 1954, cols. 260–7; CPA, CRD 2/30/12, minutes of health and social security committee, 6 December 1954.
62. CPA, CRD 2/47/2 and 3, transcripts of 'Straight from Conference', BBC Radio Light Programme, 6–8 and 10–14 October 1955.
63. CPA, CRD 2/47/3, transcript of 'Straight from Conference', BBC Radio Light Programme, 12 October 1955.
64. Roberts was quoting from *Social Services: Needs and Means*; CPA, CRD 2/47/3, transcript of 'Straight from Conference', BBC Radio Light Programme, 12 October 1955.
65. CPA, CRD 2/47/3, transcript of 'Straight from Conference', BBC Radio Light Programme, 12 October 1955.

CHAPTER 7: REACHING THE DESPATCH BOX

1. *Economist*, 25 December 1954.
2. The re-shuffle had been occasioned by Oliver Lyttelton's retirement as Colonial Secretary and Sir Thomas Dugdale's resignation over the Crichel Down affair; Butler papers, RAB G.28, f.47, Macleod to Butler, 20 July 1954; CPA, 1922 committee minute book, 25 February 1954; the Crichel Down case involved the failure of civil servants to expedite the return of land requisitioned in wartime to its previous owners.
3. CPA, CCO 150/3/2/1–4, RSG meeting of 13 April 1954; Butler papers, RAB G.28, f.47, Macleod to Butler, 20 July 1954.
4. CPA, ACP 2, ACP(55) 21st meeting, 1 September 1954.
5. Quoted in Michael Cockerell's 'The Market-place Romantic', *The Times*, 11 November 1995; conversations with Powell's former Wolverhampton acquaintances.
6. Conversations with Powell's former Wolverhampton acquaintances.
7. Butler and Sloman, 1980, p. 327; *Daily Mail*, 24 June 1993.
8. *Daily Telegraph*, 16 February 1967; CPA, CCO 4/6/151, West Midlands area meeting, 19 November 1955.
9. *World Perspectives*, CPC, London, 195, p. 39.
10. CPA, CRD 2/47/3, transcript of 'Straight from Conference', BBC Radio Light Programme, 6 October 1955.
11. CPA, CRD 2/44/1. Powell sometimes attended the Tory Home Office committee, although whether he attended the discussion on hanging on 9 February 1955 is not clear; *Express and Star*, 15 February 1955; *Spectator*, 16 July 1965.
12. *Hansard*, 4 February 1955, col. 1479; the Clean Air Bill had not completed its passage through parliament when the election was called in May 1955, but a successor became law during the 1955–56 session.
13. *Hansard*, 15 February 1955, cols. 232–40; *The Times*, 5 March 1955.
14. CPA, Powell's election address, May 1955; Roth, 1970, p. 121.

15. The broadcasts on the House of Lords were reprinted in the *Listener; Express and Star*, 31 August and October 1955; CPA, ACP 2, ACP(55) 25th meeting, 11 November 1955; the TUC had rejected such a proposal, made by their president, Geddes.

16. *Express and Star*, 3 November 1955; CPA, 1922 Committee minute book, 10 and 17 November 1955.

17. CPA, CRD 2/23/12, housing, local government and public works committee, 13 July 1955; Short, 1982, p. 49; *United for Peace and Progress*, Conservative and Unionist Central Office, 1955.

18. CPA, CRD 2/23/10–11, minutes of housing, local government and public works committee, 1951–55; Roth, 1970, p. 109.

19. *Hansard*, 30 November 1953, cols. 886–93; CPA, CRD 2/23/11, housing and local government committee, 18 and 25 November 1953, 19 May 1954; CCO 150/3/2/1–4, RSG meeting of 22 June 1954.

20. The sorry saga is expertly analysed by Dunleavy, 1981 – in particular, see p. 166, citing Ministry of Housing circulars 99/51 and 65/52; CPA, CRD 2/23/10, housing and local government committee, 11 February 1953; Central Office estimated that 'overspill' was putting seven Tory seats at risk and was consolidating Labour's hold on three marginals, 16 December 1953.

21. CPA, CRD 2/23/10, housing and local government committee, 21 January 1953.

22. CPA, CRD 2/23/10, housing and local government committee, 9 November 1955.

23. *Spectator*, 13 January 1990; *One Nation*, p. 26. The warning occurred in the chapter on population, and not in Powell's chapter on housing; CPA, CRD 2/23/10, housing and local government committee, 18 February 1953.

24. CPA, CRD, 2/23/12, housing and local government committee, 13 July and 3 November 1955; Short, 1982, p. 51.

25. *Hansard*, 17 November 1955, cols. 796–7; Dunleavy, 1981, pp. 159–65.

26. CPA, CRD 2/23/12, housing and local government committee, 9 and 16 November 1955.

27. CPA, CRD 2/23/12, housing and local government committee, 3 and 9 November 1955.

28. CPA, CRD 2/23/12, housing and local government committee, 16 November 1955; *Hansard*, 21 November 1955, cols. 1079–90.

29. *Hansard*, 21 November 1955, cols. 1079–80.

30. *LP*.

31. *Express and Star*, 21 and 24 December 1955; *Wolverhampton Chronicle*, 30 December 1955.

32. *Express and Star*, 2 January 1956 and 27 September 1956.

33. *Express and Star*, 6 February 1956.

34. *Express and Star*, 6 February 1956.

35. *Hansard*, 25 January 1956, col. 223 and 228.

36. *Hansard*, 1 February 1956, cols. 929–34; February 1956, col. 2370.

37. *Hansard*, 31 January 1956, cols. 831–2, 864.

38. Dunleavy, 1981, p. 163, 39.

39. Roth, 1970, p. 143; *Hansard*, 28 March 1956, cols. 2161–2, 10 April 1956, cols. 132, 150.

40. Conversations with and letters from officials of the Ministry of Housing and Local Government; Roth, conversation with Colonel Kenneth Post, 18 December 1995.

41. Conversations with and letters from officials of the Ministry of Housing and Local Government.

42. Conversations with and letters from officials of the Ministry of Housing and Local Government; Roth, 1970, p. 141.

43. *Express and Star*, 1 September 1956.

44. *Express and Star*, 21 May 1956; Whitehouse, 1982, p. 37.

45. Whitehouse, 1982, p. 37.

46. *WB*.

47. *WB*; conversation with Colonel Kenneth Post, 18 December 1995; *Spectator*, 26 July 1986.

48. In 1956 there were an estimated 14.3 million houses or flats in Britain, of which 4.6 million were owner-occupied; 3.2 were council houses; and 6.5 million were privately rented; CPA, CRD 2/23/3, brief of 8 November 1956; CPA, CRD 2/23/10–12, minutes of housing, local government and public works committee, 1951–56.

49. Macmillan, 6 March 1952, cited in brief, 5 November 1952, CPA, CRD 2/24/1; Timmins, 1995, p. 188; CPA, CRD 2/24/3.

50. CPA, CRD 2/24/3, quoted in brief of 8 November 1956.
51. *LP*.
52. *Hansard*, 6 November 1956, cols. 97–104.
53. CPA, CRD 2/23/12, housing and local government committee, 20 November 1956.
54. *Hansard*, 21 November 1956, cols. 1759–60.
55. *Hansard*, 21 November 1956, cols. 1761–4.
56. *Hansard*, 21 November 1956, col. 1765.
57. *Daily Telegraph*, 25 June 1957.
58. Short, 1982, pp. 177–8; CPA, CRD 2/23/12, housing and local government committee, 20 November 1956; *Hansard*, 21 November 1956, col. 1768; Timmins, 1995, pp. 189–90.
59. CPA, Minute book of the 1922 Committee, meeting of 22 November 1956; Horne, 1988, p. 455; *Spectator*, 3 April 1982; Howard, 1987, p. 241.
60. Shepherd, 1991, pp. 146–8; Roth, 1970, p. 159.

CHAPTER 8: AT ODDS WITH MACMILLAN'S COURT

1. CPA, CRD 2/53/24–8, Policy Study Group papers.
2. Speech to the Salisbury Group, 12 October 1987.
3. Speech to the Salisbury Group, 12 October 1987; *Spectator*, 3 April 1982.
4. CPA, CRD 2/53/28, PSG 3rd meeting, 1 April 1957; *Spectator*, 1 March 1980, 10 January 1987.
5. *Spectator*, 1 March 1980, 3 April 1982.
6. *Spectator*, 16 April 1981, 14 March 1987; Dickinson, 1979, pp. 91–2; Speck, 1977, pp. 4–7.
7. Dickinson, 1979, pp. 163–92; Speck, 1977, pp. 222–6.
8. CPA, CRD 2/53/26, Macleod meetings with Fraser, 18 January and 7 February 1957; CRD 2/53/25, Powell to Macleod, circulated 13 February 1957. CRD 2/53/ 28, PSG 5th meeting, 6 May 1957.
9. CPA, CRD 2/53/25, Powell to Macleod, circulated 13 February 1957.
10. CPA, CRD 2/53/25, Powell to Macleod, circulated 13 February 1957.
11. CPA, CRD 2/53/25, Powell to Macleod, circulated 13 February 1957; CRD 2/53/24, PSG 1st meeting, 15 February 1957; CRD 2/53/28, PSG 7th meeting, 3 June 1957.
12. CPA, CRD 2/53/25, Powell to Macleod, circulated 13 February 1957; CRD 2/53/24, PSG 1st meeting, 15 February 1957.
13. CPA, CRD 2/53/26, Powell, The National Insurance Scheme, 21 February 1957; Lowe, 1996 (forthcoming).
14. CPA, CRD 2/53/26, Powell, The National Insurance Scheme, 21 February 1957; Lowe, 1996 (forthcoming).
15. Crossman 1981, diary entry of 3 May 1957; CPA, CRD 2/53/28, PSG 6th meeting, 31 May 1957.
16. CPA, CRD 2/53/25, Powell to Macleod, circulated 13 February 1957.
17. Horne, 1989, p. 4; Brittan, 1971, pp. 203–7.
18. Wolverhampton, 9 January 1958; Lord Thorneycroft, *WB*.
19. House of Commons information service; *Express and Star*, 9 October 1957.
20. Turner, 1994, p. 227; PRO, T 230/408, Thorneycroft minutes, 14, 16 and 18 January 1957; T 227/ 1116, Powell, Vosper and officials meeting, 15 January 1957; T 227/485, Treasury minute 18 January 1957.
21. PRO, CAB 129/85, C(57)20, Boyd-Carpenter, 30 January 1957.
22. *Hansard*, 19 February 1957, cols. 209–12.
23. The committee stage of the Finance Bill was first taken upstairs in 1968; Brittan, 1971, p. 210; Turner, 1994, p. 230; *Hansard*, 9 April 1957, cols. 1302–17; *Economist*, 20 April 1957.
24. CPA, CRD, 2/53/28, PSG, 5th meeting, 6 May 1957.
25. CPA, CRD, 2/53/28, PSG, 9th meeting, 15 July 1957; Horne, 1989, pp. 64–5; Turner, 1994, pp. 227–8.
26. *Express and Star*, 3 and 7 June 1957, 27 August 1957.
27. *Sunday Times*, 11 May 1986.
28. Dow, 1965, p. 67; Fforde, 1992, p. 656; Cairncross, 1992, pp. 96–7.

29. *WB*.
30. Charles Kennedy, 'Monetary Policy', in Worswick and Adey, 1962, p. 318; Powell, 'Is Bigger Public Spending Really Necessary', in *The Banker*, March 1959.
31. PRO, Prime Minister (PREM), Cabinet (CAB) and Treasury (T) files for 1957–58.
32. Macleod claimed that the Chancellor was 'obsessed and dominated by Powell', Shepherd, 1994, p. 133; *WB*; Charles Kennedy, 'Monetary Policy', in Worswick and Adey, 1962, p. 318; Brittan, 1971, p. 164.
33. Lord Thorneycroft, *WB*.
34. Shepherd, 1994, pp. 108–9, 122–6.
35. Brittan, 1971, pp. 215–6; PRO, PREM 11/2878, 11/3125, Macleod to Macmillan, 27 April 1957; CAB 128/31, CC(57)55th, 19 July 1957.
36. Robert Hall, 1991, diary entry, 18 December 1957; Powell, 1960, p. 8.
37. PRO, CAB 128/31, CC(57)2nd, 21 January 1957; T 233/1369, Makins to Powell, 15 July 1957.
38. PRO, T 233/1369, Thorneycroft to Macmillan, 27 May 1957; Fraser to Hall, Hall to Fraser, 18 July 1957.
39. PRO, CAB 128/31, CC(57)55th, 19 July 1957.
40. PRO, T 233/1369, Thorneycroft to Macmillan, 30 July 1957.
41. PRO, T 233/1369, Thorneycroft to officials, 7 August 1957.
42. PRO, T 233/2369, Thorneycroft to Macmillan, 30 July 1957; PREM 11/2306, Macmillan to ministers, 10 August 1957; Lowe, 1993, pp. 518–9.
43. Roth, 1971, p. 176.
44. Robert Hall, 1991, diary entries, 22 October 1957, 27 August 1957; a new system of 'special deposits' was eventually introduced in 1958 to enable the authorities to reduce bank liquidity, Fforde, 1992, p. 690.
45. PRO, PREM 11/1824, CAB 129/88, C(57)194, Macmillan memorandum, 1 September 1957.
46. Robert Hall, 1991, diary entry, 22 October 1957; PRO, PREM 11/1824, CAB 129/88, C(57)195, Thorneycroft memorandum, 7 September 1957.
47. PRO, PREM 11/1824, CAB 129/88, C(57)195, Thorneycroft memorandum, 7 September 1957.
48. PRO, CAB 128/31, CC(57)66th, 10 September 1957; CC(57)68th, 17 September 1957; Turner, 1994, p. 233.
49. Quoted in Horne, 1989, p. 76.
50. Robert Hall, 1991, diary entry, 27 August 1957; *The Times*, 20 September 1957; Fforde, 1992, p. 690; Brittan, 1971, p. 212.
51. PRO, CAB 128/31, CC(57)66th, 10 September 1957; Brittan, 1979, pp. 216–7.
52. Report of the Parker Tribunal.
53. Conservative Conference, Brighton 10 October 1957.
54. *Express and Star*, 5 October 1957; *Express and Star*, 16 November 1957.
55. *Hansard*, 13 November 1957, cols. 1088–90, 19 November 1957, col. 217.
56. PRO, C(57)225, Macmillan memorandum, 5 October 1957.
57. PRO, T 233/1459, Padmore minute, 5 December 1957; Robert Hall, 1991, diary entry, 18 December 1957.
58. PRO, T 233/1459, Powell to Thorneycroft, 6 December 1957; Treasury minutes, 6 December 1957; Lord Croham, *WB*.
59. Lowe, 1993, pp. 518–9.
60. PRO, T 233/1459, Thorneycroft minute, 9 December 1957; Robert Hall, 1991, diary entry, 18 December 1957; CAB 130/139, GEN 625, 1st meeting, 11 December 1957.
61. PRO, T 233/1459, Powell to Thorneycroft, 16 December 1957.
62. PRO, T 233/1459, Powell to Thorneycroft, 16 December 1957; draft paper, 17 December 1957; Robert Hall, 1991, diary entry, 18 December 1957.
63. PRO, CAB 128/32, CC(58)1st, 3rd January 1958; Lowe, 1993, p. 517; CPA, election address of J. Enoch Powell, Conservative candidate for Wolverhampton South-West, May 1955.
64. *Hansard*, 11 April 1957, col. 1308; Robert Hall, 1991, diary entry, 30 December 1957.
65. Lord Sherfield, *WB*.

66. PRO, T 233/1459, Treasury minute, 1 January 1958; CAB 130/139, GEN 625, 2nd meeting, 23 December 1957; Horne, 1989, p. 71.
67. PRO, CAB 129/90, C(57)295, Thorneycroft, 27 December 1957.
68. PRO, CAB 128/32, CC(57)86th, 31 December 1957.
69. PRO, T 233/1459, Powell minute of ministerial group, 1 January 1958.
70. PRO, CAB 130/139, GEN 625, 3rd and 4th meetings, 1 and 2 January 1958; T 233/1459, Powell minute, 2 January 1958; Lamb, 1995, p. 49.
71. PRO, CAB 128/32, CC(58)1st, 3 January 1958.
72. Lord Boyd-Carpenter, *WB*; PRO, CAB 128/32, CC(58)1st, 3 January 1958.
73. Robert Hall, 1991, diary entry, 8 January 1958
74. PRO, CAB 128/32, CC(58)2nd, 3 January 1958; Boyd-Carpenter, 1980, p. 139.
75. PRO, CAB 128/32, CC(58)3rd, 5 January 1958; PREM 11/2306, Macleod to Macmillan, 5 January 1968.
76. Lord Sherfield, *WB*; Cockett, 1994, p. 165; *WB*; Lord Thorneycroft, *WB*.
77. Egremont, 1968, pp. 178–9; Lord Sherfield, *WB*.
78. Lord Sherfield, *WB*; Robbins, 1971, p. 233; Brittan, 1971, p. 156.
79. Sir Edward Heath, *WB*.
80. *Hansard*, 23 January 1958, cols. 1294–97; Robert Hall Diaries, 1991, diary entry, 30 January 1958.
81. *Express and Star*, 10 January 1958.
82. *Express and Star*, 10 January 1958.
83. *WB*.
84. Horne, 1989, pp. 78–9; Sir Edward Heath, *WB*; Lord Sherfield, *WB*.
85. PRO, CAB 130/139 and 128/32, January 1958. Mark Jarvis drew this to my attention at a seminar of the Institute of Historical Research, 17 January 1996.
86. Horne, 1989, pp. 78–9.
87. *WB*; Robert Hall Diaries, 1991, 8 January 1958.
88. Dow, 1964, p. 200–3; Brittan, 1971, pp. 219–21; Cairncross, 1992, p. 111; PRO, PREM 11/2311, Heathcoat Amory to Macmillan, 23 October 1958, with Macmillan's scrawled insults in red ink, including his comments that it was a 'very bad paper' and could have been written by 'Mr Neville Chamberlain's ghost'. Powell was amused to be shown this paper in July 1993.
89. *Spectator*, 24 April 1971; *WB*; Horne, 1989, p. 76.
90. Butler papers, G 32, notes for a speech, 7 January 1958; *Spectator*, 24 April 1971.
91. *WB*.
92. The seminar and lunch were held on 29 January 1981.
93. *Spectator*, 24 April 1971; *WB*.

CHAPTER 9: 'COMING HOME TO MOTHER'

1. *Sunday Express*, 15 September 1959; Maudling joined the Cabinet as Paymaster-General in September 1959.
2. *Express and Star*, 6 February 1958; private information.
3. *LP*; *Listener*, 20 November 1958.
4. *Hansard*, 12 February 1958, col. 436.
5. *Hansard*, 12 February 1958, col. 437.
6. *Hansard*, 12 February 1958, col. 437–41.
7. *The Times*, 7 November 1958; private information.
8. *Express and Star*, 5 April 1958 and 19 June 1959.
9. Interview with John Biffen; Howe, 1994, p.31; see for example, *The Banker*, 1959.
10. Lord Harris of High Cross, *WB*.
11. *Hansard*, 16 April 1958, cols. 214–9.
12. Reprinted as 'Tradition and Change: Contributions to the Future of the Welfare State', March 1958, CPC; *Express and Star*, 23 April 1958; CPA, CRD 2/53/28, Policy Study Group, second meeting, 15 March 1957.

13. *Daily Telegraph*, 9 June 1958.
14. *Daily Mail*, 29 March 1958; *Daily Telegraph*, 7 July 1958.
15. *Express and Star*, 7 July 1958; Oxford, 20 September 1958; *Express and Star*, 5 November 1958.
16. *WB*; interview with John Biffen.
17. Foot, 1969, pp. 32–3.
18. PRO, CAB 134/1210, Cabinet committee on Colonial Immigrants, second meeting, 25 April 1956.
19. CPA, CRD, 2/53/28, Policy Study Group, 10th meeting, 1 August 1957.
20. Roth, 1970, p. 208.
21. Foot, 1969, p. 35; Roth, 1970, pp. 210–1.
22. *Hansard*, 20 January 1959, col. 99; *Express and Star*, 17–18 February 1959.
23. CPA, CRD 2/53/24, Macleod to Powell, 19 February, Powell to Macleod, 27 February 1959.
24. CPA, CRD 2/53/28, Policy Study Group, 1 August 1957.
25. CPA, CRD 2/53/28, Policy Study Group, 1 August and 11 November 1957.
26. Rodney Lowe, Institute of Historical Research seminar, 25 October 1995; and in M. Francis et al., 1996.
27. *Hansard*, 8 April 1959, cols. 252–6.
28. CPA, CRD 2/27/16, 15 July 1959; Shepherd, 1994, pp. 155, 159.
29. *WB*; Roth, 1970, pp. 213–4.
30. *Hansard*, 27 July 1959, col. 234–7; *LP*.
31. *LP*.
32. *LP*; *Hansard*, 27 July 1959, col. 236.
33. *Hansard*, 27 July 1959, col. 237.
34. *WB*.
35. Berkeley, 1977, p. 67; *LP*.
36. Shepherd, 1994, p. 159.
37. CPA, Powell's election address, 15 September 1959.
38. CPA, Powell's election address, 15 September 1959.
39. CPA, Powell's election address, 15 September 1959.
40. CPA, Powell's election address, 15 September 1959; Conservative manifesto, October 1959.
41. Foot, 1969, pp. 35–7; Roth, 1970, p. 220.
42. *Express and Star*, 6 May 1959; Butler and Rose, 1960, pp. 202–40.
43. *Express and Star*, 22 October 1959; as Chief Whip, Heath was not a member of the Cabinet, although he attended its meetings.
44. *Daily Telegraph*, 22 October 1959; *Hansard*, 28 October 1959, col. 330.
45. CPA, 1922 Committee minute book, 12 November 1959; *The Times*, 19 November 1959.
46. *Financial Times*, 7 January 1960; 18 February 1960; speech to Hitchin Young Conservatives, *Express and Star*, 23 November 1959; quoted in Roth, 1970, p. 223.
47. *Hansard*, 7 April 1960, cols. 613–21.
48. *Spectator*, 20 February 1988.
49. *Crossbow*, April 1960.

CHAPTER 10: ARCH-PLANNER

1. PRO, PREM 11/3438, Macmillan to Powell, 1 August 1960.
2. *Observer*, 5 February 1961.
3. Roth, 1970, p. 232; Plowden Report on *Control of Public Expenditure*, Cmnd 1432, HMSO, 1961.
4. Klein, 1989, p. 66; *Spectator*, 20 February 1988.
5. *Spectator*, 20 February 1988.
6. *Spectator*, 18 July 1970.
7. *Observer*, 5 February 1961; note by Bryan Rayner, Powell's private office, 1960–62.
8. *Spectator*, 20 February 1988.
9. *Spectator*, 20 February 1988; *Independent Magazine*, 14 January 1995.
10. Powell, 1966, p. pp. 14–16.

11. Powell, 1966, p. 69.
12. CPA, CRD 2/30/14, Conservative health and social security committee, 15 November 1960; PRO, CAB 130/160, GEN 677, 14 July 1959, .
13. Over 170 Tory MPs had signed an early day motion on the issue; PRO, CAB 134/34, CC(60)15th, 8 March 1960; CPA, CRD 2/30/14, Conservative health and social security committee, 15 November 1960.
14. PRO, PREM 11/3438, Powell to Macmillan, 20 August 1960; CAB 134/1980, HA(60)19th, 22 September 1960; CAB 128/34, CC(60)53rd, 6 October 1960 (Powell's first Cabinet attendance had been at that day's morning meeting).
15. Conservative Conference, Scarborough, 15 October 1960.
16. PRO, PREM 11/3438; CAB 128/34, CC(60)56th, 27 October 1960; CPA, CRD 2/30/14, Conservative health and social security committee, 15 November 1960.
17. CPA, CRD 2/30/14, Conservative health and social security committee, 15 November 1960.
18. CPA, CRD 2/30/14, Conservative health and social security committee, 15 and 29 November 1960.
19. Powell, 1966, pp. 68–70.
20. CPA, CRD 2/30/14, Conservative health and social security committee, 29 November 1960.
21. CPA, CRD 2/30/14, Conservative health and social security committee, 29 November 1960; Llandudno, 28 October 1960.
22. Conservative election manifesto, October 1959; PRO, CAB 134/2533, Amory, SS(60)5, 9 January 1960.
23. Powell, 1966, p. 14; PRO, CAB, 129/102, C(60)150, 14 October 1960.
24. PRO, CAB 129/103, C(60)151, 17 October 1960; PREM 11/3438, Macleod to Macmillan, 18 October 1960; PREM 11/3438, briefs on C(60)148, 150, 151, 17 October 1960; CAB 128/34, CC(60)54th, 55th and 56th, 18, 25 and 27 October 1960.
25. PRO, CAB 129/102, C(60)150, 14 October 1960; Bridgen and Lowe (forthcoming); I am grateful to Charles Webster for drawing information in this section to my attention.
26. PRO, CAB 134/1983, HA(60)177, 13 December 1960; CAB 134/1980, HA(60)25th, 16 December 1960; PREM 11/3438, report for Macmillan, 16 December 1960; CAB 129/103, C(60)193, 19 December 1960; CAB 128/34, CC(60)65th, 21 December 1960; Butler papers, G 36, Butler to Macmillan, 16 December 1960; Bridgen and Lowe (forthcoming); the final package was subject to minor amendments – PRO, CAB 128/35, CC(61)3rd, 31 January 1961; *Evening Standard*, 28 November and 5 December 1960.
27. Klein, 1989, pp, 73–4; Bridgen and Lowe (forthcoming); PRO, MH 90/83, Powell to RHB chairmen, 20 December 1960; PREM 11, Capital Expenditure on Hospitals, 1954–62.
28. CPA, CRD 2/29/8, meeting on 12 January 1961.
29. *Spectator*, 20 February 1988; CPA, CRD 2/30/11, Conservative health and social security committee, 2 December 1953.
30. *The Times*, 18 January 1961; PRO, HM(61)4, 17 January 1961; *Hansard*, written answer, 25 January 1961, cols. 33–6; Bridgen and Lowe (forthcoming).
31. *The Times*, 18 and 25 January 1961.
32. *Hansard*, 1 February 1961, col. 987; Powell's first Commons' appearance as Minister of Health was on 25 October 1960; the second reading of the Human Tissues Bill was held on 20 December 1960.
33. *Hansard*, 1 February 1961, cols. 987–89.
34. *Hansard*, 1 February 1961, cols. 980–90; debates relating to the 1961 NHS measures were held in the Commons on 3, 8, 15 and 23 February; and 6, 9, 13 and 29 March.
35. CPA, CRD 2/30/15, Conservative health and social security committee, 7 February 1961; *Daily Telegraph*, 8 February 1961.
36. *Hansard*, 8 February 1961, cols. 406–44.
37. *Observer*, 5 February 1961; *Hansard*, 8 February 1961, cols. 426–44, 506–16.
38. *New Statesman*, 17 September 1960, p. 366; Crossman, 1981, diary entry of 21 February 1961; *Sunday Times*, 12 February 1961; the Rent Bill was guillotined after Powell had left the Ministry of Housing; *Sunday Telegraph*, 5 February 1961.
39. PRO, CAB 128/36 (62)46th, 12 July 1962; Selwyn Lloyd's 'little budget' was announced on 25 July 1961.

40. PRO, T, 298/115, Powell to Selwyn Lloyd, 16 September 1961. I am grateful to Rodney Lowe for drawing this to my attention.
41. PRO, T, 298/115, Powell to Selwyn Lloyd, 16 September 1961, note by Clarke, 22 September 1961.
42. Bridgen and Lowe (forthcoming); *The Times*, 24 January 1962.
43. CPA, CRD 2/30/15, Conservative health and social security committee, 25 January 1962; Powell made similar claims in the Commons, *Hansard*, 4 June 1962, cols. 151–2.
44. PRO, CAB 134/1985, 1988; HA(610)48; Bridgen and Lowe (forthcoming); CPA, CRD 2/30/15, Conservative health and social security committee, 10 July 1961; PRO, CAB 16/8/14/6–7.
45. *Hansard*, 8 February 1961, col. 429; PRO, CAB 134/1988.
46. I am grateful to Paul Bridgen for drawing this to my attention.
47. CPA, CRD 2/30/15, Conservative health and social security committee, 30 April 1963; television archive of 1963, included in *Odd Man Out*, BBC Television, 11 November 1995.
48. *Hansard*, 4 June 1964, cols. 151–60; Timmins, 1995, pp. 209–10.
49. *WB*; CPA, Selsdon weekend papers, 30 January – 1 February 1970.
50. *WB*.
51. Departmental Committee on Medical Manpower, 1955; CPA, CRD 2/30/15, Conservative health and social security committee, 26 March 1962.
52. PRO, PREM 11/3238, Sir Norman Brook to Macmillan, 24 November 1960.
53. PRO, CAB 134/1469, CCM(61)2nd, 17 May 1961; Walker, 1977, p. 51.
54. PRO, CAB 134/1469, CCM(61)1, 11 January 1961.
55. PRO, CAB 134/1469, CCM(61)1st, 16 February 1961, CCM(61)7, 11 April 1961.
56. PRO, CAB 134/1469, CCM(61)7, 11 April 1961.
57. PRO, CAB 134/1469, CCM(61)7, 11 April 1961; CCM(61)10.
58. PRO, CAB 134/1469, CCM(61)10.
59. PRO, CAB 134/1469, CCM(61)2nd, 17 May 1961; 31 July 1961.
60. PRO, CAB 134/1469, 31 July 1961.

CHAPTER 11: HUMANIZING THE NHS

1. Conservative conference, Scarborough, October 1960.
2. Speech to the National Association for Mental Health, 9 March 1961.
3. *Consequences*, BBC Radio 4, January 1996.
4. Professor Kathleen Jones, interviewed on 'Consequences', BBC Radio Four, January 1996; Murphy, 1991, pp. 57–8; CPA, CRD 2/30/15, Conservative health and social security committee, 2 December 1953.
5. Murphy, 1991, pp. 58–60; *The Welfare State*, 1961, CPC.
6. Murphy, 1991, p. 58; 'Consequences', BBC Radio Four, January 1996.
7. Timmins, 1995, pp. 212–22; Titmuss, 1968, pp. 104–9; *Sunday Telegraph*, 29 October 1961.
8. CPA, CRD 2/30/15, Conservative health and social security committee, 25 January 1962; Cmnd 1973, HMSO, 1963; CPA, CRD 2/30/15, Conservative health and social security committee, 30 April 1963, 13 November 1962.
9. *Evening Standard*, 13 July 1993.
10. I am grateful to Charles Webster for drawing this to my attention.
11. 'Consequences', BBC Radio Four, January 1996.
12. Speech at Broadmoor, 27 June 1963.
13. *The Times*, April–July 1961; CPA, CRD 2/30/15, Conservative health and social security committee, 24 July 1962.
14. CPA, CRD 2/30/15, Conservative health and social security committee, 25 January 1962.
15. *Hansard*, 10 December 1962, col. 26; PRO, CAB 128/36, CC(62)73, 6 December 1962; C(62)198, 3 December 1962; *Express and Star*, 24 September 1963.
16. *Smoking and Health*, report by the Royal College of Physicians, 1962; interviewed by Quentin Crewe in the *Daily Mail*.

17. Interviewed by Quentin Crewe in the *Daily Mail*; PRO, CAB 128/36, 6 and 8 March, 12 July 1962; CAB 130/185, GEN 762–3, 1962–64; *Hansard*, 12 March 1962.
18. Evans, 1983, p. 58; CPA, CRD 2/30/15, Conservative health and social security committee, 24 July 1962.
19. CPA, CRD 2/30/15, Conservative health and social security committee, 24 July 1962; Lord Cohen was Professor of Medicine at the University of Liverpool and President of the General Medical Council.
20. CPA, CRD 2/30/15, Conservative health and social security committee, 24 July 1962; Evans, 1983, pp. 72–3.
21. CPA, CRD 2/30/15, Conservative health and social security committee, 30 April 1963.
22. PRO, PREM 11/3438, Macmillan to Powell, 1 August 1960.
23. I am grateful to Charles Webster for this information.
24. *The Times*, 16 May 1961.
25. The Senate inquiry was chaired by Senator Estes Kefauver; Inglis, 1965, pp. 11–2, 14–5, 30–6, 120–2; Reports from the Committee of Public Accounts, session 1961–62 (HMSO, 1962); *Hansard*, 6 December 1962, cols. 1511–946.
26. Speech to the Association of the British Pharmaceutical Industry, 27 April 1961.
27. *The Times*, 18 May 1961.
28. Inglis, 1965, pp. 9–11.
29. Evans, 1981, p. 264 – Powell had been suggested as a chief of staff by Macleod and Oliver Poole, the former party chairman; *Sunday Express*, 2 April 1961.
30. *Express and Star*, 10 March 1962.
31. Selwyn Lloyd's 'little budget' was announced on 25 July 1962. A pay 'pause' was announced in the public sector, and the Chancellor invited the private sector to follow suit; PRO, CAB 128/36, CC(62)49th, 24 July 1962.
32. *Spectator*, 20 February 1988; CPA, CRD 2/30/15, minutes of the Tory committee.
33. PRO, T. 214/1295, Powell to the Treasury, 2 January 1962; Fraser to Sir Frank Lee, 2 January 1962.
34. PRO, CAB 134/2568, WN(62)1st, 8 January 1962; WN (62) 5th, 21 February 1962.
35. *Hansard*, 12 March 1962, questions to Minister of Health.
36. CPA, CRD 2/52/9, Chairman's Committee meeting, 19 March 1962.
37. CPA, CRD 2/30/15, Conservative health and social security committee, 26 March 1962.
38. *The Times*, 28 March 1962, April 1962; Roth, 1970, p. 267.
39. PRO, PREM 11/5203, Powell to Macmillan, 10 April 1962; CPA, CCO 20/8/5, Macleod to Macmillan, 27 April 1962.
40. PRO, PREM 11/3745, brief for Macmillan, 2 May 1962; CAB 134/2568, WN(62)18th, 9 May 1962; CAB 128/36, CC(62)32nd, 10 May 1962; *The Times*, 8 May 1962.
41. PRO, CAB 134/2568, WN(62)18th, 9 May 1962; CAB 128/36, CC(62)32nd, 10 May 1962; *Hansard*, 14 May 1962.
42. *Daily Telegraph*, 15 May 1962; *The Times*, 21 May 1962.
43. PRO, CAB 134/2568, WN(62)21st, 4 June 1962, WN(62)37th, 19 December 1962; PREM 11/5203, Powell to Macmillan, 13 June 1962; Industrial Court – award 2931, 3 September 1962; CPA, CRD 2/30/15, Conservative health and social security committee, 18 December 1962.
44. Powell, 1966, pp. 3–5.
45. CPA, CRD 2/52/8, 'Social Policy', note by Powell, 7 March 1962; CRD 2/52/9, Chairman's Committee meeting, 19 March 1962.
46. *Observer*, 5 February 1961.

CHAPTER 12: A DIFFICULT HORSE

1. PRO, PREM 11/3930, transcript of 28 May 1962.
2. Speech to Oxford Conservatives, 2 October 1961; PRO, PREM 11/3930, transcript of 28 May 1962.
3. PRO, PREM 11/3930, transcript of 28 May 1962.
4. *Spectator*, 1 March 1980.

5. *PM*; *Sunday Times*, 15 July 1962.
6. Horne, 1989, pp. 72, 541; *Spectator*, 3 April 1982; *WB*.
7. Hennessy, 1995, p. 82; *Spectator*, 3 April 1982; Lord Home, *PM*.
8. PRO, CAB 129/113, C(63)82, paper by Powell, 14 May 1963; CAB 128/37, CC(63)32nd, 16 May 1963.
9. Cairncross, 1991, pp. 146–8.
10. Roth, 1970, p. 256.
11. *WB*.
12. *WB*.
13. Ian Davidson, quoting Sir Frank Lee's advice to the Macmillan Cabinet in 1960, *Financial Times*, 17 April 1996.
14. PRO, PREM 11/3325, Macmillan's note, 'The Grand Design', of 29 December 1960–3 January 1961; Layton-Henry, 1980, p. 100.
15. Speech to the Salisbury Group, 12 October 1987.
16. *WB*.
17. *WB*; Horne, 1989, pp. 275–7; 432–43.
18. *Hansard*, 2 August 1961, Commons, cols. 1507–14; Lords, cols. 254–63; Labour Party Conference, Brighton, 3 October 1962.
19. *The Poisoned Chalice*, BBC 2 Television, 9 May 1996; Shepherd, 1994, p. 290; BBC Television's satirical programme, *That Was The Week That Was*, was launched in October 1962.
20. CPA, CCO 20/31/1, Macleod to Powell, 14 February 1962; CRD 2/52/8, CC/7, Powell, 7 March 1962.
21. CPA, CRD 2/52/8, CC/7, Powell, 7 March 1962; CRD 2/52/9, CC 3rd meeting, 19 March 1962.
22. CPA, CRD 2/52/8, CC/7, Powell, 7 March 1962; CRD 2/52/9, CC 3rd meeting, 19 March 1962; CCO 20/1/10, Powell to Macleod, 4 September 1962; speech at Halesowen, 13 September 1962.
23. CPA, CRD 2/52/9, CC 3rd meeting, 19 March 1962; CCO 20/31/1; CCO 20/41/1, Macleod to Powell, 11 January 1963; Butler papers, H 104, summary of meeting, 28 April 1963; Lowe, 1996 (forthcoming).
24. Butler papers, H 104, SC/63/9, for second meeting of steering committee, 26 July 1963; CPA, CCO 20/41/1, Macleod to Macmillan, 10 May 1963, Macleod to Powell, 4 October 1963. PRO, PREM 11/4686, 19 May 1964.
25. Shepherd, 1994, pp. 291–8.
26. Evans, 1981, pp. 271–4; Cosgrave, 1989, p. 182.
27. Rawlinson, 1989, p. 97.
28. PRO, CAB 128/37, CC(63)37th, 12 June 1963.
29. Evans, 1981, p. 273; *Evening Standard*, 12 June 1963.
30. Roth, 1970, p. 286; Cosgrave, 1989, p. 183; *The Times*, 17 June 1963.
31. *Hansard*, 17 June 1963, col. 99; Schoen, 1977, p. 6; Carlton, 1981, p. 476.
32. Shepherd, 1991, pp. 150–9; 1994, pp. 300–6.
33. *Spectator*, 9 October 1976; Shepherd, 1991, p. 152; 1994, p. 306; *WB*.
34. Butler papers, G 40, f. 103; Shepherd, 1994, pp. 306–12; *Spectator*, 13 October 1973.
35. Private information; Butler papers, G 32, note of 7 January 1958; Howard, 1987, pp. 185–9; *LP*.
36. Butler papers, G 37, note of 24 October 1961; G 38, note of 18/10, November 1962; peers were not yet able to renounce their titles and leave the Lords, but a joint committee of both Houses was about to report on the subject – Shepherd, 1991, p. 151.
37. Shepherd, 1994, pp. 300–18; Roth, 1970, pp. 298–9; Macleod, *Spectator*, 17 January 1964; Butler papers, G 43, Macleod to Butler, 15 January 1964: *The Times*, 17 January 1964.
38. *WB*; Shepherd, 1991, pp. 150–2, 1994, pp. 303–4.
39. Shepherd, 1994, pp. 320–1; PRO, PREM 11/5008, Macmillan's personal note, 15 October 1963.
40. Macleod, *Spectator*, 17 January 1964; Shepherd, 1994, pp. 328–9.
41. Macleod, *Spectator*, 17 January 1964; Shepherd, 1994, pp. 328–9.
42. Shepherd, 1994, pp. 330–2.
43. Macleod, *Spectator*, 17 January 1964; Shepherd, 1994, pp. 329–2; Thorpe, 1989, p. 380.
44. Shepherd, 1994, pp. 323–4. Butler had been told of the strong support for one of the younger

generation in July 1963, Butler papers, G 40, 31 July 1963; private information; Macleod, *Spectator*, 17 January 1964; Powell, speaking at a witness seminar on the 1963–64 Conservative Government, *Contemporary Record*, vol. 2, no. 5, spring 1989, p. 31; Nuffield College seminar, 22 January 1964.

45. PRO, PREM 11/5008, Dilhorne to Macmillan, 15 October 1963 – only Butler himself, Henry Brooke and Powell were listed as wanting Butler; Shepherd, 1994, pp. 325–7; Horne, 1989, 559–62.

46. *Spectator*, 13 October 1973 (Powell had refreshed his memory before writing about the crisis of October 1963 from the record that he had dictated afterwards).

47. Nuffield College seminar, 22 January 1964; *The Day Before Yesterday*, Thames Television, October 1970.

48. *Spectator*, 13 October 1973; Macleod, *Spectator*, 17 January 1964; Shepherd, 1994, pp. 332–3.

49. *LP*.

50. Shepherd, 1994, pp. 332–3; *LP*.

51. Butler papers, G 40, 25 October 1963; Home, 1976, p. 185; Shepherd, 1994, p. 335; Nuffield College seminar, 22 January 1964.

52. Shepherd, 1994, p. 335.

53. *LP*.

54. *Spectator*, 13 October 1973.

55. Shepherd, 1994, pp. 322–7; *Spectator*, 13 October 1973; Bogdanor, 1995, pp. 93–4; *Spectator*, 1 March 1980.

56. Bogdanor, 1995, p. 94–5; Shepherd, 1991, p. 159; 1994, pp. 331–2; private information; Butler papers, G 37, note of 24 October 1961.

57. *Spectator*, 9 October 1976; letter from Sir Robin Butler, Cabinet Secretary, to the author, 3 April 1996.

58. Lamb, 1995, p. 498; letter from Sir Robin Butler, Cabinet Secretary, to the author, 3 April 1996; letter from Lord Charteris of Amisfield to the author, 21 March 1996.

59. Lascelles is quoted in Bogdanor, 1995, p. 99; Hennessy, 1995, pp. 52–67.

60. *LP*.

CHAPTER 13: POWELLISM

1. On the renunciation of his title, the Earl of Home became known as Sir Alec Douglas-Home; Nuffield College seminar, 22 January 1964; *Daily Telegraph*, 1 November 1963; *The Times*, 19 November 1963.

2. Nuffield College seminar, 22 January 1964.

3. PRO, PREM 11/3930, 28 May 1962; *Political Quarterly*, October–December 1959, vol. 30, no. 4, pp. 340–1.

4. Interview with Powell about Macleod; Shepherd, 1994, pp. 338–40; *Express and Star*, 19 February 1964.

5. Nuffield College seminar, 22 January 1964; *Spectator*, 17 July 1965.

6. Interviewed by Butler and Pinto-Duschinsky for the Nuffield election study, 28 July 1970.

7. Butler papers, G 43, 15 January 1964; Shepherd, 1994, pp. 360–7; Nuffield College seminar, 22 January 1964.

8. Westminster, 28 January 1964.

9. Interviewed by Butler and Pinto-Duschinsky, Nuffield election study, 28 July 1970.

10. Speech to the parliamentary press gallery, 12 February 1964; interviewed by Butler and Pinto-Duschinsky, Nuffield election study, 28 July 1970. (Egeria was a Roman water spirit, who was considered prophetic).

11. Interviewed by Butler and Pinto-Duschinsky, Nuffield election study, 28 July 1970; *Express and Star*, 13 February 1964; conversations with Conservative MPs.

12. Interviewed by Butler and Pinto-Duschinsky, Nuffield election study, 28 July 1970; *The Times*, 7 April 1964; interview with Powell about Macleod.

13. *Express and Star*, 4 May 1964; *Spectator*, 17 April 1964; interview with John Biffen.

14. *The Times*, 1 April 1964.

15. *The Times*, 2 and 3 April 1964.
16. Glasgow, 3 April 1964; *The Times* and the *Daily Telegraph*, 4 April 1964; *Express and Star*, 4 April 1964.
17. *Spectator*, 10 April 1964.
18. *Sunday Telegraph*, 3 May 1964.
19. *Spectator*, 12 and 26 June 1964; *This Week*, Thames Television, 18 June 1964; Medlicott, 1967, pp. 582–3.
20. *Spectator*, 12 June 1964; speech to City of London Young Conservatives, 29 July 1964; speech to City of London Young Conservatives, 29 July 1964.
21. *Express and Star*, 6 October 1964.
22. CPA, Powell's election address, October 1964.
23. Walker, 1977, p. 52; Butler and King, 1965, pp. 354–5, 360–8; Foot, 1969, pp. 67–8.
24. *The Times*, 2 April 1964.
25. *Sunday Times*, 14 June 1964.
26. Speech to the Royal Society of St George, 22 April 1964; Seymour Martin Lipset has used the term 'exceptionalism' in relation to Americans' belief in their unique qualities.
27. *Sunday Times*, 14 June 1964.
28. Foot, 1969, pp. 69–70.
29. *Express and Star*, 10 October 1964.
30. *Express and Star*, 10 October 1964.
31. *Sunday Telegraph*, 18 October 1964; *Express and Star*, 19 October 1964; Gordon Walker is quoted in Walker, 1977, p. 55.
32. *Sunday Telegraph*, 18 October 1964.
33. *Express and Star*, 19 October 1964; Shepherd, 1994, pp. 378–79.
34. *Express and Star*, 6 October 1964.
35. Wolverhampton, 2 October, and Hornchurch, 5 October 1964; CPA, Election address of Enoch Powell, Conservative candidate for Wolverhampton South-West, October 1964.
36. Horne, 1989, p. 582; Shepherd, 1994, pp. 378–9.
37. I am grateful to D.R. Thorpe for telling me of Douglas-Home's proposed offer; *Express and Star*, 19 October 1964.
38. Ramsden, 1996, p. 211; *The Times*, 29 October 1964.
39. Quoted in Shepherd, p. 380.
40. *Hansard*, 4 November 1964, col. 196; *Financial Times*, 3 November 1964.
41. Speech at Trinity College, Dublin, 13 November 1964; see also, *Listener*, 29 April 1965.
42. *Express and Star*, 28 November 1964; CPA, LCC(64)7th, 2 December 1964.
43. Liverpool, 4 December 1964; Batley, 11 December 1964; *The Times*, 17 and 18 December 1964; Wolverhampton, 18 December 1964.
44. *The Times*, 16 January 1965; *Director*, February 1965.
45. *Express and Star*, 16, 19, 24 and 25 February 1965.
46. CPA, LLC(65)19th, 21st and 22nd, 15, 17 and 22 February 1965; *Listener*, 29 April 1965.
47. CPA, LLC(65)34th, 23 March 1965, LCC(65)23.
48. CPA, LLC(65)34th and 36th, 23 and 29 March 1965, LCC(65)23.
49. CPA, LLC(65)42nd, 13 April 1965, LCC(65)28.
50. CPA, LLC(65)37th, 30 March 1965.
51. *One Europe*, by the One Nation Group of MPs, April 1965; Roth, 1970, p. 372.
52. *One Europe*, by the One Nation Group of MPs, April 1965.
53. CPA, LLC(65)13th and 14th, 1 and 2 February 1965.
54. Cosgrave, 1989, pp. 235–6; CPA, LLC(65)13th and 14th, 1 and 2 February 1965.
55. *The Times*, 4 February 1965; *Wolverhampton Chronicle*, 6 February 1965.
56. CPA, LCC(65)29th, 9 March 1965.
57. CPA, LCC(65)29th, 9 March and 14 April 1965.
58. Foot, 1969, pp. 77–8.
59. CPA, CRD, 3/16/1, Immigration Policy Group meeting, 30 April 1965.
60. *Daily Telegraph*, 4 May 1965.

61. *Sunday Mercury*, 21 May 1965; *Daily Telegraph*, 22 May 1965.
62. CPA, CRD, 3/16/1, PG/9/65/22, Immigration Policy Group interim report, 14 July 1965; speech by Selwyn Lloyd, Heswell, 3 July 1965.
63. CPA, CRD, 3/16/1, Immigration Policy Group meeting, 30 April 1965.
64. CPA, LCC(65)38th, 31 March 1965.
65. Shepherd, 1994, p. 399.
66. Shepherd, 1994, pp. 400–1; *The Times*, 23 July 1965.
67. *Spectator*, 16 July 1965 – Wolfenden recommended liberalizing the laws on homosexuality and prostitution.
68. *The Times*, 26 July 1965; *Express and Star*, 26 July 1965.
69. *Spectator*, 30 July 1965; Shepherd, 1994, pp. 401–2; *The Times*, 28 July 1965.
70. Cosgrave, 1989, p. 206; Roth, 1970, p. 331; Howe, 1994, p. 39.
71. Interview with John Biffen; *Spectator*, 30 July 1965; Shepherd, 1994, p. 404.
72. Interview with J. Clement Jones; Hailsham, 1975, p. 236.
73. Private information; *Express and Star*, 21 October 1963; *Spectator*, 16 July 1965; *Express and Star*, 24 April 1966.
74. Interview with J. Clement Jones; *Spectator*, 16 July 1965; *Express and Star*, 4 August 1964 and 11 September 1965; *Daily Telegraph*, 1 July 1995; *Guardian*, 9 September 1995.
75. Interview with J. Clement Jones; *Express and Star*, 23 October 1961.
76. Interview with J. Clement Jones; *Observer*, colour magazine profile, April 1966.
77. *Observer*, colour magazine profile, April 1966; *Spectator*, 16 July 1965.

CHAPTER 14: DIVERGENCE

1. *The Times*, 5 August 1965; Shepherd, 1994, p. 405; Cosgrave, 1989, p. 208.
2. *WB*; interview with John Biffen.
3. *Economist*, 7 August and 18 September 1965; *The Times*, 2 April 1964.
4. *Odd Man Out*, BBC 2 Television, 11 November 1995.
5. *Crossbow*, April–June 1968.
6. *Swinton College Journal*, summer 1965; *WB*; CPA, PG/17/65/30; LCC/E(65)1st, 9 September 1965.
7. CPA, CRD 3/11/7, Corbyn to Douglas, 3 February 1966; Alexander and Watkins, 1970, pp. 81–3; CRD 3/11/25, Defence Policy Study file, 1966–68 contains Powell's drafts: Landward Defence Study Group 23 May 1968; Maritime Defence Study Group, 28 May 1968; The Shape of Our Future Armed Forces, 1 July 1968.
8. Shepherd, 1994, pp. 422–7; *Contemporary Record*, vol. 3, no. 3, February 1990.
9. Whitehead, 1985, pp. 32–3.
10. *Express and Star*, 4 August and 24 September 1965.
11. Dockrill, 1988, p. 86; CPA, CRD 3/11/3, draft letter to Viscount Watkinson, 29 October 1965.
12. CPA, LCC(65)65th and 68th, 15 September and 5 October 1965; Alexander and Watkins, 1970, p. 81.
13. Conservative Conference, Brighton, 14 October 1965.
14. CPA, LCC(65)56th, 23 June 1965; PG/7/65/17, 6 August 1965; see, for example, 'The Defence of Europe', in *RUSI Journal*, February 1968; Conservative Conference, Brighton, 14 October 1965.
15. Conservative Conference, Brighton, 14 October 1965.
16. Conservative Conference, Brighton, 14 October 1965; CPA, CRD 3/11/3, transcript of BBC interview between Sir Robin Day and Powell, 14 October 1965.
17. *Spectator*, 22 October 1965; CPA, LCC(65)71st, 27 October 1965.
18. *Spectator*, 22 October 1965.
19. CPA, LCC(65)71st, 27 October 1965, LCC(65)51.
20. CPA, LCC/0(65)2nd, 1 November 1965.
21. CPA, LCC/0(65)2nd, 1 November 1965; Pimlott, 1992, p. 386, citing Clive Ponting, *Breach of Promise: Labour in Power, 1964–70*, Hamish Hamilton, 1989, pp. 43–55.

22. CPA, LCC/0(65)2nd, 1 November 1965; Hemel Hempstead, 4 November 1965.
23. Dockrill, 1988, p. 93–7; CPA, LCC(66)96th, 21 February 1966; LCC/0(66)4th, 22 February 1966; LCC(66)98th, 2 March 1966; *Hansard*, 7 March 1966, cols. 1748–70.
24. Falkirk, 26 March 1966; *The Times*, 18 March 1966; Pimlott, 1992, pp. 388–9; Alexander and Watkins, 1970, pp. 81–3; Campbell, 1993, p. 228.
25. For example, CPA, CRD 3/11/5, minute of joint meeting of Foreign Affairs and Defence Committees, 27 June 1967.
26. Aislaby, 24 June 1967.
27. CPA, CRD 3/11/5 and 31, minutes of joint meeting of Foreign Affairs and Defence Committees, 27 June 1967.
28. *WB*; *LP*; *The Times*, 8 June 1987.
29. *LP*.
30. *LP*; CPA, CRD 3/11/3, transcript of BBC interview between Sir Robin Day and Powell, 14 October 1965.
31. Conservative Conference, Brighton, 14 October 1965.
32. *Listener*, 17 February 1966.
33. See, for example, *Today on Sunday*, 30 November 1986; *Listener*, 17 February 1966.
34. *Listener*, 17 February 1966.
35. CPA, CRD 3/12/1, Morton (for Fraser) to Sewill, 10 November 1965; LCC(66)78.
36. *Listener*, 17 February 1966.
37. CPA, LCC(67)149th and 153rd, 23 January and 6 February 1967.
38. CPA, LCC(67)149th and 153rd, 23 January and 6 February 1967.
39. CPA, LCC(67)149th, 23 January 1967.
40. *Hansard*, 6 March 1967, cols. 1194, 1197, 1199–1202.
41. Alexander and Watkins, 1970, p. 87; CPA, CRD files, Defence Policy, Hadley to Sewill, 30 June 1967.
42. CPA, CRD files, Defence Policy, Hadley to Sewill, 30 June 1967.
43. CPA, LCC(68)219th, 28 February 1968.
44. Bath, 15 March 1968.
45. CPA, CRD 3/12/3, Powell to Whitelaw, 15 July 1967.
46. *Spectator*, 19 November 1965.
47. *Spectator*, 19 November 1965 and 14 January 1966.
48. *The Times*, 22 November 1965; Foot, 1969, pp. 90–1.
49. *The Times*, 5 January 1966; Manchester Statistical Society, 12 January 1966.
50. CPA, LCC(66)91st, 31 January 1966.
51. CPA, LCC(66)91st, 31 January 1966.
52. Private information; *The Times*, 11 March 1966.
53. Wolverhampton, 25 March 1966.
54. Butler and Stokes, 1966, pp. 1, 259–62, 317; Shepherd, 1991, p. 166.
55. Speech to the City of London Young Conservatives, 6 April 1966.
56. Shepherd, 1994, p. 419; speech to the City of London Young Conservatives, 6 April 1966.
57. Speech to the City of London Young Conservatives, 6 April 1966; *The Times*, 14 April 1966.
58. *The Times*, 14 April 1966.
59. *Sunday Times*, 17 April 1966; *Express and Star*, 23 April 1966.
60. Edinburgh, 30 April 1966; for example, his speeches at Wolverhampton, 6 May; Wembley, 9 May; Harrogate, 6 July; Wolverhampton, 6 September; Blackpool, 5 November; Bognor Regis, 11 November; and London, 1 December 1966; 30 October 1966; Alexander and Watkins, 1970, p. 86.
61. Cosgrave, 1989, p. 226.
62. Crossman, 1976, diary entry for 3 November 1966; Shepherd, 1994, p. 457–9; *Contemporary Record*, vol. 3, no. 3, February 1990.
63. CPA, LCC(68)222nd and 224th, 7 and 13 March 1968; *Contemporary Record*, vol. 3, no. 3, February 1990; vol. 3, no. 4, April 1990; Shepherd, 1994, pp. 457–9.
64. Birmingham, 11 January 1967; Shepherd, 1994, p. 451; *Listener*, 21 March 1968.
65. See above, pp. 315–16.

66. *LP.*

CHAPTER 15: 'THE RIVER TIBER'

1. Interviewed by Butler and Austin Mirchell, 14 March 1968, and Butler and Pinto-Duschinsky, 28 July 1970 for the Nuffield election studies.
2. See above, pp. 223–26, 274–78, 286–91; *Daily Telegraph*, 16 February 1967.
3. The study was by the sociologists, John Rex and Robert Moore; *Daily Telegraph*, 16 February 1967.
4. *Daily Telegraph*, 16 February 1967.
5. The reports included one by PEP, the independent organization, the first annual report of the Race Relations Board, and Mark Bonham Carter's report on American race relations; CPA, LCC(67)169th, 24 April 1967. Powell's reference to three million as opposed to $3\frac{1}{2}$ million in his February article reflected differing estimates made at the time.
6. CPA, LCC(67)171st, 1 May 1967; LCC(67)141.
7. Foot, 1969, p. 102.
8. Deakin, 1970, p. 130; *Spectator*, 5 November 1994.
9. Foot, 1969, p. 107, quoting Wilfred Sendall, *Daily Express*, 19 October 1967; Shepherd, 1994, p. 494.
10. Deal, 18 October 1967; *Hansard*, 16 November 1961, col. 695.
11. Deal, 18 October 1967.
12. As Macleod argued in the *Spectator*, 23 February 1968.
13. PRO, CAB 134/1469, CCM(61)10, report by inter-departmental working party.
14. PRO, CAB 134/1469, CCM(61)1st – 4th meetings.
15. Tanganyika became Tanzania in 1964, following its merger with Zanzibar; Berkeley, 1977, p. 77.
16. Berkeley, 1977, pp. 77–8.
17. PRO, CAB 134/1469, CCM(61)2nd, 17 May 1961; CO/2802, Nationality and Citizenship in East Africa, 1961–62, inward telegram to Commonwealth Relations Office from Dar-es-Salaam, 23 December 1961.
18. PRO, CO/2802, Nationality and Citizenship in East Africa, 1961–62, inward telegram to Commonwealth Relations Office from Dar-es-Salaam, 23 December 1961.
19. PRO, CO/2802, Draft Brief No. 9, Kenya Constitutional Conference, February 1962.
20. *The Times*, 28 May 1971; *Hansard*, 8 March 1971, col. 145.
21. PRO, CAB 134/1468, CCI(63)3, 30 October 1963; CCI meeting, 6 November 1963.
22. PRO, CAB 134/1468, CCI(63)3, 30 October 1963; CCI meeting, 6 November 1963.
23. PRO, CAB 134/1468, CCI meeting, 6 November 1963.
24. *The Times*, 28 May 1971; *Hansard*, 8 March 1971, col. 145.
25. *Spectator*, 23 February 1968; *Hansard*, 27 February 1968, col. 1345.
26. *Spectator*, 5 November 1994; Maudling to Powell, quoted in *The Times*, 28 May 1971.
27. PRO, CAB 129/121, C(65)93, 6 July 1965; Crossman, 1977, diary entry for 24 March 1968.
28. *Panorama*, BBC Television, 12 February 1968; *The Times*, 28 May 1971.
29. *Spectator*, 5 November 1994.
30. Tomalin, *Sunday Times*, April 1968; Melville, *New York Times*, 15 December 1967; Roth, 1970, p. 341.
31. The Commons debate was on the annual renewal of the legislation to control Commonwealth immigration; CPA, LCC(67)195th, 13 November 1967.
32. *Hansard*, 15 November 1967, cols. 467–8; Lord Jenkins, speaking at IHR / ICBH witness seminar on race relations in the 1960s, 21 February 1996; Crossman, 1979, diary entry for 24 March 1968.
33. *Express and Star*, 9 December 1967.
34. *Sunday Telegraph*, 4 February 1968; CPA, LCC(68)212th, 7 February 1968.
35. Walsall, 9 February 1968; interview with J. Clement Jones; Roth, 1970, p. 346, citing the *Sunday Times*; *Express and Star*, 14 and 26 February 1968; *The Times*, 6 May 1968.
36. *Hansard*, written answer, 22 November 1967; Walsall, 9 February 1968.
37. *Express and Star*, 10 February 1968; see Hugo Young, in Jones et al, 1971, pp. 33–7.
38. Foot, 1969, p. 111; Roth, 1970, p. 346; interview with J. Clement Jones.

39. *Hansard*, 22 February 1968, col. 662; *Spectator*, 23 February 1968.
40. CPA, LCC(68)218th and 219th, 26 and 28 February 1968; *Hansard*, 27 February 1968, cols. 1298–99.
41. Shepherd, 1994, p. 498; Lapping, 1970, p. 122.
42. Crossman, 1979, diary entry for 4 March 1968.
43. Tomalin, *Sunday Times*, April 1968.
44. CPA, LCC(68)231st, 10 April 1968.
45. Walker, 1991, p. 51; Hailsham, 1990, p. 369; CPA, LCC (68) 231st, 10 April 1968.
46. *Hansard*, 23 April 1968, col. 81; Hailsham, 1990, pp. 369–70.
47. Private information.
48. Interview with J. Clement Jones.
49. Utley, 1968, pp. 16–7.
50. Roth, 1970, p. 350.
51. Birmingham, 20 April 1968.
52. Hailsham, 1990, p. 370; Whitelaw, 1989, p. 64.
53. Shepherd, 1994, p. 500; Hogg, 1975, p. 235; 1990, pp. 370–1; Whitelaw, 1989, p. 64.
54. Thatcher, 1995, pp. 146–7; Young, 1989, p. 111.
55. Thatcher, 1995, pp. 146–7; *Odd Man Out*, BBC 2 Television, 11 November 1995; Shepherd, 1994, p. 500.
56. Utley, 1969, p. 18; Roth, 1970, p. 357; Schoen, 1977, p. 32.
57. *The Times*, 23 April 1968.
58. Powell to Heath, *The Times*, 23 April 1968.
59. *The Times*, 22 April 1968; Schoen, 1977, pp. 36–7.
60. *Express and Star*, 24 April 1968.
61. Schoen, 1977, p. 37; *Express and Star*, 24 April 1968; interview with J. Clement Jones; Jones et al., 1971, pp. 19–20.
62. *Odd Man Out*, BBC 2 Television, 11 November 1995.
63. 'Enoch Powell's Postbag', in *New Society*, 9 May 1968.
64. Prior, 1986, p. 52; CPA, CCO 20/66/2–10.
65. *Express and Star*, 24 April 1968.
66. Walker, 1977, p. 110; *The Times*, 24 April 1968; Roth, 1970, pp. 360–1.
67. Castle, 1984, diary entry for 23 April 1968.
68. *The Times*, 24 April 1968; Foot, 1969, p. 126; Walker, 1977, p. 116.
69. *Odd Man Out*, BBC 2 Television, 11 November 1995; see also A.N. Wilson, *Spectator*, 23 June 1990, recalling a broadcast on the twentieth anniversary of Powell's speech.
70. Schoen, 1977, p. 39; *Hansard*, 23 April 1968, col. 75.
71. Shepherd, 1994, pp. 501–2; conversation with Keith Kyle.
72 Heath, 21 April 1968; interview with John Biffen; Howe, 1994, p. 38; Whitelaw, 1989, p. 65; *The Times*, 15 July 1968.
73. Thatcher, 1995, p. 161; interviewed by Butler and Pinto–Duschinsky for the Nuffield election studies, 9 July 1969.
74. Shepherd, 1991, p. 212.
75. Schoen, 1977, p. 38.
76. Conversations with Wolverhampton Conservatives.
77. *Express and Star*, 15 and 22 June, 23 October, 25 November, 4 and 6 December 1968; Bowen and Jacobs, 1981, pp. 201–2.
78. Interviewed by Butler and Pinto–Duschinsky for the Nuffield election studies, 9 July 1969; *Odd Man Out*, BBC 2 Television, 11 November 1995.
79. Interviewed by Butler and Pinto–Duschinsky for the Nuffield election studies, 28 July 1970.
80. Virgil's *Aeneid*, Book VI, Loeb Classical Library, 1986 edition, Heinemann, London, pp, 510–5; interview with John Biffen.
81. *LP*.
82. Eastbourne, 16 November 1968.
83. Whitelaw, 1989, p. 64; Hailsham, 1990, p. 370.

84. Hailsham, 1990, p. 370; *Odd Man Out*, BBC 2 Television, 11 November 1995; *WW*.
85. *LP*.
86. Interview with J. Clement Jones.
87. Interview with J. Clement Jones; *The Times*, 24 April 1968.
88. *The Frost Programme*, 3 January 1969, London Weekend Television; Frost, 1993, p. 427.
89. *Birmingham Post*, 4 May 1968; *LP*; conversations with Powell's friends in Wolverhampton.
90. Powell, 1977, p. 5; *LP*; *WW*; *Odd Man Out*, BBC 2 Television, 11 November 1995.
91. Powell, 1977, p. 5; Birmingham, 20 April 1968; *Social Focus on Ethnic Minorities*, HMSO, 1996.
92. *Any Questions*, BBC Radio, 29 November 1968.
93. *Odd Man Out*, BBC 2 Television, 11 November 1995; *LP*.
94. *Any Questions*, BBC Radio, 29 November 1968; *LP*.
95. *LP*. Utley, 1968, pp. 23–4.
96. *LP*.
97. Conservative Political Centre, July 1954.
98. Powell, 1977, p. 5; *LP*.
99. Layton-Henry, 1992, pp. 18–9.

CHAPTER 16: SHAKING THE TREE

1. *LP*.
2. *The Times*, 12 June 1968 – the author, whose identity has not been revealed, wrote under the pseudonym, 'C'; Prior, 1986, p. 52; interviewed on 28 July 1970 by Butler and Pinto-Duschinsky for the Nuffield election studies.
3. *The Times*, 12 June 1968.
4. *Birmingham Post*, 4 May 1968; *Express and Star*, 25 May 1968.
5. Interviewed on 9 July 1969 by Butler and Pinto-Duschinsky for the Nuffield election studies.
6. *The Times*, 15 July 1968.
7. Shepherd, 1991, pp. 107–11; Prior, 1986, p. 53.
8. *The Times*, 16 May 1968; Weybridge, 18 June 1968; CPA, CRD 3/10/16, minutes of Foreign Affairs committee, 18 and 15 June 1968.
9. *Wolverhampton Chronicle*, 5 July 1968; Norton, 1975, pp. 298–9; *The Times*, 4 July 1968.
10. Campbell, 1994, p. 245.
11. Schoen, 1977, pp. 39–40.
12. Prestatyn, 27 September 1968.
13. *The Times*, 4 and 9 October 1968; *Spectator*, 11 October 1968.
14. *The Times*, 10 October 1968.
15. *The Times*, 11 October 1968; Conservative Conference, Blackpool, 10 October 1968; *LP*.
16. *The Times*, 12 October 1968; Powell's alternative budget was attacked by Professor Alan Day and city editor, Patrick Hutber – Victor Keegan, *Guardian*, 20 July 1987; *The Times*, 12 October 1968; *Spectator*, 11 October 1968.
17. *Spectator*, 11 October 1968.
18. Eastbourne, 16 November 1968; *News of the World*, *People*. 17 November 1968.
19. Eastbourne, 16 November 1968.
20. Foot, 1969, p. 121; Campbell, 1994, p. 246; Cosgrave, 1989, p. 270; BBC Radio, *World This Weekend*, 18 January 1970; Powell, 1973, pp. 89–90; pp. 95–112; Clifford Longley, *Daily Telegraph*, 19 August 1994.
21. Heath, Walsall, 25 January 1969; Foot, 1969, p. 121.
22. CPA, PS/69/3, CRD report on General Issues Survey, 2 April 1969.
23. *The Times*, 7 December 1969.
24. *The Times*, 7 December 1969; interviewed on 9 July 1969 by Butler and Pinto-Duschinsky for the Nuffield election studies.
25. Shepherd, 1994, pp. 512–3.

26. Crossman, 1977, diary entry for 19 November 1968; CPA, LCC(67) 205th, 18 December 1967; LCC(68) 208th, 22 January 1968.
27. Shepherd, 1994, p. 513; *Hansard*, 19 November 1968, col. 1160.
28. *Hansard*, 19 November 1968, cols. 1163–70.
29. Crossman, 1977, diary entry for 19 November 1968.
30. *Hansard*, 12 February 1969, cols. 1351–4.
31. Roth, 1970, p. 363.
32. *Hansard*, 19 February 1968, cols. 428, 506.
33. Speech to Primrose League, 17 April 1969.
34. Interviewed on 9 July 1969 by Butler and Pinto-Duschinsky for the Nuffield election studies.
35. CPA, Powell's election address, March 1966; Llandudno, 6 November 1966.
36. CPA, LCC(67)149th, 23 January 1967; Wolverhampton, 5 May 1967.
37. Speech to City of London Young Conservatives, 31 May 1967; Roth, 1970, pp. 374–5; see above, pp. 372–73.
38. Kitzinger, 1973, pp. 362–3; interviewed on 9 July 1969 by Butler and Pinto-Duschinsky for the Nuffield election studies.
39. Clacton, 21 March 1969.
40. Clacton, 21 March 1969; Roth, 1970, p. 376.
41. *The Times*, 6 September 1969 reprinted the text of Powell's speech and devoted an editorial to the EEC; Shepherd, 1991. pp. 217–8.
42. Preston, 4 October 1969; *The Times*, 30 September, 3 and 4 October 1969; Ramsden, 1996, p. 296.
43. National Liberal Club, 30 September 1969.
44. Conservative Conference, Brighton, 9 October 1969.
45. Shepherd, 1994, pp. 463, 517.
46. Interviewed on 9 July 1969 and 28 July 1970 by Butler and Pinto-Duschinsky for the Nuffield election studies; *WW*.
47. *Spectator*, 25 April 1969.
48. *Hansard*, 25 February 1970, cols. 1260–70; CPA, CRD 3/10/16, Conservative Foreign Affairs committee, 18 February 1970.
49. Interview with John Biffen; interviewed on 28 July 1970 by Butler and Pinto-Duschinsky for the Nuffield election studies.
50. CPA, Powell's election address, June 1970; *LP*.
51. Interviewed by Butler and Pinto-Duschinsky, 28 July 1970, for Nuffield election studies; Ramsden, 1996, p. 311.
52. Adams, 1992, p. 307.
53. Note of Powell's meetings in Wolverhampton on 10 June 1970 by Michael Pinto-Duschinsky.
54. Rhodes James, 1972, p. 244; Campbell, 1995, p. 270; Ramsden, 1996, p. 312.
55. Interview with John Biffen.
56. CPA, election address, June 1970; *A Better Tomorrow*, Conservative 1970 election manifesto.
57. Crossman, 1977, diary entry of 7 June 1970; Benn, 1988, 3 June 1970; Adams, 1992, p. 308; BBC Television News, 3 June 1970.
58. Adams, 1992, p. 309; Benn, 1988, diary entry for 4 June 1970; Cosgrave, 1989, p. 8; Adams, 1992, p. 309.
59. Wolverhampton, 11 June 1970.
60. Crossman, 1977, diary entries for 23 July and 7 August 1969, 20 February, 11 March and 14 June 1970; *The Times*, 10 March 1970; Powell paper of 1 May 1970.
61. Alexander and Watkins, 1970, pp. 188–90, Campbell, 1995, p. 277.
62. Prior, 1986, pp. 59–60; Hurd, 1979, p. 22; Cosgrave, 1989, p. 271.
63. Prior, 1986, p. 60; *The Times*, 15 June 1970; Northfield, 13 June 1970.
64. Tamworth, 15 June 1970.
65. Wolverhampton, 16 June 1970.
66. *The Times*, 19 June 1970.
67. The Tory lead averaged 3.4 per cent throughout the United Kingdom, but 2.4 per cent in Britain (excluding the Ulster Unionists in Northern Ireland).

68. Adams, 1992, p. 309; *The Times*, 19 June 1970.
69. *The Times*, 20 June 1970.
70. Richard Rose, *The Times*, 20 June 1970; David Butler, *Sunday Times*, 21 June 1970; Nicholas Deakin and Jenny Bourne, in *Race Today*, July 1970, pp. 205–6, and *Political Quarterly*, Oct–Dec 1970, pp. 399–415; Michael Steed in Butler and Pinto-Duschinsky, 1971, pp. 406–8.
71. Deakin and Bourne, in *Race Today*, July 1970, pp. 205–6, and *Political Quarterly*, Oct–Dec 1970, pp. 399–415; *Sunday Times*, 21 June 1970; Steed in Butler and Pinto-Duschinsky, 1971, pp. 406–8.
72. Steed in Butler and Pinto-Duschinsky, 1971, pp. 406–8; R.W, Johnson and Douglas Schoen, 'The "Powell Effect": or How One Man Can Win', in *New Society*, 22 July 1976, pp. 168–72; Douglas Schoen, 1977, pp. 55–67; Donley T. Studlar, 'Policy Voting in Britain: the Colored Immigration Issue in the 1964, 1966 and 1970 General Elections', *American Political Science Review*, LXXII, 1978, p. 46–64; W.L. Miller, 'What Was the Profit in Following the Crowd?', in *British Journal of Political Science*, vol. 10, 1980, pp. 22–38.
73. Butler and Pinto-Duschinsky, 1971, pp. 232–33; Schoen, 1977, pp. 56–57.
74. Schoen, 1977, pp. 56–57; MORI's panel were interviewed during 1972–73.
75. Butler and Stokes, 1975, pp. 307–8; Donley T. Studlar, 'Policy Voting in Britain: the Colored Immigration Issue in the 1964, 1966 and 1970 General Elections', *American Political Science Review*, LXXII, 1978, p. 46–64; Schoen, 1977, pp. 55–67.
76. Donley T. Studlar, 'Policy Voting in Britain: the Colored Immigration Issue in the 1964, 1966 and 1970 General Elections', *American Political Science Review*, LXXII, 1978, p. 46–64; W.L. Miller, 'What Was the Profit in Following the Crowd?', in *British Journal of Political Science*, vol. 10, 1980, pp. 22–38; R.W. Johnson and Douglas Schoen, 'The "Powell effect": or how one man can win', in *New Society*, 22 July 1976.
77. R.W. Johnson and Douglas Schoen, ibid.
78. *Odd Man Out*, BBC 2 Television, 11 November 1995.

CHAPTER 17: REBEL WITH A CAUSE

1. Press Association interview, 5 October 1970.
2. *The Times*, 20 June 1970; *Sunday Times*, 21 June 1970; *Sunday Times*, 21 June 1970; Schoen, 1977, p. 67.
3. *Sunday Times*, 21 June 1970.
4. *Spectator*, 14 November 1970; interview with John Biffen; CPA, CCO 20/66/20, Deedes to the Chief Whip, 16 November 1972.
5. CPA, CCO, 20/60/15, Powell's speeches, 1972–73; Richard Rose, quoted in Norton, 1978, p. 326.
6. Norton, 1978, pp. 251–2; *New Statesman*, 26 March 1971.
7. Norton, 1978, p. 253; *Political Quarterly*, XLIV, 1973, p. 402.
8. *Express and Star*, 1 October 1970.
9. *Spectator*, 7 November 1970.
10. *The Times*, 22 July 1970; *New Statesman*, 31 July 1970; interviewed on 28 July 1970 by Butler and Pinto-Duschinsky for the Nuffield election studies.
11. *The Times*, 1 October 1970.
12. Campbell, 1993, pp. 307–8; Rawlinson, 1989, pp. 57–60.
13. CPA, Powell's election address, June 1970; Campbell, 1993, pp. 331–2; Norton, 1978, pp. 45–8, 54.
14. *Hansard*, 8 February 1971, cols. 105–8; Ramsden, 1996, pp. 48–9; Norton, 1978, p. 55; *WW*.
15. Carshalton, 15 February 1971; Schoen, 1977, pp. 70–1.
16. *Spectator*, 6 March 1971.
17. *Hansard*, 8 March 1971, cols. 76–85.
18. *The Times*, 2 and 7 April; 'Equality – an Impossible Utopia?' BBC Radio, 2 May 1971; *Spectator*, 22 May 1971.
19. Londonderry, 15 January 1971; Wolverhampton, 14 April 1971; *The Times*, 21 April and 8 May 1971.
20. *The Poisoned Chalice*, BBC 2 Television, 16 May 1996.
21. Whitehead, 1985, p. 63.

22. *WW*; Ramsden, 1996, pp. 335–7.
23. Doncaster, 19 June 1971; Robert Shepherd, 'Leadership, Public Opinion and the Referendum', in *Political Quarterly*, vol. 46, no.1, January – March 1975, pp. 25–35.
24. Ramsden, 1996, pp. 335–6.
25. Conservative conference, Brighton, 13 October 1971; Ramsden, 1996, pp. 336–7.
26. Whitehead, 1985, pp. 66–7.
27. *The Poisoned Chalice*, BBC 2 Television, 16 May 1996.
28. *The Poisoned Chalice*, BBC 2 Television, 16 May 1996.
29. *Hansard*, 17 February 1972, cols. 698–707.
30. *Hansard*, 17 February 1972, col. 707; Sir Hugh Rossi, *The Poisoned Chalice*, BBC 2 Television, 16 May 1996; *The Times*, 14 February 1972.
31. Cosgrave, 1989. p. 321; *WW*; Whitehead, 1985, p. 68; Norton, 1978, pp. 73–4.
32. *The Times*, 19 February 1972; Norton, 1978, p. 74.
33. Butler and Kitzinger, 1976, pp. 17–9; *Sunday Times*, 16 April 1972.
34. *The Times*, 10 April 1972.
35. *The Times*, 19 April 1972; Norton, 1975, pp. 434–6.
36. Norton, 1978. pp. 79–80; Ramsden, 1996, pp. 338–39.
37. Parliamentary Press Gallery, 13 May 1972.
38. *WW*; 8 April 1972.
39. *The Poisoned Chalice*, BBC 2 Television, 16 May 1996; *WW*; *The Times*, 19 April 1972.
40. Malvern, 26 February 1972; *Spectator*, 4 and 11 March 1972.
41. CPA, CCO 600/5/3, Carrington minute of 17 April 1972; *The Times*, 28 April 1972.
42. *Economist*, 17 June 1972; St Andrews, 26 January 1973; Cairncross, 1992, pp. 190–1; Whitehead, 1985, p. 86.
43. Ridley, 1991, p. 20; *Spectator*, 30 December 1972.
44. Norton, 1978, pp. 103–14; CPA, CCO 4/10/298, Uganda; *The Times*, 12 October 1972.
45. *The Times*, 11 October 1972; Ramsden, 1996, pp. 339–40; CPA, CCO 20/43/6, Monday Club.
46. *The Times*, 13 October 1972; Conservative conference, Blackpool, 12 October 1972.
47. *The Times*, 13 October 1972; *Economist*, 13 October 1972; Schoen, 1977, pp. 94–5.
48. Philip Norton, 'Intra-Party Dissent in the House of Commons', in *Parliamentary Affairs*, vol. XXIX, no. 4, autumn 1976, pp. 404–20; Norton, 1978, pp. 128–9.
49. Norton, 1978, pp. 128–9; *Economist*, 25 November 1972.
50. Schoen, 1977, p. 96; *The Times*, 9 and 19 December 1972; Norton, 1978, pp. 129–30.
51. Schoen, 1977, pp. 96–8; CPA, CCO 20/66/20, Deedes to Pym, 16 November 1972.
52. Wanstead and Woodford, 17 June 1972.
53. Schoen, 1977, p. 96; *The Times*, 28 September and 9 October 1972;
54. *Hansard*, 6 November 1972, col. 631; Norton, 1978, pp. 119–20.
55. Norton, 1978, pp. 120–1; interview with John Biffen.
56. Cairncross, 1992, pp. 190–91; *Hansard*, 29 January 1973, cols. 977–84.
57. Norton, 1978, pp. 121–4.
58. Flackes, 1980; Dillon, 1990; *WW*.
59. Prestatyn, 27 September 1968; Speech at Enniskillen, *The Times*, 9 February 1970; *Hansard*, 17 April 1970, cols. 288–92.
60. Northfield, Birmingham, 13 June 1970; Londonderry, 13 January 1971.
61. Anne Elizabeth Colville, *Enoch Powell: His Ulster Years*, M.S.Sc. thesis, Queen's University, Belfast, 1994, p. 16; *The Times*, 4 September 1974.
62. Beaconsfield, 19 March 1971; Omagh, 11 September 1971.
63. Omagh, 11 September 1971.
64. Colville, op. cit., p. 21.
65. *Hansard*, 28 March 1972, cols. 269–76.
66. Newtownards, 6 May 1972; CPA, CRD 3/18/1, meeting of Conservative Northern Ireland committee, 15 November 1972.
67. CPA, CRD 3/18/1, meeting of Conservative Northern Ireland committee, 12 July 1972; *Hansard*, 20 July 1972, col. 926.

68. Schoen, 1977, pp. 108–9; *Spectator*, 29 July 1972.
69. *The Future of Northern Ireland*, HMSO, October 1972; *Northern Ireland Constitutional Proposals*, Cmnd. 5259, March 1973.
70. *Hansard*, 29 March 1973, cols. 1589–95; Norton, 1978, pp. 135–7.
71. *The Times*, 31 May 1973; CPA, CCO, 20/66/15, Patten to Carrington, 26 October 1972; Yarmouth, 28 October 1972.
72. Stockport, 8 June 1973.
73. *Sunday Times*, 10 June 1973.
74. *The Times*, 9 June 1973; Pimlott, 1992, p. 611.
75. Johnson and Schoen, in *New Society*, 22 July 1976; *Tomorrow*, Young Conservatives newspaper, October 1973.
76. *WW*.
77. Schoen, 1977, p. 112; *The Times*, 15 October 1973.
78. Conservative Conference, Blackpool, 11 October 1973; *The Times*, 19 June 1973; *Daily Mirror*, 23 October 1973.
79. *The Times*, 30 November 1973.
80. *WW*; *The Times*, 30 November 1973.
81. *The Times*, 3 December 1973.
82. Flackes, 1980, pp. 220–2; Whitehead, 1985, pp. 168–9.
83. *WW*; Whitehead, 1985, p. 169.
84. *The Times*, 12 and 17 December 1973; *The Times*, 15 December 1973; Schoen, 1977, pp. 123–4.
85. Cosgrave, 1989, p. 340; *The Times*, 18 December 1973; Schoen, 1977, p. 124.
86. *The Times*, 16 January 1974.
87. Prior, 1982, p. 92; *WW*.
88. Prior, 1982, p. 93; Critchley, 1994, p. 136.
89. Powell to T.O.G. Wilkes, 7 February 1974; interviews with Wolverhampton Conservatives; Schoen, 1977, p. 125.
90. Powell, 1977, pp. 95–8; *Sunday Times*, 10 February 1974.
91. Cosgrave, 1989, p. 343; Pimlott, 1992, pp. 611–2.
92. *WW*.
93. *The Times*, 21 February 1974; Butler and Kavanagh, 1974, pp. 103–5, 150–1; Ramsden, 1996, p. 379.
94. Birmingham, 23 February 1974; *Sunday Times*, 24 February 1974.
95. *Sunday Times*, 24 February 1974; Butler and Kavanagh, 1974, pp. 103–5.
96. Shipley, 25 February 1974; *LP*.
97. *WW*; Whitehead, 1985, p. 113.
98. *The Times*, 1–5 March 1974; Butler and Kavanagh, 1974, p. 276.
99. Bowen and Jacobs, 1981, p. 266.
100. *Odd Man Out*, BBC 2 Television, 11 November 1995; Butler and Kavanagh, 1974, pp. 100–1, 107–8.
101. Schoen, 1977, pp. 138–9; Butler and Kavanagh, 1974, pp. 105, 151.
102. Butler and Kavanagh, 1974, pp. 331–3; Johnson and Schoen, ibid; Schoen, 1977, pp. 126, 129–30.
103. Campbell, 1993, p. 615; *Sunday Times*, 3 March 1973; Ramsden, 1996, p. 380.
104. Butler and Kavanagh, 1974, pp. 331–3; Johnson and Schoen, ibid.
105. Johnson and Schoen, ibid.; Schoen, 1977, pp. 129–39.

CHAPTER 18: 'LIKE THE SONG OF THE BIRDS BEFORE DAWN'

1. Anne Elizabeth Colville, *Enoch Powell: His Ulster Years*, 1994, M.S.Sc. thesis, Queen's University, Belfast. I am indebted to Frank Millar for his insights into Powell as an Ulster Unionist.
2. Campbell, 1993, p. 617; Colville, op. cit., p. 25.
3. Cosgrave, 1989, p. 356; private information; *LP*.
4. Londonderry, 18 September 1973; Belfast, 18 April 1974.
5. *The Times*, 25 April and 10 May 1974; Colville, op. cit., p. 26; Flackes, 1980, p. 247.

6. London, 18 May 1974; *Spectator*, 4 May 1974; *Sunday Times*, 19 May 1974; *The Times*, 11 and 20 May 1974.
7. *Sunday Times*, 19 May 1974; *The Times*, 2–4 May, 20 May 1974; Campbell, 1993, pp. 633–4.
8. *Sunday Times*, 19 May 1974; *The Times*, 20 May 1974.
9. CPA, CCO 20/66/16, 'Enoch Powell, 1974', Sir Richard Webster to the Chairman, 11 June 1974; Schoen, 1977, p. 141; *The Times* 25 May and 26 June 1974.
10. CPA, CCO 20/66/16, 'Enoch Powell, 1974', Whitelaw to Heath, 2 July, Waldegrave to Whitelaw, 8 July 1974; *The Times*, 8 July 1974; *New Society*, 5 August 1976; *The Times*, 31 August 1974.
11. CPA, CCO 20/66/16, 'Enoch Powell, 1974', Waldegrave to Whitelaw, 8 July 1974; Schoen, 1977, pp. 141–2; Colville, op. cit., pp. 27–8; Enniskillen, 3 June 1974; *The Times*, 4 June 1974.
12. Schoen, 1977, pp. 141–2; Colville, op. cit., pp. 27–8; *The Times*, 31 August 1974.
13. *The Times*, 2 and 4 September 1974; Colville, op. cit., p. 23.
14. *Guardian*, 4 June 1974; *Daily Express*, 20 April 1974; *Financial Times*, 18 April 1974.
15. Schoen, 1977, pp. 142–3; *The Times*, 2 and 21 September 1974.
16. Schoen, 1977, p. 144.
17. *The Times*, 27 September 1974.
18. Banbridge, 25 September; Newcastle, 7 October; Ballynahinch, 8 October 1974; Colville, op. cit., p. 32.
19. *The Times*, 4 October 1974; Colville, op. cit., p. 31.
20. Lewis, 1979, p. 211; Shepherd, 1990, pp. 89–90; *The Times*, 21 October 1974.
21. *LP*.
22. *The Times*, 4 October 1974; Butler and Kavanagh, 1975, p. 178.
23. *Sunday Telegraph*, 8 September 1974; *The Times*, 4 and 14 October, 23 November 1974, 15 February 1975.
24. *The Times*, 14 and 23 October 1974; Schoen, 1977, p. 150.
25. Colville, op. cit., p. 29; Cosgrave, 1989, p. 375; Prior, 1986, pp. 184–5.
26. *The Times*, 15 February 1975; Shepherd, 1991, p. 177; Whitehead, 1985, p. 330.
27. *The Times*, 15 and 28 February 1975.
28. Butler and Kitzinger, 1976, pp. 30–43.
29. Whitehead, 1985, p. 137; Butler and Kitzinger, 1976, pp. 144, 179.
30. Butler and Kitzinger, 1976, p. 111; Goodhart, cited in Cosgrave, 1989, p. 399.
31. *Guardian*, 12 May 1975.
32. *News of the World*, 1 June 1975; Butler and Kitzinger, 1976, pp. 178–9.
33. *Daily Telegraph*, 9 June 1975.
34. Holywood, 9 January 1975; Dromore, 25 January 1975; Downpatrick, 19 April 1975.
35. Colville, op. cit., p. 35; Cosgrave, 1989, pp. 416–7.
36. Kilkeel, County Down, 5 July 1975.
37. Shepherd, 1990, passim; Aughey, 1989, pp. 1–29.
38. *Belfast Telegraph*, 7 July 1975; *WW*; *LP*.
39. Ballyhill, County Antrim, 26 July 1975; Schoen, 1977, p. 152.
40. Belfast, 11 September 1975; Banbridge, County Down, 30 September 1975; *The Times*, 13 November 1975; *Hansard*, 9 January 1976, cols. 998–1006.
41. *Sunday Telegraph*, 7 March 1976; *Financial Times*, 23 April 1976; *Guardian*, 24 April and 10 May 1976.
42. Speech to South Down Unionist Association, 22 April 1976; Portadown, 28 May 1976.
43. Johnson and Schoen, *New Society*, 22 July 1976; Lewis, 1979, p. 241.
44. Banbridge, 16 September 1976; Lewis, 1979, p. 216; Colville, op. cit., p. 39.
45. Whitehead, 1985, pp. 262–3.
46. Colville, op. cit., pp. 42–3; Cosgrave, 1989, pp. 411–4.
47. *LP*.
48. Colville, op. cit., pp. 43–4; *Daily Mail*, 19 April 1977.
49. *WW*; Lewis, 1979, pp. 216–7; Cosgrave, 1989, p. 418.
50. *Hansard*, 8 May 1977; Colville, op. cit., p. 44; Lewis, 1979, p. 218.
51. *Irish Times*, 19 March 1979; Colville, op. cit., pp. 45–6.

52. *WW*; *The Times*, 29 March 1979.
53. Whitehead, 1985, p. 285; Colville, op. cit., p. 48.
54. Powell, 1977, p. 7; *WW*.
55. Powell, 1977, p. 6; *WW*.
56. Layton-Henry, 1992, pp. 156–7, 182–5; *Hansard*, 24 May 1976, col. 47; *The Times*, 6 and 15 January and 14 February 1976.
57. *The Times*, 25 May 1976.
58. *WW*; *LP*.
59. Layton-Henry, 1992, p. 187.
60. *Daily Telegraph*, 27 September 1979.
61. *Irish Times*, 3 July 1982; *The Times*, 28 October 1986.
62. *LP*.
63. *LP*.; Dimbleby and Reynolds, 1988, pp. 316–7, 323–5.
64. Prior, 1986, pp. 218–21.
65. *Daily Telegraph*, 31 March 1979.
66. *Irish Independent*, 10 January 1984; *The Times*, 20 and 28 October 1986; Dillon, 1990, pp. 278–9.
67. *LP*.
68. Dillon, 1990, pp. 278–9, 283–7.
69. Thatcher, 1993, pp. 386–7.
70. *Belfast Telegraph*, 4 January 1980.
71. Colville, op. cit., pp. 50–2.
72. Coleraine speech, *Irish Times* and *The Times*, 7 December 1981.
73. Prior, 1981, pp. 197–9.
74. *Daily Notes*, Conservative Research Department, 25 April 1979; *Hansard*, 22 June 1982, col. 177, 29 June 1982, col. 769; *The Times*, 2 July 1982.
75. *Hansard*, 29 June 1982, cols. 770–2.
76. *Hansard*, 29 June, col. 833, written answer, 28 July 1982, cols. 549–50, 10 December 1982, Cols. 1108–11. *Irish Times*, 3 July 1982.
77. Interviewed by Anne Colville, 2 November 1993.
78. Conversations with the author.
79. *The Times*, 17 July 1981.
80. *The Times*, 17 July 1981.
81. Cairncross, 1992, pp. 230–1.
82. Young, 1989, pp. 218–9; *The Times*, 29 October 1981.
83. *Hansard*, 28 October 1981, cols. 886–90; Cairncross, 1992, pp. 230–4.
84. Thatcher, 1993, p. 184 – Powell was later to tell MPs that the substance under test consisted of 'ferrous matter of the highest quality, and that it is of exceptional tensile strength, is highly resistant to wear and tear and to stress, and may be used to advantage for all national purposes'.
85. *LP*; Cockerell, in *The Times*, 11 November 1995; *TF*.
86. *LP*.
87. *The Times*, 11 September 1982; Dimbleby and Reynolds, 1988, pp. 312–6; *Economist*, 3 March 1984.
88. *WW*; *LP*; Cosgrave, 1989, p. 469.
89. *WW*; *LP*.
90. *The Times*, 11 September 1982.
91. Colville, op. cit., pp. 61–2.
92. *The Times*, 1 and 3 June 1983; *Sunday Times*, 5 June 1983; Colville, op. cit., p. 62.
93. Aughey, 1989, pp. 143–4.
94. Thatcher 1993, pp. 399–400.
95. *Belfast Telegraph*, 5 January and 4 March 1985; *The Times*, 5 January 1985; Colville, op. cit., pp. 64–5.
96. *Hansard*, 15 February 1985, cols. 637–41.
97. *Listener*, 18 April 1985; *The Times*, 8 and 15 June, 16 and 17 July 1985.
98. *Belfast Telegraph*, 3 August 1985.
99. Colville, op. cit., p. 68, citing interview with James Molyneaux, 2 November 1993.
100. *The Times*, 15 and 25 November 1985; *Spectator*, 11 October 1986.

101. Thatcher, 1993, p. 402.
102. Colville, op. cit., pp. 71–2.
103. Aughey, 1989, pp. 86–8; Colville, op. cit., pp. 75–6; *The Times*, 25, 26 and 27 November 1985.
104. *LP*.
105. *Hansard*, 27 November 1985, cols. 952–4.
106. *Hansard*, 27 November 1985, cols. 954–5; Colville, op. cit., pp. 78–9.
107. Brendan O'Leary and John McGarry, 1992, *The Politics of Antagonism: Understanding Northern Ireland*, The Athlone Press, cited in Colville, op. cit., p. 85.
108. Thatcher, 1993, pp. 415, 555, 741.
109. Young, 1989, pp. 480–1.
110. *Today on Sunday*, 30 November 1986.
111. *The Times*, 8 June 1987; see also RUSI Journal, February 1967.
112. *The Times*, 28 May 1987.
113. *The Times*, 28 May and 13 June 1987; *Irish Times*, 13 June 1987, Colville, op. cit., p. 81.
114. *The Times*, 15 June 1987.
115. *The Times*, 15 June 1987; private information; *LP*.
116. Alvide Lees-Milne (ed.), 1986, *The Englishman's Room*, Viking, London;
117. Conversation with Peter Hennessy and Enoch Powell, July 1993; *Spectator*, 6 June 1992; Powell, 1977, passim.
118. Clifford Longley, *Daily Telegraph*, 19 August 1994; Powell, 1973 and 1977, passim.
119. Powell, 1973, pp. 26–39; 71–80.
120. Powell, 1973, pp. 11, 43; 1977, pp. 14–9.
121. *Irish Times*, 21 September 1994; *Spectator*, July–December 1994; *Guardian*, 27 August 1994.
122. *Irish Times*, 21 September 1994; *Independent*, 16 August 1994; *Sunday Times*, 21 August 1994; *Guardian*, 27 August 1994.
123. Powell, 1994, pp. 207–8; *Daily Telegraph*, 17 August 1994; *Independent*, 16 August 1994; *The Times* 17 August 1994.
124. Powell, 1994, pp. viii, xi; *Daily Telegraph*, 17 August 1994; *Irish Times*, 21 September 1994.
125. *LP*.
126. *The Times*, 2 March 1994; *Guardian*, 22 October 1994; *The Times*, 19 May 1995.
127. *LP*.
128. Salisbury Group speech, *The Times*, 13 October 1987.
129. Salisbury Group speech, *The Times*, 13 October 1987; Powell, (ed. Richard Ritchie, 1989, passim).
130. Private information; *Odd Man Out*, BBC 2 Television, 11 November 1995; *Spectator*, 6 June 1992.
131. Powell, 1977, p. 151; *Odd Man Out*, BBC 2 Television, 11 November 1995.
132. *LP*.

Bibliography

WORKS BY ENOCH POWELL:

1936 *The Rendel Harris Papyri of Woodbrooke College, Birmingham*, edited, with translation and notes, Cambridge University Press, Cambridge.

1937 *First Poems*, Blackwell's, Oxford.

1938 *A Lexicon to Herodotus*, Cambridge University Press, Cambridge.

1939 *The History of Herodotus*, Cambridge University Press, Cambridge.
Casting-off, and Other Poems, Blackwell's, Oxford.
Herodotus, Book VIII, Cambridge University Press, Cambridge.

1942 *Llyfr Blegywryd* (with Stephen Williams), Gwasg Prifysgol Cymru, Caerdydd.

1949 *Herodotus*, Clarendon Press, Oxford.

1950 *One Nation* (jointly), CPC, London.

1951 *Dancer's End* and *The Wedding Gift*, Falcon Press, London.

1952 *The Social Services: Needs and Means* (with Iain Macleod), CPC, London (revised edition, 1954).

1954 *Change is our Ally* (jointly), CPC, London.

1955 *Biography of a Nation* (with Angus Maude), Berker, London (second edition, 1970).
Thucydidis historia, Clarendon Press, Oxford.

1960 *Great Parliamentary Occasions*, Jenkins, London.
Saving in a Free Society, Institute of Economic Affairs, Hutchinson, London.

1961 *The Welfare State*, CPC, London.

1965 *A Nation not Afraid* (edited by John Wood), Batsford, London.

1966 *A New Look at Medicine and Politics*, Pitman Medical, London.

1967 *Exchange Rates and Liquidity*, Institute of Economic Affairs, London.

1968 *The House of Lords in the Middle Ages* (with Keith Wallis), Weidenfeld and Nicolson, London.

1969 *Freedom and Reality* (edited by John Wood), Batsford, London.

1970 *Immigration and Enoch Powell* (edited by Tom Stacey), Stacey, London.
Income Tax at 4s/3d in the Pound, (edited by Anthony Lejeune), Stacey, London.

1971 *The Common Market: the Case Against*, Elliot, Kingswood.

1972 *Still to Decide* (edited by John Wood), Batsford, London.

1973 *No Easy Answers*, Sheldon Press, London.
Common Market: Re-negotiate or Come Out, Elliot Right Way Books, Tadworth.

1976 *Medicine and Politics: 1975 and After*, Pitman Medical, London.

1977 *Joseph Chamberlain*, Thames and Hudson, London.
Wrestling with the Angel, Sheldon Press, London.

1978 *A Nation or No Nation* (edited Richard Ritchie), Batsford, London.

1989 *Enoch Powell on 1992* (edited by Richard Ritchie), Anaya, London.

1990 *Collected Poems*, Bellew, London.

1991 *Reflections of a Statesman* (edited by Rex Collings), Bellew, London.

1994 *The Evolution of the Gospel*, Yale University Press, New Haven and London.

From 1933, Powell contributed to academic journals, including: *Aegyptus*; *The Bulletin of the Board of Celtic Studies*; *The Classical Quarterly*; *The Classical Review*; *Hermes*; *The Journal of Theological Studies*; *Philologische Wochenschrift*. His extensive post-war journalism appears in numerous publications.

WORKS BY OTHERS:

Jad Adams, 1992, *Tony Benn*, Macmillan, London.
Andrew Alexander and Alan Watkins, 1970, *The Making of the Prime Minister*, Macdonald, London.
B.W.E. Alford, 1988, *British Economic Performance, 1945–75*, Macmillan, London.
David Allen, 1981, 'An analysis of the factors affecting the development of the 1962 hospital plan for England and Wales', in *Social Policy and Administration*, vol. 15, no. 1.
Leo Amery, 1988, *The Leo Amery Diaries, 1929–45*, eds. John Barnes and David Nicholson, Hutchinson, London.
Kingsley Amis, 1991, *Memoirs*, Hutchinson, London.
Noel Annan, 1990, *Our Age: Portrait of a Generation*, Weidenfeld and Nicolson, London.
Arthur Aughey, 1989, *Under Siege: Ulster Unionism and the Anglo-Irish Agreement*, Hurst and Company, London.
John Barnes and David Nicholson, eds, 1988, *The Leo Amery Diaries, 1929–45*, Hutchinson, London.
Samuel H. Beer, 1965, *Modern British Politics*, Faber and Faber, London.
Tony Benn, 1987, *Out of the Wilderness: Diaries 1963–67*; 1989, *Office Without Power: Diaries 1968–72*; 1990, *Against the Tide: Diaries 1973–76*, Hutchinson, London.
Humphry Berkeley, 1977, *The Odyssey of Enoch: a Political Memoir*, Hamish Hamilton, London.
John Biffen, 1965, 'The Conservative Party Today', in Michael Wolff (ed.), *The Conservative Opportunity*, Batsford, London; 1989, *Inside the House of Commons*, Grafton, London.
Robert Blake, 1985, *The Conservative Party from Peel to Thatcher*, Fontana, London.
Vernon Bogdanor, 1995, *The Monarchy and the Constitution*, Oxford University Press, Oxford.
Vernon Bogdanor and Robert Skidelsky, 1970, *The Age of Affluence, 1951–64*, Macmillan, London.
Michael Bowen and David Jacobs, 1981, *Any Questions ?*, Robson, London.
John Boyd-Carpenter, 1980, *Way of Life*, Sidgwick and Jackson, London.
Paul Bridgen and Rodney Lowe, forthcoming, *Welfare Policy under the Conservatives*, HMSO, London.
Asa Briggs, 1952, *History of Birmingham*, volume II, 'Borough and City, 1865–1938', Oxford University Press, Oxford.
Samuel Brittan, 1971, *Steering the Economy*, Penguin Books, Harmondsworth.
Jock Bruce-Gardyne, 1974, *Whatever Happened to the Quiet Revolution*, Charles Knight, London.
David Butler, 1951, *The British General Election of 1950*; 1952, *The British General Election of 1951*; 1956, *The British General Election of 1955*; 1960, with Richard Rose, *The British General Election of 1959*; 1965, with Anthony King, *The British General Election of 1964*; 1966, with Anthony King, *The British General Election of 1966*; 1971, with Michael Pinto-Duschinsky, *The British General Election of 1970*; 1975, with Dennis Kavanagh, *The British General Election of February 1974*; 1975, with Dennis Kavanagh, *The British General Election of October 1974*; 1976, with Uwe Kitzinger, *The 1975 Referendum*; 1980, with Dennis Kavanagh, *The British General Election of 1979*; 1984, with Dennis Kavanagh, *The British General Election of 1983*; 1988, with Dennis Kavanagh, *The British General Election of 1987*, Macmillan, London / Basingstoke; 1971, *Political Change in Britain*, with Donald Stokes, Pelican, London; 1994, with Gareth Butler, *British Political Facts, 1900–94*, Macmillan, Basingstoke.
Lord Butler, 1982a, *The Art of the Possible*, Hamish Hamilton, London; 1982b, *The Art of Memory: Friends in Perspective*, Hodder and Stoughton, London.
Mollie Butler, 1987, *August and Rab: A Memoir*, Weidenfeld and Nicolson, London.
Alec Cairncross, 1991, (ed.) *The Robert Hall Diaries, 1954–61*, Unwin Hyman, London; 1992, *The British Economy since 1945*, Blackwell, Oxford.

Peter Calvocoressi and Guy Wint, 1972, *Total War: Causes and Courses of the Second World War*, Penguin, Harmondsworth.

John Campbell, 1983, *Roy Jenkins: A Biography*, Weidenfeld and Nicolson, London; 1993, *Edward Heath: a Biography*, Jonathan Cape, London.

David Carlton, 1981, *Anthony Eden: a Biography*, Allen Lane, London.

Barbara Castle, 1990, *The Barbara Castle Diaries, 1964–76*, Macmillan, London.

Randolph Churchill, 1964, *The Fight for the Tory Leadership*, Heinemann, London.

Richard Cockett, 1994, *Thinking the Unthinkable: Think-Tanks and the Economic Counter-Revolution*, HarperCollins, London.

Terry Coleman, 1987, *Movers and Shakers*, Deutsch, London.

Patrick Cosgrave, 1989, *The Lives of Enoch Powell*, The Bodley Head, London.

Richard Crossman, 1977, *The Diaries of a Cabinet Minister*, vols I–III, 1964–70; 1981, *The Backbench Diaries of Richard Crossman*; ed. Janet Morgan, Hamish Hamilton and Jonathan Cape, London.

Glyn Daniel, 1986, *Some Small Harvest*, Thames and Hudson, London.

Sir Robin Day, 1989, *Grand Inquisitor: Memoirs*, Weidenfeld and Nicolson, London.

Nicholas Deakin, 1964, *Colour and the British Electorate*, ed., Pall Mall Press, London; 1970, *Colour, Citizenship and British Society*, Panther, London.

H.T. Dickinson, 1979, *Liberty and Property*, Methuen, London.

Martin Dillon, 1990, *The Dirty War*, Hutchinson, London.

David Dimbleby and David Reynolds, 1988, *An Ocean Apart*, BBC Books / Hodder and Stoughton, London.

Michael Dockrill, 1988, *British Defence since 1945*, Blackwell, Oxford.

J.C.R. Dow, 1964, *The Management of the British Economy, 1945–60*, Cambridge University Presss, Cambridge.

Patrick Dunleavy, 1981, *The Politics of Mass Housing, 1945–75*, Oxford University Press, Oxford.

Lord Egremont, 1968, *Wyndham and Children First*, Macmillan, London.

Harold Evans, 1981, *The Macmillan Years, 1957–63*, Hodder and Stoughton, London.

Harold Evans, 1983, *Good Times, Bad Times*, Weidenfeld and Nicolson, London.

John Fforde, 1992, *The Bank of England and Public Policy, 1941–58*, Cambridge University Press, Cambridge.

W.D. Flackes, 1980, *Northern Ireland: a Political Directory*, Ariel, London.

Paul Foot, 1969, *The Rise of Enoch Powell: an Examination of Enoch Powell's Attitude to Immigration and Race*, Cornmarket Press, London.

Daniel M. Fox, 1986, *Health Policies, Health Politics: the British and American Experience, 1911–65*, Princeton University Press, Princeton, USA.

David Frost, 1993, *An Autobiography*, HarperCollins, London.

Andrew Gamble, 1974, *The Conservative Nation*, Routledge and Kegan Paul, London.

Victor George and Paul Wilding, 1976, *Ideology and Social Welfare*, Routledge and Kegan Paul, London.

Ian Gilmour, 1969, *The Body Politic*, Hutchinson, London; 1977, *Inside Right: A Study of Conservatism*, Hutchinson, London; 1992, *Dancing with Dogma: Britain under Thatcherism*, Simon and Schuster, London.

Howard Glennerster, 1995, *British Social Policy since 1945*, Blackwell, Oxford.

Philip Goodhart, 1973, *The 1922: The Story of the 1922 Committee*, Macmillan, London.

Richard Perceval Graves, 1979, *A.E. Housman: The Scholar Poet*, Routledge and Kegan Paul, London.

William Greenleaf, 1983, *The British Political Tradition*, vol. 2, 'The Ideological Heritage', Methuen, London.

Lord Hailsham, 1975, *The Door Wherein I Went*, Collins, London; 1990, *A Sparrow's Flight*, Collins, London.

Robert Hall, 1991, *The Robert Hall Diaries, 1954–61*, ed. Alec Cairncross, Unwin Hyman, London, 1992,

Nigel Harris, 1972, *Competition and the Corporate Society: British Conservatives, the State and Industry, 1945–64*, Methuen, London.

Roy Hattersley, 1972, 'Immigration', in David McKie and Chris Cook, *The Decade of Disillusion: British Politics in the Sixties*, Macmillan, London; 1995, *Who Goes Home? Scenes from a Political Life*, Little Brown, London.

Denis Healey, 1989, *The Time of My Life*, Michael Joseph, London.

Simon Heffer, 1995, *Moral Desperado: A Life of Thomas Carlyle*, Weidenfeld and Nicolson, London.

Peter Hennessy, 1992, *Never Again: Britain, 1945–51*, Jonathan Cape, London; 1995, *The Hidden Wiring: Unearthing the British Constitution*, Gollancz, London.

Peter Hennessy and Anthony Seldon (eds.), 1987, *Ruling Performance: British Governments from Attlee to Thatcher*, Blackwell, Oxford.

Lord Home, 1976, *The Way the Wind Blows*, Collins, London.

Alistair Horne, 1988, *Macmillan, 1894–1956*, and *Macmillan, 1957–86*, Macmillan, London.

A.E. Housman, 1967, *The Collected Poems of A.E. Housman*, Jonathan Cape, London.

Denis Howell, 1990, *Made in Birmingham*, Macdonald, London.

Anthony Howard, 1979, (ed.) *The Crossman Diaries, 1964–70*, Magnum, London; 1987, *RAB: The Life of R.A. Butler*, Jonathan Cape, London.

Geoffrey Howe, 1994, *Conflict of Loyalty*, Macmillan, London.

G.M.K. Hunt (editor), 1990, *Philosophy and Politics*, British Institute of Philosophy Lectures, Cambridge University Press, Cambridge.

Douglas Hurd, 1978, *An End to Promises: Sketch of a Government, 1970–74*, Collins, London.

Brian Inglis, 1965, *Drugs, Doctors and Disease*, Mayflower Books, London.

Keith Jebb, 1992, *A.E. Housman*, Seren Books, Bridgend.

Roy Jenkins, 1991, *A Life at the Centre*, Macmillan, London.

J. Clement Jones et al., 1971, *Race and the Press*, Runnymede Trust, London.

Kit Jones, 1994, *An Economist among Mandarins: a Biography of Robert Hall (1901–88)*, Cambridge University Press, Cambridge.

Dennis Kavanagh, 1989, *Consensus Politics from Attlee to Thatcher*, Blackwell, Oxford.

Uwe Kitzinger, 1973, *Diplomacy and Persuasion: How Britain Joined the Common Market*, Thames and Hudson, London.

Rudolf Klein, 1989, *The Politics of the NHS*, Longman, London.

Richard Lamb, 1987, *The Failure of the Eden Government*, Sidgwick and Jackson, London; 1995, *The Macmillan Years: the Emerging Truth*, John Murray, London.

Brian Lapping, 1970, *The Labour Government, 1964–70*, Penguin, Harmondsworth.

Zig Layton–Henry, 1980, *Conservative Party Politics* (ed.), Macmillan, London; 1992, *The Politics of Immigration*, Blackwell, Oxford.

Roy Lewis, 1979, *Enoch Powell: Principle in Politics*, Cassell, London.

Rodney Lowe, 1989, 'Resignation at the Treasury: the Social Services Committee and the failure to reform the Welfare State, 1955–57', in *Journal of Social Policy*, vol. 18, no. 4, pp. 505–26, London; 1993, *The Welfare State in Britain since 1945*, Macmillan, London; 1996, 'The Re-planning of the Welfare State, 1957–64', in M. Francis et al, *The Conservatives and British Society, 1880–1990*, University of Wales Press, Cardiff; with Paul Bridgen (forthcoming), *Welfare Policy under the Conservatives*, HMSO, London.

David McKie and Chris Cook, 1972, *Decade of Disillusion: British Politics in the Sixties*, Macmillan, London.

Harold Macmillan, 1971, *Riding the Storm, 1956–59*; 1972, *Pointing the Way, 1959–61*; 1973, *At the End of the Day, 1961–63*, Macmillan, London.

Peter Marsh, 1994, *Joseph Chamberlain: Entrepreneur in Politics*, Yale University Press, New Haven and London.

Philip Mason, 1978, *A Shaft of Sunlight*, Andre Deutsch, London.

Reginald Maudling, 1978, *Memoirs*, Sidgwick and Jackson, London.

W.N Medlicott, 1976, *Contemporary England, 1914–64*, Longman, London.

Janet Morgan, 1977, (ed.) *The Diaries of a Cabinet Minister*, vols I–III, 1964–70; 1981, (ed.) *The Backbench Diaries of Richard Crossman*, Hamish Hamilton / Jonathan Cape, London.

Elaine Murphy, 1991, *After the Asylums: Community Care for People with Mental Illness*, Faber and Faber, London.

Sir Gerald Nabarro, 1969, *NAB 1: Portrait of a Politician*, Robert Maxwell, London.

Doojen Napal, 1975, *Enoch Powell: a Study in Personality and Politics*, Part I, A.W.A.A.M. Press, Wolverhampton.

Philip Norton, 1975, *Dissension in the House of Commons: Intra-party Dissent in the House of Commons' Division Lobbies, 1945–76*, Macmillan, London; 1978, *Conservative Dissidents: Dissent within the Parliamentary Conservative party, 1970–74*, Temple Smith, London; 1980, *Dissension in the House of Commons, 1974–79*, Clarendon Press, Oxford.

Philip Norton and Arthur Aughey, 1981, *Conservatives and Conservatism*, Temple Smith, London.

Frank O'Gorman, 1986, *British Conservatism*, Longman, London.

David Owen, 1991, *Time to Declare*, Michael Joseph, London.

Chris Patten, 1983, *The Tory Case*, Longman, London.

Ben Pimlott, 1992, *Harold Wilson*, HarperCollins, London.

James Prior, 1986, *A Balance of Power*, Hamish Hamilton, London.

Timothy Raison, 1990, *Tories and the Welfare State*, Macmillan, 1990.

John Ramsden, 1980, *The Making of Conservative Party Policy*, Longman, London; 1995, *The Age of Churchill and Eden, 1940–57*, Longman, London; 1996, *The Winds of Change: Macmillan to Heath, 1957–75*, Longman, London.

Peter Rawlinson, 1989, *A Price Too High*, Weidenfeld and Nicolson, London.

Frank Reeves, 1983, *British Racial Discourse: a Study of British Political Discourse about Race and Race-related Matters*, Cambridge University Press, Cambridge.

Robert Rhodes James, 1972, *Ambitions and Realities: British Politics 1964–70*, Weidenfeld and Nicolson, London; 1986, *Anthony Eden*, Weidenfeld and Nicolson, London.

Paul B. Rich, 1986, *Race and Empire in British Politics*, Cambridge University Press, Cambridge.

Nicholas Ridley, 1991, *My Style of Government*, Hutchinson, London.

Lord Robbins, 1963, *Politics and Economics*, Macmillan, London; 1971, *Autobiography of an Economist*, Macmillan, London.

Andrew Roth, 1970, *Enoch Powell: Tory Tribune*, Macdonald, London; 1972; *Heath and the Heathmen*, Routledge and Kegan Paul, London.

Anthony Sampson, 1962, *The Anatomy of Britain*, Hodder and Stoughton, London;, 1968, *Harold Macmillan: A Study in Ambiguity*, Penguin, Harmondsworth.

Douglas E. Schoen, 1977, *Enoch Powell and the Powellites*, Macmillan, London.

Anthony Seldon and Stuart Ball (eds), 1994, *The Conservative Century*, Oxford University Press, Oxford.

Arthur Seldon, 1964, *Rebirth of Britain*, Pan, London.

Robert Shepherd, 1990, *Ireland's Fate: the Boyne and After*, Aurum, London; 1991, *The Power Brokers: the Tory Party and its Leaders*, Hutchinson, London; 1994, *Iain Macleod: a Biography*, Hutchinson, London.

John R. Short, 1982, *Housing in Britain: the Post-War Experience*, Methuen, London.

Brian Simon, 1974, *The Politics of Educational Reform, 1920–40*, Lawrence and Wishart, London.

Robert Skidelsky, 1990, *'Theory and Practice: a Response'*, in *Philosophy and Politics*, British Institute of Philosophy Lectures, edited by G.M.K. Hunt, Cambridge University Press, Cambridge; 1993, *Interests and Obsessions: selected essays*, Macmillan, London.

David Smith, 1987, *The Rise and Fall of Monetarism*, Penguin, Harmondsworth.

Robert Smith and John S. Moore (eds), 1994, *The House of Lords: a Thousand years of British Tradition*, Smith's Peerage, London.

S.A. de Smith, 1971, *Constitutional and Administrative Law*, Penguin, Harmondsworth.

Bill Smithies and Peter Fiddick, 1969, *Enoch Powell and Immigration*, Sphere, London.

W.A. Speck, 1977, *Stability and Strife*, Edward Arnold, London.

Michael Strachan, 1949, *'Teaching the Professor'*, in *Blackwood's Magazine*, May 1949.

Norman Tebbit, 1989, *Upwardly Mobile*, Futura, London.

Margaret Thatcher, 1995, *The Path to Power*, HarperCollins, London.

Lord Thorneycroft, 1960, *'Policy in Practice'*, in *Not Unanimous: a Rival Verdict to Radcliffe's on Money*, Institute of Economic Affairs, London.

D.R. Thorpe, 1980, *The Uncrowned Prime Ministers*, Darkhorse, London; 1989, *Selwyn Lloyd*, Jonathan Cape, London.

Nicholas Timmins, 1995, *The Five Giants*, HarperCollins, London.

Anthony Trott, 1992, *No Place for Fop or Idler: The Story of King Edward's School, Birmingham*, James and James, London.

John Turner, 1994, *Macmillan*, Longman, London.

T.E. Utley, 1968, *Enoch Powell: The Man and his Thinking*, William Kimber, London.

Martin Walker, 1977, *The National Front*, Fontana, London.

Peter Walker, 1991, *Staying Power*, Bloomsbury, London.

Dennis Walters, 1989, *Not Always with the Pack*, Constable, London.

Brian Watkin, 1978, *The National Health Service: the First Phase, 1948–74, and after*, George Allen & Unwin, 1978.

Charles Webster, 1988, *The Health Services Since the War*, Volume One, 'Problems of Health Care: The National Health Service before 1957'; (forthcoming) Volume Two, HMSO, London.

Phillip Whitehead, 1985, *The Writing on the Wall: Britain in the Seventies*, Michael Joseph, London.

Mary Whitehouse, 1982, *A Most Dangerous Woman?* Lion Books, Tring.

William Whitelaw, 1989, *The Whitelaw Memoirs*, Aurum, London.

Michael Wolff (ed.), 1965, *The Conservative Opportunity*, Batsford, London.

G. D. N. Worswick and P.H. Adey (eds), 1962, *The British Economy in the Nineteen-Fifties*, Clarendon Press, Oxford.

Hugo Young, 1989, *One Of Us*, Macmillan, London.

John Young, 1993, *Britain and European Unity, 1945–92*, Macmillan, London.

Index

Entries under Enoch Powell have been confined to those sub-headings which cannot be readily found under other entries. His name in other entries has been abbreviated to EP.

Index